Office 2010

THE MISSING MANUAL

*The book that
should have been
in the box*®

Funded by
MISSION COLLEGE
Carl D. Perkins Vocational and Technical Education Act Grant

Office 2010

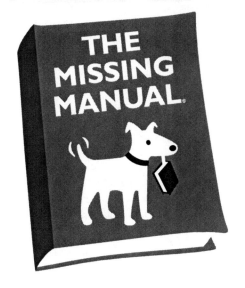

Nancy Conner and Matthew MacDonald

POGUE PRESS™
O'REILLY®

Beijing • Cambridge • Farnham • Köln • Sebastopol • Tokyo

Office 2010: The Missing Manual

by Nancy Conner and Matthew MacDonald

Copyright © 2010 Nancy Conner. All rights reserved.

Printed in the United States of America.

Published by O'Reilly Media, Inc., 1005 Gravenstein Highway North, Sebastopol, CA 95472.

O'Reilly Media books may be purchased for educational, business, or sales promotional use. Online editions are also available for most titles: *safari.oreilly.com*. For more information, contact our corporate/institutional sales department: 800-998-9938 or *corporate@oreilly.com*.

Printing History:

July 2010:   First Edition.

Nutshell Handbook, the Nutshell Handbook logo, the O'Reilly logo, and "The book that should have been in the box" are registered trademarks of O'Reilly Media, Inc. *Office 2010: The Missing Manual*, The Missing Manual logo, Pogue Press, and the Pogue Press logo are trademarks of O'Reilly Media, Inc.

Many of the designations used by manufacturers and sellers to distinguish their products are claimed as trademarks. Where those designations appear in this book, and O'Reilly Media, Inc. was aware of a trademark claim, the designations have been printed in caps or initial caps.

While every precaution has been taken in the preparation of this book, the publisher and authors assume no responsibility for errors or omissions, or for damages resulting from the use of the information contained herein.

ISBN: 978-1-449-38240-7

[LSI]   [2011-06-03]

Table of Contents

Part Two: Outlook

Part Seven: Appendix

Note: Head to this book's Missing CD page on *www.missingmanuals.com* to download four additional appendixes.

The Missing Credits

About the Authors

 Nancy Conner writes and edits tech books from her home in up-state New York. She's also worked as a medievalist, an instructional designer, and a corporate trainer. When she's not writing or messing around with someone else's prose, she likes to read mysteries, visit local wineries, and listen obsessively to opera.

Matthew MacDonald is a developer, author, and educator in all things Visual Basic and .NET. He's worked with Visual Basic and ASP since their initial versions, and has written over a dozen books on the subject, including *The Book of VB .NET* (No Starch Press) and *Visual Basic 2005: A Developer's Notebook* (O'Reilly). He has also written a number of Missing Manual titles on Excel and Access. His website is *www.prosetech.com*.

About the Creative Team

Peter Meyers (editor) is a New York City-based veteran of Team Missing Manual. He's edited more than 20 books in the series and lives with his wife and two daughters in Washington Heights, aka "upstate Manhattan".

Nellie McKesson (production editor) just bought her first home in Brockton, Mass. When not working on DIY home improvement projects, she studies graphic design and plays music with her various bands. Email: *nellie@oreilly.com*.

Julie Van Keuren (copy editor) is a freelance editor, writer, and desktop publisher who runs her "little media empire" from her home in Billings, Montana. In her free time she enjoys swimming, biking, running, and (hey, why not?) triathlons. She and her husband have two sons. Email: *little_media@yahoo.com*.

Tina Spargo (technical reviewer), her husband (and professional musician) Ed, their preschooler Max, their two silly Spaniels, Parker (Clumber), and Piper (Sussex), all share time and space in their suburban Boston home. Tina juggles being an at-home mom with promoting and marketing Ed's musical projects and freelancing as a virtual assistant. Tina has over 20 years' experience supporting top-level executives in a variety of industries. Website: *www.tinaspargo.com*.

Mitch Garvis (technical reviewer) is a Renaissance man of the IT world. He is an excellent communicator, which makes him the ideal trainer and writer. If you can't attend one of his classes or community sessions, then read his blog at *www.garvis.ca* or follow him on Twitter as @MGarvis. He makes his home outside Toronto where he has one wife, two kids, three dogs, and four minutes per day to himself.

Ellen Troutman Zaig (indexer) is a professional freelance indexer with 11 years experience in back-of-the-book indexing. Topics indexed include a wide range of subjects in computer technology and in college textbooks.

Acknowledgements

No matter whose name is on the cover, it takes a whole team of people to create a book. Thanks to Pete Meyers for discussing the original idea and guiding the manuscript through the writing process. His insightful comments and edits helped shape the chapters and add clarity to the text. Technical reviewers Tina Spargo and Mitch Garvis were diligent in double-checking instructions and technical details and helpful in contributing their own tips and tricks. Thanks to Julie Van Keuren for her thorough (and fast!) copyedit. Thanks also to production editor Nellie McKesson for keeping things moving throughout the production cycle. Finally huge thanks and appreciation to Dawn Mann, Nan Barber, and Karen Shaner for their help with reviewing galleys.

—*Nancy Conner*

The Missing Manual Series

Missing Manuals are witty, superbly written guides to computer products that don't come with printed manuals (which is just about all of them). Each book features a handcrafted index; cross-references to specific pages (not just chapters); and RepKover, a detached-spine binding that lets the book lie perfectly flat without the assistance of weights or cinder blocks.

Recent and upcoming titles include:

Access 2007: The Missing Manual by Matthew MacDonald

Access 2010: The Missing Manual by Matthew MacDonald

Buying a Home: The Missing Manual by Nancy Conner

CSS: The Missing Manual, Second Edition, by David Sawyer McFarland

Creating a Web Site: The Missing Manual, Second Edition, by Matthew MacDonald

David Pogue's Digital Photography: The Missing Manual by David Pogue

Dreamweaver CS4: The Missing Manual by David Sawyer McFarland

Dreamweaver CS5: The Missing Manual by David Sawyer McFarland

Excel 2007: The Missing Manual by Matthew MacDonald

Excel 2010: The Missing Manual by Matthew MacDonald

Facebook: The Missing Manual, Second Edition by E.A. Vander Veer

FileMaker Pro 10: The Missing Manual by Susan Prosser and Geoff Coffey

FileMaker Pro 11: The Missing Manual by Susan Prosser and Stuart Gripman

Flash CS4: The Missing Manual by Chris Grover with E.A. Vander Veer

Flash CS5: The Missing Manual by Chris Grover

Google Apps: The Missing Manual by Nancy Conner

The Internet: The Missing Manual by David Pogue and J.D. Biersdorfer

iMovie '08 & iDVD: The Missing Manual by David Pogue

iMovie '09 & iDVD: The Missing Manual by David Pogue and Aaron Miller

iPad: The Missing Manual by J.D. Biersdorfer and David Pogue

iPhone: The Missing Manual, Second Edition by David Pogue

iPhone App Development: The Missing Manual by Craig Hockenberry

iPhoto '08: The Missing Manual by David Pogue

iPhoto '09: The Missing Manual by David Pogue and J.D. Biersdorfer

iPod: The Missing Manual, Eighth Edition by J.D. Biersdorfer and David Pogue

JavaScript: The Missing Manual by David Sawyer McFarland

Living Green: The Missing Manual by Nancy Conner

Mac OS X: The Missing Manual, Leopard Edition by David Pogue

Mac OS X Snow Leopard: The Missing Manual by David Pogue

Microsoft Project 2007: The Missing Manual by Bonnie Biafore

Microsoft Project 2010: The Missing Manual by Bonnie Biafore

Netbooks: The Missing Manual by J.D. Biersdorfer

Office 2007: The Missing Manual by Chris Grover, Matthew MacDonald, and E.A. Vander Veer

Office 2008 for Macintosh: The Missing Manual by Jim Elferdink

Palm Pre: The Missing Manual by Ed Baig

PCs: The Missing Manual by Andy Rathbone

Personal Investing: The Missing Manual by Bonnie Biafore

Photoshop CS4: The Missing Manual by Lesa Snider

Photoshop CS5: The Missing Manual by Lesa Snider

Photoshop Elements 7: The Missing Manual by Barbara Brundage

Photoshop Elements 8 for Mac: The Missing Manual by Barbara Brundage

Photoshop Elements 8 for Windows: The Missing Manual by Barbara Brundage

PowerPoint 2007: The Missing Manual by E.A. Vander Veer

Premiere Elements 8: The Missing Manual by Chris Grover

QuickBase: The Missing Manual by Nancy Conner

QuickBooks 2010: The Missing Manual by Bonnie Biafore

QuickBooks 2011: The Missing Manual by Bonnie Biafore

Quicken 2009: The Missing Manual by Bonnie Biafore

Switching to the Mac: The Missing Manual, Leopard Edition by David Pogue

Switching to the Mac: The Missing Manual, Snow Leopard Edition by David Pogue

Wikipedia: The Missing Manual by John Broughton

Windows XP Home Edition: The Missing Manual, Second Edition, by David Pogue

Windows XP Pro: The Missing Manual, Second Edition, by David Pogue, Craig Zacker, and Linda Zacker

Windows Vista: The Missing Manual by David Pogue

Windows 7: The Missing Manual by David Pogue

Word 2007: The Missing Manual by Chris Grover

Your Body: The Missing Manual by Matthew MacDonald

Your Brain: The Missing Manual by Matthew MacDonald

Your Money: The Missing Manual by J.D. Roth

Introduction

Office—it's where millions of people head to work each day, and it's also how they get stuff done once they get there. Whether you're crunching numbers in a spreadsheet, writing a novel between meetings, or building a slideshow, chances are you've worked with an Office program. Microsoft's money-making powerhouse has long been the world's most popular collection of productivity tools. Office 2010—more powerful, flexible, and usable than ever—is a cinch to continue that trend.

This book shows you how to make the most of Office 2010, so you can work faster, smarter, and better. If you're brand-new to Microsoft Office, no worries. In the pages that follow, you'll learn what you need to get up and running, and soon you'll be creating documents, worksheets, and presentations like a pro. If you're coming to Office 2010 from an earlier version, you'll be impressed at the fit and finish Microsoft has applied and the new features it's added: new ways to edit graphics, for example, and online versions of the flagship programs.

What Is Office 2010?

Office 2010 is a group of programs that help you work more productively. Here's the full roster you'll find inside most versions of Office 2010:

- **Word 2010.** Write reports, memos, and manifestos. If you've owned a computer during the past 20 years, you've probably at least heard of this, the world's most ubiquitous word processor.

- **Excel 2010.** Microsoft may not have invented the spreadsheet, but Excel sure comes close to perfecting it. Crunch numbers, generate graphs and charts, or track your budget or your progress on a project.

- **PowerPoint 2010.** This presentation program has become synonymous—for better or for worse—with the slideshows speakers use to illustrate their points. Create and organize slides, and then bring them to life with animations and special effects.

- **Outlook 2010.** Use this popular program to send and receive email—but that's just the beginning. With built-in notes, a calendar, and a to-do list, you'll keep yourself organized as you communicate with friends, family, and colleagues.

- **Access 2010.** Just the word "database" is enough to make some people break out in a cold sweat. Access is Microsoft's *no*-sweat database program: Gather, track, and report on data with ease.

- **OneNote 2010.** Clip, snip, jot, doodle, and organize your thoughts with this digital notebook. You can type in notes, paste in screenshots, and even attach entire documents into this flexible program.

- **Publisher 2010.** For professional-looking publications, you can't beat this layout program. It comes with tons of built-in templates that you can use as a foundation for creating your own newsletter, greeting card, calendar, brochure, catalog—just about any kind of document you can think of.

Note: Although they're not part of the programs you install on your computer, Office Web Apps—free online versions of Word, Excel, PowerPoint, and OneNote—are also new and designed to work seamlessly with their Office 2010 counterparts. As Chapter 31 explains, Office Web Apps are free and available online at *http://home.live.com*.

Office 2010 comes in three different packages, and the programs you get depend on which package you buy. Word, Excel, PowerPoint, and OneNote form Office 2010's core, and they come with all three packages. Table I-1 has the full rundown.

Table I-1. The programs available in Office 2010 suites

	Office Home and Student	Office Home and Business	Office Professional
Word 2010	X	X	X
Excel 2010	X	X	X
PowerPoint 2010	X	X	X
OneNote 2010	X	X	X
Outlook 2010		X	X
Publisher 2010			X
Access 2010			X

Note: This book covers Office 2010, which is for Windows only. The most recent Mac version of Office is covered in *Office 2008 for Macintosh: The Missing Manual*.

What's New in Office 2010

Office 2007 represented an Office revolution, introducing the ribbon—a screen-top strip of buttons, organized around common tasks, that replaced the unwieldy collection of toolbars found in earlier versions. The ribbon forever changed the way people worked with Word, Excel, PowerPoint, and the other Office programs. Office 2010 doesn't shake things up the way its predecessor did, but it does fine-tune the entire machine and adds some pretty useful new features. Highlights include these:

- **Backstage view.** Office 2007 introduced the File menu–replacing Office button and Office menu—frustrating plenty of folks who couldn't find basic commands for things like printing and saving files. With Office 2010, Microsoft sweeps away that misstep and replaces it with Backstage view, a smart new way to work with a file. Backstage view gathers together everything you might do *with* a file (as opposed to what you might do *to* a file): Save, print, set permissions, share, and open. In Word, for example, when you're finished editing a document, you go Backstage to print it or email it to a colleague.

  You get Backstage by clicking the File tab, the leftmost tab on every ribbon. Clicking here takes you out of editing view and shows information about the file itself—which is why it's called "Backstage." Figure I-1 shows an example of Backstage view in Word.

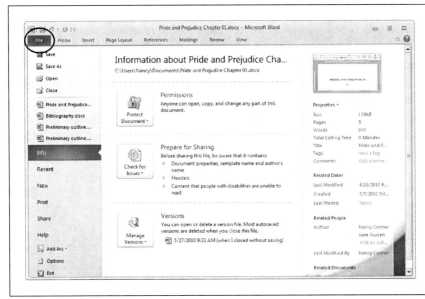

Figure I-1:
Clicking the File tab (circled) in any Office program opens Backstage view. Instead of the file's contents, you see information about the file and a slew of options for working with it, from saving to printing to sharing. Click any item on the menu to open a page of related actions.

- **Customization.** The ribbon is now completely customizable—and that's as it should be. Hand tailor the ribbon by organizing its commands in a way that makes sense to you. You can add new tabs, create your own groups, add or remove buttons, and more.

- **Temporary saving of discarded changes.** When you close a file, Office programs ask if you want to save your changes—that's nothing new. But in Office 2010, when you click Don't Save, the program saves the latest version of your file anyway, just in case. This can be a lifesaver when you inadvertently toss out changes you meant to save.

Note: To find files you closed without saving, head Backstage and look for them in your list of recent files (marked "when I closed without saving"). If you don't open the temporarily saved file within a few days, the program discards it.

- **Protected view.** Lots of people think nothing of downloading and opening files they found somewhere or other on the Internet—even when they have no idea who created these documents. To protect your computer, Office programs open downloaded files in Protected view, showing a read-only version of the file that can't do nasty things to your computer. If you trust the source from which you got the file, you're an easy click away from enabling full-fledged editing.

- **New SmartArt templates.** SmartArt graphics were a terrific and much-needed addition to Office 2007, punching up PowerPoint presentations with eye-catching diagrams. If you liked SmartArt in Office 2007, you'll love it in Office 2010. There are more templates to make your graphics even snazzier.

- **Built-in screenshot tool.** You can take a snapshot of what's on your screen right from within Word, PowerPoint, or OneNote—no need for a separate program to capture screenshots that you then must insert into an Office file.

- **Background removal in photos.** Another great feature for working with images is the ability to remove a distracting background from a photo. Word and PowerPoint both include this tool.

- **PowerPoint video trimming and bookmarks.** When you insert a video clip into a PowerPoint slide, you can edit the clip to choose its starting and ending point. You can also insert bookmarks that let you jump to the important parts.

- **Outlook Social Connector.** Keep in touch with your social networks without leaving Outlook. Outlook Social Connector offers a live portal into networks like SharePoint, Windows Live, LinkedIn, and MySpace. (Yes, yes: Twitter and Facebook are coming soon. More details are on page 302.) Know what's happening, *as* it happens, with the people in your network.

- **Office Web Apps.** Microsoft has put its most popular Office programs on the Web. With Internet access and a Windows Live ID, you can work with Web-only versions Word, Excel, PowerPoint, and OneNote from just about anywhere. Store your files on SkyDrive, which provides 25 GB of storage space, and work on them whenever and wherever you want. There's even a new Facebook application that lets you create documents online and share them with your Facebook friends.

That's just a sampling of what's new in Office 2010. Throughout this book, you'll learn your way around these and many other new features—what they are and how to put them to work for you.

About This Book

Although many things have changed with Office 2010, one thing hasn't—it still doesn't come with a manual. If you have a question about how to perform a complex task or what a mysterious button on the ribbon does, you have to turn to Microsoft's online help files. Searching those files doesn't always turn up what you're looking for—you can look through a dozen search results and still be scratching your head.

This is the book, then, that *should have* come with Office 2010. In clear, straightforward language and with a minimum of geek-speak, it tells you how to make Office work for you. The book explains what you need to know just when you need to know it, and its organization makes it easy to find the topic you're looking for.

Here's what lies ahead:

Part 1: Word 2010 starts with the very basics—how to open Word, create a document, add some text, and save it—and ends with advanced techniques for working on documents. Along the way, you'll learn everything you need to become proficient in Word, including using its proofing tools, searching with Word 2010's new Navigation pane, new tricks for working with images, merging a mailing list with a document, recording macros to automate tasks, putting Word documents on the Web, and a whole lot more.

Part 2: Outlook 2010 shows how to send, receive, and organize email messages. But Outlook is so much more than just an email program—you'll see how to manage your address book, prioritize your to-do list, and keep track of appointments with the built-in calendar.

Part 3: Excel 2010 demonstrates how to build a better worksheet. It starts off with the need-to-know essentials and gets you up to speed fast, covering formulas and functions and charts and graphics.

Part 4: PowerPoint 2010 teaches you how to create eye-catching, professional presentations—create slides, choose a theme, work with images, add notes, and liven up the show with animations and transitions. You'll also learn how to create handouts, record narration for your slideshow, insert and edit video and audio clips, give a state-of-the-art slideshow—even turn your slideshow into a video.

Part 5: Access 2010 guides you through creating, working with, and sharing a database. Sound intimidating? It shouldn't. With chapters on building and linking tables, and on how to sort, search, and filter everything you've collected, you'll have a database running in no time.

Part 6: Other Office Tools includes a chapter apiece on Publisher, OneNote, and Office Web Apps. Publisher 2010 gives you tools to create professional-looking publications, from simple greeting cards to newsletters and catalogs. You'll learn how to work with text boxes, design and lay out pages, and prepare a publication for a commercial printer. For OneNote 2010, Office's flexible, free-form note-taking program, you'll see how to create a notebook and then fill it with text, doodles, images, and clippings. And in the Office Web Apps chapter, you'll learn how to create, upload, edit, and share files you store on the Web.

Appendix: Customizing Office shows how to customize the ribbon, the Quick Access toolbar, and the status bar in all the Office 2010 programs.

Note: You can download four more appendixes from this book's Missing CD page at *www.missingmanuals.com/cds*.

The Very Basics

You'll find very little jargon or nerd terminology in this book. You will, however, run across a few terms and concepts that you'll encounter frequently in your computing life:

- **Clicking.** This book gives you four kinds of instructions that require you to use your computer's mouse or trackpad. To *click* means to point the arrow cursor at something on the screen and then—without moving the cursor at all—to press and release the clicker button on the left side of the mouse (or laptop trackpad). To *double-click* means to press and release the clicker button twice in quick succession without pausing. To *right-click* means to point the cursor and click the button on the right side of the mouse (or trackpad). And to *drag* means to move the cursor while pressing the button continuously.

- **The ribbon.** As you read earlier, the ribbon refers to the wide band of command buttons that appear at the top of the screen when you click a tab like File or Home. Each tab describes a related set of commands (Insert, Page Layout, Review, and so on); when you click a tab, the ribbon changes to show the buttons that let you use those commands: insert a picture or table, change page orientation, check spelling—you get the idea.

    Some ribbon buttons have *menus,* lists of related commands. When you click the button, the list of commands appears, as though they were written on a window shade you just pulled down. Click any option on the menu to put that command to work.

- **Keyboard shortcuts.** Whenever you take your hand off the keyboard to move the mouse, you lose time and potentially disrupt your workflow. That's why many experienced computer fans use *keystroke combinations* instead of menu commands whenever possible. Ctrl+B, for example, is a keyboard shortcut for boldface type in most word-processing programs, including Word.

  When you see a shortcut like Ctrl+C (which copies something to the Windows Clipboard), it's telling you to hold down the Ctrl key, and, while it's down, press the C key, and then release both keys.

  Office 2010 offers a keyboard shortcut for each and every command on the ribbon. To turn on these shortcuts, you press the Alt key, which makes tiny labels, each with a letter (or two), appear on the ribbon's tabs. Press a letter on the keyboard to open that tab. Then, on the ribbon, labels appear on all the command buttons in that tab, and you can press the key that corresponds to the command you want. So, for example, if you want to print a file, you'd press the keys Alt, then F, then P.

Note: You don't have to hold down the Alt key while pressing the other keys in the keyboard shortcut sequence, so this book uses a comma instead of a plus sign to indicate these shortcuts, like this: Alt, F, P. Translated: Press the Alt key and let it go; then press F and let it go; and, finally, press P and let it go.

About→These→Arrows

Throughout this book, and throughout the Missing Manual series, you'll find sentences like this one: "Select Home→Change Styles→Style Set." That's shorthand for a much longer instruction that directs you to click three commands in sequence, like this: "On your screen, you'll find a tab called Home. Click that. On the Home tab's ribbon is an option called Change Styles; click it to see a menu of related commands. On that menu is yet another option called Style Set. Click that option to open it, too." This kind of arrow shorthand helps to simplify the business of choosing commands.

About MissingManuals.com

At the Missing Manuals website (*www.missingmanuals.com*), you'll find articles, tips, and updates to this book. In fact, you're invited and encouraged to submit such corrections and updates yourself. In an effort to keep the book as up-to-date and accurate as possible, each time we publish new editions of this book, we'll make any confirmed corrections you've suggested. We'll also note such changes on the website. (Click the book's name, and then click the Errata link, to see the changes.)

While you're online, you can also register this book at *www.oreilly.com*. Registering means we can send you updates about this book, including any additions or Web-only offerings.

Safari® Books Online

 Safari® Books Online is an on-demand digital library that lets you easily search over 7,500 technology and creative reference books and videos to find the answers you need quickly.

With a subscription, you can read any page and watch any video from our library online. Read books on your cellphone and mobile devices. Access new titles before they're available for print, and get exclusive access to manuscripts in development and post feedback for the authors. Copy and paste code samples, organize your favorites, download chapters, bookmark key sections, create notes, print out pages, and benefit from tons of other time-saving features.

O'Reilly Media has uploaded this book to the Safari Books Online service. To have full digital access to this book and others on similar topics from O'Reilly and other publishers, sign up for free at *http://my.safaribooksonline.com*.

Part One: Word

1

Basic Word Processing

With Word 2007, Microsoft completely overhauled its world-famous electronic typewriter. Gone were menus that buried commands two or more levels deep. In their place were tabs and the ribbon, a dynamic, turbo-charged toolbar that put the most common tasks out in plain view as easy-to-find buttons. Word 2010 improves on this model, letting you work with documents even more efficiently and giving you easy-to-find, detailed information about your document with Backstage view.

This chapter gets you up to speed—fast—with Word 2010 basics. Learn where everything is onscreen; find out how to create, save, and open documents; and check out the different ways to view your creations. Whether you're looking for a quick refresher or a step-by-step guide to getting started with Word, you'll find it here.

Opening Word

You can open Word in several different ways, depending on how you installed it, but the most common method is clicking the lower-left Windows Start button. From the menu that appears, select All Programs→Microsoft Office→Microsoft Word 2010. Word opens, displaying the screen shown in Figure 1-1.

If you've opened Word recently, it appears as an option on the Start menu; if that's the case, save yourself some menu burrowing and just click Start→Microsoft Word 2010. You can also open Word by opening a document you've been working on. In Windows 7, click Start→Documents, and then select the one you want from the Documents library. Alternatively, click Start and then click the right-pointing arrow next to Microsoft Word 2010. This opens a list of documents you've saved recently; make your pick and Word launches automatically.

Quick Access toolbar

Title bar

Minimize Ribbon button

Minimize, Restore, and Close buttons

Tabs

The Ribbon

Help button

View Ruler button

Status bar

View buttons

Zoom controls

Figure 1-1:
The Word 2010 screen features the ribbon, which gathers together er related buttons for common tasks. Click any tab's name—File, Home, and so on—to change the ribbon to show buttons related to that tab.

If your computer has Windows Vista, then click Start→Recent Items to see a list of all the files you've worked with recently; choose a Word document from the list to open Word.

Tip: In Windows 7 and Vista, you can *pin* (permanently affix) a program you use regularly to the Start menu, making it easy to find. Click Start, right-click the program you want to pin (such as Word), and then select Pin to Start Menu from the shortcut menu that appears. Pinned programs always appear at the top of the Start menu, above a horizontal line that separates them from recently used (but unpinned) programs. In Windows 7, you can also pin a program to the taskbar, giving you one-click access to the program.

If you're a Word 2007 veteran, the biggest change you'll notice in the Word screen—and you'll notice it right away—is that the upper-left Office button has disappeared. Replacing it is the File tab, a blue tab on the left side of the screen. (It's always blue, no matter which tab you've selected.) The File tab brings back a souped-up version of the File menu you may remember from earlier versions of Word. Clicking this tab gives you what Microsoft calls the Backstage view of your document, shown in Figure 1-2; what you see on the main part of the screen depends on which menu item you select. You'll be seeing more about Word's Backstage view as you read on, but it's more or less what you'd expect: choices that let you open, print, share, and so on.

The Word 2010 Screen

Here's a quick guided tour of the Word 2010 screen, starting in the upper left:

- **The Word button.** Clicking this tiny W-in-a-box opens a menu that lets you resize the Word window or close the program entirely.

- **Quick Access toolbar.** No matter which tab you select, the Quick Access toolbar remains visible at the top of the screen, giving you easy access to frequently used buttons. The standard icons on this toolbar are Save, Undo, and Redo, but you can customize it with your own personal faves. (Page 889 tells you how.)

- **Title bar.** Across the top of the screen, the middle section shows you the name of this document—handy when you're working on several files at once. If the document is one you just created, the title bar shows Document1 or Document2 (and so on), until you've saved and named your work.

- **Minimize, Restore, and Close buttons.** These upper-right buttons give you a one-click way to work with the currently open window:

  — **Minimize.** Click this to make your document disappear from the screen without closing the file. Word shrinks your document down to nothing but leaves its button on the taskbar. To summon it again, click that taskbar button.

  — **Restore Down/Maximize.** This resizes the window that displays your document. When the button shows two overlapping windows, then the Word screen is at full size; click the button to shrink the window. When the button shows a single window (as in Figure 1-1), the window isn't taking up the full screen; click the button to maximize the window.

Tip: You can resize the Word window by hand so it's exactly the size you want. Click the Restore Down button to make the window smaller. Then position the mouse pointer along the window's border so it becomes a two-headed arrow. Click and, while holding down the mouse button, drag the window to the size you want. Then let go of the mouse button.

— **Close.** Click this button to close the current window.

Note: If you have just one document open, clicking the upper-right Close button closes Word as well as the document.

- **Minimize Ribbon button.** The ribbon (described below) takes up a fair chunk of screen space. If you want to see more of your document as you work on it, click the upper-right Minimize Ribbon button. When you do, the ribbon disappears, leaving just the tabs across the top of the screen. To bring the ribbon back, click the button again—or simply click whichever tab you want to use.

Tip: A quick way to minimize the ribbon (and expand it again): Press Ctrl+F1.

- **Help button.** Click the Help button when you want to search or browse through Microsoft's built-in Word help center.
- **Ribbon.** The ribbon shows the most commonly used buttons associated with a certain task. Each task gets its own tab name, listed along the top of the ribbon:
  - **Home.** This tab gathers together buttons you'll use most often as you write, divided into these sections: Clipboard (page 38), Font (page 47), Paragraph (page 54), Styles (page 51), and Editing (page 41).
  - **Insert.** Modern documents hold more than words and paragraphs. This tab has buttons for inserting just about anything you might want: Pages (page 155), Tables (page 81), Illustrations (page 96), Links (page 170), Header & Footer (page 73), Text (for special text effects, page 109 and page 202), and Symbols (page 61).
  - **Page Layout.** Here's where you format your writing canvas and, if you want, give it a theme, with buttons in these sections: Themes (page 181), Page Setup (page 65), Page Background (page 68), Paragraph (page 54), and Arrange (page 107). That last item has commands for positioning images and graphics in your document.
  - **References.** This tab helps you work with long, formal documents, thanks to these sections: Table of Contents (page 173), Footnotes (page 158), Citations and Bibliography (page 163), Captions (page 99), Index (page 174), and Table of Authorities, which sounds like where you don't want to sit at a school banquet but is actually a list of references common in legal documents.
  - **Mailings.** One of the great advantages of word processing is how easy it makes mass mailings. This tab makes sending out a mailing even easier, thanks to the buttons in these sections: Create (page 142 for printing envelopes and page 147 for labels), Start Mail Merge (page 148), Write & Insert Fields (page 154), Preview Results (page 154), and Finish (page 154).

— **Review.** The buttons on this tab help you check your document to make sure it's correct before sending it out into the world. It also groups together some super-helpful collaboration tools. Here's what's on it: Proofing (page 115), Language (page 128), Comments (page 219), Tracking (page 223), Changes (page 226), Compare (page 228), Protect (page 230), and One-Note (page 862).

— **View.** Click the View tab for different ways of looking at your document as you work on it. Here you'll find Document Views (page 26); Show to show or hide the ruler (page 15), table gridlines, and the Navigation pane (page 42); Zoom (page 29); and Window (page 32).

— **Add-Ins.** *Add-ins* are programs that beef up Word's ability to work even harder for you, adding custom commands and specialized features. For example, your company might add a special template for certain documents. If your copy of Word has any add-ins, they appear on this tab.

Click any tab, and the ribbon changes to show the sections and buttons on that tab.

Tip: Some sections of the ribbon have more options than the ribbon can show. When that's the case, you see a pop-out icon, which looks like a square with a diagonal arrow pointing outward, in the section's lower-right corner. Click the icon to open a dialog box that gives you all the options for that section.

- **View Ruler button.** Word's ruler measures your document and shows indenting and tabs. To display it (or hide it again), click this button on the right side of the document window.

- **Scroll bars.** Just as you'd expect: These babies let you navigate up and down through your document.

- **Status bar.** Across the bottom of the Word screen is the status bar, which gives you information about the current document. Standard info includes what page you're on and how many pages and words make up the document; you can also customize the status bar (page 893 tells you how).

- **View buttons.** As page 26 explains, Word can display your document in one of five different views: Print Layout, Full Screen Reading, Web Layout, Outline, and Draft. You can select any of these views from the View tab, or just click one of these buttons on the right-hand side of the status bar.

- **Zoom level button.** This button shows you whether you're viewing the text in the document at normal size (100%), larger, or smaller. Click the button to open the Zoom dialog box (page 30) and adjust the text viewing size.

- **Zoom controls.** To increase or decrease text size even faster than clicking the Zoom button, use this slider—just drag the pointer to the left or right. Slide to the left to zoom out (making text smaller); slide to the right to zoom in (making text bigger). For more about zooming, see page 29.

Note: Zoom controls don't change the font size of the text in your document; they just let you get a closer look or take a longer view of what's on the page.

Using Keyboard Shortcuts

If you've used earlier versions of Word, you know how much faster you can work by keeping your hands on the keyboard. (That way, you can just keep typing, rather than having to reach for the mouse, move it around, click a few times, reposition your fingers—and then repeat the whole ordeal each time you need a command.) So you may have learned certain keyboard shortcuts, such as Ctrl+C for copy and Ctrl+V for paste. You'll be pleased to know that these shortcuts work are alive and kicking in Word 2010.

Starting with Word 2007—and continuing in Word 2010—Microsoft has revamped the keyboard shortcut system, and it stars the Alt key. No longer do you have to remember dozens of keystroke combinations. Just click Alt, and Word shows you which key to press to perform the task you want, as shown in Figure 1-3. For example, if you want to choose a task from the File menu, press Alt, then F (you don't have to hold the keys down at the same time) to open that menu. Similarly, to do something on the Review tab, press Alt, then R. Each option on the menu or ribbon is labeled with its own shortcut key, so you know what to press next.

To hide the labels, simply press Alt again or click anywhere on the screen.

Figure 1-3:
When you press the Alt key, little word- and number-labels sprout onscreen, indicating keyboard shortcuts. Here, for example, press N to open the Insert tab, P to open Page Layout, and so on.

Creating a New Document

It doesn't get much easier: Just open Word from the Start menu, and a fresh, new, blank document, called Document1, appears with a blinking cursor at the beginning of the first line. All you need to do is start typing.

Note: Opening Word directly from the Start menu creates a new blank document. But if you've *already* opened Word (or if you opened Word by opening an existing document), then you need to use one of the methods below to create a new document.

To create a new document after you've opened Word, use any of these methods:

- Create a new blank document.
- Create a new document from a template.
- Create a new document from an existing document.

The sections that follow show you how.

Creating a New Blank Document

If you've already got Word open and want to create a new document, simply press Ctrl+N (think *N* for *new*). Doing so opens a window with a new blank document. Or follow these steps:

1. **Click File→New (Alt, F, N).**

   The Available Templates pane opens with "Blank document" already selected, as shown in Figure 1-4. In the right pane, Word previews what the blank document you're creating will look like. It's a big, empty rectangle, just like a blank page.

2. **In the right pane, under the blank document, click Create (or, if you've got keyboard shortcuts turned on, press N). Alternatively, you can double-click "Blank document".**

   Word creates a new blank document. You're good to go.

"Blank document" is
already selected.

Click to create a new
blank document.

Figure 1-4:
*When you create a
new document, you
can start off with a
blank document or
choose a template or
an existing document
as the basis for your
new one.*

Creating a New Document from a Template

Imagine you return from lunch to find an email from the boss in your inbox: "We need 15 award certificates for tonight's banquet. Attached is the list of recipients and awards."

Oh, great. You have an idea of what an award certificate looks like, but you've never made one before—let alone 15. Never fear. Word comes to the rescue with a huge variety of prebuilt templates. A *template* is a reusable model for a document, with specialized formatting already built in. For an award certificate, for example, the template already has formatting to make it horizontal (landscape orientation) and to center and space the text. Use the template as a starting point, tweak it to meet your needs, add your information—and you're done. You'll have the stack of award certificates printed out in no time. (Chapter 5 tells you everything you need to know about printing documents.)

Tip: Word 2010 comes with some templates built right in, but Microsoft keeps a much larger selection of Word templates online at *http://office.microsoft.com*. You can find and download these templates right from Word, so for the widest selection make sure your computer is connected to the Internet before creating a new document using a template.

To create a new document from a template, follow these steps:

1. **Click File→New (Alt, F, N).**

   The Available Templates pane (Figure 1-4) opens. Templates take up most of this pane.

2. **Click "Sample templates" to see the ones preloaded in Word. (If you've recently created a document using a template, you can also look in "Recent templates" or "My templates".) If you're connected to the Internet, look in the Office.com Templates section for a wide variety of all kinds of templates: Find a category that fits the template you want, and click that category. (If the category is a folder, it holds more than one template.)**

   Word shows you the available templates in whatever category you chose.

3. **To see what any template looks like, click it.**

   Word previews the template in the right pane, as shown in Figure 1-5.

4. **To use a template as the basis for your new document, click the Create button (for a preloaded template) or the Download button (to get the template from Office.com).**

   Word creates a new document using the template you chose. Now you can type your own information into the template.

Figure 1-5:
Templates give you preformatted documents for a wide variety of purposes, like the award certificates shown here. Click any template to see a preview of it in the right pane; if it looks good, click Download to create a new document based on that template.

Tip: If you're online, you can also search for a template. On the right side of the bar that says Office.com Templates, type the word or phrase you want to search for into the Search box. Press Enter or click the right-pointing arrow. Word shows you all templates related to your search term.

Creating a New Document from an Existing Document

If there's a document format you use frequently—such as a meeting agenda, a report, a memo, whatever—you can use an existing version of that document to create a brand new one. For example, say it's your job to create the agenda for the weekly departmental meeting. Instead of starting from scratch each week, just use an agenda you've already created as the basis for a new one. The format and some placeholder text are already there; just fill in the new information—and save yourself a lot of time. Here's how:

1. Click File→New (Alt, F, N).

    Word opens the Available Templates pane.

2. Click "New from existing" (keyboard shortcut: Press X).

    The New from Existing Document dialog box opens, showing folders and documents, as you can see in Figure 1-6.

3. **Navigate to the document you want. Double-click a folder to open it and see the documents it contains. Double-click the document you want to use to create your new document (or click the document to select it, and then click the Create New button). Alternatively, if you know the name of the document you want, type its name into the "File name" box and click Create New.**

Word opens the document you selected—but as a new document. If you selected "Agenda 10-14-10", for example, Word doesn't show that filename in the title bar. Instead, it shows "Document2" (the number will vary, depending on how many new files you've created this session). Word has made a copy of Agenda 10-14-10, so any changes you now make happen to the new file, not to the original on which Word based the copy. Type in whatever new information you want, and then save the document with a new name (the next section tells you how).

Figure 1-6:
To create a new document from an existing one, find the document you want to use as the basis for your new document (use the left-hand pane to change folders). Select a file, and then click Open.

Typing in Some Text

This part's easy. Just place your fingers on the keyboard and type away. The cursor, a blinking vertical line, shows where the text will appear as you type. You can move the cursor with the mouse (put the mouse pointer where you want it, and then click to make the cursor jump there) or by using the arrow keys and navigation keys (Page Up, Page Down, Home, and End).

As you type, Word automatically moves to the next line when you reach the end of the current one (this is called *wrapping*). To start a new paragraph, press Enter.

If you make a mistake, use the Backspace and Delete keys to erase characters. Backspace deletes the character immediately to the left of the cursor, and Delete deletes the character immediately to the right of the cursor. Or you can select text (holding down the mouse button, drag the cursor across the text you want to select) and then press either Backspace or Delete to make that text disappear. You can also delete text by typing new text over it: Select what you want to delete, and then type its replacement text.

Tip: Flip to page 35 to learn the many different ways you can select text in Word.

Saving a Document

After you've created a document and typed in some text, you need to save your work. Whether you're retaining the document for posterity or because you want to work on it again later, the advice is the same: Save early, save often. In order to do so, you need to first give it a name and tell Word where to store it. Word offers a bunch of different ways to perform this safety dance, and this section explains 'em all.

Saving a Document Using Your Mouse

You can use your computer's mouse or your laptop's touchpad to save a document using Word's menu commands. When you're ready, use one of these methods:

- **On the Quick Access toolbar, click Save.** The Save button looks like an old-fashioned floppy disk (um, maybe it's time for a new icon designer?). If you click this button to save a document that you haven't yet saved, Word opens the Save As dialog box shown in Figure 1-7. If you've already named the document and saved it once, Word does a quick save of the document as it exists right now, no dialog box required.

- **Click File→Save.** This opens the Save As dialog box (Figure 1-7), where you can name and save the file. If you've already saved the file at least once, Word saves the file *without* opening the dialog box.

- **Click File→Save As.** Whether or not you've already saved the document, this opens the Save As dialog box (Figure 1-7). This option is handy when you want to save a previously saved file with a new name or in a different file format. For example, if you opened up your novel-in-progress (a filed called, say, "Vampires.docx," and proceeded to add a new lead villain, you could use Save As to create a new file called "Wolves and Vampires.docx." That way you preserve the first vampire-only version and create a separate dual-beast version.

Saving a Document Using Keyboard Shortcuts

If you want to do a quick save to make sure Word is keeping up with you as you type, using keyboard shortcuts is the way to go; just press a couple of keys and get on with your typing. You can quickly save a document using any one of these keyboard shortcuts:

- **Press Ctrl+S.** If you haven't yet saved the document, this opens the Save As dialog box (Figure 1-7). If you've already saved it, this key combination saves the current version of your document.

- **Press Alt, 1.** This is the same as clicking the Save button on the Quick Access toolbar.

- **Press Alt, F, S.** This is the same as clicking File→Save.

- **Press Alt, F, A.** This is the same as clicking File→Save As.

Using the Save As Dialog Box

However you open the Save As dialog box, here's how to use it:

1. **Open the Save As dialog box using one of the methods described earlier.**

   The dialog box looks like the one in Figure 1-7.

Figure 1-7:
To save a file, choose a location, give the file a name, and then click Save. If the dialog box looks a little crowded to you, then click the lower-left Hide Folders button to streamline it by hiding the left-hand navigation pane.

2. In the left pane, double-click the folder where you want to store the document.

   The center pane shows all the documents in that folder.

3. In the "File name" text box, type in a name for your document.

   Word uses the first few words of your document to guess at a name, but you can call the document whatever you want.

4. From the "Save as type" menu, select the file type you want for this document. The box on page 24 explains about file types. Click Save.

   Word saves your document.

Tip: If you save a lot of documents in a format other than Word's standard .docx format, you can choose that format as the default. Click File→Options (Alt, F, I) and then choose Save. In the "Save documents" section, use the "Save files in this format" dropdown list to choose the file type you want as your standard. Click OK. From now on, Word saves all your documents as this type, unless you tell it otherwise when you save.

Closing a Document

When you're done working on a document, Word gives you several different ways to close it:

- Click the X in the upper right.
- Click the upper-left Word button, then select Close.
- Press Alt, F, C.
- Press Alt+F4.

If your document has unsaved changes, Word shows a dialog box asking if you want to save those changes. Make your pick:

- **Save.** This tells Word to save the changes and close the document.
- **Don't Save.** When you click this button, Word discards your changes and closes the document.

Note: A new feature in Word 2010 helps you avoid forehead smacks when you accidentally close a document without saving your changes. If you choose Don't Save when closing your document and Word has autosaved the document at least once, it temporarily hangs onto the autosaved version as a draft (for a week), just in case you change your mind and want it later.

To see whether there's a saved version of a document you closed without saving, click File→Recent (Alt, F, R). At the bottom of the screen, click Recover Unsaved Documents. You see the Open dialog box (Figure 1-8) with a list of all the recent documents you saved without closing. Select the document you want, and click Open to open it. If you want to keep the draft this time, save it in the usual way (page 21).

- **Cancel.** If you change your mind and don't want to close the document right now, this button keeps the document open so you can continue to work on it.

File Types in Word

Word lets you create and save documents in a variety of different formats, called *file types*. Different file types work with different programs; for example, .docx files work with Word 2007 or later, and .pdf files work with Adobe Acrobat (and other programs that can read this format). You can tell a document's file type by the file extension that appears at the end of its name, such as *Chapter 01.docx* or *Chapter 01.pdf*. In Word 2010, you can save files as any of these types:

- **Word Document (.docx).** Microsoft introduced this as the standard document format starting with Word 2007. The format made it easier for different Office 2007 programs to exchange information and enhanced security it offered, mainly by forbidding macros, a series of prerecorded commands and shortcut routines that could be abused by hackers to infect documents.

- **Word Macro-Enabled Document (.docm).** Although macros could represent a security risk, they can also be useful in helping you automate common tasks (as page 193 explains). A .docm file is a Word 2007 or 2010 document that allows you to create and use macros.

- **Word 97–2003 Document (.doc).** Pre-2007 versions of Word can't read the .docx or .docm format without a special compatibility pack installed. If you plan to share your document with someone who has an older version of Word, save the file in this format, or get your pals to install the compatibility pack; details here: *http://tinyurl.com/2xp8e3*. (Word 2010 can read .doc files just fine, so you won't have any compatibility issues with this format.)

- **Word Template (.dotx, .dotm, or .dot).** If you want to save a document as a template to use as a model for creating future documents, select one of these formats. (Flip to Chapter 7 to learn more about working with templates.) The .dotx format works with Word 2007 and 2010, as does the .dotm format, which lets you use macros in the document. If you're saving the template to work with Word 97–2003, use the .dot format.

- **PDF (.pdf).** Portable document format (PDF for short) is a standard file format that accurately preserves your formatting, making it easier to exchange documents electronically. Many of the publications and forms you can download from the Internet are in this format.

- **XPS Document (.xps).** XPS, which stands for *XML paper specification*, is another fixed-layout file format. Like PDFs, XPS files keep their format when someone views or prints them.

- **Web Page (.htm).** If you want to display a document on the Internet as a web page, this is the file type to choose. It formats the document to make it look good on the Web. Chapter 8 tells you more about publishing a document as a web page.

- **Rich Text Format (.rtf).** This format, designed to be compatible with many different word processing programs, holds the text and some formatting information.

- **Plain Text (.txt).** If you want to save your text without formatting—for compatibility with programs like Notepad and other simple text editors—use this file type.

- **Word XML Document (.xml).** XML stands for extensible markup language, which is a text format for structuring documents to make them easier to share between applications and on the Web.

- **OpenDocument Text (.odt).** This file type uses the OpenDocument standard to create a file that you can open and edit in Word, OpenOffice.org's Writer and many other word-processing programs, including StarOffice, NeoOffice Writer, AbiWord, Kword, and LotusNotes 8 or later, as well as online word processors such as Google Docs and Zoho Writer.

- **Works 6.0–9.0 (.wps).** Microsoft Works is a smaller, stripped-down version of Office that Microsoft stopped selling in 2009, replacing it with Office Starter 2010. Still, many people used Works as a cheaper alternative to Office, so if you need to share a document with someone who uses Works, save it in this format.

Opening an Existing Document

Say you're working on a report. You created the document, typed in some text, saved it, and closed it when you left work for the day. The next morning, you're ready to crack it open again. Here's how to find the document you want and open it, so you can get back to work:

1. **Click File→Open. (Ctrl+O or Alt, F, O.)**

   The Open dialog box, shown in Figure 1-8, appears.

2. **Navigate to the folder and file you want to open.**

   When you double-click a folder, Word displays its contents in the center pane. Select a file by clicking its name.

3. **Click Open.**

   Word opens the document.

Figure 1-8:
To open a document, navigate to the file you want and click the lower-right Open button.

Tip: For a shortcut to opening a document you've worked with recently, click File→Recent (Alt, F, R) to see a list of recent files. Click any file (or, if you're using keyboard shortcuts, type its number) to open the document.

When you open a document in the way just described, you open it as a normal document that you can read and edit in Word. But you also have a few *other* options. To see them, follow steps 1 and 2 above, then click the downward-pointing arrow to the right of the Open button. These are your choices:

- **Open.** This opens the document as usual, so that you can read and edit it.

- **Open Read-Only.** When you select this option, you can read the document but not make any changes to it.

- **Open as Copy.** This copies the file and opens that duplicate, rather than the original. If the original file had the title "Smith Report," the new file gets named "Copy(1)Smith Report." (When you save the new file, you can give it whatever name you like.)

- **Open in Browser.** If you saved a document as a web page (page 24), then you can open it in a web browser (like Internet Explorer or Firefox) instead of in Word.

- **Open with Transform.** When you open an XML file (page 24) in Word, this command determines which data makes it into the Word document. The Transform option works like a filter: If the Transform can't work with some of the data in the file you open, then that data doesn't make it to the open file. You might use Transform to create a list of products and prices, for example, automatically filtering out the data you don't want instead of doing it by hand. When you use Open with Transform to open an XML document, click the Transform button to choose the Transform you want to apply.

- **Open in Protected View.** When you open a file from an iffy source, like the Internet or an email attachment from someone you don't know, this option opens a read-only copy that can't run any malicious code that might harm your computer.

Note: When you open a document you downloaded from the Internet or got as an email attachment, Word automatically opens the file in Protected view, telling you this via a yellow bar above the document. If you trust the document's source, click the yellow bar's Enable Editing button to work with it in the normal way.

- **Open and Repair.** If you can't open a file because Word tells you it's been damaged, try this option.

- **Show Previous Versions.** When you choose this option, Word searches for earlier versions of the file and displays them in a list. Select a version from the list, and click Open to open the older version. See page 228 for more about comparing different versions of a document.

Different Ways to View Your Work

Word gives you numerous options for viewing your document, so you can choose the view that lets you work best on the task at hand. If you're writing the first draft of a report, for example, you want to focus on what you're writing, and you might choose Draft view. Later, when you're ready to print the report, you might switch to Print Layout view to make sure the margins, headers, and page numbers look the way you want them to on the page. Or if the report is long, with lots of headings and subheadings, and you want to check how it's shaping up, Outline view gives you a high-level look at its organization. These are just some of the ways you can view a document in Word—read on to learn about them all.

To look at a document in one of Word's views, click the View tab, shown in Figure 1-9, and then choose the view you want. Or click a view in the lower-right part of the screen—they open the same views. Going from left to right, these are Word's view options:

- **Print Layout (Alt, W, P).** This layout is the standard view for a Word document, the one you see when you start the program and the one most folks use. It shows the document laid out like a physical page, including the edges of the page, margins, headers and footers, page numbers, and so on. This what-you-see-is-what-you-print view lets you make sure the document looks the way you want it before you send it to the printer (page 135).

- **Full Screen Reading (Alt, W, F).** In Full Screen Reading View, the ribbon, its tabs, the status bar, and the scroll bars all disappear so you can concentrate on the text. The view also zooms out so you see a full page on the screen. To navigate through the pages, click the arrows at the top of the screen or in the lower-left and -right corners of the pages. To switch from this view back to Print Layout view, click the upper-right Close button. (Clicking Close doesn't close the document, only this view.)

Tip: Full Screen Reading view lets you choose what you see on the page. When you're in this view, click the upper-right View Options button to select Show One Page, Show Two Pages, or Show Printed Page.

- **Web Layout (Alt, W, L).** To see how your document would look as a web page, choose this view. It removes page breaks and shows text and images as they'd appear if you posted this document on the Web—as one long scrolling page.

- **Outline (Alt, W, U).** This view gives you an overview of your document, collapsing it into outline format. Outline view emphasizes headings and subheadings and treats paragraphs like subsections—so you need to use it in a document that has headings, or this view won't make much sense. This view can be useful when you're working on a long document; switch to Outline view to see the document's sections and check its organization, then go back to Print Layout or Draft view to work on the text.

- **Draft (Alt, W, E).** If you want to focus on what you're writing—not how it will look on the page—try Draft view. This view fits more text on the screen because it doesn't show margins, headers, footers, or page numbers, and it marks page breaks with a dotted line. Draft view does show other formatting, however, like font and line spacing, so you can see what you're doing if you apply, for example, italics or underlining.

Figure 1-9:
Your options for viewing a document appear on the left side of the View tab. The tiny illustration on each button gives you an idea of what the view looks like.

Viewing a Document in the Navigation Pane

New to Word 2010 is the Navigation pane, which provides a high-level map of your document. To turn on the Navigation pane, click View (Alt, W). In the ribbon's Show section, turn on the Navigation Pane checkbox. This opens the Navigation pane on the left side of your screen, as shown in Figure 1-10.

Outline view in the Navigation pane

If your document has headings to introduce sections and subsections, click the Navigation pane's Outline tab to see just those headings in the pane, as shown in Figure 1-10. Each heading is a button you can click to jump to that section in your document. It's a fast way to find your way through a long document.

Figure 1-10:
The Navigation pane helps you find what you're looking for with a high-level view of your document. In Outline view (shown here), click any heading to jump to that section in the document. To close the Navigation pane, click its upper-right X or turn off the View tab's Navigation Pane checkbox.

Page view in the Navigation pane

To find and jump to a particular page, click the Navigation pane's middle tab. The pane switches to a view that lets you browse your document page by page, as shown in Figure 1-11. Pages in the pane appear in Print Layout view and are numbered; click any page to move to that page in the document.

Tip: The Navigation pane is also home to Word 2010's supercharged new search function. Read more about how to find a word or phrase in your document on page 41.

Figure 1-11:
Use the Navigation pane to browse through the pages of your document; click any page to jump there.

Zooming In and Out

You don't have to get a headache squinting at the screen, trying to make out words written in a teensy-tiny font. And neither do you have to spend time scrolling back and forth to read lines written in a large font. Instead, just zoom in or out to make the text the perfect size for your peepers. Zooming doesn't change the font size; it just gives you a close-up or bird's-eye view of the words on your pages. This section will have you zooming in and out in no time.

Using the Zoom slider

The Zoom slider appears in the lower-right corner of the Word screen. A pointer indicates the current magnification. When the pointer is in the middle of the slider, the document is at 100 percent. But you can make the text appear larger or smaller:

- To **magnify** the text, click the pointer and, holding the down the mouse button, drag the pointer to the right. As you drag, the text gets bigger. When it reaches the size you want (the maximum on the slider is 500 percent), let go of the mouse button. The text remains the size you've selected.

- To **reduce** the text, click the pointer and hold down the mouse button as you drag the pointer to the left. The farther left you go, the smaller the text gets, all the way down to 10 percent. When it's the size you want, let go of the mouse button.

Tip: Instead of clicking and dragging, you can zoom in or out in 10 percent increments by clicking the plus sign (to magnify) or the minus sign (to reduce) on either end of the slider.

Using the Zoom dialog box

The Zoom slider is great for quick adjustments in and out. If you prefer, you can also zoom using the Zoom dialog box, shown in Figure 1-12, which gives you more options and more precision. To open it, click View→Zoom (Alt, W, Q). Or you can click the current zoom percentage in the lower-right part of the screen (it's just to the left of the Zoom slider).

Figure 1-12:
Use the Zoom dialog box to zoom in and out with precision, or to show multiple pages on the screen.

In the Zoom dialog box, you've got a couple of different ways to change your view:

- **By percentage.** Word offers three popular zoom settings: 200 percent, 100 percent, and 75 percent. Turn on the radio button for the size you want. Or set the size in the Percent box: Click the up and down arrows to change magnification, or double-click the number in the box and type in the percentage you want. Click OK to zoom.

- **By width/size.** If thinking in terms of percentages makes your head hurt, you can zoom using one of these plain-English options instead:

    — **Page width.** Choose this to make the page as wide as possible on your screen (you can still see the page's margins).

    — **Text width.** This option makes the text even bigger than page width by showing lines of text but not margins or the edges of the page.

    — **Whole page.** Choose this if you want to shrink down the text to display a single page, from top to bottom and left to right, on the screen. You may not be able to read the text at this size, but (believe it or not) you can still edit it.

    — **Many pages.** With this option, you can display multiple pages on the screen at one time. Click the button underneath "Many pages" (it shows a computer monitor displaying multiple pages) to select how many pages you want to see. When you click that button, a menu opens showing two rows of four pages across, as shown in Figure 1-13. Move the mouse pointer to select the number of pages you want, and then click it.

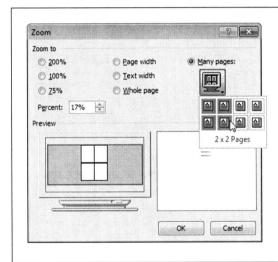

Figure 1-13:
To see multiple pages at once on your screen, use the mouse to choose the number of pages and the layout you want to see.

As you make choices in the Zoom dialog box, the Preview section gives you an idea of the size of the text and how the page will appear on your monitor. When everything looks good, click OK to apply your selection.

Working with Multiple Windows

Using multiple windows can speed up your work exponentially. Instead of having to switch back and forth between two different windows showing two different Word documents, you can show them both on the same screen. That way, you can compare different drafts of the same document or easily copy text from one document into another. You work with multiple windows from the View tab's Window section, shown in Figure 1-14. Click View (Alt, W) and then choose one of these options:

- **New Window (Alt, W, N).** This opens another copy of the current document in a new window, which can come in handy when you're working on a long document and you need to see two different sections of it at the same time. For example, if Section 3 develops a topic you touched on briefly in Section 1, you might want to see both sections at the same time to make sure they're in sync. When you open the same document in a new window, you can move through each one independently and any change you make to the document in one window also happens in the other. Nice.

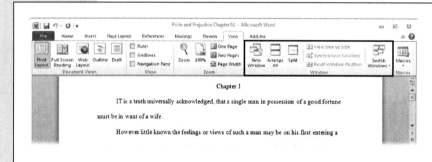

Figure 1-14:
The buttons in the View tab's Window section let you work with more than one document, or with different sections of the same document, at once.

- **Arrange All (Alt, W, A).** When you're working with two windows, it takes a lot of mouse-clicking to jump back and forth between them. It'd be a lot easier to see both windows on the same screen, and that's what the Arrange All button is for. When you click it, Word resizes the windows for all open documents and shows them on the same screen, as shown in Figure 1-15. Each resized document window gets the same amount of screen space. To devote the full screen to any one window again, click its upper-right Maximize button.

- **Split (Alt, W, S).** Use the Split button to divide a document's window horizontally, giving it an upper and a lower scroll bar. After you've split the screen, use the scroll bars to move through each part of the document independently—for example, hold your place in the document's Introduction while you check that

Chapter 2 covers the all topics it's supposed to. When you click Split (or press Alt, W, S), Word draws a horizontal line across the screen. Use the mouse to position the line where you want the screen to split, and then click there. Word splits the screen and creates a second scroll bar. To go back to a single screen, click View→Remove Split (Alt, W, S).

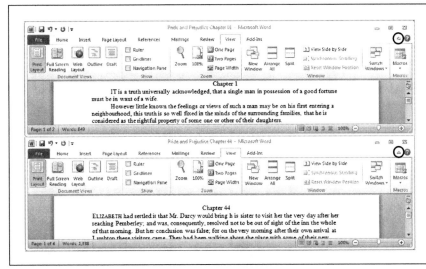

Figure 1-15:
Arrange All shows you two or more documents at once. If the screen looks a little crowded, click the upper-right Minimize Ribbon button (circled) in either or both documents so you can read more text.

- **View Side by Side (Alt, W, B).** When you choose this option, Word resizes your documents' windows and displays them side by side, as shown in Figure 1-16. When you view your documents this way, Word automatically turns on synchronous scrolling (View→Window→Synchronous Scrolling or Alt, W, ZW, VS), so that when you scroll through one window, the other window scrolls right along with it. (If you don't want synchronous scrolling, you can toggle it off by clicking View→Window→Synchronous Scrolling or pressing Alt, W, ZW, VS.) While the windows are side by side, you can resize them if you want, perhaps making one larger to see a little more of its text. To restore the side-by-side windows to their original sizes, click View→Window→Reset Window Position (Alt, W, ZW, T).

***

Tip: When you use New Window to open the same document in two different windows, use Arrange All or View Side by Side to see both windows on the same screen.

***

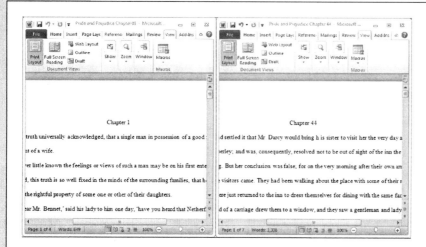

Figure 1-16:
When you view two documents side by side, Word squeezes the ribbon so you can still see all its sections. Click the arrow in any section to see its buttons.

Note: When Word arranges two document windows side by side, it has to squeeze the ribbon so everything fits. In Side by Side view, you won't see all the buttons for each section of the ribbon. To see the buttons for a particular section, click the down arrow beneath the section's name, and Word opens the toolbar for that section. And if you're using keyboard shortcuts, there'll be an extra command in the sequence to open the section before you can choose a button.

Editing and Formatting

W ay back in prehistoric times, when cave-dwellers hunted woolly mammoths by day and hunched over firelit typewriters at night, editing text was a difficult chore. If you made a mistake, you had to get out the messy correction fluid and paint over it. If you wanted to move a paragraph, you had to type your text all over again from scratch. And forget about varying fonts with italics or boldface. Not gonna happen on a typewriter.

Word processing has made life *way* easier for anyone who's ever had the urge to put words on paper. And Word 2010 takes "easy" to a whole new level. You can format your text in any font, size, or color; move words, sentences, paragraphs, and sections wherever you want 'em; and quickly search for, find, and replace words and phrases (and Word 2010's new Navigation pane makes searching faster and more powerful than ever before). This chapter shows you how to get things looking the way you want them, whether you're italicizing a single word, adding a header or footer, inserting a list, or formatting the entire document.

Selecting and Moving Text

First things first: You have to grab the text you want to move or change. The surefire, old-school way is by using your mouse. Position its pointer at the start of your selection and click. Holding down the mouse button, drag the pointer over your selection. As you drag, Word highlights the text, as shown in Figure 2-1. When you're finished dragging, let go of the mouse button.

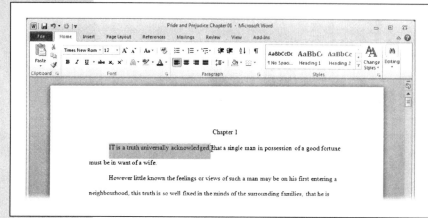

But don't forget that there are *plenty* of other options, a few of which will save your wrists some serious wear and tear. Depending on what you're selecting, you can do any of the following:

- **Select a word.** Double-click any word to highlight it.

- **Select a sentence.** Position the mouse pointer over the sentence you want, and then press the Ctrl key and click.

- **Select a line.** Move your mouse pointer into the left margin beside the line. When the pointer turns into an arrow, click. Line selected; neato.

- **Select a paragraph.** Position your mouse pointer in the left margin next to the paragraph (as though you were going to select a line). When the pointer turns into an arrow, double-click, and Word selects the entire paragraph. Alternatively, triple-click anywhere in a paragraph to select the whole thing.

- **Select any block of text.** Move the mouse pointer to the start of the text you want. Click to position the cursor there. Holding down the Shift key, move the mouse pointer to the *end* of your selection, and then click again. Word selects the text between the two spots where you clicked. This one should be in the Selection Hall of Fame; it's saved serious wordsmiths a *ton* of time.

- **Expand a selection.** You didn't drag the mouse *quite* far enough when you selected some text and left off the last couple of letters of a word. Happens to the best of us. Good news: You don't have to start over again. If you want to expand the selection beyond the end of your current selection, hold down the Shift key and use the mouse to select more text. You can either click and drag, or click at the point where you want the expanded selection to end.

- **Select the entire document.** Click Home→Select→Select All.

Tip: To select several different chunks of text in different places, select the first piece of text you want. Then hold down the Ctrl key as you make your next selection. This is a great way, for example, to italicize a bunch of different phrases in one fell swoop.

Keyboard shortcuts are another option, sparing you from having to fumble around with that sometimes-hard-to-position mouse. Here's what you can do:

- **Select one character at a time.** Place the cursor at the start of your selection, and then hold down the Shift key as you use the left or right arrow key to make a selection. As long as you continue to hold down the Shift key, you can press the arrow key multiple times (or hold it down) to expand your selection, selecting as much text as you want.

- **Select a word.** Use the arrow keys to put the cursor at the start or end of the word you want to select. Press Ctrl+Shift+left arrow to select the word to the left of the cursor; press Ctrl+Shift+right arrow to select the word to the right of the cursor.

- **Select a line.** Position the cursor at the start of the sentence you want, then press Shift+End to select the entire line. This also works the other way: Put the cursor at the end of the line you want to select and press Shift+Home.

Tip: You can also select any part of a line using the keyboard. Put the cursor where you want your selection to start, then press Shift+End to select to the end of that line or Shift+Home to select to its beginning.

- **Select a paragraph.** Put the cursor at the start of the paragraph you want to select and press Ctrl+Shift+down arrow. (Or place the cursor at the end of the paragraph and press Ctrl+Shift+up arrow.)

- **Select any block of text.** Position the cursor at the beginning or end of your selection. Holding down the Shift key, use the arrow keys or the navigation keys (Home, End, Page Up, Page Down) to select the text you want.

- **Select the entire document.** Press Ctrl+A to highlight everything in your document. Or work with the ribbon's keyboard shortcuts: Press Alt, H, SL, A.

Finally, one last way to select text using the keyboard with the F8 key, way up at the top of your keyboard:

- **Set a selection point.** When you press the F8 key, you create a starting point for selecting. From then on, if you use the arrow keys, the navigation keys, or the mouse, Word selects text from that starting point. After you've made your selection, press Esc to stop selecting.

- **Select a word.** Put the cursor on the word you want to select and press F8 twice.

- **Select a sentence.** Position the cursor on the sentence you want, and then press F8 three times to select it.

- **Select a paragraph.** With the cursor in the paragraph you're selecting, press F8 four times.

- **Select an entire document.** Press F8 (you guessed it) five times.

Tip: Although this section talks about selecting text, the methods described here work just as well for *other* elements you might have in a document, such as pictures, charts, videos, and tables. Chapter 3 explains more about working with these elements.

Four Ways to Move Text

Now that you know every single way ever invented to *select* text, what do you once you've grabbed it? Moving it—either to another place in the current document, into a new document, or even into a different program (an email, for example)—is a popular option. Here's what you need to know to make *that* happen.

If you're moving text to a spot close to its current location, the quickest route is to start by selecting the text you want and then letting go of the mouse button. Next, with the mouse pointer over your selection (anywhere over the highlighted region is fine), click and hold down the mouse button. The mouse pointer becomes an arrow with a small square at the bottom, as shown in Figure 2-2. Still holding the mouse button down, move the mouse pointer to the text's new location. Let go of the mouse button, and the text you selected jumps to the new spot. It might sound complicated, but it's simple once you try it out.

Note: Behind the scenes, Word lets you move text in this (and plenty of other) ways by temporarily placing the text on the *Clipboard*, a holding area that stores text you've cut or copied so you can insert it somewhere else. When you *copy* text, the original selection remains in place, but Word places an exact copy of it on the Clipboard. When you *cut* text, Word deletes the selection and puts a copy on the Clipboard. When you insert text from the Clipboard somewhere else, you're *pasting* that text.

Word gives you several other ways to move text around. Some use the mouse; others use the keyboard. Try them out for yourself and see which works best for you.

Option 1: Use the Ctrl key

A super-fast, super-easy way to move text is to select the text you want, and then use one of these keyboard shortcuts:

- Ctrl+C to copy.
- Ctrl+X to cut.

Then move the cursor to the place where you want to insert the text, and press Ctrl+V to paste it there.

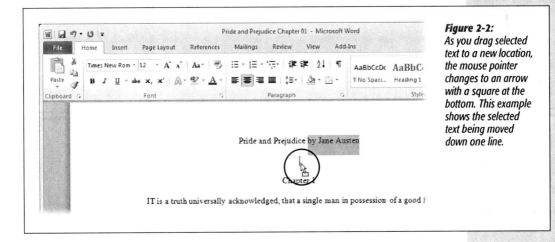

Option 2: Right-click your mouse

After you've selected the text you want to move, right-click your mouse. A shortcut menu like the one shown in Figure 2-3 appears. From the menu, select Cut (if you want to delete the selection from its current spot) or Copy (if you want to keep the selection where it is).

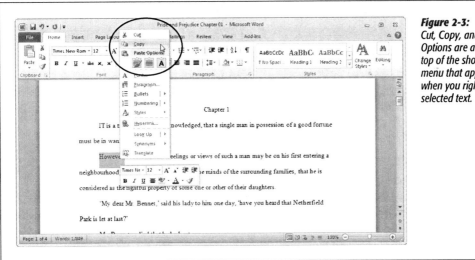

Figure 2-3:
Cut, Copy, and Paste Options are at the top of the shortcut menu that appears when you right-click selected text.

Next, position the cursor at the selection's new location. Right-click to bring up the shortcut menu again. Here you have three options for pasting:

- **Keep Source Formatting.** Choose this if you want the pasted text to keep its original formatting (font, size, and so on—page 47 tells you more about text formatting).

- **Merge Formatting.** If you want the text to *match* the formatting of the text where you're pasting it, then this is the option you want.

- **Keep Text Only.** Choose this if you want to paste words—and only words—without any fancy formatting. Keep Text Only strips out any images, as well as headings, hyperlinks, and styles. Lists and tables get converted to regular paragraphs. You end up with words and paragraphs that have the same formatting as the document you're pasting into.

Option 3: Use the Home tab

This option is for folks getting paid by the hour; it works, but it sure does take time. To copy or cut text using the ribbon, select the text you want to move and then click the Home tab (shown in Figure 2-1). In the Home tab's far-left Clipboard section, click Cut (which looks like a pair of scissors) or Copy (which looks like two sheets of paper). If you prefer, you can press Alt, H, X to cut and Alt, H, C to copy. Word copies your selection to the Clipboard.

Next, place the cursor where you want the text to appear. On the Home tab, click Paste (Alt, H, V). A button appears; click it to choose the formatting option you want: Keep Source Formatting (K), Merge Formatting (M), or Keep Text Only (T). Word applies your choice as it pastes in the selection.

Tip: If you don't want to choose one of these options every time you paste, click File→Options (Alt, F, I) to open the Word Options dialog box. There, choose Advanced and, in the "Cut, copy, and paste" section, turn off the checkbox labeled "Show Paste Options button when content is pasted." Click OK.

Option 4: Use the Clipboard pane

Word keeps track of the text you've copied or cut—up to 24 different selections—by placing it on the Clipboard. You can find any of these snippets on the Clipboard, and from there paste the text into your document. Say you're creating a program for a conference, and you're copying names from a list of speakers and pasting them into the sessions where they'll be speaking. You copy Anne Adams and paste her name into Session 1, and then go on to copy and paste the speakers' names for Sessions 2 and 3. When you get to Session 4, you see that Anne Adams is scheduled to speak again. You can open the Clipboard, find her name, and paste it in from there.

To find text you've put on the Clipboard, click the Home tab and, in the far-left Clipboard section, click the pop-out icon in the section's bottom-right corner (it's just after the word "Clipboard"). Or press Alt, H, FO. Doing so opens the Clipboard pane, shown in Figure 2-4. The pane shows text you've placed on the Clipboard by cutting or copying. Put the cursor where you want to insert the text, and then find what you want to insert (you may have to scroll down in the Clipboard pane to find it). As you move the mouse pointer over each snippet on the Clipboard, a downward-pointing arrow appears to its right. Click the arrow beside the snippet you want. When you do, two options appear:

- **Paste.** Click to paste the selection into the document at the insertion point you chose.

- **Delete.** Click to remove the text from the Clipboard.

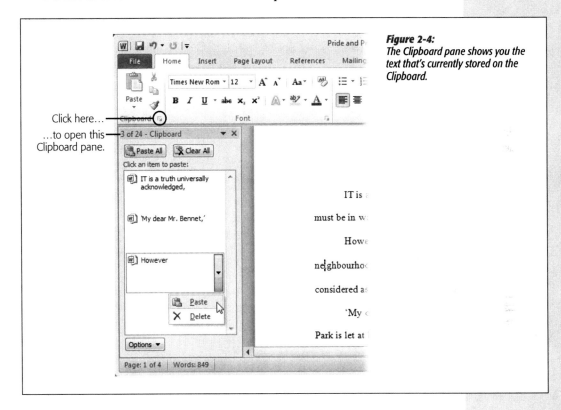

Click here...
...to open this Clipboard pane.

Figure 2-4:
The Clipboard pane shows you the text that's currently stored on the Clipboard.

Finding and Replacing Text

In a long document, manually searching for a particular word or phrase can be like hunting for the proverbial needle in a haystack. When you're seeking out every instance of a word or phrase in a printed document or book, you need a highlighter, a sharp eye, and a jumbo-sized helping of patience. But when you let Word do the searching for you, you've got that word or phrase at your fingertips in a matter of seconds. And if you're searching for text because you need to replace it—because you want to correct the spelling of someone's name, for example—you can find and replace your search term just as fast.

Searching with the Navigation Pane

New to Word 2010, the Navigation pane helps you find the word or phrase you're looking for faster and more efficiently, by showing you all instances of the term in context. Here's how to use it:

1. **In the document you're searching, click Home→Find (Alt, H, FD, F).**

    The Navigation pane opens on the left side of the screen, as shown in Figure 2-5.

2. **In the Navigation pane's Search box, type the word or phrase you want to find.**

    Even as you type, Word searches for matching text. It displays matches (in context, wherever they occur) in the main part of the Navigation pane and highlights them in the text. If you continue to type, Word refines its results when you pause again.

3. **Scroll through the Navigation pane's results to find the particular instance you're looking for. Click the result you want.**

    Word jumps to that phrase, highlighting it, in the document.

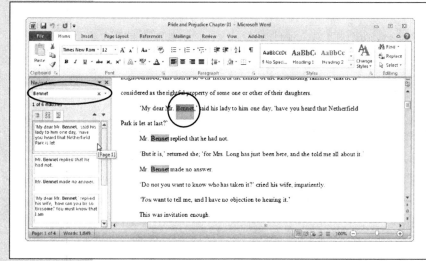

Figure 2-5:
Type a word or phrase into the Navigation pane's Search box (circled) to find all matches in the document. As you pass the mouse pointer over the results, Word shows you the page on which each result appears. Click any match to jump right to it (also circled) in the document.

Tip: One of the great benefits of the Navigation pane is that you can use it to search for more than just text. In Word 2010, you can search for graphics, tables, and equations, too. Chapter 3 tells you more about hunting down these items.

Setting Search Options

Searching for a word like "tweet" is straightforward enough. But what if you're writing a report on *The Internet and Birdcalls* and want to find just the spot where you mention your firm's Chief Tweet Officer—and not all the dozens of other instances of plain old, lowercase "tweet"? Head to the far-right side of the Navigation pane's Search box; from the shortcut menu that appears, choose Options. This opens the Find Options dialog box, shown in Figure 2-6, where you can fine-tune your search with plenty of search options:

- **Match case.** Normally, Word ignores upper- and lowercase letters when it searches. If case is important—for example, you're looking for the month "May," not the verb "may"—then turn on this checkbox.

- **Find whole words only.** A search returns partial matches if this checkbox is turned off. So a search for "but" returns "butcher," "butter," "butler," "abut," and so on. If you want your results to list *only* the word you typed, turn on this checkbox.

- **Use wildcards.** In poker, when deuces are wild, they can stand in for any card. In Word, wildcards work the same way—they stand in for any character or group of characters. When you turn on this checkbox, a question mark (?) serves as a wildcard for any character, and an asterisk (*) serves as a wildcard for any group of characters. So "wa?" returns "wad," "was," "war," and similar words, and "w*t" returns "wart," "what," "wait," "went," "warrant," "widget," "without," and so on.

- **Sounds like (English).** Not great at spelling? You'll love this option. Turn on this checkbox, type in your search term—sounding it out the best you can— and Word shows you matches that sound like what you typed. With this option turned on, a search for "poseshun" finds "possession," for example.

- **Find all word forms (English).** With this turned on, you can search for "have" and get all forms of that verb—"has," "have," "had," "having"—in your results.

- **Highlight all.** When this checkbox is turned on, Word highlights all your search term's matches in the document. If you turn it off, Word highlights a match only as you click on it in the Navigation pane's results.

- **Incremental find.** This checkbox, turned on by default, tells Word to start searching for text even as you type in your search term.

Note: To use incremental find, you have to have the "Highlight all" checkbox turned on.

- **Match prefix.** This is a good choice when you've got a word on the tip of your tongue and can only remember how it starts. Turn on this checkbox to find matches to the beginnings of words—for example, if you want a search for "pe" to return "petunia," "pert," and "pecunious," but not "ape" or "type."

- **Match suffix.** This matches the ends of words. So you'd turn it on if you want to find all words that end in "ing," such as "standing" and "running," but don't want results like "ingot" or "twinge."

- **Ignore punctuation characters.** Turn this on when you want Word to ignore hyphens, apostrophes, and other punctuation marks when searching. For example, searching for "backup" would include "back-up" in the results.

- **Ignore white-space characters.** When turned on, this checkbox tells Word to ignore spaces, tabs, paragraph marks, and other nonprinting characters in its search, so a search for "rundown" would include "run down" in the results.

Turn on the checkbox of any option you want to apply to your search. If you want your future searches to retain these options, click Set As Default. To use the settings just for this session, click OK.

Figure 2-6:
Use the Find Options box to refine your search.

Searching with the Traditional Find and Replace Dialog Box

If you prefer the familiar Find and Replace dialog box from previous versions of Word, you can still search that way in Word 2010. To bring it up, just follow these steps:

1. **Click Home→Find (Alt, H. FD, F).**

   Word opens the left-hand Navigation pane.

2. **At the right side of the Search box, click the downward-pointing arrow beside the magnifying glass.**

   A shortcut menu appears.

3. **Select Find.**

   Word opens the Find and Replace dialog box, shown in Figure 2-7, with the Find tab selected.

4. **Type in the word or phrase you want to search for, and then click Find Next.**

   Word jumps to the next match to your search term and highlights it.

5. **If this is the match you want, click Cancel to close the Find and Replace dialog box. If it's not the one you're looking for, keep clicking Find Next until Word has jumped to the right one. When you're finished, click Cancel.**

   Word closes the Find and Replace box.

Type your search term here...

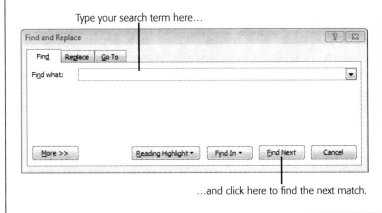

Figure 2-7:
*If you're familiar with the Find
and Replace box from earlier
versions of Word, you can still
use it to search for text in Word
2010. Type in the word or phrase
you want to find, and then click
Find Next to jump to the next
instance.*

...and click here to find the next match.

Tip: To refine your search, click the More button. The Find and Replace box expands, showing you the same choices you get when you open the Find Options dialog box in the Navigation pane (minus "Highlight all" and "Incremental find").

If you want Word to highlight all examples of your search term in the document, follow steps 1–3 above. In step 4, after you've typed in your search term, click Find In, and then select Main Document. Word highlights all matches and tells you how many it found.

Tip: To find all matches within a limited section of the document, select the part of the document you want to search, and then follow steps 1–3 above. In step 4, type in your search term, click Find In, and then choose Current Selection. Word finds all matches for the term in the part of the document you selected.

Replacing Text

You're on page 374 of your novel when inspiration strikes and you know you just *have* to change the main character's name from Eleanor to Fifi. Instead of combing through all of those hundreds of pages, hunting for each instance of "Eleanor," you can make the change globally, throughout the whole document, with just a few clicks. To find all instances of a search term and replace it with something else, follow these steps:

1. **With the document open, click Home→Replace (Alt, H, R).**

   Word opens the Find and Replace dialog box, with the Replace tab selected, as shown in Figure 2-8.

2. In the "Find what" box, type the word or phrase you want to replace. (In the novel example, you'd type *Eleanor*.) Below it, in the "Replace with" box, type the word or phrase you want to replace it with (*Fifi* in the example). Click Replace All (Alt+A).

   Word replaces all instances of the "Find what" term with the "Replace with" term and shows a dialog box telling you how many replacements it made.

3. Click OK. If you're done searching and replacing for now, click Close.

   Word closes the Find and Replace dialog box.

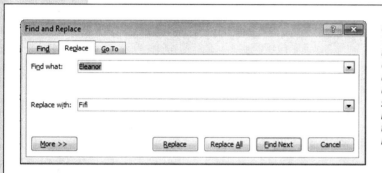

Figure 2-8:
To find all instances of a search term and replace each and every one with something different, click Replace All. To decide whether to replace the search term on a case-by-case basis, click Replace to replace this instance and then go to the next one.

What if you don't want to replace each and every instance of the search term? For example, imagine you've been working on a personnel report, and you realize that you've misspelled Bob Browne's name all the way through, typing it as "Brown." But you can't just replace all instances of "Brown" with "Browne," because then Samantha Brown's name would be wrong. You need to see each instance in context before you decide whether to replace it.

To go through a document one match at a time, replacing some instances of the search term but not others, do this:

1. With the document open, click Home→Replace (Alt, H, R).

   Word opens the Find and Replace dialog box, with the Replace tab selected, as shown in Figure 2-8.

2. In the "Find what" box, type the word or phrase you want to replace. Below it, in the "Replace with" box, type the word or phrase you want to replace it with. Click Find Next (Alt+F).

   Word jumps to the next instance of your search term, highlighting it.

3. If you want to replace this instance of the search term, click Replace (Alt+R). If you want to leave the search term as it is, click Find Next (Alt+F) again.

   When you click Replace, Word replaces the search term with the new term and jumps to the next match. When you click Find Next, Word leaves the search term as it is and jumps to the next match.

Tip: As you move through the document, the Search and Replace box jumps around quite a bit. So you don't have to keep repositioning the mouse pointer, use the keystroke combinations to move more quickly through your document.

4. **Keep clicking Replace or Find Next (or pressing Alt+R or Alt+F).**

   When Word has found all instances of your search term, it shows a dialog box that says, "Word has finished searching the document."

5. **Click OK, and then click Close.**

   Word closes the Find and Replace dialog box.

Tip: Want to jump to a particular page? You can get there via either the Navigation pane or the Find and Replace box. Open the Navigation pane (Home→Find or Alt, H, FD, F) and click the down arrow on the search box's right side, then click Go To. Or select Home→Replace (Alt, H, R); in the Find and Replace dialog box, click the Go To tab. Type in the page number you want, click Next, and you're there.

Text Formatting: Font, Size, and Style

Okay, so you've cut what needed cutting, moved those out-of-place passages to where they made more sense, and changed all the main characters' names once—and then back again. Now it's time to make all your text look as pretty as your prose sounds. Word's many formatting options let you control things like font style, size, and color. Use its powers to emphasize certain words and phrases, to add special effects, and to make your document attractive and easy to read.

The Home Tab's Control Center

The Home tab's Font section, shown in Figure 2-9, is the place to go if you're looking for every formatting option Word offers. First, select the text you want to format. Then, click Home (or press Alt, H) to make the ribbon show these options:

- **Font (Alt, H, FF).** Use this drop-down list to choose from the wide variety of fonts that come preloaded in Word. Each font name in the menu appears in that font's style, so you get a preview of how your text will appear.

- **Font Size (Alt, H, FS).** Click the arrow to choose a standard font size ranging from 8 points to 72 points, or double-click inside the box and type in a different number.

- **Grow Font (Alt, H, FG).** Click this button to increase the size of selected text. The more you click, the bigger it gets.

- **Shrink Font (Alt, H, FK).** Click this button to decrease the size of selected text, all the way down to 1 point (which is pretty much illegible).

Figure 2-9:
*The Home tab's Font
section is where you
make formatting
choices for your
document's text.*

- **Change Case (Alt, H, 7).** When you click this button, you get four choices:
  - — **Sentence case.** This option capitalizes the first word of each sentence in the selection, just like your fourth-grade teacher taught you in English.
  - — **Lower case.** The *I'm-too-cool-for-school* special: Choose this to make every letter in the selection lower case.
  - — **Upper case.** Choose this to make every letter in the selection A CAPITAL LETTER.
  - — **Capitalize each word.** This option makes the first letter of each word uppercase. (In previous versions of Word, this option was called "title case.")
  - — **Toggle case.** This option reverses the existing cases in the selection, capitalizing lowercase letters and making capital letters lowercase.
- **Clear Formatting (Alt, H, E).** Use this option to remove all formatting from the selection.
- **Bold (Alt, H, 1 or Ctrl+B).** This option makes the selection **bold**.
- **Italic (Alt, H, 2 or Ctrl+I).** This option makes the selection *italic*.
- **Underline (Alt, H, 3 or Ctrl+U).** This option adds <u>underlining</u> to the selection. If you want to get fancy with dashed, wavy, or dotted lines or by making the underlining a different color from the rest of the text, click the downward-pointing arrow to the right of the button and make your selections from the menu that opens.
- **Strikethrough (Alt, H, 4).** This button puts a horizontal line through the middle of your text, ~~like this~~.
- **Subscript (Alt, H, 5).** Handy for math and science writing, this option makes the selected text smaller and drops it below other characters: H_2O.
- **Superscript (Alt, H, 6).** This shrinks the selected text and raises it above the other characters, like this: $E = MC^2$.
- **Text Effects (Alt, H, FT).** Snazz up your text with outlining, shadows, reflections, and glow effects in different colors. When you click this button, you get a menu of choices, each one illustrated so you can see how the effect will look before you apply it.

- **Text Highlight Color (Alt, H, I).** Just like the highlighting markers that students use to draw attention to important passages in a textbook, this option gives the selected text a colored background (click the down arrow to choose the color you prefer).

- **Font Color (Alt, H, FC).** Click this button to choose a color that makes the selected text stand out.

Copy Formatting with Format Painter

It can take some work to format text: You make a selection and then keep clicking buttons until you've got the font, size, color, and any extras you want. If you've got some formatting just so in one section of your document and want that same formatting elsewhere, save yourself a boatload of time by copying the formatting and applying it where you want it. To do this, use Word's Format Painter, which copies just the formatting details of some text—not the text itself—and then "paints" that formatting onto other text.

To use the Format Painter, follow these steps:

1. **Select the text whose formatting you want to copy. Then click Home→Format Painter (Alt, H, FP).**

   The mouse pointer changes to a cursor with a paintbrush, as shown in Figure 2-10.

2. **Select the text whose formatting you want to change by clicking and dragging over the text. When you've made your selection, let go of the mouse button.**

   Word changes the formatting of the text to match the formatting you copied.

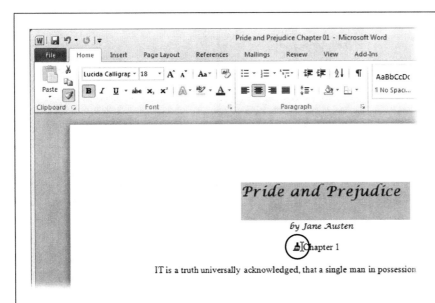

Figure 2-10:
You can tell you're using Format Painter because your cursor changes to an I-bar with a paintbrush.

Tip: To copy the same formatting to several locations in your document, select the formatting you want and then *double-click* the Format Painter button. Format Painter stays turned on until you press Esc, click Format Painter again, or save your changes.

Quick Formatting with the Mini Toolbar

Word 2007 introduced the Mini Toolbar, a fast, on-the-spot way to format text without having to click a tab and change the ribbon. When you select some text, an almost-transparent toolbar appears just above it. As you move the mouse pointer toward the toolbar, it solidifies (as shown in Figure 2-11) and you can click any of its buttons to format the text. The options on the Mini Toolbar are those that people use most commonly to format text (explained starting on page 47):

- Font
- Font Size
- Grow/Shrink Font
- Decrease/Increase Indent
- Bold
- Italic
- Underline
- Center
- Text Highlight Color
- Font Color
- Format Painter

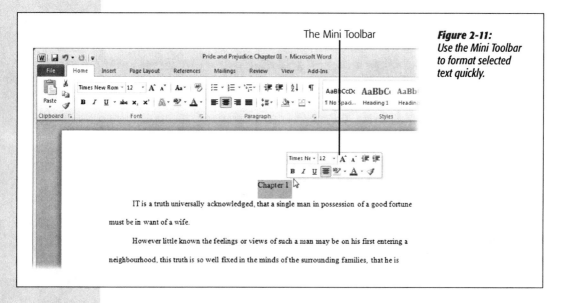

The Mini Toolbar

Figure 2-11:
Use the Mini Toolbar to format selected text quickly.

Click any button to apply the formatting to the text you've selected. To make the Mini Toolbar disappear, click elsewhere in the document. To bring it back, select some more text.

Tip: Some people don't like seeing the ghostly Mini Toolbar floating above text they've selected. To prevent it from appearing, click File→Options (Alt, F, I). In the "General options for working with Word" dialog box, turn off the "Show Mini Toolbar on selection" checkbox, and then click OK.

Formatting Power with Styles

In long documents—reports, novels, lists of George Foreman's kids named "George"—you often need to format certain elements the same way over and over again. For example: chapter and section titles, regular paragraph text, picture captions, whatever. *Styles* let you define reusable formatting collections that are great ways to help create a consistent look. Best of all, if you ever change your mind—you want a sidebar title, say, to be 18-point red Courier rather than 12-point blue Arial—just change the style definition, and those changes get made across all items using that style. What a timesaver.

Styles appear on the Home tab, as you can see in Figure 2-12. But the menu of styles that appears on the ribbon is only part of the story. Click the down arrow to scroll through styles, or the More button just below it (Alt, H, L) to see a menu of styles.

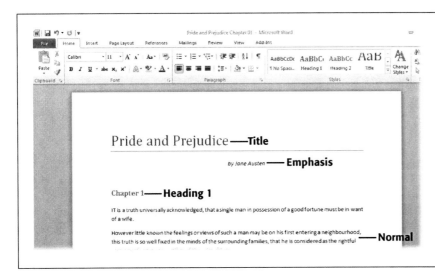

Figure 2-12:
Styles give your document a consistent look by letting you reuse predesigned formatting.

Styles work on the paragraph level, affecting all the text in that paragraph. (In Word, when you type something and then press Enter, that's a paragraph—even if you've typed only a single word or line.) To apply a style, put the cursor anywhere in the paragraph whose text you want to format (or select several paragraphs) and click

Home, and choose a style from the Styles section. (You can also press Alt, H, L and use the arrow buttons to move through the style options) As you move through the menu from one style to the next, Word changes your selected text to match that style. Click or press Enter to apply a style to your text.

Tip: To see all the styles you can apply to text in your document, open the Home tab and click the pop-out button in the Styles section's lower-right corner (Alt, H, FY) or press Alt+Ctrl+Shift+S. This opens the Styles pane, shown in Figure 2-13, which lists styles alphabetically by name. Apply any style by clicking it. When you're using a lot of styles in a document, you can work faster by keeping this window open and quickly applying styles as you need them.

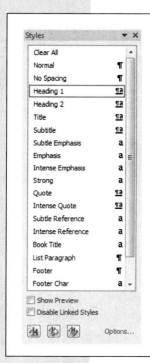

Figure 2-13:
The Styles pane lets you apply any style to your text with a single click.

Applying styles using style sets

The styles that appear in the Home tab's Styles section or in the Styles pane all belong to a *style set*—a group of predesigned and preformatted styles that work together to give your document a unified look and feel. If your document looks a bit boring to you, give it a makeover by dressing it up in a different style set.

To browse Word's style sets, click Home→Change Styles→Style Set (Alt, H, G, Y). This opens the menu shown in Figure 2-14. Each style has a name—Elegant, Fancy,

Formal, Modern, and so on—that gives you a sense of its feel. Use your mouse pointer (or use the arrow keys) to take a look at each style; when you move to a style, the document changes to show you how that style set looks in your document (Microsoft calls this Live Preview). When you find the style you want to use, click it or press Enter. Word applies the style to your document and changes the styles in the Home tab's Styles section to match your choice.

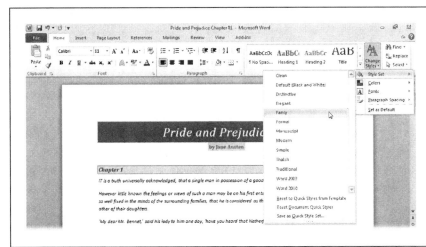

Figure 2-14:
With Live Preview, you can see how different style sets will format your document before you apply them.

Tip: The standard style set in Word 2010 is called, not all that imaginatively, Word 2010. If you find a style set you prefer, you can make it the standard for your Word documents. Apply the new style set to a document and then choose Home→Change Styles→Set as Default (Alt, H, G, S).

Creating your own style set

If none of Word's style sets meet your needs, you can let your inner text designer out to play by creating your own style set. The easiest way to do this is to start with one of Word's style sets as a baseline and then tweak it to customize.

To customize an existing style set, start by opening a document that has a bunch of different styles, such as titles, subtitles, headings, body text, and so on. Then follow these steps:

1. **Select Home→Change Styles→Style Set (Alt, H, G, Y).**

   The menu of current style sets (shown in Figure 2-14) appears.

2. **Move through the menu, using Live Preview to get a look at the different styles. When you find one that's close to the style set you want to create, select it.**

   Word uses the style set you selected to set the current document's styles.

3. **Change the style set's color scheme by selecting Home→Change Styles→Colors (Alt, H, G, C).**

   A menu appears that shows Word's built-in color schemes. Use Live Preview to see how the different schemes look. If you find one you like, click or press Enter to apply it. Or select Create New Theme Colors to create your own color scheme. (Page 182 goes into detail about how to customize theme colors in Word.)

4. **Choose the fonts you want the style set to use by selecting Home→Change Styles→Fonts (Alt, H, G, F).**

   The menu of built-in fonts shows both the name and a sample of each built-in font group. As you browse the list, you get a preview of how each group of fonts looks in the document. Select one (click or press Enter) or select Create New Theme Fonts to choose the fonts you want to use for headings and body text, creating your own font group.

5. **Set paragraph spacing by clicking Home→Change Styles→Paragraph Spacing (Alt, H, G, P).**

   Going from tightest to most open, the options include compact, tight, open, relaxed, and double. Choose one of these or select Custom Paragraph Spacing to fine-tune the line and paragraph spacing (page 58) for this style.

6. **When you're finished, click Home→Change Styles→Style Set→Save as Quick Style Set (Alt, H, G, Y, Q).**

   A dialog box opens, asking you to name the style.

7. **Type your new style's name into the "File name" text box, and then click Save.**

   Word saves your new style set and adds it to the menu of style sets, making it easy to find the next time you want to use it.

Paragraph Formatting: Aligning, Indenting, Spacing

Ever wonder what it'd be like if books and other documents featured a single, never-varying, long block of text? It's no picnic, which is why doing things like adjusting a paragraph's width, its line break style, and specially formatting its opening line all make a huge difference in the reader's experience. Your control center for such matters is the Home tab's Paragraph section, shown in Figure 2-15.

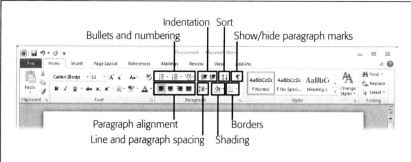

Figure 2-15:
The Home tab has several buttons you can use to format paragraphs. If you're not sure what constitutes a "paragraph" in Word, click the "Show/hide paragraph marks" button to see where each paragraph ends.

Aligning Text

Word offers four kinds of alignment options, all of them on the Home tab's Paragraph section, shown in Figure 2-15:

- **Left (Alt, H, AL).** This makes the paragraph's text line up on the left side only, leaving it ragged on the right. This is the most common kind of alignment and works well for all kinds of writing: reports, essays, school papers, letters, stories, and other documents.

- **Center (Alt, H, AC).** This lines up the paragraph down the center, so each line is of equal length to the left and right of that point. Centered text is good for titles and headings but also for invitations and programs.

- **Right (Alt, H, AR).** Right-aligned text lines up along the right side of the paragraph and is ragged on the left side. You might use right alignment to line up a column of numbers, for example, or to offset a quotation you're using as an epigraph.

- **Justified (Alt, H, AJ).** Justified text lines up along both the right and left margins. Many business documents, formal reports, and books use this kind of justification.

Figure 2-16 shows an example of each alignment style.

Figure 2-16:
Here's the same paragraph using Word's four different alignment options.

Indenting Paragraphs

Paragraphs don't always need to line up evenly along the page's left margin. This section shows you how to tweak their appearance, if you're so inclined.

Indenting the first line of a paragraph

Some document formats, such as manuscripts and academic reports, require that the first line of each paragraph be indented. (This kind of indentation often goes with double-spacing; page 58 shows you how to adjust line spacing within a paragraph.) To indent the first line of a paragraph, use one of these methods:

- **The ruler.** The ruler lets you manage indentation, tabs, and margins. To see Word's rulers (the horizontal ruler just below the ribbon and the vertical ruler along the left side—shown in Figure 2-17)—click the View Ruler button just above the vertical scroll bar. Or click View and, in the Show section, turn on the Ruler checkbox (Alt, W, R). With the ruler displayed, set indentation by clicking the First Line Indent marker and dragging it wherever you want. Do this with a new, blank document to indent every paragraph as you type.

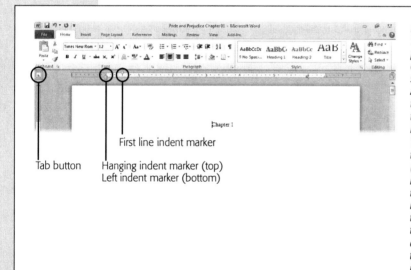

First line indent marker

Tab button   Hanging indent marker (top)
              Left indent marker (bottom)

Figure 2-17:
To indent the first line of a paragraph, use the ruler or create a tab. Word has several kinds of tab stops: A left tab (shown here) sets the start position of the text; a center tab (which looks like an upside-down T) sets the position of the text's center; a right tab (which looks like a mirror reflection of a left tab) sets the position of the text's right side—as you type, the text moves left. A decimal tab lines up numbers by decimal point, and a bar tab doesn't position text—it inserts a bar at the tab position.

- **Tabs.** If you're used to indenting paragraphs by hitting the Tab key at the start of each new paragraph, you can use that method in Word. Display the ruler and make sure that the Left Tab button (it looks like the letter L) appears at the left side of the screen. If you see a different tab button, keep clicking it until you see the L. (Those tab buttons that *don't* look like an L? Figure 2-17 has the scoop.)

Then click the horizontal ruler where you want to set the tab. A tab mark (which also looks like the letter L) appears where you clicked. Now when you start a new paragraph, pressing the Tab key makes the cursor jump to the spot where you set the tab.

- **The Paragraph dialog box.** If you find it hard to click and drag the ruler's tiny First Line Indent marker, try this method. On the Home tab, click the Paragraph section's lower-right pop-out button (Alt, H, PG) to open the Paragraph dialog box, shown in Figure 2-18. In the Indentation section, click the Special drop-down list and select "First line". Word automatically sets the indentation to half an inch; if you want, you can adjust the amount of indentation in the By box. Click OK to indent the paragraph.

Tip: You can also change a paragraph's indentation by using the Page Layout tab. Click Page Layout; in the Paragraph section, change the number in the Left box (Alt, P, IL) to increase the indentation or the Right box (Alt, P, IR) to decrease the indentation.

Indenting an entire paragraph

If you want to emphasize a paragraph by setting it off from the rest of the text, you can indent it. Block quotations often get set off in this way.

To indent a paragraph, put the cursor in the paragraph you want to indent, and then click Home→Increase Indent (Alt, H, AI). The paragraph jumps five spaces to the right—if that's not indented enough, click the button or press the shortcut keys again.

If you want to get rid of a paragraph's indentation, click Home→Decrease Indent (Alt, H, AO).

Tip: If you prefer, use the Paragraph dialog box (Figure 2-18) to indent an entire paragraph. Use the Left and Right boxes to adjust the amount you want the paragraph indented on each side, and then click OK.

Creating a hanging indent

For this kind of indent, often used in bibliographies, only the first line of the paragraph begins at the left margin, and subsequent lines are indented.

There are two ways to create a hanging indent:

- **To create a hanging indent using the ruler,** display the ruler and drag its Hanging Indent marker (shown in Figure 2-17) to the place where you want it. Release to apply the hanging indent.

- **To create a hanging indent using the Paragraph dialog box,** open the dialog box (on the Home tab, click the Paragraph section's lower-right pop-out button or press Alt, H, PG). In the Paragraph dialog box's Indentation section (shown in Figure 2-18), go to the Special drop-down list and select Hanging. If you want, adjust the size of the indentation in the By box. Click OK to indent your paragraph.

Figure 2-18:
The Paragraph dialog box lets you adjust a paragraph's indentation and spacing. At the bottom of the dialog box, the Preview pane shows how your changes will look.

Spacing Within a Paragraph

You can make your document shorter, longer, or easier to read by adjusting the spacing between a paragraph's lines. If you like to print out a hard copy of a draft (read Chapter 5 to learn about printing in Word) and edit it up with a red pen in hand, for example, then you might want to use double or even triple spacing between lines. Later, you can print out the final version with single or one-and-a-half spacing.

The Line and Paragraph Spacing button lives in the Home tab's Paragraph section, as shown back in Figure 2-15. To set the spacing for a particular paragraph, select the one you want to adjust (or press Ctrl+A to select the whole document), and then click Home→Line and Paragraph Spacing (Alt, H, K). From the menu that opens, choose the line spacing you want. As you move your mouse pointer over the choices, the paragraph changes to give you a preview of what that spacing looks like. Click the spacing you want to apply it to your document.

If you don't see the spacing option you want, click Line Spacing Options to open the Paragraph dialog box, shown in Figure 2-18, and fine-tune the line spacing in the Spacing section, keeping an eye on the Preview pane to see how your choices will appear in the document. When your spacing is all set, click OK to apply it.

Spacing Between Paragraphs

Adding a little space between paragraphs makes your pages easier on readers' eyes and improves the flow of your document, making it clear where each paragraph starts and ends. To increase or decrease the amount of space between paragraphs, click Home→Line and Paragraph Spacing→Line Spacing Options (press Alt, H, K, use the down arrow to select Line Spacing Options, and then press Enter). This opens the Paragraph dialog box (Figure 2-18). In the Spacing section, use the up and down arrows to adjust how much space Word inserts before or after each paragraph. Or you can double-click inside the Before or After box and type the number you want. Spacing between paragraphs is measured in points—to give you an idea of what that means, there are 72 points in an inch.

If you don't want Word to insert space before or after two paragraphs of the same style (page 51)—for example, you want extra space between headings and body paragraphs but not between the paragraphs themselves—turn on the checkbox labeled "Don't add space between paragraphs of the same style." Click OK to apply your spacing.

To do a quick insertion of extra space before or after a paragraph, place the cursor anywhere in the paragraph you want and then click Home→Line and Paragraph Spacing→Add Space Before Paragraph or Add Space After Paragraph (Alt, H, K, B or A). When you do, Word throws in an extra 10 points of spacing where you indicated.

Tip: You can also adjust spacing between paragraphs from the Page Layout tab. Click Page Layout and use the Paragraph section's Before box (Alt, P, SB) or After box (Alt, P, SA) to change the spacing.

Working with Lists

Some people organize their lives by lists: to-do lists, shopping lists, top 10 lists…if something crosses their mind, they put it in a list. Lists are a great way to organize information and present it in an easy-to-read format, and Word makes creating and formatting lists a snap.

Word's Home tab has buttons for three kinds of lists:

- **Bulleted list.** This kind of list marks each item with a bullet or other symbol (like an arrow or a checkmark).

- **Numbered list.** Good for instructions or expressing priorities, this kind of list begins each item with a number.

- **Multilevel list.** Choose a multilevel list to give your list hierarchical sections. Use this kind of list for an outline or a document where each new paragraph is a new section or subsection.

Whichever kind of list you choose, Word makes sure your list looks good, taking care of spacing and keeping track of any numbering or levels.

Creating a List

To create a list, click the Home tab and, in the Paragraph section, click the button for the kind of list you want, as shown in Figure 2-15. Or use these keyboard shortcuts:

- **Bulleted list:** Alt, H, U
- **Numbered list:** Alt, H, N
- **Multilevel list:** Alt, H, M

When you use keyboard shortcuts, these keystroke combinations open a formatting menu for the kind of list you chose (you can see these in Figures 2-19, 2-20, and 2-21). Use the arrow keys to choose a style, and then press Enter to apply it.

You can position the cursor on a new line, create the list, and then start typing. Each time you press Enter, Word creates a new list item. To end the list and go back to normal paragraphs, click the list button again to turn it off.

If you've already typed some text and want to turn it into a list, select the text you want to convert, and then click Home and select the kind of list you want, or use the keyboard shortcuts listed above. Word converts the selected text to the kind of list you chose.

Tip: Thanks to Word's Autoformat As You Type feature, you can also create a bulleted or numbered list by typing a special character at the beginning of each line. Page 126 tells you how.

Formatting a List

Word gives you several different options for formatting your lists. To see them, click the down arrow to the right of the button for the kind of list you're formatting, or use the keyboard shortcuts listed above. Doing so opens a menu whose options depend on the kind of list you're formatting.

Formatting a bulleted list

Figure 2-19 shows the options for the different styles of bullets Word offers. As you move the mouse pointer over the choices, the list in your document changes to show how that style looks with your list. Click any button to apply its style.

Although the Bullet Library offers several built-in choices, you're not stuck with just the ones you see in Figure 2-19. Feel free to create your own bullet and add it to the bullet library. To do that, click Home, click the Bullets button's down arrow, and then select Define New Bullet (Alt, H, U, D). The Define New Bullet dialog box has three buttons:

- **Symbol.** Click Symbol to open the Symbol dialog box, which lets you choose from dozens of different symbols and characters, from Greek letters to shapes such as hearts, diamonds, and arrows. Click the symbol you want, and then click OK to close the Symbol dialog box. Click OK again to close the Define New Bullet dialog box and insert the new symbol into your document as a bullet.

- **Picture.** Click this button to browse through a wide range of bullet shapes, colors, and styles. Select the one you want and click OK to close the Picture Bullet dialog box, and then click OK to close the Define New Bullet dialog box and use the picture you selected as a bullet.

Tip: You're not limited to the pictures Word displays in the Picture Bullet dialog box. If you want to use your own picture (such as a small version of the company logo) as a bullet, click the Import button at the bottom of the Picture Bullet dialog box. The window that opens lets you choose a picture from your computer's hard drive. Navigate to the image you want, select it, and then click Open to add that picture to the Picture Bullet dialog box.

- **Font.** To change the font of your bullet, click this button. When the Font dialog box opens, use its selections to change the color or size of the bullet. (Word shows you a preview as you make your selections.) Click OK to close the Font dialog box and go back to the Define New Bullet dialog box. There, click OK again to apply your changes.

Figure 2-19:
Choose a bullet style from the Bullet Library, or click Define New Bullet to widen your options.

Tip: To sort a list alphabetically, select the list, go to the Home tab's Paragraph section, and then click the Sort button (Alt, H, SO), as shown in Figure 2-15. The Sort Text dialog box opens, letting you choose whether you want ascending order (A–Z) or descending order (Z–A). Make your selection and then click OK to sort.

Formatting a numbered list

Word offers quite a few choices for numbered lists, some of which don't even involve numbers! To apply a numbering scheme, start on the Home tab and click the down arrow next to the Numbering button (Alt, H, N). Choose the scheme you want from the Numbering Library, shown in Figure 2-20, and click or press Enter.

To create your own numbering scheme, look below the Numbering Library and select Define New Number Format (Alt, H, N, D) to open the Define New Number Format dialog box. In this dialog box, choose from these options:

- **Number style.** Use this drop-down list to select the number style you want to use to indicate each item: I, II, III; A, B, C; 1st, 2nd, 3rd; and so on.

- **Font.** Click this button to open the Font dialog box and choose a font, style, size, and color for your numbering.

- **Number format.** If you want a punctuation mark beyond the standard choices (maybe a colon or a hyphen) after the list number or letter, click in this box and insert your change.

If your list is interrupted by other elements, such as a table, an image, or some explanatory text, you can pick up the numbering again from where you left off. In the paragraph where you want to continue numbering, click the down arrow next to the Home tab's Numbered List button, and then click Set Numbering Value (Alt, H, N, V). In the Set Numbering Value dialog box, select "Start new list" or "Continue from previous list." Use the "Set value to" box to specify the number or letter you want to use to continue the list. Click OK to continue your numbering.

Formatting a multilevel list

A multilevel list is a bulleted or numbered list made up of different levels: main items with subitems indented below them and sub-subitems indented below those—up to nine levels deep. If you've created a list and want to make it a multilevel list, the easiest way to do that is to select the items you want to make subitems and increase their indentation by clicking Home→Increase Indent (Alt, H, AI). To promote a subitem, select it and decrease its indentation: Home→Decrease Indent (Alt, H, AO).

Tip: You can also use the Mini Toolbar (page 50) to increase and decrease indentation.

To format a multilevel list, open the Home tab and click the Multilevel List button's down arrow (Alt, H, M). Select a style from the List Library, shown in Figure 2-21, to apply that style to your list.

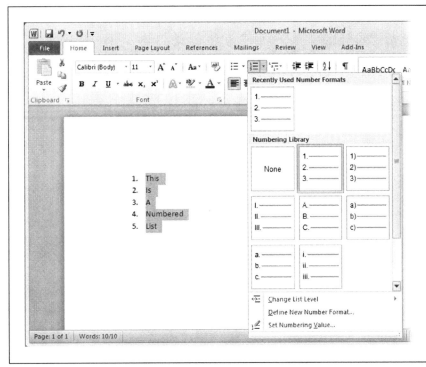

Figure 2-20:
The Numbering Library offers popular numbering formats for your lists. To create your own, choose Define New Number Format.

To define a new list style, open the List Library menu and, at the bottom, click Define New Multilevel List. The dialog box that opens gives you lots of choices for designing your multilevel list, as Figure 2-22 shows:

- **Click level to modify.** Select the level you want to change by clicking a number: 1 is the top level, and as the numbers increase, the levels decrease (so 9 is the lowest level). In the pane to the right, you can see which level you've chosen on a sample list.

- **Number format.** In this section, choose the bullet or number style and font for the level you're working with.

- **Position.** Here you tell Word how to position the bullet or number in relation to the text, refining alignment and indentation. You can apply this position just to the current level or to all levels in the list.

- **More.** Click this button to define the list even further: You can apply changes to just the level you've selected or to the whole list; link the list formatting to a style (page 51); tell Word after which level to repeat your formatting; and specify what follows the bullet or number (a tab, a space, or nothing).

After you've defined your list, click OK to apply your changes.

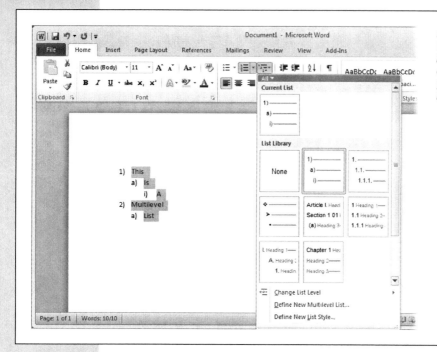

Figure 2-21:
*Whether your multi-
level list is made up
of numbers or bullets,
you can format it us-
ing the List Library.*

Figure 2-22:
*You can define formatting and positioning in a multilevel
list for the current level or for the entire list.*

Tip: For a quick way to work with lists, select all or part of a list and right-click. The shortcut menu that appears lets you increase or decrease the indentation of your selection, adjust the numbering, and open the Bullet or Numbering library to choose a different style.

Formatting a Document

When you create a new document in Word, there's actually a template that, behind the scenes, sets it up in a certain way. For example, normal.dotx, the template Word uses to create an ordinary blank document, has portrait (vertical) orientation, 1" margins on all sides, 11-point Calibri font, 10 points of white space after each paragraph, and so on. If you choose a different option from Word's template library (page 18), such as a resumé or a brochure, Word sets you up with formatting appropriate to the style you've chosen.

Of course, you can also customize a document's formatting. For example, you might widen the margins on a presentation handout so audience members have extra room to jot down notes. To make these kinds of document-wide changes, head for the Page Layout tab (Alt, P), shown in Figure 2-23.

Figure 2-23:
The Page Layout tab is where you can adjust a document's formatting—everything from margin size to page color.

Using the Page Setup Section

When you want to change how the text fits on a document's pages—tweak the margins, adjust the paper size, switch from landscape to portrait orientation or vice versa—head to the Page Layout tab's Page Setup section. That's where you'll find these buttons:

- **Margins (Alt, P, M).** Click this button to open a menu of margin choices:
  - **Normal.** 1" margins on all sides.
  - **Narrow.** 0.5" margins on all sides.

— **Moderate.** 1" margins on the document's top and bottom and 0.75" margins on the sides.

— **Wide.** 1" margins on the document's top and bottom and 2" margins on the sides.

— **Mirrored.** Choose this option when you're printing pages that will be bound in book format, so readers will see two facing pages. It sets up top, bottom, and outside margins of 1" and inside margins of 1.25" (to leave some room for the binding).

— **Office 2003 default.** This option takes you back in time to the standard for the Office 2003 documents: 1" margins on the top and bottom and 1.25" margins on the sides.

— **Custom margins.** Choose this option to open the Page Setup dialog box, where you can set the size of each margin by typing in the number of inches you want or using the up and down arrows to increase or decrease each margin in increments of a tenth of an inch.

- **Orientation (Alt, P, O).** When you click this button, a menu opens that lets you choose portrait (vertical) or landscape (horizontal) orientation for your document. Letters, reports, memos, agendas, and most written documents use portrait orientation; landscape orientation is good for certificates, tri-fold brochures, bi-fold programs, and similar documents.

- **Size (Alt, P, SZ).** Click this button to see a menu of common paper sizes, such as letter (8.5 × 11), legal (8.5 × 14), and A4 (8.27 × 11.69). For each paper size, Word gives you the name, dimensions, and a preview. Click More Paper Sizes to open the Paper tab of the Page Setup dialog box, where you can specify the paper dimensions by typing in the width and height yourself.

- **Columns (Alt, P, J).** If you need to format your document in columns, as for a newsletter, here's where to go. Select the text you want in columns and then use this button to lay it out in two or three columns. The Left option creates a narrow column on the left and a wide column on the right, and the Right option puts the wide column on the left and the narrow one on the right. Choose More Columns to open the Columns dialog box, where you can customize the number of columns, their widths, and the spacing between them.

Tip: If you've created some columns and decide that you don't want them after all, click Page Layout→Columns→One (Alt, P, J, use the arrow keys to select One, and then press Enter). This creates one continuous block of text across the width of the page in normal paragraph format.

- **Breaks (Alt, P, B).** Breaks force Word to end one textual element (a page, a column, a section, and so on) and start a new one. Position the cursor where you want the break to occur, and then choose this button to insert one of these breaks:

  — **Page (Alt, P, B, P)** ends one page and begins the next page.

  — **Column (Alt, P, B, C)** ends one column and jumps to the top of the next column.

  — **Text Wrapping (Alt, P, B, T)** lets you create image or table captions on web pages, keeping the captions separate from your document's body text.

Tip: Page 205 tells you more about working with text and images on web pages.

  — **Next Page (Alt, P, B, N)** ends the current section and starts a new section on a fresh page—useful for long documents.

  — **Continuous (Alt, P, B, O)** ends the current section and starts a new section on the same page.

  — **Even Page (Alt, P, B, E)** ends the current section and starts a new section on the next even-numbered page—handy when you're going to print out the document with facing pages, like a book.

Tip: Chapter 6 goes into detail about working with page breaks (page 155) and section breaks (page 156).

- **Line Numbers (Alt, P, LN).** Use this button to insert a number in the left margin next to each line in your document. You can number lines continuously or restart numbering with each new page or section. If you've turned line numbering on and want to turn it off for part of the document (such as a quotation or a table), select the part you don't want numbered and then use this button to suppress numbering for the selection.

- **Hyphenation (Alt, P, H).** This button tells Word how to handle words that are too long to fit at the ends of their lines. Here are its options:

  — **None (Alt, P, H, N)**, which is the default, doesn't hyphenate but puts the long word at the beginning of the next line.

  — **Automatic (Alt, P, H, U)** is helpful when you're working with a justified (page 55) document and some of the lines have spaces between words that look too wide. It lets Word fit the maximum number of characters on a line, hyphenating long words instead of pushing them to the next line.

  — **Manual (Alt, P, H, M)** tells Word to search the document for words that could be hyphenated and asks you to accept or reject hyphenation for each possibility.

— **Hyphenation Options (Alt, P, H, H)** opens the Hyphenation dialog box. Here you can specify whether you want hyphenation of words that are all in caps (such as acronyms), set the hyphenation zone (which specifies the maximum distance between the end of the last word and the edge of a column), and limit how many hyphens can appear in a stack at the ends of lines (too many hyphens can be distracting, so you might want to set this to one or two).

Using the Page Background Section

The Page Layout tab's Page Background section lets you add special effects to each page in your document, including watermarks, background color, and borders.

Adding a watermark

A watermark is a faint background image, like a company logo, that appears on each page. (It can also be text saying, for example, "CONFIDENTIAL" or "DRAFT DOCUMENT.") When you type, your words appear in the foreground, over the document, as shown in Figure 2-24.

To insert one of Word's preloaded watermarks, follow these steps:

1. **Click Page Layout→Watermark (Alt, P, PW).**

   A menu opens, displaying watermarks in a variety of categories, including Confidential, Disclaimers, Urgent, and so on.

2. **Scroll down to find the category you want, and then click a watermark.**

   Word inserts your selection on each page of the document.

Customizing a watermark with text

If Word doesn't offer the text you want as a watermark, you can compose your own watermark text and insert it. Here's how:

1. **Click Page Layout→Watermark (Alt, P, PW).**

   The watermark menu opens.

2. **Click Custom Watermark (if you have keyboard shortcuts turned on, press W).**

   Word opens the Printed Watermark dialog box, shown in Figure 2-25.

3. **Turn on the "Text watermark" radio button and make your choices from each drop-down list: Language, Text, Font, Size, and Color. To write your own text, double-click in the "Text:" box, clear the existing text, and type in what you want your watermark to say. If you want the watermark to be solid, turn off the Semitransparent checkbox (but a solid watermark makes the document harder to read, so you'll probably want to leave this on). Choose a layout—diagonal or horizontal—and then click Apply.**

   Word adds your watermark to your document.

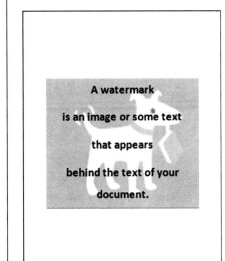

Figure 2-24:
*You can use a company logo or other image as a watermark on
your document's pages.*

Figure 2-25:
*Create a do-it-yourself watermark, using either text or an
image, in the Printed Watermark dialog box.*

Customizing a watermark with an image

You're not restricted to text for watermarking your pages. You can easily insert a
watermark that shows a background image on each page, such as a logo or some clip
art that relates to your document's theme—a ball and bat for the Little League newsletter, for example, or some flowers on flyers announcing a Garden Club meeting.

Take these steps to watermark your document with an image:

1. **Click Page Layout→Watermark (Alt, P, PW).**

   The watermark menu opens.

2. **Click Custom Watermark (if you have keyboard shortcuts turned on, press W).**

   Word opens the Printed Watermark dialog box, shown in Figure 2-25.

3. **Turn on the "Picture watermark" radio button and click Select Picture.**

   Word opens the Insert Picture dialog box.

4. **Navigate to the image you want to insert, select it, and then click Insert.**

   Word closes the Insert Picture dialog box and adds the name of the file you chose to the Printed Watermark dialog box.

5. **If you want to specify how big the image should be, choose a number (from 50% to 500%) from the Scale drop-down list. Selecting Auto lets Word size the image for you. Leave the Washout checkbox turned on to make the watermark a faint background image; if you turn it off, the image may be too dark, obscuring the text of your document. When you've made all your selections, click Apply.**

   The image appears on each page of your document.

Tip: You can have *either* text or an image for a watermark—not both. If you want an image with text, use your favorite image editor to make the text part of the image, and then insert the new image as your watermark.

Editing or deleting a watermark

If the watermark you created doesn't look right, click Page Layout→Watermark→ Custom Watermark (Alt, P, PW, W) to open the Printed Watermark dialog box (Figure 2-25) and tweak its settings. To remove a watermark from a document, select Page Layout→Watermark→Remove Watermark (Alt, P, PW, R), and it's gone.

Adding color to page backgrounds

For a document you're putting on the web, you might want to add a background color to make your document stand out. Doing so is easy:

1. **Select Page Layout→Page Color (Alt, P, PC).**

   A menu opens, displaying a palette of colors you can use for the background in your document.

2. **Move your cursor over the different colors to see how they look as a background. Click a color to select it.**

   Word gives your document the selected color as a background.

If you don't see a color you like, follow step 1 above and then do this:

1. **Click More Colors (press M if you have keyboard shortcuts turned on).**

   The Colors dialog box opens, showing dozens of colors.

2. **Click a color to select it (or click the Custom tab to choose from even more color options). Click OK.**

   Word applies your custom color.

Tip: If you want to make a single paragraph pop by coloring just its background, use the Home tab's Shading button (shown back in Figure 2-15). Select the paragraph you want to emphasize, open the Home tab, and, in the Paragraph section, click the down arrow next to the Shading button, which looks like a can of paint tipping over (Alt, H, H). From the menu that opens, choose a color, and Word paints the paragraph's background the color you chose.

Adding patterns to page backgrounds

If you like a little texture or pattern with your background color, you can add that, too:

1. **Select Page Layout→Page Layout→Fill Effects (Alt, P, PC, F).**

   The Fill Effects dialog box, shown in Figure 2-26, opens.

Figure 2-26:
Use the Fill Effects dialog box to add shading, texture, or a pattern to a document's background. If you want to add a picture, your best bet is to use a watermark (page 68).

2. **Choose one of these tabs: Gradient, Texture, or Pattern.**

— The **Gradient** tab shades the background from darker to lighter or between two colors. Choose the number of colors you want, the degree of transparency (for backgrounds, lighter is usually better) and the style of shading.

— The **Texture** tab offers a variety of textures, such as linen, burlap, granite, marble, and wood grain. Click a texture to see a preview in the Sample section.

— The **Pattern** tab has graphic patterns, such as stripes, diamonds, bricks, and checks, that can serve as page backgrounds in your document. Click a pattern and select foreground and background colors (careful not to make these too dark).

3. **When you've chosen and formatted the background you want, click OK.**

Your document now has your selection as its background.

Giving pages a border

Great for flyers and announcements, a border gives a page visual oomph and calls attention to its contents. To put a border around the pages in your document, start with the Page Layout tab:

1. **Select Page Layout→Page Borders (Alt, P, PB).**

Word opens the Page Border tab of the Borders and Shading dialog box, shown in Figure 2-27.

2. **Use the dialog box to make your selections:**

— **Setting.** Here's where you choose the type of border you want: box, shadow, 3-D, or custom.

— **Style.** Use the drop-down list to select a style of line for your border: solid, dashed, multiple lines, and so on.

— **Color.** Click the down arrow to see a menu of colors you can use for your border.

— **Width.** Select the border's width here, from a thin one-quarter point to a very thick 6 points.

— **Art.** You can use pictures, rather than a line, for your border—such as a border of hearts to announce a Valentine's Day dance or bats for a Halloween party. Click the drop-down list to scroll through the options.

— **Preview.** This section shows how your border is shaping up as you work on it. Click any of the buttons around the preview to remove or add the border to the top, bottom, left, or right of the page.

— **Apply to.** You can apply your border to the whole document or just a section (page 156 tells you more about working with sections).

As you make your choices, Word displays a preview of how your border will look on the page.

3. **When everything looks good, click OK.**

The border you created appears on your document's pages.

Figure 2-27:
You've got lots of flexibility in creating borders in Word. Choose a kind of border, define its style and appearance, and apply it to a page, to a section, or to the whole document.

Tip: You can also apply a border to a single paragraph (or group of paragraphs) from the Home tab's Paragraph section (Figure 2-15). Select the text you want the border to surround; on the Home tab, click the down arrow beside the Border button (Alt, H, B). This opens a menu that gives you a range of border choices: bottom, top, left, right, outside, inside—and any combination of these. To open the Borders and Shading dialog box and use it to format a paragraph border, go to the bottom of the menu and click Borders and Shading (Alt, H, B, O).

Inserting Headers, Footers, and Page Numbers

Headers, footers, and page numbers aren't part of the main body of your document. They live in its margins and provide running information throughout the document. In a printed report, for example, headers might show the report's title on odd-numbered pages and the author's name on even-numbered pages. A footer might contain the company name or copyright information. This information appears throughout the document, no matter how long or how short it is.

When it comes to inserting these elements, Word does a lot of the work for you, with preformatted styles. To get started, click the Insert tab (Alt, N), and head to the Header & Footer section, shown in Figure 2-28.

Figure 2-28:
To insert headers, footers, and page numbers, head for the Insert tab. Makes sense, doesn't it?

Inserting a header or footer

To insert a header or a footer, follow these steps:

1. **Select Insert→Header (Alt, N, H) or Insert→Footer (Alt, N, O).**

   Depending on what you chose, Word opens a menu of built-in, preformatted header or footer styles. Figure 2-29 shows some of the built-in headers you can choose.

Note: There's no live preview of headers or footers in your document as you scroll through the possibilities, but the menu shows a sample of each style.

---

2. **Browse through the available headers or footers using the scroll bar or the arrow keys. When you find the one you want, click it or press Enter.**

   Word inserts the header or footer into your document.

Now you can type in the information you want the header or footer to hold.

Figure 2-29:
Choose any of Word's built-in headers to insert that preformatted header into your document; you just type in the text. You also use this menu to edit a header you've already inserted.

Tip: You can format the text in a header or footer as you'd format any other text in Word—changing the font, adjusting its size, adding italics, and so on. While you're working in the header or footer, use the Mini Toolbar (page 50) or click the Home tab to access its formatting options.

Editing a header or footer

After you've inserted a header or footer, you may need to make some changes to it—maybe there's a typo that needs correcting, you need different text to appear on odd and even pages, or you want to adjust the spacing between the header or footer and the top or bottom of the page. To make any of those changes, start on the Insert tab:

1. **Click Insert→Header→Edit Header (Alt, N, H, E) or Insert→Footer→Edit Footer (Alt, N, O, E).**

   The header or footer (as you chose) becomes editable, and a new tab, Header & Footer Tools | Design, appears on the ribbon, as shown in Figure 2-30.

2. **Make any changes to the text in the header or footer itself, typing in the editable areas. To change the header or footer's formatting, use these options on the Header & Footer Tools | Design tab:**

   — **Different First Page (Alt, JH, A).** Turn on this checkbox if you want your document's first page to have a different header or footer than the rest of the pages.

   — **Different Odd & Even Pages (Alt, JH, V).** When you turn on this checkbox, Word marks each page's header or footer as odd or even, so that you can give each kind of page different text. You might choose this, for example, if you want the document's title on odd-numbered pages and the author's name on even-numbered pages.

   — **Show Document Text (Alt, JH, W).** When this checkbox is turned on, you can see slightly grayed-out text in the body of the document. When it's turned off, the body text disappears, showing just headers and footers. It's helpful to leave the checkbox turned on if you want to see how the header or footer looks in relation to the document's main text.

   — **Header from Top (Alt, JH, T).** Use this box to adjust the distance (in inches) between your header and the top of the page; use the up and down arrows, or click inside the box and type the number you want.

   — **Footer from Bottom (Alt, JH, B).** Use this box to adjust the distance (in inches) between your footer and the bottom of the page; use the up and down arrows, or click inside the box and type the number you want.

   — **Insert Alignment Tab (Alt, JH, M).** This option inserts a tab stop into the header or footer (not the body of the document) so you can line up its content the way you want it. Click the button to open the Alignment Tab dialog box; there, choose left, center, or right alignment and whether you want a leader (such as a dotted or dashed line), and then click OK.

   As you make your selections, Word applies your changes.

To close the header or footer, double-click the Header or Footer tag in the document or, on the Header & Footer Tools | Design tab, click the Close section's big red X (Alt, JH, C).

Figure 2-30:
When you're editing a header or footer, Word grays out the main document's body text and defines the area you can edit. This built-in header, designed for inserting a title, is easy to edit. Click the title and type in the text box that opens.

Tip: To move through your document's headers and footers, use the Header & Footer Tools | Design tab's Navigation section, where you can click Go to Header, Go to Footer, Previous, and Next.

Inserting the date and time into a header or footer

A *timestamp* shows when you created or updated a document, which is a great way to keep track of different versions. You can easily put a timestamp in your header or footer:

1. **Create a header or footer, and then click where you want to insert the timestamp. Open the Header & Footer Tools | Design tab, and click Date & Time (Alt, JH, D).**

    The Date and Time dialog box opens. This dialog box shows a variety of formats you can choose to display the date, time, or both, such as 1/17/11; January 17, 2011; 17-Jan-11; 2:49 PM: 1/17/11 2:49 PM; and so on.

2. **Choose a format for your timestamp. If you want Word to update the date and time automatically when you open the document, turn on the "Update automatically" checkbox. Click OK.**

    Word inserts the current date and/or time into your header or footer.

Tip: If you turn on the "Update automatically" checkbox, you don't have to close the document and open it again to make Word update the time. Open the header or footer as though you were going to edit it and click the timestamp. An Update button appears. Click it or press F9 to get an up-to-the-second update.

Inserting an image into a header or footer

Headers and footers don't have to be boring. You can liven them up with an image, such as your company logo. After you've created the header or footer, position your cursor where you want the image to appear and open the Header & Footer Tools | Design tab (Alt, JH). From there, you can insert an image from Word's clip art collection or choose an image stored on your computer.

To insert a clip art image, follow these steps:

1. **On the Header & Footer Tools | Design tab, select Clip Art (Alt, JH, F).**

    Word opens the Clip Art pane.

2. **If you're connected to the Internet, turn on the "Include Office.com content" checkbox to search both Word's built-in clip art and Microsoft's vast online collection of images. Type in a word that describes the kind of image you're looking for, and then click Go.**

    Word shows you any clip art that matches your search term.

3. **Double-click an image to insert it.**

    The image appears in your header or footer.

4. **If you need to resize the image, click it and use the sizing handles to adjust its size. When you're done, click the Clip Art pane's upper-right X.**

    The Clip Art pane closes, and you can get back to editing your document.

Tip: Chapter 3 gives you the full scoop about working with images in Word.

To select an image from your computer and insert it into a header or footer, follow these steps:

1. **On the Header & Footer Tools | Design tab, select Picture (Alt, JH, P).**

    The Insert Picture dialog box opens to your Pictures library.

2. **Navigate to the image you want and double-click to select it.**

    Word inserts the image into your header or footer.

3. **If you need to resize the image, click it and use the sizing handles to adjust its size.**

    When the image is the right size, you can close the header or footer and continue working on the document.

Tip: To remove an image from a header or footer, simply click the image and press Delete.

Removing a header or footer

Change your mind about including a header or footer in your document? No problem. You can get rid of it with just a few clicks. To remove a header or footer, select Insert→Header→Remove Header (Alt, N, H, R) or Insert→Footer→Remove Footer (Alt, N, O, R). That's it—they're gone.

Inserting page numbers

When you distribute a document for comments or discussion, the surest way to keep everyone on the same page is to number your document's pages. Word makes it a snap to put page numbers in your document:

1. **Choose Insert→Page Number (Alt, N, NU). If you've already created a header or footer, you can insert page numbers on the Header & Footer Tools | Design tab; on the left side of the ribbon, click Page Number (Alt, JH, NU).**

   You see a menu that gives you options for where the numbers will appear: at the top or bottom of the page or in a margin.

2. **Point at the position you want or use the arrow keys to move to it.**

   A menu appears, showing different styles and positions for the option you chose.

3. **Click or press Enter to select the one you want.**

   Your document now has page numbers.

Formatting page numbers

Word gives you some options for formatting page numbers in your document. To format page numbers, select either Insert→Page Number→Format Page Numbers (Alt, N, NU, F) or Insert→Header & Footer Tools | Design→Page Number→Format Page Numbers (Alt, JH, NU, F). This opens the Page Number Format dialog box shown in Figure 2-31.

The dialog box has these formatting options:

- **Number format.** Choose a number format from the drop-down list. Your options include regular numbers, Roman numerals, and even letters.

- **Include chapter number.** In a long document, you can show both the chapter number and the page number by turning on this checkbox. When you turn on this option, you have to make a couple more choices: Which heading level defines a chapter, and how to separate the chapter number from the page number (using a hyphen or a colon, for example).

- **Page numbering.** If your document has multiple sections, you can simply number the pages continuously (this is the standard choice) or start each section all over again from page 1 (or any number you choose).

When you've made your formatting choices, click OK to apply them to your document.

Figure 2-31:
Word gives you several options for formatting page numbers, including format, whether to include a chapter number (if your document has chapters), and how to treat page numbers in a long document with multiple sections.

Removing page numbers

To take page numbers out of your document, take either of these routes:

- Insert→Page Number→Remove Page Numbers (Alt, N, NU, R).
- Header & Footer Tools | Design→Page Number→Remove Page Numbers (Alt, JH, NU, R).

Poof! The page numbers disappear.

Tables, Graphics, and Charts

W ord processing isn't just about words—and neither is Word 2010. Although text probably accounts for the bulk of your documents, you can liven up the proceedings and make your points more clearly by adding other elements. Tables organize information into rows and columns so that readers can easily navigate large collections of data. Charts take the same kind of information and present it graphically, which is great when you want to make a high-impact presentation of comparisons or trends. Graphics can be any kind of image: family vacation photos, the company logo, whimsical clip art, executive portraits, product photos—if you've got a picture on your computer, you can put it in your document.

This chapter shows you how to work with nontext elements in Word: inserting them into a document, resizing them, moving them, and editing them. Your documents will be that much more interesting, and your points will come across that much better.

Creating a Table

For centuries, philosophers have puzzled over the question "Which came first, the chicken or the egg?" When you're working with tables in Word, a less mind-bending—and far more practical—question is "Which comes first, a table or its data?" The answer is entirely up to you.

When you create a table in Word, you can start by designing an empty table and adding information to it later, or you can start with the information the table will hold, and then use that to create the table. Whichever way you prefer, it's easy.

Creating a Table from Scratch

If you like to create a table by drawing it first and then filling in its cells with data, you have several options: Insert an empty table, insert one that's preformatted, or draw it yourself. And best of all, when you adopt this design-first, enter-data-later approach, you're not stuck with the table's structure if you need to change it. Later in this chapter, you'll get the scoop on how to edit a table.

Inserting a table

To quickly draw and insert a basic grid of equal-sized cells, start by putting the cursor where you want the new table to appear. Then follow these steps:

1. **Head to the Insert tab and click the Table button (Alt, N, T).**

   The Insert Table menu, shown in Figure 3-1, appears, showing a 10 × 8 grid of squares.

2. **Use your mouse pointer or your keyboard's arrow keys to move over the grid.**

   As you select the number of rows and columns, Word shows you a live preview of how the table will appear in your document.

3. **When the table is the size you want (for now), click or press Enter.**

   The table appears in your document.

Note: When you create a table, the Table Tools contextual tab appears, adding two tabs specific to working with tables—Table Tools | Design and Table Tools | Layout. When you move outside the table to work on another part of your document, these babies disappear. So you see 'em only when you need 'em.

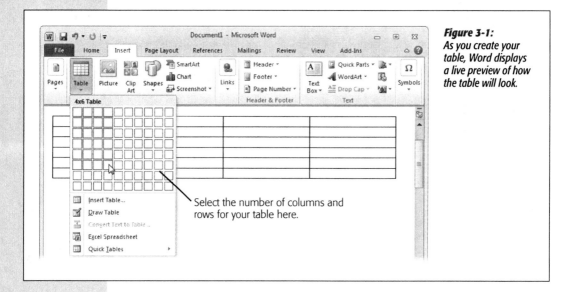

Figure 3-1:
As you create your table, Word displays a live preview of how the table will look.

Select the number of columns and rows for your table here.

Inserting a preformatted table

If you have a certain type of table in mind—like a calendar or an expense list, for example—or if you just want a nice-looking table without doing all the work of designing it yourself, take advantage of one of Word's predesigned, preformatted tables.

Position the cursor where you want this new grid to appear. From there, you're only a couple of steps away from inserting the table:

1. Select Insert→Table→Quick Tables (Alt, N, T, T).

   A fly-out menu of built-in tables appears, as shown in Figure 3-2. Use the scroll bar or arrow keys to browse through its tables.

2. **When you find the table you want, position the mouse over it and click or press Enter.**

   Word inserts the preformatted table into your document.

Preformatted tables contain some placeholder data, such as a month's name and dates for a calendar table. To clear a table's contents, select the table by clicking Table Tools | Layout→Select→Select Table (Alt, JL, K, T) and then press the Delete key. This deletes the table's data while keeping its structure and formatting.

Figure 3-2:
Word comes with a full complement of predesigned Quick Tables built right in. Your options include calendars and lists in table form. Save yourself time and formatting headaches by selecting one.

Drawing a table

If you need a table that goes beyond simple rows and columns—one with different-sized cells, for example—whip out a virtual pencil and design your own table by drawing it. Here's how:

1. **Select Insert→Table→Draw Table (Alt, N, T, D).**

    The mouse pointer changes to a pencil, as shown in Figure 3-3.

2. **Click and drag diagonally to draw the table's outer boundaries.**

    As you drag, a dotted line shows the size of the rectangle you're drawing.

3. **When the rectangle is the size you want for your table, let go of the mouse button.**

    Word creates the boundaries of your table and opens the Table Tools | Design tab.

4. **Draw gridlines between the rows and columns of your table.**

    As you draw, dotted lines snap into place, keeping your lines straight and perfectly horizontal or vertical.

5. **When you're finished drawing, click inside any cell and start typing there.**

    The drawing pencil disappears, and you've got a custom table in your document, ready and waiting for your data.

Tip: If you make a mistake as you're drawing the table, use the Eraser to get rid of any line you've drawn. Select Table Tools | Design→Eraser (Alt, JT, E), and the pointer morphs into an eraser. Click any line to erase it. When you're done, you can go back to drawing lines by selecting Table Tools | Design→Draw Table (Alt, JT, D).

Figure 3-3:
When you draw a table, Word opens the Table Tools | Design tab. Drawing tools are in the Draw Borders section (circled). Click Eraser if you make a mistake, and then click Draw Table to go back to drawing lines. You can also change the line style, width, and color with the options in this section.

Tip: When you're drawing a table, display the ruler to help measure intervals between lines. On the View tab, turn on the Ruler checkbox or press Alt, W, R.

Creating a Table from Text

Many people like to start by getting all their data down and then using it to build a table. If that's your style, Word is happy to accommodate. To begin, type in your data, using tabs to separate the info into columns and the Enter key to separate data into rows. (You can use other characters to mark your columns, but tabs make it easiest to see how your table-to-be is shaping up.) Here's a simple example:

Pet Vampire Names	Age	Preferred Food
Giselle	2	Llamas
Hercules	7	Marshmallows
Mujibar	3.5	Beer

When you're ready to convert your data into a table, follow these steps:

1. **Select the text or data you've entered and choose Insert→Table→Convert Text to Table (Alt, N, T, V).**

   The Convert Text to Table dialog box, shown in Figure 3-4, opens. Word has already filled in the number of columns and rows, based on the text you selected, but you can use the drop-down lists to adjust these numbers if necessary. There are also sections for "AutoFit behavior" (which determines the size of the table) and "Separate text at" (which tells Word how to determine when to create a new column).

2. **Choose the options you want for your table and click OK.**

   Word converts your data into a table.

Now you can edit and format your new table however you want—the rest of this chapter gives you the details on how to do that.

Tip: If you live, breathe, and think Excel (covered in Part 3 of this book), you can build a Word table by starting with an Excel-style spreadsheet. Position your cursor where you want the table to appear and then select Insert→Table→Excel Spreadsheet (Alt, N, T, X). Word inserts a spreadsheet that looks just like an Excel spreadsheet and changes the ribbon's tabs to match those in Excel. When you're done adding data, click outside the spreadsheet to turn it into a table and bring back Word's ribbon tabs. If you want to go back and work with the table's data later, double-click inside the table, and it becomes a spreadsheet-style table again.

Figure 3-4:
You can start with your data and use it to build a table. In this example, tabs separate columns and paragraph marks separate rows. The Convert Text to Table dialog boxes uses this information to set up the table.

Adding Information to a Table

When you've created a table in your document, all you have to do to add information is click any cell and start typing. You move around inside a table a little differently than you move around a document, as Table 3-1 shows, although pointing and clicking with the mouse will always put the cursor where you want it.

Table 3-1. *Keyboard shortcuts for working with tables*

Action	Keyboard Shortcut
Select next cell	Tab
Select previous cell	Shift+Tab
Jump to the first cell in a row	Alt+Home
Jump to the last cell in a row	Alt+End
Jump to the first cell in a column	Alt+Page Up
Jump to the last cell in a column	Alt+Page Down
Create a new paragraph within a cell	Enter
Insert a tab within a cell	Ctrl+Tab

Editing a Table

After you've created a table, you may find that you need to change it. You might, for example, want to make the table bigger to hold more data, or perhaps you didn't need as many rows as you thought you would. Tables are very flexible; it's easy to edit them to meet your needs.

Selecting Part or All of a Table

Just as you can select different parts of the text that makes up a document, you can select different parts of a table. Once you've made your selection, you can format, copy, or delete its contents.

Using your mouse

Here's how to make selections in a table by using your computer's mouse or touchpad:

- **Select a cell.** Move your mouse pointer to the lower-left corner of any cell. The pointer changes to a thick black arrow pointing toward the upper right, as shown in Figure 3-5. (On a compass, the arrow would be pointing toward the northeast.) Click to select the cell and its contents.

- **Select a range of cells.** Click in the first cell of the range you want. Holding down the Shift key, click in the last cell of the range. Alternatively, you can select a cell (as described in the previous bullet) and, holding down the mouse button, drag the selection cursor; let go of the mouse button when you've selected the range you want.

- **Select a row.** Move your mouse pointer to the lower-left corner of any cell in the row you want. When the pointer changes to a thick black arrow, double-click to select the entire row.

Tip: If your table spans the page, you can select one of its rows in the same way you select a line of text (page 36): Move your pointer to the left margin of the page so that it points at the row you want, and then click.

- **Select a column.** Move your mouse pointer above the column you want. When it becomes a thick black arrow pointing downward, click to select the column.

- **Select an entire table.** Pass your mouse pointer over the table. When you do, a small button containing a four-way arrow appears just outside the table's upper-left corner. This is the Select Table button, shown in Figure 3-5. Click it to select the whole enchilada.

Select table

Selection arrow

Resizing handle

Using the ribbon

You can also select all or part of a table from the Table Tools | Layout tab. Click anywhere in the table to make this tab appear, and then click Select. From the menu that appears, choose Select Cell, Select Column, Select Row, or Select Table. Or use these ribbon-based keyboard shortcuts:

- **Select a cell:** Alt, JL, K, L
- **Select a row:** Alt, JL, K, R
- **Select a column:** Alt, JL, K, C
- **Select the entire table:** Alt, JL, K, T

Inserting Rows and Columns

As you work with a table, you might discover that you need more rows or columns to hold all your information. No problem. One way to do this is from the Table Tools | Layout tab. Start by clicking in a cell *next to* where you want to insert the row or column. Then take one of these actions:

- **To insert a row above the insertion point,** select Table Tools | Layout→Insert Above (Alt, JL, A).
- **To insert a row below the insertion point,** select Table Tools | Layout→Insert Below (Alt, JL, E).

- **To insert a column to the left of the insertion point,** select Table Tools | Layout→Insert Left (Alt, JL, L).

- **To insert a column to the right of the insertion point,** select Table Tools | Layout→Insert Right (Alt, JL, R).

You can also insert rows or columns by right-clicking inside the table in a cell that will adjoin the new row or column. When you right-click, a shortcut menu appears; select Insert and then choose what you want to insert: Columns to the Left, Columns to the Right, Rows Above, Rows Below, or Cells (to insert a new cell). When you choose a column or a row, Word inserts it where you indicated. When you choose Cells, a dialog box opens with these additional options:

- **Shift cells right.** This shoves the contents of the row (after the insertion point) to the right to make room for the empty cell.

- **Shift cells down.** This moves the contents of the column (after the insertion point) down a row to make room for the empty cell.

- **Insert entire row.** This inserts a new row above the insertion point.

- **Insert entire column.** This inserts a new column to the left of the insertion point.

Tip: Here's a great timesaver when you need to insert multiple adjacent rows or columns. Start by selecting the same number of rows or columns you want to insert. If you want to insert two new columns at the right side of your table, for example, select the two columns currently at right. Then use any of the insertion methods described in this section. Word inserts the same number of rows or columns you selected.

Moving Rows and Columns

What if a row or column somehow landed in the wrong place? You can move it to its proper location with good ol' cutting and pasting. Select the row or column you want to move, and then do this:

1. **Select Home→Cut (Alt, H, X or Ctrl+X).**

   Word deletes the row or column you selected and puts a copy of it on the Clipboard.

Tip: If cutting a whole row or column with all its contents makes you a little nervous, you can *copy* the row or column for now and then go back and delete the original once the copy is in its new home. To copy, select Home→Copy (Alt, H, C or Ctrl+C).

---

2. **Click a cell adjacent to where you want to paste the row or column.**

   For a row, click in a cell in the row below where the new row will appear. For a column, click in a cell immediately to the right of where the new column will appear.

3. **Select Home→Paste (Alt, H, V or Ctrl+V).**

   The row or column appears immediately above or to the left of the insertion point.

Tip: You can select and move multiple rows and columns in the same way. Just select all the rows or columns that you want to move before cutting or copying.

Merging and Splitting Cells

You may think of a table as a perfect grid, with uniform, evenly spaced cells. But tables are more flexible than that. You can *merge* cells to make a supercell that spans multiple columns, or you can *split* a cell to divide it more narrowly than the other cells in its row or column. Whether you want to merge cells or split them, head to the Table Tools | Layout tab's Merge section:

- **To merge cells,** select the cells you want to fuse into one and then select Table Tools | Layout→Merge Cells (Alt, JL, M).

Tip: Here's another way to merge cells: Select the cells you want to merge, right-click, and then choose Merge Cells from the shortcut menu.

- **To split a single cell,** click the cell you want to divide and select Table Tools | Layout→Split Cells (Alt, JL, P). This opens the Split Cells dialog box, shown in Figure 3-6. Set the number of columns and/or rows you want the split cells to have, and then click OK.

- **To split a range of cells,** select the range you want to split and then click Table Tools | Layout→Split Cells (Alt, JL, P). When the Split Cells dialog box (Figure 3-6) opens, make sure that the "Merge cells before split" checkbox is turned on. This makes your range one big cell first, then splits that cell into the number of columns and rows you select. Click OK to split the cells.

- **To split a table,** position the cursor in the first row of what will become the new table. Select Table Tools | Layout→Split Table (Alt, JL, Q). Word splits the table into two separate ones and inserts a line between them.

Figure 3-6:
When you split a cell, you need to set the number of rows and columns you want to create. If you selected a range of cells to split, the "Merge cells before split" checkbox starts by merging the range into one big cell, then splits it according to how many columns and rows you set.

Tip: If you've ever created a table at the very top of a document and then tried to add a line of regular text *above* the table, you know it's hard to do—Word wants to put your text *into* the table. When you've got a table at the top of a document, here's a trick that lets you insert a line of text above it: Put the cursor at the beginning of the table's upper-left cell—the one that's in the first row and the first column. Select Split Table, and Word pushes the whole table down a line. Now you've got room to type above the table.

Deleting All or Part of a Table

You can delete any cell, row, or column from a table, or the table itself. First, select what you want to make go away. Then use one of the following methods:

- **To delete a cell,** select Table Tools | Layout→Delete→Delete Cells (Alt, JL, D, D). The Delete Cells dialog box opens. Select "Shift cells left" if you want the cells to the right of the deleted cell to move over to the left; select "Shift cells up" if you want the cells below the deleted cell to move up a row. (You can also choose to delete the entire row or column in which the selected cell appears.) Click OK to delete.

- **To delete a row,** select Table Tools | Layout→Delete→Delete Rows (Alt, JL, D, R).

- **To delete a column,** select Table Tools | Layout→Delete→Delete Columns (Alt, JL, D, C).

- **To delete a table,** select Table Tools | Layout→Delete→Delete Table (Alt, JL, D, T).

Tip: To delete just the *contents* of a cell, row, column, or table, without affecting the table's structure, select the table element whose contents you want to delete, and then press the Delete key.

Formatting a Table

A table is all about the information it holds. But you can make your tables eye-catching and easier to read by formatting them in various ways. For example, you might set off column headings with a different color or shade alternating rows. The easiest way to format a table is to use Word's built-in styles, but you can also format your table by hand.

Save Time with Ready-to-Use Table Styles

To make your table look good, you can choose a predesigned style and apply it to your table. When you do, Word automatically formats the table according to the style you chose. Say you want the table in shades of blue, with a dark blue row at the top to distinguish headings and alternating white and blue rows to make it easier to read each entry. Sounds like a lot of formatting work, doesn't it? Not with Table Styles. You don't have to figure out how to do all that formatting—just pick the style you want, and Word does the rest.

The Table Tools | Design Tab has two sections for table styles, as shown in Figure 3-7:

- **Table Style Options** is where you select the table elements you want to emphasize.
- **Table Styles** is where you choose a style to apply to your table.

Here's how to format your table using Table Styles:

1. **Click anywhere in the table you want to format to bring up the Table Tools contextual tabs; click the Design tab (Alt, JT).**

    The ribbon changes to show sections and buttons for formatting tables. In the Table Style Options section, you have these choices:

    — **Header Row** (Alt, JT, A) sets off the top row from the rest of your table to emphasize column headings.

    — **Total Row** (Alt, JT, T) sets off the very last row from the rest of the table—useful if you've got columns of figures to add up.

    — **Banded Row** (Alt, JT, R) alternates colors between rows—the rows may be blue, white, then blue again, and so on, for example—which is great for helping readers trace information across the table.

    — **First Column** (Alt, JT, M) emphasizes the table's far-left column. You might do this to set off names, for example, from the information about each name.

    — **Last Column** (Alt, JT, N) emphasizes the table's far-right column, which is useful if the far-right column holds totals.

    — **Banded Columns** (Alt, JT, U) alternates colors between columns. If readers are likely to read down the columns rather than across the table (if columns hold numbers you're adding up, for example), then this style helps them stay in a column as they read.

    The checkboxes you turn on determine the styles that appear in the Table Styles gallery.

2. **Turn on the checkboxes of the table style options you want for your formatted table. Then use the arrows in the Table Styles section (Figure 3-7) to view styles with the options you chose. Use the up and down arrows or click the More arrow below the down arrow (Alt, JT, S) to open a gallery where you can view more styles at once.**

    As you pass the mouse pointer over the various choices, Word displays a live preview of how your table looks in that style.

3. **Click the style you want.**

    Word gets to work and applies the formatting in a jiffy.

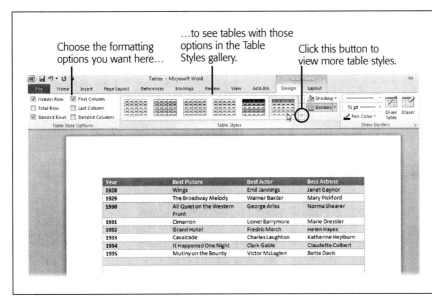

Choose the formatting options you want here...

...to see tables with those options in the Table Styles gallery.

Click this button to view more table styles.

Figure 3-7:
Choose the options you want, and then pick a table style. To pop out a larger selection of styles, click the More button (circled).

Applying Shading and Borders

If you're the do-it-yourself type, you can format a table yourself using the Shading and Borders buttons in the Table Styles section of the Table Tools | Design tab (click any table to see this tab). You can also use these buttons to change the look of a table you've formatted using Table Styles.

Shading a Table

You can shade any part of a table—a cell, a row, a column, or multiples of these—to call attention to it. You might want to set off the row that contains the column headings from the table's data, for example, or highlight a row or column that contains totals. In a table you're using as a calendar, you could use shading to highlight important dates, like project due dates.

To add shading to a table, start by selecting the part of the table you want to shade. (You can select multiple elements by holding down the Ctrl key as you make your selections.) Then add shading using this method:

1. **Select Table Tools | Design→Shading (Alt, JT, H).**

   The Shading menu, shown in Figure 3-8, appears. This menu shows Theme Colors, drawn from the theme (page 181) of your document; Standard Colors; No Color (Alt, JT, H, N); and More Colors (Alt, JT, H, M), which opens a dialog box that lets you choose from a wider range of colors. As you pass over the possibilities, Live Preview shows how that color looks in your table.

2. **Click the color you want.**

Word shades your selection with the color you chose.

Figure 3-8:
When you shade parts of a table, you can choose colors related to your document's current design using Theme Colors— or pick whatever colors you like. Click More Colors for an even broader palette.

Working with Borders

A basic table is a grid with borders around all sides and between the rows and columns to define each cell. You can show or hide any or all of those borders to give your table the look you want. (Borders still exist if you hide them—they're how Word knows where each cell begins and ends—you just make them invisible.) Select the table (or the part of it you want to work with), and then do this:

1. **Select Table Tools | Design→Borders (Alt, JT, B).**

The Borders menu, shown in Figure 3-9, opens, giving you all the possible options for showing and hiding borders, both outside and inside the table. Current borders are highlighted.

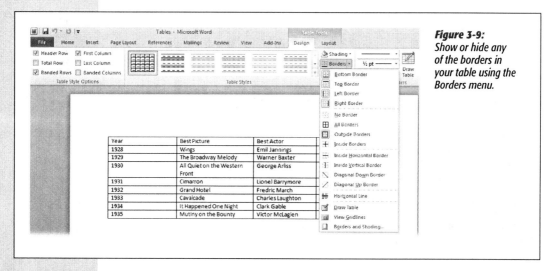

Figure 3-9:
Show or hide any of the borders in your table using the Borders menu.

2. Choose the border you want to apply (if it's currently invisible) or erase (if it's currently visible).

   Word closes the Borders menu and applies your change to the table.

Tip: To adjust the line style, width, or color, use the drop-down options in the Draw Borders section of the Table Tools | Design tab.

The Borders menu makes one change at a time, closing after each one, which can get pretty tedious if you want to alter multiple borders. Here's how to apply multiple changes without opening and reopening the Borders menu:

1. Select Table Tools | Design→Borders→Borders and Shading (Alt, JT, B, O).

   The Borders and Shading dialog box, shown in Figure 3-10, opens with the Borders tab selected.

2. In the Setting section, choose the basis for your formatted table.

   Here are your options:

   — **None** removes all external and internal borders from the table.

   — **Box** applies external borders and removes internal borders.

   — **All** applies the same borders internally and externally.

   — **Grid** applies one border style externally and standard borders internally.

   — **Custom** lets you choose and apply different border styles to different parts of your table.

Figure 3-10:
The Borders and Shading box, familiar to people who used earlier versions of Word, also works with tables in Word 2010. Separate columns and rows one border at a time to create a custom look for your table.

3. **In the middle section of the dialog box, choose how you want to format the borders.**

    The Style drop-down menu offers a selection of lines, including solid, dotted, dashed, wavy, double, triple, and so on. The Color drop-down menu gives you a choice of line colors—similar to the Shading menu shown in Figure 3-8. The Width drop-down menu is where you choose a thickness for the border.

4. **In the Preview section, use the buttons or click the diagram to apply the border where you want it to appear in your table.**

    The Preview changes as you make your selections to give you an idea of how the table will look.

5. **When you're finished, click OK.**

    Your table now has a custom-designed border.

Inserting Images

Picture this: You're writing to family members about your new puppy, trying to describe just how darn cute he is. You could write a couple of paragraphs and still not get the message across as eloquently as one big-eyed puppy photo could.

Images enliven a document, adding visual interest and illustrating key points. Whether you're adding snapshots of the kids to a holiday letter, putting flow charts into a project management plan, or showing screenshots of designs for a website, showing—not just telling—is what makes your documents stand out.

Inserting a Picture

If you've got a picture stored on your computer—like that photo of your cute puppy—you can insert it into a document. Position the cursor where you want the image to appear, and then select Insert→Picture (Alt, N, P). This opens the Insert Picture dialog box, shown in Figure 3-11. Navigate to the file, click to select it, and then click the Insert button. Word puts the picture wherever you first positioned the cursor.

Tip: Here's a quick way to get a picture into your document. Open Windows Explorer and size the window so you can see both Windows Explorer and your document on your computer screen. In Windows Explorer, find and select the image you want. Drag it into the Word document and drop it in place.

Figure 3-11:
Although Word comes with sample pictures built in, you'll probably want to use your own. Find and select a folder in the left-hand pane, choose the picture you want, and then click Insert.

Note: When Word inserts a new picture, it opens the Picture Tools | Format tab so that you can edit the picture. Keep reading to learn how to edit images in Word.

Inserting Clip Art

Clip art is a collection of images—ranging from cartoonish drawings to basic animations to photographs—that you can use to illustrate Word documents and other Office files (like PowerPoint presentations). Office comes with a bunch of built-in clip art, and you can access more at Office.com. You put clip art into your document from the Insert tab:

1. **Put the cursor wherever you want to add the art, and then select Insert→Clip Art (Alt, N, F).**

   The Clip Art pane opens, as shown in Figure 3-12. This pane lets you search for clip art images, both those that come preloaded in Microsoft Office and those on Microsoft's Office.com website.

2. Type in a search term that describes the kind of image you're looking for. If you want, click the "Results should be" drop-down list to select one or more media types: All, Illustrations, Photographs, Videos, or Audio. If you're connected to the Internet and want to see results from Office.com, turn on the "Include Office.com content" checkbox. Click Go.

   Word displays any clip art that meets your search criteria.

3. Scroll through the results and click an image to insert it.

   The image appears in your document.

If you're done inserting clip art for now, you can close the Clip Art pane by clicking its upper-right X.

Figure 3-12:
Search for built-in clip art to spruce up your document. For more options, get online, turn on the "Include Office.com content" checkbox, and then click Go to search a much larger online collection.

Inserting a Screenshot

If you've ever needed to show an image of a web page or a dialog box, you know that getting that screenshot into your document can take a lot of work: You have to use some program to take the screenshot, save it on your computer, and then insert it into your document as an image. New in Word 2010, you can now cut out the middleman by taking screenshots and inserting them directly into your document—all in Word. It really couldn't be easier:

1. **Position the cursor where you want the image to appear, and then select Insert→Screenshot (Alt, N, SC).**

   A menu called Available Windows opens, as shown in Figure 3-13. This menu shows a miniature version of each window you have open.

2. **Position the mouse over a screenshot and click or press Enter.**

   The screenshot appears as an image in your document.

Now you can work with the screenshot just as you'd edit any image in Word (the next section tells you how).

Tip: They say a picture is worth a thousand words, but sometimes even a picture needs a little explanation. To give an image a caption, select the image and then click References→Insert Caption (Alt, S, P). In the Caption dialog box that opens, type what you want the caption to say. Select whether you want the caption to appear above or below the image, and then click OK to insert the caption into your document. Bonus tip: You can insert captions for tables in the same way.

Figure 3-13:
Word can take a snapshot of any other window you have open and insert it into your document.

What if you don't want to insert the whole screen? For example, maybe you're interested in the main part of a web page but not the ads along its sides. You can select a region of the window you're shooting, then insert just that region. Position the cursor where you want to insert the image and minimize all windows except for Word and the window you want to shoot. Then proceed like this:

1. **Select Insert→Screenshot (Alt, N, SC).**

   The Available Windows menu (Figure 3-13) opens, showing just the open window.

2. **At the bottom of the Available Windows menu, click Screen Clipping (press C if you've got keyboard shortcuts turned on).**

   The window opens and grays over, and a crosshairs pointer appears, as shown in Figure 3-14.

3. **Move the pointer to the upper-left corner of the section you want to clip. Click and drag to select a region.**

   As you drag, you create a rectangle around your selection. Inside the rectangle, the section you're selecting loses the gray tint of the rest of the window, making it easier to see what you're doing.

4. **When you've selected the region you want, let go of the mouse button.**

   Word takes a snapshot of the region and inserts it into your document.

Figure 3-14:
Click and drag the crosshairs cursor (circled) to "clip" a screenshot, selecting a region of a window instead of the whole thing.

Note: To take a screenshot in Word, you must be working with a .docx file. When you open a .doc file (from Word 2003 or earlier), Word 2010 goes into Compatibility Mode, and it can't take screenshots in that mode.

Editing an Image

When you insert an image, Word automatically opens the Picture Tools | Format contextual tab, shown in Figure 3-15. This tab also appears whenever you click an image to select it, and it's what you use to edit or format an image. As you'll see in this section, Word (and the rest of Office) has more tools for working with images than ever before—and those tools are great for making minor adjustments to a document's pictures. But if you need to do some heavy-duty image editing, you still need a purpose-built program like Photoshop to do the job.

Changing an Image's Size

Resizing an image makes it fit better on the page, but there are some limits to what you can accomplish when you change a picture's size. For example, if you try to take a small image and make it much bigger, it will appear blurry and pixelated (the small squares that make up the image will become visible). Resizing works best for relatively small adjustments.

When you select an image, handles appear at the image's corners and halfway along each side, as you can see in Figure 3-15. The easiest way to make the image larger or smaller is to click a handle and hold down the mouse button as you drag to resize the image. If you use this method, work with a corner resizing handle; these handles keep the image's width and height in proportion as you change its size.

You can also resize an image using the drop-down lists of the Picture Tools | Format tab's Size section. The Shape Height (Alt, JP, H) and Shape Width (Alt, JP, W) boxes show the image's current size in inches. Change one (use the up and down arrows or type in the number you want), and the other changes to retain the image's proportion.

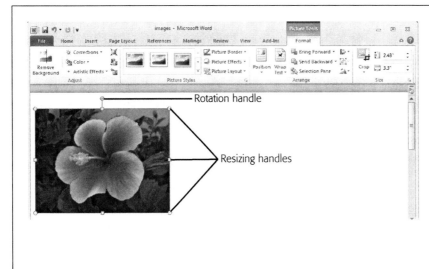

Figure 3-15:
The Picture Tools | Format tab has commands for working with images in these sections: Adjust (for brightening or sharpening an image, adjusting its color, or applying effects), Picture Styles (to frame your image or give it shadows, beveling, or other effects), Arrange (to position the image in relation to other elements in your document), and Size (to crop the image or adjust its size in inches).

Cropping an Image

Cropping is different from resizing. When you resize an image, you grow or shrink the entire image. But when you crop an image, you cut out parts of the image that you don't want. If you want only part of an image that you've inserted, you can crop the image directly in Word. Select the image to open the Picture Tools | Format Tab, and then click Crop; on the menu that opens, click Crop again (Alt, JP, V, C).

Cropping handles appear around the image. As Figure 3-16 shows, these cropping handles are at the same points as the resizing handles and look like bold black lines. Move the mouse pointer over a cropping handle until the cursor changes shape to match the cropping handle. Click (the cursor becomes a crosshairs when you do) and drag to crop out parts of the image you don't want. As you drag, the original outline of the image remains. Let go of the mouse button to finish the crop.

Tip: You can drag cropping handles both ways. So if you crop too far and want to restore some of what you've cropped, simply drag the handle back out to restore the image. You can do this even after you've finished cropping the image.

Repeat with the other cropping handles as necessary. When you're done, click outside the image to save your changes.

Tip: To add a fun effect to an image, crop it to a shape. Click the image and select Picture Tools | Format→Crop→Crop to Shape (Alt, JP, V, S). A menu opens showing shapes—hearts, triangle, arrows, lightning bolts, and more—that work like cookie cutters. When you choose a shape, Word crops the photo to that shape.

Removing a Picture's Background

Some pictures have busy backgrounds that steal the focus from the main image. It can take a keen eye, a steady hand, and a lot of concentration to remove the background from an image. But Word 2010 has made that job a whole lot easier. As you can see in Figure 3-16, you can remove an image's background after you've inserted the image into Word.

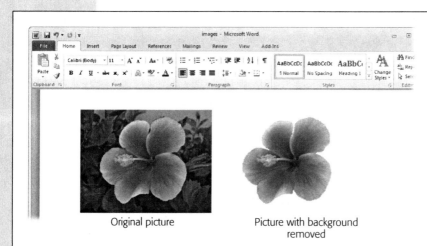

Original picture

Picture with background removed

Figure 3-16:
'fraid of Photoshop? You don't need image-editing software to remove the background from a picture—you can do it right in Word.

Note: Removing a picture's background works only with .docx files—you can't do this if Word 2010 is working with an older .doc file in Compatibility Mode.

Here's how to make the main subject of an image stand out by getting rid of the background:

1. **Click the image whose background you want to remove and then select Picture Tools | Format→Remove Background (Alt, JP, E).**

   The Background Removal tab, shown in Figure 3-17, opens. Word starts off by guessing which part of the photo you want to emphasize and places a selection area around it. Any part of the photo that Word considers background is dimmed.

Figure 3-17:
Use the handles to adjust the selection area, telling Word which part of the image is foreground—that is, which part of the image you want to keep.

2. **If necessary, adjust the selection area. You can also mark areas you want to keep or discard using the buttons on the Background Removal tab.**

   When you click the appropriate button, the pointer turns into a pencil. Use the pencil to draw lines around any part of the image you want to select or remove. If you make a mistake, press the Delete Mark button, and when the pointer changes to an arrow, click the mark you want to remove.

3. **When you're done selecting and marking the image, click Keep Changes.**

   The image's background disappears like magic, as you can see on the right back in Figure 3-16.

Background removal works best with clearly defined main images that contrast strongly with their backgrounds, but you can use the Background Removal tab's tools to fine-tune which parts of the image stay and which parts go.

Tip: You can tweak an image after you've removed its background. Click the image to select it and then choose Picture Tools | Format→Remove Background (Alt, JP, E). The image changes to background removal mode, looking something like the image in Figure 3-17. From there, you can make whatever adjustments you want; click Keep Changes to apply them.

Moving and Rotating Images

Inserting an image into your document is just the beginning. Once you've got a picture in there, you can move it to a new position or adjust its angle.

Moving an image

The easiest way is to use the Clipboard: Cut the image from its current location (Ctrl+X), move the cursor to the new location, and paste the image there (Ctrl+V).

You can also drag the image to its new home: Click the picture to select it and move your pointer over the image until it becomes a selection arrow combined with a four-way arrow. Click and drag the image to its new position; let go of the mouse button to drop it where you want it.

Tip: To position an image that's on its own line (in other words, when there's no text wrapped around it), head for the Home tab (Alt, H) and, in the Paragraph section, use the Alignment buttons to line up the image with the left or right margin or to center it.

Rotating an image

When you insert an image, it appears in either vertical (portrait) or horizontal (landscape) orientation. To tilt the image at a rakish angle or to turn it upside down, use the rotation handle. Click the image to show the sizing handles. Above the image is a green circle; that's the rotation handle. When you click it, the pointer becomes four arrows pointing in a circle, as shown in Figure 3-18. Drag the rotation handle in a circular direction, and a ghost of the image moves with you. When the ghost image is at the angle you want, let go of the mouse button to rotate the image to that angle.

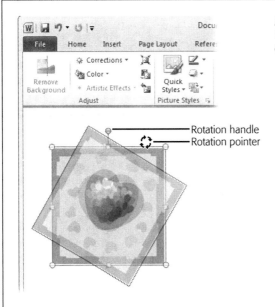

Figure 3-18:
To rotate an image, click the rotation handle and drag in a circle until you've got the angle you want.

Adjusting an Image's Appearance

Amateur and professional photographers alike adjust their pictures—sharpening here, brightening there, maybe adjusting the color saturation—to make the images look their best. You can make these adjustments right in Word; no need to mess around with photo-editing software. Adjust a picture's appearance in the Picture Tools | Format tab's Adjust section (click the image to open this tab). Here are the buttons to use:

- **Corrections (Alt, JP, R).** Use this button to sharpen (increase focus) or soften (blur) an image and to adjust its brightness and contrast.

- **Color (Alt, JP, I).** This button is where you adjust color saturation (purity) or color tone (the actual color that appears—red, blue, fuchsia, whatever). It's also where you can recolor an image—making a full-color image grayscale, for example.

- **Artistic Effects (Alt, JP, X).** Make a photograph look like a painting, a chalk sketch, an image seen through glass, and a whole bunch more. If you feel like getting creative, check out the effects here.

The basic drill for any of these adjustments is the same:

Select the image you want to adjust to open the Picture Tools | Format tab (Alt, JP). In the Adjust section, click the kind of adjustment you want to make: Corrections, Color, or Artistic Effects.

A menu like the one in Figure 3-19 opens. The menu's selections depend on the kind of adjustment you chose, but they all work the same way: You see a gallery of thumbnail images illustrating changes to the image (pass the mouse pointer over the thumbnails to see a live preview on the full-sized image). Click a thumbnail to change the image in the document.

Figure 3-19:
You don't have to guess how changes you make to brightness will affect an image; the thumbnails in the Brightness and Contrast menu show you. When you pass the mouse pointer over a thumbnail, Word tells you what you're adjusting and shows a live preview of the effect on the full-sized image.

Using Picture Styles

Picture Styles add frames and other effects—shadows, soft edges, beveling, and reflections, for example—to your images. To apply one of these effects, select the image to open the Picture Tools | Format tab (Alt, JP). Quick Styles appear in the Picture Styles section of that tab, showing you some previews of different styles. You can use the up and down arrows to scroll through the styles, but to save yourself some squinting and see all the options at once, look below the scroll down arrow and click the More button (Alt, JP, K).

Take a look at the different styles available and use your mouse pointer to see a live preview of any of them on your image. Click the one you want to give your image some style!

___

Tip: Use the Picture Border (Alt, JP, SO) and Picture Effects (Alt, JP, F) buttons to create do-it-yourself picture styles. These buttons give you more options than the quick styles, including border colors, glow colors and widths, and various options for shadows, reflections, and rotation effects.

___

Wrapping Text Around an Image

An image can be a pretty decoration, or it can be an essential part of your document. To incorporate an image into the text that it illustrates, you can wrap text around the image. Instead of inserting a lonely image sitting all by itself on its own line, the image gets surrounded by text. This makes it clear which part of the text goes with the image, saves space, and gives your document a professional-looking layout.

The two buttons you use to position an image in relation to text are in the Picture Tools | Format tab's Arrange section:

- **Position (Alt, JP, PO)** lets you left-, center-, or right-align the image at the top, middle, or bottom of the page. Thumbnails show you what each layout looks like.

- **Wrap Text (Alt, JP, TW)** tells Word how to place words in relation to the image:
  - **In Line with Text.** The bottom of the image is even with the first line of the paragraph that follows it.
  - **Square.** The text forms a neat-looking square around the image, even if the image has an irregular shape.
  - **Tight.** The text approaches the image more closely than with normal wrapping. For an irregularly shaped image, the text is straight across the top and bottom of the image but approaches the contours on the sides.
  - **Through.** When you select this option, you can place the image anywhere in your document, and the text will wrap around its edges, with a little white space between the text and image. If the image has an irregular shape, the text wraps to follow its contours.
  - **Top and Bottom.** The image appears on its own line, with text above and below it but not on either side.
  - **Behind Text.** The text runs right across the image. (Depending on your image, this can be hard to read.)
  - **In Front of Text.** The text runs behind the image, which blocks some of the text.

    As you move the mouse pointer over the various wrap options, Live Preview shows how each looks in your document, so you can select the one that looks best.

Tip: You can also find the Position and Wrap Text buttons in the Arrange Section of the Page Layout tab (Alt, P, PO for Position and Alt, P, TW for Wrap Text).

You can manually adjust how closely the text wraps around your image by selecting the image and then taking these steps:

1. **Choose Picture Tools | Format→Wrap Text→Edit Wrap Points (Alt, JP, TW, E).**

    Word shows a box around the image, with a small black square at each corner, as shown in Figure 3-20. These square are the image's *wrap points*, which determine the distance between the text and the image.

2. **Click any wrap point. Drag it closer to the image to bring the words closer; drag it away from the image to push back the text.**

    As you drag, Word shows both where the wrap point was and where you're moving it (connected to other wrap points by a dotted line).

3. **Let go of the mouse button to reposition the wrap point.**

    Word moves the text according to the new wrap point.

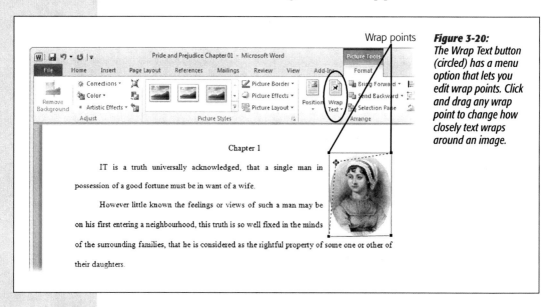

Figure 3-20:
The Wrap Text button (circled) has a menu option that lets you edit wrap points. Click and drag any wrap point to change how closely text wraps around an image.

Searching for Images

When you have multiple images, especially in a long document, it's a pain to scroll through page by page, looking for a particular picture. Word 2010's Navigation pane lets you jump from one image to the next, browsing quickly through the document until you find the image you want. Here's how:

1. **Open the Navigation pane by going to the View tab and, in the Show section, turning on the Navigation Pane checkbox (Alt, W, K). If you prefer, you can select Home→Find (Alt, H, FD).**

    The Navigation pane opens. If it's not already selected, click the Browse tab.

2. At the top of the Navigation pane is the Search Document box. Click Find Options (the down arrow at the far right of the Search Document box).

   A context menu appears.

3. In the Find section, select Graphics.

   The Navigation pane can't display previews of images as it does with text, so it tells you that a preview isn't available.

Tip: You can search for tables and equations using this method, too. Just choose the element you want to search for from the context menu.

---

4. Use the up and down arrows above the results pane to jump between images.

   As you click the arrows, Word jumps to the next (or previous) image in your document.

Fun with Fonts and Art That's Smart

You don't have to be an artist or a graphic designer to add professional-looking graphic effects to your documents. WordArt bends and twists words in all kinds of ways—it's great for an attention-getting flyer (and just plain fun to play with). SmartArt adds punch to your words and ideas by representing them visually, graphically showing relationships between ideas, such as a hierarchy chart, or steps in a process—a flowchart, for example. Both are easy to use—and you'll look good, because your document looks so good.

Creating WordArt

You can find WordArt in the Text section of the Insert tab. Here's how to use it:

1. Position the cursor where you want your WordArt. Select Insert→WordArt (Alt, N, W).

   The WordArt gallery opens, showing examples of WordArt styles.

2. Choose the style you want.

   Word inserts a text box in your document (which has some placeholder text in the style you chose) and opens the Drawing Tools | Format contextual tab, as shown in Figure 3-21.

3. Click inside the text box and start typing. As you type, the text box automatically expands to accommodate your text.

   Word overwrites the placeholder text with your new text.

When you're finished, click outside the text box to go back to working with normal text.

Tip: You can also turn existing text into WordArt. Select the word or phrase you want to convert, and then follow steps 1 and 2 in the preceding list.

Figure 3-21:
The WordArt button (circled) is in the Insert tab's Text section. After you choose a WordArt style, Word inserts a text box with placeholder text in that style. Start typing to replace that with your own text. You can adjust the size of the text box by clicking and dragging any of its handles.

Editing WordArt Text

If you need to make changes to what WordArt text says, click the WordArt to make the text box that holds it visible. Position the cursor where you need to make changes, and edit as necessary.

And here's where WordArt gets really fun: adding effects. To change the look of the WordArt, head for the Drawing Tools | Format tab's WordArt Styles section, shown in Figure 3-22. Click the WordArt in your document, and the ribbon automatically switches to that tab at the same time the text box appears. Inside the text box, select the text you want to monkey with. The WordArt Styles section gives you these options:

- **Quick Styles.** Click this button to open the gallery of WordArt styles and change the current style to a different one. If you want to change the WordArt back to plain vanilla text, select Clear WordArt beneath the gallery.

Tip: All the options in WordArt Styles show you a live preview of the different choices as you pass your pointer over those choices.

- **Text Fill.** This option changes the fill color of the letters, turning blue letters, for example, purple. Clicking it opens a menu of colors; choose a color from your document's theme (no worries about clashing; see page 181 for more about themes) or click More Fill Colors to expand your choices. The Gradient option lets you choose a pattern of lighter-and-darker shading.

- **Text Outline.** This changes the color of letters' outlines. As with text fill colors, you can select from colors related to the current theme or any color you like. Select Weight to change outlines' thickness or Dashes to pick a different line style (dotted, dashed, and so on).

- **Text Effects.** You can add a lot of special effects to WordArt, including shadows, reflections, glow, beveling, 3-D rotations, and transform effects, which warp the letters into waves, circles, and other patterns. Figure 3-22 shows an example of a wave transform effect. Select the kind of effect you want, and a fly-out menu appears to show you a gallery of options for that effect. Some of these effects make your text hard to read, so watch the live preview to make sure the *word* part of your WordArt remains legible.

Note: If you add a text effect to WordArt, when you bring up the text box to edit the text, Word temporarily removes the effect so you can see the letters clearly. When you click outside the box, the effect gets reapplied.

Figure 3-22:
There are dozens of options for adding effects to your WordArt text. Transform effects bend words into circles, waves, arcs, and much more.

To position WordArt on the page, click it to reveal its text box. Move the pointer to any of the dashed lines that make up the text box's borders so that the pointer becomes a four-way arrow. Click, and the dashed line turns solid. With the pointer still on the border, click and drag the WordArt wherever you want it.

Tip: The green rotation handle above the WordArt text box lets you change the angle of the WordArt on the page. Click and drag in an arc until the text box is at the angle you want.

To delete WordArt, click the WordArt to show its text box, click any border of the text box, and then press Delete or Backspace.

Inserting SmartArt into Word Documents

Introduced with PowerPoint 2007, SmartArt added visual interest to ho-hum Power-Point slides, replacing boring old bullets and cockeyed flowcharts with professional-looking graphics. And SmartArt can do the same for your Word documents, impressing colleagues, clients, and higher-ups with your attention-getting graphics.

Chapter 21 discusses working with SmartArt in detail (it's consistent across Office programs). So head there to see figures and read about editing and formatting SmartArt. Here's how to insert SmartArt into a Word document:

1. **Place the cursor where you want SmartArt to appear in your document, and then select Insert→SmartArt (Alt, N, M).**

   The Choose a SmartArt Graphic dialog box opens. A menu on the left lists the different kinds of graphics you can insert: list, process flow, cycle, hierarchy, and so on. A gallery of SmartArt appears in the middle of the box, and there's a preview of the selected SmartArt graphic on the right. Each preview includes commentary on when you might want to use that graphic.

2. **Choose the kind of SmartArt you want on the left, and then select a graphic from the gallery. Click OK.**

   The graphic you selected appears in your document, along with a pane where you can type the text to appear on the graphic, such as labels on a chart or points or steps on a list.

3. **Use the typing pane to add text to the graphic and the arrow keys to move between text boxes.**

   As you type, your text appears in the graphic.

4. **When you're finished adding text, click the typing pane's upper-right X to close it.**

   Your graphic shows the text you entered.

To edit what you've written on a SmartArt graphic, click its text to reveal the text box that contains it and type inside the box. Alternatively, click the tab on the left side of the frame that holds the graphic to reopen the typing pane.

Adding Charts and Diagrams

If a picture is worth a thousand words, then a good chart is probably worth 10 times that amount. Charts and diagrams take data and express it in an easy-to-understand visual form. When you insert a chart into Word, you present information that readers can easily interpret and absorb at a glance.

Here's how to insert a chart into Word:

1. **With the cursor in the spot where you want to insert the chart, select Insert→Chart (Alt, N, C).**

   The Insert Chart dialog box, shown in Figure 3-23, opens. On the left is a menu of different chart types, including column, line, pie, bar, and so on. The rest of the dialog box shows a gallery of chart styles for each type.

Figure 3-23:
Word (like the other programs in the Office suite) comes with many built-in chart styles. Select a type of chart on the left to see the available styles for that type.

2. **Select the chart style you want and click OK.**

Tip: If you tend to use the same chart style over and over again, select that style and click Set as Default Chart. The next time you open the Insert Chart dialog box, Word preselects that style for you. Of course, you can pick a different style if you want, but you won't have to hunt for your favorite.

   Word inserts the chart into your document and opens Excel in another window with some sample data, as shown in Figure 3-24.

3. **In the Excel window, replace the placeholder data with your own.**

   For example, say you were comparing quarterly sales for four different territories. You'd replace the categories in Column A with time periods: 1st Quarter, 2nd sQuarter, 3rd Quarter, and 4th Quarter. And you'd replaces the series in Row 1 with territories: say, North, South, East, and West. Then fill in your data in the appropriate cells.

   As you type, the changes you make in Excel appear immediately in your chart in Word. If you need more rows or columns, click the lower-right corner of the blue box that surrounds the data in Excel and drag it to expand the range of cells.

Figure 3-24:
When you insert a chart into Word, you store its data in Excel.

4. **When you're finished entering data, close Excel by clicking its upper-right X.**

   Excel closes, and the window containing Word expands to its full size. Your chart displays the labels and data you entered in Excel.

If you need to change the information in your chart, select Chart Tools | Design→Edit Data (Alt, JC, D) to reopen Excel to edit the chart's data. To change a chart's type, click the chart to display its frame. Right-click the frame and, from the shortcut menu that appears, select Change Chart Type. This opens a dialog box that looks just like Insert Chart; select a type and style of chart, and then click OK. Word converts the current chart to that style.

To delete a chart from a Word document, click the chart to select it, and then press Delete or Backspace.

Tip: For more about working with charts, see Chapter 19.

Proofing and Research Tools

You know what they say: Nobody's perfekt. Everyone makes spelling mistakes, typos, and grammar flubs. And nobody—yet—can cram an entire library's worth of reference information between their ears. Thanks to Word's proofing and research tools, you don't have to be perfect to produce perfect documents. Word can keep an eye on your spelling and grammar and correct common typos before you even realize your finger hit the wrong key. It takes the drudgery, too, out of common formatting tasks, like creating lists and inserting certain symbols, by automating them. It can also help you find information you need, from synonyms and definitions to translations to web searches—all without leaving Word.

Checking Spelling and Grammar

You may not have a small army of editors to make sure your spelling and grammar are up to snuff, but thanks to Word's spelling- and grammar-checking tools, you don't need them. Word is constantly on the lookout for mistakes in both departments, flagging problems and offering suggested fixes.

Catching Spelling Mistakes

Word assumes you want to catch and correct spelling errors as they occur, so it automatically checks your spelling as you type. When Word spots an error, it puts a wavy red line under the offending word. If the mistake is obvious, you can fix the spelling yourself to make the red line go away. If you're not sure how to spell the word correctly, right-click it. A shortcut menu opens, as shown in Figure 4-1, with suggested corrections at the top. Click a suggestion to replace the misspelled word with the correct one.

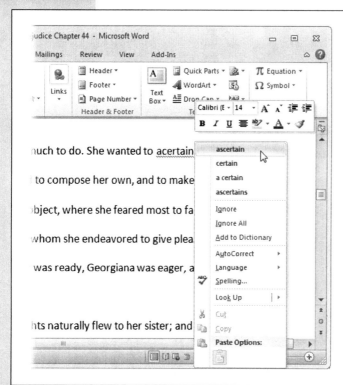

Figure 4-1:
When Word spots an iffy spelling, a wavy red line appears beneath the suspect word. To find out what the correct spelling may be, right-click the word and choose a correction from the menu.

Some people prefer to focus on getting their thoughts down as they write—they don't want to worry about fixing typos and spelling errors until later. If that's how you roll, then getting your spelling checked while you type is distracting, kind of like having someone reading over your shoulder, periodically poking you and saying, "Hey! Look there! You made a mistake!" If you prefer to focus on your thoughts as your write and clean up the text later, it's simple to turn off automatic spell checking:

1. **Click File→Options (Alt, F, I).**

    The Word Options dialog box opens.

2. **Select Proofing.**

    Options related to spell checking are in the "When correcting spelling and grammar in Word" section.

3. **Turn off the "Check spelling as you type" checkbox, and then click OK.**

    Those wavy red lines appear no more in your documents.

If you turn off the "Check spelling as you type" feature, don't forget to run a spell check on your document before you print it out or email it; page 115 shows you how.

Tip: You can hide those wavy red lines as you work on a document and then turn them back on when you're ready to see which words need fixing. To hide the marking of spelling mistakes, go Backstage by clicking File→Options (Alt, F, I); in the Word Options dialog box, select Proofing. In the "Exceptions for" section, choose the current document or All New Documents and then turn on the checkbox labeled "Hide spelling errors in this document only"; click OK. Now Word keeps track of spelling problems as you type, but doesn't point them out to you.

When you're ready to see the document's spelling mistakes, head Backstage to the Word Options Proofing page again, turn off the "Hide spelling errors…" checkbox, and then click OK. The wavy red lines are back—you can see your spelling errors without having to run a word-by-word spelling check.

Using contextual spelling

Sometimes you get the spelling right but the meaning wrong. For example, "their," "there," and "they're" are all correct spellings, but those words are not interchangeable; each has its own meaning. For example, you can't write

There going to check into they're room once they get their.

or

Their going to check into there room once they get they're.

The sentence makes sense only when you put the right spelling in the right place:

They're going to check into their room once they get there.

Word's *contextual spelling* feature sniffs out problems that regular spell checking doesn't catch. It works just like spell checking. When you type a word that might not fit the context in which it appears, Word throws a wavy blue line under it. To see Word's proposed suggestion, right-click the questioned word.

Contextual spelling isn't perfect. It does miss some mistakes. But if it catches even some of the errors that would otherwise sneak into your document, that's a good thing.

Note: Turn contextual spelling on or off in the Word Options dialog box, select File→Options (Alt, F, I), choose Proofing, and, in the "When correcting spelling and grammar in Word" section, find the "Use contextual spelling" checkbox. For Word to watch for contextual spelling errors as you type, you must also have "Check spelling as you type" turned on.

Checking spelling in an entire document

If you'd rather check your document's spelling all at once than on the fly, here's how:

1. **In the document whose spelling you want to check, select Review→Spelling & Grammar (Alt, R, S).**

   Word searches for any word that doesn't match the spellings in its built-in dictionary. When it finds one, it opens the Spelling and Grammar dialog box, shown in Figure 4-2. This box shows the misspelled word (highlighted in red) in its context and suggests a spelling. If there are several possible corrections, Word lists them all.

2. **To replace the misspelled word, select the correct replacement and click Change. If you think the misspelled word appears more than once in the document, then select Change All to replace them all at once. If the word is correct as it is, tell Word to ignore it (just this instance or all instances in the document) or to add it to the dictionary.**

   Word jumps to the next misspelled word.

3. **Keep repeating these steps until Word can find no more potential spelling errors and tells you the spelling check is complete. Click OK.**

   Word leaves spell checking mode and returns you to your document.

Note: While it checks your spelling, Word also looks for repeated words, as in "The dog chased *the the* cat." When it flags an occurrence of a repeated word, your options are to ignore just this instance or to delete the repeated word.

Figure 4-2:
When Word finds a spelling that doesn't match anything in its dictionary, it suggests one or more replacements. You can accept a replacement (click Change or Change All) or tell Word to ignore the word this time (Ignore Once) or throughout the document (Ignore All). Click Add to Dictionary if the word is one you use frequently, like your boss's last name.

Note: If you have contextual spelling (page 117) turned on, Word highlights any possible contextual mistakes in blue.

Word's Grammar Checker

Word can also play grammar cop, policing your style and working to root out embarrassing errors. Word is great at finding sentence fragments, passive voice, capitalization errors, and other grammatical no-no's.

Grammar checking works very much like spell checking. You can have Word check your grammar as you type or check the whole document at once (or both, if you're *really* a perfectionist). In fact, you can run a grammar check at the same time you have Word check your spelling.

To control whether Word checks grammar as you type, select File→Options (Alt, F, I). In the Word Options dialog box, choose Proofing; in the "When correcting spelling and grammar in Word" section, turn on the "Mark grammar errors as you type" checkbox. (When you do, Word automatically turns on the "Check grammar with spelling" checkbox as well.) Click OK.

When you have automatic grammar checking turned on, Word puts a wavy green line under any text—a word, a phrase, a sentence—that looks like it might be incorrect. Right-click any part of the text that has the wavy green underlining. The shortcut menu, shown in Figure 4-3, suggests a grammar fix (or tells you what the problem might be, such as Fragment). Replace what's underlined by clicking Word's suggestion, or leave things as they are by clicking Ignore Once.

Tip: Not sure why Word flagged the selection as a possible error? Click About This Sentence to open a dialog box that explains the suspected error, along with easy-to-understand examples of right and wrong usage.

Figure 4-3:
When Word's grammar checker finds a potential mistake, right-click the flagged word or phrase to open a shortcut menu that helps you correct the problem. Click the suggested fix to insert it in your document. Click About This Sentence for an explanation of why Word flagged it.

If you prefer to give the entire document a grammatical once-over, you can run a grammar check simultaneously with a spelling check. When you fire up the spell checker (Review→Spelling & Grammar or Alt, R, S), look in the bottom-left part of the Spelling and Grammar dialog box and make sure there's a checkmark in the "Check grammar" checkbox. This tells Word to look for grammatical problems at the same time it scours your document for spelling mistakes.

When Word finds a potential grammatical problem, the Spelling and Grammar dialog box looks something like the one in Figure 4-4. Word highlights the potential problem in green and suggests alternatives (or names the problem, as shown in Figure 4-4). Here are your options for dealing with text flagged in a grammar check:

- **Ignore Once.** Click this button to skip over this one instance and move on, while still applying the grammatical rule that flagged this instance.

- **Ignore Rule.** Maybe you're writing a novel or play, for example, and don't care if your document has sentence fragments, because people often use them in speech. If there's a grammatical rule you don't want Word to apply, click this button to skip all potential violations of the rule.

- **Change.** When Word suggests a fix, apply it to your document by clicking this button. If Word identifies a problem but can't say how to fix it in this case, you'll see something like "Fragment (consider revising)" in the Suggestions box. To fix the problem, click the flagged sentence in the Spelling and Grammar dialog box and make your changes there. Then click Change to insert your changed text into the document.

- **Next Sentence.** Click this button to leave this sentence as is and check the next sentence for errors.

Figure 4-4:
When you run a grammar check, Word offers a correction or, as here, identifies the potential problem.

Tip: If you're not sure why the highlighted text might be a problem, click Explain to open a dialog box and get a mini–grammar lesson.

When Word has finished checking the document, it tells you it's done. Click OK to go back to the document.

Getting Things Right with AutoCorrect

Typos happen. When your fingers are flying over the keyboard, sometimes they'll land on the wrong key. Spell checking roots out some typos, but why take that extra step if you don't have to? Word corrects many common typos as soon as you make them. When you type *abotu*, for example, as soon as you hit the space bar Word magically changes the word to *about*. That's thanks to AutoCorrect, which keeps a long list of common typos and their corrections—and automatically applies those corrections as you type. So if you can never remember that darn "I before E except after C" rule, you'll love AutoCorrect. This feature also converts certain combinations of letters and punctuation marks into symbols; for example, if you type :) Word converts it into a smiley face (☺), and (*c*) becomes the copyright symbol (©).

As its name implies, AutoCorrect happens automatically, and it's already turned on when you install Word. So you don't really have to do anything to take advantage of AutoCorrect. But you can tweak it in various ways, as this section explains.

Note: Word won't autocorrect any text that contains a hyperlink. So you can type website names without fear that Word will "correct" their spelling to something else.

Undoing an AutoCorrect Change

Ninety-nine percent of the time, AutoCorrect is super-helpful. Sometimes, though, it blithely goes ahead and makes a change you don't want. For example, a common typo that AutoCorrect fixes is changing "teh" to "the." As you type up a list of conference participants, you notice that Dr. Teh has become Dr. The. In this case, you don't want the correction. If you notice an AutoCorrect change immediately after it happens, you can undo the change by pressing Alt+Backspace before you go any further.

If you type on a bit further before you notice the AutoCorrect-induced error, though, Alt+Backspace won't work (that keystroke combination simply undoes your most recent action). In that case, go back and hover over the autocorrected word or symbol so that a small blue rectangle appears beneath it. Move the pointer toward the rectangle until the AutoCorrect Options button, shown in Figure 4-5, appears (the picture on the button looks like a lightning bolt). If you want to undo the change just this time, click the button and select the "Change back" option from the shortcut menu. If you want Word to stop making this correction for good, select the Stop Automatically Correcting option.

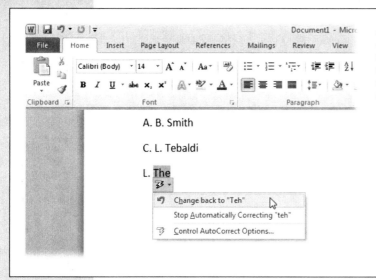

Figure 4-5:
Use the AutoCorrect Options button to undo corrections that you don't want. Click Control AutoCorrect Options to open the AutoCorrect dialog box (page 123).

Setting AutoCorrect Options

You can adjust what Word does and doesn't autocorrect. If there's a typo you make frequently that AutoCorrect doesn't already cover, for example, you can add the typo and its correction to the AutoCorrect list. Or if you want to stop Word from automatically correcting something—maybe you use (c) in lists and don't want that combination of characters to turn into a copyright symbol—you can do that, too.

To fine-tune your AutoCorrect settings, open the AutoCorrect dialog box: Select File→Options (Alt, F, I), select Proofing, and click the AutoCorrect Options button. The AutoCorrect dialog box opens to the AutoCorrect tab, shown in Figure 4-6, which gives you these options (Word has all of them turned on by default):

- **Show AutoCorrect Options buttons.** If you don't want the AutoCorrect Options button (Figure 4-5) to appear when you hover the pointer over an autocorrected word, then turn on this checkbox.

- **Correct TWo INitial CApitals.** If you tend to type faster than you can let up on the Shift key, this is a helpful correction. But you can turn it off by unchecking the box.

- **Capitalize first letter of sentences.** Basically, this tells Word to make sure that a capital letter always follows a period, question mark, or exclamation point.

Tip: If there are cases where you *want* two initial caps or a lowercase letter after a period, click the Exceptions button and tell Word what your special case is. (The next section tells you more about creating AutoCorrect exceptions.)

- **Capitalize first letter of table cells.** This setting helps you format tables consistently.

- **Capitalize names of days.** This setting does what it says, properly capitalizing the names of the days of the week.

- **Correct accidental usage of cAPS LOCK key.** When you've got Caps Lock on, it turns normal capitalization backwards: Caps Lock makes all the letters you type capital letters (unless you hit the Shift key, which makes letters lowercase). When you hit the Caps Lock key by mistake, it makes your writing look like you're shouting. This AutoCorrect option fixes the problem and turns off Caps Lock. (If you *want* to shout, you can always hit the Caps Lock key again.)

- **Replace text as you type.** Turning off this checkbox suspends AutoCorrect. If it's off and you want to correct a misspelled word, for example, you have to use the spelling checker or a good old-fashioned sharp eye. With this checkbox on, you can add new corrections to AutoCorrect (as explained later in this section).

- **Automatically use suggestions from the spelling checker.** This option uses Word's dictionary to correct common spelling errors automatically. (If you turn it off, Word autocorrects only those spellings that are in its AutoCorrect list.)

Figure 4-6:
Word comes with all these AutoCorrect options turned on, but you can pick and choose the ones you want. For any of these options you don't want Word to correct automatically, turn off the checkbox. Add custom corrections in the "Replace text as you type" section—put the typo you want corrected in the Replace text box and its correction in the With text box.

Making an exception

AutoCorrect makes you a better typist, fixing typos as they happen. Sometimes, though, you might want AutoCorrect to be a little less vigilant. You might want Word to catch the problem when you type two initial caps accidentally, for example, but wish it would make an exception for frequently used abbreviations, like "RAs" for research associates—it gets a little old having to undo the autocorrection to "Ras" every single time you type *RAs*.

You can tell Word to make specific exceptions to the things it corrects automatically. Here's how:

1. **Select File→Options→Proofing→AutoCorrect Options (Alt, F, I; use the arrow keys to select Proofing, and then press Alt+A).**

   This opens the AutoCorrect dialog box shown in Figure 4-6. (If your dialog box looks different from the one in the figure, then click the AutoCorrect tab.)

2. **Click the Exceptions button (Alt+E).**

   The AutoCorrect Exceptions dialog box has three tabs you can use to set up your specific exceptions:

   First Letter. This tab lists exceptions to the rule that a capital letter must always follow a period, question mark, or exclamation point.

   INitial CAps. Here's where you'd make "RAs" an exception. For any word you add here, Word won't correct two initial caps by making the second letter lowercase.

   Other Corrections. This is the catch-all tab for anything else you don't want Word to AutoCorrect.

3. **Select the tab you want. In the "Don't correct" text box, type your exception, using the capitalization you want (in the example, you'd type *RAs*). Click OK.**

   Word puts your addition on its exceptions list and will no longer autocorrect it.

Tip: You don't have to find your way to the AutoCorrect Exceptions box every time you want Word to make an exception to something it corrects automatically. The AutoCorrect Exceptions box has a checkbox labeled "Automatically add words to list" under the exceptions list. When this checkbox is turned on (as it is by default), Word adds an exception to the list whenever you *undo* an autocorrection.

Adding custom corrections

You can tell Word to automatically correct any of your habitual typos that aren't covered by its dictionary or AutoCorrect list, such as a name you find difficult to spell. Simply open the AutoCorrect dialog box to the AutoCorrect tab (Figure 4-6): Select File→Options (Alt, F, I), select Proofing, and then click AutoCorrect Options. If necessary, click the AutoCorrect tab.

In the dialog box, make sure the "Replace text as you type" checkbox is turned on. Then type the misspelling in the Replace text box and the correct spelling in the With text box. Click Add to add this correction to the AutoCorrect list.

Tip: AutoCorrect can be an easy way to spare your tired fingers some typing. If there's a long phrase you use frequently, you can create your own keyboard shortcut for it using AutoCorrect. For example, say you work for the Mutually Beneficial Aid and Comfort Society of Peers and Mentors, and you get really tired of typing out the organization's long name. Open the AutoCorrections dialog box and, in the Replace text box, type a keystroke combination you'd never normally use, like *#$%*. Then, in the With box, type the long phrase: in the example, *Mutually Beneficial Aid and Comfort Society of Peers and Mentors*. Click Add. Now, whenever you type *#$%* in a document, Word autocorrects it to the name of the organization.

Deleting an AutoCorrect correction

If AutoCorrect insists on making a correction you *don't* want, you can delete that correction from the AutoCorrect list. Open the AutoCorrect dialog box and find the correction in the AutoCorrect list. Corrections start with punctuation marks and symbols, followed by words in alphabetical order. Use the scroll arrows to find the correction you want to banish. Select it, and then click the Delete button.

Tip: When you use the AutoCorrect Options button (Figure 4-5) in a document to tell Word to stop making an automatic correction, that action also deletes the correction from the AutoCorrect dialog box's AutoCorrect list.

AutoFormatting in Word

Spelling and grammar aren't the only things Word corrects automatically as you type; it also makes formatting corrections and adjustments. For example, if you're on a new line and type *1.*, Word assumes you're starting a numbered list and turns what you just typed into that kind of list. The AutoFormat As You Type feature can be a great timesaver—or it can be a pain in the neck, depending on your preferences. Some people don't like it when the paragraph suddenly turns into a list, and some of Word's formatted characters—like "smart" quotes and dashes—don't translate well to other programs.

Whether you love or hate autoformatting, you're in control. Start by heading to the AutoFormat As You Type tab of the AutoCorrect dialog box. To get there, select File→Options (Alt, F, I), select Proofing, and click AutoCorrect Options. In the Auto-Correct dialog box, click the AutoFormat As You Type tab, shown in Figure 4-7.

As Figure 4-7 shows, Word turns on most of its AutoFormat options by default. Here's what they do:

- **Replace as you type.** This section contains the following replacements:

  — **"Straight quotes" with "smart quotes."** Instead of quotation marks that look like two small vertical lines, this option inserts curly quotation marks that curve toward the word they precede or follow.

  — **Fractions (1/2) with fraction character (½).** Type a common fraction as a number, followed by a slash, followed by another number, and Word inserts a single-character fraction instead.

  — ***Bold* and _italic_ with real formatting.** If you surround some text with asterisks, Word changes the text to boldface. Putting underline characters before and after text makes it italic. (This option is normally turned off, so turn on the checkbox if you want to activate it.)

  — **Internet and network paths with hyperlinks.** With this option on, whenever you type a web address (like *www.google.com*), Word inserts a hyperlink to that address into the text. So a reader who's connected to the Internet can Ctrl-click the link to open the web page. And if you publish the document as a blog post or web page, its links are already live.

  — **Ordinals (1st) with superscript.** If you'd rather write "1st" than "1st," then leave this checkbox turned on to add superscript formatting to the letters.

  — **Hyphens (--) with dash (—).** Back in the days of typewriters, two hyphens did the same job as a dash, and a typesetter would convert the hyphens into a dash as part of the publication process. Word plays typesetter for you, automatically converting two hyphens in a row into a single dash.

- **Apply as you type.** This section lists autoformatting that lets you create lists, horizontal lines, and tables by simply typing, without hitting buttons on the ribbon:

  — **Automatic bulleted lists.** This option creates a bulleted list whenever you begin a new line by typing an asterisk (*), hyphen (-), or closing angle bracket (>) followed by a space or a tab.

Tip: If you create a bulleted list using this method, press Enter twice to end the list.

  — **Border lines.** When this option is active, you can draw a specific style of horizontal line by going to a new line and typing three of the following characters one right after another and then pressing Enter:

  Tildes (~) create a wavy line.

Pound signs (#) create a triple line: a bold center line with thin lines above and below it.

Asterisks (*) create a dashed line.

Hyphens (-) create a thin line (but be careful that two consecutive hyphens don't autoformat into a dash).

Underscores (_) create a bold line.

Equal signs (=) create a double line.

— **Built-in Heading styles.** This option automatically formats a paragraph of five or fewer words as a heading when you take one of these actions:

For Heading 1, type a new line.

For Heading 2, precede the new line with a single tab.

For Heading 3, precede the new line with two tabs.

Whichever level of heading you want, be sure that the line does not end with any mark of punctuation, and then press Enter twice to apply the heading style.

— **Automatic numbered lists.** This option automatically formats your text as a numbered list when you start a new line by typing 1 followed by a period or a tab. Press Enter twice to end the list.

Figure 4-7:
These are the standard settings for AutoFormat As You Type. Turn any checkbox off or on to make your AutoFormat settings the way you want them.

— **Tables.** This option lets you create a table by using a rather cumbersome combination of plus signs (+) and hyphens (-). If you use it, begin and end each column with a plus sign and use hyphens to indicate column width. For example, typing +--------+----+--------+----+ and then pressing Enter would create a one-line table of four columns, with the first and third columns twice the width of the second and fourth columns. (Watch out for consecutive hyphens that get autoformatted into dashes.) To create a new row, place the cursor just after the row you want to insert the new row beneath, and then press Enter.

- **Automatically as you type.** This section controls these miscellaneous formatting changes:

  — **Format beginning of list item like the one before it.** If you apply formatting to the beginning of a list, such as boldfacing an introductory word or phrase (like this list does), Word keeps track of that formatting up to the first punctuation mark and applies it to the list items that follow.

  — **Set left- and first-indent with tabs and backspaces.** This option is off by default. If you turn it on, you can indent a paragraph by placing the cursor at the beginning of the paragraph's first line and pressing the Tab key. To indent an entire paragraph, place the cursor at the beginning of any line in the paragraph except the first line, and press the Tab key. To undo either kind of indentation, press the Backspace key.

  — **Define styles based on your formatting.** This options applies one of Word's built-in styles (page 51) to text you've formatted manually when your text has the same formatting as that built-in style.

Word's Built-in Research Tools

Word comes with a number of handy research tools built in, including a dictionary, thesaurus, translator, and access to several search and research websites. You access these tools in the Research pane, shown in Figure 4-8. To summon its help, click Review→Research (Alt, R, R).

Tip: If the Research pane looks a little small, you can make it bigger. Hover your mouse pointer over the Research pane's left border until it becomes a two-headed arrow, and then click and drag to resize the pane. When the pane is the size you want, let go of the mouse button.

Looking Up a Word in the Dictionary

No matter how big your vocabulary, once in a while you have to look up a word to find out (or check) its meaning. No need to leaf through a dictionary, though—you can look up words using the Research pane.

Select the word that's puzzling you and open the Research pane (Figure 4-8): Review→Research (Alt, R, R). When the pane opens, the word you selected already appears in the "Search for" text box. From the drop-down list beneath it, select the dictionary. (In the U.S., it's Encarta Dictionary: English [North America]). Word looks up the word you selected and displays its definitions; scroll down to read through them.

To look up another word, just type it into the "Search for" box and press Enter or click the green "Start searching" arrow.

Figure 4-8:
Word's Research pane puts an entire library of reference information at your fingertips. Use the drop-down list beneath the "Search for" box to select the research tool you want (here, Word's thesaurus is displaying a list of synonyms).

Using the Thesaurus

When the word you're thinking of is almost—but not quite—the word you want, you can consult a thesaurus to look up synonyms. To make that chore just a little bit easier, Word has its own thesaurus that you can check as you work, without taking the time to pull a book from the shelf.

The quickest way to get a list of synonyms is to right-click the word you want to replace. In the shortcut menu, point at Synonyms to see a fly-out list of alternatives for the word you right-clicked. Click any word on that list, and it replaces the original word.

If none of the words on the list are what you're looking for, go to the bottom of the list and click Thesaurus. This opens the thesaurus in the Research pane, shown in Figure 4-8. The Thesaurus offers a longer list of synonyms than the fly-out list. Scroll through the possibilities and click the one you want to put it in the document.

Tip: Here's another route to open the Thesaurus in the Research pane: Select the word you want and then choose Review→Thesaurus (Alt, R, E).

Getting Information about a Subject

If your computer is connected to the Internet, you can also use the Research pane to look up information. When you type a word or phrase into the "Search for" text box, choose Bing from the drop-down list to use Microsoft's search engine to find references to your search term on the web.

Note: The Search pane offers a couple of options besides Bing for researching a topic: Factiva iWorks and HighBeam Research. Both of these are subscription sites that show you a preview of an article—but you can read the whole thing only if you pay to subscribe.

The Search pane shows you a preview of each website it finds; when you want to read more, click the link that follows the preview to open that page in your web browser.

Tip: If trying to read the article previews in the Search pane gives you a headache, scroll down to find the "View all results on Live Search" link. Click it to open a window that shows the results in your web browser.

Translating Text

A foreign word or phrase can add a little *je ne sais quoi* to your writing. Word's translation tools let you translate from one language to another—with nearly two dozen languages to choose from.

Word uses its built-in bilingual dictionaries to translate words and common phrases. To translate an entire document, Word works with translation service WorldLingo (*www.worldlingo.com*) to provide a machine translation of the document. Here's how it works: Word sends a copy of your document over the Internet to the WorldLingo website, where a computer program scans and translates the text. Computers don't have quite the "ear" for human language that people do, so the translation is likely to sound stiff and, in places, may even be somewhat hard to understand. Still, you'll get the gist of the document by translating it with this method. (On the plus side, machine translation isn't yet good enough that your kids can use it to cheat on their Spanish homework.)

Getting a quick translation with the Mini Translator

Word's Mini Translator gives you a quick translation. When you point to a word or select a phrase, the translation appears in a transparent box that floats over your text. Move the mouse pointer toward the box to make it solid (and easier to read), as shown in Figure 4-9.

Here's how to set up Word's Mini Translator:

1. **In the Language section of the Review tab, select Translate (Review→Translate or Alt, R, L).**

   From the menu that appears, select Choose Translation Language at the bottom (if you've got keyboard shortcuts turned on, press L).

2. **This opens the Translation Options dialog box. In the left-hand list, select Mini Translator.**

   The main part of the dialog box shows a drop-down list of the languages available for translation.

3. **Select the language you want from the drop-down list and click OK.**

   Now, when you point to a word or select a phrase in your document, Word translates it into the language you selected, as shown in Figure 4-9.

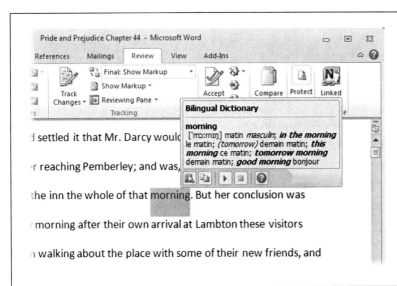

Figure 4-9:
The Mini Translator gives you an on-the-spot translation of a word or selected phrase. The buttons at the bottom are, from left to right, Expand, Copy, Play (to hear a recording of someone pronouncing the word or phrase), Stop (to stop the recording), and Help.

Tip: If the Mini Translator has lots of definitions and you can't read them all, click the lower-left Expand button to open the Research pane, with translation information about the selected word or phrase already displayed.

You probably don't need the Mini Translator turned on for every document you work with. To turn it off, select Review→Translate→Mini Translator (Alt, R, L, M). This sequence toggles the Mini Translator off and on, so when you require the Mini Translator's services again, repeat the same clicks or keystrokes, and it's back.

Note: When you open Word, the Mini Translator is off by default, so you have to turn it on to use it.

Using the Research pane for translations

If you don't like having the Mini Translator always hovering over your text, you can use the Research pane (Figure 4-8) to get a quick translation of a word or phrase. Select the phrase you want to translate, and then follow these steps:

1. **Select Review→Translate→Translate Selected Text (Alt, R, L, S).**

   The Research pane opens with the text you selected in the "Search for" box. In the Translations box, two drop-down lists show the From and To languages.

2. **Make sure the From and To languages match what you want the translator to do—for example, translate a phrase from Spanish to English. If necessary, use the drop-down lists to choose languages.**

   In the WorldLingo section (you may have to scroll down to see it), a translation of the selection appears.

Translating an entire document

If you need to translate more than just a word or phrase, you can tell Word to translate an entire document. Doing so requires two main steps: choosing the languages you're working with and then sending the document over the Internet to the translation site. So before you translate a document, make sure you're connected to the Internet. Next choose your From and To languages:

1. **Select Review→Translate→Choose Translation Language (Alt, R, L, L).**

   The Translation Language Options dialog box opens.

2. **Make sure that Translate Document is selected in the left-hand pane. Then select your From and To languages from the drop-down lists. Click OK.**

   Word sets these languages as your standard for whole-document translation. (You can always change them later by following these steps again.)

After you've selected the languages you want, here's how you tell Word to translate a document:

3. **Select Review→Translate→Translate Document (Alt, R, L, T).**

   A dialog box appears, informing you that Word will send the document over the Internet to its translation service. Word doesn't encrypt the document, which means it may be visible to third parties as it crosses the Internet—so don't use this service to translate documents that have confidential or sensitive information, like financial data or Social Security numbers.

4. **Click Send.**

   Word sends the document to WorldLingo. A browser window opens and tells you that the translation is in progress. When the translation is ready, it appears in the browser window.

Tip: If you have the research pane open (Review→Research or Alt, R, R), you can order up a whole-document translation: Select Translation from the top drop-down list, choose your From and To languages, and then click the green arrow after "Translate the whole document".

Printing Documents

Despite all the talk about becoming a paperless society, we're still plenty fond of the dead-tree route. No matter how popular email gets, there still will be times when you want to print a hard copy to mail, to pin to a bulletin board, or to hand out at a meeting.

Printing in Word 2010 is different from earlier versions of the program. You're probably familiar with the classic Print dialog box, where you told Word what to print and how many copies. Word 2010 takes you Backstage, via the File tab, to prepare a document for printing. All the familiar settings are still there, but they're better laid out and give you more options. You won't miss the Print dialog box for a minute.

This chapter gives you a tour of the Backstage Print page; shows how to send a fax and print envelopes and labels; and introduces you to Word's super-helpful wizard to do a complex mail merge—without breaking a sweat.

Getting Started with Printing

The quickest way to print something is to add the aptly named Quick Print button to the Quick Access toolbar. (Page 889 tells you how to add buttons to this toolbar.) When you've done that, clicking Quick Print sends the current document straight to the printer. If you're a frequent printer, you'll definitely want the Quick Print button at hand.

But Quick Print isn't suitable for every printing job. You might want to double-check a document's formatting first or print a certain page range or a lot of copies, for example. These tasks require more than a single click, but Word makes 'em easy.

Previewing a Document Before You Print It

Before sending a document to the printer, make sure that it's formatted correctly and that the printed version will look the way you want it to. To get a preview, head for the View tab and check out any of these ways of looking at your document:

- **Print Layout view** (View→Print Layout or Alt, W, P), as its name implies, shows you how the document will look when printed. This view includes page numbers, as well as any headers and footers, although these elements are grayed out unless you're actively working with them.

- **One Page** (View→One Page or Alt, W, 1) gives you a bird's-eye view of a page, zooming out so that the entire page fits on your screen.

- **Two Pages** (View→Two Pages or Alt, W, 2) zooms out even farther, to show two full pages side by side.

If you need to make changes to your document, you can edit it in any of these views, although the One Page and Two Pages views shrink the document so much that it's hard to see what you're doing.

Tip: See page 26 to learn more about different ways to view a document in Word.

Word also shows you a preview as part of the printing process, as shown in Figure 5-1. Select File→Print (Alt, F, P) to see it. You can't edit the document in this mode, but you can see the entire document, one page at a time, by using the right-hand scroll bar to move through it. If you need to make changes before printing, click one of the other tabs, such as Home or Review, to scoot back to editing mode.

Tip: Add the Print Preview button to your Quick Access toolbar to get a shortcut to the Backstage Print page shown in Figure 5-1.

Printing a Document

To open the Backstage Print page shown in Figure 5-1, select File→Print (Alt, F, P). Pressing Ctrl+P also gets you there. Select the number of copies and any print settings you want (the next section reviews them in detail) and click the big Print button at the top of the Print section. Word sends your document to the printer.

Figure 5-1:
*In Word 2010, you
go Backstage to print
your document by
clicking the File tab
and selecting Print.
This is where you pre-
view the document,
select a printer, and
choose print settings
like paper size and
which pages to print.*

Selecting Print Options and Settings

Word 2010 gives you a lot of flexibility in printing. Even if you've got several different printers, Word keeps them all straight, so you can easily choose the one that
works best for a particular print job. And with the Backstage mode, it's easier than
ever to make sure your settings are just so before you hit Print.

Choosing a Printer

Many people have more than one printer connected to their computer. For example,
you might use a laser printer for documents and an inkjet for glossy photos. Other
"printing" options include faxing or sending the document to another program, like
OneNote (Chapter 30).

The Print page's Printer section has a button that shows you the default printer (it
has a checkmark on the printer icon, as Figure 5-1 shows). If that's the printer you
want to use, then you're all set. To choose another one, click the printer button and
choose the option from the menu that appears.

Specifying Settings

Unlike previous versions of Word, where you set up a printing job by squinting at the Print dialog box, the Backstage Print page in Word 2010 spreads things out. In the Settings section, you'll find a stack of big buttons (as shown in Figure 5-1), each one describing a current setting. To adjust any of these, click the button, and a menu appears that lets you make a different selection.

UP TO SPEED

Setting a Default Printer in Windows

Word always uses the same printer, called the *default*, to print your documents—unless you choose a different printer for a specific job. If you find yourself swapping choices every time you print, you might want to make that printer the default instead. Here's how:

- **Windows 7.** Select Start→Devices and Printers. This opens the Control Panel to its Devices and Printers section. The Printers and Faxes section lists the printers and faxes installed on your computer—you can tell which is currently the default printer because it has a green checkmark on its picture. Find the printer you want to make the default and right-click it. A shortcut menu opens; select "Set as default printer". The checkmark jumps to the printer you selected, making it your new default. Click the upper-right X to close the Control Panel.

- **Windows Vista.** Go to the Control Panel's Classic View and open Printers. This window is basically a location in Windows Explorer that lists all the printers and faxes installed on your computer. In the list of devices, find the printer you want, right-click it, and select Set as Default Printer. Click the upper-right X to close Printers and Faxes.

- **Windows XP.** Select Start→Settings→Printers and Faxes. The Printers and Faxes window opens, showing all your faxing and printing options. In the Name column, right-click the printer you want, and select Set as Default Printer. Click the upper-right X to close the Printers and Faxes window.

Going from top to bottom in the Settings section, here's what you can adjust:

- **Which pages to print.** You can print all pages, a selection, just the current page, or a page range you specify, such as 1–4 to print the first four pages: Type the page range in the text box below the button. You can specify a range of pages (1–4, for example), specific pages (such as 4, 7, 12), or a combination (1–4, 7, 12, 15–17). If you type in a page range, the button automatically changes to say Print Custom Range.

Tip: If you want to print a specific selection that's not defined by pages, such as a bulleted list from the middle of a page, first select the portion you want, then open the Print page. Click the top button and choose Print Selection from the menu that appears. If you haven't selected some text before you open the Print page, Word grays out the Print Selection option on this menu.

- **Single- or double-sided.** Into saving paper? Here you can choose to print double-sided and use half the paper. If your printer can't handle duplex printing, Word will pause the printing job halfway through and prompt you to reload the paper to print the rest on the second side.

- **Collation.** When you're printing multiple copies, you can save yourself time shuffling pages if you choose Collated (1,2,3 1,2,3 1,2,3) over Uncollated (1,1,1 2,2,2 3,3,3).

- **Orientation.** If the Print Preview shows that your document is set for portrait orientation when you want landscape, you can fix it here.

- **Paper size.** Word can format your pages according to a wide range of paper sizes; choose the page or envelope size you want here.

- **Margins.** Adjust a document's margins and see the results in Print Preview before you print. Word has several built-in options; click Custom Margins and set the margins manually (page 65) if none of the built-ins meet your needs.

- **Pages per sheet.** Usually, you'll print a single page per sheet of paper. But for some jobs, like printing name badges for a conference, you might want to print multiple pages on a single sheet. Choose the number of pages that print on each sheet here.

Sending a Fax

Word may help you reduce the number of machines in your home. If you've got a fax modem or your computer is connected to a fax server on a network, you can call any fax number and dispatch your document directly from your computer.

Creating a Cover Page

The easiest way to create a cover page for a fax is to make it the first page of the document you're faxing. Just type the recipient's name and fax number, your name and fax number, and perhaps a subject or a notification of how many pages are following. When you send the fax—instant cover page.

If you use the same cover page over and over again, though, you can create a cover page in the Windows Fax and Scan utility program and save it for future use. Later, when you send a fax from Word, you can choose a previously created cover page from a drop-down list and send it with your fax.

Note: Windows Fax and Scan comes with all editions of Windows 7 and the Business, Enterprise, and Ultimate editions of Windows Vista.

Here's how to create a cover page in Windows Fax and Scan:

1. **Click the Windows Start button and select All Programs→Windows Fax and Scan.**

   The Windows Fax and Scan program starts up.

2. **In the lower-left part of the screen, make sure Fax is selected. Then select Tools→Cover Pages→New.**

   A window opens where you can design your cover page.

3. **Click Insert.**

   The Insert menu has three options: Recipient, Sender, and Message.

4. **For each option, select what you want to display on the cover page, such as Recipient→Name, Recipient→Fax Number, Sender→Name, Sender→ Company, Message→Subject, and so on.**

   As you select what you want to include, Fax and Scan inserts text boxes with your selection on the page. As Figure 5-2 shows, each insertion has two text boxes: a label and some placeholder text.

5. **To replace the placeholder text with your own text, click the text box and then press the Delete key.**

   The placeholder text disappears.

6. **If you want to add more text, click the Text button. When the cursor becomes a crosshairs icon, click and drag to create a new text box. Type whatever you want inside the box.**

   Repeat this process until the cover page has all the information you want.

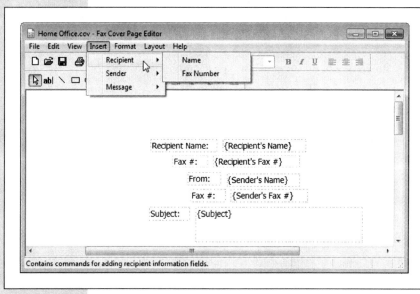

Figure 5-2:
Create a cover page by inserting labels (like Recipient Name:) and using text boxes to contain the specific information you want for the cover page. You can save cover pages to reuse later.

7. **When you're finished, click the Save button or File→Save.**

   The Save As dialog box opens.

8. **Give your cover page a name, such as "Price Quote" or "Home Office," in the "File name" box. Click Save.**

   Fax and Scan saves your cover page for use in any Office program that lets you send faxes.

When you're ready to send a fax (see the next section), you can choose a saved cover page from a drop-down list.

Sending a Fax

Word considers sending a fax a form of printing, so when you need to send a fax from your computer, head Backstage to the Print page (File→Print; Alt, F, P; or Ctrl+P). From there, sending a fax takes only a few quick steps:

Note: Before you can send a fax, you have to tell Word *how* to send faxes. The first time you choose Fax and then click Print on the Print page, the Fax Setup dialog box opens. This dialog box gives you two choices about how to send the fax: using your computer's modem or using a fax server on a network. If you send faxes using your company's network fax server, Word needs to know the server's name and network address. (You can get this info from your network administrator.)

---

1. **Open the document you want to fax and select File→Print (Alt, F, P or Ctrl+P).**

   The Print page (Figure 5-1) opens.

2. **In the Printer section, select Fax and then click Print.**

   Windows Fax and Scan's New Fax dialog box, shown in Figure 5-3, opens. Here's what it contains:

   — **Cover Page.** If you've created and saved any cover pages in Fax and Scan, they're listed in this drop-down menu. Select one if you want, or stick with the default None.

   — **To.** Type in a recipient name or click the button to select from any contacts you've added to Fax and Scan.

   — **Dialing rule.** If you need to do anything special to dial out, such as dial 9 before the number, select the rule here. Click the "New rule" button to create a dialing rule.

   — **Subject.** If you want to include a subject with your fax, type it in here.

— **Attach.** Word automatically fills in this box with an image of your document; behind the scenes it converts your document into the universally readable TIF image file format.

3. **When you've made your selections, click Send.**

   Off goes your fax to its destination.

Figure 5-3:
When you send a fax, Word saves your document as a TIF (tagged image format) file. Essentially, it takes a picture of your document and sends that as the fax. The TIF appears in this dialog box as an attachment.

Printing Envelopes

Although email is fast, convenient, and nearly instantaneous, it hasn't taken over the world quite yet. There are still times when you want to print out an old-fashioned letter—the kind you fold up, put in an envelope, stick a stamp on, and drop in the mail.

Word makes it easy to quickly print out an addressed envelope. For business correspondence, a printed envelope looks crisper and more professional than a handwritten one. The process is so simple that you'll have the envelope printed out in less time than it would take to find a pen. And check this out: If you live in the U.S., you can even pay for postage and print it right on the envelope—no need to stick on a stamp (page 146 tells you more about using Word with your electronic postage software).

Start by telling Word what your return address is:

1. **Select File→Options (Alt, F, I) and then choose Advanced.**

   This opens the "Advanced options for working with Word" dialog box.

2. **Scroll down to the General section and type your return address in the "Mailing address" text box. Click OK.**

   Word stores the address you typed as your return address for all envelopes. Now, when you prepare an envelope for printing, this address appears as the return address. (You can always edit it if necessary—for example, if you move or if you're writing a letter on someone else's behalf.)

Next, write your letter. To prepare an envelope for mailing the letter, follow these steps:

1. **With the letter open in Word, select Mailings→Envelopes (Alt, M, E).**

   The Envelopes and Labels dialog box opens to the Envelopes tab, shown in Figure 5-4. If an address appears in the "Delivery address" box, check to make sure that it's the recipient's correct address. If you don't see an address here, type in the recipient's address as you want it to appear on the envelope.

Tip: To grab an address from your Outlook Address Book (page 279), click the button with the little picture of a book just above the "Delivery address" box. The first time you do, the Choose Profile box opens, asking you to pick a source for addresses. Select your Outlook address book. Now, when you choose an existing contact, the address magically appears—with no extra typing on your part.

---

2. **Check the address in the "Return address" box and make any adjustments you want. If you don't want your return address to appear on this envelope, click Omit.**

   If you make any changes to the return address, Word asks before it closes the dialog box if you want to use the changed address as your new default return address.

3. **Check the Preview pane to make sure the envelope looks the way you want it to. Check the Feed pane so you know how to feed the envelope into your printer.**

   You can adjust envelope size, font, and address positioning (page 144), as well as the feed method for your printer (page 145) by clicking the Options button and selecting the Envelope Options or the Printing Options tab of the dialog box that opens.

4. **When everything looks good, feed an envelope into your printer and click Print.**

   Word closes the dialog box (without saving the address) and prints the envelope.

Tip: You can save the envelope right with the letter for future use. Instead of clicking Print, click Add to Document. Word inserts the formatted envelope as page 1 of the document. You can print both the letter and the envelope at the same time, or you can print just the envelope (follow the steps on page 136 for printing a document, selecting page 1 as the only page to print).

Figure 5-4:
As you prepare to print out an envelope, check the delivery address (top) and the return address (beneath it); if you need to make corrections, click inside either box to type there. If either address isn't positioned quite right in the Preview, click Options to adjust the positioning.

Formatting Envelope Addresses

When you create an addressed envelope to print out, Word automatically formats and places the text on a size 10 envelope (4⅛ × 9½ inches—the standard business size in the U.S.). You can change the font, its placement on the envelope, or the envelope size. To do that, open the Envelopes and Labels dialog box (Mailings→Envelopes or Alt, M, E) and click the Options button. This opens the Envelope Options dialog box to the Envelope Options tab, shown in Figure 5-5.

The Envelope Options tab lets you adjust these elements of an envelope:

- **Envelope size.** Use this drop-down list to select the size of the envelope you're using. When you choose a size, the Preview changes to reflect the change.

- **Address font.** Click the Font button to change a font or its size or to add special formatting (like bold or italic). There are separate sections for the delivery address and the return address, so you have to format each address separately.

- **Address position.** The "From left" and "From top" drop-down lists let you choose how far each address is from the envelope's left and top edges. Auto, the default, lets Word determine the distance. Use the up and down arrows to change an address's distance (in inches) from either edge. The Preview shows the new positioning as you make your selections.

When you're done making changes, click OK to return to the Envelopes and Labels dialog box, where you can click Print, Add to Document, or Close to return to your document.

Figure 5-5:
Use the Envelope Options box to change the envelope size or to adjust the position of either address. Click a Font button to choose a different font for an address.

Selecting a Feed Method

If the Feed section of the Envelopes and Labels dialog box (Figure 5-4) doesn't match the way you feed envelopes into your printer, you need to change the feed method in Word so the envelope prints correctly. Open the Envelopes and Labels dialog box (Mailings→Envelopes or Alt, M, E), click Options, and then select the Printing Options tab, shown in Figure 5-6.

The dialog box shows pictures of different ways you can feed an envelope into your printer. Select the one that looks like your printer's feed method. Turn on the "Face up" or "Face down" radio button as appropriate. Turn the "Clockwise rotation" dialog box on to feed the envelope into the printer with the left (return-address) edge first or off to feed it through with the right (stamp) edge first. Choose a feed tray if necessary, and then click OK to save your changes.

Figure 5-6:
Choose the picture that represents the way you feed envelopes into your printer, and make sure Word knows whether the printer prints face up or face down.

Adding Electronic Postage

Save yourself a step by paying for and printing postage when you print an envelope. No more having to make a trip to the Post Office because you've run out of stamps.

Before you can use electronic postage with Word, you need to subscribe to an electronic postage service, such as Stamps.com (*www.stamps.com*), and install its software on your computer. When you've done that, printing postage is easy:

1. **On the Envelopes tab of the Envelopes and Labels dialog box, turn on the "Add electronic postage" checkbox (Figure 5-4).**

   If you haven't yet installed an electronic postage program, Word lets you know that you need one and offers to take you to the Microsoft Office Online website for more information.

2. **To adjust your electronic postage setup, click the E-postage Properties button.**

   This takes you to your electronic postage program, where you can adjust the postage amount, add a special service (like Priority Mail or delivery confirmation), or change the date. How this works depends on the postage service you use.

3. **Back in the Envelopes and Labels dialog box, click Print.**

   Your postage-paid envelope prints.

Printing Labels

Whether you're printing just one or an entire sheet's worth, labels require special handling. You have to make sure the text appears in exactly the right position, without spilling over the edge and making the label useless. Word eliminates the guesswork. It knows the specifications of different manufacturers' products, so it can line up your text perfectly.

Note: If you're doing a big mailing and plan on printing an address label for each name on a large mailing list, jump over to page 148, which gives step-by-step instructions on mail merging in Word.

Here's what you do to print out a single label or a sheet of identical labels (return address labels, for example):

1. **Select Mailings→Labels (Alt, M, L).**

   The Envelopes and Labels dialog box opens displaying the Labels tab, as shown in Figure 5-7.

2. **In the Address box, type the address you want to print on the label.**

   If you prefer, you can click the small book above the Address box and choose a contact from your Outlook address book.

Figure 5-7:
You can print out a single label or a full page of the same label using the Labels tab of the Envelopes and Labels dialog box.

Tip: If you've given Word a default return address (page 143) and want to print out a sheet of return address labels, turn on the upper-right "Use return address" checkbox.

3. **In the Print section, choose whether you want Word to print a full page of identical labels or a single label by turning on the appropriate radio button.**

   If you choose Single label, choose the label's row and column to tell Word where on the sheet to print the label.

4. **If necessary, click Options to select the brand and product number for the labels you're using.**

   The Label Options dialog box opens. Choose the brand of label you use from the "Label vendors" drop-down menu. When you do, the "Product number" menu changes to display products from that company. When you've made your choices, click OK to return to the Envelopes and Labels dialog box.

5. **Make sure you've put the label sheet in your printer's feed tray, and then click Print.**

   Word sends your labels to the printer.

Merging Names and Addresses with Documents

When you open a letter that's addressed to "Dear Sir or Madam," you probably toss it into the recycling bin. Most people do. An impersonal letter that's not even addressed to you isn't much of an attention-getter. That's why Mail Merge was invented. It lets you send the same letter to multiple recipients with personalized touches: individual addresses, custom salutations, and more. So when you're sending a form letter to a bunch of different people—for example a fund-raising letter for your nonprofit, a new product list, or a quarterly update for clients—Mail Merge individualizes each printed letter for its recipient.

No matter how big your mailing, Word makes it a snap with an easy-to-use Mail Merge wizard that walks you through the process, one step at a time. To begin, select Mailings→Start Mail Merge→Step by Step Mail Merge Wizard (Alt, M, S, W). This opens the Mail Merge window, shown in Figure 5-8. There are six steps to doing a mail merge. If you're not sure where you are in the process, just glance at the bottom of the window.

Tip: The Mail Merge wizard is the easiest way to do a mail merge, whether you're working with letters, envelopes, or mailing labels. Whichever kind of document you choose, you follow the same six steps described in this section.

Click this button…   …to start the Mail Merge wizard in this pane.

Figure 5-8:
The Mail Merge wizard breaks up a complex mail merge into a series of simple steps.

Step 1: Select Document Type

The first step of the Mail Merge wizard, shown in Figure 5-8, is to choose the kind of document you're going to merge. Turn on the radio button for one of these options:

- **Letters.** Choose this option to send personalized versions of the same basic letter to multiple recipients.

- **E-mail messages.** If you want to send your multi-recipient letter via email instead of printing out copies, this is the way to go.

- **Envelopes.** Print addressed envelopes to send out your letters.

- **Labels.** Choose this option to print addresses on labels, rather than on envelopes.

- **Directory.** Use this option when you want to create and print out a list of addresses.

In this example, you're using Mail Merge to create and print personalized letters, so turn on the Letters radio button and, at the bottom of the window, click "Next: Starting document."

Tip: To make the Mail Merge window easier to read, click the upper-right down arrow, which lets you move and resize the window.

Step 2: Select Starting Document

In this step, you choose or create a letter to work with. If you've got a letter all ready to go, that's great—but you don't have to have a completed letter all written (and this example supposes you don't) to start a mail merge.

Here are your options in step 2:

- **Use the current document.** If you've already written your letter and have it open in this window, turn on this radio button.

- **Start from a template.** Choose this option to open a template that's already formatted for mail merging and use that template as the basis for your letter.

- **Start from existing document.** If you've sent mail merge letters in the past and want to use one of these as the basis for your letter, turn on this radio button. When you do, a drop-down list appears that lets you select and open the file you want.

If you've never done a mail merge before, then "Start from a template" is your best choice. When you turn on that radio button, a "Select template" link appears. Click it to open the Select Template dialog box, click the Letters tab, and then scroll through the available templates to find one to use as the basis of your letter. When you click a template, a bird's-eye view of it appears in the Preview pane. In the Create New section, make sure Document is turned on, and then click OK.

The document based on the template you selected appears in Word's Document pane. In the Mail Merge window, click "Next: Select recipients" to move on to step 3.

Step 3: Select Recipients

In this step, you tell Word the names and addresses of the letter's recipients. You've got three options for selecting recipients:

- **Use an existing list.** Turn on this radio button to use an existing list of names and addresses, such as an Excel spreadsheet or a table in Word. Click the Browse button to open a dialog box where you can navigate to and select the file that holds your mailing list.

- **Select from Outlook contacts.** When you turn on this radio button, a Choose Contacts Folder link appears. Click it to open a dialog box where you can select one of your Outlook Contacts folders and get recipients from that.

Note: In Outlook, the people in your address book are called Contacts, and you can put contacts into related groups, such as work contacts, family, and friends. Chapter 11 tells you all about working with contacts in Outlook.

- **Type a new list.** If you don't have an existing mailing list to use, you can create one now. Turn on this radio button and click the Create link. The New Address List dialog box opens. In this dialog box, you create a table to hold your mailing list by typing information into fields: Title, First Name, Last Name, Company Name, Address Line 1, and so on. Press Tab to move from one field to the next. Press New Entry to start a new line for the next entry. When you're done typing in information, click OK. Word prompts you to save your new address list as a file.

When you've selected a source for your letter's recipients, Word opens the Mail Merge Recipients dialog box, shown in Figure 5-9. To remove a recipient from the mailing, turn off the checkbox at the start of that recipient's record. If you want to send the mailing to some of the people on the list but not others—for example, to send the letter only to people in a certain city or Zip code—you can sort the list and then deselect people who shouldn't receive the letter.

To do a quick sort, click any column heading: Click once for an ascending sort (A→Z) and again for a descending sort (Z→A). If you need your sort to be more complex—say you want the letter to go to women between the ages of 24 and 40 who live in Boston—click the Sort link, which lets you sort by three criteria.

When you've selected the recipients you want, click OK. Back in the Mail Merge window, click the "Next: Write your letter" link to go to the next step.

Figure 5-9:
The Mail Merge Recipients dialog box lists the names and addresses on your mailing list. If you don't want someone on the list to receive the letter, turn off the checkbox next to that person's name. Use the links in the "Refine recipient list" section to sort and filter records or winnow out duplicates.

Step 4: Write Your Letter

In this step, you write your letter (if you haven't done so already) and add recipient information in the appropriate places. To do that, click the location in your document where you want to insert information from your mailing list. Then, in the Mail Merge window, click one of these links:

- **Address block.** When you click this link, the Insert Address Block dialog box, shown in Figure 5-10, opens. Here you tell Word what to insert (such as the recipient's name and postal address) and how to format it (such as "Mr. Bill Smith," "Bill Smith," or "The Smith Family"). The Preview pane shows how the formatted address block will look. Use the arrows to check the address block formatting for each name on your mailing list.

- **Greeting line.** This opens the Insert Greeting Line dialog box, where you format and insert recipient information into the letter's salutation: "Dear Bill," "Dear Mr. Smith," "Dear Mr. Bill Smith," and so on.

- **Electronic postage.** If you've got electronic postage software installed on your computer (page 146), you can add postage to your letters by clicking this link.

- **More items.** If other items appear on your mailing list that you want to insert into the letter, such as a product the recipient recently purchased from your company, you can add it to your letter by clicking this link. The Insert Merge Field dialog box opens, listing all the fields (column headings) that make up your data source (the spreadsheet or table you're using to supply information for the mail merge). Click any field on the list to insert it into your letter.

Whichever Insert dialog box you're using, click OK to insert the formatted info into the spot you selected in your letter. To insert a different kind of information, click the place in the letter where you want the information to appear, and then click the appropriate link. Keep doing this until you've personalized the letter the way you want it. Then click "Next: Preview your letters."

Step 5: Preview Your Letters

Word shows you a merged letter in the document pane, so you can review the final version and make sure it looks good. You can edit the letter's static content (the text that's the same in each letter) in the document pane, but if you want to make changes to the merged content, click the "Previous: Write your letter" link at the bottom of the Mail Merge window.

Figure 5-10:
*The Insert Address
Block dialog box is
where you specify
and format different
elements that go into
the address block
at the top of each
letter, such as how
recipients' names will
appear.*

In this step, go to the Mail Merge window to scroll through recipients, using the forward and back arrows on either side of the recipient number. To find a particular recipient, click the "Find a recipient" link and type information that identifies the recipient you want to find (such as last name or street address). Next, tell Word where to look for that info—in all fields or in a specific field—and click Find Next. Word finds the first letter that matches your criteria and displays it in the document pane. (If that's not the one you want, click Find Next again.) To remove a recipient from the mailing, click the button labeled "Exclude this recipient" in the Mail Merge window.

You're almost done. When you're satisfied with the preview, click "Next: Complete the merge."

Step 6: Complete the Merge

Word is now ready to print your merged letters. If you're ready, too, click Print. The Merge to Printer dialog box opens; select the letters you want to print: all of them, just the current one, or a range that you specify (Recipients 1 to 10, for example). Click OK to open the Print dialog box. Choose a printer and a number of copies, and then click OK to send the batch of letters to your printer.

If you want to personalize individual letters further before you print them—for example to add a P.S. to some recipients' letters but not to others—you can do that by opening a new document that contains some or all of your merged letters. Click the "Edit individual letters" link to open the Merge to New Document dialog box, where you select whether you want the new document to hold all your merged letters, just the one that currently appears in the document pane, or letters to a range of recipients. Click OK. Word opens a new document in which each letter of your mail merge begins on its own page. In this document, you can edit any letter without making changes to all the other letters. When you're done, print the document as you would any other document (page 135).

Do-It-Yourself Mail Merge with the Mailings Tab's Buttons

Although the wizard is by far the easiest and most foolproof way to do a mail merge, the buttons on the Mailings tab let you do a mail merge on your own, if for example you want to jump in and make an adjustment in the middle of the process (rather than going through the whole thing step by step). To do a wizard-free mail merge, follow the same process, going from right to left on the Mailings ribbon:

- Begin with Start Mail Merge (Alt, M, S) and select the kind of merge you want to do (letters, envelopes, labels, and so on).

- Then click Select Recipients (Alt, M, R) to choose the source of your data, followed by Edit Recipient List (Alt, M, D) to fine-tune that data.

- To insert fields, use the Address Block (Alt, M, A), Greeting Line (Alt, M, G), and Insert Merge Field (Alt, M, I) buttons.

- To preview your documents, click Preview Result (Alt, M, P).

- To finish the merge and print your documents, click Finish & Merge (Alt, M, F).

Reports and Long Documents

Long documents are the Mount Everest of word processing: a lofty goal full of special challenges. From research papers to marketing reports, from software specifications to the Great American Novel, you can ease readers' long treks by breaking long stretches of writing into manageable chunks. Chapters and sections, for starters, are simple ways to mark off discrete topics. A table of contents and an index can help speed navigation. And for some documents—such as academic and scientific papers—citations and a bibliography are a must.

Word 2010 handles lots of this heavy lifting for you, saving time and frustration. This chapter shows you how to make your opus more manageable, with a little help from Word.

Inserting Page Breaks

In the days of typewriters, starting a new chapter was easy: Remove the current sheet of paper, roll in a fresh, clean one, and type the new chapter's title on the first line. But when a single word-processing file can easily hold an entire book, starting a new chapter is less straightforward. Some writers keep hitting Enter until they're at the top of a new page. Don't do that! If you make any changes later (adding or deleting a paragraph, for example), subsequent chapter titles can jump around so that they're no longer at the top of a new page.

The easiest way to end an old chapter and start a new one is to insert a *page break* between chapters. The advantage to this method is clear: the page break stays in place, no matter how you change the text that comes before and after it. The first line of your new chapter always appears at the top of a new page.

To insert a page break, put the cursor at the beginning of the line that you want on top of the new page. Then take one of these routes:

- Insert→Page Break (Alt, N, B).
- Page Layout→ Breaks→Page (Alt, P, B, P).
- Ctrl+Enter.

How the resulting page break looks depends on what view you're in:

- **Print Layout View** (Alt, W, P) gives a clear sense of where pages break by showing you the bottom of one page and the top of the next. (Of course you need to scroll up or down to see this if you're in the middle of the page.)
- **Full Screen Reading View** (Alt, W, F) also shows page breaks clearly by displaying one or two pages, all laid out for printing, on the screen.
- **Web Layout View** (Alt, W, L) doesn't have page breaks (it treats a document as one long web page), but inserting a page break inserts white space between paragraphs.
- **Outline View** (Alt, W, U) treats each heading and paragraph as an item in a bulleted list. It shows page breaks by inserting a blank line between bullets.
- **Draft View** uses a dotted line across the page to indicate where each page ends naturally, but if you insert a page break as described earlier, it indicates that with a blank line.

Tip: To get the clearest picture of where you've inserted page breaks, tell Word to show hidden formatting characters by selecting Home→Show/Hide ¶ (Alt, H, 8) or by pressing Ctrl+* (Ctrl+Shift+8). When you do this, a short dotted line interrupted by the words Page Break appears at inserted page breaks, no matter which view you're in.

To delete a page break, turn on hidden characters (see the previous Tip) so you can easily find the page break you want to delete. Once you've located it, move the pointer to the left margin so it becomes a fat white arrow. Click to select the line that holds the page break and then press Delete or Backspace. Word removes the page break.

Breaking a Document into Sections

Sections offer more flexibility than page breaks. You can format a section differently from the rest of the document—helpful, for example, when you want to show a large table in landscape orientation when the rest of the document has portrait orientation. You can also format page numbers differently in different sections.

Kinds of Section Breaks

Before you insert a section break, it's helpful to understand the kinds of section breaks Word offers. You'll find these in the Page Layout tab's Page Setup section. Select Page Layout→Breaks to see these options:

- **Next Page (Alt, P, B, N).** This combines a section break with a page break; Word starts the new section on a new page.

- **Continuous (Alt, P, B, O).** When you insert a continuous section break, Word starts the new section on the current page.

- **Even Page (Alt, P, B, E).** This option begins the new section on the next even-numbered page. So if the current section ends on an even-numbered page, Word inserts a blank, odd-numbered page at the end of one section and before the beginning of the next.

- **Odd Page (Alt, P, B, D).** This works just like an Even Page section break, except the new section begins on the next odd-numbered page. You might use this kind of section break when you're laying out pages for a book and you want to start each new section or chapter on a right-hand page.

Inserting a Section Break

To insert a section break, position the cursor at the beginning of the first line of the new section. Open the Section Breaks menu by selecting Page Layout→Breaks (Alt, P, B), and then choose one of the options listed in the previous section.

Word inserts a section break and starts the next section where you indicated. (To see the section break, press Ctrl+* to make Word show hidden characters.) The cursor is blinking away in your new section; start typing to add content to the new section.

Changing the Orientation of a New Section

After you've inserted a section break, make sure the cursor is in the new section. Then select Page Layout→Orientation (Alt, P, O) and choose either Portrait or Landscape. To switch back to the document's usual orientation, insert another new section and repeat the process.

Changing the Page Numbering of a New Section

One good reason to start a new section is to separate preliminary material, like a prologue, from the rest of a document. You might want the prologue to use Roman numerals for page numbers, for example, and Chapter 1 to start on page 1.

Create a document and insert page numbers into it (page 78 tells you how to do that). Then follow these steps:

1. **Insert a section break between the two sections you want numbered differently (for this example, say the sections are a prologue and Chapter 1).**

   Choose any kind of section break that starts the next section on a new page: Next Page, Even Page, or Odd Page.

2. Click to position the cursor anywhere in the prologue. Then select Insert→Page Number→Format Page Numbers (Alt, N, NU, F).

   The Page Number Format dialog box, shown in Figure 6-1, opens.

3. Use the "Number format" drop-down list to select the numbering style you want. (For a prologue, you might select "i, ii, iii".) In the "Page numbering" section, turn on the "Start at" radio button and select the number you want for the first page; for the example, you'd choose i. Click OK.

   Now the pages in the prologue use Roman numerals for their numbering, while the page numbers in the next section use the numbering style you chose (such as 1, 2, 3) when you inserted page numbers into the document. The next step is to begin Chapter 1 on page 1.

4. Put the cursor in the section that contains Chapter 1 and open the Page Format Number dialog box again (Insert→Page Number→Format Page Numbers or Alt, N, NU, F).

   The Page Number Format dialog box (Figure 6-1) opens, showing the current formatting selections for this section.

5. If you want, choose a different number format. In the "Page numbering" section, turn on the "Start at" radio button and select 1. Click OK.

   Word starts the new section on page 1. The prologue and Chapter 1 now have separate numbering systems, using different styles and each beginning on page 1.

Figure 6-1:
Use page number formatting options to create different page numbering for different sections of your document. To select the page number that appears on the first page of a new section, turn on the "Start at" radio button and tell Word the page number you want.

Footnotes and Endnotes

Notes let you add commentary and tangential information to the main flow of text—you can add an explanation, elaborate on a point, or ask your readers to leave a tip in the PayPal jar. In Word, it doesn't matter whether you prefer footnotes (which appear at the bottom of the page) or endnotes (which appear all together at the end of a document or a section). Both are easy. You can even convert one to the other if you change your preference. Best of all, Word handles all the numbering and formatting for you.

You insert footnotes and endnotes from the Footnotes section of the References tab (Alt, S), shown in Figure 6-2.

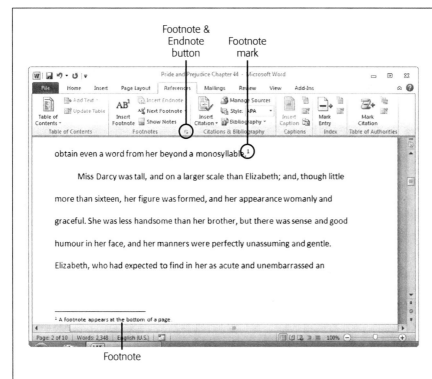

Figure 6-2:
To insert a footnote or endnote, go to the References tab's Footnotes section. This figure shows what a footnote looks like in Print Layout view.

Inserting a Footnote

First make sure your document is in Print Layout view and then position the cursor where you want the footnote mark to appear. Select References→Insert Footnote (Alt, S, F). Two things happen:

- Word inserts a superscript number as a footnote mark at your insertion point.
- At the bottom of the page, Word inserts a corresponding footnote number and puts the cursor just after it, so you can start typing your footnote.

When you've finished typing your note, click in the main body of the document and continue writing or editing.

Note: If you insert a footnote while you're working in Web Layout, Outline, or Draft view, the Footnotes pane opens at the bottom of the screen. Type your footnote in that rectangular window. When you're done, close the Footnotes pane by clicking its upper-right X.

Inserting an Endnote

This works pretty much the same way as inserting a footnote. Put the cursor wherever you want the endnote mark to appear and then select References→Insert Endnote (Alt, S, E). Word sticks the endnote mark there and then immediately jumps to the end of the document, where it adds the corresponding note number and positions the cursor. Just type to write your note.

Tip: To find your way back from an endnote to its reference in the text, double-click the number or symbol that appears at the beginning of the endnote. Word jumps right back to the corresponding endnote mark in the text. This works for footnotes, too.

Editing a Note

After you've inserted a note, double-click the note mark in the text to jump to that note. If you're in Print Layout view, Word jumps to the position of the note in the document. If you're in Draft or another view, Word opens the Footnotes or Endnotes pane and places the cursor at the corresponding note. Either way, you can edit the note just as you'd edit any other text.

Navigating Notes

To find the next footnote in your document, use the Next Footnote button: References→Next Footnote. Or click the down arrow at the right of the Next Footnote button. This opens a menu showing you these options:

- **Next Footnote** (Alt, S, O, N) jumps forward to the next footnote in your document.
- **Previous Footnote** (Alt, S, O, P) jumps back to the closest previous footnote.
- **Next Endnote** (Alt, S, O, X) moves to the document's next endnote.
- **Previous Endnote** (Alt, S, O, V) moves to the previous endnote.

Choosing one of these options takes you to the footnote or endnote mark in the text. Hover your mouse pointer over the note mark to read the associated note as a ScreenTip (pop-up window), or double-click the marker to go to the note itself.

Another way to move through your notes is to open the Footnote or Endnote pane. In Draft view, select References→Show Notes (Alt, S, H). The pane opens at the bottom of the screen, where you can scroll through it to read all footnotes or endnotes.

Tip: To make the Footnotes or Endnotes pane bigger, hover your mouse pointer over the border between the main document and the pane. When the pointer changes to the Resize indicator (two parallel lines with arrows above and below them), click and drag to resize the pane. Ah, now you've got some breathing room while working with your notes.

Having both footnotes and endnotes is probably overkill, but if your document has both, you can't open both the Footnotes and Endnotes pane at the same time. When you select References→Show Notes (Alt, S, H), a dialog box appears asking whether you want to see the footnotes or the endnotes. Turn on the radio button you want, and then click OK.

Changing the Position of Footnotes or Endnotes

You have a couple of options for where footnotes or endnotes appear in your document. Start by going to the References tab's Footnotes section, and then click the pop-out Footnote and Endnote button (Alt, S, Q). This opens the Footnote and Endnote dialog box, shown in Figure 6-3.

The Location section has two radio buttons: Footnotes and Endnotes. Turn on the radio button of the kind of notes you want to position, and then make one of these choices from the drop-down list:

- **Footnotes:** Bottom of page (the default) or below text.
- **Endnotes:** End of section or end of document (the default).

In the Apply changes section, make sure the "Apply changes to" drop-down menu shows "Whole document". Click Apply to change the position of your notes.

Figure 6-3:
Use the Footnote and Endnote dialog box to change the location of your notes, to convert one kind of note to the other, or to format the note markers in the text.

Converting Footnotes to Endnotes (or Vice Versa)

Say you've formatted all the notes in your research paper as footnotes, but then you find out that the professor wants them formatted as endnotes. Changing them sounds like a lot of work—but it's not. It takes only a couple of clicks:

1. Select References→Footnote and Endnote (Alt, S, Q).

   The Footnote and Endnote dialog box (Figure 6-3) opens. At the bottom of the Location section is a button labeled Convert.

2. **Click the Convert button.**

   The Convert Notes dialog box opens with three options: "Convert all footnotes to endnotes", "Convert all endnotes to footnotes", and "Swap footnotes and endnotes".

3. **Turn on the radio button of the option you want, and then click OK. Close the Footnote and Endnote dialog box by clicking Apply or the upper-right X.**

   That's it! You've converted your notes.

Changing Footnote or Endnote Markers

If you want to use a different style of marker from the standard ones Word uses (1, 2, 3 for footnotes and i, ii, iii for endnotes), you can do that from the Footnote and Endnote dialog box (Figure 6-3). Here's how:

1. Select References→Footnote and Endnote (Alt, S, Q).

   The Footnote and Endnote dialog box (Figure 6-3) opens.

2. **In the Format section, choose a numbering scheme from the "Number format" drop-down list.**

   You can choose from different formats using numbers, letters, Roman numerals, or symbols.

3. **In the "Start at" box, choose the starting number, letter, or symbol for your markers. Then, from the Numbering drop-down menu, choose whether you want note numbering to be continuous, to restart with each new section, or to restart on each page. Click Apply.**

   Word changes your document's note markers as you specified.

Deleting a Note

To delete a note, find the marker for the note you want to delete. Select it, and then press Delete or Backspace. The marker and the note it referred to both go away.

Citations and Bibliographies

When you're writing a research paper or report that cites other people's work—books, articles, interviews, and so on—you need to keep track of those citations and give credit where it's due. Word is ready to help and, later, to construct a bibliography. It's like having your own personal research assistant.

Creating and Inserting a Citation

How you present your sources depends on what citation style you use. Various professional groups, such as the American Psychological Association (APA) or the Modern Language Association (MLA) define the standard style for citations, including required information and formatting. Which style you work with depends on the purpose of your document. Academics use APA style for papers in the social sciences and MLA style for paper in the humanities, while engineers use ISO 690 (from the International Organization for Standardization) for technical papers.

To begin, head over to the References tab's Citations & Bibliography section and pick the style you want from the Style drop-down list (Alt, S, L). Your choice applies throughout the document and affects the information that Word collects when you add a new source.

After you've selected a citation style, here's how to create a source:

1. **Select References→Insert Citation→Add New Source (Alt, S, C, S).**

   Word opens the Create Source dialog box, shown in Figure 6-4. This dialog box has fields that collect information about the source—things like the author's name, the source's title, and the year it was published. Word uses these fields to build your bibliography entry.

2. **From the Type of Source drop-down list, select the kind of source you're citing: book, journal article, website, conference proceedings, and so on.**

   The fields in the Create Source dialog box change to match your selection.

3. **Type in information about the source.**

   When you click inside a field, Word shows you an example of what goes in that field. (These examples appear near the bottom of the dialog box.) For example, when you click inside the Author field, the example shows two author names in the proper format. Use the examples to make sure you're setting up each field correctly. In the lower-left corner, Word suggests a tag name based on information about this source, such as author and year of publication. Tags are useful for sorting your citations when you're looking for a particular citation to insert into a document. You can change the tag name if you want. If you do, though, make sure the tag clearly identifies the source.

Tip: Sometimes you might want to enter more bibliographical information than Word shows in the Create Source dialog box. For example, maybe your source is a book translated from another language—there's a field for the author's name, but not for the translator. To see more fields, turn on the lower-right Show All Bibliography Fields checkbox. When you do, the Create Source dialog box expands to show more fields, including Translator. So you don't get overwhelmed by all the fields, Word puts a red asterisk (*) next to fields recommended for the citation style you're using.

4. **When you've filled in all the necessary information about your source, click OK.**

   Word inserts the citation into your document and adds it to the Citation Gallery, a list of citations on the Insert Citation menu. If you want to insert the same citation elsewhere in the document, put the cursor where you want the citation to appear, select References→Insert Citation (Alt, S, C) and choose the citation you want from the list.

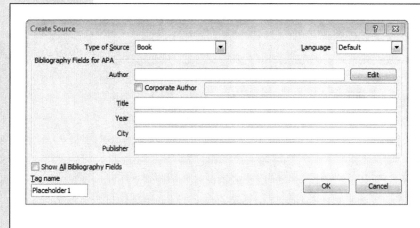

Figure 6-4:
The Create Source dialog captures the information you need to insert a citation into the text and, later, to create a bibliography. Be sure to fill out the fields required for bibliography entries. (If you don't see a field you need, such as Editor, turn on the lower-left Show All Bibliography Fields checkbox to display them.)

Tip: Get easy access to your list of citations by clicking References→Insert Citation, right-clicking any citation that appears on the menu, and then clicking Add Gallery to Quick Access Toolbar. This adds the Insert Citation button to the Quick Access toolbar that's always visible, no matter which ribbon tab is active.

Inserting an Existing Citation

When you create a citation, Word adds it to the Source Manager's master list, shown in Figure 6-5. The sources shown here are available to any document you create in Word. So if you use the same source in two or more papers, you don't have to create it again for each document. Instead, just fire up the Source Manager.

Here's how to add an existing citation to a new document:

1. **Open the document to which you want to add the source. Select References→ Manage Sources (Alt, S, M).**

   The Source Manager, shown in Figure 6-5, opens. On the left is the Master List of sources you've created. (You can sort these items by author, tag, title, or year—use the upper-right drop-down list to select your sort criterion.) On the right is a list of sources available in the current document. At the bottom, the Preview area shows you how the selected citation looks in the style you selected (APA, MLA, and so on), both as an in-text note and as a bibliography entry.

Tip: If you can't find the source you want in the Master List, click the Browse button. In the Open Source List dialog box that opens, find and select the source file you want, and then click OK to show it in the Master List.

---

2. **Select a source from the Master List, and then click Copy.**

   The source you selected appears in the Current List box. Word also adds the source to the current document's Source Gallery.

3. **When you're done adding sources to the current document, click Close.**

   The Source Manager closes.

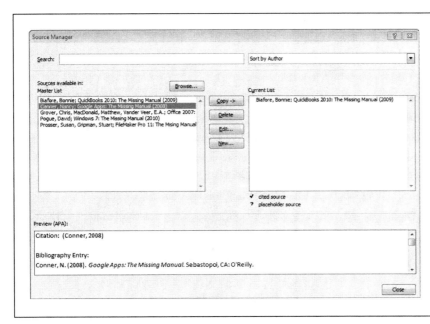

Figure 6-5:
Select any item from the Master List to use as a source in the current document (click Copy to add it). If the Master List is jam-packed, you can find the one you're looking for using the Search box at the top of the Source Manager. You can sort sources by author, tag, title, or year.

4. **When you want to add a citation to your document, position the cursor where you want the citation to appear. Select References→Insert Citation (Alt, S, C).**

    The Source Gallery appears, showing sources available to this document.

5. **Select the source you want to cite.**

    The citation appears in your document.

Tip: You can also create a new source right from the Source Manager. Click the New button to open the Create Source dialog box (Figure 6-4). Word adds the new source to both the Master List and the Current List.

Inserting a Placeholder

Sometimes you know you need to insert a citation but don't have the source information at hand. When that happens, there's no need to stop everything and make an emergency trip to the library. Just insert a placeholder for the citation and keep working. Later, when you have the info you need, you can fill it in.

Here's what to do:

1. **Put the cursor where you want the citation to appear, and then select References→Insert Citation→Add New Placeholder (Alt, S, C, P).**

    The Placeholder Name dialog box opens. This dialog box simply asks you for a name for the placeholder.

2. **Enter a name (or accept the one Word suggests, which is along the lines of "Placeholder1"). Click OK.**

    Word inserts the placeholder in your text.

3. **When you've gathered the info you need to fill in the source, open the Source Manager (References→Manage Sources or Alt, S, M.)**

    Your placeholder name appears in the right-hand Current List, preceded by a question mark, like this: ? Placeholder1.

4. **Select the placeholder and then click the Edit button.**

    The Edit Source dialog box opens. This looks just like the Create Source dialog box shown in Figure 6-4.

5. **Add the information about the source. When you're done, click OK.**

    Word replaces the placeholder with whatever you added.

6. **Click Close to dismiss the Source Manager.**

    Back in your document, Word has replaced the placeholder with the new information. If you've used the same placeholder in more than one spot, then the new citation appears in all of them.

Note: In the Source Manager's Current List, Word marks placeholders with a question mark and sources that you've cited in the document with a checkmark. So before you print or email a document, you can double-check to make sure that you've replaced all placeholders and cited all sources.

Editing a Citation or Its Source

When Word inserts a citation into your document, it doesn't put the citation in as plain old text; it holds the citation in what's known as a "content control frame"—a mini-database that Word uses to update all citations if you change the source information. So if you need to correct a source—maybe you misspelled an author's name or typed in the wrong year—you don't have to go through the document and fix the problem one instance at a time. Instead, change the source information and let Word hunt down and correct all the related citations.

The quickest way to edit a source is to click the citation in your document. A content control frame like the one shown in Figure 6-6 opens; click Citation Options (the down arrow in its lower-right corner) and then choose one of these options:

- **Edit Citation.** Select this if you want to make a change just to this citation. In the Edit Citation box, you can add page numbers to the citation or suppress the author, year, or title. (Suppressing information means that the piece of information doesn't appear in this citation. It doesn't affect other citations in the document or the source that's the basis for the citation.)

- **Edit Source.** Select this if you want to change the underlying source information.

- **Convert citation to static text.** This changes the citation from dynamically updated content to regular text. You might choose this option if you're going to save the document in a format other than Word's .docx format (see page 24 to learn about document formats).

Note: If you convert a citation to static text, Word can't use that citation when it creates a bibliography automatically (page xx6).

Figure 6-6:
Citations are content enclosed in a frame. When you want to edit or delete a citation, click the citation to make the frame appear.

Click this tab to select the frame.   Citation Options button

You can also edit sources using the Source Manager (Figure 6-5). Select References→Manage Sources (Alt, S, M) and, in either the Master List or the Current List, select the source you want. Click the Edit button.

The Edit Source dialog box opens. This looks just like the Create Source dialog box (Figure 6-4), except that it has the information for this source already filled in. Make your changes, and then click OK to update the source.

If the source appears in both the Master List and the Current List, Word shows a dialog box asking whether you want to update both lists with the changes you just made. Click Yes, and Word updates both lists. (If you click No, Word updates the source info only in the list from which you selected the source.)

When you update a source using the Source Manager, Word automatically updates all citations drawn from that source.

Tip: Maybe you created all your sources using Chicago style and then found out that your professor requires MLA style. Don't panic. To change the style of a document's citations, use the References tab's Style drop-down menu (Alt, S, L). Select a style from the list, and Word takes care of the rest, automatically changing all citations to the new style.

Deleting a Citation

To remove a particular citation from your document, click the citation to show its frame (Figure 6-6). Click the tab on the frame's left side to highlight the frame. Then press Backspace or Delete to remove the citation from your text.

Deleting a Source

If there's a source that you're unlikely ever to need again, you can delete it. You do this in the Source Manager. Open it (References→Manage Sources or Alt, S, M), select the item you want to delete, and then click the Delete button. That's it.

Note: Deleting a source from the Current List doesn't delete it from the Master List (or vice versa). If you want the source to be really and truly gone, you have to delete it separately from each list.

Building a Bibliography

A document that contains citations needs a bibliography at the end to give readers full information about the sources cited in the text. Building a bibliography would be a daunting task if you had to type in each and every entry. But Word automates bibliography creation for you—it does all the work, and you get all the credit.

After you've written your document and added all its citations, go to the end of the document (or section) and insert a page break (page 155) so your bibliography begins on its own page. Then follow these steps:

1. **Make sure the cursor is where you want the bibliography to appear. Select References→Bibliography (Alt, S, B).**

   A menu of built-in bibliography styles appears.

2. **Click the option you want.**

   Word inserts a bibliography—alphabetized and properly formatted—that includes full source information for all the citations in the document.

How easy was that?

Updating a Bibliography

If you've already generated a bibliography, you can update it when you add a new source or edit an existing one. Like a citation, a bibliography appears inside a frame so that Word can automatically make behind-the-scenes changes when your source information changes.

To update a bibliography, click the bibliography to select it. A frame appears around it, like the one shown in Figure 6-7. In the tab at the top of the frame, click "Update Citations and Bibliography." That's it—Word updates your bibliography with the most current source and citation information.

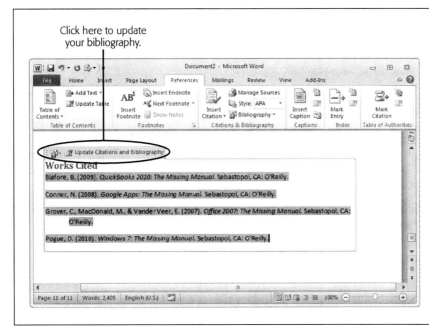

Click here to update
your bibliography.

Figure 6-7:
At the top of the frame, click Update Citations and Bibliography, and Word revises your bibliography to include the latest citation and source info.

Helping Readers Navigate Your Document

A long document is like a long journey—it's hard to find your way without signposts and a map. Word gives you several tools to help readers make that trip through your document, including bookmarks, cross-references, tables of contents, and indexes.

Inserting Bookmarks and Cross-References

Bookmarks and cross-references help you find what you're looking for in a long document. Just like its physical counterpart, a *bookmark* marks a particular place in the document so you can go back to it later. A *cross-reference* directs readers to a related spot in the document—such as a figure, section, or chapter—to help them find targeted information that illustrates or expands on what they're reading about now.

Note: Although bookmarks are useful for jumping to a particular point in your document, they also do a lot more. Bookmarks can come into play when you create an index (page 174), insert a hyperlink, record a macro (page 193), or insert a cross-reference (page 171).

Creating a bookmark

There are several reasons why you might want to create a bookmark in a long document: to mark an important point so you can easily find it again later, to find your place if you have to stop reading now, or to tell Word how to find a specific part of the text (for example when you're creating an index and need to indicate a range of pages for a particular entry—page 175 tells you more).

To insert a bookmark, follow these steps:

1. **Select what you want to bookmark.**

   You can select some text to bookmark or simply position the cursor at the spot you want.

2. **Go to Insert→Bookmark (Alt, N, K).**

   The Bookmark dialog box opens, displaying any previous bookmarks you've created.

3. **Type a name for your bookmark into the "Bookmark name" text box.**

   Make it descriptive to help pick out this bookmark from a list later on. Bookmark names can't have spaces in them. To distinguish words in your bookmark, you can use capital letters, underscores or hyphens, like so: Really_Important-POINT.

4. **Click the Add button.**

   Word inserts your bookmark and adds it to a running list for future reference.

Jumping to a bookmark

After you've inserted a bookmark, here's how to jump to it:

1. Select Insert→Bookmark (Alt, N, K).

    The Bookmark dialog box opens. This time, instead of adding a new bookmark, you'll go to an existing one.

2. **From the list of bookmarks, find the one you want. Select it and click the Go To button.**

    Word whisks you off to the bookmark.

3. **Click Close to close the Bookmark box.**

Tip: Here's another way to jump to a bookmark. Press the F5 key to open the Find and Replace dialog box with the Go To tab selected. In the "Go to what" drop-down list, select Bookmark, and then select a bookmark from the "Enter bookmark name" list. (Or you can type in a bookmark name here.) Click Go To, and you're there.

Deleting a bookmark

You can have as many bookmarks as you want in a document. But if you find that the bookmarks list is getting a little crowded, making it harder to find a specific bookmark, just delete any old bookmarks you no longer use. Open the Bookmarks dialog box (Insert→Bookmark or Alt, N, K), select the bookmark you no longer want from the list of bookmarks, and then click Delete. The bookmark disappears from the list and from your document.

Creating cross-references

In a printed book like this one, a cross-reference directs you to a specific figure, page, section, or chapter; it's up to you to flip the pages to get there. When you insert a cross-reference into a Word document, though, someone who's reading the document on a computer can jump to whatever you've cross-referenced simply by pressing the Ctrl key as he clicks the cross-reference. Word keeps track of cross-references so they're always current, even if you add, delete, or move material after you've created the cross-reference.

You've got tons of options for cross-references, which can point to any of these items in your document:

*   **Bookmark.** As explained earlier, a bookmark marks a specific location in the text. Bookmarks are great for creating cross-references, because you can stick them anywhere. If you want your cross-reference to jump to an element that's not on this list—a glossary definition, for example, or a particular word or sentence—just bookmark that element and then create a cross-reference to the bookmark.

- **Heading.** If you applied the Heading 1 or Heading 2 style to a paragraph, you can create a cross-reference to that heading.

- **Figure.** If you insert a picture and give it a caption (page 99), Word keeps track of the figure numbers. That means any cross-references you make to figures stay current, even if you add, move, or delete images and the figure numbers change.

- **Table.** Any table you create in Word (whether or not you give it a caption) can be the target for a cross-reference.

- **Equation.** Word's built-in equation editor keeps track of any equations you put into the document and lets you cross-reference them.

- **Numbered item.** If you create a numbered list (Home→Numbering or Alt, H, N), you can create a cross-reference that jumps to the list—even to a particular item on the list.

- **Footnote or endnote.** Word tracks your notes by location and number, making them easy to cross-reference.

When you want to create a cross-reference, here's what to do:

1. **Type the text that introduces the cross-reference.**

   For example, you might type *For more information, see* or *As illustrated by.* Type whatever text you want up to the point where the cross-reference will appear.

2. **Select Insert→Cross-reference (Alt, N, RF).**

   The Cross-reference dialog box, shown in Figure 6-8, opens. This dialog box has three main sections:

   — **Reference type.** This drop-down menu lists the different kinds of references you can link to (numbered item, heading, bookmark, and so on). What you choose here determines the contents of the other lists in the box.

   — **Insert reference to.** Here's where you select the text that will make up your cross-reference; that is, the text that readers will jump to when they click the reference. If you're cross-referencing a heading, for example, you can choose the text of the heading, the page number on which the heading appears, or the heading number (if it has one). So if you select "Page number" here, your cross-reference will say something like "For more information, see page 42," and the page number will be a Ctrl-clickable link.

   — **For which.** In this list you'll find all the document's references of the type you selected; here's where you pick the item you want to link to.

3. **Make your selections, and then click Insert.**

   Word inserts the cross-reference you chose. Now, when a reader hovers the cursor over the cross-reference, a ScreenTip appears advising the reader to Ctrl-click to follow the link.

Figure 6-8:
To create a cross-reference to a heading, as in this example, select Heading as the reference type to make Word display all of the document's level 1 and level 2 headings. Then select the specific heading you want the cross-reference to point to. By default, Word inserts cross-references as hyperlinks—on a computer, readers can find what's referenced by Ctrl-clicking the cross-reference. If you prefer, though, you can insert a cross-reference as plain old text by turning off the "Insert as hyperlink" checkbox.

Creating a Table of Contents

A table of contents gives readers an at-a-glance overview of what's in a long document. If you picked up this book looking for a chapter on formatting documents in Word or using formulas in Excel, for example, you'd naturally begin with the table of contents.

Word can automatically create and format a table of contents for you. The secret is to work with Word's styles (page 51), so that Word knows which headings to include in the table of contents and how to organize and format them. You can include paragraphs formatted in the Heading 1, Heading 2, or (if it exists in the style set you're using) Heading 3 style in your table of contents.

So the first step in creating a table of contents is to check the heading styles. View your document in Outline view (click the lower-right Outline button on the status bar, which makes the Outlining tab appear on the ribbon). As you scroll through the document, make sure that all headings you want to appear in the table of contents appear as level 1, 2, or 3. To see just the headings, use the Outline tab's Show Level drop-down list (Alt, U, V) to select the heading level you want. If you select Level 3, for example, the document changes to show levels up to and including level 3.

Tip: If there's any level 1, 2, or 3 paragraph that you don't want in the table of contents, click somewhere in that paragraph and select References→Add Text (Alt, S, A) and then choose Do Not Show in Table of Contents.

If your headings look OK, switch to Print Layout view. Put the cursor where you want the table of contents to appear. Select References→Table of Contents (Alt, S, T). From the menu that opens, select the style for the table of contents you want to insert. (If you're online, you can browse additional styles on Office.com and download your preference by clicking More Tables of Contents from Office.com.)

Word inserts your table of contents, complete with relevant page numbers for each heading. To keep those page numbers (and other information) accurate, you can update the table of contents if you later make changes to the document. After you've edited the document, click References→Update Table (Alt, S, U). In the Update Table of Contents dialog box, select whether you want to update the entire table of contents (if you've reworded a heading, for example) or just its page numbers. Click OK, and your table of contents is up to date.

Creating an Index

A table of contents gives an overview of what's in a document, but an index helps readers locate specific topics. For example, the table of contents in an employee handbook tells readers that Chapter 4 is all about company policies, but if you're looking for specifics about the dress code, the index takes you to the page you want.

An index should be your last step in creating a document (except for maybe a final spell check, page 115) before you print it out and distribute it. Creating an index is a two-part process:

- Mark index entries in your document.
- Generate an index.

The first part, marking index entries, is the more time-consuming of the two, because you have to go through the document, decide what topics belong in the index, and mark them so that Word knows to include them. The second part is a snap, because Word does all the work for you.

Marking index entries

Before Word can generate your index, you need to spend some time going through the document, page by page, marking the topics that belong in the index. In an employee handbook, for example, you might create index entries for "dress code"; "dress code, women"; "dress code, men"; "dress code, casual Fridays"; and so on. The box on page 177 has tips for creating good index entries.

To mark an index entry, select the word or phrase you want to appear in the index. Then head to the References tab's Index section (References→Mark Entry or Alt, S, N). This opens the Mark Index Entry dialog box, shown in Figure 6-9, with the phrase you selected already filled in as the main entry (you can edit this phrase in the Mark Index Entry box; doing so won't affect the actual text in your document).

Here's what's in the Mark Index Entry dialog box:

- **Main entry.** This is the main topic that readers will look for in the index.

- **Subentry.** Each main topic may have one or more subtopics. In the index, these subtopics appear under the main entry.

- **Options.** In this section, you choose the type of index entry you want:

  — **Cross-reference.** This option directs readers to another index entry. For example, the index entry for Thanksgiving might say "See company holidays."

  — **Current page.** If you choose this option, the index lists the current page number for this entry in the index. Current page numbers update automatically when you update the index (page 179).

  — **Page range.** When your discussion of a topic spans several pages, you don't want to clutter up the entry with individual page numbers. If information about health benefits starts on page 45 and ends on page 50, the index looks much cleaner (and is easier to read) if the entry lists pages 45–50 instead of 45, 46, 47, 48, 49, 50.

Note: Before you can mark a page range for the index, you need to do a little prep work. To find and keep track of page ranges, Word needs to use bookmarks. To create a bookmark, select the text that makes up the range (so you might select several pages) and then go to Insert→Bookmark (Alt, N, K). After you've inserted the bookmark, choose the one you want from the Bookmark drop-down list in the Mark Index Entry dialog box. To learn more about working with bookmarks in Word, see page 170.

- **Page number format.** In this section, tell Word if you want page numbers in the index to be bold, italic, or both. In most indexes, bold indicates the page (or pages) that hold the most important information about the topic, as opposed to a passing mention of it, and italics indicate that the page has a figure or illustration related to the topic. But of course you can set up any scheme you like. If you leave the checkboxes in this section turned off, Word uses regular formatting for page numbers.

Tip: Use a page range for a main topic that spans several pages and individual page numbers for subtopics within that main topic.

When you've set up the index entry the way you want it, click Mark, which marks instances of the word or phrase to include in the index. Marking is how Word knows where to find terms to put their page numbers in the index. If you want Word to find and mark every instance of your selected word or phrase throughout the document, click Mark All. Word keeps the Mark Index Entry dialog box open after you've marked an entry, figuring that you'll mark multiple entries before you're done. When you're finished marking entries, click Cancel to close the dialog box.

Tip: Go easy on the Mark All button. It finds and marks every single occurrence of the selected word or phrase, which can clutter up the index and add page references that aren't terribly helpful—such as when a marked word is used in a different sense. For example, you might be thinking about "benefits" as a noun, but if you click Mark All, Word will also index instances where the word appears as a verb, as in "Employee participation benefits the company by…" Instead of clicking Mark All, use the Mark Index Entry dialog box together with the Navigation pane (page 42) to quickly find all occurrences of a word or phrase, check the context of each, and then mark the ones you want listed in the index.

When you mark a word or phrase in the text as an index entry, Word inserts a data marker called a *field code* into the document at your marking point that looks something like this:

    { XE "company holidays" }

This field code is how Word knows what page the entry is on, and it's visible only when you tell Word to show hidden characters (Home→Show/Hide ¶; Alt, H, 8; or Ctrl+*). Field codes don't appear in the final, printed document. You can edit the code to correct a typo or change the wording of your index entry, as page 179 explains.

Figure 6-9:
As you go through your document page by page, this dialog box stays open so you can mark as many index entries as you need.

Generating an index

After you've done all the work of finding and marking index entries, it's time to sit back and let Word take over to create the actual index. Start by putting the cursor where you want the index to appear. (The best place is on a new page after the last page of text in your document—that's where you'd look for an index, right? So go to the end of the document and insert a page break so the cursor appears at the top of the new page.) Then, type *Index* to identify it to readers and press Enter.

Tip: If you want the index to be listed in your document's table of contents (always a good idea so readers know it's there), then make "Index" a top-level heading. Select it and then choose Home→Heading 1.

Now you're ready to create the index. Here's all you need to do:

1. **Select References→Insert Index (Alt, S, X).**

    The Index dialog box, shown in Figure 6-10, opens. This is where you tell Word how to set up the index. As you make your choices, watch the Print Preview box to show how they'll look in the printed document. Here are your formatting choices:

    — **Type.** Entries can be either indented, in which each subentry appears on its own line indented under the main entry, or run-in, in which all subentries appear as a paragraph that's part of the main entry. Indented is easier to read, but run-in can save you space if you have a lot of subentries throughout the index.

    — **Columns.** Standard index format is two columns, which is the default here, but you can select the number of columns you want.

    — **Language.** The default here is the default language you use with Word.

    — **Right-align page numbers.** When you turn on this checkbox, page numbers line up along the right side of the column, and you can select a tab leader to make it easy to see which page numbers go with which entries. When this checkbox is turned off, relevant page numbers appear immediately after entries.

Figure 6-10:
Format the index you're creating in the Index dialog box. As you make selections, keep an eye on the Print Preview box to get an idea of how your choices will look once your index goes live.

— **Tab leader.** If you choose to right-align page numbers, you can pick a leader style to connect each entry with its page number(s): dots, dashes, or underlining. You can also opt for no leader.

— **Formats.** Choose an index style from this drop-down list (the Print Preview shows you what each option looks like). If you choose "From template", then Word applies the current template's default formatting (line spacing and so on) to your index.

2. **Make your selections and click OK.**

   Word creates your index and inserts it into your document, automatically alphabetizing entries and applying the formatting you chose. Your index looks something like the example in Figure 6-11.

WORD TO THE WISE

Tips for Creating a Good Index

Word does a great job of alphabetizing, organizing, and formatting index entries, as well as matching up each entry with the appropriate pages in the document. But it can never know or understand your document the way you do. A computer doesn't create a good index—you do.

These tips will help you create an effective index:

- **Think like a reader.** What information does someone approaching the topic for the first time need to know? What are the core topics of each chapter or section of the document? If you created the document from an outline, use the outline now to help you identify the important topics. (Looking at your document's headings achieves the same purpose.)

- **Know the difference between entries and subentries.** A main entry is a key idea, name, concept, or term. Subentries break down main entries into their important elements. The point of subentries is to help readers zero in on some aspect of a main entry.

- **Don't get carried away with index entries.** Don't try to turn every word in the document into an index entry. Focus on main topics and their most important elements.

- **Avoid clutter.** Make your index as easy as possible to read. For example, showing a range of pages is less cluttered than listing each page in the range individually.

- **Be consistent.** Use the same terminology and the same format throughout the index. For example, avoid listing people's last names first in some instances and first names first in others.

- **Use cross-references—but don't overdo it.** Cross-references direct readers to a main topic that expands on or defines what they're looking up. But too many cross-references can be annoying. It's hard to use an index that's always referring you to another topic instead of just giving you the information you're looking for.

- **Know what to leave out.** An index applies to the body of the book, so there's no need to index the table of contents, prologue, list of contributors, glossary, and so on.

Undoubtedly you've used indexes as a tool. Take some time to look over a professionally produced index to see how it works—what makes a good entry vs. a subentry, when to use cross-references, how to format entries. Understanding what makes an index useful to readers will help you create an effective one.

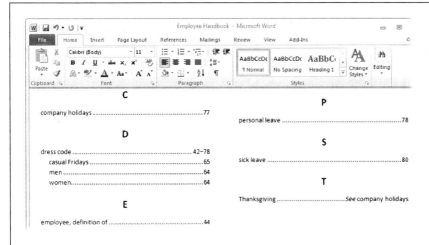

Figure 6-11:
This example of an index has the page numbers right-aligned and uses dots as tab leaders to show which page number goes with which index entry.

Updating an index

If your document changes before you print it, you can update its index to make sure the document's final version is accurate. If you've marked more terms to include or created new entries, for example, you want to make sure that information appears in the index.

Updating the index is simple. Click anywhere in the index to highlight it, and then select References→Update Index (Alt, S, D). Word rebuilds your index (in a long document, this might take a minute), updating it automatically.

Editing index entries

As you look over your index, you may notice a typo or that some entries start with lowercase letters and others are capitalized. You can fix such problems by editing the index entry field code in your document. Start by showing the document's hidden characters: Click Home→Show/Hide ¶; press Alt, H, 8; or use the Ctrl+* keyboard shortcut. Now you can see the field code that marks each index entry, which looks something like this:

```
{ XE "index entry" }
```

(Of course, you see the actual index term in place of the words "index entry.")

To change the entry, you can edit anything inside the quotation marks. Just click and make your changes, as you would any other text in your document. When you're finished, update the index to implement your edits.

Tip: You can use the Navigation pane (page 42) to find index entries. Make sure your document is showing its hidden characters, open the Navigation pane, and search for "XE". The Navigation pane displays all the code that marks index entries, and you can scroll through them to find the one you want.

Deleting an index entry

To remove an entry from the index, select the field code that creates the entry you want to delete (including both curly brackets) and press Delete or Backspace. Update the index, and the entry is gone.

Deleting an index

If you decide you don't want an index after all, here's how to delete it: Right-click the index and select Toggle Field Codes from the shortcut menu. The index disappears, replaced by a field code that looks something like this:

```
{ INDEX \h "A" \c "2" \ z "1033" }
```

Select that field code (including the curly brackets) and then press Delete. No more index.

Customizing Your Documents with Themes, Templates, and Macros

Word power users do more than master what's on the ribbon; they make Word their own by customizing documents with themes, templates, and macros. *Themes* give your documents a consistent look and sense of style, making sure you produce attractive, easy-to-read documents. *Templates* set up documents' formatting so you don't have to fuss with page layout, line spacing, paper orientation, and the like every time you create a new document. Many of the templates available in Word even include sample text that you can replace with your own, so you don't have to worry about what goes where. And if themes and templates take the bother out of making your documents look good, *macros* help you avoid mind-numbing drudge work by automating actions that you perform frequently.

Themes: The Way to Better Designs

Ever watch a 3-year-old pick out her own clothes? She might choose a favorite orange-and-blue striped T-shirt to go with a flowered skirt in pinks and purples and a couple of mismatched knee socks. Cute, but you probably don't want her to go to preschool dressed that way.

Thanks to Word's themes, you don't have to send your documents out into the world looking like a self-dressed toddler. A *theme* pulls your document together, giving it a unified look. Each theme is a predesigned, preformatted set of fonts, sizes, and colors, letting you create professional-looking documents without giving a thought to formatting. Word offers dozens of themes to choose from. (Of course, you can tweak a theme's formatting any way you like. Chapter 2 tells you all about do-it-yourself formatting in Word.)

Note: To use themes, you must be working with a .docx file. If you're working with an older .doc file in Word 2010's Compatibility Mode, themes are turned off.

Here are some examples of the nitty gritty formatting a theme handles for you:

- **Headings.** Font size, style, and color.
- **Body text.** Font size, style, and color.
- **Tables.** Colors and shading; border and line styles; and font size, style, and color.
- **Charts.** Colors; chart styles; border and line styles; and font size, style, and color.
- **Images and clip art.** Border colors.
- **WordArt.** Font colors.
- **SmartArt.** Colors and font size, style, and color.

In Word, the standard theme is called Office. It uses 11-point Calibri font for the body text and Cambria in different sizes and shades of blue for headings—the different fonts and colors for different purposes are called *styles*. You can see all the styles associated with a particular theme by selecting it (see the next section) and then going to the Home tab's Styles section; click the More button (Alt, H, L) to see all of its text styles.

Choosing a Theme

To select a theme, head to the Page Layout tab and click the far-left Themes button (Alt, P, TH). This opens a gallery of Word's built-in themes, as shown in Figure 7-1. As you move your pointer over the different options, Live Preview shows you how your document looks with each theme. When you find one you like, click it. Word applies that theme to your document.

Tip: If you don't see a preview of changes to your document as you browse through the menu, turn on Live Preview by selecting Select File→Options (Alt, F, I). In the General section of the Word Options dialog box, turn on the Enable Live Preview checkbox.

Customizing a Theme

You might like everything about a theme except for, say, the color scheme or the fonts. You can customize any theme and save it as your own creation so you can use it again for future documents.

Figure 7-1:
After Office, the standard theme, the Themes gallery shows Word's built-in choices in alphabetical order by name. Scroll down to see more.

Whether you're using Word's standard Office theme or you've chosen a different one, you can tweak it to suit your needs. Go to the Page Layout tab's Themes section (it's at the far left end of the ribbon), and then choose one of these commands:

- **Theme Colors (Alt, P, TC).** This button shows you a menu of theme colors so you can change them without changing any of the theme's other elements. Choose a preselected set of colors or click Create New Theme Colors to open the dialog box shown in Figure 7-2, where you can select your own.

- **Theme Fonts (Alt, P, TF).** Choose the fonts most pleasing to your eye for headings and for body text. You can pick one of Word's built-in pairings, or click Create New Theme Fonts to open a dialog box where you choose a heading font and a body font from drop-down lists. (A preview in the Sample pane shows how your choices look together).

- **Theme Effects (Alt, P, TE).** Each theme includes graphic effects, such as shadows and line styles. (If your document is just text with no graphics, you don't have to worry about the options here.) You can take the effects from one theme and apply them to another. Click this button, scrutinize the examples to see which effects you want, then and select any theme to grab its goodies.

Figure 7-2:
If you've got a good eye for color, you can create a new color scheme for a theme. The labels tell you what the color is for, such as text/background and hyperlink; use the drop-down list to choose the color for that element. As you select a new color, the sample image on the right changes so you can see how changing that color affects documents. Give your color scheme a name and click Save to add it to the Theme Colors menu for future use.

Saving a Theme

After you've created a custom theme, you'll probably want to save it for reuse. Here's how:

1. **Create a custom theme and select Page Layout→Themes→Save Current Theme (Alt, P, TH, A).**

   The Save Current Theme dialog box opens. It looks just like the dialog box you use to save a document, but it's got the Document Themes folder open and Office Theme as the type of file you're saving.

2. **Type a name for your theme in the "File name" box. If you want to save your theme in a folder other than the Document Themes folder, navigate to and open the folder you want. Click Save.**

   Word saves your theme and adds it to the Themes menu. Now it's available for any document you work with in Word.

Finding a Saved Theme

When you've saved a theme, Word adds it to the Themes gallery, which opens when you select Page Layout→Themes or press (Alt, P, TH). If you've saved a custom theme, it appears in the Custom section at the top of the Themes gallery.

If you've got a lot of custom themes, the easiest way to find a theme is to browse for it. If you don't see the one you want in the Custom section of the Themes menu, try this:

1. **Select Page Layout→Themes→Browse for Themes (Alt, P, TH, B).**

   The Choose Theme or Themed Document dialog box opens.

2. **Navigate to the folder where you saved the theme or a document that uses the theme. Select the theme or themed document you want. Click Open.**

   If you selected a theme, Word applies it to the current document. If you selected a themed document, Word opens the file you chose.

Templates: Reusable Document Blueprints

A *template* is a pattern or mold used to produce consistent objects. A cookie cutter is an example—when you use one, you know that each cookie in the batch will be the same size and shape. In word processing, a template serves a similar purpose. Its predesigned formatting is automatically applied to every document you create using it, so fonts, colors, heading styles, page layout, spacing, and so on are consistent in your documents. There are also templates for special-purpose documents, like flyers, mailing labels, memos, newsletters, invitations—if you can create it in Word, there's probably a template for it.

Choosing a Template

As page 18 explains, when you create a new document (File→New or Alt, F, N) you can select a template to create a specific kind of document, such as a resumé or an expense report. So if you haven't yet read about choosing a template to create a new document, flip back to Chapter 1 to see how that works.

When you use a template to create a new document, you're not stuck with that template forever. Sometimes you might be working on a document when it suddenly occurs to you that your job would be easier if you'd created the document with a different template. No need to start from scratch. You can attach a new template to an existing document. When you do, all the styles and formatting that make up the attached template become available in the document.

Note: All Word documents are based on a template. If you don't select a specific template when creating a new document, then Word uses its default template, Normal.dotm.

To attach a template to an existing document, you need to work with the Developer tab, and Word hides that tab in its default display. So before you can attach a template, you need to make the Developer tab visible: Right-click the ribbon; from the shortcut menu that appears, select Customize the Ribbon. This opens the Word Options dialog box to its Customize Ribbon Options. In the right-hand Main Tabs box, find Developer and turn on its checkbox. Click OK, and the Developer tab appears on your ribbon. (Page 891 tells you more about customizing Word's ribbon.)

Once you can see the Developer tab on the ribbon, follow these steps to attach a template to your document:

1. **Go to the Templates section on Word's Developer tab and click Document Template (Alt, L, U).**

   The Templates and Add-ins dialog box opens, showing the Templates tab. In the Document template box, you see the name of the template currently used for this document. To the right of that is a button labeled Attach.

2. **Click the Attach button.**

   Word opens the Attach Template dialog box.

3. **Find and select the template you want. Click Open.**

   Word takes you back to the Templates and Add-ins dialog box. Now the name of the template you chose appears as the document's template.

4. **Turn on the checkbox labeled "Automatically update document styles".**

   Turning on this checkbox tells Word to transfer the styles in the template to your document.

5. **Click OK.**

   Your document has a new template.

Creating Your Own Template

Word offers a huge variety of templates, some built into Word and others that you can download from Office.com (page 18) and use to create new documents. You can also create and save a template of your own design. This is useful when you frequently create documents whose formatting needs to be just so, and none of Word's templates quite suits your needs. There are three ways to create a do-it-yourself template: build it from scratch, model it on an existing document, or tweak an existing template.

Creating a template from scratch

To design and save your own template, create a new blank document (page 17) and set up the formatting the way you want it (Chapter 2 tells you all about formatting). When you've done that, follow these steps to save your new template:

1. **Click File→Save As (Alt, F, A).**

   The Save As dialog box opens. This is the same dialog box, shown back in Figure 1-7 (page 22), that you use to save any Word file.

2. **In the Save As dialog box, choose the folder where you want to save your template.**

   To make your new template appear in "My templates" the next time you're looking for it, save it here:

   For Windows 7 and Vista, save the template in *C:\Users\[YourName]\AppData\ Roaming\Microsoft\Templates.*

For Windows XP, save the template in *C:\Documents and Settings\[YourName]\ Application Data\Microsoft\Templates.*

For Windows 95, 98, 2000, and ME, save the template in one of these folders: *C:\Windows\Application Data\Microsoft\Templates, C:\Windows\Profiles\ [YourName]\Application Data\Microsoft\Templates,* or *C:\Documents and Settings\[YourName]\Application Data\Microsoft\Templates.*

Note: Replace [YourName] with the name you use on your computer.

---

3. **Give the template a name and, from the "Save as type" drop-down menu, select Word Template. Click Save.**

   Word saves your new template in the folder you selected.

Tip: Can't find the AppData folder (in Windows 7 and Vista) or the Application Data folder (in Windows XP) under your name? Try this: Open the Control Panel (from the Start menu in Windows 7 and Vista or by selecting Start→Settings→Control Panel in XP). There, select Folder Options (to find this in Windows 7, set "View by" to either large or small icons). In the Folder Options dialog box, click the View tab. In the "Advanced settings" list, find "Hidden files and folders" and turn on the "Show hidden files, folders, and drives" radio button. Click OK. Now you can dig down and find the folder to store your template.

Creating a template from a document

If there's a document whose formatting you like, you can use it as the basis of a new template. Open the document you want to use as a template. You can save the document's current contents as boilerplate text (if you don't want to, clear the text by pressing Ctrl+A and then Delete). Click File→Save As (Alt, F, A) and then proceed as though you were saving a template you created from scratch.

Creating a template from an existing template

You can use an existing template as the basis for a new one. Select File→New→"New from existing" (Alt, F, N, X). Word opens the New from Existing Document dialog box to the Templates folder. Select the template you want as the basis for your new template, and then click Create New. Word opens a new document from the template you selected. Save it as a template, following the steps listed earlier.

If the template you want to use appears Backstage in the "Sample templates" or "My templates" categories, you can create a new template like this: Select File→ New→"Sample templates" (Alt, F, N, A) or File→New→"My templates" (Alt, F, N, M). In the dialog box that opens, select the template you want, turn on the lower-right Template radio button, and then click Create (if you're in "Sample templates") or OK (if you're in "My templates"). Save your new template using the steps for saving a template created from scratch.

Customizing a Template

After you've been working with a particular template, you might want to make some changes to it. This section shows you how.

Changing an existing style within a template

If you want, you can tweak any style within an existing style set (recall that style sets are a theme's preformatted fonts for different kinds of text: titles, headings, body text, and so on). To do this, start on the Home tab. In the Styles section, click the lower-right Styles button (Alt, H, FY or Alt+Ctrl+Shift+S) to open the Styles pane, shown in Figure 7-3. This window lists all the styles in the current set: normal (regular body text), headings, emphasis, and so on.

As you pass your mouse over the styles, a ScreenTip appears to show you the specifications of each (font, size, color, any special formatting or spacing).

Tip: To see what the style looks like, instead of just reading a description of it, turn on the Show Preview checkbox just below the list of styles.

Figure 7-3:
The Styles pane shows you all the styles in the current style set (turn on the Show Preview checkbox to see how they look in the document). At the bottom of the windows are these buttons: New Style (for building your own style), Style Inspector (which gives you a detailed look at a style's formatting), and Manage Styles (where you can edit existing styles).

To change a style, hover the pointer over it so the symbol to the right of the style's name becomes a downward-pointing arrow. Click the arrow and, from the menu that appears, select Modify. The Modify Style dialog box opens, as shown in Figure 7-4. This dialog box has the name of the style you selected already filled in, along with its properties and formatting. Here's what you can change:

- **Name.** When you modify an existing style, this box displays the name of the style you selected. If you like, rename the style to something that's easier for you to remember.

- **Style type.** Word has five style categories:

  - **Paragraph.** This sets the style for an entire paragraph, up to the final paragraph mark (¶) that Word inserts when you hit the Enter key. For a paragraph style, you can set font, paragraph, tabs, border, language, frame (text wrapping), bullets and numbering, and text effects. Many of these settings appear in the Formatting section; if you don't see the formatting option you want, click the lower-left Format button and select a setting from the menu that appears.

  - **Character.** This applies to specific text within a paragraph, such as *foreign words you want to italicize* or `computer code`. When you select text and apply a character style to it, the selected text appears in that style, whatever the style of the rest of the paragraph. You can set font, border, language, and text effects for character styles.

  - **Linked (paragraph and character).** This is a hybrid of a paragraph style and a character style. If you select only part of a paragraph and apply a linked style to it, the selected text takes on the linked style's formatting, but the rest of the paragraph remains unchanged. If you simply click in a paragraph without selecting and apply a linked style, then the entire paragraph takes on the formatting. Linked styles appear in the Style window as a paragraph mark (¶) followed by the letter *a*.

Tip: All of Word's built-in heading styles are linked styles. Here's a neat trick for working with them: Select the first word or phrase of a paragraph and apply a heading style to it. This makes the first few words stand out in the text—and now those opening words can show up in Outline view (page 27), appear in a table of contents (page 173), or be cross-referenced (page 171).

  - **Table.** This applies to the text and formatting of tables. You can set table properties, borders and shading, banding (number of rows or columns in a band), font, paragraph, tabs, and text effects for table styles.

  - **List.** As you might guess, this style formats both bulleted and numbered lists. Style settings include font, bullets and numbering, and text effects.

In the Modify Style dialog box, the "Style type" field shows the kind of style you've chosen.

Figure 7-4:
The Modify Style dialog box lets you change the formatting of an existing style. As you make changes, a preview gives you an idea of how they'll affect the text in your document.

- **Style based on.** If the style is a modification of another style within the style set—for example, a character style like Emphasis is based on the style of the paragraph in which it appears.

- **Style for following paragraph.** Sometimes, you might want a certain style to follow another whenever it appears. A common example is the first body paragraph after a heading, which often has different formatting than subsequent body paragraphs. If you select a style here, the paragraph that follows the style automatically gets the style you specify. This option isn't enabled for character styles.

- **Formatting.** This section gives you toolbar-like buttons and drop-down menus you can use to format the style. The options depend on the type of style you're working with. As you format the style, you see a preview of it in the Sample Text box beneath the formatting options.

Tip: For an alternative way to adjust formatting, click the lower-left Format button, choose a type of formatting from the menu, and make your changes in the resulting dialog box.

- **Add to Quick Style list.** If you want this style to appear in the Styles gallery, Styles pane, and the Apply Styles pane, make sure that this checkbox is turned on.

- **Automatically update.** For paragraph and linked styles only, turning on this checkbox tells Word to change the whole style whenever you make a formatting change to a paragraph that uses this style. That means that a formatting change you make to one paragraph—indenting the paragraph, for example—automatically alters *all other* paragraphs using that style to reflect the change. Most folks keep this option turned off.

- **Only in this document/New documents based on this template.** Here's where you decide whether you want this style only for the document you're working with right now or for all documents created from this template.

After you've modified the style, click OK to save your changes.

Creating a new style for a template

You're not limited to the styles that come with Word. You can build your own style from the ground up. When you do, you can make the new style a part of the template you're using, so it's always available for any document you create using that template.

To create a brand-new style, go to the Home tab's Styles section and click the lower-right Styles button (Alt, H, FY) to pop out the Styles pane (Figure 7-3). There, click the lower-left New Style button. The Create New Style from Formatting dialog box opens; it looks just like the Modify Style box shown in Figure 7-4. Give your new style a name and type and set up the formatting options you want for it. Click OK, and you've got yourself a new style.

Tip: To make your new style available to all documents created from the current template, be sure to turn on the "New documents based on this template" radio button before you click OK.

Copying a style from one template to another

If there's a style you really like in one template that you want to use in a different template, you don't have to try to rebuild that style from the ground up—you can simply copy it from one template to the other. Start by opening a document that has the style (or styles) you want to copy. Then take these steps:

1. **In the Home tab's Styles section, click the lower-right pop-out button (Alt, H, FY).**

   The Styles pane (Figure 7-3) opens.

2. **At the bottom of the window, click the Manage Styles button.**

   Word opens the Manage Styles dialog box. Select the Edit tab (if it's not already selected).

3. **In the Edit tab's lower-left corner, click the Import/Export button.**

   The Organizer dialog box opens to the Styles tab, as shown in Figure 7-5. On the left is a list of the styles available in the open document. On the right is a list of styles available in the current template.

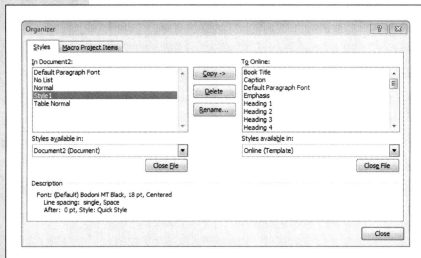

Figure 7-5:
To copy a style from one document or template to another, click the style you want to copy in the left-hand box and click Copy to add it to the template shown on the right. You can also delete or rename styles here.

4. **On the right side of the Organizer, click the Close File button.**

   What you're doing here is choosing a different template so you can use its styles in the current document. The current template's styles disappear, and the button changes its name to Open File.

5. **Click the Open File button.**

   The Open dialog box appears, displaying Word templates.

6. **Navigate to the template to which you want to copy the style(s). Select it and click Open.**

   The template you opened now appears on the right side of the Organizer, with its styles listed in the box there.

7. **In the left-hand list, select the style you want to copy. (You can select multiple styles by holding down Ctrl or Shift as you make your choices.) In the middle of the Organizer, click the Copy button.**

   The selected styles appear in the template's list on the Organizer's left side. If any of the styles already in that template have the same name as a style you're copying, a dialog box appears, asking if you want to overwrite the existing style. Select Yes, Yes to All, No, or Cancel.

8. **When you're finished copying styles, click Close.**

   Word closes the Organizer; the styles you copied are now available to any document created using that template (including existing documents).

Deleting a style from a template

To remove a style from a template, start by selecting Home and clicking the Styles section's lower-right Styles button (Alt, H, FY). When the Styles pane opens, go to the bottom and click the Manage Styles button. This opens the Manage Styles dialog box; if necessary, select the Edit tab.

At the bottom of the box, turn on the radio button labeled "New documents based on this template". Then select the style you want to delete and click the Delete button. Word asks you to confirm the deletion; click Yes, and the style disappears. Click OK to close the Manage Styles box.

Save Time with Macros

For certain tasks you do a lot, a macro can save you time and spare you the tedium of doing the same repetitive task over and over (and over) again. Macros let you automate your work, creating your own custom buttons or keyboard shortcuts for a specific chore. For example, say your company recently changed its name from Robert X. Smith & Sons to BobSonCo. Whenever you work on a document, you need to make sure that the new name replaces the old one. You could do a Find and Replace (page 41), typing in the old name and the new one each time. But by recording a macro, you can create a button, add it to the Quick Access toolbar, and replace all instances of the old name with a single click—and then get on with your work.

Recording a Macro

In Word 2007, macros were hidden away on the Developer tab, which doesn't appear in the default version of the ribbon. Word 2010 brings macros out in the open, putting them on the View tab. (Why View? Who knows? Maybe because there was room there. Macros are really all about automating tasks, not viewing a document.)

Recording a macro means telling Word the sequence of actions (keystrokes and mouse clicks) you want it to take when you click a certain button or press a certain combination of keys. Here's how to cook one up:

1. Select View→Macros→Record Macro (Alt, W, M, R).

   The Record Macro dialog box, shown in Figure 7-6, opens.

2. Type a name for your macro in the "Macro name" box. If you want, you can also type a brief description of what the macro does in the Description box.

   Give the macro an easy-to-remember, descriptive name, like "RemoveFormatting" or "ReplaceOldName" (macro names can't contain spaces).

Note: If you give your new macro the name of an existing macro, your new macro will overwrite the old one.

Figure 7-6:
Before you record a macro, choose whether you'll run that macro by clicking a button or by pressing a combination of keys on the keyboard.

3. **Select where you want to store the macro, either in all documents or just in this document.**

   The default is All Documents, which stores the macro in the Normal.dotm template, so the macro works with any document created using the Normal template.

4. **In the "Assign macro to" section, choose how you'll run the macro: by clicking a button or by using a keyboard shortcut.**

   If you click Button, the Word Options dialog box opens to the Quick Access toolbar section, as shown in Figure 7-7. Your new button appears in the left-hand box. Click Add to put it on the Quick Access toolbar. (Page 889 tells you more about customizing the Quick Access toolbar.) Click OK.

Figure 7-7:
When you create a button to run a macro, put it on the Quick Access toolbar for easy access. Select your macro from the left box and click Add to put it on the toolbar. All macro buttons look the same, but the name you gave the macro appears as a tooltip when you point at the button.

If you click Keyboard, the Customize Keyboard dialog box, shown in Figure
7-8, appears. In the "Press new shortcut key" section, press the combination of
keys you want to use to run your macro. If that keystroke combination already
belongs to another shortcut, Word tells you; Figure 7-8 explains your options.
Once you've settled on a keystroke combo you like, click Assign.

Figure 7-8:
*If the keystroke combination you want to
use for your macro already does another
job, Word tells you in the "Currently assigned to" section (circled). You can try a
combination of different keys, or you can
overwrite the current task with your new
macro.*

Word starts recording your macro. You know it's recording because the pointer
changes to show an arrow with an antique, 1980s-style cassette. (Memo to Microsoft: Does that icon even mean anything to people under 30?)

5. **Go through the sequence of actions you want Word to record—in other
   words, do what you want to happen automatically when you click the button
   or press the keystroke combination.**

   For example, to record a macro to find all instances of Robert X. Smith & Sons
   with BobSonCo, you'd select Home→Replace to open the Find and Replace box,
   where you'd type *Robert X. Smith & Sons* in the "Find what" box and *BobSonCo*
   in the "Replace with" box; click Replace All; click OK; and then click Close.

6. **When you've completed the task you want the macro to automate, stop recording by select View→Macros→Stop Recording (Alt, W, M, R).**

   Word stops recording your macro.

Now your macro is ready to use.

Tip: Don't rush as you record a macro. Word records your actions—not how long it takes you to do them.
And if you make a mistake, don't worry. You can always delete the faulty macro (page 197) and start again.

Tip: Can't find your macro button on the Quick Access toolbar? Here's how to display it. Select File→Options (Alt, F, I) and, in the Word Options dialog box, select Quick Access Toolbar. From the "Choose commands from" drop-down list, click Macros. This displays all your macros in the left list box. Select your macro, click Add, and then click OK, and your button shows up on the toolbar.

Running a Macro

After you've created a macro, run it by clicking the button you created or by pressing the combination of keys you assigned. You can also run any macro from the Macros dialog box:

1. **Select View→Macro→View Macros (Alt, W, M, V).**

   The Macros dialog box, shown in Figure 7-9, opens.

2. **Find the macro you want in the list of macros. Select it and then click the Run button.**

   Like magic, the macro performs the task you recorded.

Figure 7-9:
As you create macros, Word adds them to the Macros dialog box. You can always find and run a macro from here.

Copying a Macro Between Templates

If you've got a macro that works beautifully in one template and want the same macro in a different template, you can simply copy it from one template to the other, using the Organizer (Figure 7-5). Open the Organizer to the Macro Project Items tab by selecting View→Macros→View Macros (Alt, W, M, V) and clicking the Organizer button.

Copying a macro from one template to another works just like copying a style between templates (page 191). Find and select the macro you want to copy (from a template or a document) on the left side, and find and select the template you want to copy to on the right side. (If you need to hunt for either template, click Close File and then Open File to find the template you want.) Click Copy to copy the macro, and then click Close to close the Organizer.

Deleting a Macro

If a macro has outlived its usefulness, simply delete it from the Macros dialog box. Select View→Macro→View Macros (Alt, W, M, V), find the macro you no longer need, select it, and click Delete. A dialog box appears, checking to make sure you *really* want to delete the macro. Click Yes, and no more macro.

Note: When you delete a macro that lived in a button on the Quick Access toolbar, Word deletes the macro but not the button. To get rid of the button, right-click it. From the shortcut menu that appears, select Remove from Quick Access Toolbar.

Desktop and Web Publishing

S ome documents, like a personal journal, are meant for you alone. Others are meant for public consumption: a sales brochure, a website, that memo to extra-terrestrials you've been working on. When you create a document for the public at large, you want it to look professional—well laid out and attractively designed. Word is ready to help.

The program offers plenty of tools for designing publications, whether you're publishing on paper or on the Web. Choose from a large array of predesigned templates for creating newsletters and brochures, or use columns and text boxes to lay out your own. If you're designing a website, you can create it in Word and save it as an HTML file (the format that tells web browsers how to display a file); this chapter gives you step-by-step instructions for creating a document that will look sharp as a web page.

Note: Bloggers can even use Word to write posts and upload them directly from Word. Check out the online Appendix B, "From Word to Your Blog," on this book's Missing CD page for the full scoop.

Newsletters and Brochures

Word makes it super-easy for you to lay out newsletters and brochures by providing a rich, varied collection of templates that you can use or modify for your own publication. To choose one, select File→New (Alt, F, N), which opens the Available Templates page Backstage. In the Office.com Templates section, click either the Brochures or the Newsletters folder.

The page changes to show you available templates. Scroll through them and click any design to see a preview of it in the right pane. When you find one you like, click

Download. Word opens a new document based on the template; Figure 8-1 shows an example.

The template has placeholder text showing you what goes where. Click any place-holder and start typing to replace it with your own content.

Text box

Figure 8-1:
This newsletter template consists of a series of text boxes filled with temporary, placeholder text. Click any box (like the newsletter's title here) and type in your own content.

Note: If you create a wide range of publications—newsletters, calendars, greeting cards, brochures, and so on—or if you plan to send your publishing job to a commercial printer, consider using Publisher, Microsoft's professional-level publishing program, covered in Chapter 29. Publisher lets you create, format, and customize a wide variety of publications, from greeting cards and calendars to brochures, newsletters, and business cards. Publisher comes with Office Professional, but it's not included in the Office Home and Student or the Office Home and Business suite. (Don't worry—if that's your version of Office, you can still create great-looking documents with Word.)

Laying Out Text in Columns

By using one of Word's templates, you can create a tri-fold brochure or a multicol-umn newsletter without even thinking about how to set up columns—the template takes care of that for you. If you're designing your own document, though, it's easy enough to lay out your text in columns:

1. **Select Page Layout→Columns (Alt, P, J).**

   A menu appears, as shown in Figure 8-2, that gives you a choice of layouts: one column (the normal page layout in Word), two or three columns of equal width, Left (a narrow column on the left side of the page and a wide column to its right), or Right (vice versa).

2. **Click the option you want.**

   Word applies that layout to your document.

Now, when you type in your text, Word lays it out in the column format you chose. When you get to the end of one column, the text continues at the top of the next column.

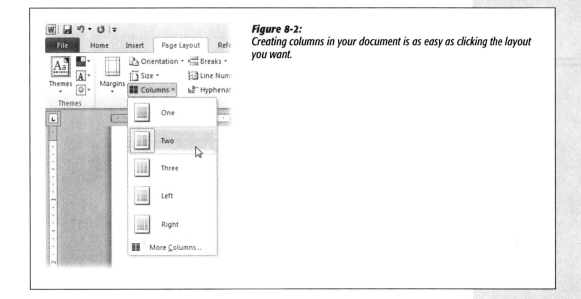

Figure 8-2:
Creating columns in your document is as easy as clicking the layout you want.

Tip: You can change the layout of text you've already written, changing single-column text to two columns, for example. Select the text whose layout you want to change, go to the Page Layout tab, and then click the Columns button (Alt, P, J). Pick the new layout, and Word applies it to the text you selected.

Formatting Columns

You may never need to do more than select one of the canned designs described in the previous section; Word has already measured and laid out the columns so they look good on the page. If you do, however, want to adjust the width, spacing, or appearance of your document's columns, select Page Layout→Columns→More Columns (Alt, P, J, C) to open the Columns dialog box, shown in Figure 8-3.

Here's what you can do in this dialog box:

- **Change the number of columns.** Select a different setting at the top of the box, or change the number in the "Number of columns" box.

- **Adjust the column width and the spacing between columns.** Use the arrow controls in the "Width and spacing" section to adjusts these aspects of your layout. Leave the "Equal column width" checkbox on if you want Word to keep the columns the same width. If you want a different look, say a three-column layout with narrow columns on the right and left and a wide middle column, turn off this checkbox before adjusting the individual columns' width and spacing.

- **Insert a vertical line between columns.** Turn on the "Line between" checkbox.

As you make changes, the Preview section's sample layout reflects them. When your layout looks good, click OK to apply it to your document.

Figure 8-3:
Create your own custom layout in the Columns dialog box.

Tip: To create a trifold brochure using columns, go to the Page Layout tab (Alt, P) and set the orientation to Landscape and set half-inch margins on all sides. Open the Columns dialog box (Figure 8-3) and, in the Preset section, select Three. Make sure the "Equal column width" checkbox is turned on, and then set the spacing for Column #1 to 1.0". Click OK, and you've set up three columns that are perfectly spaced for a trifold brochure.

Inserting a Text Box

Another way to create columns for your newsletter or brochure is to use text boxes, which let you place the text with more precision than columns do. If you've ever worked on a PowerPoint presentation, you've used text boxes to place words on your slides (Chapter 20 has details on that maneuver). In Word, text boxes work the same way; you position a text box on the page and then type inside it to add text. You can move text boxes around and change their sizes as you design the page.

To insert a text box into a Word document, select Insert→Text Box (Alt, N, X). A menu of predesigned text boxes appears, as shown in Figure 8-4. The menu features *sidebars* (brief articles that run alongside the main text) and *pull quotes* (phrases from the main text you want to feature prominently) in many different styles. Select any text box to insert it—with the formatting and positioning shown in the menu—into your document. Once it's there, click inside the box to type in your own text. You can click and drag the text box to put it wherever you like on the page.

Figure 8-4:
If you want a sidebar or a pull quote (called "quotes" in this menu) for your newsletter, check out the ones that Word has already designed for you. Each style of text box has a name, such as Alphabet or Austere, so you can choose text box styles that work together—you'll know, for example, that the Annual Sidebar and the Annual Quote will look good together on the page.

You can also draw your own text boxes. You might do this to position the main text of your brochure or newsletter, and then use one of Word's preformatted text boxes to add a pull quote or sidebar. To draw a text box, follow these steps:

1. **Select Insert→Text Box→Draw Text Box (Alt, X, D).**

   The mouse pointer changes to a crosshairs.

2. **Click and, holding down the mouse button, drag to create a rectangle.**

   As you move the mouse, the text box expands or contracts.

3. **When the text box is the size you want, release the mouse button.**

   Word creates a text box for you to type in. The cursor is already inside it, so go ahead and start typing. Or, if you prefer to lay out the page before adding content, go ahead and draw another text box.

When you select a text box, the Drawing Tools | Format contextual tab appears. You format text boxes in Word in the same way you would in PowerPoint. To read about positioning text with these boxes, see page 568. For information on formatting text boxes, flip ahead to page 569.

Images and Text Wrapping

Adding images to your newsletter or brochure breaks up the text, illustrates your points, and catches the reader's eye. Chapter 3 is all about working with images, so head back there if you need a refresher. Here, read on to see how to integrate images with columns and text boxes.

Inserting an image into a document with columns

You can insert an image into a column or have it appear between two columns. The first maneuver is easy: It's just like inserting an image in a paragraph. Click where you want the image to appear, and then select Insert→Picture (or whatever kind of graphic you want). In the dialog box that opens, find and select your image, and then click Insert. Word puts your picture into the column at the point you selected; resize and align the picture as you like.

To insert an image between two columns, click approximately where you want the image to appear, and then follow these steps:

1. **Go to the Insert tab (Alt, N) and select the kind of image you want to insert—you can insert any kind of graphic.**

   Word inserts the image and displays the Picture Tools | Format contextual tab. The image probably isn't quite where you want it to appear, but you'll fix that in the next step.

2. **Select Picture Tools | Format→Wrap Text.**

   Wrapping text is a way of telling Word how to position text in relation to a picture. A menu appears, showing the different ways you can position the image in relation to the text.

3. **Select an option such as Square, Tight, or Through.**

   Word applies the kind of wrapping you chose. Square is a good choice for a square or rectangular image that appears between two columns. Page 107 describes text wrapping options.

4. **Click the image to select it, and then drag and position it where you want it to appear between the columns.**

   If the wrapping doesn't look quite right, you can click the image and click Wrap Text again to select a different wrapping style. Or see the instructions for adjusting the image's wrap points on page 108.

Inserting an image into a document with text boxes

If you've laid out your newsletter or brochure using text boxes, you'll want to position any images you insert in relation to those text boxes. You can drag both images and text boxes around the page and drop them into place. To make your layout look professional, head to the Drawing Tools | Format tab, where you can pretty up your layout in the following ways:

- **Align text boxes and images.** Select the objects you want to line up, and then click the Align button (Alt, JD, AA). A menu opens, letting you choose how you want to align the selections: left, center, right, top, middle, bottom, and so on. Page 569 explains more about these alignment options.

- **Group objects.** If you want to treat two or more objects as a single entity, select them and click Group, and then select Group from the menu that opens (Alt, JD, AG, G). Word glues them together (so to speak) so you can work with them as a single object—moving or resizing everything in the group with one action. To unglue the grouped objects, select the group, click the Group button again, and choose Ungroup (Alt, JD, AG, U).

- **Rotate objects.** Select an object and click Rotate (Alt, JD, AY) to rotate or flip it.

- **Order objects.** You can put text boxes and other objects on top of one another— insert a shape, for example, and then put a text box on top of it so the shape becomes a background for the text. To change the order of objects, use the Bring Forward and Send Backward buttons:

  — **Bring Forward (Alt, JD, AF, F)** moves the object forward one place in the stack.

  — **Bring to Front (Alt, JD, AF, R)** moves the object to the top of a stack of objects, in front of all other objects.

  — **Bring in Front of Text (Alt, JD, AF, T)** places the selected object in front of any text.

  — **Send Backward (Alt, JD, AE, B)** moves the object back one place in the stack.

  — **Send to Back (Alt, JD, AE, K)** moves the object to the bottom of the stack, behind all other objects.

  — **Send Behind Text (Alt, JD, AE, H)** places the selected object behind any text.

Web Page Design

Most people don't think of Word as a web page editor, but if you like working with Word, you can use it to create pages to post to your website. The trick is in knowing how to format the page so it'll look good on the Web—and not like a couple of manuscript pages you decided to post. This section explains your options for saving the files you'll put up on the Web and shows you how to set up a template for creating multiple web pages that share the same design.

Saving a Word Document as a Web Page

Normally, when you save a Word document, you save it as a .docx or .doc file. Those file formats are for working with Word (and a few other word processors, like Open-Office.org Writer, that can also read them), but they're no good for files you put on the Web. If you intend to turn your document into a web page, you need to save it as an HTML file. *HTML* (hypertext markup language) is a formatting language specifically meant for web pages—it tells web browsers how to display the page.

Word offers these Web-friendly file formats:

- **Single File Web Page (.mht, .mhtml).** This format, originally designed as a way to archive web-page files, saves all the separate files that make up a web page in a single package. Files in this format don't display properly in all web browsers, so stick with the next two choices if you're looking to publish a page online (as opposed to emailing to a friend).

- **Web Page (.htm, .html).** This is the format to use if you're not yet finished working with a page in Word. It retains special codes that Word uses to work with your file; if you're going to edit the file in Word, you want to keep those codes in place.

- **Web Page, Filtered (.htm, .html).** What *filtered* means is that those Word-specific codes just mentioned get stripped out of the saved file. This makes the file leaner, so it loads faster when someone views it in a web browser. When you're ready to upload your document to your website, choose this option.

When you save a Word document as a web page, Microsoft saves your file in the HTML format and creates a folder with associated files. The HTML file has the name you chose for the filename, such as *index.htm*. The folder name is the filename plus the word "files," such as *index_files*. The folder holds formatting information, any images you include in the page, and a list of the files associated with the page.

Creating a Web Page from Scratch

The best way to create a Word document that will look good on the Web is to create a table to hold all the elements that make up the page. Tables let you control placement of the page's header, navigation bar, text, and images. When you type some content into a table, the width of the cell keeps the lines of text from getting too long—which is good, because viewers don't like having to scroll horizontally to read what's on a web page. You can give your website a consistent look across all its pages by saving the table as a template. This section walks you through the process of building a web page from scratch, one step at a time.

Creating your site's home page

Start by creating the first page your visitors will see: your site's home page. This page welcomes folks and gives them an idea of what your site is about.

Step 1: Set up a table

To make sure that web browsers will display your page as you want it to look, use a table to control each page's layout. Here's how:

1. Select Insert→Table (Alt, N, T) and create a 3 × 3 table (three columns and three rows).

   Why a 3 × 3 table? The top row will hold your web page's header, the banner that announces your site's name. Most of the left column will become the navigation bar that lets visitors jump to other pages. The bottom row holds your footer, which might include a copyright notice or a Contact Me link, and the rest of the table is for your content. As you go through the steps, you'll see how this table creates a place for each element on the page.

   Tip: For details about working with tables in Word, see page 81.

   ---

2. Select the entire table, and then click Table Tools | Design→Borders→No Border (Alt, JT, B, N).

   You're using a table to help with layout, but you don't actually want lines between its columns and rows to appear on the final page.

3. On the Table Tools | Layout tab, click the View Gridlines button (Alt, JL, TG) to turn on gridlines.

   Gridlines are dotted lines that appear between a table's rows and columns. They help you see what you're doing as you work with the table, but they're not visible when you upload the final table to your site.

4. Center your table: Selecting the whole table, go to the Home tab's Paragraph section, and then click the Center button (Alt, H, AC).

   This centers the table when a web browser displays it. If you don't center the table, it appears shoved over to the left side of visitors' screens.

5. Give your page some style. On the Table Tools | Design tab, go to the Table Style Options section and turn on the Header Row checkbox (Alt, JT, A) and the First Column checkbox (Alt, JT, M). Make sure all the other checkboxes in that section are off. From the Table Styles gallery (Alt, JT, S), choose a style whose color scheme you like.

   Figure 8-5 shows an example of a style that makes a good background for a web page.

6. Choose one of Word's themes to unify the look of your page. Select Page Layout→Themes (Alt, P, TH) to open the Themes gallery.

   As you pass your cursor over the different theme options, your table changes to reflect each theme.

7. Select Page Layout→Page Color (Alt, P, PC) to set a background color for your web page.

   Choose a color from the same theme you applied to the table. This is the background against which your text will appear, so choose a light color that's easy on the eyes and that provides good contrast to your theme's font color.

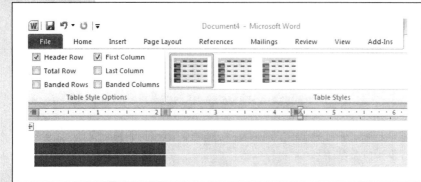

Figure 8-5:
This 3 × 3 table has one color for the top row (which will serve as the web page's header), another for the left column (soon to become the navigation bar), and a third for the rest of the table, which will hold text and images.

Step 2: Create a header

The header is the banner across the top of a web page that announces the name and purpose of the site. It's a good idea to use a header consistently across all pages in your website, so viewers never lose track of where they are.

Create your web page's header by focusing on your table's top row:

1. **Select the first row of the table, and then click Table Tools | Layout→Merge Cells (Alt, JL, M).**

   The cells merge into a single cell that stretches across the entire row.

2. **Type and format the heading for your web page, such as *My Web Page*.**

   To format the text, use the Home tab's formatting buttons or go to the Styles gallery (Alt, H, L) and select Title (or another style you like for your heading). Center the header (Alt, H, AC) and, to make it a good size for a web page, choose a font size of about 36 points. Figure 8-6 gives you an idea of how the header might look.

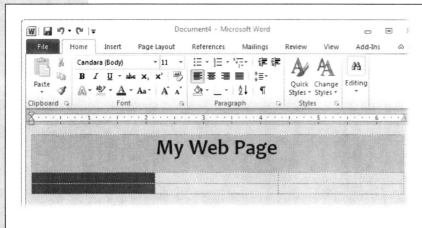

Figure 8-6:
Use a large font for your header to make it clear and easily visible.

Step 3: Add a navigation bar

When you visit a website, navigation buttons provide links that jump to the sites' various pages. In this step, you'll add a navigation bar to your own page:

1. **Merge the lower two cells in the far-left column; select them and then click Table Tools | Layout→Merge Cells (Alt, JL, M).**

   The two cells fuse together into a column that will hold your navigation bar.

2. **Click inside the column and type the names of the pages that will make up your website. Your entries here will link to those pages.**

   For example, a personal website might have pages called Home, About Me, My Blog, My Photos, and so on.

3. **Format the text in your navigation bar.**

   Adjust the line spacing (Home→Alt, H, K) to double or triple spacing so there's ample room to see and click the options. If you want, center the text in the cell using the alignment buttons on the Home tab or the Table Tools | Layout tab.

4. **Link Home in the navigation bar to your home page (that's the same page you're working on now). Select the word "Home" and then select Insert→Hyperlink (Alt, N, I).**

   The Insert Hyperlink dialog box, shown in Figure 8-7, opens. This is where you specify what you're linking to.

5. **In the "Link to" box, select Existing File or Web Page. Navigate to the folder where you saved *index.htm*, select it, and then click OK.**

   Word inserts the hyperlink and underlines "Home," as shown in Figure 8-8, to show that it's a link viewers can click.

6. **Create a link to the next page in your navigation bar. Select the next entry (About Me in Figure 8-8) and click Insert→Hyperlink (Alt, N, I).**

   Again, the Insert Hyperlink box (Figure 8-7) opens.

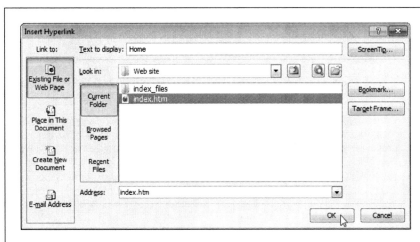

Figure 8-7:
Your navigation bar's Home link always jumps back to the website's home page (usually called index. htm).

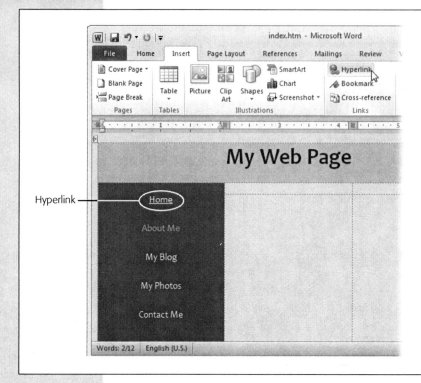

Figure 8-8:
As you add links to your navigation bar, Word underlines any text that contains a link. (For this reason, it's a good idea to reserve underlining only for links.)

Hyperlink

7. **This time, you're linking to a page that doesn't yet exist, so in the "Link to" box, select Create New Document.**

   The Insert Hyperlink box changes to look like the one in Figure 8-9.

8. **In the "Name of new document" text box, type in the name you'll use for the page, such as *aboutme.htm*. Below, in the "When to edit" section, turn on the radio button labeled "Edit the new document later." Click OK.**

   Word creates a new, empty HTML file and links to it. Later, you can create a new page (see page 206) and save it with this name.

9. **Repeat steps 6–8 until you've created links for all the terms in your navigation bar.**

   You've now got a navigation bar to help visitors get around your site.

Tip: If you'd prefer a line of links across the top of the page instead of a left-hand navigation bar, follow these steps *after* you've created the page's header: Insert a row into your table just under the header and use the Table Tools | Design tab's Shading button to give it a stand-out color. Split the row (Table Tools | Layout→Split Cells or Alt, JL, P) into the number of cells you need for your navigation links. For example, if your website has six pages, including Home, split the row into six cells. Type in the names of your website's pages, one per cell. Then create links as described in steps 4–9 above.

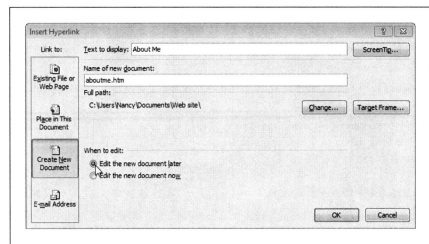

Figure 8-9:
As you create links for the navigation bar, you create new, empty files. Later, you'll create a page for each link.

Step 4: Add a footer

You've probably seen websites that show a copyright notice or other information, like the website designer's name or a link to a privacy policy, at the very bottom of each page (Figure 8-10 shows an example). Creating a footer lets you put the same, boilerplate text at the bottom of each page in your site. Here's how to do it:

1. **In the table's last row, select the two cells to the right of the navigation bar; click Table Tools | Layout→Merge Cells (Alt, JL, M).**

   The two cells merge into one.

2. **Type your copyright notice into the merged cell:** *Copyright © 2010 Jane Smith.*

   If you want to include any other information at the bottom of every page, include that, too. Choose a smaller font size than you plan to use for the page's main content: 8 or 10 points is about right.

3. **Select your text and press Ctrl+E (or select Home→Center or Alt, H, AC).**

   Word centers your text within the cell.

Step 5: Save the page as a template

Now that you've got a layout for your website's pages, you should save the design as a template. Doing so lets you reuse the template whenever you create a new page for your site, ensuring that all the pages on your site have a consistent look.

After all the hard work you've done laying out your page, saving it as a template is easy:

1. **Select File→Save As (Alt, F, A).**

   The familiar Save As dialog box opens.

2. **Navigate to the folder where you want to save the template (such as with the individual pages for this website). Give it a name that indicates it's a template, like *my site template.htm*. Select Web Page (.htm, .html) as the file type, and then click Save.**

   Word saves your template.

3. **Close *my site template.htm* (or whatever you named your new template) and reopen *index.htm*.**

   Now you can finish working on your site's home page, adding text and images. Use your saved template as a starting point for creating more pages (the next section shows you how).

Step 6: Adding text and images

Use the table's middle and right columns to position the text and images you add to your page, as shown in Figure 8-10. To add text, click inside a cell and start typing. To insert a photo, click in the column where you want the image to appear and select Insert→Picture (Alt, N, P). Then find and insert the image you want.

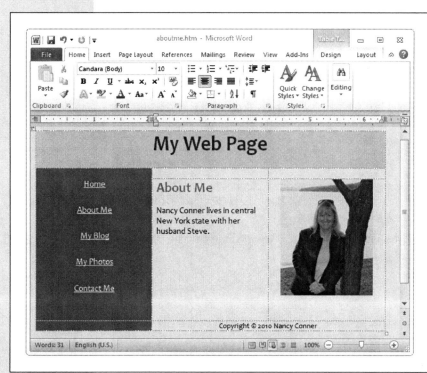

Figure 8-10:
Now you can see the benefit of using a table to lay out your page; the table's cells ensure even spacing.

Format text and images in the same way you'd format them in any other Word document. If you need a refresher, Chapter 2 is all about working with text in Word, and the discussion of formatting images starts on page 100.

Tip: To see a preview of how the page will look when you post it on the Web, open your favorite web browser and use it to view the page. In Firefox, for example, click File→Open File; in the Open File dialog box, find the HTML file on your computer, select it, and then click Open. If you make changes to the page in Word, click Save (Ctrl+S), and then refresh the page in your browser to see how it looks.

Creating More Pages for Your Site

When you created your web page template's navigation bar (page 209), you created a new, empty document for each link and opted to edit it later. Now is the time to add some content to those documents.

1. Select File→Open (Alt, F, O).

   Word's Open dialog box appears.

2. **Find and select the template for your site's pages (*my site template.htm* in the example). Click Open.**

   "Wait a second," you might be thinking. "Why am I creating a new document, when I've already got one (or more) waiting for a fresh helping of new content?" Patience, Grasshopper; you'll see why in a moment. Meanwhile, your template gives birth to a new, untitled document.

3. **Before you do anything else, select File→Save As (Alt, F, A).**

   The Save As dialog box opens.

4. **Find and select the page you want to create. For example, if you're going to work on your About Me page, select *aboutme.htm* (or whatever you named the file when you created the navigation bar's link). Click Save.**

   Word presents you with a dialog box telling that you the file already exists. (You already know that, because you created it when you set up the navigation links.)

5. **Make sure that the "Replace existing file" radio button is on, and then click OK.**

   Your template is now the basis for the page you selected. (Now do you see the thinking behind creating that new template-based file?) Add whatever text and images you want to put on this page. Save the file when you're done working on the page.

Note: Unlike blog posts, Word can't upload pages to your website. The procedure for doing that depends on the requirements laid out by whoever's hosting your website—check their help files for instructions on how to upload HTML files.

10 Tips for a Better Web Page

When you're designing your own website, think about your own experiences surfing the Web. Which sites made you want to stay and look around? Which couldn't you leave fast enough? Thinking like a visitor will help you design web pages that are interesting and user-friendly. These tips will help, too:

- **Keep it legible.** Don't use an image for your web page's background; it makes the text much harder to read. Along the same lines, dark backgrounds and low-contrast font colors leave visitors squinting—and they won't hang around long if they can't make out the text.

- **Don't make your pages too long—or too short.** Many visitors look only at the first screen of text, never bothering to scroll down the page. If you've got a lot of information, break it up into several pages. But don't go to the other extreme, either. If visitors have to click through to a new page every couple of sentences, they might lose interest and go elsewhere.

- **Don't clutter up the page.** Make your pages inviting. Most visitors skim web pages, for example, rather than reading them carefully, so avoid big blocks of tightly packed words. And instead of putting up a dozen photos of your new puppy, pick the best shot or two.

- **Avoid flashing, blinking graphics.** Animated GIFs—those images that bounce and jump around—are distracting and, to many people, annoying. Word has some cute animated clip art, but think twice before setting it loose on your web page.

- **Test links.** Links that don't work are frustrating to visitors and make your site seem out of date and poorly maintained. When you put your page on the Web, test any links to make sure they work. That goes

for both internal links (those that jump to other pages within your site) and external links (those that open web pages outside your site).

- **Compress graphics.** Large images can take a long time to load, even when the viewer has a fast connection—and web surfers aren't known for their patience. To compress a picture in Word, select the image and click the Picture Tools | Format tab's Compress Pictures button (Alt, JP, M). In the Compress Pictures dialog box, choose Screen (150 ppi) to optimize the picture for web viewing.

- **Clean up your spelling and grammar.** This is just plain common sense whenever you share your writing. Use Word's proofreading tools (see Chapter 4) to make your text as error-free as possible.

- **Make it easy for visitors to contact you.** Put a Contact Me link in your pages' footer. Create the footer (page 211), type *Contact Me*, and then insert a hyperlink to your email address: Select Contact Me and click Insert→Hyperlink (Alt, N, I). In the Insert Hyperlink box (Figure 8-7), choose E-mail Address, and then type your address in the address box. Click OK to insert the link.

- **Go beyond Word.** Word is fine for creating basic pages. But if you're going to be building a large site, consider using alternatives designed specifically for designing web pages. Many website hosts offer easy-to-use web page editors as part of their service. Or consider buying dedicated software such as Adobe Dreamweaver or Microsoft Expression Web. And it never hurts to buy a good reference book, such as *Creating a Web Site: The Missing Manual*.

Tip: If you use your website host's HTML editor to work with your site's pages, here's a great shortcut for generating clean HTML directly from a Word document. Point your web browser to *http://word2cleanhtml. com*. Copy the Word document, and then paste it into the site's big text box. Click the "convert to clean html" button. Copy the results and paste them into your HTML editor.

Sharing and Collaborating on Documents

W e've all heard it over and over from the time we were preschoolers: It's nice to share. When it comes to documents, you can be the nicest person around, thanks to Word's many sharing options. You can email a document right from Word or upload it to the Web and share it there.

Of course, sharing documents is about more than passing them around for others to read. Want to collaborate with others on a document-in-progress? Word gives you tons of options there, too: inserting comments, tracking changes that different people make to a document, comparing and combining different versions of a document. And since some things weren't meant to be shared, you can also protect your creations in various ways to ensure that no one makes changes they shouldn't.

Sharing a Document

Besides printing out and handing readers a hard copy, there are many other ways to share your work. So many, in fact, that Word has a special Backstage section (Figure 9-1) just for sharing. To find it, select File→Share (Alt, F, H).

Tip: Before sharing a document, make sure it doesn't contain any personal or hidden information that you don't want others to see. Flip to page 230 to read about how Word's Document Inspector cleans up your documents before you share them.

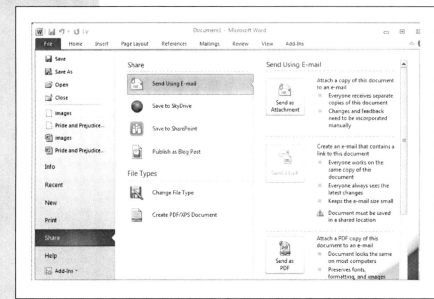

Figure 9-1:
Select File→Share (Alt, F, H) to see your options for sharing a document. Select an item in the middle of the screen (such as Send Using E-mail in this figure) to get more information about sharing your document that way. You can attach the document to an email or, if you've stored it online, send a link.

Emailing a Document

To email a document, go to the Backstage Share section (File→Share) and select Send Using E-mail (Alt, F, H, E). The right side of the screen gives you these options:

- **Send as Attachment.** When you send a document as an attachment, you send a copy of the document along with your email. If you send the attachment to multiple people, each recipient gets his own, separate copy of the file. So if your readers make comments or changes, you have to incorporate those back into your copy by hand. (Page 230 tells you how to easily combine different versions of a Word document into one.)

- **Send a Link.** If you've stored the document in a shared location, like SkyDrive or SharePoint, you can send an email that contains a link to the document. Unlike emailing an attached document, this method points everyone to a centralized copy of the document so that readers can find it online and work on a single copy—no need to combine versions later. (More details on SkyDrive and SharePoint in a moment.)

- **Send as PDF or XPS.** Portable document format (PDF) and Microsoft's XML paper specification (XPS) are file formats that keep your document looking the same—preserving formatting, images, layout, and fonts—on a variety of computers. When you send a document as an attachment in one of these formats, multiple recipients each get their own copy. The downside? It's not easy to make changes to the document. These formats are a good choice when you're sending a document for the recipients' information, not for their feedback.

- **Send as Internet Fax.** You can send a fax directly from Word. You don't even need a fax machine—but you do need a fax service provider. (If you don't have one, Word offers to take you to a page on Office.com where you can choose one.)

Note: Chapter 5 gives you the lowdown on faxing a document from your computer.

Emailing a document as an attachment

To email a document as an attachment, follow these steps:

1. **Open the file you want to send and choose File→Share→Send Using Email→Send as an Attachment (Alt, F, H, E, A).**

   Word launches your main email program (this book assumes it's Outlook, which is discussed in Part 2) with the document already attached. Your email address appears in the From line, and the document's title provides the Subject line.

2. **Type your recipient's email address in the To line (if you're sending the email to multiple people, put commas between the addresses to separate them). Leave the Subject line as is, or change it if you want. Add an email message (this is optional, but it's courteous to write up a quick a note explaining what's in the attachment). When your email is ready to go, click the Send button on the left.**

   Your email zips off through cyberspace with copies of your document tagging along.

Note: Emailing the document as a PDF (Alt, F, H, E, F) or as an XPS (Alt, F, H, E, X) works the same way as attaching the document. The only difference is behind the scenes: Word converts your document to the file format you chose before opening Outlook and attaching the file to a new email.

Emailing a link to a document

If you've stored a document on SkyDrive (see the next section) or on SharePoint (see page 219), you can email a link to the online document. With the document open in Word, select File→Share→Send Using Email→Send a Link (Alt, F, H, E, L).

Just like when you send a document as an attachment, Outlook opens a new email message with your address in the From line and the document's title in the Subject line. In the body of the message is a link to the online document. Type in a recipient, add a message explaining the link, and click Send. Your message and its link are on their way.

Saving a Document to SkyDrive

You've probably heard of "cloud computing," which lets you store files on distant servers and access them over the Internet. Cloud computing must have been what Microsoft had in mind when it named SkyDrive, which is home to Office Web Apps and offers 25 GB of free online storage. (Chapter 31 tells you all about working with Office on the Web.) When you store a file on SkyDrive, you can access it from any-where—all you need is an Internet connection and a web browser. When you save a document on SkyDrive, you can read and edit it from any computer online. Or you can download the document and open it in Word, edit it, and save the edited file on your computer or in SkyDrive.

Note: Whenever you download a document from the Internet, Word opens that document in Protected View (which means you can't edit it) and warns you that files you find on the Internet might harm your computer. If you're simply retrieving a file you stored on SkyDrive, you don't have to worry that it's malicious. Click Enable Editing to edit the document.

Before you can store documents on SkyDrive, you need a Windows Live ID. If you've got a Hotmail, Messenger, or Xbox Live account, you already have one—you can sign into SkyDrive with the username and password you use for that account. If you don't yet have a Windows Live ID and you want to use SkyDrive, go to *http://home. live.com* and click the Sign Up button to create an account and get your ID.

To save a document to SkyDrive, make sure your computer is connected to the Internet, and then do this:

1. **Open the document you want to save on SkyDrive and select File→Share→Save to SkyDrive (Alt, F, H, K). On the right side of the screen, click the big Sign In button (or press Y3 if you're using keyboard shortcuts).**

   A dialog box opens, asking for your Windows Live ID username and password.

2. **Type the requested info and, if you're on a computer that's for your own personal use (that is, not a public or shared computer), turn on the "Remember my credentials" checkbox—it'll save you typing them in again in the future. Click OK.**

   The right side of the screen changes to list your SkyDrive folders.

Note: The first time you use SkyDrive, you have to agree to the Windows Live service agreement and privacy statement before you can proceed. Click the links to read these policies, and then click the button labeled "I accept".

---

3. **Choose the folder where you want to store this document, and then click the Save As button.**

   The familiar Save As dialog box opens, with a SkyDrive folder as the location for saving the document.

4. **If you need to make any adjustments (such as changing the document's name), do so. Then click Save.**

   Windows uploads the file to the folder you selected in SkyDrive.

To see your document on SkyDrive, go to *http://skydrive.live.com* and sign in (if you're not signed in already). Find the folder where you uploaded the file and click it; your document is there.

Tip: You can also get to SkyDrive right from Word. Select File→Share→Save to SkyDrive→Go to SkyDrive (Alt, F, H, K, Y1). Your default web browser opens and takes you to a sign-in page or, if you're already signed in, to your "Recent folders" page.

Saving a Document to SharePoint

SharePoint is what Microsoft calls a "comprehensive content management" system. In plain English, that means it's a central location where you can upload, share, and keep track of files. You can check out a document, work on it, and then check it back in so others can use it. In principle, SharePoint is similar to SkyDrive, but it's typically installed by a corporation's IT department to serve as a kind of private employees-only service.

Saving a document to SharePoint works the same way as saving one to SkyDrive. When you want to upload a document to SharePoint, open the file and then select File→Share→Save to SharePoint (Alt, F, H, S). In the right part of the screen, find and sign into the SharePoint location you want. The Save As dialog box opens, allowing you to save the document at that location.

Note: Word's Backstage Share options also let you publish a document as a blog post. For detailed information about uploading a Word document to your blog, see online Appendix B.

Adding Comments

One of the main reasons for sharing a document is to get feedback. Having several other pairs of eyes go over your writing can raise issues you need to address, point out confusing parts, or just shower you with praise. In Word, reviewers provide feedback in the form of comments that appear in your document's margin and point to the relevant parts of your text. It's kind of like putting a sticky note on the page.

Inserting a Comment

Adding comments to a document is easy; it takes just a couple of steps:

1. **Highlight the text you're commenting on (if you don't select any text, Word selects it for you, highlighting the word immediately after the cursor). Select Review→New Comment (Alt, R, C).**

   What happens next depends on the view you're in:

   — **In Draft and Outline views,** the Reviewing pane opens, as shown in Figure 9-2.

   — **In Print Layout and Web Layout views,** a balloon appears in the right margin, as shown in Figure 9-3.

   In either case, Word assigns the comment a number and puts the cursor in the spot where you can offer your feedback.

Figure 9-2:
In Draft view, when you insert a comment, Word automatically opens the Reviewing pane. Comments appear at the top of the pane (circled), along with any tracked changes (223) in the document.

Reviewing pane

2. **Type your comment. When you're finished, click anywhere in the document.**

   In Draft and Outline views, the Reviewing pane stays open until you close it. In Print and Web Layout views, Word dims the highlighting and the comment balloon to show that the comment isn't active right now. Comments are marked in the text with highlighting and your initials.

Figure 9-3:
In Print Layout view, type your comment into the balloon that appears in the right margin.

Tip: Word uses your name and initials to label comments. Occasionally, you might want to change how word marks your comments—for example, in a project where each team member identifies him- or herself by role (AU for author, ED for editor, CE for copyeditor, and so on), rather than by name. To change the name or initials Word uses, go Backstage: Select File→Options (Alt, F, I). In the General section of the Word Options box, find "Personalize your copy of Microsoft Office"—that's where you can change this info. Click OK to apply.

Viewing Comments

When you want to see the comments in a document, it's easiest to read them in Print Layout or Web Layout views. Just look for a comment balloon in the right margin. A dotted line connects the comment to the highlighted text it refers to. That way, in a document with lots of comments, you'll never get confused about which comment refers to what.

In Print Layout and Web Layout views, you can proceed through the comments by scrolling down the page. Or you can jump from one comment to the next by using the Next Comment and Previous Comment buttons in the Review tab's Comments section. Click the button you want to move forward or backward, or press Alt, R, N to move forward to the next comment or Alt, R, V to go back to the previous comment.

Note: Outline view isn't a good choice for viewing comments, because it shows only the first line of body paragraphs. Use a different view when you're working with comments.

When you're reading a document in Draft view, highlighting and the commenter's initials indicate that there's a comment, but the comment itself is hidden. There are two ways to read a comment in Draft view:

- **Hover your mouse pointer over the commenter's initials.** The comment appears as a ScreenTip.

- **Open the Reviewing pane.** This pane lists all a document's comments in its "Main document changes and comments" section, so you can scroll down the list to read the comments. To open the Reviewing pane, select Review→Reviewing Pane (Alt, R, TP and then either V to see a vertical Reviewing pane on the left side of the screen or H to see a horizontal Reviewing pane at the bottom of the screen).

You can tell Word to display the Reviewing pane either horizontally or vertically: Click the Reviewing Pane button's right-hand down arrow and then select your preference: Reviewing Pane Vertical or Reviewing Pane Horizontal. Word remembers your preference and displays the Reviewing pane in the orientation you chose the next time you open it.

Tip: Here's a shortcut to opening the Reviewing pane: Right-click any text that has a comment attached to it. From the shortcut menu that pops up, choose Edit Comment.

To move through comments in the Reviewing pane, you can use the pane's scroll bar or the Review tab's Next and Previous Comment buttons.

Tip: To switch views, use the View buttons on the right side of the status bar.

Editing a Comment

At some point, you might want to clarify feedback or fix a typo in a comment you previously made, or perhaps respond to a comment someone else has made. If you're in Print Layout or Web Layout view, simply click inside the balloon where you want the cursor to appear and make your edits. Click outside the balloon when you're done.

To edit a comment in Draft view, open the Reviewing pane (Review→Reviewing Pane or Alt, R, TP), click the comment you want to edit, and type away. Click anywhere in the document to return to it.

Deleting a Comment

If you want to clean up old comments (after you've taken care of the issues they raised, for example), start by right-clicking the text related to the comment you want to delete. From the shortcut menu, select Delete Comment. Everything about the comment—the highlighting, the balloon or text in the comment pane, the commenter's initials—disappears.

Tracking Changes

If you've got several people working on one document—adding sections here, making corrections and changes there—it's easy to lose track of who did what. To keep everyone's contributions straight, use Word's Track Changes feature.

Track Changes does exactly what its name says: When you turn it on, Word tracks each and every change any author or reviewer makes: Jane's additions, deletions, and comments might show up in red; Pete's in blue; Tammy's in orange; and so on. When you hover the mouse pointer over a change, a ScreenTip appears, listing the name of the reviewer and the time and date of the change.

To start tracking changes, head for the Review tab: Select Review→Track Changes (Alt, R, G, G). Word colors the Track Changes button so you know that it's now tracking all changes that you or anyone else makes to the document. Figure 9-4 shows an example of a document with Track Changes turned on.

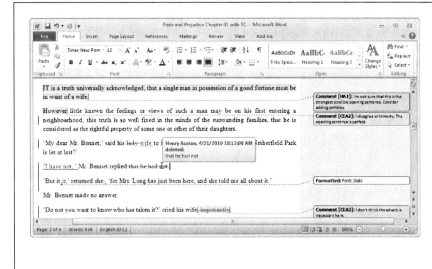

Figure 9-4:
Everyone is a critic when you track changes. When multiple people edit a document, Word keeps track of who did what. Comments appear in different colors (although that's hard to see in this black-and-white image) and marked with the commenter's initials. Word underlines additions and strikes through deletions. It also marks formatting changes. Hover your mouse pointer over any change to see who made it.

When it's tracking changes, Word marks everything you do to the document in a different color from the document's normal text:

- When you **add** text, Word underlines it.
- When you **delete** text, Word uses strikethrough formatting for that text.
- When you **move** text, Word double-underlines the text you moved and uses double-strikethrough formatting for the text in its original location.

- When you **change text's formatting,** Word describes the formatting change (such as Font: Italic or Indent: Left: 0.5") in a balloon visible in Print Layout and Web Layout views.

- When you **make any kind of change,** Word adds a vertical line in the left margin to mark it.

If the formatting of these options displeases you, you can customize the appearance of any type of tracked changes; page 227 has the details.

Word also tracks all your changes, one by one, in the Reviewing pane's "Main document changes and comments" section. You can review changes there; to see a change in its context, click it in the Reviewing pane, and Word jumps to that change in the document.

Selecting Which Changes to View

When you've got several people making changes, all those strikethroughs and underlines and different colors can quickly make a document hard to read. You can make the document more legible—or focus on a particular kind of change—by telling Word to show only certain kinds of changes. For example, maybe you just want to see the changes made by a certain reviewer, hiding everyone else's. Or you can show only formatting changes or only insertions and deletions. You can even hide all changes and comments without actually deleting them from the document.

In the Tracking section of the Review tab, the Display for Review drop-down list (Alt, R, TD) gives you these options:

- **Final: Show Markup.** Choose this option to see the most recent version of the document in all its marked-up glory, including additions, deletions, comments, and formatting changes.

- **Final.** Choose this option to see what the document would look like if you were to accept all changes. (Word doesn't actually incorporate the changes into the document; that comes later, as explained on page 226.) This option also hides comments and balloons.

- **Original: Show Markup.** If you've set Word to show all revisions in balloons (see the next bulleted list), this option shows insertions in balloons, as though an editor has written suggested changes in the margin. Deletions appear in the text. For the other Show Markup settings, this option looks just like Final: Show Markup.

- **Original.** If you want to temporarily clear away all comments and changes, choose this option. It hides comments and shows how the document would look if you rejected all changes and returned the document to its original, pristine state. (The changes are still in the document; they just don't show in this display.)

You can also display only certain kinds of changes. Make sure that the Display for Review drop-down menu shows Final: Show Markup, and then click the Show Markup button and uncheck any type of change that you *don't* want to see. Here are the kinds of changes you can turn on and off, as shown in Figure 9-5:

- **Comments (Alt, R, TM, C).** If you don't want to see comments or the high-lighting and initials that show that they're there, uncheck this option.

- **Ink (Alt, R, TM, K).** This option is for showing or hiding comments added to a document by writing on a tablet PC.

- **Insertions and Deletions (Alt, R, TM, I).** Insertions and deletions come as a set; you can show them both or hide them both.

- **Formatting (Alt, R, TM, F).** Turning off this option leaves the formatting in place but removes the balloon that marks it.

- **Markup Area Highlight (Alt, R, TM, H).** The markup area is where Word displays balloons on the right side of the page in Print Layout and Web Layout views. When this is turned on, the markup area is set off from the document with light blue highlighting. When it's off, the markup area has a white background, just like the document proper.

- **Balloons (Alt, R, TM, B).** You've got some flexibility about what balloons can display. When you point at this option, a fly-out menu appears, giving you the choice of one of these uses for balloons:

  — **Show Revisions in Balloons.** This makes the markup area work like the Reviewing pane; all changes—comments, insertions, deletions, formatting changes, you name it—get flagged in balloons.

  — **Show All Revisions Inline.** Some people don't like balloons. If that's you, choose this option to hide balloons in all views (even Print Layout and Web Layout).

  — **Show Only Comments and Formatting in Balloons.** This is Word's default choice. In Print Layout and Web Layout views, comments and formatting appear in balloons, but other changes appear in the text.

- **Reviewers (Alt, R, TM, R).** If several people are working on the same document, you can focus on the changes made by just one reviewer. You might want to review your boss's changes extra carefully, for example, or tone down the flowery prose of that Shakespeare wannabe two cubicles over.

Figure 9-5:
A document with lots of tracked changes can be difficult to read. Focus on a particular kind of change—or changes from a particular reviewer—by turning Show Markup options on and off.

- **Highlight Updates (Alt, R, TM, U).** When you're working on a document that's stored on a server that supports simultaneous editing (at work, for example), then whenever someone saves the file, Word saves it on the server and updates the document for anyone viewing it now. (It also saves the previous version, just to be safe.) When Highlight Updates is turned on, Word brings other people's updates to the document to your attention, helping you keep track of who's doing what.

- **Other Authors (Alt, R, TM, O).** When a document has multiple authors, you can show only the work of a particular author. To do that, you must be working on a document that's stored on a server that supports simultaneous editing. So you might use this option at work, but probably not on your personal, home version of Word.

Tip: Flip to the end of this chapter to read more about coauthoring and simultaneous editing in Word 2010. Chapter 31 covers editing in Office Web Apps.

Accepting or Rejecting Changes

When someone reviews or edits your work, you'll find changes you agree with and others you don't. Word lets you accept changes, incorporating them into the document, or reject them, keeping the text in its original form.

To accept or reject a particular change, highlight the change and go to the Review tab:

- To **accept the change,** select Review→Accept (Alt, R, A, C), or right-click the change and choose Accept Change.

- To **accept this change and jump to the next change in the document,** select Review, click the down arrow at the bottom of the Accept button, and then select Accept and Move to Next (Alt, R, A, M).

- To **reject the change,** select Review→Reject (Alt, R, J, R), or right-click the change and choose Reject Change.

- To **reject this change and jump to the next change in the document,** select Review, click the down arrow to the right of the Reject button, and then select Reject and Move to Next (Alt, R, J, M).

You don't have to pick your way through a document's changes one by one. If you've reviewed everything and want to make all the proposed changes permanent—or get rid of them all in one fell swoop—you can accept or reject all changes at once:

- To **accept all changes,** select Review, click the down arrow at the bottom of the Accept button, and then choose Accept All Changes in Document (Alt, R, A, D).

- To **reject all changes,** select Review, click the down arrow to the right of the Reject button, and then choose Reject All Changes in Document (Alt, R, J, D).

Tip: If you want to accept or reject all instances of a particular kind of change, such as all formatting changes, while leaving other changes tracked, click the Show Markup button and make sure that only the kind of change you want to accept or reject en masse is checked. Then, on the Review tab, click the down arrow for the Accept or the Reject button and select Accept All Changes Shown (Alt, R, A, A) or Reject All Changes Shown (Alt, R, J, A).

Setting Track Changes Options

Like so many aspects of Word, Track Changes is highly customizable. If you'd rather show insertions by making them bold (rather than underlining them), for example, you can do that. Or if you don't want Word to track formatting changes, you can turn that off. It's up to you.

To set your Track Changes options, select Review, click the down arrow at the bottom of the Track Changes button, and then select Change Tracking Options (Alt, R, G, O). This opens the Track Changes Options dialog box, shown in Figure 9-6, where you can set these options:

- **Insertions.** Use the drop-down menus to select how Word indicates that a reviewer has inserted new text. Your options include formatting and color.

- **Deletions.** Choose the formatting and color for deleted text.

Figure 9-6:
Customize how Word tracks changes to reflect the way you work best.

- **Changed lines.** Word shows that someone has made changes to the text by inserting a vertical line in the outside border on the line with the change. If you prefer, you can tell Word to show this line always on the left or the right, or to not show it at all.

- **Comments.** Usually, Word assigns each commenter a different color, making it easy to see who made which comment. If you prefer, however, you can set a single color for all comments.

- **Track moves.** If you don't want Word to mark moved text, turn off the "Track moves" checkbox. You can also set formatting and color options for the text in its original ("Moved from") and new ("Moved to") locations.

- **Tables.** Word tracks the text in tables the same way it does text in a paragraph. If a reviewer makes changes to the table itself, though, Word tracks it by assigning inserted, deleted, merged, and split cells different colors. If you want, you can change the default colors here.

- **Track formatting.** If you don't want to know about formatting changes, turn off the "Track formatting" checkbox. Or you can set the formatting and color options that indicate that someone has changed the formatting.

- **Balloons.** Here you can specify when to use balloons (the options are the same as in the Show Markup menu). You can also set the width and position of balloons.

- **Paper orientation.** When you print a marked-up document, Word usually preserves the same orientation that you see on the screen. If you prefer, however, you can let Word decide on the best orientation for printing or force landscape orientation, which can be useful in a document that has lots of comments in the margins.

Comparing Documents

When multiple people work on the same document, you often end up with a tangle of conflicting changes. Even worse, if you're dealing with multiple versions that don't have Track Changes turned on, you're in for a mind-numbing, line-by-line review to spot the differences. Fortunately, Word can help by marking the variations using the same tracked changes formatting you learned about earlier in this chapter. Here's how to make that happen:

1. Select Review→Compare→Compare (Alt, R, M, C).

    This opens the Compare Documents dialog box, shown in Figure 9-7.

2. From the "Original document" and "Revised document" drop-down lists, select the two versions you want to compare.

    When you select a document from the "Revised document" list, Word fills in your name in the "Label changes with" text box. You'll probably want to leave your name as the label, because it identifies the changes you made. But if you want a different label, click inside the box and type what you want.

Tip: If you've got several different saved versions of a document, it may not be clear from the drop-down lists which ones you want. Click the Open button to the right of either drop-down list to find and choose a file in the Open dialog box.

3. **If you want to fine-tune the kinds of changes Word shows, then click the More button.**

   The dialog box expands to show two sections:

   — **Comparison settings.** In this section, turn off the checkboxes of any changes you don't care about. You can turn on or off just about anything that can change in a document, including comments, formatting changes, case changes, headers and footers, and so on.

   — **Show changes.** Word normally shows changes at the level of words, but you can take the granularity down to the level of characters if you prefer. Your other option in this section is how to show the changes: in a newly created document (the default), in the original version, or in the revised version.

4. **When your settings are the way you want them, click OK.**

   Word shows you the difference between the original and revised versions. The result looks like a document showing markup (like the one shown in Figure 9-4), except that Word marks all changes with the label you assigned in the Compare Documents dialog box.

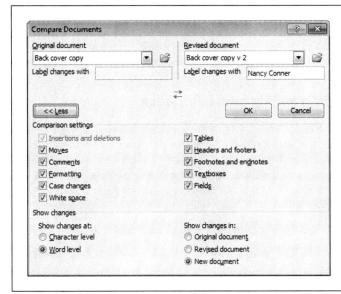

Figure 9-7:
When you're comparing two versions of a document, click the More button to expand the Compare Documents dialog box so it looks like the one shown here. The "Comparison settings" section lets you focus on finding only the changes you're interested in.

Tip: You can also compare two documents by opening them both and then viewing them side by side. Word even lets you scroll though both at the same time. See page 33 for more about side-by-side viewing and synchronous scrolling.

Combining Documents

It used to be that, if you wanted to combine multiple versions into a single document, you were in for a long and tedious session of careful copying and pasting. No more. Word compares and combines documents for you, showing the differences as tracked changes you can accept or reject.

The process for combining documents is almost identical to the process for comparing them, discussed in the previous section. Start by selecting Review→Compare→ Combine (Alt, R, M, M) to open the Combine Documents dialog box. This looks exactly like the Compare Documents dialog box shown in Figure 9-7, except for the name at the top. In the Combine Documents dialog box, follow steps 2–4 for comparing documents.

In the document that combines the two versions, review the revised document's changes and accept or reject them as you wish.

Protecting Your Documents

Sending a document out into the world can be a risky venture. You might get feedback you don't want or—worse—changes made to a finished document. It's even possible that others might be able to see hidden or personal information that you don't want them to, like comments and revisions or your name as the original author.

Word gives you several ways to protect the documents you share with others. Document Inspector removes hidden data and personal information. You can also restrict others' ability to format or edit a document, protect a document by requiring a password to open it, or add a digital signature so you know that a document is authentic. This section tells you how to protect your Word documents in all these ways and more.

Removing Hidden Data and Personal Information

Even a document that looks squeaky clean may contain information you don't want to share. For example, there may be tracked changes you didn't spot or headers that were only for your working version. Even the sharpest-eyed reviewer can miss something occasionally. That's why it's a good idea to have Word give your document a final once-over before you share it. Document Inspector knows what to look for. When it finds hidden or personal information, you can remove it from the document.

When you've finalized the document, save it. Then put Document Inspector to work:

1. **Select File→Info (Alt, F, E) and take a look at the Prepare for Sharing section.**

   This is where Word lists any issues that you might want to clear up before you share a document.

2. **Click Check for Issues→Inspect Document (press I and then Enter if you've got keyboard shortcuts turned on).**

   The Document Inspector, shown in Figure 9-8, opens.

Figure 9-8:
*This dialog box shows the differ-
ent kinds of content the Document
Inspector can look for when it
scours your document. For any
item you want the Document
Inspector to find, make sure its
checkbox is turned on.*

The Document Inspector lists different kinds of content you might want to find
and remove from your document:

— **Comments, Revisions, Versions, and Annotations.** If any of these linger
in your document, Word smokes them out. If you decide to remove them,
Word accepts revisions and annotations and removes comments and other
versions.

Note: *Annotations* refers to ink annotations made on a tablet PC.

— **Document Properties and Personal Information.** This category includes
information like the author's name and the name of the template you used
to create the document. You can view Document Properties on the right
side of Word's Backstage info section. (Click the Properties button and select Show All Properties to see just how much information travels with
your document—properties could include your company name and manager, for example.)

— **Custom XML Data.** Your company might use custom XML data that you
can't see simply by looking at a document—but others who know how to
look for it can find it.

— **Headers, Footers, and Watermarks.** You might have a header or footer that contains information about the document in process that you don't need to share with outsiders. Or your company's watermark may be proprietary. If you need to remove this kind of information, the Document Inspector will make sure it's gone.

— **Invisible Content.** This doesn't apply to Word documents, but you can format objects as invisible in Excel workbooks and PowerPoint presentations.

— **Hidden Text.** You can use the Font dialog box (Alt, H, FN) to format selected text as hidden. When you do, the Document Inspector finds it and reminds you it's there. If you decide to remove this hidden text, Word deletes it from the document.

Note: *If you're trying to run the Document Inspector on a file that has unsaved changes, Word warns you to save changes before proceeding. That's because the Document Inspector may remove information that you can't restore if you decide later that you wanted it. Click Yes to save the file or No to proceed without saving.*

---

3. **For each item you want the Document Inspector to look for, make sure its checkbox is turned on. Then click Inspect.**

   The Document Inspector conducts its inspection. While this is happening (for a long document, it can take awhile), you see a dialog box with a progress bar. When the Inspector is done checking, it changes to look something like Figure 9-9. If the Inspector finds a particular kind of comment, it tells you and displays a Remove All button. (You can't pick and choose which instances of the content you want to get rid of.) If it doesn't find any content, it tells you that, too.

4. **For any kind of content you want to remove, click the Remove All button.**

   Word removes the content, and the Document Inspector box changes to tell you that it's gone.

5. **When you're done removing content, you can click Reinspect to have the Document Inspector take a final sweep of the document. When you're finished, click Close.**

   The Document Inspector closes, and your document is squeaky clean and ready to share.

Restricting Formatting and Editing

If too many cooks spoil the broth, then too many authors can wreak complete havoc with your documents. Sometimes you want to share a document, but you don't want others putting their messy fingerprints all over your prose. Word offers a lot of options for collaborating, but it also lets you protect your documents against changes you don't want.

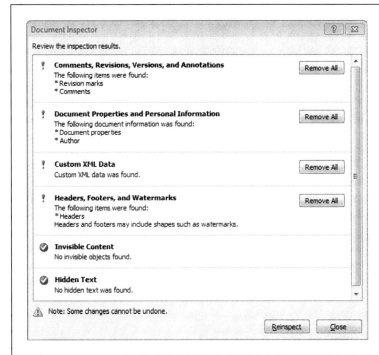

You can prevent other people from editing or formatting your document (or both) in the Review tab's Protect section. Click Review→Restrict Editing (Alt, R, PE) to open the Restrict Formatting and Editing pane, shown in Figure 9-10.

The Restrict Formatting and Editing pane lets you set these restrictions:

- **Formatting restrictions.** To let others use only those styles you approve to for-mat the document, turn on the checkbox labeled "Limit formatting to a selec-tion of styles" and then click Settings. The Formatting Restrictions dialog box opens with a list of styles currently allowed for the document—each permitted style has a check in the box next to it. You can go through the list and turn off the checkbox for any style you don't want, or you can use the buttons beneath the list to make your selection:

  — **All** turns on all checkboxes in the list, allowing all styles.

  — **Recommended Minimum** turns on the checkboxes of only those styles Word recommends.

  — **None** turns off all checkboxes in the list, so reviewers can't do any format-ting at all.

At the bottom of the Formatting Restrictions dialog box are three checkboxes. These are off by default; turn on any that meet your needs:

— **Allow AutoFormat to override formatting restrictions.** Usually you'll leave this off. But if you want AutoFormat to have the final say about formatting, turn on this checkbox.

— **Block Theme or Scheme switching.** This prevents anyone reading the document from changing its theme. So if you created the document with Word's Executive theme and you want it to stay that way, turn on this checkbox.

— **Block Quick Style set switching.** Turning on this checkbox prevents readers from changing the document's current style set.

Tip: Chapter 7 discusses themes (page 181), and you can read about styles sets in Chapter 2 (page 51).

Click OK to apply the formatting restrictions you chose.

Figure 9-10:
The Restrict Formatting and Editing pane is where you set limits on what others can do with your document.

- **Editing restrictions.** Here's where you limit the kinds of changes others can make to a document's content. Turn on the checkbox labeled "Allow only this type of editing in the document" and then choose one of these options from the drop-down list:
  - **Tracked changes.** When you select this option, Track Changes is on by default. Others can't be sneaky and turn it off to hide any changes they might make.
  - **Comments.** This option lets readers insert comments into the document but not make any changes to the text.
  - **Filling in forms.** If the document contains forms (a web page might, for example), this option lets others submit information to the forms but not change the document.
  - **No changes (Read only).** This option prevents others from making any changes whatsoever to the document.

Tip: If it's okay for some readers to edit but not others, you can create exceptions to editing restrictions. When you turn on editing restrictions, the Restrict Formatting and Editing pane expands to include a section for exceptions. Select a part of the document where editing is OK, and then turn on the checkbox for the group who can edit it. To add people who aren't listed in the Groups box, click the "More users" link.

After you've set up the formatting and editing restrictions you want, you're ready to enforce those restrictions. So click the button labeled Yes, Start Enforcing Protection. Word opens a dialog box asking you to choose a protection method for this document. Here you tell Word how to know who can turn restrictions on and off. Pick one of these methods:

- **Password.** Turn on this radio button to require a password from anyone who tries to remove restrictions from the document. If this is the first time you're protecting the document, type a password and confirm it in the appropriate boxes.

- **User authentication.** This method is more secure than password protection, but to use it you need to have a Windows Live ID and sign up for Microsoft's Information Rights Management Service (it's free). If you want to do that, then turn on the "User authentication" radio button and click OK. A wizard opens and takes you through the steps of signing up.

After you've selected a protection method, click OK. Word applies the restrictions to the document.

Later, if you want to remove the restrictions (temporarily or for good), open the Restrict Formatting and Editing pane again and click Stop Protection. Depending on the protection method you chose, Word requests a password or authenticates you as a user. If you pass muster, Word stops protecting the document.

Restricting Permissions

You can also go Backstage to restrict who can do what in a document. Click File→Info (Alt, F, E) and take a look in the Permissions section to see whether there are any restrictions on the document. Click Protect Document (or press P if you've got keyboard shortcuts on), and then select one of these Permissions options:

- **Mark as Final.** This option makes the document read-only and marks it as final. When you mark a document as final, Word hides the ribbon and places the Marked as Final icon on the status bar (it looks like a rubber stamp marking a document). When you choose this option, a dialog box opens telling you that Word is about to mark the document as final and save it. Click OK.

Note: Marking a document as final doesn't necessarily give you the last word. When a reader opens the document, a yellow bar at the top of the screen displays this message: "An author has marked this document as final to discourage editing." There's also an Edit Anyway button that the reader can click to turn editing back on. If you want to make sure a document is really and truly read-only, set it that way using the Restrict Formatting and Editing pane (Figure 9-10).

- **Encrypt with Password.** When you choose this option, readers need to know the password to open the file. To set a password, click Encrypt with Password; Word opens the Encrypt Document dialog box, which asks you to set the password for this document. Type it in (passwords are case-sensitive) and then click OK. Word asks you to re-enter the password to confirm it. Type it again and click OK.

  Later, if you want to remove the password, come back here (Review→Info→ Protect Document→Encrypt with Password) and clear the password from the Encrypt Document dialog box.

Warning: When you password-protect a document, write down the password—and keep it in a location that's safe from prying eyes! If you forget it, there's no way for anyone to open the document—not even Bill Gates himself. It's a good idea to keep a list of passwords and the documents they protect.

- **Restrict Editing.** This opens the Restrict Formatting and Editing pane (Figure 9-10) so you can set restrictions there. (The previous section tells you how to do that.)
- **Restrict Permission by People.** You need to sign up for Microsoft's Information Rights Management Service to use this option, which lets you allow certain people or groups to open the document but not edit, copy, or print it.

- **Add a Digital Signature.** Think of the number of business and legal documents that require a signature: checks, wills, sales contracts, leases, credit card receipts.... You sign a document to show that you approve it or agree to its terms. A forged signature makes the document invalid, so some documents require a witness to confirm that you're the one who signed it.

When you email or share some documents, you want to be able to prove they come from you. But you can't whip out a pen and dash off your signature on an email. That's where digital signatures come in. A *digital signature* is an electronic tag that verifies a document's authenticity—it proves that the document comes from you and that nobody has tampered with it since it left your desk.

To put your electronic John Hancock on a document, choose Add a Digital Signature from the Protect Document menu. A dialog box opens, offering two ways to add a digital signature to your document:

— **Get a digital ID from a Microsoft partner.** A third-party digital signature is like getting someone to witness your signature—it guarantees that you're the one who signed the document. If you choose this option, your web browser opens and takes you to the Office Marketplace, where you can choose a digital ID provider, such as GlobalSign.

— **Create your own digital ID.** When you choose this option, it's like signing a check or a credit card slip without anyone standing by to verify that you're you; it's less secure than third-party verification, but it shows to your own satisfaction that the document is yours and not altered by anyone since you signed it.

The first time you select this option and click OK, Word opens a dialog box where you can set up your digital signature: name (required), email address, organization, and location (optional). Type in your signature information and click Create. Now you've got a digital signature to attach to documents.

Next time you opt to create your own digital ID, Word opens the Sign dialog box, shown in Figure 9-11. Type in a brief description of your purpose for signing the document, and then click Sign. Word makes your document read-only (to prevent any changes); attaches your digital signature; and adds a Signatures button, which looks like a document seal, to the status bar.

Note: You can also attach digital signatures to Excel workbooks and PowerPoint presentations.

Figure 9-11:
When you attach a digital ID to a document, Word asks you to enter your reason for signing it.

FREQUENTLY ASKED QUESTION

Signing on the Bottom Line

How do I add a signature line to a Word document?

When you want someone else to acknowledge or verify a document, you can add a signature line for that person to sign. Say you send Joe a memo and want him to sign and return it, acknowledging that he read it. You can insert a digital signature line—when Joe reads the memo, he double-clicks the signature line and inserts his digital signature. At the same time, Word verifies that Joe is the signer.

Here's how it works:

1. In the document you want signed, click to place the cursor wherever you want the signature line to appear.
2. Select Insert→Signature Line (Alt, N, G) to open the Signature Setup dialog box.
3. In the box, type in the name, title, and email address of the person who'll sign the document. Type any directions into the "Instructions to the signer" box. If you want to let the signer add comments, then turn on the checkbox labeled "Allow the Signer to add comments in the Sign dialog". Leave the "Show sign date in signature line" checkbox on to date the signature. Click OK.
4. Word inserts a signature line, marked by a big, black X, with the signer's name beneath.

After Joe has read the memo, he double-clicks the signature line to open the Sign dialog box.

In the box, he can type in his name, select an image of his pen-and-ink signature (if he's got one stored on his computer), or sign it with a stylus (if he's using a tablet PC). When he's done that, he clicks the Sign button to add his signature to the document.

You can add signature lines to Word documents and Excel workbooks.

Coauthoring and Simultaneous Editing

They say writing is a lonely occupation, conjuring images of a solitary author scribbling away by candlelight in a drafty garret. But that kind of writing is so 19th century. Today, writing is more and more a collaboration. Several authors might work together to draft a report or even a novel, for example, or relatives might share memories for a family history.

Word 2010 is up to speed with how people write in the 21st century. Now you can write and edit documents collaboratively—in real time—over the company network.

Note: Real-time collaboration works only for desktop versions of Office 2010. The Windows Live version of Office Web Apps, which lets you store files on the Web and access them from anywhere, allows real-time, collaborative editing only for Excel workbooks. For Word documents, only one author can work on a document at a time. See Chapter 31 for more about using Word on the Web.

If you're collaborating on a document—say, a report for work or school—you probably divide up the workload among your coauthors. For example, you might volunteer to write the introduction and background, while Sara tackles research methods, and Jim compiles the results and writes a conclusion. In the past, you might have passed around the document by email, checked it out one at a time from a central file-management repository like SharePoint, or worked on separate versions of the document and merged them later.

But if your organization has Office Web Apps set up on its own SharePoint servers (or a Microsoft-hosted subscription version of SharePoint), you, Sara, and Jim can all work on the same document at the same time. You'd sign into the network and open the file as usual. If Jim does the same thing, he opens the same document you're working on. When that happens, an icon appears on the status bar, showing a couple of people, and a message appears to tell you that someone else is also editing the document. Click the message balloon or the icon to see who else is working on the document.

Tip: When Word displays the names of the other authors currently editing the document, you can contact any of them right from Word. Hover the pointer over a person's name, and a box opens with ways to contact that person. Click the email icon to send an email, or sign into your favorite instant messaging program to send an IM or call.

As you work, you can see which paragraphs the other authors are working in; when an author edits a paragraph, Word labels that paragraph with his name in the left margin. (The other authors see the same kind of label on the paragraph where you're working.) You don't have to worry about showing your coworkers what a lousy typist you are, though. Even though Word shows other authors where you're working, it doesn't show your actual work until you save it.

When you or another author saves a file, Word notifies everyone with an update in the status bar. The next time you save the document, those changes appear in your copy. That way, you're not distracted by what others are doing while you're in the middle of working.

Part Two: Outlook

2

Getting Started with Outlook

I f you think of Outlook as Microsoft's email program, then you haven't seen Outlook lately. Sure, you can use Outlook to send, receive, and organize email, but it does a whole lot more. It's also a supercharged address book, a calendar to keep track of appointments, a virtual notepad, and a personal assistant that reminds you of tasks and keeps you organized.

This chapter provides a quick overview of what you can do with Outlook. Then, since email is the first thing most people work with in Outlook, you'll get right down to business learning the ins and outs of sending and receiving email messages—from the basics to more advanced maneuvers, like creating rules to sort incoming emails, using and creating Quick Steps (new in 2010), and managing multiple email accounts. In Outlook 2010, the ribbon is standard throughout all windows, making it easier to find the commands you want. You'll see where to find your favorite shortcuts when working with email—and maybe learn a few new ones.

Setting Up Outlook

Before you can start using Outlook 2010, you have to set it up. Microsoft lends a hand by providing a startup wizard that guides you through these steps:

1. **Make sure your computer is connected to the Internet. Then fire up Outlook from the Windows Start menu (Start→All Programs→Microsoft Office→ Microsoft Outlook 2010).**

   The Microsoft Outlook 2010 Startup wizard opens, telling you that it's going to walk you through the process of configuring Outlook so you can use it to send and receive email.

2. **Click Next.**

   To configure Outlook to send and receive email messages, you need to connect it to an email account. You can use Outlook with Internet email services (like Gmail or Yahoo Mail), Microsoft Exchange (if your organization uses it), or another email server (like a local Internet service provider). The wizard asks if you want to configure an email account now.

3. **Turn on the Yes radio button and click Next.**

   The wizard takes you to the Auto Account Setup step, shown in Figure 10-1, which asks for your name, email address, and password.

4. **Type in the requested information, and then click Next.**

   Outlook connects to your email server and tests your email address. When it's finished, it lets you know that it's configured your email account to work with Outlook.

5. **If you want, you can add another email account to Outlook at this point—a personal email, for instance, in addition to your work email. Click "Add another account" to go through the process again. Otherwise, click Finish.**

   Outlook opens your inbox, shown in Figure 10-2. You've already got one message—the test message Outlook sent to make sure your account is all set up.

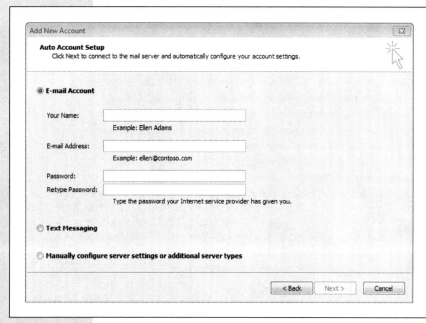

Figure 10-1:
The Outlook startup wizard helps you set up your Outlook account to work with your current email address, perhaps the one you use for work or school.

Taking a Quick Look Around

When you start up Outlook, you see a window that looks something like the one shown in Figure 10-2.

Navigation pane   Inbox   Reading pane

Figure 10-2:
If your Outlook setup goes well, you get a test message showing that you've added your email address successfully. The main Outlook window has a Navigation pane on the left so you can easily switch from, say, reading your email to working with your calendar.

Mail

You use Outlook, of course, to send, receive, and organize email messages. The program puts related email exchanges into a group called a *conversation*. Say your boss emails you asking for an update on your project. You reply to that email, outlining the work you've done in the past week. She responds with another email that says, "Good job!" (hey, it could happen) and suggests a couple of priorities for next week. That's a conversation. You can expand any conversation in your inbox to see all its messages, then click the message you want to read.

To further organize your emails, you can sort them into folders. Outlook comes with basic folders already built in, but the real power of folders comes when you create your own. Chapter 12 is all about that topic.

Calendar

Outlook's calendar lets you keep track of meetings, appointments, dinner dates, the kids' concerts and soccer games—anything you want to be sure you don't forget. After you've scheduled some events, you can check the calendar to see what's up on a given day. You can also send yourself automatic reminders. Chapter 13 tells all.

Contacts

Outlook provides an electronic address book where you can store, organize, and find contact information for everyone you know. Having contacts makes it easier to send emails and share information with colleagues, family, friends, neighbors, the members of your book club—anyone. Create groups so you can be sure everyone gets the message when you email your project team at work or invite relatives to the family reunion. See Chapter 11 for more on your 21st century Rolodex.

Tasks

Tasks are like items on an electronic to-do list. Whether you're keeping track of upcoming deadlines or reminding yourself to pick up the dry cleaning, you can list and organize tasks so you're always on top of what you need to do. Because they're so closely related to your schedule, they're also covered in Chapter 13, as are Notes.

Notes

Outlook also has a built-in notepad where you can write notes, musings, reminders, or whatever you feel like jotting down to think about later. They're like sticky notes without the paper.

Composing and Sending Email

After you've got Outlook set up, you'll probably want to use email right away. This section tells all about sending email messages, from the basics—sending a message, inserting a picture, attaching a file—to the fancier stuff, like creating virtual stationery and scheduling when to send an email.

When you want to compose and send an email message, start from the main Outlook window, with Mail selected in the Navigation pane. Then follow these steps:

1. **When you're in Outlook's Mail section, take the speedy route by pressing Ctrl+N. Or select Home→New Email (Alt, H, N). Ctrl+Shift+M is yet another option.**

   A message window opens (like the one shown in Figure 10-3), ready for you to write your email. Your email address shows in the From line. (If you're using more than one email address with Outlook, you can click the From button and choose the sender address you want for this email. Page 276 tells you more about managing multiple email accounts with Outlook.)

Note: You may not see a From line in the email you're composing. To show or hide it, select Options→From (Alt, P, F).

---

2. **In the To text box, type the recipient's email address.**

   If you want to send the email to more than one person, use semicolons (;) or commas (,) to separate addresses. The box on page 248 lists other ways to address an email message.

3. **In the Subject text box, type the subject of your message.**

   A subject is like an email's title. Because the subject line is the first thing a recipient sees when your email lands in her inbox, make it descriptive.

4. **Type your message into the main text box.**

   You format text in an email message the same way you'd format it in Word or PowerPoint. Formatting buttons appear on the Message tab (Alt, H) and the Format Text tab (Alt, O).

5. **When your message is ready to go, click Send. For a shortcut, press Ctrl+Enter or Alt+S.**

   Off whizzes your message, zipping through cyberspace to the recipient's inbox.

Outlook automatically saves a copy of every email you send in your Sent Items folder. To see those messages, click Sent Items in the Navigation pane.

Figure 10-3:
When you compose an email message in Outlook, a new window opens. The message window's ribbon is loaded with tabs related to creating and sending email messages, but everything you need to send a basic email appears on the Message tab, shown here.

Tip: When you compose an email message, Outlook periodically saves it. If you're interrupted while writing an email and want to finish it later, press Ctrl+S to save it. Outlook stores saved messages in the Drafts folder; look for any unfinished email messages there.

One Address, Many Ways to Insert It

Typing an address directly into the To box is only one way to make sure your email message reaches its recipient. In fact, Outlook's many options for addressing an email message are so convenient that you'll rarely find yourself typing in the whole address. Check out these alternatives:

- **Start typing.** If you've emailed the recipient before, Outlook tries to guess the address as soon as you start typing. Type a few letters, and a list of addresses beginning with those letters appears. Click any address on the list to insert it into the To line.

- **Choose a recipient from the Address Book.** The Address Book holds the contacts you've added to Outlook. You can use the Address Book to insert a contact's address straight into an email message. Start a new message and click either the To button or the Message tab's Address Book button (Alt, H, AB). Either option opens the Select Names: Contacts dialog box, shown in Figure 10-4. Use the Search box to find the name you want, and then click the button that corresponds with where you want the address to

appear: To, Cc, or Bcc. Click OK to insert your choices into your email.

- **Use the Check Names button.** For people you've added as contacts, you can type a first or last name and then click the Message tab's Check Names button (Alt, H, M). If Outlook recognizes the name from your Contacts, it will fill in that person's email address. If there's more than one possibility (say, for a common name like Smith), Outlook shows you the options so you can pick the one you want.

- **Reply to a message you received.** If someone sent you an email and you want to answer it, open the email you received and select Home→Reply (Alt, H, RP) to reply to the sender or Home→Reply All (Alt, H, RA) to reply to the sender and any other recipients. Outlook opens a message window with the address line and the subject line already filled in. Outlook also quotes the original message in the area where you write your reply.

Sending an Email to More Than One Recipient

You can send an email message to multiple recipients by typing all the addresses in the To line, one by one (separating the addresses with semicolons or commas). If you've created a Contact Group (page 296), then you can put the group in the To line, and your email goes to all the group members.

Besides putting all recipients front and center in the To line, you can also use the Cc or Bcc line to hold some recipients' addresses. These terms come from the days of typewriters and paper letters:

- **Cc** means *carbon copy* and indicates that an exact copy of the message is going to someone other than the person to whom the message is addressed. The address of the Cc recipient is visible to all recipients. It's a good idea to Cc an email when you just want to keep someone in the loop about the subject of your email—a manager, for example, who needs to stay informed about the topic but doesn't have to act on it. Cc-ing is also useful when you want message recipients to know that the manager is keeping an eye on the issue.

Figure 10-4:
When you use Outlook's Address Book, select a contact and click the button to put that person's email address in the To, Cc, or Bcc line of your email.

Select an address...

...and choose the line where you want it to appear.

- **Bcc** means *blind carbon copy*. Entering an address here sends a copy to whomever's listed in the Bcc line, but the address is invisible to those folks whose addresses appear in the To and Cc lines. You might use the Bcc line when you're sending an email message to a large number of people and don't want to reveal all their email addresses—put your own address in the To line and then the list of other recipients in the Bcc line. This method protects recipients' privacy by hiding their email addresses from everyone else on the mailing list.

To add a Cc address, simply add the address you want to the Cc line at the top of the message. (Type it in or click the Cc button to open your Outlook Address Book and find it there.)

To add a Bcc address, select Options→Bcc (Alt, P, B). This adds a Bcc line to the top of your message; enter the address as usual. Even though you can see this address line when you compose your message, the email's recipients can't see it in the message they receive.

Proofreading a Message

Nothing is more embarrassing than sending an email that's riddled with typos and spelling mistakes. (Well, okay, there are some Facebook pages with pictures that are way more embarrassing than a typo or two.) It's a good idea to give a new email message the once-over before you send it. Outlook has the same proofing and research tools as other Office programs, so you can find everything you need to know about proofing your work in Chapter 4. Table 10-1 tells you where to look.

Note: To get to Outlook's proofing options, select File→Options (Alt, F, I), choose Mail, and then click the Spelling and Autocorrect button.

Table 10-1. *Where to find information about proofing and research tools*

Topic	Page Number
Catching spelling mistakes	115
Using contextual spelling	117
Checking spelling in an entire message	117
Checking grammar	118
Undoing an AutoCorrect change	121
Setting AutoCorrect options	122
AutoFormatting	125
Looking up a word in the dictionary	129
Using the thesaurus	129
Getting information about a subject	130

Tip: Want to make spell checking automatic before you send an email? In the main Outlook window, select File→Options→Mail (Alt, F, I, then use the arrow keys to select Mail). In the "Compose messages" section, turn on the checkbox labeled "Always check spelling before sending" and then click OK.

Attaching a File to an Email Message

Email is a fast, convenient way to send documents and other files: Just compose your message, attach a file, and send. The recipient gets your message, along with the attachment, which he can open in an appropriate program such as Word for a word-processing file or Excel for a spreadsheet.

Here's the quickest way to attach a file to an email message: Compose the email and then open Windows Explorer and resize the window so you can see both Windows Explorer and your Outlook message window. Next, click the file you want to attach, drag it into your email message, and drop it there. Presto—instant attachment.

You can also attach a file by taking one of these paths:

- In the Message tab's Include section, click Attach File (Alt, H, AF).
- Select Insert→Attach File (Alt, N, AF).

Either path opens the Insert File dialog box, where you can find and select your file; click Insert to attach it to your email.

Tip: When you're working in another Office program, you can email a file right from that program. Open the file you want to send and select File→Share→Send Using E-mail (Alt, F, H, E). Select Send as Attachment (A if you're using keyboard shortcuts) to open an email-message-in-progress in Outlook with the file already attached. You can also convert the file to a PDF or XPS (page 24) before you attach it or email a link to a file that's saved in SkyDrive or another shared location.

Inserting a Picture into an Email Message

People love to email photos, whether vacation snaps, new baby photos, or pictures from the company's annual meeting. You can send a photo as an attachment (see the previous section), but that means the recipient has to open it using a separate image-viewing program. To make sure your recipient sees your picture, you can insert it into the body of the email instead.

To insert a picture (or any other kind of images, like shapes, charts, and clip art), go to the Insert tab. In the Illustrations section, click the Picture button (Alt, N, P). When the Insert Picture dialog box opens, navigate to the picture you want, select it, and click Insert. Your picture appears in the email, and Outlook opens the Picture Tools | Format contextual tab so you can edit the image before you send it.

Tip: You can also insert a picture into an email message by dragging it from Windows Explorer and dropping it into the email.

Formatting pictures in Outlook works the same way as in Word. Table 10-2 lists the different ways you can edit and format images, along with where you can find instructions for doing different tasks.

Table 10-2. Where to find information about working with images

Topic	Page Number
Inserting a picture	96
Inserting clip art	97
Inserting a screenshot	98
Changing an image's size	101
Cropping an image	101
Removing a picture's background	102
Moving an image	104
Rotating an image	104
Adjusting an image's appearance	105

Tip: Create high-impact emails with SmartArt graphics. Outlook now lets you insert and format SmartArt right in the body of an email message. Click Insert→SmartArt (Alt, N, M) to begin. Page 588 tells you all about working with SmartArt.

Adding a Signature

An email *signature* is text that Outlook adds to the end of every email you send. This might be contact information for business emails, or your favorite witty quote for personal emails. In Outlook, you can have different signatures for different purposes. This section shows you how to create and work with signatures.

Creating a signature

Before you can stamp your signature on outgoing emails, you need to create one or more of these mini memos. Here's how:

1. **Open the Signatures and Stationery dialog box. Outlook offers several different paths there:**

   — If you have a message window open in which you're composing an email, select Message→Signature→Signatures (Alt, H, G, S).

   — An alternative path when you're composing an email is to click Insert→ Signature→Signatures (Alt, N, G, S).

   — If you're in the main Outlook window, select File→Options→Mail (Alt, F, I, and select Mail), and click the Signatures button.

   Whichever path you take, the Signatures and Stationery dialog box, shown in Figure 10-5, opens with the E-mail Signature tab selected. This dialog box is where you compose, edit, and work with signatures.

2. **Click the New button.**

   A small dialog box appears, asking for a name for the signature you're creating.

3. **Type in a name for the signature and click OK.**

   Pick a name that makes it easy to find the signature you want, such as "Standard," "Work," "Holiday greeting," and so on.

4. **The main part of the dialog box is the big "Edit signature" text box. Click inside this box and type your signature.**

   You can format the signature's text using the buttons above the text box. The far-right buttons let you add a picture or a link to your signature.

5. **In the "Choose default signature" section, tell Outlook which messages to add this signature to:**

   — If you use more than one email account with Outlook, then select the email account for this signature.

— If you want this signature to be part of all new messages you send, then select it from the "New messages" drop-down list.

— If you want this signature to be part of all emails you forward or create in response to an email you received, then select it from the "Replies/forwards" drop-down list.

6. **When everything looks good, click OK.**

Outlook saves your new signature.

If you've made your signature the default for outgoing messages, then the signature automatically appears in the message area when you compose an email. (You can edit the signature inside the email message, but your changes apply only to that email. If you want to edit a signature for all outgoing email, see the next section.)

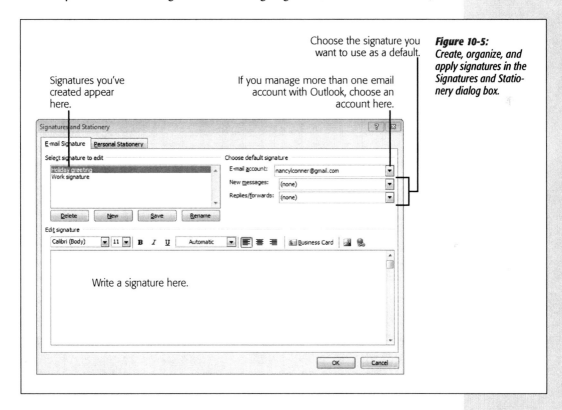

Choose the signature you want to use as a default.

Signatures you've created appear here.

If you manage more than one email account with Outlook, choose an account here.

Figure 10-5:
Create, organize, and apply signatures in the Signatures and Stationery dialog box.

Editing a signature

If you need to edit a signature, go back to the Signatures and Stationery dialog box (make sure the Signature tab is selected). Choose a signature from the "Select signature to edit" list, and it appears in the "Edit signature" text box. Make your changes, and then click OK to save them.

Choosing a signature to add

If you select a default signature in the Signatures and Stationery box (Figure 10-5), Outlook inserts that signature in all emails you send (of the type you selected: new, replies/forwards, or both). If you've created more than one signature, you can choose a signature to suit the occasion. For example, you might set your job title and work phone as the default signature, but for some emails you might prefer a different signature, such as a holiday greeting or an announcement of an upcoming event.

If you've created alternative signatures, you can select the one you want to add to the current email message. Select Message→Signature. A menu appears, listing the names of the signatures you've saved. Click the signature you want, and Outlook inserts it into your email message.

Note: When you insert a signature this way, Outlook inserts the signature wherever the cursor happens to be, so make sure the cursor is where you want it before making your selection.

Deleting a signature

If there's a signature you won't use again—maybe you had one advertising a company promotion that's now over—here's how to delete it: Click Message→Signature→ Signatures (Alt, H, G, S) to open the Signatures and Stationery dialog box (Figure 10-5). Select the name of the signature you want to delete, and click the Delete button. So long, signature.

Adding a Theme or Stationery

Like other Office programs, Outlook has themes you can use to customize the look of your email messages. Each theme combines a color scheme with easy-on-the-eyes fonts to give your emails an attractive design. (The content, of course, is still up to you.)

To select or customize a theme for an email you're composing, head to the message window's Options tab and work these buttons:

- **Themes (Alt, P, TH).** Outlook shows you a gallery of themes; click one to apply it to your message.

- **Colors (Alt, P, TC).** To pick a different color scheme, click this button and select the one you want.

- **Fonts (Alt, P, TF).** Themes use a combination of fonts and sizes for different text levels—for example, the default Office theme uses Cambria for headings and Calibri for regular text, and the Office Classic theme uses Arial for headings and Times New Roman for regular text. Click this button to select a font combo.

- **Effects (Alt, P, TE).** Each theme has built-in effects associated with it for shapes and SmartArt. To change a theme's effects, use this button.

- **Page Color (Alt, P, PC).** If you want to give your message a background color, click this button and select the color you want.

Tip: For more about working with Office themes, see page 181.

The days of handwritten notes on perfumed stationery may be over (and good riddance if you have allergies), but you can design virtual stationery for email messages you send from Outlook. They're not perfumed, but they have a fun, elegant, or funky look.

Note: For stationery to be visible, you must send the message in HTML format (that's Outlook's default). The box on page 257 tells you more about email formats.

Here's how to design your own email stationery:

1. **In the email's message window, select Message→Signature→Signatures (Alt, H, G, S)**

   This opens the Signatures and Stationery dialog box.

2. **Click the Personal Stationery tab.**

   The dialog box changes to look like the one shown in Figure 10-6. The Personal Stationery tab is where you choose a design and tell Outlook when to use that design.

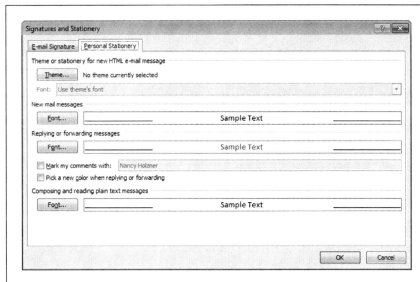

Figure 10-6:
Personalize the look of your emails by creating your own stationery.

3. **Click the Theme button.**

   The Theme or Stationery box opens, as shown in Figure 10-7. In this dialog box, *themes* include a background and styles for fonts, bullets, horizontal lines, and hyperlinks. Stationery is just a background without any styles for the text. When you select a theme, you can see what it looks like in the right-hand Sample pane.

4. **Choose a design and click OK.**

   Outlook saves your choice and returns you to the Personal Stationery tab.

5. **If you chose stationery, use the Font buttons to select a font for new messages and messages you reply to or forward. When you're finished designing your stationery, click OK.**

   Outlook applies your newly designed stationery to the next email message you compose.

Tip: If you want to apply a theme to *all* your outgoing email messages, head Backstage. Select File→Options (Alt, F, I) and click Mail. In the "Compose messages" section, click the Stationery and Fonts button. This opens the Signatures and Stationery dialog box to its Personal Stationery tab, shown in Figure 10-6, where you can choose a theme and fonts to decorate all your messages.

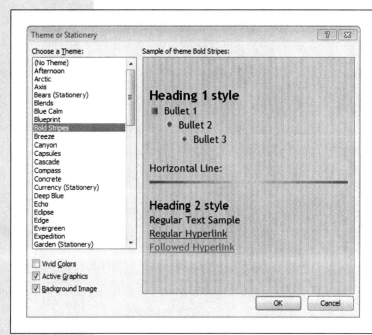

Figure 10-7:
This example of an Outlook theme shows the background, fonts, and other styles that will add a certain style to your email messages.

Email Message Formats

Outlook sends email in any of these formats:

- **HTML** stands for *hypertext markup language*, which is what tells web browsers how to display web pages. Sending an email message in HTML format lets you format and align your text to make it look good. It also lets you include images and graphics in the body of the email. Many email messages nowadays use HTML format, but some recipients might have trouble viewing the email if they've set their email programs to view emails as plain text (see the next option).

- **Plain text** sends text but removes all formatting, such as fonts and text alignment. And forget about anything fancy like symbols, shapes, or WordArt. But some people prefer to set their email programs to read only plain text, because it's the highest-security way to read email messages.

- **Rich text** maintains the formatting that plain text strips out. The problem with the Outlook Rich Text

email format is that Microsoft owns it, and it doesn't work in any email programs besides Outlook and Microsoft Exchange Client. Unless you're sure your recipients use Outlook or Exchange to read email (such as coworkers), don't send in this format.

HTML format is Outlook's default for sending email messages, and you probably won't have to change it. There are rare occasions when you might want to send an email in a different format. For example, maybe a recipient tells you that the formatting of an email you sent was messed up and he couldn't read the text. That's not your fault—it has to do with his email program's settings. But if you want to make sure he gets the message, the best bet in this case would be to send plain text next time.

To change the format of an email you're writing, go to the Format Text tab and then select HTML (Alt, O, H1), Plain Text (Alt, O, L1), or Rich Text (Alt, O, R1).

Setting a Message's Priority and Confidentiality

With the volume of email most people get, it's easy for an important message to get lost in an overcrowded inbox. To get a recipient's attention, you can set both a priority and a sensitivity level. You can do this using the Properties dialog box, shown in Figure 10-8. To open this dialog box, on the Message tab, click the Tags section's lower-right Message Options button.

In the Settings section at the top of the Properties box, click the Importance button to select an option: Low, Normal (no mark), or High. If you want, you can also let the recipient know the email's level of confidentiality. Click the Sensitivity button and pick a confidentiality level: Normal (no label), Personal, Private, or Confidential.

When a recipient opens your email, its sensitivity level appears above the message, like this: "Sensitivity: Personal" (or whatever level you chose). Emails with Normal sensitivity don't show a sensitivity level.

How your importance and sensitivity display on the recipient's email depends on the email program she uses. In Outlook, for example, priority icons appear in the inbox, to the right of the subject: High-priority messages show an exclamation point, and low-priority messages a blue, downward-pointing arrow. Sensitivity labels appear in the message, between the sender's address and the date sent. Other email programs may show these labels differently (or not at all).

Figure 10-8:
The Properties box lets you work with outgoing email messages in various ways: You can note the message's urgency or confidentiality level, create voting buttons (page 260), request delivery receipts, schedule a sending time, and more.

Making Sure They Got the Message

Between overzealous spam filters and overcrowded inboxes, you might want to make extra-sure that your recipient received and read an important message. Here's how to get confirmation: When you compose your message, click the Options tab and, in the Tracking section, turn on one or both of these checkboxes:

- **Request a Delivery Receipt (Alt, P, U)** to get notification when your email successfully reaches the recipient's account.

- **Request a Read Receipt (Alt, P, Q)** to get notification when the recipient has actually opened your email.

Notifications are sent via emails with a subject line of "Notification for <Subject of email that requested the receipt>," so if you send out several receipt requests, you can keep track of which ones reached their targets. Notice that you don't *demand* these receipts; you *request* them. Not all email servers will respond to the receipt request, and the recipient may tell her email program not to send a receipt. Still, it's worth a try.

Setting a Delivery Time

When you write an email message and click Send, Outlook sends your message on its way immediately. Sometimes, though, you might get a little bit ahead on your correspondence and compose an email that you want to send at some point in the future—like birthday wishes, next month's email newsletter, or that resignation note for the day after the bonus arrives.

To schedule a message and send it at a scheduled date and time, select Options→Delay Delivery (Alt, P, D). This opens the Properties dialog box (Figure 10-8). In the "Delivery options" section, turn on the "Do not deliver before" checkbox and choose the delivery date and time from the drop-down lists. Click Close to save your selections.

Now when you click Send, Outlook waits until the time you specified before it sends the email. Outlook must be running to send a scheduled message; if you've closed the program or turned off your computer, it sends the message the next time you open Outlook after the scheduled time has passed.

Tip: If you sent an email and the recipient hasn't gotten it within a few minutes, open the Properties box and make sure that the "Do not deliver before" checkbox is off.

Directing Replies to Another Address

When you send an email, you might not want recipients' replies to come back to you. For example, you might send out a marketing newsletter to subscribers but prefer that any replies to go to the guys and gals in sales. Here's how to set that up:

1. **Compose your email, and then select Options→Direct Replies To (Alt, P, I).**

   The Properties box (Figure 10-8) opens. In the "Delivery options" section, Outlook has already turned on the "Have replies sent to" checkbox.

2. **In the "Have replies sent to" text box, type in the address where you want to direct replies.**

   To find the address in your Address Book, click the Select Names button.

3. **Click Close.**

   Outlook closes the Properties box and returns you to the message you're composing.

When you send the email, any recipient who hits Reply will open a message addressed to the email address you inserted in the "Have replies sent to" text box. Nice way to pass the buck!

Adding Voting Buttons

There are times when the only reply you want is a yes or no answer. Maybe you've sent around a final copy of a proposal or specification and simply want recipients to vote whether to accept or reject the final version. That's what voting buttons are for.

When you add voting buttons to an email, people who receive the email and read it in Outlook see a Vote button added to their Message tab. Clicking that button opens a menu of voting options, such as approve/reject, yes/no, or whatever you specify. When the recipient votes, Outlook sends a special email message back to you that logs the vote. Votes stay within the conversation, so you can easily keep track of them.

To add voting buttons to an email, compose your email and then select Options→Use Voting Buttons (Alt, P, V). Pick the voting options you want from the menu that opens.

If you want to create custom voting options—such as people's names to vote for Employee of the Month—then choose Custom (C) from the Use Voting Buttons menu to open the Properties dialog box (Figure 10-8). In the Voting and Tracking options section, make sure the "Use voting buttons" checkbox is on, and then type in the voting choices you want, separated by semicolons. Click Close to add your custom voting options to the email. (Outlook also adds them to the Use Voting Buttons menu in case you want to use them again in the future.)

Note: Voting buttons won't work if a recipient uses a program other than Outlook to read her email.

Working Offline

Even the most accomplished multitasker needs to focus sometimes. If you want to work uninterrupted by a barrage of incoming emails, go to the main Outlook window and select Send/Receive→Work Offline (Alt, S, W). Outlook disconnects from the server (although your computer remains online, so you can still use the Internet).

You know that Outlook is offline because there's a Working Offline notification in the status bar and a big red X on Outlook's taskbar button. To take Outlook back online and start receiving emails again, repeat what you did before: Select Send/Receive→Work Offline (Alt, S, W). This toggles the connection back on and changes the status bar notification to Connected.

Note: Going offline means you won't be disturbed by incoming emails, but you can't send email when you're offline, either. If you try to send an email when you're offline, Outlook sends it automatically after you reconnect.

Receiving Email

When someone sends you an email, it lands in your inbox, shown back in Figure 10-1. (Depending on what you're doing in Outlook when an email message arrives, you may have to click Mail or Inbox in the navigation pane to see the new email.) Click any email in the inbox to display it in the right-hand Reading pane.

If the Reading pane feels a bit cramped, or if you want to reply to a message, double-click the message in the inbox to open it in its own window, as shown in Figure 10-9. The message window for a received email has just two tabs: File and Message. The Message tab takes care of most of what you need to do with messages you receive.

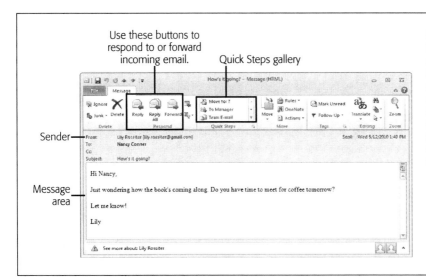

Use these buttons to respond to or forward incoming email.

Quick Steps gallery

Sender

Message area

Figure 10-9:
When you open a received email message in its own window, use the Message tab's buttons to reply or to forward it to someone else. The customizable Quick Steps gallery shows common actions for dealing with received mail.

Replying to or Forwarding an Email

To answer an email, open it in a message window (as shown in Figure 10-9) and click Reply (Alt, H, RP). Outlook opens a new window for you to compose your reply, which has some information already filled in:

- **From.** Your email address.
- **To.** The email address you're replying to.
- **Subject.** "RE:" followed by the original email's subject.
- **Message.** The original message, reproduced below the area where you write your reply.

The cursor is already blinking in the message area, waiting for you to start typing. Write your message and, if you want, change any of the prefilled info—you might want to add another email address, for example. Then click Send (or press Alt+S or Ctrl+Enter) to deliver your reply.

If the original email went to multiple recipients and you want to respond to the whole gang, then click Reply All (Alt, H, RA).

Note: If the email you're replying to had any Bcc recipients, those recipients don't receive your reply if you click Reply All.

When you *forward* an email message you received, you send the message—exactly as you received it—to another recipient. If you want, you can add your own commentary to the forwarded email. Open the email in a message window and click Forward (Alt, H, FW).

The message opens in a new window, with your address, the subject line (marked "FW" for forward), and the quoted message already filled in. Add the address of the person you're forwarding to, along with any text you want to add to the forwarded message, and then send.

Tip: Here's a shortcut for forwarding or replying to an email straight from your inbox. Right-click any email and then choose Reply, Reply All, or Forward from the shortcut menu.

Opening an Attachment

When an email arrives with an attached file, such as a photo or a document, you can tell it has an attachment by looking at it in the inbox; messages with attachments have a paper clip icon to the right of the subject.

When you open an email with an attached file, a bar with two tabs appears in the subject line: One says "Message," and the other sports the name of the attached file. Click Message to read the email message; click the filename to view the attachment. Outlook displays the attachment right in the message window.

When you view an attachment in a message window, as shown in Figure 10-10, the Attachment Tools | Attachments tab appears. This tab has a handful of buttons for dealing with attachments:

- **Open (Alt, JA, OP)** opens the file in an appropriate program, such as Word for a document or Windows Photo Viewer for a picture.

Note: Because attached files may contain viruses, Windows opens any at-risk files in Protected View, a read-only view that protects your computer. If you trust the source of the file, click Enable Editing to work with the file.

- **Quick Print (Alt, JA, Q)** sends the attached file to your default printer.

- **Save As (Alt, JA, AV)** saves the file on your computer in whatever location you select.

- **Remove Attachment (Alt, JA, R)** detaches the attachment from the email and gets rid of it—helpful if you want to slim down hard drive clutter after you've read and saved that 10 MB PowerPoint attachment. (After all, no need to save it in Outlook *and* in another folder on your hard drive, right?) Careful, though: You can't undo removing an attachment, and there's no confirmation before Outlook acts.

- **Select All (Alt, JA, SA)** selects all files when a message has multiple attachments. If you want to copy, save, or remove all of an email's attachments, use this button to select them first, and then click the appropriate button.

- **Copy Attachments (Alt, JA, C)** makes a copy of the attachment and puts it on the Clipboard, so you can paste it elsewhere—you might want to paste a picture into a Word document or a PowerPoint slide, for example.

- **Show Message (Alt, JA, M)** closes the attachment and returns you to the email message it came with.

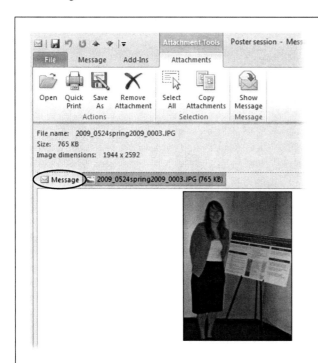

Figure 10-10:
The Attachment Tools | Attachments contextual tab lets you open, save, or remove an attached file. To stop viewing the attachment and go back to the email message, click the Show Message button or Message in the bar above the reading area (circled).

Getting Notified

Outlook gets pretty excited when a new email arrives: It plays a sound, changes the mouse pointer, displays a picture of an envelope in the taskbar, and displays an alert on your desktop for several seconds. If that's more notification than you need, you can tone it down a bit.

From the main Outlook window, click File→Options (Alt, F, I), and then select Mail. Scroll down to find the "Message arrival" section. Turn off the checkbox of any notification method you don't want. Click OK to save your changes.

Deleting a Message

You probably won't want to hang onto every email you receive. Often you can open an email, read its contents, and be done with it. When you delete a message from Outlook, you move it to the Deleted Items folder. Deleted messages sit there until you empty the trash, which removes them permanently.

If you've got a message open in its own window, press Ctrl+D or click the Message tab's Delete button (Alt, H, D) to send the message to the Deleted Items folder. From the inbox, right-click the message you want to delete and choose Delete from the bottom of the shortcut menu.

After a while, your Deleted Items folder fills up with items you don't want. There are two ways to empty all items from the trash:

- In the Navigation pane, right-click Deleted Items. From the shortcut menu, choose Empty Folder.
- Select File→Info→Cleanup Tools (Alt, F, E, T). Then choose Empty Deleted Items Folder.

In either case, Outlook checks to make sure you really want to get rid of *everything* in the folder. Click Yes, and you've taken out the trash.

Marking a Message as Unread

In your inbox, the subject of any message you haven't read yet appears as bold text. When you open a message in the Reading pane or in its own message window, the inbox no longer displays that message's subject as bold; it's just normal text.

If you want to mark a message as unread, making it easier to find when you scan what's in your inbox, use one of these methods:

- If you have the message open in its own window, go to the Message tab's Tags section and click Mark Unread (Alt, H, U).
- In the inbox, select a message and click the Home tab's Unread/Read button (Alt, H, W).

- In the inbox, you can also right-click the message and select Mark as Unread from the shortcut menu.

Outlook restores bold formatting to that message in the inbox.

Flagging a Message

Flagging a message means marking it so you'll remember to deal with it later. In the inbox or other mailbox, flagged messages show a colored flag to the right of the subject. (Messages you haven't flagged show the dim outline of a flag.)

Flagging a message you've received

When you receive an important message and want to make sure you remember to act on it later, you can click the message's flag icon right in your inbox. Alternatively, select the message and, on the Home tab, click Follow Up→Flag Message (Alt, H, U, M). The flag turns red so you'll notice it.

Later, when you've attended to the message, clear the flag by clicking it again in the mailbox. Or you can select the message, go to the Home tab, and click Follow Up→Clear Flag (Alt, H, U, E). The flag goes back to its original, ghostly gray appearance.

If you're reading the message in a message window and want to flag it, select Message→Follow Up→Flag Message (Alt, H, W, M). This puts a reminder to follow up above the message's From line. To unflag a message, select Message→Follow Up→Clear Flag (Alt, H, W, E). The reminder disappears.

Flagging an outgoing message

When you send an email message, you can flag it for yourself, for recipients, or for both. Compose your email, and then follow these steps:

1. Select Message→Follow Up→Custom (Alt, H, W, C).

   Outlook opens the Custom dialog box, shown in Figure 10-11. The dialog box has a section where you can flag the message for yourself and another section where you can add a flag for the recipient. (The recipient has to use Outlook to see your flag.)

2. **If you want the flag to appear on your copy of the sent email, turn on the "Flag for Me" checkbox.**

   This marks the message in your Sent Items folder, so you can remember to follow up on it.

3. **Turn on the "Flag for Recipients" checkbox, and then choose the flag you want.**

   Flags include Follow Up, For Your Information, Forward, No Response Necessary, Read, and Reply.

4. **If you want to send recipients a reminder, turn on the Reminder checkbox and pick the date and time for Outlook to remind them.**

   For more about reminders in Outlook, see page 333.

5. **Click OK.**

   Outlook sets the flags you chose.

Send your email as usual, and your flags go with it.

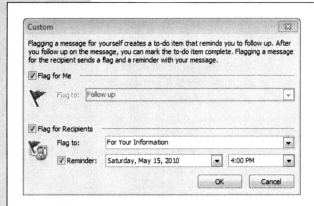

Figure 10-11:
When you add a flag to an email you're sending, you can flag both the email in your Sent Items folder and the one heading to the recipient.

Finding flagged messages

To make a folder display only its flagged messages, use the Home tab's far-right Filter E-mail button; click it and select Flagged (Alt, H, L, F). Outlook searches the folder for all flagged messages and displays only those. When you find the message you want, return the folder to normal by clicking the Search Tools | Search tab's Close Search button (Alt, JS, CS).

Tip: Flags aren't the only filter you can apply to a folder. For more about filtering a folder's contents, see page 315.

Organizing Messages

Received messages pile up in your inbox unless you move them into a different folder. Outlook comes with a number of folders built right in, such as Trash, Starred, All Mail, and Spam. (You can also create your own—Chapter 12 tells you all about folders.)

When you're reading a message in its own window, you can move that message out of the inbox and to a different folder by following these steps:

1. **Select Message→Move (Alt, H, MV).**

   A menu appears, giving you three options:

   — **Other Folder (O).** This option removes the message from its current folder (for a new message, that's the inbox) and places it in a different folder.

   — **Copy to Folder (C).** This option keeps the message in its current folder and places an exact copy in a different folder.

   — **Always Move Messages in This Conversation (A).** This option removes the message from its current folder and places it (along with any follow-up messages) in a different folder.

2. **Select the option that reflects what you want to do with this message.**

   A dialog box like the one shown in Figure 10-12 opens. The box looks the same whether you're moving, copying, or always moving—the only difference is its name in the title bar. The main part of the box lists your folders, with the message's current folder selected.

3. **Select the folder you want to move or copy the message to, and then click OK.**

   Outlook moves your message to the new folder (or puts a copy of the message there, depending on what you chose in step 2).

Figure 10-12:
Select the folder that will become the message's new home. To create a new folder and move the message there, click New.

Tip: If you want to create a new folder in which to store this message, click the New button in step 3. Chapter 12 tells you more about creating and working with folders in Outlook.

Routing Incoming Messages

Most of the time, you'll probably want new messages to land in your inbox, because that's where you'll look for and notice them. But you can tell Outlook to bypass the inbox and send some messages straight to a different folder. For example, maybe you sent out invitations to a party and want RSVP replies to go into a special folder. In Outlook, you create *rules* to send incoming emails to the folders where you want them to go.

Note: Rules are a great way to sort your email automatically. You can set up rules to filter out spam messages, but you probably won't have to, because Outlook has some advanced spam-busting tools that fight spam for you—read about those on page 270.

When you receive an email you want to create a rule for, open it in its own message window and do this:

1. **On the Message tab, click Rules→Create Rule (Alt, H, RR, U).**

   This opens the Create Rule dialog box, shown in Figure 10-13. In this dialog box, you tell Outlook how to handle similar messages.

2. **In the top section, tell Outlook which messages the rule applies to by turning on the appropriate checkboxes.**

   You can create a rule based on sender, subject line, recipient (sent only to you or to a particular group), or a combination of these.

3. **In the bottom section, tell Outlook what to do with these messages by turning on the checkboxes you want.**

   Here are your choices:

   — **Display in the New Item Alert window.** This calls attention to a message you're watching for by opening it in a brand-new window when it arrives.

   — **Play a selected sound.** If some emails make you feel like cheering and others make you groan, you can apply the appropriate sounds when those emails arrive. Turn on this checkbox and select a sound. (Use the Browse button to find and select a sound file stored on your computer.)

   — **Move the item to folder.** When you turn on this checkbox and select a folder, Outlook always moves emails with the characteristics you chose above to this folder.

4. **After you've made your choices, click OK.**

   Outlook creates a new rule based on your criteria. A dialog box appears, asking if you want to apply this rule to messages you've already received.

5. **If you want, turn on the "Run this rule now on messages already in the current folder" checkbox. You'd do this, for example, when you just created a new, special-purpose folder and want to file all similar messages there. Click OK.**

   Now Outlook is on the alert for messages that fit your rule's criteria.

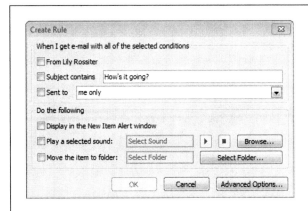

Translating a Message

Whether you're composing or reading an email, you can translate the message from one language to another. The only difference is where you find the Translate button:

- If you're composing a message, select Review→Translate (Alt, R, L).

- If you're reading a message, select Message→Translate (Alt, H, L).

Outlook's translation tools work just like Word's—which is to say, pretty good for quick-and-dirty jobs, but definitely not well enough to convince anyone that you're a native speaker. Table 10-3 shows you where to find information about using translation tools.

Table 10-3. *Where to find information about working with the Office translation tools*

Topic	Page number
Translating text	130
Using the Mini Translator	131
Using the Research pane for translations	132
Translating an entire message	132

Printing a Message

In Outlook, printing a message works like printing from the other Office programs— you go Backstage to do it. Where you start from depends on what you want to print:

- If you want to print a particular message, you can print it from its folder or open it in a message window.

- If you want to print a list showing the contents of a folder (such as your inbox), select that folder in Outlook's main window.

Select what you want to print, and then click File→Print (Alt, F, P) to go to the Backstage Print Settings page. There, choose a printer (or simply use the default that appears in the Printer section). Click Print Options if you want to adjust the number of copies, select a page range, or print any files attached to the email message. Next, use the Print What section to select what you're printing (a preview shows on the right):

- If you're printing from a message window, your only option is Memo Style.

- If you're printing from a folder, choose Table Style to print a list of the folder's messages or Memo style to print a single message you've selected.

Click the big Print button at the top of the Print Settings page to send your selections to the printer.

Fighting Spam

Nobody likes getting junk email, popularly called *spam*, those messages promising everything from a date this weekend to cheap meds to untold millions won in a foreign lottery. (Sorry, but that's a scam—no big checks are headed your way from Nigeria.)

Outlook watches for messages that are clearly spam—such as emails with telltale words or phrases in their subject lines, like "pharmacy" or "100% customer satisfaction"—and automatically routes them to your Junk E-mail folder, keeping them out of your inbox. (You can check that folder once in a while to see if a legitimate message has slipped through.) If some spam does find its way into your inbox, you can mark it as junk to send it to the Junk folder and prevent similar messages from getting through in the future.

If you open a message and realize it's spam, click the Message tab's far-left Junk button and select Block Sender (Alt, H, J, B). Outlook dumps the message into your Junk E-mail folder and adds the sender to your Blocked Senders list. In the future, anything that comes your way from this sender goes straight into the Junk E-mail folder.

Sometimes you can tell an email is junk just by looking at it in your inbox. To label an email as junk from a mailbox, select the email and, on the Home tab, select Junk→Block Sender (Alt, H, J, B). Alternatively, right-click the offending message and select Junk→Block Sender from the shortcut menu.

What If It's Not Spam?

Just because a message looks like junk to Outlook doesn't necessarily mean it *is* junk. It's a good idea to scan your Junk E-mail folder periodically to make sure a legit message didn't land there by mistake. If you find a non-spam message in your Junk E-mail folder, select it and then select Home→Not Junk (Alt, H, J, N). A dialog box appears, telling you that Outlook is about to move the message back to your inbox. If you want to add the sender to your Safe Senders list so Outlook will always send the sender's messages to your inbox, turn on the checkbox labeled "Always trust email from <sender's address>." Click OK.

If you've opened the junked email in a message window, you can remove it from the Junk E-mail folder by clicking the Message tab's Junk button and then selecting Not Junk.

Setting Up a Safe Senders List

If you want to make sure that email from a certain sender always gets through, you can add that person to your Safe Senders list. Select or open an email from that person and click the Junk button (Alt, H, J). Then pick an option:

- **Never Block Sender (S).** Choose this to make sure that emails coming from this address always land in your inbox and never get sent to the Junk E-mail folder.

- **Never Block Sender's Domain (D).** The second part of an email address (the part that comes after the @ symbol) is called the *domain*. In the email address *sender@gmail.com,* for example, *gmail.com* is the domain. You may want to make sure that all emails from a certain domain, such as your company's or school's domain, always arrive in your inbox. If so, choose this option.

- **Never Block This Group or Mailing List (M).** Maybe you look forward to your monthly newsletter from the Tricities Needlepoint Society and want to make sure you don't miss it. When you get regular mailings from a group, you can make sure their messages get through by choosing this option.

Tip: You can ignore a conversation without blocking the sender. For example, say you get an email sent to a group of coworkers about setting up a meeting. You respond, the meeting is scheduled, and you're done with that topic. But two people on the list get into a long back-and-forth about a movie they saw over the weekend. You don't want to block them entirely, but you also don't want to hear the fine points of their plot analysis. Go ahead and ignore any new emails in the thread by selecting the conversation and clicking Home→Ignore (Alt, H, X). Outlook dumps the conversation into your Deleted Items folder—and sends any future additions to the conversation there, too.

Managing Junk Email

Outlook gives you flexibility in telling it how to deal with spam. To manage your junk email settings, select Home→Junk (or Message→Junk if you're in a message window) and then choose Junk E-mail Options (Alt, H, J, O) to open the Junk E-mail Options dialog box shown in Figure 10-14.

The Junk E-mail Options dialog box has these tabs for controlling and managing your settings:

- **Options.** Here you can set the level of junk-mail filtering (from none to allowing through only messages from preapproved addresses) and fine-tune how Outlook handles messages it perceives as junk.

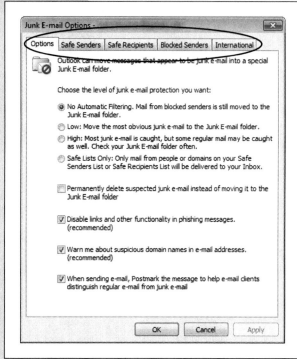

Figure 10-14:
Use the Junk E-mail Options box to manage you settings for dealing with spam and other email you don't want. The tabs (circled) let you manage lists that tell Outlook to always let certain messages through and to always block others.

- **Safe Senders.** When you tell Outlook to never block email from a certain address, that address ends up in this list. Come here to add, edit, or remove addresses.

- **Safe Recipients.** This list is for mailing lists you're on. Often, a mailing list message is addressed to a group, not individual recipients. When this kind of message arrives, Outlook may look at the To address and assume it's spam. To make sure mailing list messages you want get through, add them to this list. (You can do that on this tab or by using the Junk button's Never Block This Group or Mailing List option.)

- **Blocked Senders.** When you block a sender, the sender's address goes on this tab's list. If you need to manage the list (adding, editing, or deleting addresses), use this tab.

- **International.** Spam has gone global, and it may arrive from a country where you know no one or written in a language you don't speak. This tab maintains two lists of blocked items:

  — **Blocked Top-Level Domain List.** Email addresses in different countries may use a country-specific domain, ending with abbreviations such as .nl (Netherlands), .ru (Russia), .cn (China), .ca (Canada), and so on. If you never want to receive email from an email address that ends in one of these top-level domains, click this button and turn on the checkbox of any top-level domain you want to block.

— **Blocked Encodings List.** Encoding allows emails to display characters from a particular language. If you don't want to receive emails whose characters you can't read, click this button and turn on the checkbox of any character set you don't want.

After you've made changes to your junk email settings, click OK to save them.

Saving Time with Quick Steps

Quick Steps are a great new feature in Outlook 2010, designed to make working with email faster and more efficient. A quick step takes several actions and combines them into one, saving you time and mouse clicks. For example, you can mark an email as read and move it to a specified folder, or reply to an email and delete it, with just one click.

Outlook 2010 includes prebuilt Quick Steps, but you can also create your own, making it faster to perform repetitive tasks when dealing with email.

Applying a Quick Step

You can select and apply Quick Steps from any folder that holds email messages (such as your inbox) or while you're reading a received message in a message window:

- If you're in a folder, the Quick Steps gallery appears on the Home tab. The gallery displays a bunch of different Quick Steps, so you can quickly choose the one you want. (*Quickly* is the whole point, right?)

- If you're in a message window, the Quick Steps gallery appears on the Message tab.

Figure 10-15 shows what the Quick Steps gallery looks like. To apply a Quick Step, select the email you want (if you're in a folder), go to the gallery, and then click the action you want. And that's all there is to it—Outlook performs the action you chose. There's a reason why they call these Quick Steps.

Figure 10-15:
The Quick Steps gallery offers one-click options for dealing with email messages.

Note: The first time you use certain Quick Steps, such as "Move to" or "To Manager", a dialog box opens, asking you to set up the Quick Step by giving Outlook the specifics it needs to complete the action, such as the folder name or the manager's email address.

Customizing a Quick Step

Outlook's built-in Quick Steps are a great start, but even the smart folks at Microsoft can't know exactly how you do your day-to-day work. That's why you can customize any Quick Step to tweak it so it works for you. Here's how:

1. **In the Quick Steps section of the Home or Message tab, click the lower-right Manage Quick Steps button (Alt, H, QQ).**

   The Manage Quick Steps dialog box opens. Quick Steps are listed in the left pane; when you select a Quick Step, its description appears in the right pane.

2. **Select the Quick Step you want to customize, and then click the Edit button.**

   The Edit Quick Step dialog box, shown in Figure 10-16, opens. Here's where you tell Outlook what to do when you apply this Quick Step. The name you see in the gallery appears at the top of the box; below it are the actions that make up the step. Each action appears as a drop-down list; click the list to select an action from one of these categories: Filing; Change Status; Categories, Tasks, and Flags; Respond; Appointment.

3. **To remove an action from this Quick Step, click the X to its right. To add a new action, click the Add Action button.**

   When you click Add Action, a new drop-down list appears.

4. **Choose your new action. Repeat until you've customized the Quick Step the way you want it. When you're done, click Save.**

   Outlook customizes the Quick Step with your changes.

Tip: If you want to keep the original Quick Step and create a new Quick Step that's based on it, select Duplicate (not Edit) in the Manage Quick Steps dialog box.

Creating Your Own Quick Step

You can also build your very own Quick Step from scratch. In the Quick Step gallery, click Create New. Or you can open the Manage Quick Steps dialog box (Alt, H, QQ). Below the list of Quick Steps is a New button; click that and select Custom.

The Edit Quick Step dialog box (Figure 10-16) opens. Type a descriptive name in the Name box, and then Add Actions as you would when customizing a Quick Step. When you're done, click Finish—and you've got yourself a brand-new Quick Step for the gallery.

Figure 10-16:
*To customize a Quick
Step, you can remove
any action you don't
want and add new
actions.*

Click to remove
this action.

Click this button to
add a new drop-down
list and choose an
action.

Tip: To change the order in which Quick Steps appear in the gallery, open the Manage Quick Steps dialog box. In the list of Quick Steps, select a step to move, and then use the up and down button beneath the list to change the steps' order.

Deleting a Quick Step

If there's a Quick Step you never use, you can remove it from the gallery. Open the Manage Quick Steps dialog box, select the Quick Step you want to get rid of, and then click the Delete button. Outlook removes it from the Quick Steps list and gallery.

Managing Multiple Email Accounts

These days, lots of people have more than one email account: one for work, one for personal use, one for your moonlighting business. You can manage all of these accounts from Outlook, centralizing your correspondence.

Adding Another Email Account

To add a new email account to Outlook, select File→Info→Account Settings (Alt, F, E, S), and then click the Account Settings menu item. In the Account Settings dialog box, make sure the E-mail tab is selected, and then click New.

The Add New Account dialog box opens, with POP3 or IMAP selected. The option that's already selected is probably what you want, so click Next. (This steps looks like the dialog box shown in Figure 10-1, which you used to set up your original account.) Make sure the E-mail Account radio button is on, then type in your name and the email address and password of the account you want to add. Click Next.

Outlook does the rest. It checks with the email account you added to make sure the address and password are correct. If all's well, your new account gets a test message, just like when you first set up Outlook. Click Finish when you're done adding accounts.

Keeping Accounts Straight

When you use Outlook to manage multiple email accounts, the different accounts appear, listed by email address, in the Navigation pane. Use the arrows beside each address to expand that account, showing its folders, or to collapse it, showing just its address.

To see what's in a particular folder in one of your accounts, find the folder in the Navigation pane and click it. The contents of the folder appear in the center pane, so you can select a message to view in the Reading pane.

Choosing Which Account to Send From

When you're managing several different email accounts, you want to make sure each message you send heads out into the great beyond bearing the email address from the right account. Otherwise, recipients could get confused and their replies could end up in the wrong Outlook folder.

When you click the New E-mail button or press Ctrl+N to compose a new message, Outlook sends it from your default address. Here's how to choose that default address:

1. **Select File→Info→Account Settings (Alt, F, E, S), and choose the Account Settings menu item.**

   The Account Settings dialog box appears, listing the email accounts you've added to Outlook. The account that has a checkmark to its left is your default account.

2. **To change the default, select the account you want, and then click Set as Default.**

   The account you selected jumps to the top of the list, and a checkmark appears beside it.

3. **Click Close.**

Now, when you compose a new email, it's sent from that account.

Sometimes, you'll compose a new email but want to send it from one of your other accounts, not the default. In that case, click the From button. A menu appears listing your accounts. Select the account you want to put it in the From line.

Note: When you reply to an email that someone sent you, the reply always comes from the account that received the original email, no matter which account is the default. If you want your reply to come from a different account, click your reply's From button to select a different email address.

Outlook's Address Book

Outlook is all about helping you stay in touch with the people you know. You do that with *contacts,* which is what Outlook calls the folks who fill up your Address Book. The program makes it easy to collect a biography's worth of information for each person: name, job info, phone numbers, email and postal addresses, notes, birthday—pretty much anything you want to track.

This chapter shows you how to work with contacts, starting off with adding a new one and keeping it current. You can also import contacts from another address book (Outlook makes that easy). And once you've stocked your Outlook Address Book, you can view its contacts in different ways and find that special someone you're looking for. If you need to send emails to a group of people, like your project team, book club, or friends who owe you money, you can gather individual contacts into a contact group and email them all at once. And if you need a printed directory, you can select a layout and print your own little portable address book.

New in Outlook 2010 is the People pane, which lets you view information about a contact, including recent interactions and upcoming appointments. And thanks to Outlook Social Connector, the People pane can be a hub for social networking with your contacts.

Adding and Editing Contacts

An empty address book isn't much help when you need to send out a memo, an announcement, or the latest family news. Filling up and fine-tuning your Outlook Contacts folder—where you store information about the people you communicate with—is the first step.

Adding Contacts

You can stock Outlook's Contact form with everything from the barest basics (name and email address) to a fully fleshed-out address book entry: company, job title, multiple phone numbers and addresses, even a photo. When someone sends you an email, you can instantly transform that person into a contact. As you create new contacts, Outlook automatically builds a virtual business card for those people, giving you at-a-glance access to the info you need.

Creating a new contact from scratch

What you need to do here is really pretty simple; just follow these steps:

1. **In Outlook's Navigation pane, click Contacts. Select Home→New Contact (Alt, H, N) or press Ctrl+N.**

   The Contact window, shown in Figure 11-1, opens. This window is where you create and work with individual contacts. You can save a ton of information here, including the contact's name and company, Internet info (email, web address, instant messaging ID), phone numbers, and physical addresses. You can also create a virtual business card—an online card within Outlook that holds a person's contact information—and add a photo.

2. **In the top section, fill in the person's name and personal information.**

   Type directly into the text boxes, or click the Full Name button to enter the name by field: Title, First Name, Last Name, and so on. The information you fill in appears on the virtual business card to the right.

3. **Take a look at the "File as" box, which tells Outlook how to display this contact—most people go for Last Name, First Name. If that's not how you'd look for this person, then click the down arrow and select a different category.**

   You might want to look up certain contacts by their company, rather than their names, for example. You can select how you want to file any contact when you create or edit that contact.

4. **If you want, add a photo. To do so, click the silhouette to the right of the contact's name.**

   A dialog box opens where you can navigate to and select a photo from your computer. Find the photo you want, and then click Open to insert it.

5. **In the Internet section, type in an email, website address, and IM screen name (or as much of this as you have and want to save).**

   Each contact can have up to three email addresses. To add a second (or third) address, click the E-mail button's down arrow and select E-mail 2 (or E-mail 3) and enter the address.

6. **In the Phone numbers section, type in any telephone numbers you want to include.**

   As Figure 11-1 shows, the default phone number fields are Business, Home, Business Fax, and Mobile, but these labels are flexible. Click the down arrow next to any phone number label to select from a list of kinds of numbers: Assistant, Business 2, Pager, Other, and so on.

Business card

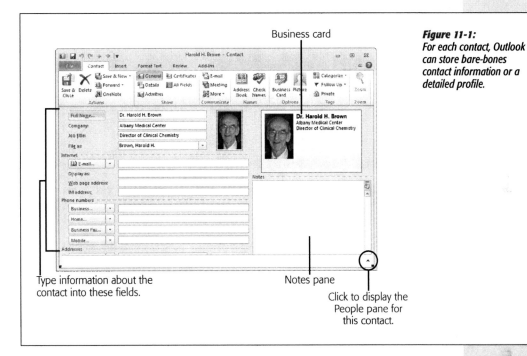

Figure 11-1:
For each contact, Outlook can store bare-bones contact information or a detailed profile.

Type information about the
contact into these fields.

Notes pane

Click to display the
People pane for
this contact.

7. **Next, add info to the Addresses section.**

   As with the labels for phone numbers, you've got more than one option here. Click the down arrow to change the address from Business, say, to Home. When you add more than one address, turn on the "This is the mailing address" checkbox for the one you'd use to send mail.

Tip: If you want to see the address on a map, click the Map It button. Clicking this button opens your web browser and goes to Bing Maps with the address displayed.

---

8. **In the Notes box, add any other information you want to remember about this contact.**

   You might include names of the person's spouse and children, birthday, preferred name (maybe William *hates* to be called Bill), professional associations you both belong to—the info you include here is entirely up to you.

9. **When you're finished, click Save & New if you want to add another contact. If you're done for now, click Save & Close.**

   Outlook creates your new contact.

You can come back to your new contact's card at any time. In Outlook's main Contacts window, find the person you want and double-click his or her name.

Creating a new contact from an email message

When you receive an email, Outlook makes it easy to add the sender to your contacts. Just open the email in a Message pane, right-click the contact's address in the From line, and select Add to Outlook Contacts.

The Contact page opens in a new window, with the person's name and email address already filled in. Add whatever information you want, and then click Save & Close. Presto: a new contact.

Importing Email Addresses from Another Program

If you're switching to Outlook from another email program, forget about wasting hours typing in all those contacts one by one. Outlook is ready to help with some handy importing tools. The process usually entails two steps:

1. **In the email program whose address book you want to grab, export the addresses and save them in a file.**

2. **Import the file into Outlook, which sucks in the data and uses it to create contacts there.**

The file that saves the data is most often a *CSV* (comma-separated values) or a *TSV* (tab-separated values) file. In these formats, commas or tabs separate pieces of information; Outlook can read the file and create new contacts from it.

Tip: Before importing address book contacts into Outlook, take a few minutes to go through your other email program and weed out any contacts you don't want.

Importing from Outlook Express, Windows Mail, or Eudora

If you're importing from Outlook Express, Windows Mail, or Eudora, there's even better news: You don't have to worry about those geeky-sounding CSV files. Outlook can find and use the information it needs with a few simple details from you.

Note: For this method to work, both Outlook and the program you're importing from must be on the same computer.

Here's what you need to do:

1. Select File→Open→Import (Alt, F, O, I).

   The Import Wizard starts up.

2. Choose Import Internet Mail and Addresses, and then click Next.

   The wizard asks which email program you're importing from.

3. Make your choice and tell Outlook whether you also want to import mail messages, or just the address book. Click Next.

   The wizard asks how you want to handle any duplicate addresses. You can choose to replace the contact information in Outlook with the imported information, allow duplicates, or not import any duplicates. If you tell Outlook to import email messages, it grabs the 30 most recent messages in your inbox.

4. Turn on the radio button that indicates how you want to deal with duplicates, and then click Finish.

   If you're importing from Outlook Express or Windows Mail, you're done. Outlook finds the information and imports it into Outlook. If you're importing from Eudora, you have one more step: A Browse dialog box opens, listing the drives and folders on your computer.

5. Find and select the mail folder for Eudora. Click OK.

   Outlook imports your data.

After Outlook is finished, it presents you with an Import Summary listing how many addresses and contact groups (and messages if you chose to import mail) it imported.

Importing from another email program

If the email program you're importing from isn't one covered by the previous steps, you've got to expend a little more time and effort (but only a little). Different email programs have different steps for exporting addresses, but the overall process is usually quite similar to the two-step dance described on page 282. As an example, here's how to export contacts from Gmail:

1. Sign in to your Gmail account and click the left-hand Contacts link.

   Your Contacts page opens.

2. Click the upper-right Export link.

   Gmail opens the Export page.

3. Choose which contacts you want to transfer to Outlook, and then choose the export format. In this case, turn on the "Outlook CSV format" radio button to save your contact info in a comma-separated-value file. Click Export.

   Gmail creates a file named *contacts.csv*, and your web browser opens a dialog box so you can download it to your computer.

4. Download the file to a location where you can find it when you import the contacts into Outlook.

That's the export phase of the operation. To import your contacts, open Outlook and follow these steps:

1. **In Outlook, select File→Open→Import (Alt, F, O, I).**

   The Import Wizard opens.

2. **Select "Import from another program or file", and then click Next.**

   The wizard shows a list of file types.

3. **Select Comma Separated Values (Windows) as the type of file you're importing from. Click Next.**

   Outlook asks where to find the file you're importing.

4. **Click the Browse button, and then find and select your CSV file (in the Gmail example, that's *contacts.csv*). In the wizard, turn on the radio button that reflects how you want to deal with any duplicate addresses. Click Next.**

   Outlook asks where you want to store the imported contacts.

5. **Select Contacts, click Next, and then click Finish.**

   Outlook imports your contacts (which can take a few minutes if you have lots of contacts) and stores them in your Contacts folder.

Tip: After you've imported contacts, open the Contacts window and look through the contacts Outlook imported. You might want to add details to some of the contacts, change the way Outlook files them, or weed some out.

Editing a Contact's Information

People move, change jobs, and get married all the time. To update your Outlook records, head back to the same page you used to create the contact in the first place. From the main Outlook window, double-click the contact you want to edit. Click any field, select what you want to change, and then enter the new info. If you need to change anything on the Details page, don't forget to click the Contact tab's Details button and update what you see there.

Editing all fields

To avoid hopscotching through the many fields on the Contact and Details pages—and to make sure you change everything you want—try clicking the Contact tab's All Fields button (you can find it in the Show section, or just press Alt, H, AE). Use the "Select from" drop-down list to pick what you want to change, such as address, email, or frequently used fields, and the page changes to look like Figure 11-2. Select any field to edit it; scroll down the page to make sure all the info is accurate.

Creating a new field

If you need to keep track of specialized information that Outlook doesn't cover—
Employee ID or Favorite Sibling, for example—you can create your own field. Open
any contact and select Contact→All Fields (Alt, H, AE) as shown in Figure 11-2. At
the bottom of the page, click the New button.

In the dialog box that opens, give the field a name (this becomes its label). Choose a
type (such as text, number, or yes/no) and then click OK. To see your new field, open
the contact and click the All Fields button. Your new category appears in the "Select
from" drop-down menu's "User-defined fields in this item" category.

Adding details

The Notes pane is great for jotting random, non-database-y info (where you first
met, topics to avoid talking about, and so on). Microsoft has already created categories for a few popular entries, things like manager's name, assistant's name, spouse/
partner, birthday, anniversary, and more. Summon these via the Contact tab's Details button (Alt, H, TA). Details you add here don't show up on the main contact
page; you have to click the Details button to see them.

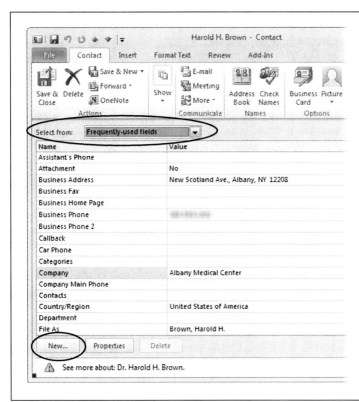

Figure 11-2:
*Select a category from the drop-down
list (circled) to see fields in that category, and then change any info that
needs editing. To create a new field,
click the New button (also circled).*

Note: If you've ever been in hot water for forgetting a birthday or anniversary, that's a thing of the past. When you add those dates using the Details button, Outlook automatically slots them into your Outlook Calendar.

Editing business cards

If a contact's virtual business card is too crowded, have Outlook present the salient details front and center by editing the business card to show only what you want to see.

Open any contact and either double-click the business card or click the Contact tab's Business Card button (Alt, H, B). The Edit Business Card dialog box, shown in Figure 11-3, is where you can change just about anything:

- **Card Design.** Adjust the layout, background color, or how much room the photo takes up and where it appears on the card. Click Change to choose a different picture.

- **Fields.** Customize the fields that display on the card. For example, you may not want a business contact's home phone number displayed on the card. (It's still in the contact's information; it just doesn't appear when you look at the card in Business Card view.) Use the Add, Remove, and arrow buttons to customize the fields on the card and where they appear.

- **Edit.** Use this section to change the look of the text on the card. Choose a field from the Fields list, and it appears in the Edit text box. Now you can apply different fonts, sizes, formatting, and alignment.

As you edit the business card, the upper-left preview reflects your changes. If you want to go back to the card's original appearance, click Reset Card to undo all changes. Otherwise, click OK to apply your edits to the card and close the dialog box.

Back in the Contact window, click Save & Close to save your changes.

Deleting a contact

Friendships end, coworkers get fired. Life goes on, but your address book doesn't have to remain cluttered with every person you've ever been in touch with. To do a little contact pruning, open the main Contacts window, select the entry you want, and then click the Delete button (Alt, H, D). Outlook vaporizes it immediately, without asking you to confirm. (If you accidentally delete the wrong contact, immediately click Undo or press Alt, 2 to resurrect it.)

You can also delete a contact from that person's Contact page. Click the Contact tab's Delete button (Alt, H, D). When you delete a contact this way, though, you can't undo the deletion.

Finding a Contact

As you add contacts, it's easy for any one of them to get lost in the crowd. Outlook gives you lots of ways to find whomever you're looking for. From the main Contacts page, try any of these:

- **Search.** Click inside the Search box at the top of the page and start typing. As your fingers fly across the keys, Outlook narrows down the contacts it displays, so it may take just a few letters to find the contact. To fine-tune your search, click the Search Tools | Search tab (Alt, JS), shown in Figure 11-4, and get more specific by searching within a specific category or other search parameter, such as a particular city or company.

- **Search by category.** Use this method when you've assigned a contact to a category (page 308) and want to narrow your search by looking only in that category. Press Ctrl+E to open the Search Tools | Search tab (Figure 11-4). Click the Categorized button (Alt, JS, G) and select the category you want.

Tip: For even more details about searching in Outlook—how to repeat a search or do an advanced search, for example—see page 313.

- **Search from the Home tab.** If you happen to be here when you want to find a contact, look in the far-right Find section for the Find a Contact search box. Type the contact's name, and then press Enter. Outlook opens the page for that contact.

Note: The Find a Contact search box appears on the right side of the Home tab no matter what you're doing in Outlook. The Home tabs of the Mail, Calendar, Contacts, Tasks, and Notes windows all display Find a Contact there.

- **Scroll down.** There's a scroll bar to the right of the contacts; use it to move through them.

- **Use the index.** To the right of the contacts in Business Card and Card views is an index you can use to jump to contacts filed under a certain letter—actually a letter pair. So if you click "rs", for example, the display changes to show you the first contact filed under R. Scroll up or down from there. This method is helpful when you've got a full Contacts folder and want to jump to a specific letter.

- **Switch to Phone or List view and sort by name, company, or other category.** As the next section explains, you've got loads of different options for viewing your contacts. Views arranged in a list format allow you to sort and filter your entries in various ways, making it easier to find the particular person you're looking for.

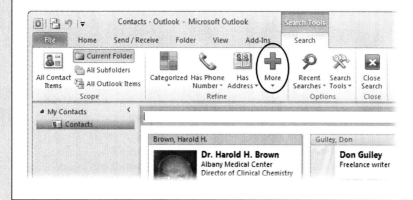

Figure 11-4:
Press Ctrl+E for instant access to Outlook's Search Tools | Search contextual tab. Use this tab to widen your search (looking in more folders) or narrow it by searching by category or other criterion. Click More (circled) to see a list of specific fields to search, such as First Name and Job Title.

Viewing Contacts

It might not be as much fun as watching TV or surfing the Web, but sometimes you need to browse your Contacts list. Outlook gives you plenty of display options, which it calls *views*. Each one shows all your contacts, but in noticeably different ways. Some give more information about each contact but minimize the number of listings that fit on the screen; others show more contacts but give minimal details about them.

Start by selecting Contacts from the Navigation pane; the Contacts window's Home tab displays a Views gallery, shown in Figure 11-5. Click a view to select it, or click the lower-right More button to expand the gallery and see all its options.

Tip: You can also select a view from the View tab. Select View→Change View (Alt, W, CV) to see the gallery of view options and pick the one you want.

- **Business Card.** This view (Figure 11-5) displays your contacts as business cards, arranged alphabetically, with a photo (if you added one), name, job, and contact info.

- **Card.** In Card view, your contacts look more like index cards, as shown in Figure 11-6. This view arranges cards alphabetically in columns, so you can see more contacts on a page.

- **Phone.** Shown in Figure 11-7, this view emphasizes phone numbers by showing contacts in a list with all their key digits to the right of the full names.

- **List.** As its name implies, this view shows contacts in a list. No photos, no card format—each contact gets a single line. This view is more like looking at a full spreadsheet listing of everything that's in an entry.

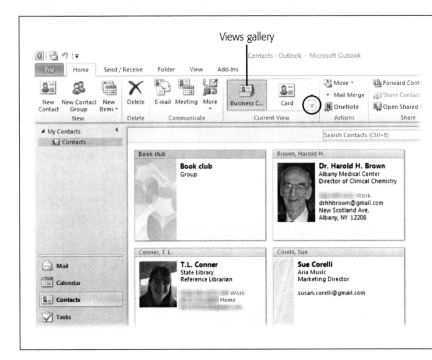

Views gallery

Figure 11-5:
In Business Card view, Outlook lays out your contacts' virtual business cards. Use the Views gallery to select a view; click the More button (circled) to see more choices.

Figure 11-6:
Card view shows less information for each contact but fits more cards onto the screen.

Figure 11-7:
Phone view shows a line of info for each contact. List view is similar but shows slightly different information in each line. This figure shows the View tab, whose Arrangement section offers lots of options for sorting and filtering contacts in these views.

Sorting and Grouping Contacts

Displaying all your contacts is only a start. You need to be able to sort through 'em and find the one(s) you're looking for. To do that, head to the View tab's Arrangement section (you can see it in Figure 11-7).

Sorting contacts

In Phone and List views, you can quickly sort your contacts by any field by clicking a column header. For example, to sort by company, click the Company header above the list of contacts. Outlook sorts the contacts in ascending (A–Z) order. Click again to sort in descending (Z–A) order. Sort any column in this way.

If you're looking at your contacts in Business Card or Card view, there are no column headers to sort by. You can still change the order of the contacts, though, by selecting View→Reverse Sort (Alt, W, RS). If your contacts currently appear in ascending order, clicking Reverse Sort displays them in descending order (and vice versa).

Grouping contacts

Another helpful way to view contacts is by grouping them by some common criterion, such as company or location. If you want to find all the contacts in a certain city, for example, grouping is the way to go.

Grouping works only with list-style views, so start by showing your contacts in Phone or List view. Then choose what you want to group by: The Groups gallery has several options built in. When you click a group, such as Company, Outlook rearranges the list, grouping together all contacts that have the same entry in the Company column. Find the firm you want, and you find all your contacts who work there.

Tip: To see only what you need to see in the list of contacts, use the View tab's Expand/Collapse button (Alt, W, E). You can choose to expand or collapse all groups or just the currently selected one.

Customizing a View

If one of Outlook's views doesn't show the information you want, you can change the view to suit your preferences. This is a great help if you're looking to sort or group by some category that doesn't appear in the current view.

Start by displaying the view you want to customize. On the View tab, click View Settings (Alt, W, V) to open the dialog box shown in Figure 11-8. Here's where you can tweak these settings:

- **Columns.** Click this button to change which columns appear in the view. For example, you might want to include website addresses or notes.

Tip: For a quick way to customize columns in a view, select View→Add Columns (Alt, W, AC). In the dialog box that opens, choose and arrange the columns you want to display.

- **Group By.** When Outlook groups your contacts, it lumps them together according to a common characteristic that you choose, such as company. You can nest groups, as well. For example, you might group by company and then by department and finally by job title.

Figure 11-8:
You can customize a view by changing any of these settings.

- **Sort.** Click this button to tell Outlook how to organize the contacts in the view. You might sort by company, last name, or city, for example. You can do nested sorts, just as you can do nested groupings.

- **Filter.** Grouping and sorting display all your contacts, To winnow them out and see only selected contacts, click the Filter button. Then tell Outlook which keywords to search for and where to look for them when it applies the filter.

Note: When you apply a filter to a view you're customizing, you never see the contacts that get filtered out in that view. If you're just looking for certain contacts, do a search instead.

- **Other Settings.** Here's where you can customize a view by changing its look, such as the fonts and grid lines displayed.

- **Conditional Formatting.** What a hidden gem this one is. It lets you change a contact's display font when a certain condition is met. For example, if a contact's job title is Manager, you can display the information for that contact in red. To add a new rule for conditional formatting, click this button and, in the Conditional Formatting dialog box, click Add. Outlook adds a new condition called Untitled. Change the name to something descriptive, and then click the Condition button. This opens the Filter dialog box, where you can specify the condition that triggers the formatting change. Tell Outlook what condition to look for—such as ABC Company in the Company field—and click OK. Back in the Conditional Formatting box, click the Font button to choose the font, style, size, and color to use when Outlook finds a match to the condition. Click OK.

- **Format Columns.** Set the view's column widths here.

Note: If you're customizing a Business Card or Card view, only some of these View Settings options are available.

After you've customized the settings, click OK to apply them to the current view. If you don't like the results, select View→Reset View (Alt, W, X) and click Yes to confirm, to change everything back to its original settings. Reset View undoes *all* your custom changes, so if you want to adjust only one custom setting, click the View Settings button and redo the setting from there.

Saving a View

If you like the custom view you've set up but don't want to get rid of the original view you built it from, save the hand-tailored view separately. Here's how:

1. **On the Home tab, go to the Current View section and click the View gallery's lower-right More button. Then select Save Current View As a New View (Alt, H, CV, S).**

   The Copy View dialog box opens.

2. **Give your new view a name, and choose where the view can be used—in the current folder or in all your Contacts folders. Click OK.**

   If a view is useful only for this folder, select "This folder, visible to everyone" or "This folder, visible only to me", depending on whether you want to share the view or keep it to yourself. If the view is one you find yourself using over and over, no matter which Contacts folder you're in, select "All Contact folders". After you've clicked OK, Outlook saves your new view and adds it to the View gallery.

Now go back to the original view you used as the basis for the custom view. Select View→Reset View (Alt, W, X), and then click Yes to confirm. That view returns to its original formatting.

Tip: If you prefer, you can copy a view first, and then adjust the settings of the new view.

Deleting a View

If you've saved a custom view but no longer need it, open Outlook's main Contacts page and click the Home tab. In the View gallery (Alt, H, CV), find the view you want to delete and right-click it. Choose Delete. Outlook asks whether you really want to delete this view. Click Yes, and it's a goner.

The People Pane

New in Outlook 2010 is the People pane—an assembled-on-the-fly dashboard of info about each of your contacts. The People pane brings together up-to-date information about a contact: recent email messages, email attachments you've exchanged, upcoming meetings you've both got scheduled. A single click opens any of these items.

But the People pane does more than that. If you use Outlook Social Connector (see the box on page 302), you can add a contact as a friend on social networking sites like MySpace or LinkedIn (with other sites, like Facebook, Windows Live, and Twitter to come), see his profile photo, and keep track of status messages and activities—right from Outlook. So, for example, you can see if someone in your Windows Live network has added a new item to a shared SkyDrive folder or posted a new status message on Facebook.

To open the People pane, select an email either from your inbox or another mail folder or, open a contact's window. In the lower-right corner of the screen is an up arrow. Click that to expand the People pane (Figure 11-9 shows an example).

Figure 11-9:
A look at the People pane tucked inside your inbox. Click any tab inside the pane to see information about a contact's activities, mail, attachments, meetings, or status updates.

The People pane

Some early users feel that the People pane takes up a lot of screen real estate. If you're not using the pane, you can collapse it by clicking the down arrow in its upper-right corner. You can also turn it off altogether. In the main Outlook window, select View→People Pane→Off (Alt, W, PP, O).

Later, if you get lonely and want this fella back, head to the View tab; click People Pane and then select either Normal (Alt, W, PP, N), to restore the full-sized pane, or Minimized (Alt, W, PP, M), to restore the small bar at the bottom of the Reading pane.

POWER USERS' CLINIC

Contacts and Mail Merge

Your Outlook Contacts folder holds tons of information about the people you communicate with—so it makes sense to use these contacts when you need to do a mail merge. Here's what you need to do:

1. Create a view that shows the contacts for the mailing. Select Home→Mail Merge (Alt, H, RG).

2. The Mail Merge Contacts dialog box opens. Make sure the "All contacts in current view" radio button is on, and then specify whether you want to use all contact fields in the merge or only those appearing in the current view.

3. If you haven't yet written your form letter, turn on the "New document" radio button; if your letter is ready

to go, turn on the "Existing document" radio button, click Browse, and then locate and select the letter.

4. If you want to save these contacts in a separate file to use later (for a mail merge within Word, perhaps), turn on the "Permanent file" checkbox and specify a name for the file.

5. In the "Merge options" section, choose a document type (form letter, mailing label, or whatever) and a merge destination (new document, printer, email).

6. Click OK to fire up Word and begin your mail merge. Page 148 walks you through the process of doing a mail merge in Word.

Tip: If you turn off the People pane, you can still see what a contact has been up to recently. Open any contact page and select Contact→Activities. Click the Show drop-down list and choose the category you want to see. The Activities button doesn't show RSS activities or status message updates, but you can find recent emails, upcoming tasks and appointments, and similar info here.

Communicating with a Contact

They don't call them *contacts* for nothing. The reason you've collected all these names, addresses (both virtual and physical), phone numbers, and other info is so you can get in touch with anyone in your contacts folder. No matter which part of Outlook you're working with, it's easy to click a button and contact a contact.

Start by selecting anyone in the Contacts window, and then use one of these buttons on the Home tab:

• **E-mail (Alt, H, E).** Click this button, and a message window opens with the address already filled in.

• **Meeting (Alt, H, TI).** This button opens a new Meeting window, with an email preaddressed to the person you've selected. Now you just need to pick a time and location, add it to your calendar, and send off the invite. (See page 326 for more about setting up meetings with Outlook.)

• **More (Alt, H, J).** This button holds these contact options:

— **Assign Task (T).** Outlook opens a Task window that lets you assign a chore and notify the contact. (Page 339 has full details.)

— **Journal Entry (J).** The little-used Outlook Journal automatically tracks shared Office documents and emails associated with a contact, but the Activities page (page 295) and the People pane (page 294) do the same thing and are easier to find. If you want to use the Journal, you have to customize the ribbon (page 891) to add its buttons and then turn it on. Most people are unlikely to use this option.

— **Call (A).** If your phone is hooked up to your computer through an automatic phone dialer, you can make calls right from Outlook. When you pick this option, Outlook displays a list of phone numbers for this contact. Choose one, and the new Call dialog box opens. Click Open Contact if you want to see the person's detailed information during the conversation. Click Start Call to place the call.

Note: Before you can make a call using Outlook, you have to specify information for your location, including country, area code, and other details.

Contact cards also offer a quick way to get in touch with a contact. When you're working with email, hover the mouse pointer over a contact's email address in the Reading pane or a message window. The person's contact card appears, as shown in Figure 11-10. Click one of the icons at the bottom to email, send an instant message, call, or schedule a meeting with the contact.

Contact card

Figure 11-10:
When you get an email from a contact, you can quickly get a glimpse of its key details thanks to this tiny pop-up window. Hover over the contact's email address to see it. Use the upper-right pin icon to keep the contact card visible until you unpin it; click the lower-left down arrow to expand it and see more info.

Gathering Contacts into a Group

Emailing groups of people is a remarkably common activity—sending off that monthly newsletter, scheduling your kickball league, issuing reports on the kids to adoring grandparents. When you routinely send emails to multiple recipients, don't waste time entering their email addresses one by one. Instead, create a group that gathers together all the contacts into a single entity; when you email the group, you email everyone in it.

Creating a Contact Group

To create a group of contacts, follow these steps:

1. **Select Home→New Contact Group (Alt, H, CG).**

   Outlook opens the Contact Group window, shown in Figure 11-11, with the Contact Group tab displayed.

Figure 11-11:
The Contact Group window lists the individual contacts that make up a group. Click Add Members (circled) to populate the group.

2. **In the Name text box, type in a name for your group.**

   Pick something descriptive, like "Book Group," "Softball Team," "Koala Bear Lovers"—whatever makes it easy to remember the purpose of the group.

3. **Click the Add Members button (Alt, H, M).**

   A menu appears so you can choose where to find everyone:

   — **From Outlook Contacts.** When you choose this option, Outlook opens the Select Members: Contacts dialog box, shown in Figure 11-12.

   — **From Address Book.** The Outlook Address Book is a collection of address lists created from your Outlook Contacts folders.

   — **New E-mail Contact.** Click this to add someone who's not already in your Contacts. Outlook asks for a name and email address and turns on the Add to Contacts checkbox. Provide the requested info and click OK.

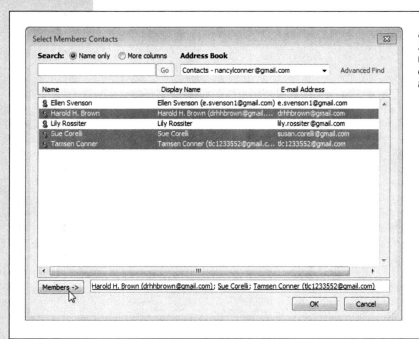

Figure 11-12:
Select the contacts you
want to add, and then
click Members to group
them together.

4. **If you chose From Outlook Contacts or From Address Book, select the contacts you want and click OK.**

   You can select multiple contacts by pressing Shift or Ctrl as you click.

5. **Click the lower-left Members button.**

   The contacts you chose appear in the Members text box.

6. **Click OK.**

   The contacts you selected appear in your group's list of members.

7. **When you're done populating your group, click Save & Close.**

   Outlook creates your new group.

Groups you've created join the list of contacts on Outlook's main Contacts page. In Phone and List views, groups show up in boldface; in Business Card and Card views, the group's name appears as the contact's name.

Groups have a special icon, which looks like two tiny people, so in List and Phone views you can easily move all your groups to the top of the list by sorting the contacts by icon. In these views, icons appear at the far right side of each contact; click the Sort by Icon button to do this sort.

***

Note: All your Outlook Contacts folders are automatically available to you in your Address Book—each Contacts folder is its own mini–address book within the Outlook Address Book.

***

Sending Email to a Contact Group

The whole point of creating a group is being able to email everyone en masse. Whatever you're sending, you've got these options when it's time to reach out to the gang:

- **From the Outlook Contacts window, method 1.** Select the group you want to email, and then click Home→E-mail (Alt, H, E). A new message window opens, ready for you to write your email.

- **From the Outlook Contacts window, method 2.** Right-click a group, and then select Create→E-mail. As with the first method, a new message window opens.

- **From the Contact Group window.** If you have the group open (maybe you just added a new member), you can start an email from the Contact Group tab by clicking the E-mail button (Alt, H, E). This also opens a new message window.

- **From your inbox or other mailbox.** If you're already working with email, start by creating a new email message as you normally would: Press Ctrl+N or select Home→New E-mail (Alt, H, N). A new message window opens. Click the To button or the Message tab's Address Book button (Alt, H, AB) to open the Select Names: Contacts dialog box. Here, select the group you want and click the To button, and then click OK.

Wherever you started from, Outlook inserts the name of the group in the message's To line. Compose and send your message in the usual way. Recipients who get your message can see all group members' email addresses displayed in the To line, so don't send an email this way if you want to keep the address private or make multiple recipients invisible. If that's the case, put the group in the Bcc line instead.

Managing a Contact Group

Groups change. People change jobs or email providers, move away, stop attending a club. To update the contacts in a group, go to the main Outlook Contacts window and find the group you want. Double-click it, and the window that opens looks just like the one in Figure 11-11, with the group's information already filled in. Here's what you can do from the Contact Group tab on this page:

- **Add new members.** This works in the same way as adding members while creating the group. Click the Add Members button (Alt, H, M) and choose a source to add a new member to the current group.

- **Remove members.** To say buh-bye, select the member you want to remove and then click Remove Member (Alt, H, X). There's no confirmation and no undo, so make sure you've selected the right person. (If you nix someone by mistake, click the Add Members button to bring her back into the fold.)

Note: Removing a contact from a group doesn't delete the contact from Outlook. If you want to delete a contact entirely, follow the instructions on page 286.

- **Rename the group.** To change the group's name, click inside the Name text box and type in the new name.

- **Update the group.** This updates your Contact Group with the contacts' most recent information.

- **Add notes.** You can add notes to a group just as you can to any individual contact. Click the Notes button (Alt, H, O) and jot down whatever you want to keep in mind about this group. To view or edit the notes later, open the group's page, and then click the Notes button.

- **Share group details.** If you need someone else to do some work with the group, such as send out bulletins while you're on vacation, you can share the group's details with that person. How you share depends on whether the person you're sharing with uses Outlook. Click Forward Group (Alt, H, N), and then choose one of these options:

  — **In Internet Format (vCard).** A vCard is a virtual business card. In this case, it means you send the contact info as a text file that the recipient can open with a word processing program. Use this option when you're not sure whether the recipient uses Outlook.

  — **As an Outlook Contact.** If you know that the person you're sharing with uses Outlook, then choose this option, which shares the contacts as a list of Outlook Contacts. The recipient can then use this list to create the group.

  After you've chosen how to share the group, Outlook opens a message window with your group as an attachment. Address, compose, and send the email to the person with whom you're sharing the group.

- **Delete the group.** The Garden Show was a big success, and the committee has disbanded. If a contacts group has outlived its usefulness, you can delete it. As with removing a contact from a group, deleting a group doesn't delete its members from your Contacts—it just undoes the ties that bind them into the group. Click the Delete Group button (Alt, H, D), click Yes to confirm that you want to delete the group, and you're done.

Tip: You can also delete a group from the main Contacts page. Select the group and click the Home tab's Delete button; then confirm the deletion.

Except for deleting a group, you need to click Save & Close to apply any changes you make in the Contact Group window. So after you've finished managing the group, don't forget to click Save & Close (Alt, H, AV). If you try to close the window without saving, Outlook asks whether you want to save the changes you made. Click yes to save them and close the Contact Group window.

Printing Your Contacts

Outlook offers various options for printing information about your contacts: You can print info for a single contact, a group, or all your contacts. Whatever you want to print, start by opening it in a window. Then follow these steps:

1. **Select File→Print (Alt, F, P).**

   The Backstage Print Settings page opens. Figure 11-13 shows an example.

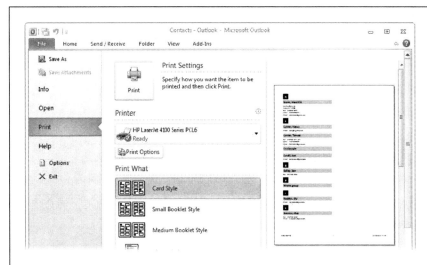

Figure 11-13:
When you print your contacts list, you have numerous layout options.

2. **Select a printer.**

   You'll probably use your default printer, but if you want to select a different one, click the Printer button and choose it from the list.

3. **Optionally, click Print Options.**

   This opens the Print dialog box, where you can specify which pages you want to print, the number of copies, and whether to collate the printed pages. Click Preview to return to the Print Settings page, or click Print if you're all set.

4. **In the Print What section, select a layout.**

   If you're printing an individual contact or group, you don't have much choice here: Your only option is Memo Style. If you're printing a list of contacts from the main Contacts window, though, you've got a bunch of choices. Select an option to see how it looks in the right preview pane.

Tip: Some options, such as Card Style, have more than one layout—if you see "1 of 2" below the preview, then click the right arrow to see the alternative layout for this style.

5. **When you're ready to print, click the big Print button at the top of the page.**

   Outlook sends your document to the printer.

GEM IN THE ROUGH

Contacts and Social Networking: Outlook Social Connector

Outlook is aiming to become *the* social networking tool for busy professionals. With the explosion of services like Twitter, LinkedIn, Facebook, and MySpace (to name just a few) Outlook Social Connector aims to gather up all your contacts' latest posts, so you can see what's up right from your inbox.

In Outlook Mail, social networking info appears in the People pane (page 294). In addition to seeing the Outlook information you have in common (such as emails and upcoming meetings), you can see your pals' latest status updates. That way you don't have to jump around between windows to see what's up with a particular contact. Social Connector makes keeping track of your contacts easier and more efficient.

At this writing, Outlook Social Connector works with SharePoint 2010's new social capabilities. It also works with LinkedIn and MySpace, and other sites, including Facebook, Windows Live, and Twitter, are scheduled to come on board soon. To get updates from third-party sites on Outlook, you need to download an add-in so the site can communicate with Outlook. Get LinkedIn for Outlook at *www.linkedin.com/outlook* and MySpace for Outlook at *www.myspace.com/msoutlook*.

Getting Organized with Folders

O utlook is built on folders. No matter what you're working with—an email message, a contact, a task, or an appointment—it gets stored in a folder. Learn how folders work in Outlook, and you'll work faster and more efficiently.

This chapter covers how to find folders in Outlook's Navigation pane, how to create and manage folders, and how to move items between folders. It's also got techniques to make working with folders easier: Categories help you organize items within folders; customizing Outlook's panes puts folder items at your fingertips; and search techniques zero in on what you're looking for, no matter what folder it's in. Finally, because virtual folders can fill up and get messy just as fast as their physical counterparts, this chapter closes by showing how to clean out your Outlook folders and archive their information.

Finding Folders in the Navigation Pane

Outlook's Navigation pane is the place to go when you're looking for a folder. The bottom part of the pane shows Outlook's main offerings: Mail, Calendar, Contacts, and Tasks. Click any of these links to open that folder and whatever items it holds.

The top part of the Navigation pane displays the currently selected task's subfolders. When you're working in the Mail folder, for example, you'll see Inbox, Drafts, Sent Mail, Deleted Items, Junk E-mail, and so on. Figure 12-1 shows what the Navigation pane looks like when Mail is on center stage. Other folders, like Calendar and Contacts, don't have any related folders built in (although you can create some).

Tip: You can see a list of *all* your Outlook folders if you like. At the bottom of the Navigation pane, click the Folder List button (or press Ctrl+6), and the entire list of folders appears in the top half of the pane.

Figure 12-1:
Use the Navigation pane to find folders in Outlook. To show a list of all folders, click the Folder List button (circled).

Tip: When opened, Outlook presents you with a view of your inbox. If you'd prefer a different folder to greet you, select File→Options (Alt, F, I); click Advanced. In the Outlook "Start and exit" section, click the Browse button to open a Select Folder dialog box. Choose the folder you want, and then click OK in this window and the next to save your new choice.

Creating a New Folder

Outlook's built-in folders are a good start for organizing your Outlook items. But you'll probably want to create a few of your own. For example, maybe you'd like to keep email messages from your family all together. Outlook lets you create new folders to store any kind of item—email messages, tasks, notes, whatever—so you can save related items in one place and easily find them.

To create a new folder, start by going to the Navigation pane and choosing one of the top-level folders: Mail, Calendar, Contacts, Tasks, or Notes. Then follow these steps:

1. **Select Folder→New Folder (Alt, D, N). Alternatively, you can right-click any folder in the Folder List.**

    The Create New Folder dialog box, shown in Figure 12-2, appears.

Note: If you're in the Calendar folder, the button's name is New Calendar. It still opens the Create New Folder dialog box (Figure 12-2).

---

2. **Type a name for your folder into the Name text box.**

    Make it descriptive; you'll appreciate having done so as your folder collection grows.

3. **If the "Folder contains" drop-down list *doesn't* show the kind of item you want in your new folder, then click the list and pick another option. Then tell Outlook where to place your new folder.**

    Your new folder will become a subfolder of the folder you choose. For example, if you're creating a new folder to collect emails related to a work project, then select Outlook Data File to put it with the other mail folders (at the same level as Inbox, Drafts, and so on). Similarly, if you want your new folder to be a subfolder of Contacts, select Contacts.

4. **Click OK.**

    Outlook adds your new creation to the Folder List, which is organized alphabetically.

Figure 12-2:
The Create New Folder dialog box asks for three pieces of information: the folder's name, the type of items it will contain, and its location within Outlook.

Note: When you're working with Calendars, the Folders tab is a little different. Instead of a New Folder button, there's a New Calendar button. That's because a calendar works like a folder, storing different appointments, meetings, and events.

Filling Up and Managing Folders

The reason for creating a folder, of course, is to put items in it. If you didn't use separate folders for email, for example, all your messages would stuff your inbox, making it hard to find a particular message. To keep your items organized, put each in its proper place.

To move an item from one folder to another (an email message from the inbox to a custom folder, for example), select the email and click the Home tab's Move button (Alt, H, MV). A menu opens, showing a list of other folders. Select the one you want. If you don't see it on the menu, click Other Folder (O) to open a dialog box showing all your Outlook folders.

As you read individual email messages, you can quickly move them to other folders without closing the message window. Use the Message tab's Move button (Alt, H, MV) to choose the new folder.

Tip: If you're moving an email message, you can make sure that all future messages in the same conversation automatically follow the same path to the new folder. From the Move menu, select Always Move Messages in This Conversation (Alt, H, MV, A).

Copying a Folder

To copy an entire folder (to create a record of what was in the folder as of a certain date, for example), select the folder you want to duplicate, and then head to the Folder tab. There, click the Action section's Copy Folder button (Alt, D, CF). The dialog box shown in Figure 12-3 opens; it's got a list of all your Outlook folders. Select the one you want to hold the folder you're copying, and then click OK.

Moving a Folder

From the Navigation pane's Folder List, select the one you want to move, and then click Folder→Move Folder (Alt, D, MF). The Move Folder dialog box opens; like the Copy Folder dialog box (Figure 12-3), it shows a list of possible destinations. From the list, select where you want to move the new folder *to* (the moved item becomes a subfolder of the folder you choose).

Figure 12-3:
From the list of folders, select the one that will hold the folder you're copying.

Renaming a Folder

Renaming a folder is simple. Select any item in the Folders List and then click the Folder tab's Rename Folder button (Alt, D, RN). The current name temporarily becomes a text box. Type in the name you want. When you click outside the text box, the new name sticks.

Deleting a Folder

Select the folder you want to nix and, on the Folder tab, click Delete Folder (Alt, D, DF). Outlook asks whether you're sure you want to do this. Click Yes if you're ready. Helpful tip: When you ax a folder, Outlook gets rid of it and then moves its contents to the Deleted Items folder. (Good to know, in case you regret your decision later on.)

Categorizing Items

Folders provide a certain amount of neatness, but categories add a whole 'nother level of organization. A category is a color-coded label that you stick onto items you want to group together. A category can link together different *kinds* of Outlook items, and it can help you find what you're looking for within a folder.

Say you're starting a new project at work. You can pick (or create) a category for all items related to that project. Perhaps you pick the Blue category, change its name to Paperless Office Project, and use it to categorize all your Outlook items related to that daunting mission: emails, contacts who are also working on the project, meetings, tasks, and notes. When you're looking for items related to the project, you can easily find them in any folder, thanks to the blue label.

You can also assign an item to more than one category. If one of your colleagues is on the paper reduction project *and* on the company's Lumberjack Team, you can assign that person to both categories. In sum, it's a flexible way to organize your Outlook items.

Assigning a Category

Outlook comes with half a dozen categories already built in. (You can also create your own, as explained in the next section.) Assigning a category takes just a couple of clicks:

1. **Select the item you want to categorize (pick multiple items by pressing Shift or Ctrl as you select). Click the Home tab's Categorize button (Alt, H, G).**

    A menu of categories appears, as shown in Figure 12-4.

2. **Select the category you want to assign.**

    When you open an item, its category appears across the top: a bar of color and the category name.

Note: The first time you work with a new category, Outlook asks if you want to rename it. (After all, "Blue Category" isn't very descriptive.) You can also select a shortcut key (such as Ctrl+F2) for the category, making it even faster to associate items with it.

Figure 12-4:
The quick way to assign an item to a category is to choose from the Categorize button's menu.

Note: The Calendar folder works a little differently than Outlook's other folders. You can assign meetings to categories, but you do it from the Calendar Tools | Meeting contextual tab, which appears when you select a meeting. The keyboard shortcut for that tab is Alt, H2. So when you see "Alt, H" in the following sections, think "Alt, H2" if you're working with a meeting.

OFFICE 2010: THE MISSING MANUAL

Creating a New Category

Outlook starts you out with six categories, but you might find that it doesn't take long to use them all up. When that happens, go ahead and create a new category by following these steps:

1. **Select an item that you want to assign to the new category, and then select Home→Categorize (Alt, H, G).**

   The menu of categories (Figure 12-4) opens.

2. **Select All Categories (A).**

   The Color Categories dialog box opens (Figure 12-5).

Tip: You can assign a category from the Color Categories box. This is particularly helpful when you want to put an item in more than one category. Turn on as many of the checkboxes as you want, and then click OK.

---

3. **Click New.**

   The Add New Category dialog box opens.

4. **Give your new category a descriptive name, and select a color from the drop-down list. You can also select a shortcut key for assigning items. Click OK.**

The next time you click the Categorize button, your new category is on the menu.

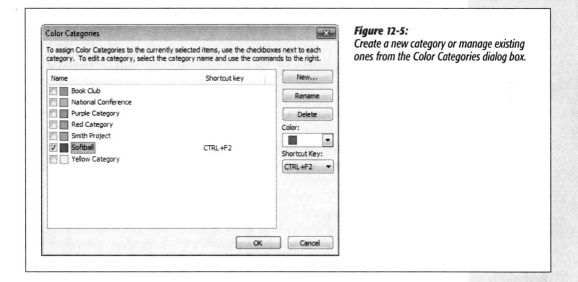

Figure 12-5:
Create a new category or manage existing ones from the Color Categories dialog box.

Viewing Items by Category

The whole point of using categories is to make similarly labeled items easier to find. To view a folder's items by category, go to the Navigation pane and select the folder you want. Then use one of these methods:

- **Click the View tab.** In the Arrangement section, select Categories from the Group gallery.

- **Arrange a list.** If you're looking at items in a list—viewing your contacts in List or Phone view, for example—click the Categories column header to arrange the list by category. (You may have to scroll to the right to see the Categories column.)

- **Arrange a list of search results.** After you've run a search, you can group the results by category: Click Search Tools | Search→Categorized (Alt, JS, G) and select a category to group by.

Clearing Categories

Sometimes you'll want to remove an item from a category—a colleague left the Paperless Office Project, for example, and you want to remove her contact info from that category. Outlook offers two routes:

- **Clear all categories.** If you want to clear any and all categories from an item, select it and, on the Home tab, click Categorize→Clear All Categories (Alt, H, G, C). This immediately scrubs any categories associated with the item.

- **Clear a single category.** You might come across a situation where an item is in multiple categories but you only want to clear one—your colleague left the Paperless Office Project, but she's still on the Lumberjack Team. In a case like that, select the item, head for the Home tab, and click Categorize→All Categories (Alt, H, G, A) to open the Color Categories dialog box (Figure 12-5). Turn off the checkbox of whichever category you want to clear, and then click OK.

Renaming a Category

Giving a category a new name is simple. Open the Color Categories dialog box (Figure 12-5), and then select whatever you want to rename. Click the Rename button to enter your new label.

Customizing Views

Like all of Office 2010, Outlook is highly customizable. You can set up your workspace however it makes sense to you. The Navigation pane crowding your inbox? Minimize it. Like seeing a list of what's on your plate for today? Maximize the To-Do Bar. This section looks at ways to adjust Outlook's layout, keeping important folders and items right at your fingertips.

Note: Each of Outlook's main folders offers options for viewing the items in that folder: Email conversations are covered on page 245, contacts on page 279, calendars on page 325, tasks on page 336, and notes on page 343.

Customizing the Navigation Pane

To tweak the Navigation pane's appearance, click View→Navigation Pane (Alt, W, N). Here's where you can minimize the pane, making it just wide enough to display icon buttons for your folders, or turn it off. (To turn it back on, click the Navigation Pane button and select Normal or Minimized, as you prefer.)

Note: Changes you make to the Navigation pane apply to all your Outlook folders.

Other, more cosmetic, options await. You can, for example, change the buttons that appear on the Navigation pane by selecting View→Navigation Pane→Options (Alt, W, N, N). This opens a dialog box from which you can perform any of the following actions:

- **Remove a button.** Turn off the checkbox of the button you *don't* want to appear in the pane.
- **Add a button.** Turn on the checkbox of the button you want to add.
- **Reorder buttons.** Select any button and use the Move Up or Move Down buttons to change where it appears in the pane.
- **Change the font.** To add a little style to the Navigation pane, select a new font for your items and Folder List.
- **Reset.** If you've made changes to the Navigation pane and decide you preferred its original configuration, just click Reset.

After you've made your changes, click OK to apply them.

Tip: A quick way to minimize the Navigation pane (or the To-Do Bar) is to click the arrow at the top of the pane that points toward the side of the screen. After you've minimized the pane, the arrow points the other way, toward the middle of the screen; click that arrow to maximize the pane again.

Customizing the Reading Pane

The Reading pane lets you preview an item without opening it in a new window. When you select View→Reading Pane (Alt, W, PN), you can reposition the Reading pane from its current location (the choices are Bottom and Right) or turn it off. The position of the Reading pane is specific to each folder, so you can have the Reading pane appear on the bottom of your Mail folder, on the right side of your Tasks folder, and not at all in your Contacts folder. It's up to you.

Select View→Reading Pane→Options (Alt, W, PN, N) to open the Reading Pane dialog box and adjust these settings:

- **Mark items as read when viewed in the Reading Pane.** Outlook lets you know which items you haven't yet read by showing them in boldface; that way they stand out from those messages you've already looked at, as a reminder that these items still need your attention. Turn on this checkbox to mark an item as read after it's been in the Reading pane for a certain number of seconds (you specify the number). Using this option means that Outlook marks the item as read, removing its bold formatting, after the specified time has passed, whether you've actually read the item or not.

Tip: After you've given the items in your email inbox a quick scan, mark any messages you want to read more closely as unread. That'll remind you that you need to take another look at those emails.

- **Mark item as read when selection changes.** This option is on by default; when you select a new item to display in the Reading pane, Outlook assumes you're done with the item that was previously shown there—so it marks it as read.
- **Single key reading using space bar.** This option, on by default, lets you press the space bar to scroll through a long item in the Reading pane. If you turn it off, you'll have to use the pane's scroll bar to scroll down.

Pick your options and click OK to put them to work.

Note: Unlike Reading pane positions, which are folder-specific, the choices you make in the Reading Pane dialog box apply across all folders.

Customizing the To-Do Bar

Outlook's To-Do Bar appears on the right side of your screen. When you maximize it, you see a calendar, any upcoming meetings, and your task list. Minimizing it narrows the bar so it's wide enough to show a calendar icon and upcoming meetings and tasks written sideways—click any of these elements to pop out the To-Do Bar temporarily and see the details.

When you click the View tab's To-Do Bar button (Alt, W, B), you can set the bar's size (normal or minimized) or turn it off altogether. You can also select what appears on the To-Do Bar:

- **Date Navigator.** The Date Navigator is Outlook's fancy name for a calendar. Click any date to see it in your Calendar folder.
- **Appointments.** This section of the To-Do Bar shows upcoming meetings you've scheduled.
- **Task List.** As you add tasks to your Task List (page 336), they also appear here.

When you click the To-Do Bar button and choose Options (Alt, W, B, N), you can add or remove any section of the To-Do Bar and adjust these settings:

- **Choose the number of calendars to show in the Date Navigator section.** Normally, this section shows one month. If you want it to show more, then type the number you want in the "Number of month rows" text box.

- **Show or hide certain kinds of appointments.** By default, Outlook shows all upcoming appointments here. If you want to hide either all-day events or appointments you've marked as private, then turn off the appropriate checkbox.

Click OK to save your settings.

Tip: You can also customize the To-Do Bar's task list. Click Arrange By at the top of the list and select the option you want, such as type, start date, importance, and so on.

Searching Folders

It doesn't take very long to build up a huge stockpile of Outlook items: email messages sent and received; a growing number of contacts and appointments; an endless collection of tasks and notes. Looking for a single item in all that stuff can be like searching for the proverbial needle in a haystack. That's why Outlook has a powerful search feature that helps you find exactly what you're looking for. You can specify which folders to search, look only for items in a certain category or modified within the past week, and specify multiple criteria (such as who sent an email and the approximate time you received it) in an advanced search.

Needle? Haystack? No problem.

Searching the Current Folder

You can do a quick search—so quick, in fact, that Outlook calls it an *instant search*—from any folder. Try an instant search when you just want to type in a keyword or two and get a fast result.

To search for an item in the folder you're in right now, find the Search box (it's somewhere at the top of the folder, but below the ribbon), click inside it, and type your search term. (If you have trouble locating the Search box, press Ctrl+E to highlight it.) Outlook starts searching even as you type, so pause after you've typed a few characters and scan the results list to see if it shows what you're looking for. Outlook highlights your search term in the results. Double-click an item to view it.

Repeating a Search

When you search for an item, Outlook opens the Search Tools | Search contextual tab (Figure 12-6). In the Options section is the Recent Searches button. When you want to get another look at the results of a search you did recently, go to the folder

---

where you conducted the search and click Search Tools | Search→Recent Searches (Alt, JS, N).

Tip: If you don't see the Search Tools | Search contextual tab in a folder, press Ctrl+E to open it.

The Recent Searches menu (click the button with the same name to show it) lists your six most recent searches. Select any search to see its results.

Figure 12-6:
This is the Search Tools | Search tab that appears when you're searching a mail folder. The Scope section lets you broaden your search, whereas the Refine section narrows it. Click Recent Searches to see your six most recent searches. When you're done searching, you can close this tab by clicking Close Search.

Expanding Your Search

It's frustrating when you can't find an item you *know* is in Outlook…somewhere. If the item doesn't turn up in a quick search of the current folder, you may want to broaden your search to look for the item in more places. Enter the Search Tools: | Search tab's Scope section, where you can choose any of these options:

- **All Items (Alt, JS, A).** The name of this button depends on the folder you're currently in; if you're searching the Mail folder, for example, the button says All Mail Items. Choose this option when you want Outlook to search a main folder and all its related folders. So if you search All Mail Items, Outlook searches the folders that contain email messages, including Inbox, Drafts, Sent Items, and so on.

Tip: When you search with the All Items button, hover your mouse pointer over any item in the results list to see which folder Outlook found that item in.

- **Current Folder (Alt, JS, CF).** This is the default search option. It searches the folder you selected in the Navigation pane—and only that folder.

- **All Subfolders (Alt, JS, SU).** If the folder you picked in the Navigation pane has subfolders, such as custom folders you created to hold related items, then this option searches those subfolders in addition to the parent folder.

- **All Outlook Items (Alt, JS, OL).** This is the broadest search option, searching all Outlook folders.

Refining Your Search

If you've run an instant search and haven't found the item you're looking for, use the Search Tools | Search tab to refine the search. The buttons on this tab's ribbon are specific to the folder you're in. For example, when you search in the Mail folder, the ribbon lets you search by From line, Subject line, or messages with attachments. In the Tasks folder, the ribbon has buttons to search by the start date, due date, or the date someone last modified the task; by status or importance; and more. Press Ctrl+E to open the tab and see what your search options are for a particular folder.

Here's how these buttons work to refine your search: Say you're helping to plan an industry convention in Las Vegas, and you're looking for the draft of the program you received as an attachment a while back. You do an instant search of email messages using "convention" and "Vegas" as keywords, but there are too many results. So you click the Search Tools | Search tab's Has Attachments button. Now Outlook looks for messages that mention "convention" and "Vegas" and also have an attachment. That narrows down the results, and you find the message you wanted.

Doing an Advanced Search

Sometimes the best way to find exactly what you're looking for is to search for multiple criteria. For example, you might want to find a task with the keyword "sign-off" whose status is in progress and that was sent to you by your boss. You can add such criteria, one click at a time, using the Tasks folder's Search Tools | Search tab. Or you can specify your criteria all at once using Advanced Find. Advanced Find speeds up your search by putting multiple criteria up front, making the list of results more precise.

Here's how to use it:

1. **On the Search Tools | Search contextual tab, click Search Tools→Advanced Find (Alt, JS, SS, F).**

   The Advanced Find dialog box opens, displaying options related to the folder from which you opened it. Figure 12-7 shows an example.

2. **In the "Look for" drop-down menu, select the type of item you want to find (if necessary).**

   The dialog box's options change to match the kind of item you're looking for.

3. **In the In text box, tell Outlook where to search.**

   You can type in the name of a folder or click the Browse button and select the folder from a list.

4. **Type in a search term and choose your search criteria.**

   The criteria depend on the kind of item you're looking for. If you're searching for an appointment, for example, you can search by the organizer who created the event or by the names of contacts who are attending. For email messages, you can search for messages from or to a particular contact and within a time range of when the message was sent or received.

5. **When you've set all the criteria you want to use for the search, click Find Now.**

   Outlook searches for your item using the criteria you set up and returns any results, which appear in a pane at the bottom of the Advanced Find box.

Figure 12-7:
Advanced Find lets you set multiple criteria for your search. Options depend on the kind of item you're looking for. This example does an advanced search for an email message.

Changing Search Settings

When you do an instant search, Outlook conducts that search in a certain way: going through just the current folder, anticipating what you're searching for as you type, and highlighting your search term in the results. You can change any of these settings to customize your instant searches.

To change how Outlook does an instant search, follow either of these paths:

— On the Search Tools | Search tab, click Search Tools→Search Options (Alt, JS, SS, O).

— Select File→Options (Alt, F, I), and then select Search.

A dialog box showing Outlook's search options opens, as shown in Figure 12-8. Here are the options you can adjust:

— **Searching the current folder or all folders.** Outlook's default setting is to speed up the search by looking in just the current folder. If you'd prefer to always search *all* folders, then turn on the "All folders" radio button. To make rummaging through the trash part of an instant search, turn on the "Include messages from the Deleted items folder…" checkbox.

— **Displaying search results as you type the search term.** If you don't like the way Outlook jumps the gun and tries to anticipate your keyword as you type, turn off the checkbox labeled "When possible, display results as the query is typed".

— **Limiting the number of results to allow faster searching.** Your choice here is between faster or more thorough. If you opt for the latter, turn off the "Improve search speed by limiting the number of results shown" checkbox.

— **Highlighting search terms in results.** You *know* the search results contain your keyword, so maybe you don't want that keyword highlighted in each and every result. If that's the case, turn off the "Highlight search terms in the results" checkbox. If you want highlighting but yellow isn't your color, click the Highlight color drop-down list to choose a more flattering shade.

— **Notifying you when search results may be incomplete.** If the list of results may come up short because Outlook hasn't completed indexing the search, Outlook lets you know.

Figure 12-8:
You can adjust how Outlook performs an instant search by tweaking the settings in the Search tab of the Outlook Options dialog box.

Cleaning Out Folders

Picture an overly full file cabinet, so stuffed with papers that you can't close its drawers. How many of those crammed-in papers do you actually need? How many are just taking up space, never to be looked at again?

With Outlook, you don't see overcrowded folders like you would with a physical file cabinet. But those folders may need a good cleaning out anyway. Attachments (especially images and videos) can take up a lot of storage space—do you really *have* to keep them? And why clutter up folders with obsolete items you no longer need? A leaner folder makes it easier to find essential items.

Outlook helps clean out your folders with automatic archiving (which works like boxing up old files and putting them in storage) and the Mailbox Cleanup tool. Email folders fill up particularly fast, so you'll appreciate this tool, which simplifies clearing out old messages.

Tip: You might have to nag family members to take out the trash, but you can tell Outlook to do it automatically, dumping all the trash from your Deleted Items folder whenever you close Outlook. Select File→Options (Alt, F, I) to open the Outlook Options dialog box. In the "Outlook start and exit" section, turn on the checkbox labeled "Empty Deleted Items folder when exiting Outlook". Click OK to save the change. No nagging required.

Archiving Old Data

In a library, an *archive* is a collection of items that aren't in circulation but are worth keeping. Outlook's archive works according to the same idea. After a while, you'll have items in your folders that are no longer current but that you don't want to delete. You might use them again later, or maybe you just like having them around. With AutoArchive, Outlook can automatically clear out email messages, appointments, and tasks that are past their prime—say, older than 90 days—and store them in the Archive folder. Once you've set up your AutoArchive rules, you never have to think about dealing with old, out-of-date items, because Outlook takes care of them for you.

Note: Contact info doesn't go stale just because a certain number of days have passed. A contact you added a year ago will still be up to date if the person hasn't moved or changed jobs. So Outlook doesn't AutoArchive contacts.

Setting up AutoArchive

To set up AutoArchive, you need to tell Outlook how and when to archive your old items. To do that, go Backstage:

1. Select File→Options (Alt, F, I).

   The Outlook Options dialog box opens.

2. Select Advanced and, in the AutoArchive section, click the AutoArchive Settings button.

   You see the AutoArchive dialog box, shown in Figure 12-9.

Figure 12-9:
Keep your folders free of old, outdated items with Auto-Archive. Set how often you want AutoArchive to run, what it looks for, and what it does with old items.

3. Turn on the "Run AutoArchive every __ days" checkbox, and then select how often you want AutoArchive to run.

   When you turn on the Run AutoArchive checkbox, Outlook enables these other options:

   — **Prompt before AutoArchive runs.** If you want to get a notification from Outlook before it AutoArchives old items from your folders, leave this checkbox turned on. When Outlook is about to run an AutoArchive, it asks for your okay before starting.

   — **Delete expired items (email folders only).** When this checkbox is on, Outlook deletes any of your email messages that have an expiration date attached, instead of moving them to the Archive folder.

   — **Archive or delete old items.** If you don't want to archive old items, turn off this checkbox.

   — **Show Archive folder in folder list.** Leave this checkbox turned on if you want to be able to easily find the Archive folder.

   — **Clean out items older than.** Here's where you tell Outlook how old an item must be to go to the Archive folder. You can specify the age in days, weeks, or months.

— **Move old items to/Permanently delete old items.** Turn on one of these radio buttons to tell Outlook what to do with old items: Store them in the Archive folder (or click the Browse button to pick a different storage location) or delete them for good.

4. **Make your selections. If you want to run an AutoArchive based on these settings right now (you don't have to), click the button labeled "Apply these settings to all folders now". Click OK.**

   Outlook saves your AutoArchive settings and returns you to the Outlook Options dialog box.

5. **Click OK to close Outlook Options.**

   Now Outlook will AutoArchive old items based on your settings.

Adjusting AutoArchive settings for a specific folder

AutoArchiving is great for keeping your standard folders, like the Inbox and Sent Mail folders, manageable. But there may be some folders you'd prefer that Auto-Archive leave alone. Say you created a folder for storing love notes from your spouse—you might not want to archive those love notes at all. Or you might have a folder that you want Outlook to AutoArchive but want the settings a bit different from the standard AutoArchive procedure.

To turn off AutoArchive or tweak its settings for a particular folder, follow these steps:

1. **Select Folder→AutoArchive Settings (Alt, D, A).**

   The Properties dialog box for that folder opens, with the AutoArchive tab selected, as shown in Figure 12-10.

Tip: Some folders don't display the AutoArchive button on the Folder tab. If you don't see it there, then click the Properties button (Alt, D, P) to open the folder's Properties box, and then click the AutoArchive tab.

---

2. **Select a radio button to tell Outlook how you want AutoArchive to work with items in this folder.**

   Here are your choices:

   — **Do not archive items in this folder.** If you never want Outlook to sweep old items out of this folder, then turn on this radio button.

   — **Archive items in this folder using the default settings.** Turning on this radio button tells Outlook to AutoArchive items in this folder based on the settings you selected in the previous set of steps.

   — **Archive this folder using these settings.** If you want AutoArchive to treat items in this folder differently from other AutoArchived folders, then turn on this radio button and adjust the settings: how often AutoArchive cleans out this particular folder and what it does with old items.

3. **Click OK.**

   For this individual folder, AutoArchive now follows the settings you've established for it.

Archiving manually

You can also archive items in any folder yourself from Backstage, without waiting around for AutoArchive to do it. To archive items right now, select File→Info→ Cleanup Tools (Alt, F, E, T), and then select Archive.

In the Archive dialog box, you can run an archive right now based on your Auto-Archive settings, or you can specify special settings for running this particular archive. Click OK, and Outlook archives the items you told it to.

Tip: To look through items you've archived, head for the Navigation pane and expand Archives–this shows all archived folders. If you're searching for an archived item, select Archives in the Navigation pane and then press Ctrl+E to search archived folders. Searching All Items (press Ctrl+E and then select Search Tools | Search→All Items (Alt, JS, A) also searches archived items. (When you search All Items, the All Items button reflects what you're searching: Mail, Calendar, Task, and so on.)

Figure 12-10:
If you don't want Outlook to ever AutoArchive items in a particular folder, you can make that selection in this dialog box.

Cleaning up Your Mailbox

You don't have to wait for April to do a good spring cleaning—you can roll up your sleeves and get busy cleaning up any time of year. And whenever your Mail folder needs that kind of cleanup, Outlook is ready to help. Mailbox Cleanup helps you keep your mail folders from getting overcrowded.

Here's how to clean up your mailbox:

1. **Select File→Info→Cleanup Tools (Alt, F, E, T), and then choose Mailbox Cleanup.**

   The Mailbox Cleanup dialog box, shown in Figure 12-11, opens, offering these options:

   — **View Mailbox Size.** When you click this button, you see a new dialog box that lists your Outlook mail folders, along with the total size of each, indicating how much space that folder is taking up on your computer's hard drive.

   — **Find items by age or size.** If you want to clean up messages by getting rid of the out-of-date ones or those that take up a lot of storage space, choose which you want to find and your criterion for searching (say, items older than 60 days or larger than 250 KB). Click Find to open the Advanced Find dialog box (Figure 12-7), showing your search results at the bottom. Delete the messages you don't want by right-clicking them and choosing Delete.

   — **AutoArchive.** If you've set up AutoArchiving (page 318), click this button to run AutoArchive now.

   — **Empty Deleted Items.** Old messages and attachments do tend to pile up in the Deleted Items folder. To get rid of what's in there right now, click the Empty button.

   — **Delete Conflicts.** You may end up with different versions of the same item in your mailbox—Outlook calls these conflicting items and stores them all in a Conflicts folder, so you can choose the correct version. When you have items in the Conflicts folder, you can see the size of that folder by clicking the View Conflicts Size button. To clean out the Conflicts folder, click the Delete button.

2. **After you've finished cleaning up your mailbox, click Close.**

   Feels good to have your Mail folder nice and tidy now, doesn't it?

Figure 12-11:
Just like spring cleaning involves lots of different tasks, so does a Mailbox Cleanup. Check folder sizes, find items by age or size, run an AutoArchive, dump out the trash, and get rid of conflicting items—all from one dialog box.

PST! Back Up Your Outlook Data

Outlook saves all your information in a .pst file (that stands for *personal storage table*) where it makes copies of your messages, contacts, appointments, and other items and stores them in this file. It's a good idea to back it up on a flash drive, external hard drive, or other storage device.

Your .pst file is stored somewhere on your computer; exactly where depends on factors like which version of Windows you have and whether you upgraded to Office 2010 from an earlier version of Office. To back up this ultra-important file, here's what you need to do:

1. Select File→Info→Account Settings (Alt, F, E, S), and then click the Account Settings menu item.

   The Account Settings dialog box opens.

2. Click the Data Files tab.

   This tab shows the location of your Outlook Data File (*Outlook.pst*) and also any data files related to secondary email accounts.

3. Select your Outlook Data File and click Open File Location.

   Windows Explorer opens to the location of your data file, with *Outlook.pst* selected.

4. Back up *Outlook.pst*. If you're saving a copy on a flash drive, for example, insert the flash drive in your computer's USB port and drag *Outlook.pst* to the flash drive to make a copy. Or right-click *Outlook.pst* and, from the shortcut menu, select the destination where you're backing up the file.

   You may have to close Outlook before you can copy the file. (If so, Windows will tell you.)

   Later, if something happens to your computer and you need to restore your .pst file, open Windows Explorer and copy the file you saved into the folder that stores *Outlook.pst.*.

Getting Organized with Outlook's Calendar, Tasks, and Notes

B usy people can use a little help keeping track of all they have to do. Emails fly into your Inbox, inviting you to meetings and "asking" you to get things done. Your boss sends a list of to-do's; your coworker needs help with a project; and you've got so many conference calls lined up that it's only a matter of time before you forget to call your honey.

Outlook brings together the tools you need to get organized, keep up with your busy schedule, and stay on top of your to-do list:

- **Calendar** lets you schedule and view appointments, meetings, and other events. You can see what's on tap for today or take a longer view, keeping an eye on events by week or month. Invite others to attend a meeting, set real-time reminders so you won't be late, and schedule recurring events with ease.

- **Tasks** are super-helpful for list makers, thanks to an easy-to-manage To-Do List. Outlook organizes your tasks by their due date—helpful for spotting deadlines. You can even assign a task to someone else—lucky them.

- **Notes** are a flexible way to jot down things you need to remember—and easily find again. They're quick to write, and you can view and group them in different ways, just like you were arranging sticky notes on a bulletin board.

These tools all work together (and with Outlook Mail), so you won't get buried under a mountain of to-do's and shoulda-done's.

Your Schedule, Your Calendar

To see your Outlook calendar, click the Navigation pane's Calendar button or press Ctrl+2. When you open its folder, the view you see looks something like Figure 13-1.

The main calendar shown there divides days into hours, and each hour can hold any events you've scheduled for that time.

Use the buttons in the Home tab's Arrange sections to change this view (to list things by day, week, and so on), and click the navigation buttons (Figure 13-1, circled) to move forward or backward from the current date range.

If you've got the Navigation pane or the To-Do Bar maximized, the Date Navigator appears at the top, marking today's date with a red square. Dates for which you've scheduled an event appear in boldface. Click any date to view its details in the main window.

Create a new calendar item

Navigation buttons

Calendar views

All-day event

Date Navigator

Date range showing in calendar   Today's date

Figure 13-1:
Display your calendar by day, work week, week, or month (this example shows Week view). Choose a date or a date range in the Date Navigator, or use the navigation arrows to move backward and forward. Appointments show up in the block of time you've assigned to them; all-day events appear at the top of their day. To open any appointment and check out its details, double-click it.

Creating an Appointment or Meeting

An empty calendar can tell you what the date is, but not much else. To make your calendar useful, you need to fill it up with your meetings, appointments, and other events.

An *appointment* is something you put on your calendar, reserving a block of time on a particular day. It could be a checkup at your doctor's office, a lunch date, a scheduled talk with someone in human resources, a day off, even a block of quiet time when you don't want any distractions.

A *meeting* is just like an appointment—a discrete block of time set aside for a specific purpose—but it involves other people. When you create a meeting in Outlook, you send participants an email invitation with details of the meeting.

Scheduling an Appointment

To put an appointment on your calendar, follow these steps:

1. **Select Home→New Appointment (Alt, H1, N) or press Ctrl+N. Alternatively, you can double-click an empty time slot on the calendar.**

   Outlook opens an Appointment window, as shown in Figure 13-2.

Figure 13-2:
When you create an appointment, record its essential details: the reason for the meeting, its location, and its start and end times. If you need to block out the whole day, turn on the "All-day event" checkbox.

Tip: When you select an empty time slot on the calendar before taking step 1, the Appointment window opens with the date, start time, and end time already filled in.

---

2. **Enter the appointment's basic information.**

   Subject. The reason for having the appointment: a lunch date, a birthday party, a meeting with your ice cream consultant—whatever you're setting aside time for. The subject appears on your calendar, so choose something that reminds you of the appointment's purpose at a glance.

   Location. It's no good showing up in Conference Room A when the meeting is happening across town. List the location so you know where you need to be.

   Start Time/End Time. The start time is, of course, when the meeting kicks off. If the appointment is scheduled to end at a certain time, like a two-hour seminar, you can reserve the whole block on your calendar by selecting an end time. If you're scheduling a business trip or vacation days, set the end time for the end of the final day of the event.

Note: If you don't set an end time, Outlook assigns half an hour to the appointment.

All day event. When you need to set aside a whole day—maybe you're going to a wedding—turn on the "All day event" checkbox instead of selecting start and end times.

Notes. Use the big text box to record any notes or need-to-know info about the appointment.

3. **Click Save & Close (Alt, H, AV).**

Outlook creates the appointment and adds it to your calendar.

Back in the Calendar folder, your new appointment appears in the date and time slot you assigned it, as shown back in Figure 13-1. To open the appointment and view its details, double-click it.

Setting up a Meeting

When you set up a meeting, you can schedule it and invite others to attend, all in one step. Just follow these steps:

1. **Select Home→New Meeting (Alt, H1, MR).**

A Meeting window opens. As you can see in Figure 13-3, this window looks just like what you see for an appointment, except it has fields and buttons to send out email invitations.

Email controls

Figure 13-3:
The form for creating a meeting looks like an Appointment window, except it adds a From line, a To line, and a Send button—that way you can send out an email message inviting others. Outlook uses the meeting's subject as the Subject line of the invitation.

2. **Enter participants' email addresses in the To line.**

    You can type them in or select addresses from the Address Book, shown in Figure 13-4. If you're using the Address Book, select a contact (choose multiple contacts by pressing Shift or Ctrl as you select) and then click Required (for participants you expect to attend) or Optional (for participants you'd like to attend, like consultants). If you're requesting a room or equipment, put that contact in the Resources line.

Tip: The box on page 248 lists ways to address an email.

---

3. **Fill in the rest of the information just as you would for creating an appointment.**

    The previous list of steps tells you how to set up an appointment.

Tip: If you're scheduling a phone or video conference among far-flung participants, it's helpful to specify a time zone when you send out invitations, to avoid confusion about what time the meeting *really* starts. On the Meeting tab, click the Time Zones button (Alt, H, OS). Time zone fields appear after the start and end times, with your current time zone already selected. You can click the drop-down arrow if you need to specify a different time zone.

---

4. **When everything looks good, click the Send button (or press Ctrl+Enter).**

    Outlook sends out your invitations with details of the meeting.

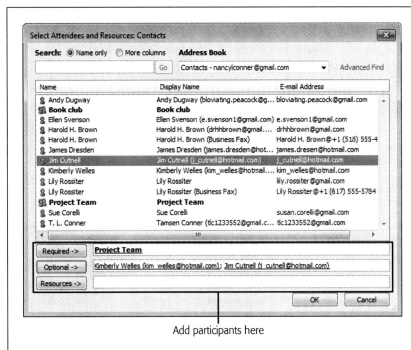

Figure 13-4:
When you select meeting attendees from your Outlook Address Book, click the buttons at the bottom to add their email addresses to your meeting invitation. The status you assign (Required, Optional, or Resources) appears in your tracking list for the meeting.

Add participants here

People you've invited can accept or decline. To see how to keep track of who's planning on attending the meeting, skip ahead to page 331.

Accepting an Invitation to a Meeting

When you receive an invitation to a meeting, the email shows a preview of your calendar, so you can see how the meeting fits in with the rest of your day. When you've determined whether you can attend, click one of these buttons on the Meeting tab:

- **Accept.** Adds the meeting to your calendar and shoots off an email confirming that you'll be there.

- **Tentative.** Adds the meeting to your calendar and notifies the organizer that you're not sure whether you'll make it.

- **Decline.** Lets the organizer know you won't be there.

- **Propose New Time.** If you want to attend the meeting but have a conflict, choose this response to suggest an alternative date and time (Outlook lists you as Tentative in the organizer's response list).

Tip: Don't see a Propose New Time button? That's because the meeting's organizer disabled it. You can still send a tentative response and suggest a different time in the email.

- **Respond.** Click this button if you have any questions or comments about the meeting before you RSVP. You can reply to the organizer or to all participants, or you can forward the invitation to someone else.

If you have a message for the organizer (such as the reason why you can't attend), select Edit Response to add your comment. When you've made your choice from the items listed above, click Send, and your response is on its way.

Adding or Removing Attendees

After you've created a meeting, you may have to adjust the attendance list. To do so, open your calendar, select the meeting you want, and then choose Calendar Tools | Meeting→Add or Remove Attendees (Alt, H2, AA).

A list of your Outlook contacts opens, as shown in Figure 13-4. Meeting participants and their contact info appear at the bottom, where you can take one of these actions:

- To **add** an attendee, select the person's name from the Address Book list, and then click Required or Optional to add that person to the meeting.

- To **remove** an attendee, find the person's contact info in the Required or Optional field; select and delete it.

Click OK when you're done. Outlook opens a Meeting window (Figure 13-3) so you can email attendees and update them about the changes.

Keeping Track of Who's Attending

It's important to know who's coming to your party. As people respond to your invitation, you get emails letting you know whether they've accepted or declined. To get an overview of who'll be there and who won't, go to your calendar and open the meeting. In the Meeting window, click Tracking (Alt, H, T, V) to open a list of people you've invited along with their responses, as shown in Figure 13-5. Outlook automatically updates the Response column as invitees make their decisions.

Tip: If you need to get in touch with participants, first turn off the left-hand checkbox of anybody you *don't* want to include in the mailing (such as those who declined to attend). Then select Meeting→Contact Attendees→New E-mail to Attendees (Alt, H, AM, S). A message window opens so you can fire off an email.

If you need to contact just one participant, hover your mouse pointer over that contact's name, and a contact card appears—use it to send an email or instant message, or place a phone call (page 296 tells you how).

Figure 13-5:
After you've invited people to your meeting, Outlook helps keep track of their RSVPs.

Canceling a Meeting

Even when you've been meticulous in organizing a meeting, sometimes you have to cancel—the best laid plans and all that. When you need to cancel, follow these steps:

1. **In your Calendar, select the meeting you're canceling, and then select Calendar Tools | Meeting→Cancel Meeting (Alt, H2, C).**

   Outlook opens a Meeting window; it's already addressed to the meeting's participants.

2. **If you want, write a message explaining why you're calling things off. Click Send Cancellation.**

   Outlook sends the cancellation email and removes the meeting from your calendar.

When participants get word of the cancellation, they can click a button in the email to remove the meeting from their own calendars.

Editing Events

The doctor's office calls to change your Wednesday checkup to Thursday. A colleague emails with news that her 4:30 meeting got bumped to 3:30. Welcome to real-world scheduling. As your calendar fills up with events, there'll be times when you have to make a change or cancel a meeting.

When that happens, find the appointment on your calendar and double-click it. The window that opens looks just like the one you used to create the appointment, except that its information is already all filled in.

You can change any of the existing information—subject, location, start and end times, notes—by clicking in a text box and editing what's there. Click Save & Close (Alt, H, AV) to record your changes. The rest of this section describes other ways to edit an appointment.

Turning an Appointment into a Meeting

Imagine you've scheduled an appointment for yourself, like a meeting with a consultant, and then you remember a couple of colleagues who might want to come along. You don't have to create a new meeting from scratch to invite them—just turn your existing appointment into a meeting.

Open the appointment to which you want to invite others. On the Appointment tab, click Invite Attendees (Alt, H, I). When you do, the appointment magically morphs into a meeting: The Appointment tab becomes the Meeting tab, and its ribbon reflects all the options you see when setting up a meeting. Outlook also adds From and To lines and a Send button for emailing invitations.

Fill in the recipients' email addresses, add a message if you like, and then click Send. From then on, you handle the event as you would any other meeting.

Making an Event Recur

Some events happen on a regular basis, like a weekly manicure or a department meeting on the second Tuesday of each month. You can make an appointment or meeting recur when you create it, or edit the event to accomplish the same thing. In the Appointment or Meeting window, click the Options section's Recurrence button (Alt, H, E). The dialog box shown in Figure 13-6 opens.

Tip: In the main Calendar window, when you click any event, the Recurrence button appears on the Calendar Tools contextual tab. (Press Alt, H2, E if you're using keyboard shortcuts.)

The Appointment Recurrence dialog box has three sections:

- **Appointment time.** Set the start and end times for the recurring appointment. When you do, Outlook automatically adjusts the duration.

- **Recurrence pattern.** In this section, tell Outlook how often the event occurs and on which day. For example, you might have a meeting that happens every Monday at the same time.

- **Range of recurrence.** This section specifies how long the recurring event goes on. Pick a start date and specify a number of occurrences or an actual end date, or tell Outlook to keep rescheduling the recurring event indefinitely.

When you've specified the event's pattern and range, click OK to create the event.

Figure 13-6:
Tell Outlook how often and for how long an event recurs, and Outlook takes care of adding the event to your schedule.

Getting Reminders

Every memory needs a little jogging now and then. Even when you've faithfully added all your upcoming meetings to your calendar and every task you can think of to your to-do list, you might forget to check or just lose track of the time. That's when you'll be glad of Outlook's reminders.

When you add an event to your calendar, Outlook automatically sets a reminder for it. At a preset time (usually 15 minutes before the event's scheduled start), Outlook reminds you that you've got an appointment or a meeting coming up. Outlook sounds a chime and displays a reminder like the one shown in Figure 13-7.

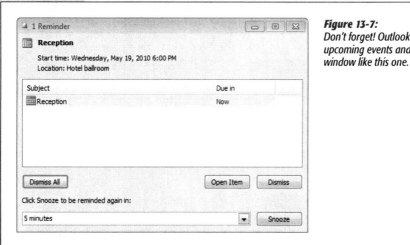

Figure 13-7:
Don't forget! Outlook can remind you of upcoming events and tasks with a Reminder window like this one.

You can adjust the amount of warning time you get when you create or edit an event. With the event open, look in the Appointment tab's Options section for the Reminder drop-down list. The number you see there tells you how long before the event's scheduled start time the Reminder window will appear. Click the drop-down menu to change the interval—you can set it anywhere from zero minutes (you get the reminder right at the start time) to two weeks. If the event is something you don't need a reminder for, like your birthday, select None.

When the Reminder window pops open to nudge you, choose from any of the following options:

- **Open the item.** If you need more details about the event, click Open Item.

- **Hit the Snooze button.** When the alarm clock shatters your sleep in the morning, you can grab an extra 5 minutes' shut-eye by hitting the snooze button. The Snooze button in Outlook's Reminder window does the same thing. When you click it, the Reminder window goes away and leaves you in peace for a little bit—but comes back again after a specified interval, usually 5 minutes. (To adjust how long the Reminder window goes away, click the drop-down list to the Snooze button's left.)

- **Dismiss the reminder.** If you're on your way to your appointment, click Dismiss. This removes the event and closes the Reminder window.

Note: You must have Outlook open for reminders to appear. If it's closed when a reminder is due, the reminder appears the next time you open Outlook.

- **Ignore it for now.** You can also simply close the Reminder window by clicking its upper-right X. This shuts up the Reminder window but doesn't erase the event. When it's time for your next reminder, the box lists this event as well as the new one it's reminding you about. If the Reminder window shows you multiple reminders and you want to clear them all out, click Dismiss All.

Tip: If reminders feel like the nagging pain that they're, uh, designed to be and you'd rather not deal with them at all, you can turn them off Backstage. Select File→Options (Alt, F, I) and then choose Calendar. In the Calendar Options section, turn off the "Default reminders" checkbox, then click OK to apply the change.

Deleting an Appointment

To remove a meeting from your calendar, select it and, on the Calendar Tools | Appointment contextual tab, click Delete (Alt, H2, D). Or, if you've got the appointment open, click the Appointment tab's Delete button (Alt, H, D).

Viewing Your Schedule

Sometimes you need to know what's on your plate for today, and sometimes you need to get an overview of what's coming up during the next week or month. The Home tab's Arrange section lets you quickly switch from one calendar view to another, so you can see the events for a single day (Alt, H, R), a Monday–Friday work week (Alt, H, K), a full seven-day week (Alt, H, W), or an entire month (Alt, H, T).

Tip: These views are also available as buttons on the View tab's ribbon.

For a quick look at just today's appointments and meetings, click the Today button (Alt, H, OD). And to see what events are looming on the horizon, click Next 7 Days (Alt, H, X), which shows your events relative to today's date, rather than using a standard Monday–Friday or Sunday–Saturday format.

You can also tweak your calendar's view in these ways:

- **Lengthen or shorten the time slots.** Most views of your calendar divide the day into half-hour segments: Each hour has two time slots. You can adjust how many events you can schedule for an hour, from just one event all the way up to 12 (that's 5-minute increments).

- **Change the color.** To choose a different color scheme for your calendar, select View→Color (Alt, W, CR). A menu appears showing a palette of colors. Click the one you like to apply it to the calendar.

- **See your events in a list.** This is a great way to find a particular event—display all entries in a list, and then sort or group them to find what you're looking for. Select View→Change View (Alt, W, CV), and then select List.

Tip: List view shows *all* the events on your calendar. To show only current and upcoming events, select Active from the Change View menu.

Tasks

Some people live their lives by lists: shopping lists, to-do lists, lists of Ways I Can Outshine My Sister. If you're a list maker, you'll love what Outlook's Tasks folder can do for you. Even if you're not big on lists, it's worth giving Tasks a try. You'll feel more on top of what you have to do and get a sense of accomplishment when you cross off a task well done.

To open your Outlook Tasks folder, click the Navigation pane's Tasks button or press Ctrl+4. The Tasks folder looks something like Figure 13-8. At the top of the Navigation pane is your My Tasks list, with two built-in views:

- **To-Do List.** Your To-Do List shows your tasks organized by date. Tasks that are due today appear at the top of the list. Overdue tasks (those that were due on an earlier date but you haven't marked as completed) appear here, too—those are in red so you'll remember they're overdue.

- **Tasks.** This shows *all* your Outlook tasks in list form, so you can see the entire collection at once and sort them in various ways. Tasks you've marked as completed appear in this list in strike-through font to indicate that they're done.

In Outlook's default view, your To-Do List appears in the center pane, and the Reading pane, which shows information about any task you select, appears on the right.

Adding a Task

You've got two options here: Create the task yourself, or accept a task that someone has assigned to you. This section shows you how to do both.

Creating a Task

To create a new task and add it to your To-Do List, open your Tasks folder and press Ctrl+N or use the ribbon: Select Home→New Task (Alt, H, N1). A Task window, shown in Figure 13-9, opens.

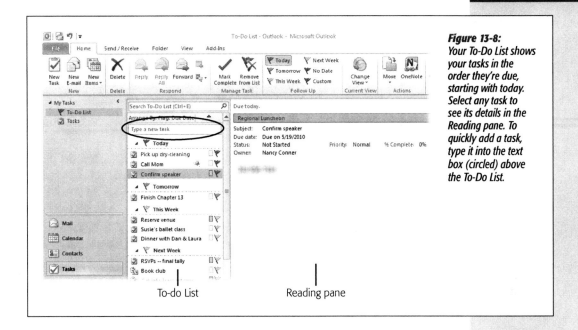

Figure 13-8:
Your To-Do List shows your tasks in the order they're due, starting with today. Select any task to see its details in the Reading pane. To quickly add a task, type it into the text box (circled) above the To-Do List.

To-do List   Reading pane

Figure 13-9:
You create and edit chores you want to tackle in a Task window like this one.

***

Tip: If there's something you have to do today, the quickest way to add it to your To-Do List is to type it into the "Type a new task" text box just above the To-Do List. Press Enter, and Outlook adds the task to today's chores. You can then open and edit it like any other task.

***

Here are the fields you can fill in when creating your task:

- **Subject.** This sums up what the chore is: "Pick up dry cleaning" or "Organize hundred-dollar bill collection."

- **Start date.** You might be laying out the timeline for a project that takes place in several phases. For a task that will start at some point in the future, click the drop-down arrow and select the projected start date from the calendar.

- **Due date.** If you've got to complete the task by a certain date, click the drop-down arrow and select the finish line from the calendar.

- **Status.** Where are you in the process of completing this task? Click the drop-down arrow and select the phrase that best describes the project's current status: Not Started, In Progress, Completed, Waiting for Someone Else, Deferred. Currently there's no option for "Oh please, make this go away."

- **Priority.** When your To-Do List is brimming with tasks, all of them demanding your attention, sometimes you've got to do a little triage. Assigning a priority helps you decide what to tackle first.

- **% Complete.** If the task is brand-new, you don't have to worry about this yet. But you might get around to adding the task after it's already begun or inherit a task that someone else has started. When that happens, you can estimate how close the task is to completion by putting a number in this dialog box.

- **Reminder.** Turn on the checkbox and set a date and time for getting a reminder about this task from Outlook. Page 333 explains how to get the most out of reminders.

- **Notes.** Write a description of the task or jot down any relevant notes in the big text box that takes up most of the Task window. For example, if you need to call someone, it's handy to put the phone number here.

Note: All fields are optional. At a minimum, though, you'll probably want to give your task a subject and a due date, so Outlook knows what to call it and where to put it on your To-Do List.

When you've filled out the relevant fields for your new task, click Save & Close (Alt, H, AV); that adds it to your To-Do List.

Creating a recurring task

Ever feel like you'll never cross everything off your list? It doesn't help that some tasks recur on a regular basis, like your daughter's weekly ballet class or a standing lunch date every other Wednesday. You want to keep these tasks on your To-Do List so they don't slip your mind, but it's a pain to enter the same task over and over again.

Outlook can't drive your little girl to ballet, but it can save you some time by putting recurring tasks on your To-Do List automatically, at an interval you specify. To set up a recurring task, create or open the task and click the Task tab's Recurrence button

(Alt, H, E). The dialog box that opens is similar to the Appointment Recurrence box (Figure 13-6), and it works the same way. Set the task's recurrence pattern and range (page 332 explains about those) and then click OK. Outlook keeps adding the task to your list for as long as you've specified.

Assigning a task

When you create a task, the real fun lies in passing it to somebody else. Of course, the person you assign a task to can always refuse it, but this feature is helpful for project managers, Big Cheeses, and others who delegate work.

To assign a task, start by pressing Ctrl+N or selecting Home→New Task (Alt, H, N1). When the Task window opens, click the Task tab's Assign Task button (Alt, H, B). The Task window changes, morphing the task you're creating into an email message. Fill in the email address of the person you're assigning the task to and take a look at these checkboxes (both are on by default):

- **Keep an updated copy of this task on my task list.** This option lets you track a task's progress as the person you assigned it to updates the task—just check your own Tasks list and To-Do List to see how it's going. If you don't want to keep tabs on the task, turn off this checkbox.

- **Send me a status report when this task is complete.** When the person doing the task crosses it off her list by marking it as completed, you get an email letting you know it's done. If you'd prefer not to get the status report, turn off the checkbox.

When you've created the task, click Send to email it to the person you assigned it to. If you told Outlook to keep a copy of the task on your Task list, it appears there as well. Tasks you've assigned to someone else have a special icon: a clipboard and a blue arrow pointing to a person (like the picture on the Assign Task button).

Note: Assigning a task transfers ownership of that task to the other person, so that person can overwrite any changes you make to the task.

Accepting a Task

The second way to put a task on your To-Do List is to accept a task that somebody else assigns to you. When someone does this, you get an email from that person with Task Request and the task's name in the Subject line. Inside the email are buttons labeled Accept and Decline, circled in Figure 13-10. Click Accept to add it to your To-Do List or Decline if you aren't willing and able.

Outlook sends an email to the person who assigned you the task, notifying him of your response.

Figure 13-10:
When someone as-
signs you a task, click
Accept to add the
Task to your To-Do
List or Decline to turn
it down.

Managing Tasks

Adding tasks to your To-Do List is the easy part—the hard part, of course, is getting them done. You've got to do the work yourself, but Outlook helps keep track of
your progress. You can edit a task to change its details or update its status, email it,
categorize it, add a custom flag, and more. And when you're done, you can cross it
off your list (that's the best part).

Editing a Task

By their very nature, tasks change. You make progress (or extend the due date if
not). Priority goes up or down. Maybe someone else offers to take on a task. You can
double-click the left-hand icon of any task on your To-Do List to open it, and then
make whatever changes you want. Here are some common changes you might make:

- **Rename a task.** You can open a task and type a new name in its Subject box.
  Even faster, right-click the task and select Rename Task from the shortcut menu;
  the task's name changes to a text box where you can type the new name.

- **Add notes.** If you get new information about a task or want to record something
  about its progress (notes summarizing a phone conversation, for example), type
  whatever you want in the Notes area.

- **Add details.** Plenty of people need to keep track of things like billable hours or
  mileage. In an open task, click the Task tab's Details button (Alt, H, L1) to record
  info in any of these fields: "Date completed", "Total work" (number of hours
  spent working for a given client), "Actual work" (time spent on this specific
  task), "Mileage", "Billing information", and "Company".

- **Change a task's status.** Making progress? Give yourself credit by reflecting how much you've accomplished in the task's Status and % Complete fields.

- **Send a status report.** When you've changed a task's status, you can update others by emailing a status report. On the Task tab, select Send Status Report (Alt, H, O1—that's the letter O, not a zero). A message window opens so you can send the new status to any interested parties (like your boss). Status reports automatically include the task's subject, as well as its current priority, due date, status, percent complete, and actual work info.

- **Change a task's start and due dates.** Schedules slip—it's a fact of business life. When a project's schedule changes, open the task and select a new due date and (if the task hasn't yet begun) a new start date.

- **Email a task.** To send someone an email message with the task as an attachment, select the task in the To-Do List or open it in its Task window, and then click Forward (Alt, H, FW). A message window opens, with the task already attached. Compose and address your email, and then click Send.

- **Assign the task to someone else.** During a busy week, the words "I'll do it" can be music to your harried ears. If someone steps forward to take on a task from your To-Do List, open the task and click the Assign Task button (Alt, H, B). Then follow the instructions for assigning a task on page 339.

- **Categorize a task.** You can do this either from the To-Do List or in an open Task window. From the To-Do List, select the task and click Home→Categorize (Alt, H, G), and then choose the category you want to assign. (Alternatively, you can right-click the task, choose Categorize from the shortcut menu, and assign a category from there.) If you've got the task open, select Task→Categorize (Alt, H, G) to assign a category.

Note: When you've assigned a task to a category, that category's color appears on your To-Do List to the right of the task name. For more about working with categories, see page 307.

- **Make a task recurring.** Maybe you attended a meeting you thought was a one-off, only to learn that you'd be meeting at the same time each week for the foreseeable future. In the Task window, click the Recurrence button (Alt, H, E) and fill out the Task Recurrence box's fields (they're just like the ones shown in Figure 13-6).

- **Delete a task.** As page 343 explains, you don't need to delete a task if you've marked it as completed—Outlook takes those tasks off your To-Do List automatically. But if there's a task that, for some reason, you no longer need to attend to—a meeting or dinner party gets canceled, for example—you can delete it. Select the item on your To-Do List or open it in a Task window, and then click Delete (Alt, H, D).

After you've made any of these changes, don't forget to click Save & Close (Alt, H, AV).

Flagging Tasks

Outlook automatically assigns a flag to each task, based on its due date. Flags are different shades of red, from bright crimson to pale pink: The redder the flag, the closer its due date. (One exception: If a task has no specific due date, Outlook still gives it a bright red flag.) You don't have to do a thing to manage your tasks' flags—Outlook assigns them and adjusts their color based on when each task is due.

Tip: Here's an easy way to change a task's due date. Select the task in the To-Do List and, in the Home tab's Follow Up section, select a flag, such as Today, Tomorrow, or No Date.

If you're flagging a task for a reason other than to keep an eye on its due date, you can create a *custom flag*. A custom flag adds a label to an item, such as Follow Up or Review (useful when you're emailing a task). You can apply custom flags to tasks, contacts, or email messages. Here's how:

1. **In your To-Do List, select a task and, in the Home tab's Follow Up section, click Custom (Alt, H, Q). If you have the task open in its Task window, click the Task tab's Follow Up button, and then choose Custom (Alt, H, W, C).**

    The Custom dialog box, shown in Figure 13-11, opens.

2. **Choose a reason for the flag from the "Flag to" drop-down list.**

    You can pick from a list of labels including Follow Up, Call, For Your Information, Read, Review, and so on.

3. **Select a start and due date for the flagged task. Click OK.**

    Outlook closes the Custom box and takes you to the item's Task window.

4. **Click Save & Close (Alt, H, AV).**

    Outlook saves your custom flag.

Now when you view the task in the Reading pane or in its Task window, it's flagged with the label you chose. If you selected Follow Up, for example, that label appears at the top of the task.

Figure 13-11:
Create a custom flag to add a wide variety of labels to a task.

Marking a Task as Completed

Few things in life are as satisfying as crossing a bunch of chores off your to-do list. When you've finished a task, select it in your Task folder's To-Do List and click the Home tab's Mark Complete button (Alt, H, C1). Outlook removes the item from your To-Do List and strikes it through on your Tasks list, placing a checkmark in the Flag Status column.

If you marked something as done by mistake, you can put it back on your To-Do List: Find the item in your Tasks list and click its far-left icon to select it. Click Mark Complete (Alt, H, C1) again. Outlook removes the strike-through formatting from the task and returns it to your To-Do List.

Viewing Tasks

As with all Outlook folders, you can change how your tasks look on the screen:

- To sort the items in your Tasks list, click any column header.
- To add columns to the Tasks list, click the View tab's Add Columns button (Alt, W, AC) to open the Show Columns dialog box. There, choose and arrange the columns you want to display.
- To group tasks by date, category, importance, type, and so on, select a grouping criterion from the View tab's Group gallery.

You can also click View→Change View (Alt, W, CV) to open a gallery of different views; what you select here shows only those tasks that match your selection. If deadlines are bearing down on you, you might pick Overdue or Today to focus only on what you need to do now. You can view tasks by their priority or get a preview of how the coming week looks by restricting your view to tasks due in the next seven days. Or if you need a sense of accomplishment, view only your Completed tasks.

Taking Notes in Outlook

Some people fill their world with sticky notes, jotting down thoughts, reminders, and musings and sticking them all over the office, the refrigerator, the bathroom mirror…. If you like using notes but would prefer not to live life covered with paper, you'll love Outlook Notes. Notes are a flexible tool for writing down whatever is on your mind so you can remember it later. There's no fancy formatting to mess around with—just a text area and the words you type, the virtual equivalent of a notepad and a pencil.

To open Outlook's Notes folder, shown in Figure 13-12, click the Notes button at the bottom of the Navigation pane or press Ctrl+5. Your notes appear in the Notes pane. In Figure 13-12, notes appear in Icon view, each note looking like a sticky note. Double-click any note to read it.

Notes button   Notes pane

Adding a Note

Creating a new note is as simple as opening the Notes folder and pressing Ctrl+N. (If
you prefer using the ribbon, select Home→New Note or press Alt, H, N). Outlook
opens a new note in its own window, as shown in Figure 13-13; start typing to create
your note. The first line you type becomes the note's name in the Notes pane, so start
off with something like "Grocery List" that will help you find the note later.

Tip: If the Note window feels a bit cramped for typing, you can expand it by clicking the lower-right
corner and dragging it to a more comfortable size.

When you're done typing, click the upper-right X to close the note. Outlook adds
your new note to the Notes pane.

Figure 13-13:
*When you create a new note, it opens in its
own small window. Type inside the window
to write the note; when you're finished,
click the upper-right X to close the note's
window.*

Working with Notes

After you've added a new note to your Notes folder, you can work with it in any of
these ways:

- **Read it.** Double-click a note to reopen it in its own window so you can read its
  full text.

- **Edit it.** Double-click the note. When it opens, click the part you want to edit
  and make your changes.

- **Copy it.** You can make an exact copy of a note by right-clicking it and selecting Copy from the shortcut menu. You can then paste the copy into the Notes
  pane, into another Office program, or onto your Desktop. Press Ctrl+V to paste
  the copied note into the location you want. A copy of a note is a separate entity
  from the original—any changes you make to the original won't affect the copy,
  and vice versa.

Tip: The fastest way to copy a note to the Desktop or another Office program is to click the note, drag it
to the window where you want the copy to appear, and drop it there.

- **Categorize it.** You can assign notes to a category, just like any other Outlook
  item. Select a note and, on the Home tab, click Categorize (Alt, H, G) to pick the
  category you want for the item. See page 307 for more about using categories to
  organize Outlook items.

Note: When you assign a note to a category, the note's icon becomes the color of that category.

- **Email it.** When you email someone a note, Outlook sends it as an attachment. Click a note to select it, and then choose Home→Forward (Alt, H, FW). Outlook opens a message window with the note already attached; the name of your note serves as the subject line. Type in an address, type something in the body of the email if you like, and send your message—along with the note—to the recipient.

- **Print it.** The fastest way to print a note is to right-click it and select Quick Print—Outlook immediately sends the note to your default printer. If you need to choose a different printer or set print options (like specifying a number of copies), select File→Print (Alt, F, P) and make your selections on the Backstage Print Settings page.

- **Delete it.** When you're done with a note, remove it from your Notes pane by selecting it and clicking Home→Delete (Alt, H, D). If you made a mistake and deleted the wrong note, click the Quick Access Toolbar's Undo button (Alt, 2) to bring it back.

Viewing Notes

Whether you write only an occasional note or clutter up the Notes pane with several books' worth of jottings, it's easy to arrange your notes and find the one you're looking for. Use the Home tab's View gallery or the View tab's Change View button (Alt, W, CV) to select a view for your notes. Outlook has three built-in options: Icon, Notes List, or Last 7 Days. The sections that follow describe each view.

Icon view

Icon view shows your notes as sticky-note icons. One advantage to this view is that you can drag the icons around and place them wherever you want in the Notes pane—helpful when you want to group related notes together.

In Icon view, Outlook offers three ways to arrange your notes (all in the View tab's Arrangement section):

- **Large Icons (Alt, W, L).** This is Outlook's default setting for displaying notes—you can see an example in Figure 13-12. The icons appear as eye-catching squares, with the text underneath.

- **Small Icons (Alt, W, S).** This option shrinks the icons, and the text for each note appears to the right of the icon.

- **List (Alt, W, T).** This option displays notes with small icons and lines them up in a list. Unlike the other two options, List doesn't let you drag icons to reposition them.

Tip: If you've been dragging notes around and want them all lined up nice and pretty again, select View→Line Up Icons (Alt, W, I).

Notes List view

This view displays the notes in a list, as shown in Figure 13-14. Each note takes up two or more lines in the list: You see the name of the note and a preview of its text. Notes List view makes it faster to find the note you're looking for, because you get a sneak peek at each note's contents. Another advantage of this view is that you can sort the list by clicking any column header to sort by subject, date created, or category.

Tip: To add columns to Notes List view, select View→Add Columns (Alt, W, AC) to open the Show Columns dialog box. There, select "All Note fields" from the drop-down list. Select a field from the "Available columns" list and click Add to display it in your list. Click OK when you're done.

In Notes List view, you can group similar notes by date, category, or date—go to the View tab's Group gallery to choose.

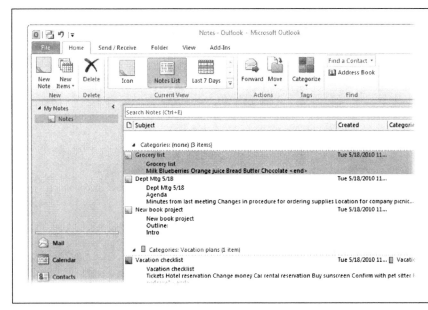

Figure 13-14:
When you look at your notes in Notes List view, you get a preview of each note's contents. Click any column header to sort the notes.

Last 7 Days view

This view is identical to Notes List view, except it displays notes from the past week, rather than all your notes. Sort and group notes in this view in the same way you would in Notes List view.

Part Three: Excel

3

Creating Your First Spreadsheet

Every Excel grandmaster needs to start somewhere. In this chapter, you'll learn how to create a basic spreadsheet.

First, you'll learn to move around Excel's grid of cells, typing in numbers and text as you go. Next, you'll take a quick tour of the Excel window, stopping to meet the different tabs in the ribbon and take a quick peek at the formula bar. Finally, you'll get a tour of Excel's innovative *Backstage view*—the file-management hub where you can print your creations, save your work for posterity, open recent files, and tweak Excel options.

Note: Even if you're an Excel old-timer, don't bypass this chapter. Although you already know how to fill in a simple spreadsheet, you haven't seen Excel's Backstage view, which is a completely new feature in Excel 2010. It gives you a single, streamlined place to perform a whole variety of tasks, most of which have to do with managing your files.

Creating a Basic Worksheet

When you first launch Excel, it starts you off with a new, blank *worksheet*, as shown in Figure 14-1. A worksheet is the grid of cells where you type your information and formulas. This grid takes up most of the Excel window. It's where you'll perform all your work, such as entering data, writing formulas, and reviewing the results.

Here are a few basics about Excel's grid:

- **The grid divides your worksheet into rows and columns.** Columns are identified with letters (A, B, C…), while rows are identified with numbers (1, 2, 3…).

- **The smallest unit in your worksheet is the** *cell*. Cells are identified by column and row. For example, C6 is the address of a cell in column C (the third column) and row 6 (the sixth row). Figure 14-2 shows this cell, which looks like a rectangular box. Incidentally, an Excel cell can hold up to 32,000 characters.

- **A worksheet can span an eye-popping 16,000 columns and 1 million rows**. In the unlikely case that you want to go beyond those limits—say you're tracking blades of grass on the White House lawn—you'll need to create a new worksheet. Every spreadsheet file can hold a virtually unlimited number of worksheets.

- **When you enter information, you enter it one cell at a time**. However, you don't have to follow any set order. For example, you can start by typing information into cell A40 without worrying about filling any data in the cells that appear in the earlier rows.

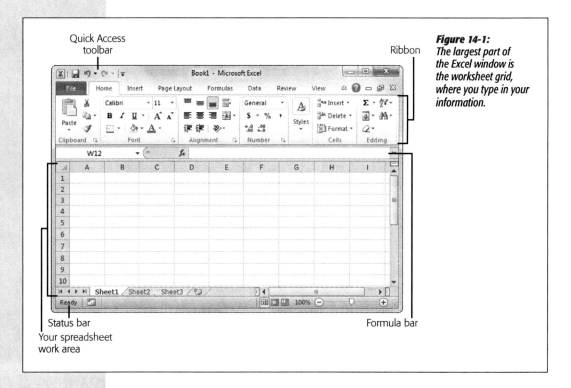

Figure 14-1:
The largest part of the Excel window is the worksheet grid, where you type in your information.

Quick Access toolbar

Ribbon

Status bar

Formula bar

Your spreadsheet work area

Note: Obviously, once you go beyond 26 columns, you run out of letters. Excel handles this by doubling up (and then tripling up) letters. For example, column Z is followed by column AA, then AB, then AC, all the way to AZ and then BA, BB, BC—you get the picture. And if you create a ridiculously large worksheet, you'll find that column ZZ is followed by AAA, AAB, AAC, and so on.

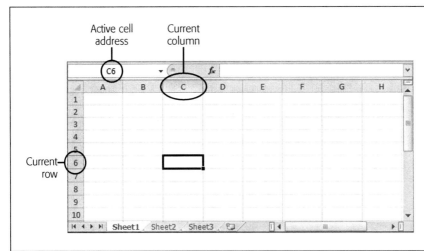

Active cell address

Current column

Current row

C6

A B C D E F G H

1
2
3
4
5
6
7
8
9
10

Sheet1 Sheet2 Sheet3

Figure 14-2:
Here, the current cell is C6. You can recognize the current (or active) cell based on its heavy black border. You'll also notice that the corresponding column letter (C) and row number (6) are high-lighted at the edges of the worksheet. Just above the worksheet, on the left side of the window, the formula bar tells you the active cell address.

The best way to get a feel for Excel is to dive right in and start putting together a worksheet. The following sections cover each step that goes into assembling a simple worksheet. This one tracks household expenses, but you can use the same approach to create any basic worksheet.

Starting a New Workbook

When you fire up Excel, it opens a fresh workbook file. If you've already got Excel open and want to create *another* workbook, just choose File→New. You'll see a variety of options for creating specialized types of spreadsheets. But to get started with a blank canvas, keep "Blank workbook" selected and click the Create button, as shown Figure 14-3.

Note: A workbook is a collection of one or more worksheets. That distinction isn't terribly important now because you're using only a single worksheet in each workbook you create. For now, all you need to know is that the worksheet is the grid of cells where you place your data, and the workbook is the spreadsheet file that you save on your computer.

You don't need to pick the file name for your workbook when you first create it. Instead, that decision happens later, when you *save* your workbook (page 369). For now, you start with a blank canvas that's ready to receive your numerical insights.

Note: Creating new workbooks doesn't disturb what you've already done. Whatever workbook you were using remains open in another window. You can use the taskbar to move from one workbook to the other.

Figure 14-3:
Excel lets you create a new, blank workbook or a ready-made workbook from a template—just like the ones you learned about for Word back in Chapter 7. For now, choose "Blank workbook" and then click the big Create button in the bottom-right corner.

Adding the Column Titles

Excel allows you to arrange information in whatever way you like. There's nothing to stop you from scattering numbers left and right, across as many cells as you can. However, one of the most common (and most useful) ways to arrange your information is as a table, with headings for each column.

It's important to remember that even for the simplest worksheet, the decisions you make about what's going to go in each column can have a big effect on how easy it is to manipulate your information. For example, in a worksheet that stores a mailing list, you *could* have two columns: one for names and another for addresses. But if you create more than two columns, your life will probably be easier since you can separate first names from street addresses from Zip codes, and so on. Figure 14-4 shows the difference.

You can, of course, always add or remove columns later. But you can avoid getting gray hairs by starting a worksheet with all the columns you think you'll need.

The first step in creating your worksheet is to add your headings in the row of cells at the top of the worksheet (row 1). Technically, you don't need to start right in the first row, but unless you want to add more information before your table—like a title for the chart or today's date—there's no point in wasting the space. Adding information is easy—just click the cell you want and start typing. When you're finished, hit Tab to complete your entry and move to the next cell to the right (or Enter to head to the cell just underneath).

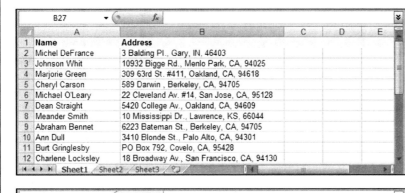

Figure 14-4:
Top: If you enter the first and last names together in one column, Excel can sort only by the first names. And if you clump the addresses and Zip codes together, you give Excel no way to count how many people live in a certain town or neighborhood because Excel can't extract the Zip codes.

Bottom: The benefit of a six-column table is significant: It lets you sort (reorganize) your list according to people's last names or where they live. It also allows you to filter out individual bits of information when you start using functions later in this book.

Note: The information you put in an Excel worksheet doesn't need to be in neat, ordered columns. Nothing stops you from scattering numbers and text in random cells. However, most Excel worksheets resemble some sort of table, because that's the easiest and most effective way to deal with large amounts of structured information.

For a simple expense worksheet designed to keep a record of your most prudent and extravagant purchases, try the following three headings:

- **Date Purchased** stores the date when you spent the money.

- **Item** stores the name of the product that you bought.

- **Price** records how much it cost.

Right away, you face your first glitch: awkwardly crowded text. Figure 14-5 shows how you can adjust column width for proper breathing room.

Figure 14-5:
Top: The standard width of an Excel column is 8.43 characters, which hardly allows you to get a word in edgewise. To solve this problem, position your mouse on the right border of the column header you want to expand so that the mouse pointer changes to the resize icon (it looks like a double-headed arrow). Now drag the column border to the right as far as you want. As you drag, a tooltip appears, telling you the character size and pixel width of the column. Both of these pieces of information play the same role—they tell you how wide the column is—only the unit of measurement changes.

Bottom: When you release the mouse, the entire column of cells is resized to the new width.

Note: A column's character width doesn't really reflect how many characters (or letters) fit in a cell. Excel uses *proportional* fonts, in which different letters take up different amounts of room. For example, the letter W is typically much wider than the letter 1. All this means is that the character width Excel shows you isn't a real indication of how many letters can fit in the column, but it's still a useful measurement that you can use to compare different columns.

Adding Data

You can now begin adding your data: simply fill in the rows under the column titles. Each row in the expense worksheet represents a separate purchase you've made. (If you're familiar with databases, you can think of each row as a separate record.)

As Figure 14-6 shows, the first column is for dates, the second column is for text, and the third column holds numbers. Keep in mind that Excel doesn't impose any rules on what you type, so you're free to put text in the Price column. But if you don't keep a consistent kind of data in each column, you won't be able to easily analyze (or understand) your information later.

	A	B	C	D	E	F	
1	Date Purchased	Item	Price				
2	7/7/2007	Cowbell	$43.99				
3	7/7/2007	Fresh Fruit	$3.00				
4	7/10/2007	IBM Laptop	$750.00				
5							
6							
7							
8							

Sheet1   Sheet2   Sheet3

Figure 14-6:
This rudimentary expense list has three items (in rows 2, 3, and 4). The alignment of each column reflects the data type (by default, numbers and dates are right-aligned, while text is left-aligned), indicating that Excel understands your date and price information.

That's it. You've now created a living, breathing worksheet. The next section explains how you can edit the data you've entered.

Editing Data

Every time you start typing in a cell, Excel erases any existing content in that cell. (You can also quickly remove the contents of a cell by just moving to it and pressing Delete, which clears its contents.)

If you want to edit cell data instead of replacing it, you need to put the cell in *edit mode*, like this:

1. **Move to the cell you want to edit.**

   Use the mouse or the arrow keys to get to the correct cell.

2. **Put the cell in edit mode by pressing F2.**

   Edit mode looks almost the same as ordinary text entry mode. The only difference is that you can use the arrow keys to move through the text you're typing and make changes. (When you aren't in edit mode, pressing these keys just moves you to another cell.) If you don't want to use F2, you can also get a cell into edit mode by double-clicking it.

3. **Complete your edit.**

   Once you've modified the cell content, press Enter to make your change or Esc to cancel your edit and leave the old value in the cell. Alternatively, you can click on another cell to accept the current value and go somewhere else. But while you're in edit mode, you can't use the arrow keys to move out of the cell.

Tip: If you start typing new information into a cell and decide you want to move to an earlier position in your entry (to make an alteration, for instance), just press F2. The cell box still looks the same, but you're now in edit mode, which means that you can use the arrow keys to move within the cell (instead of moving from cell to cell). You can press F2 again to return to the normal data entry mode, which allows you to use the arrow keys to move to another cell.

As you enter data, you may discover the Bigtime Excel Display Problem (known to aficionados as BEDP): Cells in adjacent columns can overlap one another. Figure 14-7 shows the problem. One way to fix BEDP is to manually resize the column, as shown in Figure 14-5. Another option is to use wrapping to fit multiple lines of text in a single cell, as described on page 453.

Figure 14-7:
Overlapping cells can create big headaches. For example, if you type a large amount of text into A1, and then you type some text into B1, you see only part of the data in A1 on your worksheet (as shown here). The rest is hidden from view. But if, say, A3 contains a large amount of text and B3 is empty, the content in A3 is displayed over both columns, and you don't have a problem.

Moving Around the Grid

Learning how to move around the Excel grid quickly and confidently is an indispensable skill. To move from cell to cell, you have two fairly obvious choices:

- **Use the arrow keys on the keyboard**. Keystrokes move you one cell at a time in any direction.

- **Click the cell with the mouse**. A mouse click jumps you directly to the cell you've clicked.

As you move from cell to cell, you see the black focus box move to highlight the currently active cell.

In some cases, you might want to cover ground a little quicker. One option is to use the scrollbars at the bottom and on the right side of the window to scroll off into the uncharted regions of your worksheet. Excel also provides two more powerful features—shortcut keys and the Go To feature—which are described in the following sections.

Shortcut Keys

Excel provides a number of handy key combinations that can transport you across your worksheet in great leaps and bounds (see Table 14-1). The most useful shortcut keys include the Home key combinations, which bring you back to the beginning of a row or the top of your worksheet.

Note: Shortcut key combinations that use the + sign must be entered together. For example, "Ctrl+Home" means you hold down Ctrl and press Home at the same time. Key combinations with a comma work in sequence. For example, the key combination "End, Home" means press End first, release it, and then press Home.

Table 14-1. *Shortcut keys for moving around a worksheet*

Key Combination	Result
→ (or Tab)	Moves one cell to the right.
← (or Shift+Tab)	Moves one cell to the left.
↑	Moves one cell up.
↓ (or Enter)	Moves one cell down.
Page Up	Moves up one screen. Thus, if the grid shows 10 cells at a time, this key moves to a cell in the same column, 10 rows up (unless you are already at the top of the worksheet).
Page Down	Moves down one screen. Thus, if the grid shows 10 cells at a time, this key moves to a cell in the same column, 10 rows down.
Home	Moves to the first cell (column A) of the current row.
Ctrl+Home	Moves to the first cell in the top row, which is A1.
Ctrl+End (or End, Home)	Moves to the last column of the last occupied row. This cell is at the bottom-right edge of your data.

Excel also lets you cross great distances in a single bound using a *Ctrl+arrow* key combination. These key combinations jump to the *edges* of your data. Edge cells include cells that are next to other blank cells. For example, if you press Ctrl+→ while you're inside a group of cells with information in them, you'll skip to the right, over all filled cells, and stop just before the next blank cell. If you press Ctrl+→ again, you'll skip over all the nearby blank cells and land in the next cell to the right that has information in it. If there aren't any more cells with data on the right, you'll wind up on the very edge of your worksheet.

The *Ctrl+arrow key* combinations are useful if you have more than one table of data in the same worksheet. For example, imagine you have two tables of data, one at the top of a worksheet and one at the bottom. If you are at the top of the first table, you can use Ctrl+→ to jump to the bottom of the first table, skipping all the rows in between. Press Ctrl+→ again, and you leap over all the blank rows, winding up at the beginning of the second table.

The Go To Feature

If you're fortunate enough to know exactly where you need to go, you can use the Go To feature to make the jump. Go To moves to the cell address you specify. It comes in useful in extremely large spreadsheets, where just scrolling through the worksheet takes half a day.

To bring up the Go To dialog box (shown in Figure 14-8), choose Home→Editing→ Find & Select→Go To. Or you can do yourself a favor and just press Ctrl+G. Enter the cell address (such as C32), and then click OK.

Figure 14-8:
You'll notice that in the Go To list, cell addresses are written a little differently than the format you use when you type them in. Namely, dollar signs are added before the row number and column letter. Thus, C32 becomes $C$32, which is simply the convention that Excel uses for fixed cell references. (You'll learn much more about the different types of cell references in Chapter 17.)

The Go To feature becomes more useful the more you use it. That's because the Go To window maintains a list of the most recent cell addresses that you've entered. In addition, every time you open the Go To window, Excel automatically adds the current cell to the list. This feature makes it easy to jump to a far-off cell and quickly return to your starting location by selecting the last entry in the list.

The Go To window isn't your only option for leaping through a worksheet in a single bound. If you look at the Home→Editing→Find & Select menu, you'll find more specialized commands that let you jump straight to cells that contains formulas, comments, conditional formatting, and other advanced Excel ingredients that you haven't learned about yet. And if you want to hunt down cells that have specific text, you need the popular Find command (Home→Editing→Find & Select→Find).

A Tour of the Excel Window

Finding your way around a worksheet is a fundamental part of mastering Excel. Knowing your way around the larger program window is no less important. The next few sections help you get oriented in the Excel window, pointing out the important stuff and letting you know what you can usually ignore.

The Tabs of the Ribbon

Back in Chapter 1, you learned about the ribbon, the super-toolbar that offers one-stop shopping for all of Word's features. Turns out, all the most important Office applications—including Access, PowerPoint, and Excel—use the ribbon. However, each program has a different set of tabs and buttons.

Throughout the Excel portion of this book, you'll dig through the different tabs of the ribbon to find important features. But before you start your journey, it's nice to get a quick overview of what each tab provides. Here's the lowdown:

- **File** isn't really a toolbar tab, even though it appears first in the list. Instead, it's your gateway to Excel's Backstage view, as described on page 367.

- **Home** includes some of the most commonly used buttons, like those for cutting and pasting information, formatting your data, and hunting down important bits of information with search tools.

- **Insert** lets you add special ingredients like tables, graphics, charts, and hyperlinks.

- **Page Layout** is all about getting your worksheet ready for the printer. You can tweak margins, paper orientation, and other page settings.

- **Formulas** are mathematical instructions that you use to perform calculations. This tab helps you build super-smart formulas and resolve mind-bending errors.

- **Data** lets you get information from an outside data source (like a heavy-duty database) so you can analyze it in Excel. It also includes tools for dealing with large amounts of information, like sorting, filtering, and subgrouping.

- **Review** includes the familiar Office proofing tools (like the spell checker). It also has buttons that let you add comments to a worksheet and manage revisions.

- **View** lets you switch on and off a variety of viewing options. It also lets you pull off a few fancy tricks if you want to view several separate Excel spreadsheet files at the same time.

Note: In some circumstances, you may see tabs that aren't listed here. Macro programmers and other highly technical types use the Developer tab. The Add-Ins tab appears when you're viewing workbooks that were created in previous versions of Excel and used custom toolbars.

GEM IN THE ROUGH

Collapsing the Ribbon

Most people are happy to have the ribbon sit at the top of the Excel window, with all its buttons on hand. However, serious number crunchers demand maximum space for their data. They'd rather look at another row of numbers than a pumped-up toolbar. If this describes you, then you'll be happy to find out you can *collapse* the ribbon, which shrinks it down to a single row of tab titles, as shown Figure 14-9. To collapse it, just double-click any tab title. (Or, you can click the tiny up-pointing icon that appears in the top-right corner of the ribbon, right next to the help icon.)

Even when the ribbon is collapsed, you can still use all its features. All you need to do is click a tab. For example, if you click Home, the Home tab pops up over your worksheet.

As soon as you click the button you want in the Home tab (or click a cell in your worksheet), the ribbon collapses itself again. The same trick works if you trigger a command in the ribbon using the keyboard.

If you use the ribbon only occasionally, or if you prefer to use keyboard shortcuts, it makes sense to collapse the ribbon. Even when collapsed, the ribbon commands are available—it just takes an extra click to open the tab. On the other hand, if you make frequent trips to the ribbon or you're learning about Excel and like to browse the ribbon to see what features are available, don't bother collapsing it. The two or three rows that you'll lose are well worth it.

Figure 14-9:
Do you want to use every square inch of screen space for your cells? You can collapse the ribbon (as shown here) by double-clicking any tab. Click a tab to pop it open temporarily, or double-click a tab to bring the ribbon back for good. And if you want to perform the same trick without raising your fingers from the keyboard, you can use the shortcut key Ctrl+F1.

The Formula Bar

The *formula bar* appears above the worksheet grid but below the ribbon (Figure 14-10). It displays the address of the active cell (like A1) on the left edge, and it also shows you the current cell's contents.

Figure 14-10:
The formula bar (just above the grid) shows information about the active cell. In this example, the formula bar shows that the current cell is B4 and that it contains the number 592. Instead of editing this value in the worksheet, you can click anywhere in the formula bar and make your changes there.

You can use the formula bar to enter and edit data, instead of editing directly in your worksheet. This approach is particularly useful when a cell contains a formula or a large amount of information. That's because the formula bar gives you more work room than a typical cell. Just as with in-cell edits, you press Enter to confirm your changes or Esc to cancel them. Or you can use the mouse: When you start tying in the formula bar, a checkmark and an "X" icon appear just to the left of the box where you're typing. Click the checkmark to confirm your entry or "X" to roll it back.

Note: You can hide (or show) the formula bar by choosing View→Show→Formula Bar. But the formula bar is such a basic part of Excel that you'd be unwise to get rid of it. Instead, keep it around until Chapter 17, when you'll learn how to build formulas.

Ordinarily, the formula bar is a single line. If you have a *really* long entry in a cell (like a paragraph's worth of text), you need to scroll from one side to the other. However, there's another option—you can resize the formula bar so it fits more information, as shown in Figure 14-11.

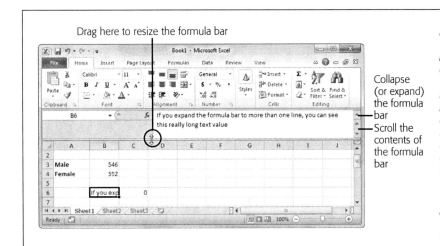

Drag here to resize the formula bar

Collapse (or expand) the formula bar

Scroll the contents of the formula bar

Figure 14-11:
To enlarge the formula bar, click the bottom edge and pull down. You can make it two, three, four, or many more lines large. Best of all, once you get the size you want, you can use the expand/collapse button on the right side of the formula bar to quickly expand it to your preferred size and collapse it back to the single-line view.

The Status Bar

Though people often overlook it, the status bar (Figure 14-12) is a good way to keep on top of Excel's current state. For example, if you save or print a document, the status bar shows the progress of the printing process. If you're performing a quick action, the progress indicator may disappear before you have a chance to even notice it. But if you're performing a time-consuming operation—say, printing out an 87-page table of the airline silverware you happen to own—you can look to the status bar to see how things are coming along.

Figure 14-12:
In the status bar, you can see the basic status text (which just says "Ready" in this example), the view buttons (which are useful when you're preparing a spreadsheet for printing), and the zoom slider bar (which lets you enlarge or shrink the current worksheet view).

The status bar combines several different types of information. The leftmost part of the status bar shows the Cell Mode, which displays one of three indicators:

- The word "Ready" means that Excel isn't doing anything much at the moment, other than waiting for you to take some action.

- The word "Enter" appears when you start typing a new value into a cell.

- The word "Edit" means the cell is currently in edit mode, and pressing the left and right arrow keys moves through the cell data, instead of moving from cell to cell. As discussed on page 357, you can place a cell in edit mode or take it out of edit mode by pressing F2.

Just to the right of the Cell Mode information, you may see a small button that lets you start recording a macro. (A *macro* is a series of steps you can replay as often as you need to automate tiresome chores; they're typically created by Excel jockeys who, for example, design corporate expense report forms.)

Farther to the right on the status bar are the view buttons, which let you switch to Page Layout View or Page Break Preview. These different views help you see what your worksheet will look like when you print it. They're covered later in this chapter, starting on page 403.

The zoom slider is next to the view buttons, at the far right edge of the status bar. You can slide it to the left to zoom out (which fits more information into your Excel window at once) or slide it to the right to zoom in (and take a closer look at fewer cells).

In addition, the status bar displays other miscellaneous indicators. For example, if you press the Scroll Lock key, a Scroll Lock indicator appears on the status bar (next to the "Ready" text). This indicator tells you that you're in *scroll mode*. In scroll mode, the arrow keys don't move you from one cell to another; instead, they scroll the entire worksheet up, down, or to the side. Scroll mode is a great way to check out another part of your spreadsheet without leaving your current position.

You can control what indicators appear in the status bar by configuring it. To see a full list of possibilities, right-click the status bar. A huge list of options appears, as shown in Figure 14-13. Table 14-2 describes the different status bar options.

Note: The Caps Lock indicator doesn't determine whether or not you can use the Caps Lock key—that feature always works. The Caps Lock indicator just lets you know when Caps Lock mode is on. That way you won't be surprised by an accidental keystroke that turns your next data entry INTO ALL CAPITALS.

Figure 14-13:
Every item that has a checkmark appears in the status bar when you need it. For example, if you choose Caps Lock, the text "Caps Lock" appears in the status bar whenever you hit the Caps Lock key to switch to all-capital typing. The text that appears on the right side of the list tells you the current value of the indicator. In this example, Caps Lock mode is currently off and the Cell Mode text says "Ready."

Table 14-2. *Status bar indicators*

Indicator	Meaning
Cell Mode	Shows Ready, Edit, or Enter depending on the state of the current cell, as described on page 364.
Signatures, Information Management Policy, and Permissions	Displays information about the rights and restrictions of the current spreadsheet. These features come into play only if you're using Office SharePoint Server to share spreadsheets among groups of people (usually in a corporate environment).

Caps Lock	Indicates whether Caps Lock mode is on. When Caps Lock is on, every letter you type is automatically capitalized. To turn Caps Lock mode on or off, hit Caps Lock.
Num Lock	Indicates whether Num Lock mode is on. When this mode is on, you can use the numeric keypad (typically at the right side of your keyboard) to type in numbers more quickly. When this sign's off, the numeric keypad controls cell navigation instead. To turn Num Lock on or off, press Num Lock.
Scroll Lock	Indicates whether Scroll Lock mode is on. When it's on, you can use the arrow keys to scroll through the worksheet without changing the active cell. (In other words, you can control your scrollbars by just using your keyboard.) This feature lets you look at all the information you have in your worksheet without losing track of the cell you're currently in. You can turn Scroll Lock mode on or off by pressing Scroll Lock.
Fixed Decimal	Indicates when Fixed Decimal mode is on. When this mode is on, Excel automatically adds a set number of decimal places to the values you enter in any cell. For example, if you set Excel to use two fixed decimal places and you type the number 5 into a cell, Excel actually enters 0.05. This seldom-used featured is handy for speed typists who need to enter reams of data in a fixed format. You can turn this feature on or off by selecting File→Options, choosing the Advanced section, and then looking under "Editing options" to find the "Automatically insert a decimal point" setting. Once you turn this checkbox on, you can choose the number of decimal places (the standard option is two).
Overtype Mode	Indicates when Overwrite mode is turned on. Overwrite mode changes how cell edits work. When you edit a cell and Overwrite mode is on, the new characters that you type overwrite existing characters (rather than displacing them). You can turn Overwrite mode on or off by pressing Insert.
End Mode	Indicates that you've pressed End, which is the first key in many two-key combinations; the next key determines what happens. For example, hit End and then Home to move to the bottom-right cell in your worksheet. See Table Table 14-1 for a list of key combinations, some of which use End.
Macro Recording	Macros are automated routines that perform some task in an Excel spreadsheet. The Macro Recording indicator shows a record button (which looks like a red circle superimposed on a worksheet) that lets you start recording a new macro.
Selection Mode	Indicates the current Selection mode. You have two options: normal mode and *extended selection*. When you press the arrows keys and extended selection is on, Excel automatically selects all the rows and columns you cross. Extended selection is a useful keyboard alternative to dragging your mouse to select swaths of the grid. To turn extended selection on or off, press F8.
Page Number	Shows the current page and the total number of pages (as in "Page 1 of 4"). This indicator appears only in Page Layout view (as described on page 403).

Average, Count, Numerical Count, Minimum, Maximum, Sum	Show the result of a calculation on the selected cells. For example, the Sum indicator shows the total of all the numeric cells that are currently selected.
Upload Status	Does nothing (that we know of). Excel does show a handy indicator in the status bar when you're uploading files to the Web. However, the upload status is always shown, and this setting doesn't seem to have any effect.
View Shortcuts	Shows the three view buttons that let you switch between Normal view, Page Layout View (page 403), and Page Break Preview (page 411).
Zoom	Shows the current zoom percentage (like 100 percent for a normal-sized spreadsheet, and 200 percent for a spreadsheet that's blown up to twice the magnification).
Zoom Slider	Shows a slider that lets you zoom in closer (by sliding it to the right) or out to see more information at once (by sliding it to the left).

Going Backstage

Your data is the star of the show. That's why the creators of Excel refer to your worksheet as being "on stage." The auditorium is the Excel main window, which—as you've just seen—includes the handy ribbon, formula bar, and status bar. Sure, it's a strange metaphor. But once you understand it, you'll realize the rationale for Excel's *Backstage view*, which temporarily takes you away from your worksheet and lets you concentrate on other tasks that don't involve entering or editing data. These tasks include saving your spreadsheet, opening more spreadsheets, printing your work, and changing Excel settings.

To switch to Backstage view, click the File button that's just to the left of the Home ribbon tab. Excel temporarily tucks your worksheet out of sight (although it's still open and waiting for you). This gives it space to show extra information related to the task you want to perform, as shown in Figure 14-14. For example, if you plan to print your spreadsheet, Excel's Backstage view has room to show a preview of the printout. Or if you want to open an existing spreadsheet, Excel can show a detailed list of files you've recently worked on.

To get out of Backstage view and return to your worksheet, just click the File button again, or press Esc.

Excel Options

The Excel Options window provides a central hub where you can adjust how Excel looks, behaves, and calculates (see Figure 14-15). To get to this window, choose File→Options.

Figure 14-14:
When you first switch to Backstage view, Excel shows the Info page, which provides some basic information about your workbook file, its size, when it was last edited, who edited it, and so on (see the column on the far right). The Info page also provides the gateway to important features like compatibility checking (page 373) and AutoRecover backups (page 380). To go to another section, click a different command in the column on the far left.

Figure 14-15:
The Excel Options window is divided into 10 sections. To pick which section to look at, choose an entry from the list on the left. In this example, you're looking at the General settings group. In each section, the settings are further subdivided into titled groups. You may need to scroll down to find the setting you want.

The various sections in the Excel Options window let you tweak a wide variety of different details. Some of these details are truly handy, like the options for opening and saving files (which are described at the end of this chapter). Others are seldom-used holdovers from the past, like the option that lets Excel act like Lotus—an ancient piece of spreadsheet software—when you hit the / key.

Tip: Some important options have a small i-in-a-circle icon next to them, which stands for "information." Hover over this icon, and you see a tooltip that gives you a brief description about that setting.

While you're getting to know Excel, you can comfortably ignore most of what's in the Excel Options window. Later on, though, you might want to return to adjust these settings and fine-tune the way Excel works.

Saving Files

As everyone who's been alive for at least three days knows, you should save your work early and often. Excel is no exception. You have two choices for saving a spreadsheet file:

- **Save As**. This choice allows you to save your spreadsheet file with a new name. You can use Save As the first time you save a new spreadsheet, or you can use it to save a copy of your current spreadsheet with a new name, in a new folder, or as a different file type. (Alternate file formats are discussed starting on page 374.) To use Save As, select File→Save As, or press F12.

- **Save & Send**. The File→Save & Send page in Excel's backstage view provides several of the same options you get from the Save As dialog box. The difference is that it makes them a bit more convenient. Figure 14-16 shows what to look for.

- **Save**. This option updates the spreadsheet file with your most recent changes. If you use Save on a new file that hasn't been saved before, it has the same effect as Save As: Excel prompts you to choose a folder and file name. To use Save, select File→Save, or press Ctrl+S. Or look up at the top of the Excel window in the Quick Access toolbar for the tiny Save button, which looks like an old-style diskette.

Tip: Resaving a spreadsheet is an almost instantaneous operation, and you should get used to doing it regularly. After you've made any significant change, just hit Ctrl+S to make sure you've stored the latest version of your data.

Figure 14-16:
Using File→Save & Send, you can email a copy of your workbook , transfer it to the Excel Web App (page 867), or upload it to SharePoint (page 219). But ignore these options for now and focus on the File Types section, which gives you shortcuts for saving your work in alternative file formats. If you click Change File Type, you get a list with the most common file formats (on the right). Double-click an entry to open the Save As dialog box with that selection.

The Excel File Format

Since time immemorial, Excel fans have been saving their lovingly crafted spreadsheets in *.xls* files (as in *AirlineSilverware.xls*). But when Excel 2007 hit the streets, it introduced a completely new file format, with the extension *.xlsx* (as in *AirlineSilverware.xlsx*). Excel 2010 keeps the *.xlsx* revamped format, without introducing any more changes.

As an Excel user, you need to decide whether you want to save your spreadsheets in the latest and greatest *.xlsx* format or in the older *.xls* format. But before you make that decision, it helps to know a bit more about the advantages of the .xlsx format:

- **It's compact**. The .xlsx format uses Zip file compression, so spreadsheet files are smaller—way smaller (as much as 75 percent smaller than their original sizes). And even though the average hard drive is already large enough to swallow thousands of old-fashioned Excel files, the new compact format is easier to email around.

- **It's less error-prone**. The .xlsx format carefully separates ordinary content, pictures, and macro code into separate sections. Microsoft claims that this change makes for tougher files. Now, if a part of your Excel file is damaged (for example, due to a faulty hard drive), there's a much better chance that you can still retrieve the rest of the information. (You'll learn about Excel disaster recovery on page 380.)

- **It's extensible.** The .xlsx format uses XML (the eXtensible Markup Language), which is a standardized way to store information. XML storage doesn't benefit the average person, but it's sure to earn a lot of love from companies that plan to build custom software that uses Excel documents. As long as Excel documents are stored in XML, these companies can create automated programs that pull the information they need straight out of a spreadsheet, without going through Excel. These programs can also generate made-to-measure Excel documents all on their own.

For all these reasons, .xlsx is the format of choice for Excel 2010. However, Microsoft prefers to give people all the choices they could ever need (rather than make life really simple), and Excel file formats are no exception. In fact, the .xlsx file format actually has *two* additional flavors.

First, there's the closely related .xls*m* cousin, which adds the ability to store macro code. If you've added any macros to your spreadsheet, Excel prompts you to use this file type when you save your spreadsheet.

Second, there's the optimized .xls*b* format, which is a specialized option that just might be faster when you're opening and saving gargantuan spreadsheets. The .xlsb format has the same automatic compression and error-resistance as .xlsx, but it doesn't use XML. Instead, it stores information in raw *binary* form (good ol' ones and zeroes), which is speedier in some situations. To use the .xlsb format, choose File→Save As, and then, from the "Save as type" list, choose Excel Binary Workbook (.xlsb).

POWER USERS' CLINIC

Under the Hood with .xlsx Files

Here's a shocking secret: The new .xlsx file format is actually a Zip file in disguise. It's composed of several files that are compressed and then packaged together as a single unit. With a little know-how, you can take a look at these hidden files-within-a-file, which makes for a great Excel party trick. Here's how:

1. Save your Excel spreadsheet in .xlsx format.

2. Browse to the file (using My Computer, Windows Explorer, or your favorite file management tool). If you're lazy, you can save the file on the desktop so you can manipulate it right there.

3. Right-click the file, and then choose Rename.

4. Change the file extension to .zip. So if you start with BlackMarketDinnerware.xlsx, change it to BlackMarketDinnerware.zip.

5. Now, open the Zip file by double-clicking the file.

6. You can now see the files that are hidden inside your Excel file. They're organized into several folders (Figure 14-17). To find the actual content from your spreadsheet, head to xl→worksheets→sheet1.xml. Double-click it to open it up and take a look at what's inside.

7. When you're finished, rename the file using its .xlsx extension so you can open it in Excel.

To learn way more about the technical details of this type of file storage, you can read the Microsoft white paper at *http://msdn.microsoft.com/en-us/library/aa338205.aspx*.

Figure 14-17:
Inside every .xlsx file lurks a number of compressed files, each with different information. For example, separate files store printer settings, styles, the name of the person who created the document, the composition of your workbook, and each individual worksheet.

Most of the time, you don't need to think about Excel's file format. You can just create your spreadsheets, save them, and let Excel take care of the rest. The only time you need to stop and think twice is when you need to share your work with other, less fortunate people who have older versions of Excel, such as Excel 2003. You'll learn how to deal with this challenge in the following sections.

Tip: Don't use the .xlsb format unless you've tried it out and find it really does give better performance for one of your spreadsheets. Usually, .xlsx and .xlsb are just as fast. And remember, the only time you'll see any improvement is when you're loading or saving a file. Once your spreadsheet is open in Excel, everything else (like scrolling around and performing calculations) happens at the same speed.

Preparing Your Spreadsheet for Excel 2007

As you've just learned, Excel 2007 uses the same .xlsx file format as Excel 2010. That means that an Excel 2010 fan can exchange files with an Excel 2007 devotee, and there won't be any technical problems.

However, there are still a few issues that can trip you up when sharing spreadsheets between Excel 2010 and Excel 2007. For example, Excel 2010 introduces a few new high-powered formula functions, such as RANK.AVG. If you write a calculation that uses this function in Excel 2010, it won't work when someone else opens the spreadsheet in Excel 2007. Instead of seeing the numeric result that you saw, they'll see an error code mixed in with the rest of the spreadsheet data.

To avoid this sort of problem, you need the help of an Excel tool called the Compatibility Checker. The Compatibility Checker scans your spreadsheet to find features and formulas that will cause a problem in Excel 2007.

To use the Compatibility Checker, follow these steps:

1. **Choose File→Info.**

   Excel switches into backstage view.

2. **Click the Check for Issues button, and choose Check Compatibility.**

   The Compatibility Checker scans your spreadsheet, looking for signs of trouble. It then reports any problems back to you (Figure 14-18).

Figure 14-18:
In this example, the Compatibility Checker has found two potential problems. One will affect only Excel 2003 users, while the other will affect both Excel 2007 and Excel 2003 users.

3. **Optionally, you can hide problems that don't affect Excel 2007.**

   The Compatibility Checker reports on two types of problems. The first type of problems affect anyone who doesn't have Excel 2010. These problems appear with the text "Excel 97-2003" and "Excel 2007" in the column on the right. The second problems affect Excel 2003 users but not Excel 2007 users. These problems appear with the text "Excel 97-2003" in the right column.

   If you plan to share your spreadsheet file with Excel 2007 only, there's no need to worry about Excel 2003 compatibility. You can hide these messages from the list by clicking the "Select versions to show" button and turning off Excel 97-2003.

4. **Review the problems.**

You can choose to ignore the Compatibility Checker issues, click Find to hunt each one down, or click Help to figure out the exact problem. You can also click Copy to New Sheet to insert a full compatibility report into your spreadsheet as a separate worksheet. This way, you can print it up and review it in the comfort of your cubicle. (To get back to the worksheet with your data, click the Sheet1 tab at the bottom of the window.)

Note: The problems that the Compatibility Checker finds won't cause serious errors, like crashing your computer or corrupting your data. That's because Excel is designed to *degrade gracefully*. That means you can still open a spreadsheet that uses newer, unsupported features in an old version of Excel. However, you may receive a warning message and part of the spreadsheet may seem broken—that is, it won't work as you intended.

5. **Optionally, you can set the Compatibility Checker to run automatically for this workbook.**

Turn on the "Check compatibility when saving this workbook" checkbox. Now, the Compatibility Checker will run each time you save your spreadsheet, just before the file is updated.

Saving Your Spreadsheet for Excel 2003

If you want to share your workbook with people who are using Excel 2003, the process is a bit more involved, because Excel 2003 uses the older .xls format instead of .xlsx.

When you find yourself in this situation, you have two choices:

- **Save your spreadsheet in the old format.** You can save a copy of your spreadsheet in the traditional .xls Excel standard that's been supported since Excel 97. To do so, choose File→Save As, and then, from the "Save as type" list, choose Excel 97-2003 Workbook.

- **Use a free add-in for older versions of Excel.** People who are stuck with Excel 2000, Excel 2002, or Excel 2003 *can* read your Excel 2010 files—they just need a free add-in that's provided by Microsoft. This is a good solution because it's doesn't require any work on your part. People with past-its-prime versions of Excel can find the add-in they need by surfing to *www.microsoft.com/downloads* and searching for "compatibility pack file formats" (or use the shortcut *http://tinyurl.com/y5w78r*). However, you should still run the Compatibility Checker (page 373) to find out if your spreadsheet uses features that aren't supported in Excel 2003.

Tip: When you save your Excel spreadsheet in another format, make sure you keep a copy in the standard .xlsx format. Why bother? Because other formats aren't guaranteed to retain all your information, particularly if you choose a format that doesn't support some of Excel's newer features.

As you already know, each version of Excel introduces a small set of new features. Older versions of Excel don't support these features. The differences between Excel 2007 and Excel 2010 are quite small. But the differences between Excel 2003 and Excel 2010 are more significant.

Excel tries to help you out in two ways. First, whenever you save a file in .xls format, Excel automatically runs the Compatibility Checker (page 373) to review your spreadsheet and detect compatibility issues. Second, whenever you open a spreadsheet that's in the old .xls file format, Excel switches into *compatibility mode*. While the Compatibility Checker points out potential problems after the fact, compatibility mode is designed to prevent you from using unsupported features in the first place. For example, in compatibility mode you'll face these restrictions:

- Excel limits you to a smaller grid of cells (65,536 rows instead of 1,048,576).

- Excel prevents you from using really long or deeply nested formulas.

- Excel doesn't let you use some pivot table features.

In compatibility mode, these missing features aren't anywhere to be found. In fact, compatibility mode is so seamless that you might not even notice you're being limited. The only clear indication is the title bar at the top of the Excel window. Instead of seeing something like "CateringList.xlsx", you'll see "CateringList.xls [Compatibility Mode]".

Note: When you save an Excel workbook in .xls format, Excel won't switch into compatibility mode right away. Instead, you need to close the workbook and reopen it.

If you decide at some point that you're ready to move into the modern world and convert your file to the .xlsx format favored by Excel 2010, you can use the trusty File→Save As command. However, there's an even quicker shortcut. Just choose File→Info, and click the Convert button. This saves an Excel 2010 version of your file with the same name but with the extension .xlsx, and reloads the file so you get out of compatibility mode. It's up to you to delete your old .xls original if you don't need it anymore.

Saving a Spreadsheet in Other Formats

Some eccentric individuals have even older or stranger spreadsheet software on their computers. If you want to save a copy of your spreadsheet in a more exotic file type, you can choose File→Save As, and then find the desired format in the "Save as type" drop-down list (Figure 14-19). Excel lets you save your spreadsheet using a variety of different formats, including the classic Excel 95 format from more than a decade ago. If you're looking to view your spreadsheet using a mystery program, use the CSV file type, which produces a comma-delimited text file that almost all spreadsheet applications on any operating system can read (comma-delimited means the information has commas separating each cell).

Figure 14-19:
Excel offers a few useful file type options in the "Save as type" list. CSV format is the best choice for compatibility with truly old software (or when nothing else seems to work). The four most commonly used formats—regular workbooks, macro-enabled workbooks, binary workbooks, and old-style Excel 2003 workbooks—sit at the top of the list.

Saving Your Spreadsheet As a PDF

Sometimes you want to save a copy of your spreadsheet so that people can read it even if they don't have Excel (and even if they're running a different operating system, like Linux or Apple's OS X). In this situation, you have several choices:

- **Use the Excel Viewer**. Even if you don't have Excel, you can install a separate tool called the Excel Viewer, which is available from Microsoft's website (search for "Excel Viewer" at *www.microsoft.com/downloads*). However, few people have the viewer, and even though it's free, few want to bother installing it. And it doesn't work on non-Windows computers.

- **Save your workbook as an HTML web page**. That way, all you need to view the workbook is a web browser (and who doesn't have one of those?). The only disadvantage is that you could lose complex formatting. Some worksheets may make the transition to HTML gracefully, while others don't look very good when they're squashed into a browser window. And if you're planning to let other people print the exported worksheet, the results might be unsatisfactory. The next section has more about saving your worksheet as a web page.

- **Save your workbook as a PDF file**. This gets you the best of both worlds—you keep all the rich formatting (so your workbook can be printed), and you let people who don't have Excel (and possibly don't even have Windows) view your workbook.

Excel 2007 introduced the Save As PDF feature, but it forced Excel fans to download an add-in to get it. Excel 2010 has no such limitation. To save your spreadsheet as a PDF, you simply need to File→Save As, and then pick PDF from the "Save as type" list.

When you choose the PDF file type, you'll see a few more options appear in the Save As dialog box (Figure 14-20).

Figure 14-20:
PDF files can be saved with different resolution and quality settings (which mostly affect any graphical objects like pictures and charts that you've placed in your workbook). Normally, you use higher quality settings if you're planning to print your PDF file, because printers use higher resolutions than computer monitors.

The "Publish as PDF" dialog box gives you some control over the quality settings with the "Optimize for" options. If you're just saving a PDF copy so other people can *view* the information in your workbook, choose "Minimum size (publishing online)" to save some space. On the other hand, if there's a possibility that the people reading your PDF might want to print it out, choose "Standard (publishing online and printing)" to save a slightly larger PDF that makes for a better printout.

You can switch on the "Open file after publishing" setting to tell Excel to open the PDF file in Adobe Reader (assuming you have it installed) after the publishing process is complete, so you can check the result.

Finally, if you want to publish only a portion of your spreadsheet as a PDF file, click the Options button to open a dialog box with even more settings. You can choose to publish just a fixed number of pages, just the selected cells, and so on. These options mirror the choices you get when sending a spreadsheet to the printer. You also see a few more cryptic options, most of which you can safely ignore. (They're intended for PDF nerds.) One exception is the "Document properties" option—turn this off if you don't want the PDF to keep track of certain information that identifies you, like your name.

Learning to Love PDFs

You've probably heard about PDFs, Adobe's popular format for sharing formatted, print-ready documents. People use PDFs to pass around product manuals, brochures, and all sorts of electronic documents. Unlike a document format like .xlsx, PDF files are designed to be viewed and printed, but not edited.

The best part about PDFs is that you can view them on just about any type of computer and operating system using the free Adobe Reader. You can download Adobe Reader at *http://get.adobe.com/reader*, but you probably don't need to. Most computers already have Adobe Reader installed, because it comes bundled with so many different programs (usually so you can view their electronic documentation). It's also widely used on the Web.

Incidentally, PDF isn't the only kid on the block. Microsoft's newer operating systems, Windows Vista and Windows 7, include another electronic paper format called XPS (XML Paper Specification). In time, as XPS is integrated into more and more products, it might become a true PDF competitor. But for now, PDF is dramatically more popular and widespread, so it's the one to stick with. (If you're interested in saving an Excel document as a XPS file, you can do that too—just choose XPS from the "Save as type" list.)

Saving Your Spreadsheet with a Password

Occasionally, you might want to add confidential information to a spreadsheet—for example, a list of the airlines from which you've stolen spoons. If your computer is on a network, the solution may be as simple as storing your file in the correct, protected location. But if you're afraid that you might inadvertently email the spreadsheet to the wrong people (say, executives at American Airlines), or if you're about to expose systematic accounting irregularities in your company's year-end statements, you'll be happy to know that Excel provides a tighter degree of security. It allows you to *password-protect* your spreadsheets, which means anyone who wants to open them has to know the password you've set.

Excel actually has two layers of password protection that you can apply to a spreadsheet:

- You can prevent others from *opening* your spreadsheet unless they know the correct password. This level of security, which scrambles your data for anyone without the password (a process known as *encryption*), is the strongest.

- You can let others read a spreadsheet, but you can prevent them from *modifying* it unless they know the correct password.

You can apply one or both of these restrictions to a spreadsheet. Applying them is easy. Just follow these steps:

1. **Choose File→Save As.**

   The Save As dialog box appears.

2. **Click the Tools button, and then, from the pop-up menu, choose General Options.**

   If you're using a Windows XP computer, you'll find the Tools button in the bottom-left corner of the Save As dialog box. But if you're running Windows Vista or Windows 7, it's at the bottom right, just next to the Save button.

   The General Options dialog box appears.

3. **Type a password next to the security level you want to turn on (as shown in Figure 14-21). Then click OK.**

   The General Options dialog box also gives you a couple of other unrelated options:

   — Turn on the "Always create backup" checkbox if you want an extra copy of your file, just in case something goes wrong. (Think of it as insurance.) Excel creates a backup that has the file extension *.xlk*. For example, if you're saving a workbook named SimpleExpenses.xlsx and you use the "Always create backup" option, Excel creates a file named "Backup of *SimpleExpenses.xlk*" every time you save your spreadsheet. You can open the .xlk file in Excel just like an ordinary Excel file. When you do, you see that it has an exact copy of your work.

   — Turn on the "Read-only recommended" checkbox to prevent other people from accidentally making changes to your spreadsheet. When you use this option, Excel shows a message every time you (or anyone else) opens the file. This message politely suggests that you open the spreadsheet in *read-only mode*, in which case Excel won't allow any changes. Of course, it's entirely up to the person opening the file whether to accept this recommendation.

Figure 14-21:
You can use any sequence of letters and numbers as a password. Passwords are case-sensitive (which means that PanAm is different from panam), and they are masked (which means that all that appears in the window as you type is a series of asterisks).

4. **Click Save to store the file.**

   If you use a password to restrict people from opening the spreadsheet, Excel prompts you to supply the "password to open" the next time you open the file (Figure 14-22, top).

   If you use a password to restrict people from modifying the spreadsheet, the next time you open this file you'll be given the choice—shown in Figure 14-22, bottom—to open it in *read-only mode* (which requires no password) or to open it in full edit mode (in which case you'll need to supply the "password to modify").

Figure 14-22:
Top: You can give a spreadsheet two layers of protection. Assign a "password to open," and you'll see this window when you open the file.

Bottom: If you assign a "password to modify," you'll see the choices in this window. If you use both passwords, you'll see both windows, one after the other.

Disaster Recovery

The corollary to the edict "Save your data early and often" is the truism "Sometimes things fall apart quickly…before you've even had a chance to back up." Fortunately, Excel includes an invaluable safety net called AutoRecover.

AutoRecover periodically saves backup copies of your spreadsheet while you work. If you suffer a system crash, you can retrieve the last AutoRecover backup even if you never managed to save the file yourself. Of course, even the AutoRecover backup won't necessarily have *all* the information you entered in your spreadsheet before the problem occurred. But if AutoRecover saves a backup every 10 minutes (the standard), at most you'll lose 10 minutes of work.

If your computer does crash, when you get it running again, you can easily retrieve your last AutoRecover backup. In fact, the next time you launch Excel, it automatically checks the backup folder and, if it finds a backup, it opens a Document Recovery panel on the left of the Excel window.

OFFICE 2010: THE MISSING MANUAL

If your computer crashes in mid-edit, the next time you open Excel you'll probably see the same file listed twice in the Document Recovery window, as shown in Figure 14-23. The difference is the status. The status [AutoSaved] indicates the most recent backup created by Excel. The status [Original] indicates the last version of the file that *you* saved (which is safely stored on your hard drive, right where you expect it).

Figure 14-23:
You can save or open an AutoRecover backup just as you would an ordinary Excel file; simply click the item in the list. Once you've dealt with all the backup files, close the Document Recovery window by clicking the Close button. If you haven't saved your backup, Excel asks you at this point whether you want to save it permanently or delete the backup.

To open a file that's in the Document Recovery window, just click it. You can also use a drop-down menu with additional options (Figure 14-23). Make sure you save the file before you leave Excel. After all, it's just a temporary backup.

If you attempt to open a backup file that's somehow been scrambled (technically known as *corrupted*), Excel automatically attempts to repair it. You can choose Show Repairs to display a list of any changes Excel had to make to recover the file.

AutoRecover settings

AutoRecover comes switched on when you install Excel, but you can tweak its settings. Choose File→Options, and then choose the Save section. Under the "Save workbooks" section, make sure that "Save AutoRecover information" is turned on.

You can also make a few other changes to AutoRecover settings:

- You can adjust the backup frequency in minutes. (See Figure 14-24 for tips on timing.)

Figure 14-24:
You can configure how often AutoRecover saves backups. There's really no danger in being too frequent. Unless you work with extremely complex or large spreadsheets—which might suck up a lot of computing power and take a long time to save—you can set Excel to save the document every five minutes with no appreciable slowdown.

- You can control whether Excel keeps a backup if you create a new spreadsheet, work on it for at least 10 minutes, and then close it without saving your work. This sort of AutoRecover backup is called a *draft*. Ordinarily, the setting "Keep the last Auto Recovered file if I exit without saving" is switched on, and Excel keeps drafts. (To find all the drafts that Excel has saved for you, choose File→Recent and click the Recover Unsaved Workbooks link at the bottom of the window.)

- You can choose the folder where you'd like Excel to save backup files. The standard folder works fine for most people, but feel free to pick some other place. Unfortunately, there's no handy Browse button to help you find the folder, so you need to find the folder you want in advance (using a tool like Windows Explorer), write it down somewhere, and then copy the full folder path into this dialog box.

- Under the "AutoRecover exceptions" heading, you can tell Excel not to bother saving a backup of a specific spreadsheet. Pick the spreadsheet name from the list (which shows all the currently open spreadsheet files), and then turn on the "Disable AutoRecover for this workbook only" setting. This setting is exceedingly uncommon, but you might use it if you have a gargantuan spreadsheet full of data that doesn't need to be backed up. For example, this spreadsheet might hold records that you've pulled out of a central database so you can take a closer look. In this case, there's no need to create a backup because your spreadsheet just has a copy of the data that's in the database.

Opening Files

Opening existing files in Excel works much the same as it does in any Windows program. To get to the standard Open dialog box, choose File→Open (or use the keyboard shortcut Ctrl+O). Using the Open dialog box, you can browse to find the spreadsheet file you want, and then click Open to load it into Excel.

Excel can open many file types other than its native .xlsx format. To learn the other formats it supports, launch the Open dialog box and, at the bottom, open the "Files of type" menu, which shows you the whole list. If you want to open a file but you don't know what format it's in, try using the first option on the menu, "All Files." Once you choose a file, Excel scans the beginning of the file and informs you about the type of conversion it will attempt to perform (based on what type of file Excel thinks it is).

Note: Depending on your computer settings, Windows might hide file extensions. That means that instead of seeing the Excel spreadsheet file MyCoalMiningFortune.xlsx, you'll just see the name MyCoalMiningFortune (without the .xlsx part on the end). In this case, you can still tell what the file type is by looking at the icon. If you see a small Excel icon next to the file name, that means Windows recognizes that the file is an Excel spreadsheet. If you see something else (like a tiny paint palette, for example), you need to make a logical guess about what type of file it is.

Opening Recent Documents

Plan to take another crack at a recent spreadsheet? You can find the most recently opened documents in Excel's Recent Documents list. To see this list, just choose File→Recent. The list holds 20 files. The best part about the Recent Documents list is the way you can *pin* a document there so it stays forever, as shown in Figure 14-25.

You can put recent documents even closer at hand by switching on the "Quickly access this number of Recent Workbooks" checkbox, which you'll find underneath the list of recent documents. You can then enter a number in the adjacent box. For example, if you use 4 (the standard value), the four most recently used workbooks will appear directly in the column of commands on the left side of Excel's backstage view. That means that if one of them is named *MyFavoriteFile.xlsx*, you can open it by choosing File→MyFavoriteFile.xlsx, rather than choosing File→Recent, and then clicking MyFavoriteFile.xlsx in the recent files list.

Tip: Do you want to hide your recent editing work? You can remove any file from the recent document list by right-clicking it and choosing "Remove from list." And if the clutter is keeping you from finding the workbooks you want, just pin the important files, then right-click any file and choose "Clear unpinned workbooks." This action removes every file that isn't pinned down.

Figure 14-25:
To keep a spreadsheet around on the Recent Documents list, click the thumbtack on the right. Excel moves your workbook to the top of the list and pins it in place. That means it won't ever leave the list, no matter how many documents you open. If you decide to stop working with it later on, just click the thumbtack again to release it. Pinning is a great trick for keeping your most important files at your fingertips.

Just to the right of the Recent Documents list is the Recent Places list. It keeps track of the folders where you store your Excel files. So if you like to place Excel spreadsheets on your desktop and in your documents folder, you'll see both folders in the list (as in in Figure 14-25). When you click a location, Excel heads to the appropriate location and shows the standard Open dialog box.

If you store your work in several different locations, far and wide, this feature can save you from digging through the directory tree. It's particularly handy if you store documents on different drives or on a network. And just like the Recent Documents list, you can pin folders to the Recent Places list.

Protected View

Even something that seems as innocent as an Excel file can't always be trusted. Protected view is a new security feature in Excel 2010. It opens potentially risky Excel files in a specially limited Excel window. You'll know that you're in protected view because Excel doesn't allow you to edit any of the data in the workbook, and it displays a message bar at the top of the window (Figure 14-26).

Excel automatically uses protected view when you download a spreadsheet from the Web or open it from your email inbox. This is actually a huge convenience, because

Excel doesn't need to hassle you with questions when you try to view the file (such as "are you sure you want to open this file?"). Because Excel's protected view has bulletproof security, it's a safe way to view the most suspicious spreadsheet.

At this point, you're probably wondering about the risks of rogue spreadsheets. Truthfully, they're quite small. The most obvious danger is *macro code*: miniature programs that are stored in a spreadsheet file and can perform Excel tasks. Poorly written or malicious macro code can tamper with your Excel settings, lock up the program, and even scramble your data. But before you panic, consider this: Excel macro viruses are very rare, and the .xlsx file format doesn't even allow macro code. Instead, macro-containing files must be saved as .xlsm or .xlsb files.

The more subtle danger is that crafty hackers could create corrupted Excel files that might exploit tiny security holes in the program. One of these files could scramble Excel's brains in a dangerous way, possibly causing it to execute a scrap of malicious computer code that could do almost anything. Once again, this sort of attack is extremely rare. It might not even be possible with the up-to-date .xlsx file format. But protected view completely removes any chance of an attack, which helps corporate bigwigs sleep at night.

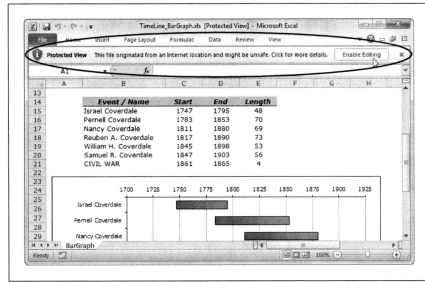

Figure 14-26:
Currently, this file is in protected view. If you decide that it's safe and you need to edit its content, click the Enable Editing button to open in the normal Excel window with no security safeguards.

Opening Files—with a Twist

The Open dialog box harbors a few tricks. To see these hidden secrets, first select the file you want to use (by clicking it once, not twice), and then click the dropdown arrow on the right-side of the Open button. A menu with several additional options appears, as shown in Figure 14-27.

Figure 14-27:
Why settle for the plain-vanilla Open command when you have all these other choices?

Here's what these different choices do:

- **Open** opens the file in the normal way.

- **Open Read-Only** opens the file, but won't let you *save* changes. This option is great if you want to make sure you don't accidentally overwrite an existing file. (For example, if you're using last month's sales invoice as a starting point for this month's sales invoice, you might use Open Read-Only to make sure you can't accidentally wipe out the existing file.) If you open a document in read-only mode, you can still make changes—you just have to save the file with a new file name (choose File→Save As).

- **Open as Copy** creates a copy of the spreadsheet file in the same folder. If your file is named Book1.xlsx, the copy will be named "Copy of Book1.xlsx". This feature comes in handy if you're about to start editing a spreadsheet and want to be able to look at the last version you saved. Excel won't let you open the same file twice. However, you can load the previous version by selecting the same file and using "Open as Copy". (Of course, this technique only works when you have changes you haven't saved yet. Once you save the current version of a file, the older version is overwritten and lost forever.)

- **Open in Browser** is only available when you select an HTML file. This option allows you to open the HTML file in your computer's web browser, which is something you'll only want to attempt when trying to convert Excel files to web pages (page 376).

- **Open in Protected View** prevents a potentially dangerous file from running any code. However, you'll also be restrained from editing the file, as explained on page 384.

- **Open and Repair** is useful if you need to open a file that's corrupted. If you try to open a corrupted file by just clicking Open, Excel warns you that the file has problems and refuses to open it. To get around this problem, you can open the file using the "Open and Repair" option, which prompts Excel to make the necessary corrections, display them for you in a list, and then open the document. Depending on the type of problem, you might not lose any information at all.

Opening Multiple Spreadsheets at Once

As you open multiple spreadsheets, Excel creates a new window for each one. Although this helps keep your work separated, it can clause a bit of clutter and make it harder to track down the window you really want. Fortunately, Excel provides a couple of shortcuts that are indispensable when dealing with several spreadsheets at a time:

- To jump from one spreadsheet to another, find the window in the View→ Window→Switch Windows list, which includes the file name of all the currently open spreadsheets (Figure 14-28).

Figure 14-28:
When you have multiple spreadsheets open at the same time, you can easily move from one to the other using the Switch Windows list.

- To move to the next spreadsheet, use the keyboard shortcut Ctrl+Tab or Ctrl+F6.

- To move to the previous spreadsheet, use the shortcut key Ctrl+Shift+Tab or Ctrl+Shift+F6.

When you have multiple spreadsheets open at the same time, you need to take a little more care when closing a window so you don't accidentally close the entire Excel application—unless you want to. Here are your choices:

- **You can close all the spreadsheets at once.** To do so, you need to close the Excel window. Select File→Exit from any active spreadsheet, or just hold down Shift while you click the close icon (the infamous X button) in the top-right corner of the Excel window.

- **You can close a single spreadsheet.** To do so, right-click the spreadsheet on the taskbar and click Close. Or switch to the spreadsheet you want to close (by clicking the matching taskbar button) and then choose File→Close.

Note: One of the weirdest limitations in Excel occurs if you try to open more than one file with the same name. No matter what steps you take, you can't coax Excel to open both of them at once. It doesn't matter if the files have different content or if they're in different folders or even different drives. When you try to open a file that has the same name as a file that's already open, Excel displays an error message and refuses to go any further. Sadly, the only solution is to open the files one at a time, or rename one of them.

Adding Different Types of Data

Now that you've created a basic worksheet, and you're acquainted with Excel's spiffy interface, it's time to get down and dirty adding data. Whether you want to plan your household budget, build a sales invoice, or graph your soaring (or plunging) net worth, you first need to understand how Excel interprets the information you put in your worksheet.

Depending on what kind of data you type into a cell, Excel classifies it as a date, a number, or a piece of text. Over the next few pages, you'll learn how Excel makes up its mind and how you can make sure it makes the right decision.

One of Excel's most important features is its ability to distinguish between different types of information. A typical worksheet contains both text and numbers. There isn't a lot you can do in Excel with ordinary text (other than alphabetize a list, perform a simple spell check, and apply some basic formatting). On the other hand, Excel gives you a wide range of options for numeric data. For example, you can string your numbers together into complex calculations and formulas, or you can graph them on a chart. Programs that don't distinguish between text and numbers— like Microsoft Word, for example—can't provide these features.

Most of the time, when you enter information in Excel, you don't explicitly indicate the type of data. Instead, Excel examines the information you've typed in and, based on your formatting and other clues, classifies it automatically. Excel distinguishes between four core data types:

- **Ordinary text**. This data type includes column headings, descriptions, and any content that Excel can't identify as one of the other data types.

- **Numbers**. This data type includes currency values, integers, fractions, percentages, and every other type of numeric data. Numbers are the basic ingredient of most Excel worksheets.

- **Dates and times**. This data type includes dates (like Oct 3, 2010), times (like 4:30 p.m.), and combined date and time information (like Oct 3, 2010, 4:30 p.m.). You can enter date and time information in a variety of formats.

- **True or false values**. This data type (known in geekdom as a *Boolean* value) can contain one of two things: TRUE or FALSE (displayed in all capitals). You don't need Boolean data types in most worksheets, but they're useful in worksheets that use complex formulas.

One useful way to tell how Excel is interpreting your data is to look at cell alignment, as explained in Figure 14-29.

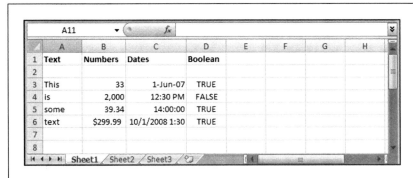

Figure 14-29:
Unless you explicitly change the alignment, Excel always left-aligns text (that is, it lines it up against the left edge of a cell), as in column A. On the other hand, it always right-aligns numbers and dates, as in columns B and C. And it centers Boolean values, as in column D.

Note: The standard alignment of text and numbers doesn't just represent the whims of Excel—it also matches the behavior you want most of the time. For example, when you type in text, you usually want to start at the left edge so that subsequent entries in a column line up. But when entering numbers, you usually want them to line up on the *decimal point* so that it's easier to scan a list of numbers and quickly spot small and large values. Of course, if you don't like Excel's standard formatting, you're free to change it, as you'll see in Chapter 16.

As Figure 14-29 shows, Excel can display numbers and dates in several different ways. For example, some of the numbers include decimal places, one uses a comma, and one has a currency symbol. Similarly, one of the time values uses the 12-hour clock while another uses the 24-hour clock. Other entries include only date information or both date and time information. You assume that when you type in a number, it will appear in the cell exactly the way you typed it. For example, when you type 3-comma-0-0-0 you expect to see 3,000. However, that doesn't always happen. To see the problem in action, try typing *3,000* in a cell. It shows up exactly the way you entered it. Then, type over that value with *2000*. The new number appears as 2,000.

In this example, Excel remembers your first entry, and assumes that you want to use thousand separators in this cell *all the time*.

These differences may seem like a spreadsheet free-for-all, but don't despair—you can easily set the formatting of numbers and dates. (In fact, that's the subject of Chapter 16.) At this point, all you need to know is that the values Excel *stores* in each cell don't need to match exactly the values that it *displays* in each cell. For example, the number 4300 could be formatted as plain old 4300 or as the dollar amount $4,300. Excel lets you format your numbers so you have exactly the representation you want. At the same time, Excel treats all numbers equivalently, no matter how they're formatted, which lets you combine them together in calculations. Figure 14-30 shows you how to find the underlying stored value of a cell.

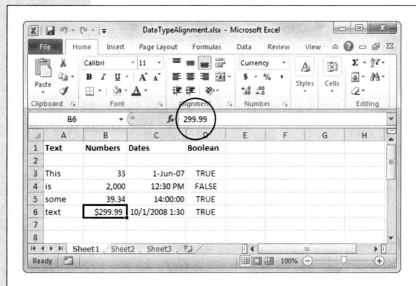

Figure 14-30:
You can see the underlying value that Excel is storing for a cell by selecting the cell and then glancing at the formula bar. In this sheet, you can see that the value $299.99 is actually stored without the dollar currency symbol, which Excel applied only as part of the display format. Similarly, Excel stores the number 2,000 without the comma; it stores the date 1-Jun-10 as 6/1/2010; the time 12:30 p.m. as 12:30:00 PM, and the time 14:00:00 as 2:00:00 PM.

Note: Excel assigns data types to each cell in your worksheet, and you can't mix more than one data type in the same cell. For example, when you type in *44 fat cats*, Excel interprets the whole thing as text because it contains letters. If you want to treat 44 as a number (so that you can perform calculations with it, say), then you need to split this content into two cells—one that contains the number 44 and one that contains the remaining text.

By looking at cell alignment, you can easily tell how Excel is interpreting your data. That's helpful. But what happens when Excel's interpretation is at odds with your wishes? For example, what if you type in something you consider a *number* but Excel freakishly treats it as *text* or vice versa? The first step to solving this problem is grasping the logic behind Excel's automatic decision-making process.

How Excel Identifies Text

If your cell meets any of the following criteria, Excel automatically treats the content as ordinary *text*:

- **It contains any letters**. Thus, C123 is text, not a number.

- **It contains any punctuation that Excel can't interpret numerically**. Punctuation allowed in numbers and dates includes the comma (,), the decimal point (.), and the forward slash (/) or dash (-) for dates. When you type in any other punctuation, Excel treats the cell as text. Thus, 14! is text, not a number.

Occasionally, Excel reads your data the wrong way. For example, you may have a value—like a social security number or a credit card number—that's made up entirely of numeric characters but that you want to treat like text because you don't ever want to perform calculations with it. In this case, Excel doesn't know what you're up to, and so it automatically treats the value as a number. You can also run into problems when you precede text with the equal sign (which tells Excel that you have a formula in progress), or when you use a series of numbers and dashes that you don't intend to be part of a date (for example, you want to enter 1-2-3 but you don't want Excel to read it as January 2, 2003—which is what it wants to do).

In all these cases, the solution's simple. Before you type the cell value, start by typing an apostrophe ('). The apostrophe tells Excel to treat the cell content as text. Figure 14-31 shows you how it works.

Figure 14-31:
To have Excel treat any number, date, or time as text, just precede the value with an apostrophe (you can see the apostrophe in the formula bar but not in the cell). This worksheet shows the result of typing 1-2-3, both with and without the initial apostrophe. When you store 1-2-3 as text, Excel left-aligns it, as if it were an all-text cell (and puts a tiny green triangle in the corner of the cell to let you know you may have made a mistake). The date, on the other hand, is right-aligned.

When you precede a numeric value with an apostrophe, Excel checks out the cell to see what's going on. When Excel determines that it can represent the content as a number, it places a green triangle in the top left corner of the cell and gives you a few options for dealing with the cell, as shown in Figure 14-32.

Tip: When you type in either *false* or *true* (using any capitalization you like), Excel automatically recognizes the data type as Boolean value instead of text, converts it to the uppercase word FALSE or TRUE, and centers it in the cell. If you want to make a cell that contains *false* or *true* as text and *not* as Boolean data, start by typing an apostrophe (') at the beginning of the cell.

Figure 14-32:
In this worksheet, the number 42 is stored as text, thanks to the apostrophe that precedes it. Excel notices the apostrophe, wonders if it's an unintentional error, and flags the cell by putting a tiny green triangle in the top-left corner. If you move to the cell, an exclamation mark icon appears, and, if you click that, a menu appears, letting you choose to convert the number or ignore the issue for this cell. Excel provides a similar menu if you enter a text date that has a two-digit year, as in '1-1-07. In this case, the menu allows you to convert the two-digit date to a four-digit date that has a year starting with 19 or 20.

How Excel Identifies Numbers

Excel automatically interprets any cell that contains only numeric characters as a number. In addition, you can add the following non-numeric characters to a number without causing a problem:

- One decimal point (but not two). For example, 42.1 is a number, but 42.1.1 is text.

- One or more commas, provided you use them to separate groups of three numbers (like thousands, millions, and so on). Thus 1,200,200 is a valid number, but 1,200,20 is text.

- A currency sign ($ for U.S. dollars), provided it's at the beginning of the number.

- A percent symbol at the beginning or end of the number (but not both).

- A plus (+) or minus (−) sign before the number. You can also create a negative number by putting it in parentheses. In other words, entering (33) is the same as entering −33.

- An equal sign at the start of the cell. This tells Excel that you're starting a formula (page 763).

The most important thing to understand about entering numbers is that when you choose to add other details like commas or the dollar sign, you're actually doing two things at once: You're entering a value for the cell *and* you're setting the format for the cell, which affects how Excel displays the cell. Chapter 16 provides more information about number styles and shows how you can completely control cell formatting.

How Excel Identifies Dates and Times

When typing in a date, you have a choice of formats. You can type in a full date (like *July 4, 2010*) or you can type in an abbreviated date using dashes or slashes (like *7-4-2010* or *7/4/2010*), which is generally easier. If you enter some numbers formatted as a date, but the date you entered doesn't exist (like the 30th day in February or the 13th month), then Excel interprets it as text. Figure 14-33 shows you the options.

Figure 14-33:
Whichever way you type the date in a cell, it always appears the same on the formula bar (the specific formula bar display depends on the regional settings on your computer, explained next). To fine-tune the way the date appears in the worksheet, you can use the formatting features discussed on page 448.

Because you can represent dates a few different ways, working with them can be tricky, and you're likely to encounter some unexpected behavior from Excel. Here are some tips for using dates, trouble-free:

- **Instead of using a number for the month, you can use a three-letter month abbreviation, but you must put the month in the middle.** In other words, you can use *7/4/2010* and *4/Jul/2010* interchangeably.

- **When you use a two-digit year as part of a date, Excel tries to guess whether the first two digits of the year should be 20 or 19.** When the two-digit year is from 00 to 29, Excel assumes it belongs to the 21st century. If the year is from 30 to 99, Excel plants it in the 1900s. In other words, Excel translates 7/4/29 into 7/4/2029, while 7/4/30 becomes 7/4/1930.

Tip: If you're a mere mortal and forget where the cutoff point is, then enter the year as a four-digit number, which prevents any confusion.

- **If you don't type in any year at all, Excel automatically assumes you mean the current year**. For example, when you enter 7/4, Excel inserts the date 7/4/2010 (assuming it's currently 2010 on your computer's internal clock). When you enter a date this way, the year component doesn't show up in the cell, but it's still stored in the worksheet (and visible on the formula bar).

- **Excel understands and displays dates differently depending on the regional settings on your computer**. Windows has a setting that determines how your computer interprets dates (see the next section, page 395). On a computer that's configured with U.S settings, Month-Day-Year is the standard progression. But on a UK-configured computer, Day-Month-Year is the deal. For example, in the U.S., either 11-7-09 or 11/7/09 is shorthand for November 7, 2009. In the UK or in Canada, the same notations refer to July 11, 2009.

  Thus, if your computer has U.S. regional settings turned on, and you type in *11/7/09*, then Excel understands it as November 7, 2009, and the formula bar displays 11/7/2009.

Note: The way Excel *recognizes* and *displays* dates varies according to the regional settings on your computer, but the way Excel *stores* dates does not. This feature comes in handy when you save a worksheet on one computer and then open it on another computer with different regional settings. Because Excel stores every date the same way, the date information remains accurate on the new computer, and Excel can display it according to the current regional settings.

Typing in times is more straightforward than typing in dates. You simply use numbers, separated by a colon (:). You need to include an hour and minute component at minimum (as in 7:30), but you can also add seconds (as in 7:30:10). You can use values from 1 to 24 for the hour part, though if your system's set to use a 12-hour clock, Excel converts the time accordingly (in other words, 19:30 becomes 7:30 PM). If you want to use the 12-hour clock when you type in a time, follow your time with a space and the letters P or PM (or A or AM).

Finally, you can create cells that have both date and time information. To do so, just type the date portion first, followed by a space, and then the time portion. For example, Excel happily accepts this combo: 7/4/2010 1:30 PM.

Behind the scenes, Excel stores dates as *serial numbers*. It considers the date January 1, 1900 to be day 1. January 2, 1900 is day 2, and so on, up through the year 9999. This system is quite nifty because if you use Excel to subtract one date from another, then you actually end up calculating the difference in days, which is exactly what you want. On the other hand, it means you can't enter a date in Excel that's earlier than January 1, 1900 (if you do, Excel treats your date like text).

Similarly, Excel stores times as fractional numbers from 0 to 1. The number 0 represents 12:00 a.m. (the start of the day) and 0.99999 represents 11:59:59 p.m. (the end of the day). As with dates, this system allows you to subtract one time value from another.

Regional Dating

Windows has regional settings for your computer, which affect the way Microsoft programs understand things like dates and currency. You can change the settings, and they don't have to correspond to where you live—you can set them for your company headquarters on another continent, for instance. But keep in mind that these affect all the programs on your computer.

Every version of Windows uses the same system for regional settings. (Note for tech nerds: You can find them in the Region and Language section of the Control Panel.) But if you're not used to digging into your computer's Control Panel, you'll face a small problem, because every version of Windows puts them in a slightly different place. Here's the easiest way to find them:

- **If you're using Windows 7 or Windows Vista:** Click the Start button. Then, in the search box at the bottom of the Start menu, type *region*. When Region and Language Options appears in the list of matches, click it.

- **If you're using Windows XP:** Click the Start button and choose Run. In the Run window, type *intl.cpl* and click OK.

Either way, the Region and Language window will appear (see Figure 14-34). The most important setting is in the first box, which has a drop-down list you can use to pick the region you want, like English (United States) or Swedish (Finland).

Figure 14-34:
In the Region and Language window, you choose a geographical region and your computer stores a set of preferences about number and date display. Excel heeds these settings.

If you want to fine-tune the settings in your region, click the "Additional settings" button (in Windows 7), the "Customize this format" button (in Windows Vista), or the Customize button (in Windows XP). Although the name has changed over the years, it's still the same button.

You might decide to customize your region's settings if you have a particular preference that doesn't match the standard options. For example, you might decide that you want UK-formatted dates on a computer that's set to use US-region settings for everything else.

When you customize a region, a new window appears (Figure 14-35) with a long list of settings.

Figure 14-35:
Tweaking the regional settings on your computer gives you complete control over how Excel recognizes dates. Use the drop-down lists to specify the date separator, order of month, day, and year components in a date, and how Excel should interpret two-digit years. You can mix and match these settings freely, although you could wind up with a computer that's completely counterintuitive to other people.

Tip: No matter what the regional settings are, you can always use the international date standard when typing dates into Excel, which is Year/Month/Day, though you must supply a four-digit year (as in 2008/7/4). If you use a two-digit year, Excel assumes you're trying to use the Month-Day-Year or Day-Month-Year pattern.

Printing

Printing in Excel is pretty straightforward—as long as your spreadsheet fits on a normal 8.5 × 11-inch piece of paper. If you're one of the millions of spreadsheet owners who don't belong to that club, welcome to the world of Multiple Page Disorder: the phenomenon in which pages and pages of apparently unrelated and noncontiguous columns start spewing from your printer. Fortunately, Excel comes with a slew of print-tweaking tools designed to help you control what you're printing. First off, though, it helps to understand the standard settings that Excel uses.

Note: You can change most of the settings listed; this is just a list of what happens if you *don't* adjust any settings before printing a spreadsheet.

- In the printout, Excel uses all the formatting characteristics you've applied to the cells, including fonts, fills, and borders. However, Excel's gridlines, row headers, and column headers *don't* appear in the printout.

- If your data is too long (all the rows won't fit on one page) or too wide (all the columns won't fit), Excel prints the data on multiple pages. If your data is both too long *and* too wide, Excel prints in the following order: all the rows for the first set of columns that fit on a printed page, then all the rows for the next set of columns that fit, and so on (this is known as "down, then over"). When printing on multiple pages, Excel never prints *part* of an individual column or row.

- Excel prints your file in color if you use colors and you have a color printer.

- Excel sets margins to 0.75 inches at the top and bottom of the page, and 0.7 inches on the left and right sides of the page. Ordinarily, Excel doesn't include headers and footers (so you don't see any page numbers).

- Excel doesn't include hidden rows and columns in the printout.

How to Print an Excel File

Excel 2010 uses its Backstage view to make printing a whole lot less confusing. Its key feature is a built-in preview that shows you what the on-paper printout will look like before you click Print.

If you're in a tremendous hurry to get your printout and you're not interested in playing with print settings, just choose File→Print, and then click the big Print button shown in Figure 14-36.

Figure 14-36:
When it comes to printing, Excel's Backstage view is a small miracle of efficiency. Not only does it let you tweak the most common print settings, but it also shows you the effect in an instantly updated preview.

If this no-fuss printing approach doesn't give you the results you want, you need to take a closer look at the print settings you can tweak. Here's a walkthrough that takes you through all your options:

1. **Choose File→Print (or press Ctrl+P).**

   Excel switches into Backstage view, and shows a two-part display that puts printing options on the left and a print preview on the right (Figure 14-36).

2. **If you want to print multiple copies of your data, use the Copies box.**

   If you want to print more than one identical copy of your data, change the Copies box accordingly. (This is automatically set at 1 to print a single copy of your work.)

   If you're printing more than one copy and your worksheet has multiple pages, you should also review the collating setting, which appears further down. This setting determines whether Excel duplicates each page separately. For example, if you print 10 pages and your printout is set to Uncollated, Excel prints 10 copies of page 1, 10 copies of page 2, and so on. If your printout it set to Collated, Excel prints the entire 10-page document, then prints out another copy, and so on. You'll still end up with 10 copies of each page, but they'll be grouped together for added convenience.

3. **Select a printer from the drop-down list under the Printer heading.**

   Excel automatically selects your regular printer. If you have more than one printer installed and you want to use a different printer, you need to select this printer yourself. You can also adjust printer settings by clicking the Printer Properties link. Every printer has its own set of options here, but common Properties settings include print quality and paper handling (like double-sided printing for those lucky enough to have a printer that supports it).

4. **Choose what you want to print from the first list under the Settings heading.**

   Print Active Sheets prints the current worksheet. Print Entire Workbook prints all the worksheets in your file. Print Selection prints out just a portion of a worksheet. To make this feature work, you need to start by selecting a range of cells, columns, or rows before you start your print out, and *then* choose File→Print.

5. **If you want to print just some pages, use the two Pages boxes.**

   By default, Excel prints as many pages as it needs to output all the data you've chosen to print. Alternately, you can choose a range of pages using the Pages option. For example, you can choose to print only the first three pages by typing 1 into the first box and 3 instead the second. You can also print just the fourth page by printing from 4 to 4.

Note: In order to use the "Print range" box effectively, you need to know how many pages you need to print your worksheet and what data will appear on each page. You can step through all the pages in your printout using the handy print preview shown in Figure 14-36.

---

6. **Set the orientation and paper size.**

   Orientation is one of the all-time most useful print settings. It lets you control whether you're printing on pages that are upright (choose Portrait Orientation) or turned horizontally on their sides (choose Landscape Orientation). If Excel is splitting your rows across multiple pages when you print your worksheet, it makes good sense to switch to landscape orientation. That way, Excel prints your columns across a page's long edge, which accommodates more columns (but fewer rows per page).

   If you're fed up with trying to fit all your data on an ordinary sheet no matter which way you turn it, you may be tempted to try using a longer sheet of paper. You can then tell Excel what paper you've decided to use by choosing it from the list just under the orientation setting. (Of course, the paper needs to fit into your printer.) Letter is the standard 8.5 × 11-inch sheet size, while Legal is another common choice—it's just as wide but comes in a bit longer at 8.5 × 14 inches.

7. **Adjust your margins.**

   Beneath the options for page orientation and paper size is the margin setting, which determines the amount of space between your worksheet content and the edges of the page.

You can set the margin setting in two ways. The easiest approach is to pick one of the presets (Normal, Wide, or Narrow), as shown in Figure 14-37.

Figure 14-37:
Each margin preset includes several numbers. The Top, Bottom, Left, and Right values measure the amount of space between your work-sheet content and the top, bottom, left, and right edges of the page, respectively.

For more control, you can choose Custom Margins and fill in your own margin values (Figure 14-38). Logically enough, when you reduce the size of your margins, you can accommodate more information. However, you can't *completely* eliminate your margins. Most printers require at least a little space (usually no less than .25 inches) to grip onto the page, and you won't be able to print on this part (the very edge of the page). If you try to make the margins too small, Excel won't inform you of the problem; instead, it'll just stick with the smallest margin your current printer allows.

If you have only a few rows or columns of information, you may want to use one of the "Center on page" options. Select Horizontally to center your columns between the left and right margins. Select Vertically to center your data between the top and bottom of the page.

Tip: A good rule of thumb is to adjust margins symmetrically (printouts tend to look nicest that way). Thus, if you shrink the left margin to 0.5, make the same change to the right margin. Generally, if you want to fit more data and you don't need any header or footer space, then you can safely reduce all your margins to 0.5. If you really want to cram in the maximum amount of data you can try 0.25, but that's the minimum margin that most printers allow.

Figure 14-38:
Excel allocates space at the top and bottom of your printout for a header or footer (page 407). In this example, the header margin is set to 0.5, which means that any header information will appear half an inch below the top of the page. The top margin is set to 1, meaning the worksheet data will appear one inch below the top of the page. When adjusting either of these settings, be careful to make sure the top margin is always larger than the header margin; otherwise, your worksheet's data will print on top of your header. The same holds true with footers when changing the bottom margin. (But if you aren't using headers or footers, their margin settings don't matter.)

8. **If you need to shrink your printout and cram more information into each page, pick a scaling option.**

   No matter how drastically you reduce your margins, you'll only be able to fit a few extra rows and columns in a page. A more powerful approach for fitting mass amounts of data into a smaller number of pages is to use *scaling*. Page 410 gives more detail, but for now, you can try one of the handy scaling presets:

   — **Fit All Columns on One Page** squashes your page width-wise, making it narrower. This way, the columns won't leak off the edge into a separate page.

   — **Fit All Rows on One Page** squashes your page height-wise, making it shorter. This way, all your rows will appear on the same page.

   — **Fit Sheet on One Page** squashes your page both ways, making sure all your data fits on a single sheet.

Note: Excel performs scaling by reducing the font size in the printout. If you try to cram too much data into too small a space, your text might shrink into near-oblivion. It can be hard to judge just how small your text is from the print preview, so you might need to print your worksheet to see how much scaling is too much.

---

9. **If you still want more options, click the Page Setup link.**

This shows the Page Setup dialog box (Figure 14-38), which holds a few of Excel's more specialized print settings. The Page Setup dialog box is organized into several tabs. The Page and Margins tabs duplicate settings that are provided elsewhere in Backstage view. The Header/Footer tab isn't the most convenient way to add a header or footer (instead, see page 407). However, the Sheet tab has a number of options you won't find anywhere else:

— **Print area** lets you specify the range of cells you want to print. While this tool definitely gets the job done, it's easier to use the Print Area tool (described in the box on page 404). And some people find that the Print dialog box's Selection setting (step 4) is an easier approach to printing small groups of cells.

— **Print titles** lets you print specific rows at the top of every page, or specific columns on the left side of every page (see Figure 14-39). For example, you could use this setting to print column titles on the top of every page.

— **Gridlines** prints the grid of lines separating columns and rows that you see on your worksheet.

— **Row and column headings** prints the column headers (which contain the column letters) at the top of each page and the row headers (with the row numbers) on the left side of each page.

— **Black and white** tells Excel to render all colors as a shade of gray, regardless of your printer settings.

— **Draft quality** tells Excel to use lower-quality printer settings to save toner and speed up printing, assuming your printer has these features, of course.

— **Comments** lets you print any comments that you've added to a worksheet. Excel can either append them to the cells in the printout or add them at the end of the printout, depending on the option you select.

— **Cell errors** lets you configure how Excel should print a cell if it contains a formula with an error. You can choose to print the error that's shown (the standard option), or replace the error with a blank value, two dashes (--), or the error code #N/A (meaning not available). You'll learn much more about formulas in Chapter 17.

— **Page order** sets the way Excel handles a large worksheet that's too wide and too long for the printed page's boundaries. When you choose "Down, then over" (the standard option), Excel starts by printing all the rows in the first batch of columns. Once it's finished this batch, Excel then moves on to the next set of columns, and prints those columns for all the rows in your worksheet, and so on. When you chose "Over, then down," Excel moves across your worksheet first. That means it prints all the columns in the first set of rows. After it's printed these pages, it moves to the next set of rows, and so on.

Figure 14-39:
In this example, Excel uses the "Print titles" section to ensure that every page in this printout will display the first row of the spreadsheet as well as the first column.

10. **Now that all your configuration is complete, click the Print button to send the spreadsheet to the printer.**

Excel prints your document using the settings you've selected.

If you're printing a very large worksheet, Excel shows a Printing dialog box for a few seconds as it sends the pages to the printer. If you decide to cancel the printing process—and you're quick enough—you can click the Cancel button in this Printing dialog box to stop the operation. If you don't possess the cat-like reflexes you once did, you can also open your printer queue to cancel the process. Look for your printer icon in the notification area at the bottom-right of your screen, and double-click that icon to open a print window. Select the offending print job in the list, and then press Delete (or choose Document→Cancel from the print window's menu). Some printers also provide their own cancel button that lets you stop a print job even after it's left your computer.

Page Layout View: A Better Print Preview

When you're preparing to print that 142-page company budget monstrosity, there's no reason to go in blind. Instead, prudent Excel fans use Page Layout view to check out what their printouts look like *before* they appear on paper.

GEM IN THE ROUGH

Printing Parts of a Spreadsheet

When working with large worksheets, you'll often want to print only a small portion of your total data. Excel gives you several ways to limit your printout. You can hide the rows or columns you aren't interested in, or you can select the cells you want to print, and, in the Print dialog box's "Print what" box, choose Selection. But if you frequently need to print the same area, you're better off defining and using a *print area*.

A print area designates a portion of your worksheet as the only region that Excel will print. (The one exception is if you choose Selection from the "Print what" box, in which case Excel prints the selected cells, not the print area.) Once you define a print area, Excel retains it until you remove it. That means you can make changes, save, close, and open your spreadsheet, and the same print area remains in place.

To set a print area, select the rows, columns, or group of cells, and then choose Page Layout→Page Setup→Print Area→Set Print Area. The portion of the worksheet that you've highlighted now has a thin dashed outline, indicating that this is the only region Excel will print. You can only have one print area at a time, and setting a new one always clears the previous one. To remove your print area so that you can print the entire worksheet, choose Page Layout→Page Setup→Print Area→Clear Print Area.

Page Layout view is a bit like the print preview that you saw Backstage (Figure 14-36), but it's more powerful. First, it's bigger and easier to navigate. More importantly, it lets you do a few things that aren't possible in backstage view, like setting headers and footers, editing cell values, and tweaking other page layout settings from the ribbon.

To see the Page Layout view for a worksheet, choose View→Workbook Views→Page Layout View. Or, for an even quicker alternative, use the tiny Page Layout View button in the status bar, which appears immediately to the left of the zoom slider. Either way, you see a nicely formatted preview (Figure 14-40).

How does Page Layout view differ from Normal view? For starters, Page Layout view:

- Paginates your data. You see exactly what fits on each page, and how many pages your printout requires.

- Reveals any headers and footers you've set as part of the page setup. These details don't appear in the Normal worksheet view.

- Shows the margins that Excel will use for your pages.

- Doesn't show anything that Excel won't print (like the letters at the top of each column). The only exception is the cell gridlines, which are shown to help you move around your worksheet.

- Includes a bit of text in the Status bar that tells you where you are, page-wise, in a large spreadsheet. For example, you might see the text "Page: 5 of 26."

Figure 14-40:
The Page Layout view shows the first (and part of the second) page of this worksheet's 64 printed pages. This worksheet has 19 columns, but since they're wider than the width of a single printed page, the first page includes only the leftmost seven columns, as shown here. You can scroll to the right to see the additional columns that'll turn up on other pages, or scroll down to see more rows.

Note: Don't confuse Page Layout view with an ordinary print preview (like the one you see when you choose File→Print). A print preview provides a fixed "snapshot" of your printout. You can look, but you can't touch. Page Layout view is vastly better because it shows what your printout will look like *and* it lets you edit data, change margins, set headers and footers, create charts, draw pictures—you get the idea. In fact, you can do everything you do in Normal view mode in Page Layout view. The only difference is you can't squeeze quite as much data into the view at once.

If you aren't particularly concerned with your margin settings, you can hide your margins in Page Layout view so you can fit more information into the Excel window. Figure 14-41 shows you how.

Here are some of the tasks you may want to perform in Page Layout view:

- **To tweak print settings and see the effect,** choose the Page Layout tab in the ribbon. The most important print-related sections are Page Setup (which lets you change orientation and margin settings), Scale to Fit (which lets you cram more information into your printed pages), and Sheet Options (which lets you control whether gridlines and column headers appear on the printout).

- **To move from page to page,** you can use the scroll bar at the side of the window, or you can use the keyboard (like Page Up, Page Down, and the arrow keys). When you reach the edge of your data, you see shaded pages with the text "Click to add data" superimposed. If you want to add information further down the worksheet, just click one of these pages, and then start typing.

Figure 14-41:
Move your mouse between the pages and your mouse pointer changes into this strange two-arrow beast. You can then click to hide the margins in between pages (as shown here), and click again to show them (as shown in Figure 14-40). Either way, you see an exact replica of your printout. The only difference is whether you see the empty margin space.

- To **adjust the page margins,** first make sure the ruler is visible by turning on the View→Show→Ruler checkbox. Then, drag one of the margin lines on the ruler, as shown in Figure 14-42. If you want to set page margins by typing in the exact margin width, use the Page Layout tab of the ribbon instead.

When you're ready to return to the Normal worksheet view, choose View→Workbook Views→Normal (or just click the Status bar's tiny Normal View button).

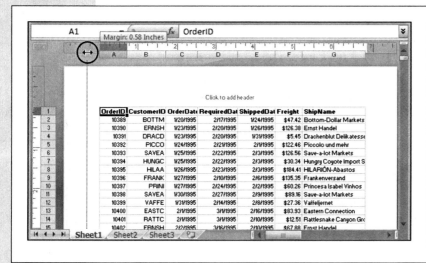

Figure 14-42:
The Page Layout view lets you set margins by dragging the margin edge with your mouse. Here, the left margin (circled) is about to be narrowed down to 0.58 inches. If you're also using a header or footer (below), make sure you don't drag the page margin above the header or below the footer. If you do, then your header or footer will overlap your worksheet's data.

Creating Headers and Footers

A *header* is a bit of text that's printed at the top of every page in your printout. A *footer* is a bit of text that's printed at the bottom of every page. You can use one, both, or neither in a printout.

Ordinarily, every new workbook starts out without a header or footer. However, Page Layout view gives you an easy way to add either one (or both). Just scroll up to the top of any page to create a header (or the bottom to create a footer), and then look for the box with the text "Click to add header" or "Click to add footer". Click inside this box, and you can type the header or footer text you want.

Note: You won't see the header or footer boxes if you've drastically compressed your margins. That's because the header and footer don't fit. To get them back, resize the margins so that they're larger. When you're finished adding the header or footer, you can try adjusting the margins again to see just how small you can get them.

Of course, a good header or footer isn't just an ordinary piece of text. Instead, it contains information that changes dynamically, like the file name, current page, or the date you printed it. You can get these pieces of information using specialized header and footer *codes*, which are distinguished by their use of square brackets. For example, if you enter the code *[Page]* into a footer, Excel replaces it with the current page number. If you use the code *[Date]*, Excel substitutes the current date (when you fire off your printout). Of course, no one wants to memorize a long list of cryptic header and footer codes. To help you get these important details right, Excel adds a new tab to the ribbon named Header & Footer Tools | Design (Figure 14-43) when you edit a header or footer.

The quickest way to get a header or footer is to go to the Header & Footer Tools | Design→Header & Footer section (shown in Figure 14-43), and then choose one of the Header or Footer list's ready-made options. Some of the options you can use for a header or footer include:

- Page numbering (for example, Page 1 or Page 1 of 10).
- Worksheet name (for example, Sheet 1).
- File name (for example, *myfile.xlsx* or *C:\MyDocuments\myfile.xlsx*).
- The person who created the document, and the date it was created.
- A combination of the above information.

Oddly enough, the header and footer options are the same. It's up to you to decide whether you want page numbering at the bottom and a title at the top, or vice versa.

The header area

Figure 14-43:
The Header & Footer
Tools | Design tab is
chock-full of useful
ingredients you can
add to a header or
footer. Click a button
in the Header & Foot-
er Elements section to
insert a special Excel
code that represents
a dynamic value, like
the current page.

If none of the standard options match what you need, you can edit the automatic header or footer, or you can create your own from scratch. Start typing in the header or footer box, and use the buttons in the Header & Footer Elements section to paste in the code you need for a dynamic value. And if you want to get more creative, switch to the Home tab of the ribbon, and then use the formatting buttons to change the font, size, alignment, and color of your header or footer.

Finally, Excel gives you a few high-powered options in the Header & Footer Tools | Design→Options section. These include:

- **Different First Page**. This option lets you create one header and footer for the first page, and use a different pair for all subsequent pages. Once you've checked this option, fill in the first page header and footer on the first page, and then head to the second page to create a new header and footer that Excel can use for all subsequent pages.

- **Different Odd & Even pages**. This option lets you create two different headers (and footers)—one for all even-numbered pages and one for all odd-numbered pages. (If you're printing a bunch of double-sided pages, you can use this option to make sure the page number appears in the correct corner.) Use the first page to fill in the odd-numbered header and footer, and then use the second page to fill in the even-numbered header and footer.

- **Scale with Document**. If you select this option, then when you change the print scale to fit in more or less information on your printout (page 410), Excel adjusts the headers and footers proportionally.

- **Align with Page Margins**. If you select this option, Excel moves the header and footer so that they're centered in relation to the margins. If you don't select this option, Excel centers them in relation to the whole page. The only time you'll notice a difference is if your left and right margins are significantly different sizes.

All these settings affect both headers and footers.

Controlling Pagination

Sooner or later it will happen to you—you'll face an intimidatingly large worksheet that, when printed, is hacked into dozens of apparently unconnected pages. You could spend a lot of time assembling this jigsaw printout (using a bulletin board and lots of tape), or you could take control of the printing process and tell Excel exactly where to split your data into pages. In the following sections, you'll learn several techniques to do just that.

Page Breaks

One of Excel's often overlooked but surprisingly handy features is *manual page breaks*. The idea is that you tell Excel explicitly where to start a new page. For example, you can tell Excel to start a new page between subsequent tables on a worksheet (rather than print a page that has the end of the first one and the beginning of the next).

To insert a page break, move to the leftmost column (column A), and then scroll down to the first cell that you want to appear on the new page. Then, choose Page Layout→Page Setup→Breaks→Insert Page Break. You see a dotted line that indicates the dividing lines in between pages (Figure 14-44).

Note: There's no limit to how many page breaks you can add to a worksheet—if you have a dozen tables that appear one after the other, you can place a page break after each one to make sure they all start on a new page.

You can also insert page breaks to split your worksheet vertically into pages. This is useful if your worksheet is too wide to fit on one page, but you want to control exactly where the page break will fall. To do so, move to the first row, scroll to the column where the new page should begin, and then choose Page Layout→Page Setup→Breaks→Insert Page Break.

You can remove page breaks one at a time by moving to an adjacent cell and choosing Page Layout→Page Setup→Breaks→Remove Page Break. Or you can clear them all using Page Layout→Page Setup→Breaks→Reset All Page Breaks.

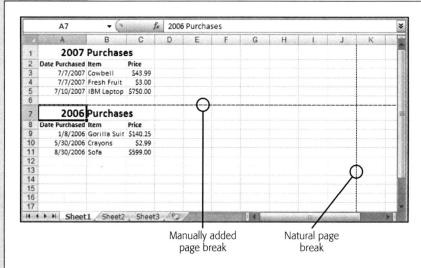

Figure 14-44:
Using a page break,
you can make sure
the second table
(2010 Purchases)
always begins on a
new page. The dotted
line shows where
one page ends and
the new page starts.
When you add a
page break, you see
a dotted line for it,
and you see a dotted
line that shows you
where additional
page breaks naturally
fall, based on your
margins, page orien-
tation, and paper size
settings.

Manually added
page break

Natural page
break

Scaling

Page breaks are a nifty feature for making sure you paginate your printouts just the way you want them. However, they can't help you fit more information on a page. They simply let you place page breaks earlier than they would ordinarily appear, so they fall in a more appropriate place.

If you want to fit more on a page, you need to shrink your information down to a smaller size. Excel includes a scaling feature that lets you take this step easily without forcing you to reformat your worksheet.

Scaling lets you fit more rows and columns on a page, by shrinking everything proportionally. For example, if you reduce scaling to 50 percent, you fit twice as many columns and rows on a page. Conversely, you can use scaling to enlarge your data.

To change the scaling percentage, just type a new percentage into the Page Layout→Scale to Fit→Scale box. The data still appears just as big on your worksheet, but Excel shrinks or expands it in the printout. To gauge the effect, you can use the Page Layout view (page 403) to preview your printout.

Rather than fiddling with the scaling percentage (and then seeing what its effect is on your worksheet by trial and error), you may want to force your data to fit into a fixed number of pages. To do this, you set the values in the Page Layout→Scale to Fit→Width box and the Page Layout→Scale to Fit→Height box. Excel performs a few behind-the-scenes calculations and adjusts the scaling percentage accordingly. For example, if you choose one page tall and one page wide, then Excel shrinks your entire worksheet so that everything fits into one page. This scaling is tricky to get right (and can lead to hopelessly small text), so make sure you review your worksheet in the Page Layout view before you print it.

Tip: Page Break Preview mode, described next, gives you yet another way to squeeze more data onto a single page.

Page Break Preview: A Bird's-Eye View of Your Worksheet

You don't must be a tree-hugging environmentalist to want to minimize the number of pages you print out. Enter the Page Break Preview, which gives you a bird's-eye view of how an entire worksheet's going to print. Page Break Preview is particularly useful if your worksheet has lots of columns. That's because Page Break Preview zooms out so you can see a large amount of data at once, and it uses thick blue dashed lines to show you where page breaks will happen, as shown in Figure 14-45. In addition, the Page Break Preview numbers every page, placing the label "Page X" (where "X" is the page number) in large gray lettering in the middle of each page.

Figure 14-45:
This example shows a large worksheet in Page Break Preview mode. The worksheet is too wide to fit on one page (at least in portrait orientation), and the thick dotted line clearly indicates that the page breaks after column G and after row 47. (Excel never breaks a printout in the middle of a column or row.)

To preview the page breaks in your data, select View→Workbook Views→Page Break Preview, or use the tiny Page Break Preview button in the Status bar. A window appears, informing you that you can use Page Break Preview mode to move page breaks. You can choose whether you want to see this message again; if not, turn on the "Do not show this dialog again" checkbox before clicking OK.

Once you're in Page Break Preview mode, you can do all of the things you do in Normal view mode, including editing data, formatting cells, and changing the zoom percentage to reveal more or fewer pages. You can also click the blue dashed lines that represent page breaks, and drag them to include more or less rows and columns in your page.

Excel lets you make two types of changes using page breaks:

- **You can make *less* data fit onto a page**. To do so, drag the bottom page break up or the right-side page break to the left. Usually, you'll perform these steps if you notice that a page break is in an awkward place, like just before a row with some kind of summary or subtotal.

- **You can make *more* data fit onto a page**. To do so, drag the bottom page break down or the right-side page break to the right.

Of course, everyone wants to fit more information onto their printouts, but there's only so much space on the page. So what does Excel do when you expand a page by dragging the page break? It simply adjusts the scaling setting you learned about earlier (page 410). The larger you make the page, the smaller the Scaling percentage setting becomes. That means your printed text may end up too tiny for you to read. (The text on your computer's display doesn't change, however, so you don't have any indication of just how small your text has become until you print out your data, or take a look at it in Page Layout view.)

Note: Scaling affects all the pages in your printout. That means when you drag one page break to expand a page, you actually end up compressing *all* the pages in your workbook. However, the page *breaks* don't change for other pages, which means you may end up with empty, unused space on some of the pages.

The best advice: If your goal is merely to fit more information into an entire printout, change the scaling percentage manually (page 410) instead of using the Page Break Preview. On the other hand, if you need to squeeze just a little bit more data onto a specific page, use the Page Break Preview.

Moving Data and Managing Worksheets

S imple spreadsheets are a good way to get a handle on Excel. But in the real world, you often need a spreadsheet that's more sophisticated—one that can grow and change as you start to track more information. For example, on the expenses worksheet you created in Chapter 14, perhaps you'd like to add information about which stores you've been shopping in. Or maybe you'd like to swap the order in which your columns appear. To make changes like these, you need to add a few more skills to your Excel repertoire.

This chapter covers the basics of spreadsheet modification, including how to select cells, how to move data from one place to another, and how to change the structure of your worksheet. What you learn here will make you a master of spreadsheet manipulation.

Selecting Cells

First things first: Before you can make any changes to an existing worksheet, you need to select the cells you want to modify. Happily, selecting cells in Excel—try saying that five times fast—is easy. You can do it many different ways, and it's worth learning them all. Different selection techniques come in handy in different situations, and if you master all of them in conjunction with the formatting features described in Chapter 16, you'll be able to transform the look of any worksheet in seconds.

Making Continuous Range Selections

Simplest of all is selecting a *continuous range* of cells. A continuous range is a block of cells that has the shape of a rectangle (high school math reminder: a square is a kind of rectangle), as shown in Figure 15-1. The easiest way to select a continuous range is to click the top-left cell you want to select. Then drag to the right (to select more columns) or down (to select more rows). As you go, Excel highlights the selected cells in blue. Once you've highlighted all the cells you want, release the mouse button. Now you can perform an action, like copying the cells' contents, formatting the cells, or pasting new values into the selected cells.

Figure 15-1:

Top: The three selected cells (A1, B1, and C1) cover the column titles.

Bottom: This selection covers the nine cells that make up the rest of the worksheet. Notice that Excel doesn't highlight the first cell you select. In fact, Excel knows you've selected it (as you can see by the thick black border that surrounds it), but it has a white background to indicate that it's the active cell. When you start typing, Excel inserts your text in this cell.

In the simple expense worksheet, for example, you could first select the cells in the top row and then apply bold formatting to make the column titles stand out. (Once you've selected the top three cells, press Ctrl+B, or chose Home→Font→Bold.)

Note: When you select some cells and then press an arrow key or click into another cell *before* you perform any action, Excel clears your selection.

You have a few useful shortcuts for making continuous range selections (some of these are illustrated in Figure 15-2):

- Instead of clicking and dragging to select a range, you can use a two-step technique. First, click the top-left cell. Then hold down Shift and click the cell at the bottom-right corner of the area you want to select. Excel highlights all the cells in between automatically. This technique works even if both cells aren't visible at the same time; just scroll to the second cell using the scroll bars, and make sure you don't click any other cell on your way there.

- If you want to select an entire column, click the header at the top of the column (as shown in Figure 15-2). For example, if you want to select the second column, then click the gray "B" box above the column. Excel selects all the cells in this column, right down to row 1,048,576.

- If you want to select an entire row, click the numbered row header on the left edge of the row. For example, you can select the second row by clicking the gray "2" box to the left of the row. All the columns in this row will be selected.

Figure 15-2:
Top: Click a column header to select that entire column.

Middle: Click a row number to select that entire row.

Bottom: To select every cell in the worksheet, click the gray box near the top-left corner of the worksheet (circled).

In all these figures, the ribbon is collapsed to give more room, as described in the box on page 361.

- If you want to select multiple adjacent columns, click the leftmost column header and then drag to the right until all the columns you want are selected. As you drag, a tooltip appears indicating how many columns you've selected. For example, if you've selected three columns, you'll see a tooltip with the text 3C (C stands for "column").

- If you want to select multiple adjacent rows, click the topmost row header and then drag down until all the rows you want are selected. As you drag, a tooltip appears indicating how many rows you've selected. For example, if you've selected two rows, you'll see a tooltip with the text 2R (R stands for "row").

- If you want to select all the cells in the entire worksheet, click the blank gray box that's just outside the top-left corner of the worksheet. This box is immediately to the left of the column headers and just above the row headers.

Tip: When you're selecting multiple rows or columns, make sure you click *between* the column header's left and right edges, not on either edge. When you click the edge of the column header, you end up resizing the column instead of making a selection.

A Truly Great Calculation Trick

Excel provides a seriously nifty calculation tool in the status bar. Just select two or more cells and look down to the status bar, where you'll see the number of cells you've selected (the count) along with their sum and their average (shown in Figure 15-3).

To choose what calculations appear in the status bar, right-click anywhere on the status bar and then, in the menu that appears, choose one of the following options:

- **Average.** The average of all the selected numbers or dates.

- **Count.** The number of selected cells that aren't blank.

- **Numerical Count.** The number of selected cells that contain numbers or dates.

- **Minimum.** The selected number or date with the smallest value (for dates this means the earliest date).

- **Maximum.** The selected number or date with the largest value (for dates this means the latest date).

- **Sum.** The sum of all selected numbers. Although you can use Sum with date values, because of the way Excel stores date values, adding dates together generates meaningless results.

Most of the status bar calculations don't work properly if you select both date and numeric information. For example, when you're attempting to add up a list of numbers and dates, Excel computes the value using both date values—which it stores internally as numbers, as explained on page 445—and the ordinary numbers; Excel then displays the final count using the formatting of the first selected cell. That adds up, alas, to a number that doesn't really mean anything.

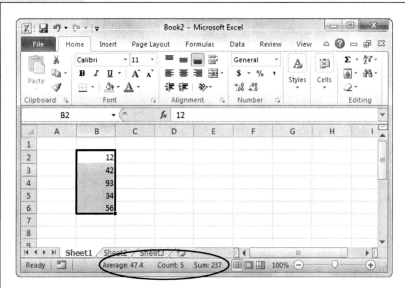

Figure 15-3:
The nicest detail about the status bar's quick calculations is that you can mix and match several at a time. Here, you see the count, average, and sum of the selected cells.

Making Noncontiguous Selections

In some cases, you may want to select cells that are *noncontiguous* (also known as nonadjacent), which means they don't form a neat rectangle. For example, you might want to select columns A and C, but not column B. Or you might want to select a handful of cells scattered throughout the worksheet.

The trick to noncontiguous cell selection is using the Ctrl key. All you need to do is select the cells you want while holding down Ctrl. You can select individual cells by Ctrl-clicking them, or you can select multiple blocks of cells on different parts of the sheet by clicking and dragging in several different places while holding down Ctrl. You can also combine the Ctrl key with any of the shortcuts discussed earlier to select entire columns or rows as a part of your selection. Excel highlights in blue the cells you select (except for the last cell selected, which, as shown in Figure 15-4, isn't highlighted because it becomes the active cell).

Figure 15-4:
This figure shows a noncontiguous selection that includes four cells (A1, B2, C3, and B4). The last selected cell (B4) isn't highlighted because it's the active cell. This behavior is a little bit different from a continuous selection, in which the first selected cell is always the active cell. With a noncontiguous selection, the last selected cell becomes the active cell. Either way, the active cell is still a part of the selection.

Automatically Selecting Your Data

Excel provides a nifty shortcut that can help you select a series of cells without dragging or Shift-clicking anything. It's called AutoSelect, and its special power is to select all the data values in a given row or column until it encounters an empty cell.

To use AutoSelect, follow these steps:

1. **Move to the first cell that you want to select.**

   Before continuing, decide which direction you want to extend the selection.

2. **Hold down Shift. Now, double-click whichever edge of the active cell corresponds to the direction you want to AutoSelect.**

   For example, if you want to select the cells below the active cell, then double-click its bottom edge. (You'll know you're in the right place when the mouse pointer changes to a four-way arrow.)

3. **Excel completes your selection automatically.**

   AutoSelection selects every cell in the direction you choose until it reaches the first blank cell. The blank cell (and any cells beyond it) won't be selected.

Making Selections with the Keyboard

The mouse can be an intuitive way to navigate around a worksheet and select cells. It can also be a tremendous time-suck, especially for nimble-fingered typists who've grown fond of the keyboard shortcuts that let them speed through actions in other programs. Fortunately, Excel is ready to let you use the keyboard to select cells in a worksheet. Just follow these steps:

1. **Start by moving to the first cell you want to select.**

   Whichever cell you begin on becomes the anchor point from which your selected area grows. Think of this cell as the corner of a rectangle you're about to draw.

2. **Now, hold down Shift and move to the right or left (to select columns) and down or up (to select more rows), using the arrow keys.**

   As you move, the selection grows. Instead of holding down Shift, you can also just press F8 once, which turns on extend mode. When extend mode is on, you'll see the text Extend Selection in the status bar. As you move, Excel selects cells just as though you were holding down Shift. You can turn off extend mode by pressing F8 once you've finished marking your range.

Tip: If you really want to perform some selection magic, you can throw in one of Excel's powerful keyboard shortcuts. Use Ctrl+Space to select an entire column or Shift+Space to select the entire row. Or use the remarkable Ctrl+Shift+Space, which selects a block that includes the current cell and all the nearby contiguous cells (stopping only at the edges where it finds a blank cell). Finally, you can hit Ctrl+Shift+Space twice in a row to select the entire worksheet.

Making a noncontiguous selection is almost as easy. The trick is you need to switch between extend mode and another mode called add mode. Just follow these steps:

1. **Move to the first cell you want to select.**

   You can add cells to a noncontiguous range one at a time or add multiple continuous ranges. Either way, you start with the first cell you want to select.

2. **Press F8.**

   This key turns on extend mode. You'll see the text Extend Selection appear in the status bar to let you know extend mode is turned on.

3. **If you want to select more than one cell, use the arrow keys to extend your selection.**

   If you just want to select the currently active cell, do nothing; you're ready to go onto the next step. When you want to add a whole block of cells, you can mark out your selection now. Remember, at this point you're still selecting a continuous range. In the steps that follow, you can add several distinct continuous ranges to make a noncontiguous selection.

4. **Press Shift+F8 to add the highlighted cells to your noncontiguous range.**

   When you hit Shift+F8, you switch to add mode, and you see the text "Add to Selection" appear in the status bar.

5. **You now have two choices: You can repeat steps 1 to 4 to add more cells to your selection, or you can perform an action with the current selection, like applying new formatting.**

   You can repeat steps 1 to 4 as many times as you need to add more groups of cells to your noncontiguous range. These new cells (either individuals or groups) don't need to be near each other or in any way connected to the other cells you've selected. If you change your mind and decide you don't want to do anything with your selection after all, press F8 twice—once to move back into extend mode and then again to return to normal mode. Now, the next time you press an arrow key, Excel releases the current selection.

Tip: You can also use the keyboard to activate AutoSelect. Just hold down the Shift key and use one of the shortcut key combinations that automatically jumps over a range of cells. For example, when you hold down Shift and then press Ctrl+→, you'll automatically jump to the last occupied cell in the current row with all the cells in between selected. For more information about the shortcut keys, refer to Table 14-1 on page 359.

POWER USERS' CLINIC

Selecting Cells with the Go To Feature

In Chapter 14 (on page 359), you learned how you could use the Go To feature to jump from one position in a cell to another. A little known Excel secret also allows you to use the Go To feature to select a range of cells.

It works like this: Start off at the top-left cell of the range you want to select. Then, open the Go To window by selecting Home→Editing→Find & Select→Go To or pressing Ctrl+G. Type in the address of the bottom-right cell in the selection you want to highlight. Now, here's the secret: Hold down Shift when you click the OK button. This action tells Excel to select the range of cells as it moves to the new cell.

For example, if you start in cell A1 and use the Go To window to jump to B3, then you'll select a block of six cells: A1, A2, A3, B1, B2, and B3.

Moving Cells Around

One of the most common reasons to select groups of cells on a worksheet is to copy or move them from one place to another. Excel is a champion of the basic cut-and-paste feature, and it also gives you worthwhile enhancements that let you do things like drag and drop blocks of cells and copy multiple selections to the clipboard at the same time.

Before you get started shuffling data from one place to another, here are a few points to keep in mind:

- Excel lets you cut or copy a single cell or a continuous range of cells. Ordinarily, when you cut or copy a cell, *everything* goes with it, including the data and the current formatting. However, Excel also has tricks that let you copy data without formatting (or even just the formatting). You'll learn about those on page 423.

- When you paste cells onto your worksheet, you have two basic choices. You can paste the cells into a new, blank area of the worksheet, or you can paste the cells in a place that already contains data. In this second case, Excel overwrites the existing cells with the new pasted data.

- Cutting and copying cells works almost exactly the same way. The only difference you'll see is that when you perform a cut-and-paste operation (as opposed to a copy-and-paste operation), Excel erases the source data once the operation is complete. However, Excel doesn't remove the source cells from the worksheet. Instead, it just leaves them empty. (Page 428 shows you what to do if you do want to remove or insert cells, not just the data they contain.)

A Simple Cut-and-Paste or Copy-and-Paste

Here's the basic procedure for any cut-and-paste or copy-and-paste operation.

1. **Select the cells you want to cut or copy.**

    You can use any of the tricks you learned in the previous section to highlight a continuous range of cells. (You can't cut and paste noncontiguous selections.)

    When you want to cut or copy only a single cell, just move to the cell—you don't actually need to select it.

2. **If you want to cut your selection, choose Home→Clipboard→Cut (or Ctrl+X). When you want to copy your selection, choose Home→Clipboard→Copy (or Ctrl+C).**

    Excel highlights your selection with a *marquee border* (Figure 15-5), so called because the border blinks like the twinkling lights around an old-style movie theater marquee. At the same time, the text "Select destination and press ENTER or choose Paste" appears in the status bar (if it fits).

3. **Move to the new location in the spreadsheet where you want to paste the cells.**

   If you selected one cell, move to the new cell where you want to place the data. If you selected multiple cells, then move to the top-left corner of the area where you want to paste your selection. If you have existing data below or to the right of this cell, Excel overwrites it with the new content you're pasting.

   It's perfectly acceptable to paste over part of the data you're copying. For example, you could make a selection that consists of columns A, B, and C and paste that selection starting at column B. In this case, the pasted data appears in columns B, C, and D, and Excel overwrites the original content in these columns (although the original content remains in column A).

Figure 15-5:
In this example, cells A1 to A4 have been copied. The next step is to move to the place where you want to paste the cells and then press Enter to complete the operation. Excel treats cut and copy operations in the same way. In both cases, the selection remains on the spreadsheet, surrounded by the marquee border. When you perform a cut operation, Excel doesn't empty the cells until you paste them somewhere else.

Tip: In some cases, you want to paste without overwriting part of your worksheet. For example, you might want to paste a column in a new position and shift everything else out of the way. To pull this trick off, you need the Insert Copied Cells command, which is described on page 429.

4. **Paste the data by selecting Home→Clipboard→Paste (or press Ctrl+V or Enter on the keyboard).**

   If you're performing a cut-and-paste, Excel removes the original data from the spreadsheet just before pasting it in the new location.

   If you're performing a copy-and-paste, a tiny clipboard icon appears in the bottom-right corner of your pasted cells, with the text "(Ctrl)" next to it. Click this icon and you'll get a menu of specialized paste options (described on page 424).

The Mysterious Number Signs

What does it mean when I see ####### in a cell?

A series of number signs is Excel's way of telling you that a column isn't wide enough to display the number or date that it contains (see Figure 15-6). Sometimes these signs appear when you're copying a big number into smaller cell.

The problem here is that Excel needs a certain amount of space to show your number. It's not acceptable to show just the first two digits from the number 412, for example, because that will look like the completely different number 41. However, Excel will trim off decimal places, if it can, which means that it will show 412.22344364 as 412.223 in a narrow column, while storing the full value with all the decimal places behind the scenes. But when the column is too narrow to show the whole number part of your value, or if you've set a required number of decimal places for your cell and the column is too narrow to accommodate them, Excel shows the number signs to flag the problem.

Fortunately, it's easy to solve this problem—just position the mouse pointer at the right edge of the cell header and drag it to the right to enlarge the column. Provided you've made the column large enough, the missing number reappears.

For a quicker solution, double-click the right edge of the column to automatically make it large enough.

This error doesn't usually occur while you're entering information for the first time because Excel automatically resizes columns to accommodate any numbers you type in. The problem is more likely to crop up if you shrink a column afterward, or if you cut some numeric cells from a wide column and paste them into a much narrower column. To verify the source of your problem, just move to the offending cell and then check the formula bar to see your complete number or date. Excel doesn't use the number signs with text cells—if those cells aren't large enough to hold their data, the words simply spill over to the adjacent cell (if it's blank) or become truncated (if the adjacent cell has some content).

There's one other situation that can cause a cell to display #######. If you create a formula that subtracts one time from another and the result is a *negative* time value, you see the same series of number signs. (Chapter 17 has more about formulas.) But, in this case, column resizing doesn't help.

Figure 15-6:
Cell C4 has a wide number in an overly narrow column. You can see the mystery number if you move to the cell and check out the formula bar (it's 10,042.01), or you can expand the column to a more reasonable width.

A Quicker Cut-and-Paste or Copy-and-Paste

If you want a really quick way to cut and paste data, you can use Excel's drag-and-drop feature. It works like this:

1. **Select the cells you want to move.**

   Just drag your pointer over the block of cells you want to select.

2. **Click the border of the selection box and don't release the mouse button.**

   You'll know that you're in the right place when the mouse pointer changes to a four-way arrow. You can click any edge, but *don't* click in the corner.

3. **Drag the selection box to its new location. If you want to copy (not move) the text, hold down the Ctrl key while you drag.**

   As you drag, a light gray box shows you where Excel will paste the cells.

4. **Release the mouse button to move the cells.**

   If you drop the cells into a region that overlaps with other data, Excel prompts you to make sure that you want to overwrite the existing cells. This convenience isn't provided with ordinary cut-and-paste operations. (Excel uses it for drag-and-drop operations because it's all too easy to inadvertently drop your cells in the wrong place, especially while you're still getting used to this feature.)

Tip: Excel has a hidden dragging trick that impresses even the most seasoned users. To use it, follow the steps listed above but click on the border of the selection box with the *right* mouse button instead of the left. When you release the mouse button to finish the operation, a pop-up menu appears with a slew of options. Using this menu, you can perform a copy instead of a move, shift the existing cells out of the way, or use a special pasting option to copy values, formats, or links (explained next).

Fancy Pasting Tricks

When you copy cells, *everything* comes along for the ride, including text, numbers, and formatting. For example, if you copy a column that has one cell filled with bold text and several other cells filled with dollar amounts (including the dollar sign), when you paste this column into its new location, the numbers will still have the dollar sign and the text will still have bold formatting. If you want to change this behavior, you can use one of Excel's fancy paste options.

In the past, these options could be intimidatingly complex. But Excel 2010 improves life with a new *paste preview* feature. This allows you to preview what your pasted cells will look like before you've actually pasted them into your worksheet.

Here's how to try it out. First, copy your cells in the normal way. (Don't cut them, or the Paste Special feature won't work.) Then, move to where you want to paste the information, go to the Home→Clipboard section of the ribbon, and click the drop-down arrow at the bottom of the Paste button. You'll see a menu full of tiny pictures, each of which represents a different type of paste (see Figure 15-7).

Here's where things get interesting. When you hover over one of these pictures (but don't click it), the name of the paste option pops up, and Excel shows you a preview of what the pasted data will look in your worksheet. If you're happy with the result, click the picture to finish the paste. Or move your mouse over a different option to preview *its* results. And if you get cold feet, you can call the whole thing off by clicking any cell on the worksheet, in which case the preview will disappear and the worksheet will return to its previous state.

Figure 15-7:
In this example, the original data is in cells C1 to C6. The paste preview is shown in cells E1 to E6. Here, the preview is for the Values paste option, which copies all the numbers but none of the formatting. You can move to a different paste option and get a different preview or click a cell in the worksheet to banish the preview and cancel the paste operation.

When you copy Excel cells (as opposed to data from another program), the list of paste options includes fourteen choices arranged into three groups. In the first group, named Paste, you'll find these choices:

- **Paste**. This option is the same as a normal paste operation, and it pastes both formatting and numbers.

- **Formulas**. This option pastes only cell content—numbers, dates, and text—without any formatting. If your source range includes any formulas, Excel also copies the formulas.

- **Formulas and Number Formatting**. This option is the same as Formulas, except it also copies the settings that control how numbers appear. (In other words, numbers that have currency signs, percentage signs, or thousands separators will remain formatted. However, you'll lose other formatting details, like fancy fonts, colors, and borders.)

- **Keep Source Formatting**. This option copies all the data and the formatting. In fact, it's the same as the ordinary Paste option, which is an unexplained Excel quirk.

- **No Borders**. This option copies all the data and formatting (just like an ordinary paste), except it ignores any borders that you've drawn around the cells.

- **Keep Source Column Widths**. This option copies all the data and formatting (just like an ordinary paste), but it also adjusts the columns in the paste region so that it has the same widths as the source columns.

- **Transpose**. This option inverts your information before it pastes it, so that all the columns become rows and the rows become columns. Figure 15-8 shows an example.

Figure 15-8:
With the Transpose option (from the Paste Special dialog box), Excel pastes the table at the top and transposes it on the bottom.

The second group of paste options, called Paste Values, includes three choices:

- **Values**. This option pastes only cell content—numbers, dates, and text—without any formatting. If your source range includes any formulas, Excel pastes the *result* of those formulas (the calculated number) but not the actual formulas. (You'll learn everything you need to know about formulas in Chapter 17.)

- **Values and Number Formatting**. This option pastes the cell content and the formatting settings that control how numbers appear. If your source range includes any formulas, Excel pastes the calculated result of those formulas but not the actual formulas.

- **Values and Source Formatting**. This option is the same as a normal paste operation, except it doesn't copy formulas. Instead, it pastes the calculated result of any formulas.

The third group of paste options, called Other Paste Options, includes four choices that are little more specialized and a little less common:

- **Formatting**. This option applies the formatting from the source selection, but it doesn't actually copy any data.

- **Paste Link**. This option pastes a *link* in each cell that refers to the original data. (By comparison, an ordinary paste creates a duplicate *copy* of the source content.) If you use this option and then modify a value in one of the source cells, Excel automatically modifies the copy, too. (In fact, if you take a closer look at the copied cells in the formula bar, you'll find that they don't contain the actual data. Instead, they contain a formula that points to the source cell. For example, if you paste cell A2 as a link into cell B4, the cell B4 contains the reference =A2. You'll learn more about cell references and get to the bottom of this strange trick in Chapter 17.)

• **Picture.** This option pastes a *picture* of your cell, which is more than a little odd. The picture is placed right in the worksheet, with the formatting and borders you'd expect. In fact, if you don't look closely, this picture looks almost exactly like ordinary Excel data. The only way you'll know that it isn't is to click it. Unlike ordinary Excel data, you can't edit the data in a picture; instead, you're limited to resizing it, dragging it around your worksheet, and changing its borders.

Note: Although it might make sense to copy a picture of your worksheet into other programs, there's little reason to use the picture-pasting feature inside an Excel spreadsheet.

• **Linked Picture.** This option is the same as Picture, except Excel regenerates the picture whenever you modify the values of formatting in the source cells. This way, the picture always matches the source cells. Excel experts sometimes use this feature to create a summary that shows the important parts of a massive spreadsheet in one place. But in the wrong hands, this feature is a head-scratching trick that confuses everyone.

At the very bottom of the menu with paste options is a command named Paste Special. This brings up another window, with more esoteric pasting options. You'll take a peek in the next section.

Once you become familiar with the different paste options, you don't need to rely on the ribbon to use them. Instead, you can use them after a normal copy-and-paste. After you insert your data (by pressing Enter or using the Ctrl+V shortcut), look for the small paste icon that appears near the bottom-right corner of the pasted region. (Excel nerds know this icon as a *smart tag*.) If you click this icon (or press the Ctrl key), Excel pops open a menu (Figure 15-9) with the same set of paste options you saw earlier.

Note: The paste icon appears only after a copy-and-paste operation, not a cut-and-paste operation. If you paste cells from the Clipboard panel, the paste icon still appears, but it provides just two options: keeping the source formatting or pasting the data only.

Paste Special

The paste options in the ribbon are practical and powerful. But Excel has even more paste options for those who have the need. To see them all, choose Home→Clipboard→Paste→Paste Special to pop open a dialog box with a slew of options (Figure 15-10).

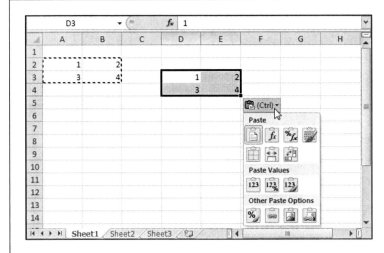

Figure 15-9:
The paste icon appears following the completion of every paste operation, letting you control a number of options, including whether the formatting matches the source or destination cells. The icon remains until you start typing in another cell, which means you can change the type of paste several times, until you get exactly the result you want. The only disadvantage is that this menu doesn't have the same preview feature that the ribbon offers.

Figure 15-10:
The Paste Special dialog box allows you to choose exactly what Excel will paste, and it also lets you apply a few other settings. The big drawback is that you don't get a preview, and some of the options are less than clear. In this example, Excel will perform an ordinary paste with a twist; it won't bother to copy any blank cells.

Paste Special is a bit of a holdover from the past. Many of its options are duplicated in the ribbon's drop-down Paste list. However, the Paste Special dialog box allows you to do a few things that aren't possible from the ribbon, including:

- **Paste comments**. Choose Comments in the Paste section, and click OK. This leaves all the text and formatting behind but copies any comments you've added to the cells.

- **Paste validation**. Choose Validation in the Paste section and click OK. This leaves all the text and formatting behind but copies any validation settings that you've applied to the cells. (Validation is an advanced spreadsheet protection maneuver used mainly by Excel power users.)

- **Combine source and destination cells**. Choose All in the Paste section, choose Add, Subtract, Multiply, or Divide from the Operation section, and then click OK. For example, if you choose Subtract and paste the number 4 into a cell that currently has the number 6, Excel will change the cell to 2 (because *6–2=4*). It's an intriguing idea, but few people use the Operation settings, because they're not intuitive.

- **Refrain from copying blank cells.** Choose All in the Paste section, click the "Skip blanks" checkbox at the bottom of the dialog box and click OK. Now, if any of the cells you're copying are blank, Excel ignores them and leaves the current contents of the destination cell intact. (With an ordinary paste, Excel would overwrite the existing value, leaving a blank cell.)

Adding and Moving Columns or Rows

The cut-and-paste and copy-and-paste operations let you move data from one cell (or group of cells) to another. But what happens if you want to make some *major* changes to your worksheet itself? For example, imagine you have a spreadsheet with 10 filled columns (A to J) and decide you want to add a new column between columns C and D. You could cut all the columns from D to J and then paste them starting at E. That would solve the problem and leave the C column free for your new data. But the actual task of selecting these columns can be a little awkward, and it only becomes more difficult as your spreadsheet grows in size.

A much easier option is to use two dedicated Excel commands designed for inserting new columns and rows into an existing spreadsheet. If you use these features, you won't need to disturb your existing cells at all.

Inserting Columns

To insert a new column, follow these steps:

1. **Find the column immediately to the *right* of where you want to place the new column.**

    That means that if you want to insert a new, blank column between columns A and B, start by looking at the existing column B.

2. **Right-click the column header (the gray box with the column letter in it) and choose Insert.**

    Excel inserts a new column and automatically moves all the columns to the right of column A (so column B becomes column C, column C becomes column D, and so on).

Inserting Rows

Inserting rows is just as easy as inserting new columns. Just follow these steps:

1. **Find the row that's immediately *below* where you want to place the new row.**

   That means that if you want to insert a new, blank row between rows 6 and 7, start by looking at the existing row 7.

2. **Right-click on the row header (the numbered box at the far left of the row) and choose Insert.**

   Excel inserts a new row, and all the rows beneath it are automatically moved down one row.

Note: In the unlikely event that you have data at the extreme right edge of the spreadsheet, in column XFD, Excel doesn't let you insert a new column anywhere in the spreadsheet because the data would be pushed off into the region Beyond The Spreadsheet's Edges. Similarly, if you have data in the very last row (row 1,048,576), Excel doesn't let you insert more rows. If you do have data in either of these spots and try to insert a new column or row, Excel displays a warning message.

Inserting Copied or Cut Cells

Usually, inserting entirely new rows and columns is the most straightforward way to change the structure of your spreadsheet. You can then cut and paste new information into the blank rows or columns. However, in some cases, you may simply want to insert cells into an *existing* row or column.

To do so, begin by copying or cutting a cell or group of cells and then select the spot you want to paste into. Next, choose Home→Cells→Insert→Insert Copied Cells from the menu (or Home→Cells→Insert→Insert Cut Cells if you're performing a cut instead of a copy operation). Unlike the cut-and-paste feature, when you insert cells, you won't overwrite the existing data. Instead, Excel asks you whether the existing cells should be shifted down or to the right to make way for the new cells (as shown in Figure 15-11).

Figure 15-11:
When you insert copied cells, Excel asks whether it should move the existing cells down or to the right.

You need to be careful when you use the Insert Copied Cells feature. Because you're shifting only certain parts of your worksheet, it's possible to mangle your data, splitting the information that should be in one row or one column into multiple rows or columns! Fortunately, you can always back out of a tight spot using Undo. Figure 15-12 shows the sort of problem you could encounter.

Figure 15-12:
Top: Here, two price cells ($43.99 and $3.00) were copied and pasted before the picture was taken, and the existing price cells were shifted down to accommodate the new entries. But the prices now no longer line up with the appropriate item names, which is probably not what you want.

Bottom: It makes much more sense to use the Insert Copied Cells command when you're copying a whole row's worth of data. Here's worksheet where two new rows have been pasted, and Excel politely moves the original set of items out of the way.

Deleting Columns and Rows

In Chapter 14, you learned that you can quickly remove cell values by moving to the cell and hitting the Delete key. You can also delete an entire range of values by selecting multiple cells and hitting the Delete key. Using this technique, you can quickly wipe out an entire row or column.

However, using delete simply clears the cell content. It doesn't remove the cells or change the structure of your worksheet. If you want to simultaneously clear cell values and adjust the rest of your spreadsheet to fill in the gap, you need to use the Home→Cell→Delete command.

For example, if you select a column by clicking the column header, you can either clear all the cells (by pressing the Delete key) or remove the column (by choosing Home→Cells→Delete). Deleting a column in this way is the reverse of inserting a column. All the columns to the right are automatically moved one column to the left to fill in the gap left by the column you removed. Thus, if you delete column B, column C becomes the new column B, column D becomes column C, and so on. If you take out row 3, row 4 moves up to fill the void, row 5 becomes row 4, and so on.

Usually, you'll use Home→Cells→Delete to remove entire rows or columns. However, you can also use it just to remove specific cells in a column or row. In this case, Excel prompts you with a dialog box asking whether you want to fill in the gap by moving cells in the current column up or by moving cells in the current row to the left. This feature is the reverse of the Insert Copied Cells feature, and you'll need to take special care to make sure you don't scramble the structure of your spreadsheet when you use this approach.

Worksheets and Workbooks

So far you've learned how to create a basic worksheet with a table of data. That's great for getting started, but as power users, professional accountants, and other Excel jockeys quickly learn, some of the most compelling reasons to use Excel involve *multiple* tables that share information and interact with each other.

For example, say you want to track the performance of your company: you create one table summarizing your firm's yearly sales, another listing expenses, and a third analyzing profitability and making predictions for the coming year. If you create these tables in different spreadsheet files, you must copy shared information from one location to another, all without misplacing a number or making a mistake. And what's worse, with data scattered in multiple places, you're missing the chance to use some of Excel's niftiest charting and analytical tools. But cramming a bunch of tables onto the same worksheet page isn't the solution. Not only are you likely to lose your spot in the avalanche of data, you'll also face a host of formatting and cell management problems.

Fortunately, a better solution exists. Excel lets you create spreadsheets with multiple pages of data, each of which can conveniently exchange information with other pages. Each page is called a worksheet, and a collection of one or more worksheets is called a *workbook* (which is also sometimes called a *spreadsheet file*).

In the following pages, you'll learn how to manage the worksheets in a workbook.

Many workbooks contain more than one table of information. For example, you might have a list of your bank account balances and a list of items repossessed from your home in the same financial planning spreadsheet. You might find it a bit challenging to arrange these different tables. You could stack them (Figure 15-13) or place them side by side (Figure 15-14), but neither solution is perfect.

Most Excel masters agree that the best way to arrange different tables of information is to use separate worksheets for each table. When you create a new workbook, Excel automatically fills it with three blank worksheets named Sheet1, Sheet2, and Sheet3. Often, you'll work exclusively with the first worksheet (Sheet1), and not even realize that you have two more blank worksheets to play with—not to mention the ability to add plenty more.

	A	B	C	D
1	**2007 Purchases**			.
2	Date	Item	Price	
3	7/7/2007	Cowbell	$43.99	
4	7/7/2007	Fresh Fruit	$3.00	
5	7/10/2007	IBM Laptop	$750.00	
6				
7	**2006 Purchases**			
8	Date	Item	Price	
9	1/8/2006	Gorilla Suit	$140.25	
10	5/30/2006	Crayons	$2.99	
11	8/30/2006	Sofa	$599.00	
12				

Figure 15-13:
Stacking tables on top of each other is usually a bad idea. If you need to add more data to the first table, then you must move the second table. You'll also have trouble properly resizing or formatting columns because each column contains data from two different tables.

	A	B	C	D	E	F	G	H
1	**2007 Purchases**				**2006 Purchases**			
2	Date	Item	Price		Date	Item	Price	
3	7/7/2007	Cowbell	$43.99		1/8/2006	Gorilla Suit	$140.25	
4	7/7/2007	Fresh Fruit	$3.00		5/30/2006	Crayons	$2.99	
5	7/10/2007	IBM Laptop	$750.00		8/30/2006	Sofa	$599.00	
6								

Figure 15-14:
You're somewhat better off putting tables side by side, separated by a blank column, than you are stacking them, but this method can create problems if you need to add more columns to the first table. It also makes for a lot of side-to-side scrolling.

To move from one worksheet to another, you have a few choices:

- Click the worksheet tabs at the bottom of Excel's grid window (just above the status bar), as shown in Figure 15-15.

- Press Ctrl+Page Down to move to the next worksheet. For example, if you're currently in Sheet1, this key sequence jumps you to Sheet2.

- Press Ctrl+Page Up to move to the previous worksheet. For example, if you're currently in Sheet2, this key sequence takes you back to Sheet1.

Figure 15-15:
Worksheets provide a good way to organize multiple tables of data. To move from one worksheet to another, click the appropriate Worksheet tab at the bottom of the grid. Each worksheet contains a fresh grid of cells—from A1 all the way to XFD1048576.

Excel keeps track of the active cell in each worksheet. That means if you're in cell B9 in Sheet1, and then move to Sheet2, when you jump back to Sheet1 you'll automatically return to cell B9.

Adding and Removing Worksheets

When you start a fresh workbook in Excel, you automatically get three blank worksheets in it. You can easily add more worksheets. Just click the Insert Worksheet button, which appears immediately to the right of your last worksheet tab (Figure 15-16). You can also use the Home→Cells→Insert→Insert Sheet command, which works the same way but inserts a new worksheet immediately to the *left* of the current worksheet. (Don't panic: page 435 shows how you can rearrange worksheets after the fact.)

Figure 15-16:
Every time you click the Insert Worksheet button, Excel inserts a new worksheet after your existing worksheets and assigns it a new name. For example, if you start with the standard Sheet1, Sheet2, and Sheet3 and click the Insert Worksheet button, then Excel adds a new worksheet named—you guessed it—Sheet4.

Insert worksheet

If you continue adding worksheets, you'll eventually find that all the worksheet tabs won't fit at the bottom of your workbook window. If you run out of space, you need to use the scroll buttons (which are immediately to the left of the worksheet tabs) to scroll through the list of worksheets. Figure 15-17 shows the scroll buttons.

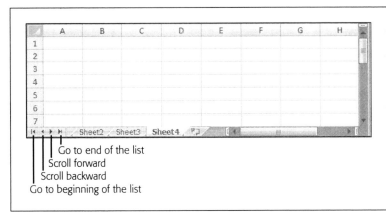

Figure 15-17:
Using the scroll buttons, you can move between worksheets one at a time or jump straight to the first or last tab. These scroll buttons control only which tabs you see—you still need to click the appropriate tab to move to the worksheet you want to work on.

Go to end of the list
Scroll forward
Scroll backward
Go to beginning of the list

Removing a worksheet is just as easy as adding one. Simply move to the worksheet you want to get rid of, and then choose Home→Cells→Delete→Delete Sheet (you can also right-click a worksheet tab, and then choose Delete). Excel won't complain if you ask it to remove a blank worksheet, but if you try to remove a sheet that contains any data, it presents a warning message asking for your confirmation. Also, if you're down to one last worksheet, Excel won't let you remove it. Doing so would create a tough existential dilemma for Excel—a workbook that holds no worksheets—so the program prevents you from taking this step.

Excel starts you off with three worksheets for each workbook, but changing this setting's easy. You can configure Excel to start with fewer worksheets (as few as one), or many more (up to 255). Select File→Options, and then choose the General section. Under the heading "When creating new workbooks" change the number in the "Include this many sheets" box, and then click OK. This setting takes effect the next time you create a new workbook.

Hiding Worksheets

Deleting worksheets isn't the only way to tidy up a workbook or get rid of information you don't want. You can also choose to *hide* a worksheet temporarily.

When you hide a worksheet, its tab disappears but the worksheet itself remains part of your spreadsheet file, available whenever you choose to unhide it. Hidden worksheets also don't appear on printouts. To hide a worksheet, right-click the worksheet tab, and then choose Hide. (Or, for a more long-winded approach, choose Home→Cells→Format→Hide & Unhide→Hide Sheet.)

To redisplay a hidden worksheet, right-click any worksheet tab, and then choose Unhide. The Unhide dialog box appears along with a list of all hidden sheets, as shown in Figure 15-18. Select a sheet from the list, and then click OK to unhide it. (Once again, the ribbon can get you the same window—just point yourself to Home→Cells→Format→Hide & Unhide→Unhide Sheet.)

Figure 15-18:
This workbook contains two hidden worksheets. To restore one, just select it from the list, and then click OK. Unfortunately, if you want to show multiple hidden sheets, you must use the Unhide Sheet command multiple times. Excel has no shortcut for unhiding multiple sheets at once.

Naming and Rearranging Worksheets

The standard names Excel assigns to new worksheets—Sheet1, Sheet2, Sheet3, and so on—aren't very helpful for identifying what they contain. And they become even less helpful if you start adding new worksheets, since the new sheet numbers don't necessarily indicate the position of the sheets, just the order in which you created them.

For example, if you're on Sheet 3 and you add a new worksheet (by choosing Home→Cells→Insert→Insert Sheet), then the worksheet tabs read: Sheet1, Sheet2, Sheet4, Sheet3. (That's because the Insert Sheet command inserts the new sheet just before your current sheet.) Excel doesn't expect you to stick with these auto-generated names. Instead, you can rename them by right-clicking the worksheet tab and selecting Rename, or just double-click the sheet name. Either way, Excel highlights the worksheet tab, and you can type a new name directly onto the tab. Figure 15-19 shows worksheet tabs with better names.

Figure 15-19:
Worksheet names can be up to 31 characters long and can include letters, numbers, some symbols, and spaces. Remember, though, the longer the worksheet name, the fewer worksheet tabs you'll be able to see at once, and the more you'll need to rely on the scroll buttons to the left of the worksheet tabs. For convenience's sake, try to keep your names brief by using titles like Sales04, Purchases, and Jet_Mileage.

Note: Excel has a small set of reserved names that you can never use. To witness this problem, try to create a worksheet named History. Excel doesn't let you because it uses the History worksheet as part of its change tracking features. Use this Excel oddity to impress your friends.

Sometimes Excel refuses to insert new worksheets exactly where you'd like them. Fortunately, you can easily rearrange any of your worksheets just by dragging their tabs from one place to another, as shown in Figure 15-20.

Figure 15-20:
When you drag a worksheet tab, a tiny page appears beneath the arrow cursor. As you move the cursor around, you'll see a black triangle appear, indicating where the worksheet will land when you release the mouse button.

Tip: You can use a similar technique to create *copies* of a worksheet. Click the worksheet tab and begin dragging, just as you would to move the worksheet. However, before releasing the mouse button, press the Ctrl key (you'll see a plus sign [+] appear). When you let go, Excel creates a copy of the worksheet in the new location. The original worksheet remains in its original location. Excel gives the new worksheet a name with a number in parentheses. For example, a copy of Sheet1 is named Sheet1 (2). As with any other worksheet tab, you can change this name.

GEM IN THE ROUGH

Colorful Worksheet Tabs

Names aren't the only thing you can change when it comes to newly added worksheets. Excel also lets you modify a worksheet tab's background color. This minor convenience has no effect on your data or your printout, but it can help you quickly find an important worksheet if it has lots of neighbors.

To change the background color of a worksheet tab, right-click the tab, and then select Tab Color (or move to the appropriate worksheet and Home→Cells→Format→Tab Color). A list of color choices appears; make your selection by clicking the color you want.

Moving Worksheets from one Workbook to Another

Once you get the hang of creating different worksheets for different types of information, your Excel files can quickly fill up with more sheets than a linens store. What happens when you want to shift some of these worksheets around? For instance, you may want to move (or copy) a worksheet from one Excel file to another. Here's how:

1. **Open both spreadsheet files in Excel.**

    The file that contains the worksheet you want to move or copy is called the *source* file; the other file (where you want to move or copy the worksheet to) is known as the *destination* file.

2. **Go to the source workbook.**

   Remember, you can move from one window to another using the Windows task bar, or by choosing the file's name from the ribbon's View→Windows→Switch Windows list.

3. **Right-click the worksheet you want to transfer, and then, from the shortcut menu that appears, choose Move or Copy.**

   If you want, you can transfer multiple worksheets at once. Just hold down the Ctrl key, and select all the worksheets you want to move or copy. Excel highlights all the worksheets you select (and groups them together). Right-click the selection, and then choose Move or Copy.

   When you choose Move or Copy, the Move or Copy dialog box appears (as shown in Figure 15-21).

Figure 15-21:
Here, the selected worksheet is about to be moved into the SimpleExpenses.xlsx workbook. (The source workbook isn't shown.) The SimpleExpenses workbook already contains three worksheets (named Sheet1, Sheet2, and Sheet3). Excel inserts the new worksheet just before the first sheet. Because the "Create a copy" checkbox isn't turned on, Excel removes the worksheet from the source workbook when it completes the transfer.

4. **Choose the destination file from the "To book" list.**

   The "To book" drop-down list shows all the currently open workbooks (including the source workbook).

Tip: Excel also lets you move your worksheets to a new workbook, which it automatically creates for you. To move them to a new workbook, choose the "(new book)" item in the "To book" list. The new workbook won't have the standard three worksheets. Instead, it'll have only the worksheets you've transferred.

---

5. **Specify the position where you want the worksheet inserted.**

   Choose a destination worksheet from the "Before sheet" list. Excel places the copied worksheets just *before* the worksheet you select. If you want to place the worksheets at the end of the destination workbook, select "(move to end)." Of course, you can always rearrange the worksheets after you transfer them, so you don't need to worry too much about getting the perfect placement.

6. **If you want to copy the worksheet, turn on the "Create a copy" checkbox at the bottom of the window.**

    If you don't turn this option on, then Excel copies the worksheet to the destination workbook and removes it from the source workbook. If you *do* turn this option on, you'll end up with a copy of the worksheet in both workbooks.

7. **Click OK.**

    This final step closes the Move or Copy dialog box and transfers the worksheet (or worksheets).

Note: If there are any worksheet name conflicts, Excel adds a number in parentheses after the moved sheet's name. For example, if you try to copy a worksheet named Sheet1 to a workbook that already has a Sheet1, Excel names the copied worksheet Sheet1 (2).

Formatting Cells

W hen you create a basic workbook, you've taken only the first step toward mastering Excel. If you plan to print your data, email it to colleagues, or show it off to friends, you need to think about whether you've formatted your worksheets in a viewer-friendly way. The careful use of color, shading, borders, and fonts can make the difference between a messy glob of data and a worksheet that's easy to work with and understand.

But formatting isn't just about deciding, say, where and how to make your text bold. Excel also lets you control the formatting of numerical values. In fact, two aspects of formatting are fundamental in any worksheet:

- **Cell appearance** formatting is all about cosmetic details like color, typeface, alignment, and borders. When most people think of formatting, they think of cell appearance first.

- **Cell value** formatting controls the way Excel displays numbers, dates, and times. For numbers, this includes details like whether to use scientific notation, the number of decimal places displayed, and the use of currency symbols, percent signs, and commas. With dates, cell value formatting determines what parts of the date the cell displays, and in what order.

In many ways, cell value formatting is more significant than cell appearance formatting because it can change the meaning of your data. For example, even though 45%, $0.45, and 0.450 are all the same number (just formatted differently), your spreadsheet readers will see a failing test score, a cheap price for chewing gum, and a world-class batting average.

Note: Keep in mind that regardless of how you *format* your cell values, Excel maintains an unalterable *value* for every number entered. For more on how Excel internally stores numbers, see the box on page 445.

In this chapter, you'll learn about cell value formatting, and then unleash your inner artist with cell appearance formatting.

Formatting Cell Values

The basic principle behind cell value formatting is this: the cell value that Excel *stores* doesn't necessarily match the cell value it *displays*. This gives you the best of both worlds. Your cells can store super-accurate values, but you don't need to clutter your worksheet with numbers that have 13 decimal places.

To make your worksheet's as clear and readable as possible, you need to make sure that the display value is in a form that makes sense for your spreadsheet. Figure 16-1 shows how Excel can show the same number in a variety of different ways.

Figure 16-1:
This worksheet shows how different formatting can affect the appearance of the same data. Each of the cells B2, B3, and B4 contain the same number: 5.18518518518519. In the formula bar, Excel always displays the exact number it's storing, as you see here with cell B2. However, in the work-sheet itself, each cell's appearance differs depending on how you format the cell.

The first time you type a number or date into a blank cell, Excel makes an educated guess about the number format you want. For example, if you type in a currency value like $34.99, Excel assumes you want a number format that uses the dollar sign. If you then type in a new number in the same cell without a dollar sign (say, 18.75), Excel adds the dollar sign automatically (making it $18.75).

Changing the Cell Value Format

Before long, you'll need to change a cell value format, or you'll want to fine-tune it. The basic process unfolds like this:

1. **Select the cells you want to format.**

   You can apply formatting to individual cells or a collection of cells. Usually, you'll want to format an entire column at once because all the values in a column typically contain the same type of data. Remember, to select a column, you simply need to click the column header (the gray box at the top with the column letter) or press Ctrl+Space.

Note: Technically, a column contains *two* types of data: the values you're storing within the actual cells and the column header in the topmost cell (where the text is). However, you don't need to worry about unintentionally formatting the column title because Excel applies number formats only to numeric cells (cells that contain dates, times, or numbers). Excel doesn't use the number format for the column header cell because it contains text.

---

2. **Select Home→Cells→Format→Format Cells, or just right-click the selection, and then choose Format Cells.**

   In either case, the Format Cells dialog box appears, as shown in Figure 16-2.

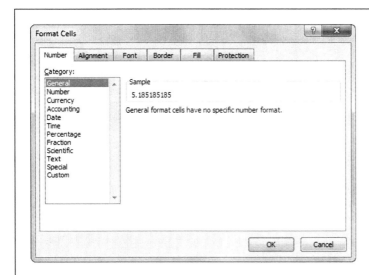

Figure 16-2:
The Format Cells dialog box provides one-stop shopping for cell value and cell appearance formatting. The Number tab lets you configure numeric value formatting. The Alignment, Font, Border, and Fill tabs control the cell's appearance.

3. **Set the format options.**

   The Number tab's options let you choose how Excel translates the cell value into a display value. For example, you can change the number of decimal places that Excel uses to show the number. (The next section covers number formatting choices in much more detail.)

Most of the Format Cells dialog box's other tabs are for cell appearance formatting, which is covered later in this chapter.

Note: Once you apply formatting to a cell, it retains that formatting even if you clear the cell's contents (by selecting it, and then pressing Delete). In addition, formatting comes along for the ride if you copy a cell, so if you copy the content from cell A1 to cell A2, the formatting comes with it. Formatting includes both cell value formatting *and* cell appearance.

The only way to remove formatting is to highlight the cell and select Home→Editing→Clear→Clear Formats. This command removes the formatting, restoring the cell to its original, General number format (which you'll learn more about next), but it doesn't remove any of the cell's content.

---

4. **Click OK.**

Excel applies your formatting changes and changes how it displays the values of the selected cells accordingly.

You'll spend a lot of time in this chapter at the Format Cells dialog box. As you've already seen, the most obvious way to get there is to choose Home→Format→Cells→Format Cells. However, your mouse finger is sure to tire out with that method. Fortunately, there's a quicker route—you can use one of three *dialog box launchers*. Figure 16-3 shows the way.

Figure 16-3:
The ribbon's Home tab gives you a quick way to open the Format Cells dialog box from three different spots: the Font, the Alignment, or the Number tab.

Tip: If you don't want to take your fingers off the keyboard, you can use the shortcut Ctrl+1 to show the Format Cells dialog box at any time.

Formatting Numbers

In the Format Cells dialog box, the Number tab lets you control how Excel displays numeric data in a cell. Excel gives you a lengthy list of predefined formats (as shown in Figure 16-4), and also lets you design your own formats. Remember, Excel uses number formats when the cell contains only numeric information. Otherwise, Excel simply ignores the number format. For example, if you enter *Half past 12* in a column full of times, Excel considers it plain ol' text—although, under the hood, the cell's numerical formatting stays put, and Excel uses it if you change the cell content to a time.

Figure 16-4:
You can learn about the different number formats by selecting a cell that already has a number in it, and then choosing a new number format from the Category list (Home→Cells→Format→Format Cells). When you do so, Excel uses the Format Cells dialog box to show how it'll display the number if you apply that format. In this example, you see that the cell value, 5.18518518518519, will appear as 5.19E+00, which is scientific notation with two decimal places.

When you create a new spreadsheet, every cell starts out with the same number format: General. This format comes with a couple of basic rules:

- If a number has any decimal places, Excel displays them, provided they fit in the column. If the number has more decimal places than Excel can display, it leaves out the ones that don't fit. (It rounds up the last displayed digit, when appropriate.) If you change a column width, Excel automatically adjusts the amount of digits it displays.

- Excel removes leading and trailing zeros. Thus, 004.00 becomes 4. The only exception to this rule happens with numbers between –1 and 1, which retain the 0 before the decimal point. For example, Excel displays the number .42 as 0.42.

As you saw in Chapter 14, the way you type in a number can change a cell's formatting. For example, if you enter a number with a currency symbol, the number format of the cell changes automatically to Currency. Similarly, if you enter three numbers separated by dashes (-) or forward slashes (/), Excel assumes you're entering a date, and adjusts the number format to Date.

However, rather than rely on this automatic process, it's far better just to enter ordinary numbers and set the formatting explicitly for the whole column. This approach prevents you from having different formatting in different cells (which can confuse even the sharpest spreadsheet reader), and it makes sure you get exactly the formatting and precision you want. You can apply formatting to the column before or after you enter the numbers. And it doesn't matter if a cell is currently empty; Excel still keeps track of the number format you've applied.

Different number formats provide different options. For example, if you choose the Currency format, then you can choose from dozens of currency symbols. When you use the Number format, you can choose to add commas (to separate groups of three digits) or parentheses (to indicate negative numbers). Most number formats let you set the number of decimal places.

The following sections give a quick tour of the predefined number formats available in the Format Cells dialog box's Number tab. Figure 16-5 gives you an overview of how different number formats affect similar numbers.

Figure 16-5:
Each column contains the same list of numbers. Although this worksheet shows an example for each number format (except dates and times), it doesn't show all your options. Each number format has its own settings (like the number of decimal places) that affect how Excel displays data.

General

The General format is Excel's standard number format; it applies no special formatting other than the basic rules described on page 443. General is the only number format (other than Text) that doesn't limit your data to a fixed number of decimal places. That means if you want to display numbers that differ wildly in precision (like 0.5, 12.334, and 0.120986398), it makes sense to use General format. On the other hand, if your numbers have a similar degree of precision (for example, if you're logging the number of miles you run each day), the Number format makes more sense.

Number

The Number format is like the General format but with three refinements. First, it uses a fixed number of decimal places (which you set). That means that the decimal point always lines up (assuming you've formatted an entire column). The Number format also lets you use commas as a separator between groups of three digits, which is handy if you're working with really long numbers. Finally, you can choose to have negative numbers displayed with the negative sign, in parentheses, or in red lettering.

The Relationship Between Formatting and Values

The format that you choose for a number doesn't affect Excel's internal storage of that number. For example, if a cell contains the fraction 1/3, then Excel stores this value as 0.333333333333333. (The exact number of decimal places varies, depending on the number you've entered, due to the slight approximations computers need to make when converting fractional numbers into 0s and 1s.) When deciding how to format a cell, you may choose to show only two decimal places, in which case the number appears in your worksheet as 0.33. Or, maybe you choose just one decimal place, in which case the number is simply 0.3. In both cases, Excel still keeps the full 15 or so decimal places on hand. To tell the difference between the displayed number and the real number that Excel stores behind the scenes, just move to the cell. Then look at the formula bar, which always shows you the real deal.

Because of this difference between the stored value and the displayed number, there may be some situations where it looks like Excel's making a mistake. For example, imagine you have three cells, and each stores 0.333333333333333 but displays only 0.3. When you add these three cell values

together, you won't end up with 0.3 + 0.3 + 0.3 = 0.9. Instead, you'll add the more precise stored values and end up with a number that's infinitesimally close to, but not quite, 1. Excel rounds this number up to 1.

This is almost always the way you want Excel to work because you know full well that if you add up 1/3 three times you end up with 1. But, if you need to, you can change this behavior.

To change what Excel does, select File→Options, choose the Advanced section, and then scroll down to the "When calculating this workbook" group of settings. A "Set precision as displayed" checkbox appears. When you turn on this checkbox, Excel adjusts all the values in your current spreadsheet so that the stored value matches the displayed value. Unfortunately, with this choice, you get less precise data. For example, if you use this option with the 1/3 example, Excel stores the display value 0.3 instead of 0.333333333333333. Because you can't reverse this change, Excel warns you and asks for a final confirmation when you try to apply the "Precision as displayed" setting.

Currency

The Currency format closely matches the Number format, with two differences. First, you can choose a currency symbol (like the dollar sign, pound symbol, Euro symbol, and so on) from an extensive list; Excel displays the currency symbol before the number. Second, the Currency format always includes commas. The Currency format also supports a fixed number of decimal places (chosen by you), and it lets you customize how negative numbers are displayed.

Accounting

The Accounting format is modeled on the Currency format. It also lets you choose a currency symbol, uses commas, and has a fixed number of decimal places. The difference is that the Accounting format uses a slightly different alignment. The currency symbol's always at the far left of the cell (away from the number), and there's always an extra space that pads the right side of the cell. Also, the Accounting format always shows negative numbers in parentheses, which is an accounting standard. Finally, the Accountancy format never shows the number 0. Instead, a dash (-) is displayed in its place. There's really no reason to prefer the Currency or the Accounting format. Think of it as a personal decision, and choose whichever looks nicest on your worksheet. The only exception is if you happen to *be* an accountant, in which case you really have no choice in the matter—stick with your namesake.

Percentage

The Percentage format displays fractional numbers as percentages. For example, if you enter 0.5, that translates to 50%. You can choose the number of decimal places to display.

There's one trick to watch out for with the Percentage format. If you forget to start your number with a decimal, Excel quietly "corrects" your numbers. For example, if you type 4 into a cell that uses the Percentage format, Excel interprets this as 4%. As a result, it actually stores the value 0.04. A side-effect of this quirkiness is that if you want to enter percentages larger than 100%, you can't enter them as decimals. For example, to enter 200%, you need to type in 200 (not 2.00).

Fraction

The Fraction format displays your number as a fraction instead of a number with decimal places. The Fraction format doesn't mean you must enter the number as a fraction (although you can if you want by using the forward slash, like 3/4). Instead it means that Excel converts any number you enter and displays it as a fraction. Thus, to have 1/4 appear you can either enter .25 or 1/4.

Note: If you try to enter 1/4 and you *haven't* formatted the cell to use the Fraction number format, you won't get the result you want. Excel assumes you're trying to enter a date (in this case, January 4 of the current year). To avoid this misunderstanding, change the number format *before* you type in your fraction. Or, enter it as *0 1/4* (zero and one quarter).

People often use the Fraction format for stock market quotes, but it's also handy for certain types of measurements (like weights and temperatures). When using the Fraction format, Excel does its best to calculate the closest fraction, which depends on a few factors including whether an exact match exists (entering .5 always gets you 1/2, for example) and what type of precision level you've picked when selecting the Fraction formatting.

You can choose to have fractions with three digits (for example, 100/200), two digits (10/20), or just one digit (1/2), using the top three choices in the Type list. For example, if you enter the number 0.51, then Excel shows it as 1/2 in one-digit mode, and the more precise 51/100 in three-digit mode. In some cases, you may want all numbers to use the same denominator (the bottom number in the fraction) so that it's easy to compare different numbers. (Don't you wish Excel had been around when you were in grammar school?) In this case, you can choose to show all fractions as halves (with a denominator of 2), quarters (a denominator of 4), eighths (8), sixteenths (16), tenths (10), and hundredths (100). For example, the number 0.51 displays as 2/4 if you choose quarters.

Tip: Entering a fraction in Excel can be awkward because Excel may attempt to convert it to a date. To prevent this confusion, always start by entering 0, and then a space. For example, instead of typing *2/3* enter *0 2/3* (which means zero and two-thirds). If you have a whole number and a fraction, like 1 2/3, you'll also be able to duck the date confusion.

Scientific

The Scientific format displays numbers using scientific notation, which is ideal when you need to handle numbers that range widely in size (like 0.0003 and 300) *in the same column*. Scientific notation displays the first non-zero digit of a number, followed by a fixed number of digits, and then indicates what power of 10 that number needs to be multiplied by to generate the original number. For example, 0.0003 becomes 3.00×10^{-4} (displayed in Excel as 3.00E-04). The number 300, on the other hand, becomes 3.00×10^{2} (displayed in Excel as 3.00E02). Scientists—surprise, surprise—like the Scientific format for doing things like recording experimental data or creating mathematical models to predict when an incoming meteor will strike the Earth.

TIMESAVING TIP

Shortcuts in the Ribbon

You don't need to waste hours jumping between your worksheet and the Format Cells dialog box. The ribbon gets you to some of the most commonly used number formats in the Home →Number section.

The Home→Number section's most prominent part is the drop-down list of number formats (Figure 16-6). Just underneath are buttons that let you apply one of the three most common formats: Accounting, Percent, or Number. Just to the right are two buttons that let you increase or decrease the number of decimal places that you see at once.

One of the neatest features is the list of currency options for the Accounting button. If you click the drop-down arrow on the Accounting button (which looks like a dollar sign), you see a list with different currency symbols you can choose (like Pounds, Euros, Chinese Yuan, and so on). But if you click the other portion of the Accounting button (not the arrow), you get the currency symbol that's appropriate, based on your computer's regional settings.

Figure 16-6:
The all-around quickest way to apply a number format is to select some cells, and then, from the number format list, choose an option. Best of all, you see a small preview of what the value in the first selected cell will look like if you apply the format.

Text

Few people use the Text format for numbers, but it's certainly possible to do so. The Text format simply displays a number as though it were text, although you can still perform calculations with it. Excel shows the number exactly as it's stored internally, positioning it against the left edge of the column. You can get the same effect by placing an apostrophe before the number (although that approach won't let you use the number in calculations).

Formatting Dates and Times

Excel gives you lots of options here. You can use everything from compact styles like 3/13/10 to longer formats that include the day of the week, like Saturday, March 13, 2010. Time formats give you a similar range of options, including the ability to use a 12-hour or 24-hour clock, show seconds, show fractional seconds, and include the date information.

To format dates and times, first open the Format Cells dialog box shown in Figure 16-7 (Home→Cells→Format→Format Cells). Choose Date or Time from the column on the left, and then choose the format from the list on the right. Date and Time both provide a slew of options.

Figure 16-7:
Excel gives you dozens of different ways to format dates and times. You can choose between formats that modify the date's appearance depending on the regional settings of the computer viewing the Excel file, or you can choose a fixed date format. When using a fixed date format, you don't have to stick to the U.S. standard. Instead, choose the appropriate region from the Locale list box. Each locale provides its own set of customized date formats.

Excel has essentially two types of date and time formats:

- **Formats that take the regional settings of the spreadsheet viewer's computer into account**. With these formats, dates display differently depending on the computer that's running Excel. This choice is a good one because it lets everyone see dates in just the way they want to, which means no time-consuming arguments about month-day-year or day-month-year ordering.

- **Formats that *ignore* the regional settings of individual computers**. These formats define a fixed pattern for month, day, year, and time components, and display date-related information in exactly the same way on all computers. If you need to absolutely make sure a date is in a certain format, you should use this choice.

The first group (the formats that rely on a computer's regional settings) is the smallest. It includes two date formats (a compact, number-only format and a long, more descriptive format) and one time format. In the Type list, these formats are at the top and have an asterisk next to them.

The second group (the formats that are independent of a computer's regional settings) is much more extensive. In order to choose one of these formats, you first select a region from the Locale list, and then you select the appropriate date or time format (that isn't preceded by an asterisk). Some examples of locales include "English (U.S.)" and "English (U.K.)."

If you enter a date without specifically formatting the cell, Excel usually uses the short region-specific date format. That means that the order of the month and year vary depending on the regional settings of the current computer. If you incorporate the month name (for example, January 1, 2010), instead of the month number (for example, 1/1/2010), Excel uses a medium date format that includes a month abbreviation, like 1-Jan-2010.

Note: You may remember from Chapter 14 that Excel stores a date internally as the cumulative number of days that have elapsed since a certain long-ago date. You can take a peek at this internal number using the Format Cells dialog box. First, enter your date. Then, format the cell using one of the number formats (like General or Number). The underlying date number appears in your worksheet where the date used to be.

Special Formats for Special Numbers

You wouldn't ever want to perform mathematical operations with some types of numeric information. For example, it's hard to image a situation where you'd want to add or multiply phone numbers or Social Security numbers.

When entering these types of numbers, therefore, you may choose to format them as plain old text. For example, you could enter the text (555) 123-4567 to represent a phone number. Because of the parentheses and the dash (-), Excel won't interpret this information as a number. Alternatively, you could just precede your value with an apostrophe (') to explicitly tell Excel that it should be treated as text (you might do this if you don't use parentheses or dashes in a phone number).

But whichever solution you choose, you're potentially creating more work for yourself because you must enter the parentheses and the dash for each phone number you enter (or the apostrophe). You also increase the likelihood of creating inconsistently formatted numbers, especially if you're entering a long list of them. For example, some phone numbers may end up entered in slightly similar but somewhat different formats, like 555-123-4567 and (555)1234567.

To avoid these problems, apply Excel's Special number format (shown in Figure 16-8), which converts numbers into common patterns. And lucky you: In the Special number format, one of the Type options is Phone Number (other formats are for Zip codes and Social Security numbers).

Figure 16-8:
Special number formats are ideal for formatting sequences of digits into a common pattern. For example, in the Type list, if you choose Phone Number, then Excel converts the sequence of digits 5551234567 into the proper phone number style—(555) 123-4567—with no extra work required on your part.

Formatting Cell Appearance

Formatting cell values is important because it helps maintain consistency among your numbers. But to really make your spreadsheet readable (and even beautiful), you'll need to enlist some of Excel's tools for controlling things like alignment, color, and borders and shading.

You can format a cell's appearance in two ways. You can find the button you need on the Home tab of the ribbon, or you can go back to the more comprehensive Format Cells dialog box. Just select the single cell or group of cells that you want to work with, and then choose Home→Cells→Format→Format Cells. Or, right-click the selection, and then choose Format Cells. The following sections walk you through the options in the Format Cells dialog box.

Tip: Even a small amount of formatting can make a worksheet easier to interpret by drawing the viewer's eye to important information. Of course, as with formatting a Word document or designing a web page, a little goes a long way. Don't feel the need to bury your worksheet in exotic colors and styles just because you can.

Alignment and Orientation

As you learned in the previous chapter, Excel automatically aligns cells according to the type of information you've entered. But what if this automatic alignment isn't what you want? Fortunately, in the Format Cells dialog box, the Alignment tab lets you easily change alignment as well as control some other interesting settings, like the ability to rotate text.

Excel lets you control the position of content between a cell's left and right borders, known as the *horizontal alignment*. Excel offers the following choices for horizontal alignment, some of which are shown in Figure 16-9:

- **General** is the standard type of alignment; it aligns cells to the right if they hold numbers or dates and to the left if they hold text.

- **Left (Indent)** tells Excel to always line up content with the left edge of the cell. You can also choose an indent value to add some extra space between the content and the left border.

- **Center** tells Excel to always center content between the left and right edges of the cell.

- **Right (Indent)** tells Excel to always line up content with the right edge of the cell. You can also choose an indent value to add some extra space between the content and the right border.

- **Fill** copies content multiple times across the width of the cell, which is almost never what you want.

- **Justify** is the same as Left if the cell content fits on a single line. When you insert text that spans more than one line, Excel *justifies* every line except the last one, which means Excel adjusts the space between words to try and ensure that both the right and left edges line up.

- **Center Across Selection** is a bit of an oddity. When you apply this option to a single cell, it has the same effect as Center. If you select more than one adjacent cell in a row (for example, cell A1, A2, A3), this option centers the value in the first cell so that it appears to be centered over the full width of all cells. However, this happens only as long as the other cells are blank. This setting may confuse you a bit at first because it can lead to cell values being displayed over cells in which they aren't stored. Another approach to centering large text titles and headings is to merge cells (as described on page 454), but Excel purists prefer Center Across Selection because it doesn't muck with the worksheet's structure.

- **Distributed (Indent)** is the same as Center—if the cell contains a numeric value or a single word. If you add more than one word, then Excel enlarges the spaces between words so that the text content fills the cell perfectly (from the left edge to the right edge).

Vertical alignment controls the position of content between a cell's top and bottom border. Vertical alignment becomes important only if you enlarge a row's height so that it becomes taller than the contents it contains. To change the height of a row, click the bottom edge of the row header (the numbered cell on the left side of the work-sheet), and drag it up or down. As you resize the row, the content stays fixed at the bottom. The vertical alignment setting lets you adjust the cell content's positioning.

Excel gives you the following vertical alignment choices, some of which are shown in Figure 16-9:

- **Top** tells Excel that the first line of text should start at the top of the cell.

- **Center** tells Excel to center the block of text between the top and bottom border of the cell.

- **Bottom** tells Excel that the last line of text should end at the bottom of the cell. If the text doesn't fill the cell exactly, then Excel adds some padding to the top.

- **Justify** is the same as Top for a single line of text. When you have more than one line of text, Excel increases the spaces between each line so that the text fills the cell completely from the top edge to the bottom edge.

- **Distributed** is the same as Justify for multiple lines of text. If you have a single line of text, this is the same as Center.

Figure 16-9:
Left: Horizontal alignment options in action.

Right: This sheet shows how vertical alignment and cell wrapping work with cell content.

If you have a cell containing a large amount of text, you may want to increase the row's height so you can display multiple lines. Unfortunately, you'll notice that en-larging a cell doesn't automatically cause the text to flow into multiple lines and fill the newly available space. But there's a simple solution: just turn on the "Wrap text" checkbox (on the Alignment tab of the Format Cells dialog box). Now, long passages of text flow across multiple lines. You can use this option in conjunction with the vertical alignment setting to control whether Excel centers a block of text, or lines it up at the bottom or top of the cell. Another option is to explicitly split your text into lines. Whenever you want to insert a line break, just press Alt+Enter, and then start typing the new line.

Tip: After you've expanded a row, you can shrink it back by double-clicking the bottom edge of the row header. Assuming you haven't turned on text wrapping, this action shrinks the row back to its standard single-line height.

Finally, the Alignment tab lets you rotate content in a cell up to 180 degrees, as shown in Figure 16-10. You can set the number of degrees in the Orientation box on the right of the Alignment tab. Rotating cell content automatically changes the size of the cell. Usually, you'll see it become narrower and taller to accommodate the rotated content.

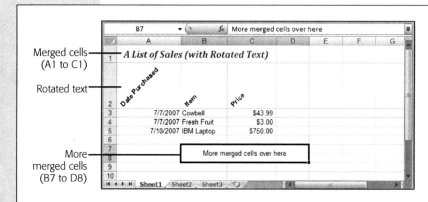

Figure 16-10:
Here's a worksheet that shows one of Excel's most commonly used formatting tricks (merged cells), along with one of its most exotic (rotated text).

Merged cells (A1 to C1)

Rotated text

More merged cells (B7 to D8)

Tip: You can use the Home→Alignment section of the ribbon to quickly change alignment, indenting, rotation, and wrapping, without opening the Format Cells dialog box.

FREQUENTLY ASKED QUESTION

Shrinking Text and Merging Cells So You Can Fit More Text into a Cell

I'm frequently writing out big chunks of text that I'd love to scrunch into a single cell. Do I have any options other than text wrapping?

You betcha. When you need to store a large amount of text in one cell, text wrapping is a good choice. But it's not your only option. You can also shrink the size of the text or merge multiple cells, both from the Format Cells dialog box's Alignment tab.

To shrink a cell's contents, select the "Shrink to fit" checkbox. Be warned, however, that if you have a small column that doesn't use wrapping, this option can quickly reduce your text to vanishingly small proportions.

Joining multiple cells together removes the cells' shared borders and creates one mega-sized cell. Usually, you'll do this to accommodate a large amount of content that can't

fit in a single cell (like a long title that you want to display over every column). For example, if you merge cells A1, B1, and C1, you end up with a single cell named A1 that stretches over the full width of the A, B, and C columns, as shown in Figure 16-11.

To merge cells, select the cells you want to join, choose Home→Cells→Format→Format Cells, and then, on the Alignment tab, turn on the "Merge cells" checkbox. There's no limit to how many cells you can merge. (In fact, you can actually convert your entire worksheet into a single cell if you want to go crazy.) And if you change your mind, don't worry—you simply need to select the single merged cell, choose Home→Cells→Format→Format Cells again, and then turn off the "Merge cells" checkbox to redraw the original cells.

Fonts and Color

As in almost any Windows program, you can customize the text in Excel, applying a dazzling assortment of colors and fancy typefaces. You can do everything from enlarging headings to colorizing big numbers. Here are the individual font details you can change:

- **The font style**. (For example, Arial, Times New Roman, or something a little more shocking, like Futura Extra Bold.) Calibri is the standard font for new worksheets. If you have an old-school workbook created by Excel 2003, you'll notice that it uses 10-point Arial instead.

- **The font size, in points**. The standard point size is 11, but you can choose anything from a minuscule 1-point to a monstrous 409-point. Excel automatically enlarges the row height to accommodate the font.

- **Various font attributes, like italics, underlining, and bold**. Some fonts have complimentary italic and bold typefaces, while others don't (in which case Windows uses its own algorithm to make the font bold or italicize it).

- **The font color**. This option controls the color of the text. (Page 459 covers how to change the color of the entire cell.)

To change font settings, first highlight the cells you want to format, choose Home→Cells→Format→Format Cells, and then click the Font tab (Figure 16-11).

Figure 16-11:
Here's an example of how to apply an exotic font through the Format Cells dialog box. Keep in mind that when displaying data, and especially numbers, sans-serif fonts are usually clearer and look more professional than serif fonts. (Serif fonts have little embellishments, like tiny curls, on the ends of the letters; sans-serif fonts don't.) Arial, the default spreadsheet font, is a sans-serif font. Adobe Minion, the font used for the body text of this book, is clearly a serif font, which works best for large amounts of text.

Tip: Thanks to Excel's handy Redo feature, you can repeatedly apply a series of formatting changes to different cells. After you make your changes in the Format Cells dialog box, simply select the new cell you want to format in the same way, and then hit Ctrl+Y to repeat the last action.

Rather than heading to the Format Cells dialog box every time you want to tweak a font, you can use the ribbon's handy shortcuts. The Home→Font section displays buttons for changing the font and font size. You also get a load of tiny buttons for applying basics like bold, italic, and underline, applying borders, and changing the text and background colors. (Truth be told, the formatting toolbar is way more convenient for setting fonts because its drop-down menu shows a long list of font names, whereas the font list in the Format Cells dialog box is limited to showing an impossibly restrictive six fonts at a time. Scrolling through that cramped space is like reading the phone book on index cards.)

Without a doubt, the ribbon's most useful formatting feature is *live preview*, a frill that shows you the result of a change *before* you've even applied it. Figure 16-12 shows live preview in action.

Figure 16-12:
Right now, this spreadsheet's creator is just thinking about using the stylish Baskerville Old Face font for this table. However, the moment she hovers over Arial (higher up in the font list), Excel switches the currently selected cells on the worksheet to that font, providing a preview of the change. The best part: When she moves the mouse pointer away, the formatting disappears instantaneously. To make the changes stick, all she needs to do is click the font. This live preview feature works with font names, font sizes, and colors.

Note: No matter what font you apply, Excel, thankfully, always displays the cell contents in the formula bar in easy-to-read Calibri font. That makes things easier if you're working with cells that've been formatted using difficult-to-decipher script fonts, or really large or small text sizes.

Formatting Individual Characters

The ribbon lets you perform one task that you can't with the Format Cells dialog box: applying formatting to just a part of a cell. For example, if a cell contains the text "New low price", you could apply a new color or bold format to the word "low."

To apply formatting to a portion of a cell, follow these steps:

1. **Move to the appropriate cell, and then put it into edit mode by pressing F2.**

    You can also put a cell into edit mode by double-clicking it, or by moving to it, and then clicking the text inside the formula bar.

2. **Select the text you want to format.**

    You can select the text by highlighting it with the mouse, or by holding down Shift while using the arrow keys to mark your selection.

3. **Choose a font option from the ribbon's Home→Font section.**

    You can also change the size, the color, or the bold, italic, or underline settings. And if you don't want to waste time choosing the Home tab if you're currently somewhere else in the ribbon, then you can simply right-click the selected text to show a pop-up toolbar with font options.

    Applying multiple types of text formatting to the same cell can get tricky. The formula bar doesn't show the difference, and, when you edit the cell, you may not end up entering text in the font you want. Also, be careful that you don't apply new font formatting to the cell later; if you do, you'll wipe out all the font information you've added to the cell.

Special characters

Most fonts contain not only digits and the common letters of the alphabet, but also some special symbols that you can type directly on your keyboard. One example is the copyright symbol ©, which you can insert into a cell by entering the text *(C)*, and letting AutoCorrect do its work. Other symbols, however, aren't as readily available. One example is the special arrow character →. To use this symbol, you'll need the help of Excel's symbols. Simply follow these steps:

1. Choose Insert→Symbols→Symbol.

    The Symbol dialog box opens, as shown in Figure 16-13. Now it's time to hunt for the symbol you need.

2. Choose the font and subset (the group of symbols you want to explore).

    If you're looking for a fairly common symbol (like a mathematical sign, an arrow, an accented letter, or a fraction), you probably don't need to change the font. In the Font box, keep the automatic selection of "(normal text)", and then, from the Subset box at the right, choose the type of default. For example, choose the Arrows subset to see arrow symbols that point in different directions.

Figure 16-13:
The Symbol dialog box lets you insert one or more special characters. You can choose extended characters that are supported by most fonts (like currency symbols, non-English letters, arrows, and so on). Alternatively, you can use a font that's all about fancy characters, like the Wingdings font that's chock full of tiny graphical icons.

If you want funkier alternatives, choose a fancy font from the Font box on the left. You should be able to find at least one version of the Wingdings font in the list. Wingdings has the most interesting symbols to use. It's also the most likely to be on other people's computers, which makes a difference if you're planning to email your worksheet to other people. If you get your symbols from a really bizarre font that other people don't have, they won't be able to see your symbols.

Note: Wingdings is a special font included with Windows that's made up entirely of symbols like happy faces and stars, none of which you find in standard fonts. You can try to apply the Wingdings font on your own (by picking it from the font list), but you won't know which character to press on your keyboard to get the symbol you want. You're better off using Excel's Symbol dialog box.

3. **Select the character, and then click Insert.**

   Alternatively, if you need to insert multiple special characters, just double-click each one; doing so inserts each symbol right next to each other in the same cell without having to close the window.

Tip: If you're looking for an extremely common special character (like the copyright symbol), you can shorten this whole process. Instead of using the Symbols tab, just click over to the Special Characters tab in the Symbol dialog box. Then, look through the small list of commonly used symbols. If you find what you want, just select it, and then click Insert.

There's one idiosyncrasy that you should be aware of if you choose to insert symbols from another font. For example, if you insert a symbol from the Wingdings font into a cell that already has text, then you actually end up with a cell that has two fonts—one for the symbol character and one that's used for the rest of your text. This system works perfectly well, but it can cause some confusion. For example, if you apply a new font to the cell after inserting a special character, Excel adjusts the entire contents of the cell to use the new font, and your symbol changes into the corresponding character in the new font (which usually isn't what you want). These problems can crop up any time you deal with a cell that has more than one font.

On the other hand, if you kept the font selection on "(normal text)" when you picked your symbol, then you won't see this behavior. That's because you picked a more commonplace symbol that's included in the font you're already using for the cell. In this case, Excel doesn't need to use two fonts at once.

Note: When you look at the cell contents in the formula bar, you always see the cell data in the standard Calibri font. This consistency means, for example, that a Wingdings symbol doesn't appear as the icon that shows up in your worksheet. Instead, you see an ordinary letter or some type of extended non-English character, like æ.

Borders and Fills

The best way to call attention to important information isn't to change fonts or alignment. Instead, place borders around key cells or groups of cells and use shading to highlight important columns and rows. Excel provides dozens of different ways to outline and highlight any selection of cells.

Once again, the trusty Format Cells dialog box is your control center. Just follow these steps:

1. **Select the cells you want to fill or outline.**

   Your selected cells appear highlighted.

2. **Select Home→Cells→Format→Format Cells, or just right-click the selection, and then choose Format Cells.**

   The Format Cells dialog box appears.

3. **Head directly to the Border tab. (If you don't want to apply any borders, skip straight to step 4.)**

   Applying a border is a multistep process (see Figure 16-14). Begin by choosing the line style you want (dotted, dashed, thick, double, and so on), followed by the color. (Automatic picks black.) Both these options are on the left side of the tab. Next, choose where your border lines are going to appear. The Border box (the square that contains the word "Text") functions as a nifty interactive test canvas that shows you where your lines will appear. Make your selection either by clicking one of the eight Border buttons (which contain a single bold horizontal, vertical, or diagonal line), or click directly inside the Border box. If you change your mind, clicking a border line makes it disappear.

1. Choose the type of border line here

2. Choose the border color here

3. Apply the border where you want it by clicking in here

For example, if you want to apply a border to the top of your selection, click the top of the Border box. If you want to apply a line between columns inside the selection, click between the cell columns in the Border box. The line appears indicating your choice.

Tip: The Border tab also provides two shortcuts in the tab's Presets section. If you want to apply a border style around your entire selection, select Outline after choosing your border style and color. Choose Inside to apply the border between the rows and columns of your selection. Choosing None removes all border lines.

4. **Click the Fill tab.**

    Here you can select the background color, pattern color, and pattern style to apply shading to the cells in the selection (see Figure 16-15). Click the No Color box to clear any current color or pattern in the selected cells. When picking a pattern color, you may notice that certain colors are described as *theme colors*. These theme colors are a set of coordinated colors that change whenever you pick a new theme for your workbook, as described in the Tip on page 532.

2. Choose the pattern color here

3. Choose the pattern style here

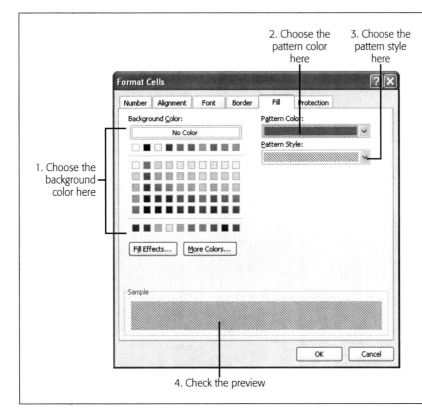

1. Choose the background color here

4. Check the preview

To get a really fancy fill, you can use a *gradient*, which is a blend of two colors. For example, with gradients you can create a fill that starts out white on one side of a cell and gradually darkens to blue on the other. To use a gradient fill, click the Fill Effects button, and then follow the instructions in Figure 16-16.

5. **Click OK to apply your changes.**

   If you don't like the modifications you've just applied, you can roll back time by pressing Ctrl+Z to trigger the indispensable Undo command.

Tip: You can remove a worksheet's gridlines, which is handy when you want to more easily see any custom borders you've added. To remove gridlines, select View→Show→Gridlines. (This action affects only the current file, and won't apply to new spreadsheets.)

Figure 16-16:
Top: To create a gradient, you need to pick the two colors you want to use to create the blend, and you need to choose the way Excel does the blending (from one side to another, from the top to the bottom, and so on). When applying a gradient fill to a stack of cells, a vertical fill makes the most sense, because that way the gradients in each cell line up and they look like one seamless shaded region. When applying a gradient fill to a row of cells, a horizontal fill looks better for the same reason.

Bottom: A gradient fill on cells A2 to A5.

Building Basic Formulas

M ost Excel fans don't turn to the world's leading spreadsheet software just to create nicely formatted tables. Instead, they rely on Excel's industrial-strength computing muscle, which lets you reduce reams of numbers to neat subtotals and averages. Performing these calculations is the first step to extracting meaningful information out of raw data.

Excel provides a number of different ways to build formulas, letting you craft them by hand or point-and-click them into existence. In this chapter, you'll learn about all of these techniques. You'll start by examining the basic ingredients that make up any formula, and then take a close look at the rules Excel uses when evaluating a formula.

Creating a Basic Formula

First things first: what exactly do formulas do in Excel? A *formula* is a series of instructions that you place in a cell in order to perform some kind of calculation. These instructions may be as simple as telling Excel to sum up a column of numbers, or they may incorporate advanced statistical functions to spot trends and make predictions. But in all cases, all formulas share the same basic characteristics:

- You enter each formula into a single cell.
- Excel calculates the result of a formula every time you open a spreadsheet or change the data a formula uses.
- Formula results are usually numbers, although you can create formulas that have text or Boolean (true or false) results.

- To view any formula (for example, to gain some insight into how Excel produced a displayed result), you must move to the cell containing the formula, and then look in the *formula bar* (see Figure 17-1). The formula bar also doubles as a handy tool for editing your formulas.

- Formulas can evaluate a combination of numbers you input (useful when you want to use Excel as a handy calculator) or, more powerfully, the contents of other cells. Formulas can even process an entire group of cells when using certain functions.

One of the simplest formulas you can create is this one:

=1+1

The equal sign's how you tell Excel that you're entering a formula (as opposed to a string of text or numbers). The formula that follows is what you want Excel to calculate. Note that the formula doesn't include the *result*. When creating a formula in Excel, you write the question, and then Excel coughs up the answer, as shown in Figure 17-1.

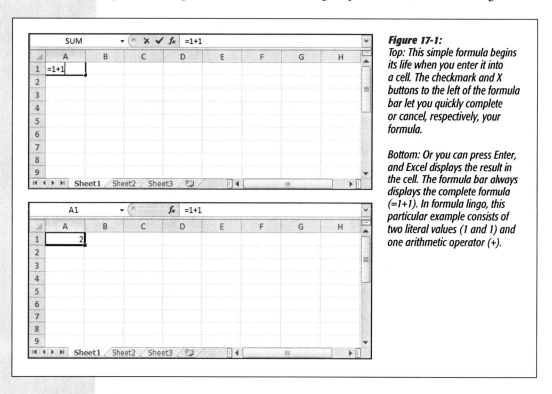

Figure 17-1:
Top: This simple formula begins its life when you enter it into a cell. The checkmark and X buttons to the left of the formula bar let you quickly complete or cancel, respectively, your formula.

Bottom: Or you can press Enter, and Excel displays the result in the cell. The formula bar always displays the complete formula (=1+1). In formula lingo, this particular example consists of two literal values (1 and 1) and one arithmetic operator (+).

All formulas use some combination of the following ingredients:

- **The equal sign** (=). Every formula must begin with the equal sign. It signals to Excel that the cell contains a formula, not just ordinary text.

- **The simple operators**. These ingredients include everything you fondly remember from high-school math class, including addition (+), subtraction (−), multiplication (*), division (/), and exponentiation (^). Table 17-1 lists these ingredients, also known as *arithmetic operators*.

- **Numbers**. These ingredients are known as constants or *literal values*, because they never change (unless you edit the formula).

- **Cell references**. These references point to another cell, or a range of cells, that you need data from in order to perform a calculation. For example, say you have a list of 10 numbers. A formula in the cell beneath this list may refer to all 10 of the cells above it in order to calculate their average.

- **Functions**. Functions are specialized formulas built into Excel that let you perform a wide range of calculations. For example, Excel provides dedicated functions that calculate sums and averages, standard deviations, yields, cosines and tangents, and much more.

- **Spaces**. Excel ignores these. However, you can use them to make a formula easier to read. For example, you can write the formula *=3*5 + 6*2* instead of *=3*5+6*2*. (The only exception to this rule applies to cell ranges, where spaces have a special meaning. You'll see this described on page 473.)

Table 17-1. Excel's arithmetic operators

Operator	Name	Example	Result
+	Addition	=1+1	2
–	Subtraction	=1–1	0
*	Multiplication	=2*2	4
/	Division	=4/2	2
^	Exponentiation	=2^3	8
%	Percent	=20%	0.20

Note: The percentage (%) operator divides a number by 100.

Excel's Order of Operations

For computer programs and human beings alike, one of the basic challenges when it comes to reading and calculating formula results is figuring out the *order of operations*—mathematician-speak for deciding which calculations to perform first when there's more than one calculation in a formula. For example, given the formula:

```
=10 - 8 * 7
```

the result, depending on your order of operations, is either 14 or -46. Fortunately, Excel abides by the standard rules for order of operations, meaning it doesn't necessarily process your formulas from left to right. Instead, it evaluates complex formulas piece-by-piece in this order:

1. Parentheses (any calculations within parentheses are always performed first)

2. Percent

3. Exponents

4. Division and Multiplication

5. Addition and Subtraction

Note: When Excel encounters formulas that contain operators of equal *precedence* (that is, the same order of operation priority level), it evaluates these operators from left to right. However, in basic mathematical formulas, this has no effect on the result.

For example, consider the following formula:

```
=5 + 2 * 2 ^ 3 - 1
```

To arrive at the answer of 20, Excel first performs the exponentiation (2 to the power of 3):

```
=5 + 2 * 8 - 1
```

And then the multiplication:

```
=5 + 16 - 1
```

And then the addition and subtraction:

```
=20
```

To control this order, you can add parentheses. For example, notice how adding parentheses affects the result in the following formulas:

```
5 + 2 * 2 ^ (3 - 1) = 13
(5 + 2) * 2 ^ 3 - 1 = 55
(5 + 2) * 2 ^ (3 - 1) = 28
5 + (2 * (2 ^ 3)) - 1 = 20
```

You must always use parentheses in pairs (one open parenthesis for every closing parenthesis). If you don't, then Excel gets confused and lets you know you need to fix things, as shown in Figure 17-2.

Tip: Remember, when you're working with a lengthy formula, you can expand the formula bar to see several lines at a time. To do so, click the down arrow at the far right of the formula bar (to make it three lines tall), or drag the bottom edge of the formula bar to make it as many lines large as you'd like.

Cell References

Excel's formulas are handy when you want to perform a quick calculation. But if you want to take full advantage of Excel's power, then you're going to want to use formulas to perform calculations on the information that's already in your worksheet. To do that you need to use *cell references*—Excel's way of pointing to one or more cells in a worksheet.

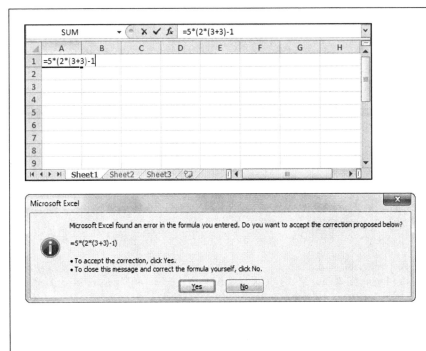

Figure 17-2:
Top: If you create a formula with a mismatched number of opening and closing parentheses (like this one), Excel won't accept it.

Bottom: Excel offers to correct the formula by adding the missing parentheses at the end. You may not want this addition, though. If not, cancel the suggestion, and then edit your formula by hand. Excel helps a bit by highlighting matched sets of parentheses. For example, as you move to the opening parenthesis, Excel automatically bolds both the opening and closing parentheses in the formula bar.

For example, say you want to calculate the cost of your Amazonian adventure holiday, based on information like the number of days your trip will last, the price of food and lodging, and the cost of vaccination shots at a travel clinic. If you use cell references, you can enter all this information into different cells, and then write a formula that calculates a grand total. This approach buys you unlimited flexibility because you can change the cell data whenever you want (for example, turning your three-day getaway into a month-long odyssey), and Excel automatically refreshes the formula results.

Cell references are a great way to save a *ton* of time. They come in handy when you want to create a formula that involves a bunch of widely scattered cells whose values frequently change. For example, rather than manually adding up a bunch of subtotals to create a grand total, you can create a grand total formula that uses cell references to point to a handful of subtotal cells. They also let you refer to large groups of cells by specifying a *range*. For example, using the cell reference lingo you'll learn on page 472, you can specify all the cells in the first column between the second and 100th rows.

Every cell reference points to another cell. For example, if you want a reference that points to cell A1 (the cell in column A, row 1), then use this cell reference:

```
=A1
```

In Excel-speak, this reference translates to "get the value from cell A1, and insert it in the current cell." So if you put this formula in cell B1, then it displays whatever value's currently in cell A1. In other words, these two cells are now linked.

Cell references work within formulas just as regular numbers do. For example, the following formula calculates the sum of two cells, A1 and A2:

```
=A1+A2
```

Note: In Excel lingo, A1 and A2 are *precedents*, which means another cell needs them to perform a calculation. Cell B1, which contains the formula, is called the *dependent*, because it depends on A1 and A2 to do its work. These terms become important when you need to hunt for errors in a complex calculation using Excel's error-checking tools (page 476).

Provided both cells contain numbers, you'll see the total appear in the cell that contains the formula. If one of the cells contains text, then you'll see an error code instead that starts with a # symbol. Errors are described in more detail on page 475.

GEM IN THE ROUGH

Excel As a Pocket Calculator

Sometimes you need to calculate a value before you enter it into your worksheet. Before you reach for your pocket calculator, you may like to know that Excel lets you enter a formula in a cell, and then use the result in that same cell. This way, the formula disappears and you're left with the result of the calculated value.

Start by typing your formula into the cell (for example =65*88). Next, press F9 to perform the calculation. Finally, just hit Enter to insert this value into the cell.

Remember, when you use this technique, you replace your formula with the calculated value. If your calculation is based on the values of other cells, then Excel won't update

the result if you change those other cells' values. That's the difference between a cell that has a value, and a cell that has a formula.

Excel has a similar trick that's helpful if you want to take a whole batch of formulas (in different cells), and replace them all with values. It's the Paste Values command. To try it out, select the cells that have the formulas you want to change, copy them (Home→Clipboard→Copy), and then paste them somewhere in your worksheet using the Home→Clipboard→Paste→Paste Values command. The pasted cells now have the numbers, not the formulas.

How Excel Formats Cells That Contain Cell References

As you learned in Chapter 16, the way you format a cell affects how Excel displays the cell's value. When you create a formula that references other cells, Excel attempts to simplify your life by applying automatic formatting. It reads the number format that the *source cells* (that is, the cells being referred *to*) use, and applies that to the cell with the formula. If you add two numbers and you've formatted both with the Currency number format, then your result also has the Currency number format. Of course, you're always free to change the formatting of the cell after you've entered the formula.

Usually, Excel's automatic formatting is quite handy. Like all automatic features, however, it's a little annoying if you don't understand how it works when it springs into action. Here are a few points to consider:

- Excel copies only the number format to the formula cell. It ignores other details, like fonts, fill colors, alignment, and so on.

- If your formula uses more than one cell reference, and the different cells use different number formats, Excel uses its own rules of precedence to decide which number format to use. For example, if you add a cell that uses the Currency number format with one that uses the Scientific number format, then the destination cell has the Scientific number format. Sadly, these rules aren't spelled out anywhere, so if you don't see the result you want, it's best to just set your own formatting.

- If you change the formatting of the source cells *after* you enter the formula, it won't have any effect on the formula cell.

- Excel copies source cell formatting only if the cell that contains the formula uses the General number format (which is the format that all cells begin with). If you apply another number format to the cell *before* you enter the formula, then Excel doesn't copy any formatting from the source cells. Similarly, if you change a formula to refer to new source cells, then Excel doesn't copy the format information from the new source cells.

Functions

A good deal of Excel's popularity is due to the collection of *functions* it provides. Functions are built-in, specialized algorithms that you can incorporate into your own formulas to perform powerful calculations. Functions work like miniature computer programs—you supply the data, and the function performs a calculation and gives you the result.

In some cases, functions just simplify calculations that you could probably perform on your own. For example, most people know how to calculate the average of several values, but when you're feeling a bit lazy, Excel's built-in AVERAGE() function automatically gives you the average of any cell range. Even more usefully, Excel functions perform feats that you probably wouldn't have a hope of coding on your own, including complex mathematical and statistical calculations that predict *trends*—hidden relationships in your data that you can use to make guesses or predict the future.

Every function provides a slightly different service. For example, one of Excel's statistical functions is named COMBIN(). It's a specialized tool used by probability mathematicians to calculate the number of ways a set of items can be combined.

Although this sounds technical, even ordinary folks can use COMBIN() to get some interesting information. You can use the COMBIN() function, for example, to count the number of possible combinations there are in certain games of chance.

The following formula uses COMBIN() to calculate how many different five-card combinations there are in a standard deck of 52 playing cards:

```
=COMBIN(52,5)
```

Functions are always written in all-capitals. (More in a moment on what those numbers inside the parentheses are doing.) However, you don't need to worry about the capitalization of function names because Excel automatically capitalizes the function names that you type in.

Learning New Functions

This book will introduce you to a "greatest hits" tour of new functions. Sometimes you'll start off by looking at a sample formula that uses the function, but for more complex functions, start by considering the *function description*.

The function description assigns a name to each argument. You can learn about the type of data the function requires before you start wading into an example with real numbers. For example, here's the function description for the COMBIN() function:

```
COMBIN(number_in_set, number_chosen)
```

You can tell the difference between a sample formula and the function description by the fact that the function description doesn't include the initial equal sign (=) that you need in all formulas.

Sometimes a function takes an *optional argument*. The argument isn't required, but it may be important depending on the behavior you want. Optional arguments are always shown in square brackets. (Excel uses the same convention in its help and formula tooltips.)

You'll see plenty of function descriptions in this book. You can look up function descriptions in Excel. Figure 17-9 (page 484) shows you where to look.

Using a Function in a Formula

Functions alone don't actually *do* anything in Excel. Functions need to be part of a formula to produce a result. For example, COMBIN() is a function name. But it actually *does* something—that is, give you a result—only when you've inserted it into a formula, like so: *=COMBIN(52,5)*.

Whether you're using the simplest or the most complicated function, the *syntax*—or, rules for including a function within a formula—is always similar. To use a function, start by entering the function name. Excel helps you out by showing a pop-up list with possible candidates as you type, as shown in Figure 17-3. This handy feature is called Formula AutoComplete.

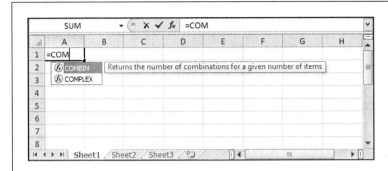

Figure 17-3:
After you type =COM, Excel helpfully points out that it knows only two functions that start that way: COMBIN() and COMPLEX(). If your fingers are getting tired, use the arrow keys to pick the right one out of the list, and then click Tab to pop it into your formula. (Or, you can just double-click it.)

After you type the function name, add a pair of parentheses. Then, inside the parentheses, put all the information the function needs to perform its calculations.

In the case of the COMBIN() function, Excel needs two pieces of information, or *arguments*. The first is the number of items in the set (the 52-card deck), and the second's the number of items you're randomly selecting (in this case, 5). Most functions, like COMBIN(), require two or three arguments. However, some functions can accept many more, while a few don't need any arguments at all. Once again, Formula AutoComplete guides you by telling you what arguments you need, as shown in Figure 17-4.

Figure 17-4:
When you type the opening parenthesis after a function name, Excel automatically displays a tooltip indicating what arguments the function requires. The argument you're currently entering is bolded in the tooltip. The argument names aren't crystal clear, but if you already know how the function works, they're usually enough to jog your memory.

Once you type this formula into a cell, the result (2598960) appears in your worksheet. In other words, there are 2,598,960 different possible five-card combinations in any deck of cards. Rather than having to calculate this fact using probability theory—or, heaven forbid, trying to count out the possibilities manually—the COMBIN() function handled it for you.

Note: Even if a function doesn't take any arguments, you still need to supply an empty set of parentheses after the function name. One example is the RAND() function, which generates a random fractional number. The formula =RAND() works fine, but if you forget the parentheses and merely enter =*RAND*, then Excel displays an error message (*#NAME?*). That's Excelian for: "Hey! You got the function's name wrong." See Table 17-2 for more information about Excel's error messages.

Using Cell References with a Function

One of the particularly powerful things about functions is that they don't necessarily need to use literal values in their arguments. They can also use cell references. For example, you could rewrite the five-card combination formula (mentioned above) so that it specifies the number of cards that'll be drawn from the deck based on a number that you've typed in somewhere else in the spreadsheet. Assuming this information's entered into cell B2, the formula would become:

    =COMBIN(52,**B2**)

Building on this formula, you can calculate the probability (albeit astronomically low) of getting the exact hand you want in one draw:

    =1/COMBIN(52,B2)

You could even multiply this number by 100 or use the Percent number style to see your percentage chance of getting the cards you want.

Tip: Excel gives you a detailed function reference to find functions and learn about them. Excel's information doesn't make for light reading, though; for the most part, it's in IRS-speak. You'll learn more about using this reference on page 486.

Using Cell Ranges with a Function

In many cases, you don't want to refer to just a single cell, but rather a *range* of cells. A range is simply a grouping of multiple cells. These cells may be next to each other (say, a range that includes all the cells in a single column), or they could be scattered across your worksheet. Ranges are useful for computing averages, totals, and many other calculations.

To group together a series of cells, use one of the three following reference operators:

- **The comma (,) separates more than one cell**. For example, the series *A1, B7, H9* is a cell range that contains three cells. The comma's known as the *union operator*. You can add spaces before or after a comma, but Excel just ignores or removes them (depending on its mood).

- **The colon (:) separates the top-left and bottom-right corners of a block of cells**. You're telling Excel: "Hey, use *this* block of cells in my formula." For example, *A1:A5* is a range that includes cells A1, A2, A3, A4, and A5. The range *A2:B3* is a grid that contains cells A2, A3, B2, and B3. The colon is the *range operator*—by far the most powerful way to select multiple cells.

- **The space can find cells that are common to two or more different cell ranges**. For example, the expression *A1:A3 A1:B10* is a range that consists of only three cells: A1, A2, and A3 (because those three cells are the only ones found in both ranges). The space is technically the *intersection operator*, and it's not used terribly often.

Tip: As you might expect, Excel lets you specify ranges by selecting cells with your mouse, instead of typing in the range manually. You'll see this trick later in this chapter on page 486.

You can't enter ranges directly into formulas that just use the simple operators. For example, the formula *=A1:B1+5* doesn't work, because Excel doesn't know what to do with the range A1:B1. (Should it sum up the range? Or average it? Excel has no way of knowing.) Instead, you need to use ranges with functions that know how to use them. For instance, one of Excel's most basic functions is named SUM(); it calculates the total for a group of cells. To use the SUM() function, you enter its name, an open parenthesis, the cell range you want to add up, and then a closed parenthesis.

Here's how you can use the SUM() function to add together three cells, A1, A2, and A3:

    =SUM(A1,A2,A3)

And here's a more compact syntax that performs the same calculation using the range operator:

    =SUM(A1:A3)

A similar SUM() calculation is shown in Figure 17-5. Clearly, if you want to total a column with hundreds of values, it's far easier to specify the first and last cell using the range operator rather than including each cell reference in your formula!

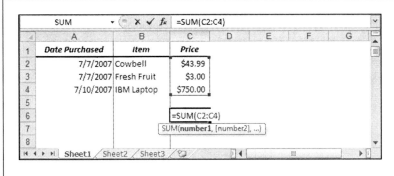

Figure 17-5:
Using a cell range as the argument in the SUM() function is a quick way to add up a series of numbers in a column. Note that when you enter or edit a formula, Excel highlights all the cells that formula uses with different colored borders. In this example, you see the range of cells C2, C3, and C4 in a blue box.

Sometimes your worksheet may have a list with unlimited growth potential, like a list of expenses or a catalog of products. In this case, you can code your formulas to include an *entire* column by leaving out the row number. For example, the range A:A includes all the cells in column A (and, similarly, the range 2:2 includes all the cells in row 2).

Excel Compatibility Functions

Some of Excel's functions use extraordinarily complex logic behind the scenes. Over the years, Excel experts have found minor flaws and quirks in some functions, like cases where the functions deviate from mathematical standards.

Correcting these problems is a bit messy. If different versions of Excel use subtly different calculation logic, you could find that your numbers change unpredictably—for example, when you upgrade your software or when you pass your spreadsheet to a colleague with a different version of Excel. In this case, consistency is more important than absolute, theoretical accuracy.

To avoid this sort of situation, the designers of Excel rarely change an existing function. Instead, in Excel 2010 they've added new functions that have similar names but incorporate a period. For example, in Excel 2010 the RANK.AVG() and RANK.EQ() functions replace the old-school RANK() function. Although RANK() still works, Microsoft recommends you use one of its replacements in new worksheets. Because RANK() is only kicking around to ensure that old worksheets keep working, it's called a *compatibility function*.

So how do you recognize compatibility functions, to make sure you don't accidentally use one when you actually want the more modern replacement? The trick is to read the function tooltip, which clearly identifies compatibility functions, as shown in Figure 17-6.

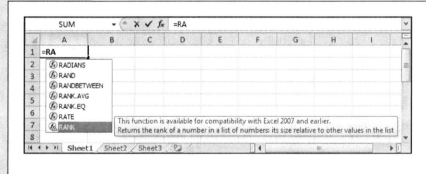

Figure 17-6:
The RANK() function is included for compatibility with old worksheets. Compatibility functions always appear at the bottom of the Formula AutoComplete list, and they're further distinguished by an icon with a yellow exclamation mark.

Unfortunately, the case for ditching compatibility functions isn't as clear-cut as it seems. The problem is that the new functions won't work in older versions of Excel. For example, imagine you use a function like RANK.EQ() and send your spreadsheet to a colleague who's using Excel 2007. Because Excel doesn't know anything about this function, it can't evaluate the formula. Instead, it shows the infamous #NAME? error (page 476) in the cell.

So the bottom line is this: for now, it's safer to keep using compatibility functions instead of their newer replacements. But if a replacement has the behavior you really want, and you don't expect to share your work with other people, you can use the new functions.

Note: Almost all of the functions you'll learn about in this book are traditional functions that have been with Excel for generations. You'll get a clear warning when we discuss new Excel 2010 functions (those with a period in their names), so you don't use them unknowingly.

Formula Errors

If you make a syntax mistake when entering a formula (like leaving out a function argument or including a mismatched number of parentheses), Excel lets you know right away. Moreover, like a stubborn schoolteacher, Excel won't accept the formula until you've corrected it. It's also possible, though, to write a perfectly legitimate formula that doesn't return a valid answer. Here's an example:

```
=A1/A2
```

If both A1 and A2 have numbers, this formula works without a hitch. However, if you leave A2 blank, or if you enter text instead of numbers, then Excel can't evaluate the formula, and it reminds you with an error message.

Excel lets you know about formula errors by using an *error code* that begins with the number sign (#) and ends with an exclamation point (!), as shown in Figure 17-7. In order to remove this error, you need to track down the problem and resolve it, which may mean correcting the formula or changing the cells it references.

Figure 17-7:
When Excel spots an error, it inserts a tiny green triangle into the cell's top-left corner. When you move to the offending cell, Excel displays an exclamation mark icon next to it (a smart tag). Hover over the exclamation mark to view a description of the error (which appears in a tooltip), or click the exclamation icon to see a list of menu options.

When you click the exclamation mark icon next to an error, you see a menu of choices (as shown in Figure 17-7):

- **Help on this error** pops open Excel's online help, with a (sometimes cryptic) description of the problem and what could have caused it.

- **Show Calculation Steps** pops open the Evaluate Formula dialog box, where you can work your way through a complex formula one step at a time.

- **Ignore Error** tells Excel to stop bothering you about this problem, in any worksheet you create. You won't see the green triangle for this error again (although you'll still see the error code in the cell).

- **Edit in Formula Bar** brings you to the formula bar, where you can change the formula to fix a mistake.

- **Error Checking Options** opens up the Excel Options dialog box, and brings you to the section where you can configure the settings Excel uses for alerting you about errors. You can turn off *background error checking*, or change the color of the tiny error triangles using the settings under the Error Checking heading. (Background error checking is the feature that flags cells with tiny green triangles when the cells contain a problem.) You can also tell Excel to start paying attention to errors you previously told it ignore by clicking the Reset Ignored Errors button. Underneath that button is a section named "Error checking rules" that has a number of options that focus on specific types of errors. For example, you can choose to have Excel ignore numbers stored as text, formulas that ignore part of a range, and other situations that technically aren't errors, but usually indicate that you've done something you didn't mean to. Excel *always* reports genuine errors, like #VALUE! and #NAME? regardless of what choices you make in this dialog box.

Note: Sometimes a problem isn't an error, but simply the result of data that hasn't yet been entered. In this case, you can solve the problem by using a conditional *error-trapping formula*. This conditional formula checks if the data's present, and it performs the calculation only if it is. The next section shows one way to use an error-trapping formula.

Table 17-2 lists the error codes that Excel uses.

Table 17-2. Excel's error codes

Error Code	Description
#VALUE!	You used the wrong type of data. Maybe your function expects a single value and you submitted a whole range. Or, more commonly, you might have used a function or created a simple arithmetic formula with a cell that contains text instead of numbers.
#NAME?	Excel can't find the name of the function you used. This error code usually means you misspelled a function's name, although it can indicate you used text without quotation marks or left out the empty parentheses after the function name. This error will also happen if you try to use a new Excel 2010 function in older version of Excel.

#NUM!	There's a problem with one of the numbers you're using. For example, this error code appears when a calculation produces a number that's too large or too small for Excel to deal with.
#DIV/0	You tried to divide by zero. This error code also appears if you try to divide by a cell that's blank, because Excel treats a blank cell as though it contains the number 0 for the purpose of simple calculations with the arithmetic operators. (Some functions, like AVERAGE(), are a little more intelligent and ignore blank cells.)
#REF!	Your cell reference is invalid. This error most often happens if you delete or paste over the cells you were using, or if you try to copy a cell from one worksheet to another.
#N/A	The value isn't available. This error can happen if you try to perform certain types of lookup or statistical functions that work with cell ranges. For example, if you use a function to search a range and it can't find what you need, you may get this result. Sometimes people enter a #N/A value manually in order to tell Excel to ignore a particular cell when creating charts and graphs. The easiest way to do this is to use the NA() function (rather than entering the text #N/A).
#NULL!	You used the intersection operator incorrectly. Remember, the intersection operator finds cells that two ranges share in common. This error results if there are no cells in common. Oftentimes, people use the intersection operator by accident, as the operator's just a single space character.
########	This code isn't actually an error condition—in all likelihood, Excel has successfully calculated your formula. However, the formula can't be displayed in the cell using the current number format. To solve this problem, you can widen the column, or possibly change the number format (page 441) if you require a certain number of fixed decimal places.

TROUBLESHOOTING MOMENT

Circular References

One of the more aggravating problems that can happen with formulas is the infamous *circular reference*. A circular reference happens when you create a formula that depends, indirectly or directly, on its own value. For example, consider what happens if you enter the following formula in cell B1.

```
=B1+10
```

In order for this formula to work, Excel would need to take the current B1 value, and add 10. However, this operation *changes* the value of B1, which means Excel needs to recalculate the formula. If unchecked, this process would continue in an endless loop without ever producing a value.

More subtle forms of circular references are possible. For example, you can create a formula in one cell that refers to a cell in another cell that refers back to the original cell. This is what's known as an *indirect circular reference*, but the problem is the same.

Ordinarily, Excel doesn't allow circular references. When you enter a formula that contains a circular reference, Excel displays an error message and forces you to edit the formula until you've removed the circular reference. However, you can configure Excel to allow circular references by modifying the calculation settings, as described in the Formulas section of the Excel Options dialog box. In this case, Excel repeats the loop a fixed number of times, or until the value seems to settle down and stop changing.

Logical Operators

So far, you've seen the basic arithmetic operators (which are used for addition, subtraction, division, and so on) and the cell reference operators (used to specify one or more cells). There's one final category of operators that's useful when creating formulas: *logical operators*.

Logical operators let you build conditions into your formulas so the formulas produce different values depending on the value of the data they encounter. You can use a condition with cell references or literal values.

For example, the condition A2=A4 is true if cell A2 contains the same value as cell A4. On the other hand, if these cells contain different values (say 2 and 3), then the formula generates a false value. Using conditions is a stepping-stone to using conditional logic. Conditional logic lets you perform different calculations based on different scenarios.

For example, you can use conditional logic to see how large an order is, and provide a discount if the total order cost's over $5,000. Excel *evaluates* the condition, meaning it determines if the condition's true or false. You can then tell Excel what to do, based on that evaluation.

Table 17-3 lists all the logical operators you can use to build formulas.

Table 17-3. Logical operators

Operator	Name	Example	Result
=	Equal to	1=2	FALSE
>	Greater than	1>2	FALSE
<	Less than	1<2	TRUE
>=	Greater than or equal to	1>=1	TRUE
<=	Less than or equal to	1<=1	TRUE
<>	Not equal to	1<>1	FALSE

You can use logical operators to build standalone formulas, but that's not particularly useful. For example, here's a formula that tests whether cell A1 contains the number 3:

    =(A2=3)

The parentheses aren't actually required, but they make the formula a little bit clearer, emphasizing the fact that Excel evaluates the condition first, and then displays the result in the cell. If you type this formula into the cell, then you see either the uppercase word TRUE or FALSE, depending on the content in cell A2.

On their own, logical operators don't accomplish much. However, they really shine when you start combining them with other functions to build conditional logic. For example, you can use the SUMIF() function, which totals the value of certain rows, depending on whether the row matches a set condition. Or you can use the IF() function to determine what calculation you should perform.

The IF() function has the following function description:

```
IF(condition, [value_if_true], [value_if_false])
```

In English, this line of code translates to: If the condition is true, display the second argument in the cell; if the condition is false, display the third argument.

Consider this formula:

```
=IF(A1=B2, "These numbers are equal", "These numbers are not equal")
```

This formula tests if the value in cell A1 equals the value in cell B2. If this is true, you'll see the message "These numbers are equal" displayed in the cell. Otherwise, you'll see "These numbers are not equal".

Note: If you see a quotation mark in a formula, it's because that formula uses text. You must surround all literal text values with quotation marks. (Numbers are different: You can enter them directly into a formula.)

People often use the IF() function to prevent Excel from performing a calculation if some of the data is missing. Consider the following formula:

```
=A1/A2
```

This formula causes a divide-by-zero error if A2 contains a 0 value. Excel then displays an error code in the cell. To prevent this from happening, you can replace this formula with the conditional formula shown here:

```
=IF(A2=0, 0, A1/A2)
```

This formula checks if cell A2 is empty or contains a 0. If so, the condition's true, and the formula simply gives you a 0. If it isn't, then the condition's false, and Excel performs the calculation A1/A2.

FREQUENTLY ASKED QUESTION

Showing and Printing Formulas

How in the world do I print out formulas that appear in my cells?

When you print a worksheet, Excel prints the calculated value in each cell rather than any formula that happens to be inside a cell. Usually, that's what you want to happen. But in some cases, rather than a printout of the formula's results, you want a record of the calculations used to generate the results.

Excel gives you a view setting so you can get this record. Just choose Formulas→Formula Auditing→Show Formulas. Now, Excel displays the cells' formula contents instead of the results—but on the current worksheet only. Excel also widens the columns so they can show more information (as formulas tend to be longer than their results). Repeat this process, and then uncheck the setting to return to normal life.

Formula Shortcuts

So far, you've learned how to build a formula by entering it manually. That's a good way to start out because it forces you to understand the basics of formula writing. But writing formulas by hand is a drag; plus, it's easy to type in the wrong cell address. For example, if you type A2 instead of A3, you can end up with incorrect data, and you won't necessarily notice your mistake.

As you become more comfortable with formulas, you'll find that Excel gives you a few tools—like point-and-click formula creation and the Insert Function button—to speed up your formula writing and reduce your mistakes. You'll learn about these features in the following sections.

Point-and-Click Formula Creation

Instead of entering a formula by typing it out letter-by-letter, Excel lets you create formulas by clicking the cells you want to use. For example, consider this simple formula that totals the numbers in two cells:

```
=A1+A2
```

To build this formula by clicking, just follow these steps:

1. **Move to the cell where you want to enter the formula.**

   This cell's where the result of your formula's calculation will appear. While you can pick any cell on the worksheet, A3 works nicely because it's directly below the two cells you're adding.

2. **Press the equal sign (=) key.**

   The equal sign tells Excel you're going to enter a formula.

3. **Move to the first cell you want to use in your formula (in this case, A1).**

   You can move to this first cell by pressing the up arrow key twice, or by clicking it with the mouse. You'll notice that moving to another cell doesn't cancel your edit, as it would normally, because Excel recognizes that you're building a formula. When you move to the new cell, the cell reference appears automatically in the formula (which Excel displays in cell A3, as well as in the formula bar just above your worksheet). If you move to another cell, Excel changes the cell reference accordingly.

4. **Press the + key.**

   Excel adds the + sign to your formula so that it now reads *=A1+*.

5. **Finish the formula by moving to cell A2, and then pressing Enter.**

   Again, you can move to A2 either by pressing the up arrow key or by clicking the cell directly. Remember, you can't just finish the formula by moving somewhere else; you need to press Enter to tell Excel you're finished writing the formula.

Another way to complete your edit is to click the checkmark that appears on the formula bar, to the left of the current formula. Even experienced Excel fans get frustrated with this step. If you click another cell before you press Enter, then you won't move to the cell—instead, Excel inserts the cell into your formula.

Tip: You can use this technique with any formula. Just type in the operators, function names, and so on, and use the mouse to select the cell references. If you need to select a range of cells, then just drag your mouse to highlight the whole group of cells. You can practice this technique with the SUM() function. Start by typing =SUM(into the cell, and then selecting the range of cells you want to add. Finish by adding a final closing parenthesis, and then press Enter.

Point-and-Click Formula Editing

You can use a similar approach to edit formulas, although it's slightly trickier.

1. **Move to the cell that contains the formula you want to edit, and then put it in edit mode by double-clicking it or pressing F2.**

   Excel highlights all the cells that this formula uses with a colored outline. Excel's even clever enough to use a helpful color-coding system. Each cell reference uses the same color as the outline surrounding the cell it's referring to. This can help you pick out where each reference is.

2. **Click the outline of the cell you want to change. (Your pointer changes from a fat plus sign to a four-headed arrow when you're over the outline.) With the mouse button still held down, drag this outline over to the new cell (or cells) you want to use.**

   Excel updates the formula automatically. You can also expand and shrink cell range references. To do so, put the formula-holding cell into edit mode, and then click any corner of the border that surrounds the range you want to change. Next, drag the border to change the size of the range. If you want to move the range, click any part of the range border, and then drag the outline in the same way as you would with a cell reference.

3. **Press Enter or click the formula bar checkmark to accept your changes.**

   That's it.

The Formulas Tab

The ribbon is stocked with a few buttons that make formula writing easier. To take a look, click the Formulas tab.

The most important part of the Formulas tab is the Function Library section at the left. It includes the indispensable Insert Function button, which you'll take for a spin in the next section. It also includes many more buttons that arrange Excel's vast catalog of functions into related categories for easier access. Figure 17-8 shows how it works.

Figure 17-8:
Each button in the Function Library section (other than Insert Function) pops up a mini menu of function choices. Choose one, and Excel inserts that function into the current formula. You can use this technique to find functions that you've used recently, or to browse the main function categories. This example shows some of the functions in the Math & Trig section, which you'll explore in the next chapter.

The Function Library divides its functions into the following categories:

- **AutoSum** has a few shortcuts that let you quickly add, average, or otherwise deal with a list of numbers.

- **Recently Used** has exactly what you'd expect—functions that you've recently chosen from the Function Library. If you're just starting out with functions, you'll see that Excel fills the Recently Used list with a small set of commonly used functions, like SUM().

- **Financial** functions let you track your car loan payments and calculate how many more years until you can retire rich.

- **Logical** functions let you create conditional logic for even smarter spreadsheets that make calculation decisions. You already had a quick introduction to conditional logic earlier in this chapter.

- **Text** functions manipulate words, sentences, and other non-numeric information.

- **Date & Time** functions perform calendar math, and can help you sort out ages, due dates, and more.

- **Lookup & Reference** functions perform the slightly mind-bending feat of searching for information in other cells.

- **Math & Trig** functions are the mathematic basics, including sums, rounding, and all the other high-school trigonometry you're trying to forget.

- **More Functions** groups together some heavy-duty Excel functions intended for specialized purposes. This category includes high-powered statistical and engineering functions. It also includes *cube* functions, which are designed for working in highly technical OLAP (*online analytical processing*) databases, and information functions, which get "information" about the other cells in your worksheet.

Using the Insert Function Button

Excel provides more than 300 built-in functions. In order to use a function, however, you need to type its name *exactly*. That means that every time you want to employ a function, you'll need to refer to this book, call on your own incredible powers of recollection, or click over to the convenient Insert Function button.

To use the Insert Function feature, choose Formulas→Function Library→Insert Function. However, formula pros skip straight to the action by clicking the *fx* button that appears just to the left of the formula bar. (Or, they press the Shift+F3 shortcut key.)

No matter which approach you use, Excel displays the Insert Function dialog box (shown in Figure 17-9), which offers three ways to search for and insert any of Excel's functions.

Figure 17-9:
Top: The Insert Function dialog box lets you quickly find the function you need. You can choose a category that seems likely to have the functions you're interested in.

Bottom: You can also try to search by entering keywords in the "Search for a function" box. Either way, when you click one of the functions in the list, Excel presents you with a description of the function at the bottom of the window.

- If you're looking for a function, the easiest way to find one is to choose a category from the "Or select a category" drop-down list. For example, when you select the Math & Trig category, you see a list of functions with names like SIN() and COS(), which perform basic trigonometric calculations.

- If you choose the Most Recently Used category, you'll see a list of functions you've recently picked from the ribbon or the Insert Function dialog box.

- If you're really ambitious, you can type a couple of keywords into the "Search for a function" text box. Next, click Go to perform the search. Excel gives you a list of functions that match your keywords.

When you spot a function that looks promising, click it once to highlight its name. Excel then displays a brief description of the function at the bottom of the window. For more information, you can click the "Help on this function" link in the bottom-left corner of the window. To build a formula using this function, click OK.

Excel then inserts the function into the currently active cell, followed by a set of parentheses. Next, it closes the Insert Function dialog box, and then opens the Function Arguments dialog box (Figure 17-10).

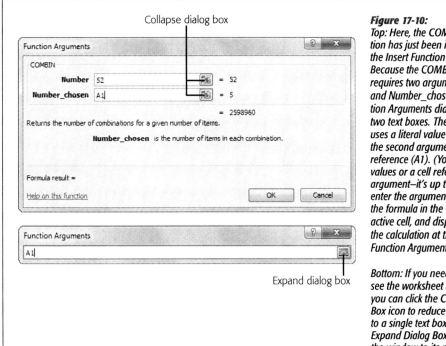

Collapse dialog box

Expand dialog box

Figure 17-10:
Top: Here, the COMBIN() function has just been inserted via the Insert Function dialog box. Because the COMBIN() function requires two arguments (Number and Number_chosen), the Function Arguments dialog box shows two text boxes. The first argument uses a literal value (52), while the second argument uses a cell reference (A1). (You can use literal values or a cell reference for either argument—it's up to you.) As you enter the arguments, Excel updates the formula in the worksheet's active cell, and displays the result the calculation at the bottom of the Function Arguments dialog box.

Bottom: If you need more room to see the worksheet and select cells, you can click the Collapse Dialog Box icon to reduce the window to a single text box. Clicking the Expand Dialog Box icon restores the window to its normal size.

Note: Depending on the function you're using, Excel may make a (somewhat wild) guess about which arguments you want to supply. For example, if you use the Insert Function dialog box to add a SUM() function, you'll see that Excel picks a nearby range of cells. If this isn't what you want, just replace the range with the correct values.

Now you can finish creating your formula by using the Function Arguments dialog box, which includes a text box for every argument in the function. It also includes a help link for detailed information about the function, as shown in Figure 17-11.

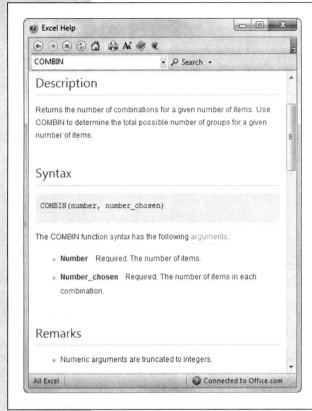

Figure 17-11:
Both the Insert Function and Function Arguments dialog boxes make it easy to get detailed reference information about any function by clicking the "Help on this function" link at the bottom left of the window. The help page shown here shows the reference for the trigonometric SIN() function, which calculates the sine of an angle. Excel's help page includes a brief description, important notes, and a couple of sample formulas that use the function, complete with results.

To complete your formula, follow these steps:

1. **Click the text box for the first argument.**

   A brief sentence describing the argument appears in the Function Arguments dialog box.

   Some functions don't require any arguments. In this case, you don't see any text boxes, although you still see some basic information about the function. Skip directly to step 4.

2. **Enter the value for the argument.**

   If you want to enter a literal value (like the number 52), type it in now. To enter a cell reference, you can type it in manually, or click the appropriate cell on the worksheet. To enter a range, drag the cursor to select a group of cells.

   You may need to move the Function Arguments dialog box to the side to expose the part of the worksheet you want to click. The Collapse Dialog Box icon (located to the immediate right of each text box) is helpful since clicking it shrinks the window's size. This way, you'll have an easier time selecting cells from your worksheet. To return the window to normal, click the Expand Dialog Box icon, which is to the right of the text box.

3. **Repeat step 2 for each argument in the function.**

   As you enter the arguments, Excel updates the formula automatically.

4. **Once you've specified a value for every required argument, click OK.**

   Excel closes the window and returns you to your worksheet.

Functions That Return Arrays

A few exotic functions actually give you *multiple* results, so rather than simply generating a single value, as a function like SUM() would, these functions generate more than one value. To use these functions properly, you need to create a special type of formula called an *array formula*. (An array is a group of numbers.) You can create an array formula quite easily. Simply select all the cells that Excel will use to display the results, type in the formula, and then end by pressing Ctrl+Shift+Enter. It's this final keystroke that actually creates the array formula and links the cells together. Usually, you'll you see a different result appear in each cell.

Technically, when you create an array formula, you have a single formula that's shared between several cells. You know that you have an array formula because the formula appears in the formula bar with curly braces { } around it whenever you move into any one of the linked cells. However, you can't edit the individual cells in the array formula. (If you try, Excel warns you that you can't change part of an array.) To make a change to an array formula, you need to select all the cells in the array, edit the formula, and then press Ctrl+Shift+Enter to recreate the array formula.

Copying Formulas

Sometimes you need to perform similar calculations in different cells throughout a worksheet. For example, say you want to calculate sales tax on each item in a product catalog, the monthly sales in each store of a company, or the final grade for each student in a class. In this section, you'll learn how Excel makes it easy with *relative cell references*. Relative cell references are cell references that Excel updates automatically when you copy them from one cell into another. They're the standard kind of references that Excel uses (as opposed to absolute cell references, which are covered in the next section). In fact, all the references you've used so far have been relative references, but you haven't yet seen how they work with copy-and-paste operations.

Consider the worksheet shown in Figure 17-12, which contains a teacher's grade book. In this example, each student has three grades: two tests and one assignment. A student's final grade is based on the following percentages: 25 percent for each of the two tests, and 50 percent for the assignment.

The following formula calculates the final grade for the first student (Edith Abbott):

    =B2*25% + C2*25% + D2*50%

The formula that calculates the final mark for the second student (Grace DeWitt) is almost identical. The only change is that all the cell references are offset by one row, so that B2 becomes B3, C2 becomes C3, and D2 becomes D3:

    =B3*25% + C3*25% + D3*50%

Figure 17-12:
This worksheet shows a list of students in a class, and calculates the final grade for each student using two test scores and an assignment score. So far, the only formula that's been added is for the first student (in cell E2).

You may get fed-up entering all these formulas by hand. A far easier approach is to copy the formula from one cell to another. Here's how:

1. **Move to the cell containing the formula you want to copy.**

   In this example, you'd move to cell E2.

2. **Copy the formula to the clipboard by pressing Ctrl+C.**

   You can also copy the formula by choosing Home→Clipboard→Copy.

3. **Select the range of cells you want to copy the formula into.**

   Select cells E3 to E10.

4. **Paste in the new formulas by pressing Ctrl+V.**

   You can also paste the formula by choosing Home→Clipboard→Paste.

   When you paste a formula, Excel magically copies an appropriate version of the formula into each of the cells from E3 to E10. These automatic formula adjustments happen for any formula, whether it uses functions or just simple operators. Excel then automatically calculates and displays the results, as shown in Figure 17-13.

Tip: There's an even quicker way to copy a formula to multiple cells by using the AutoFill feature. In the student grade example, start by moving to cell E2, which contains the original formula. Click and hold the small square at the bottom-right corner of the cell outline, and then drag the outline down until it covers all cells from E3 to E10. When you release the mouse button, Excel inserts the formula copies in the AutoFill region.

Figure 17-13:
When you paste the formula into one or more new cells, each Final Grade formula operates on the data in its own row. This means that you don't must tweak the formula for each student. The formula bar shows the formula contained in cell E3.

Absolute Cell References

Relative references are a true convenience since they let you create formula copies that don't need the slightest bit of editing. But you've probably already realized that relative references don't always work. For example, what if you have a value in a specific cell that you want to use in multiple calculations? You may have a currency conversion ratio that you want to use in a list of expenses. Each item in the list needs to use the same cell to perform the conversion correctly. But if you make copies of the formula using relative cell references, then you'll find that Excel adjusts this reference automatically and the formula ends up referring to the wrong cell (and therefore the wrong conversion value).

Figure 17-14 shows the problem with the worksheet of student grades. In this example, the test and assignment scores aren't all graded out of 100 possible points; each item has a different total score available (listed in row 12). In order to calculate the percentage a student earned on a test, you need to divide the test score by the total score available. This formula, for example, calculates the percentage for Edith Abbott's performance on Test B:

    =B2/B12*100%

To calculate Edith's final grade for the class, you use the following formula:

    =B2/B12*25% + C2/C12*25% + D2/D12*50%

Like many formulas, this one contains a mix of cells that should be relative (the individual scores in cells B2, C2, and D2) and those that should be absolute (the possible totals in cell B12, C12, and D12). As you copy this formula to subsequent rows, Excel incorrectly changes all the cell references, causing a calculation error.

Figure 17-14:
In this version of the student grade book, both the tests and the assignment are graded on different scales (as listed in row 12). Thus, the formula for calculating the final class grade uses the values in cells B12, C12, and D12. When you copy the Final Grade formula from the first row (cell E2) to the rows below it, Excel offsets the formula to use B13, C13, and D13—none of which exist. Thus a problem happens—shown here as a divide-by-zero error. To fix this, you need to use absolute cell references.

Fortunately, Excel provides a perfect solution. It lets you use *absolute cell references*— cell references that always refer to the same cell. When you create a copy of a formula that contains an absolute cell reference, Excel doesn't change the reference (as it does when you use *relative* cell references; see the previous section). To indicate that a cell reference is absolute, use the dollar sign ($) character. For example, to change B12 into an absolute reference, you add the $ character twice, once in front of the column and once in front of the row, which changes it to $B$12.

Here's the corrected class grade formula (for Edith) using absolute cell references:

```
=B2/$B$12*25% + C2/$C$12*25% + D2/$D$12*50%
```

This formula still produces the same result for the first student. However, you can now copy it correctly for use with the other students. To copy this formula into all the cells in column E, use the same procedure described in the previous section on relative cell references.

Partially Fixed References

You might wonder why you need to use the $ character twice in an absolute reference (before the column letter *and* the row number). The reason is that Excel lets you create *partially* fixed references. To understand partially fixed references, it helps to remember that every cell reference consists of a column letter and a row number.

With a partial fixed reference, Excel updates one component (say, the column part) but not the other (the row) when you copy the formula. If this sounds complex (or a little bizarre), consider a few examples:

- You have a loan rate in cell A1, and you want all loans on an entire worksheet to use that rate in calculations. If you refer to the cell as $A$1, its column and row always stay the same when you copy the formula to another cell.

- You have several rows of loan information. The first column of a row always contains the loan rate for all loans on that row. In your formula cell, if you refer to cell $A1, then when you copy the formula across columns and rows, the row changes (2, 3, 4, etc.) but the column doesn't (A2, A3, A4, etc.).

- You have a table of loan rates organized by the length of the loan (10-year, 15-year, 20-year, etc.) along the top of a worksheet. Loans in each column are calculated using the rate specified at the top of that column. If you refer to the rate cell as A$1 in your first column's formula, then the row stays constant (1), but the column changes (B1, C1, D1, etc.) as you copy the formula across columns and down rows.

Tip: You can quickly change formula references into absolute or partially fixed references. Just put the cell into edit mode (by double-clicking it or pressing F2). Then, move through the formula until you've highlighted the appropriate cell reference. Now, press F4 to change the cell reference. Each time you press F4, the reference changes. If the reference is A1, for instance, it becomes $A$1, then A$1, then $A1, and then A1 again.

Creating an Exact Formula Copy

There's another way to copy a formula that prevents Excel from automatically changing the formula's cell references. The trick is to copy the formula itself rather than copy the whole cell (which is what you do when performing a basic copy-and-paste operation on a formula).

The process takes a few more steps, and it lets you paste only one copy at a time, but it can still come in handy if you don't want Excel to use relative references. Here's how it works:

1. First, move to the cell that contains the formula you want to copy.

2. Place this cell in edit mode by double-clicking it or pressing F2.

3. Select all the text in the cell. You can use the mouse, or you can use the arrow keys (just hold down Shift as you scroll from the beginning to the end of the cell).

4. Once you've selected the complete formula, press Ctrl+C to copy it.

5. Press Esc to leave edit mode once you're finished.

6. Move to the new cell, and then press Ctrl+V to paste it.

Keep in mind that when you use this approach, you create an exact copy of the formula. That means this technique doesn't help in situations where some cell references need to be absolute, and others need to be relative.

Referring to Other Worksheets

To reference a cell in another worksheet, you simply need to preface the cell with the worksheet name, followed by an exclamation mark. For example, say you've created a formula to double the value of the number in cell A1 on a worksheet named Sheet1. You'd use this formula:

```
=A1*2
```

If you want to use the same formula in another worksheet (in the same workbook), you'd insert this formula in the new worksheet:

```
=Sheet1!A1*2
```

Note: If you use the point-and-click method to build formulas, you'll find that you don't need to worry about the syntax for referring to cells on other worksheets. If you switch to another worksheet, and then click a cell in it, while you're building a formula, Excel automatically inserts the correct reference with the worksheet name.

How Changing the Location of Cells Affects Formulas

OK, I know how Excel adjusts a formula when I copy it to another location. But what happens if I move cells around after I've created a formula?

No worries. It turns out that Excel is surprisingly intelligent. Consider the following simple formula:

```
=B1+A2
```

If you cut and paste the contents of A2 to A3, Excel automatically updates your formula to point to the new cell, without complaining once. It also performs the same automatic cleanup if you drag the contents of a cell to another location (although if you simply make a duplicate copy of the cell, Excel won't change your formula). Excel is also on the ball when you insert and delete rows and columns.

If at any time Excel can't find your cells, the formula changes to show the error code #REF!. You can then take a closer look at the formula to find out what really went wrong. For example, if you delete column B from your spreadsheet (by selecting the column and using the Home→Cells→Delete command), the formula changes to this:

```
=#REF!+A2
```

Even though there's still a B1 cell in your worksheet (it's the cell that was formerly named C1), Excel modifies the formula to make it clear that you've lost your original data.

A Function Sampler and Formula Troubleshooting

Excel is packed with dozens and dozens of functions. It's like having a team of number- and text-crunching spreadsheet jockeys by your desk, ready to help. (Yep, functions can also work their magic on your prose, doing things like joining together words, trimming out unwanted spaces, and serving as a kind of super-powered find-and-replace tool.) This chapter dips its toe into the giant pool of built-in functions. You'll take a "greatest hits"-style tour and then wind things up with a look at a related and similarly helpful aid: the program's formula evaluation and error-checking tools.

Rounding Numbers

Most people don't devote enough thought to *rounding*, the process by which you adjust fractional numbers so they're less precise but more manageable. For example, rounding can transform the unwieldy number 1.984323125 to 2. Excel has two ways to use rounding:

- **Modify the number format of the cell.** With this method, Excel rounds the displayed value, but it doesn't change the underlying value. The advantage to this approach is that you can use the value in other calculations without losing any precision. When Excel rounds your numbers using this method, it simply rounds to the last displayed digit (rounding up if the next digit is 5 or greater).

  For example, if you tell Excel to show the number 3.145 using two decimal places, then Excel displays the rounded value of 3.15. (Cell value formatting is described in Chapter 16.)

- **Use a rounding function**. This approach gives you more control. For example, you can round a number *before* you use it in another calculation, and you can round numbers to a multiple you choose, like 500 or 1,000. The drawback is that when you use a rounding function, you may lose precision. This doesn't happen when you change the number format, which simply tweaks the way the number is displayed.

With classic overkill, Microsoft includes no fewer than 10 functions designed specifically for rounding numbers; what follows is a look at the most useful ones.

ROUND(), ROUNDDOWN(), ROUNDUP(): Rounding Numbers

The most basic (and most commonly used) of Excel's rounding functions is ROUND(), which rounds a numeric value to whatever level of precision you choose. The ROUND() function needs two arguments: the actual number you want to round, and the number of digits you want to keep to the right of the decimal point. Here's what it looks like:

```
ROUND(number_to_round, number_of_digits)
```

For example, the following formula rounds the number 3.987 to two decimal places. The result is 3.99.

```
=ROUND(3.987, 2)
```

If you specify 0 for the number of digits, then Excel rounds to the nearest whole number. Interestingly, you can also round to the nearest 10, 100, 1000, and so on by using negative numbers for the second argument. For example, if you use –2 for the number of digits, then Excel rounds two digits to the *left* of the decimal place, which means your number gets rounded to the nearest 100.

Here's an example:

```
=ROUND(34655.7, -2)
```

This formula produces a result of 34,700.

Note: The ROUND() function always rounds the positive values 1 through 4 *down*; 5 through 9 get rounded *up*. If you round 1.5 to the nearest whole number, for instance, the result is 2. When dealing with negative numbers, Excel rounds the digits 5 through 9 down (toward the larger negative value). Similarly, –1 through –4 get rounded up. For example, –1.5 gets rounded to –2, while –1.4 gets rounded up to –1.

The ROUNDDOWN() and ROUNDUP() functions work similarly to ROUND(). Like ROUND(), they take two arguments: the number you want to round, and the number of decimal places you want the final, rounded number to use. The difference is that ROUNDDOWN() always rounds numbers down, while ROUNDUP() always rounds numbers up.

For example, the result of ROUNDUP(1.1, 0) is 2, even though 1.1 is only slightly above 1. Similarly, the result of ROUNDDOWN(1.9, 0) is 1, even though 1.9 is almost 2. The only time that ROUNDUP() and ROUNDDOWN() don't change a number is if it's already rounded to the appropriate precision. For example, the result of ROUND-UP(2, 0) and ROUNDDOWN(2, 0) is the same: 2.

When most people learn about ROUNDUP() and ROUNDDOWN() they often wonder why anyone would want to use a rounding function that's *less* precise than ol' reliable ROUND(). The answer, not surprisingly, must do with making more money. If you're selling discounted Beanie Babies, say, then you might set the price at 60 percent of the original list price. However, this formula produces prices like $8.43423411 that you need to round to the nearest penny. Rather than rounding down (and giving up your fractional cents), you can use ROUNDUP() to make sure the price is always rounded up, ensuring that you keep every last penny and even collect a few extra. Never say Microsoft didn't try to help you make a buck.

Manipulating Text

You can't use arithmetic operators like + and – with text. If you try to perform a calculation by referring to one or more cells containing text, Excel displays a *#VALUE* error message. However, there's one operator you can use: the *concatenation* operator (&), which joins together text. For example, imagine you have an individual's first name in cell A1, and a last name in cell A2. You could join the values from these two cells to create a full name with this formula:

```
=A1 & A2
```

This approach has one drawback. In all likelihood, the first and last name cells don't include any leading or trailing spaces. This trait means when you join them, they'll get fused into one word, like JohnSmith. One solution is to explicitly add a space (between quotation marks) into your formula, like so:

```
=A1 & " " & A2
```

The important concept in this example is that you can enter *string literals*—fixed pieces of text (including spaces)—as easily as you can enter literal numbers. The only difference between entering literal text and literal numbers is that you have to place all text between quotation marks. You can stitch together as many pieces of text together at a time as you want; there's no limit. The next group of functions showcases the many different ways that Excel lets you manipulate text.

CONCATENATE(): Joining Strings of Text Together

The CONCATENATE() function lets you join text in exactly the same way the & operator does. CONCATENATE() joins all the parameters that you supply into one long piece of text, in the order you specify them.

Here's an equivalent way to rewrite the aforementioned name-joining formula by using CONCATENATE() with two pieces of text:

```
=CONCATENATE(A1, " ", A2)
```

LEFT(), MID(), and RIGHT(): Copying Portions of a Text String

Just as you can join pieces of text, you can also split up a string of text. The LEFT(), MID(), and RIGHT() functions let you extract a portion from a larger text string. For example, the LEFT() function takes two arguments: the text you want to examine, and the number of characters that Excel should extract, starting from the string's left side:

```
LEFT(text, num_characters)
```

To take the first four letters from the text in cell A1, you'd use the formula:

```
=LEFT(A1, 4)
```

Assuming the cell contains the text *tofurkey*, the result of this formula would be the shortened text *tofu*.

The RIGHT() function performs the same operation, but it extracts letters starting from the right side of a string. For example, consider the following formula:

```
=RIGHT(A1, 5)
```

If you use this function with the same string, you'll simply end up with the text *urkey*.

The MID() function is more powerful than the LEFT() and RIGHT() functions, as it has the ability to extract a consecutive series of characters from anywhere inside a string. When using the MID() function, you need to supply *three* arguments: the text you're evaluating, the starting position, and the number of characters. Excel numbers each letter in a string (it also counts spaces), starting with 1 for the first letter, 2 for the second letter, and so on. That means if you specify a starting position of 3 and a length of 2, Excel extracts the third and fourth characters. The basic formula looks like this:

```
MID(text, start_position, number_of_characters)
```

Here's an example that copies characters from the middle of a string. If the cell A1 contains the text *Swanky Franks*, the following formula returns the value Frank.

```
=MID(A1, 8, 5)
```

Note: LEFT(), MID(), and RIGHT() all pluck out the strings you specify, but they leave the original contents of the cell you're examining unchanged.

TRIM() and CLEAN(): Removing Unwanted Spaces and Non-Printing Characters

The TRIM() and CLEAN() functions perform minor cleanup on any strings of text you run through them. TRIM() removes any leading and trailing spaces; it also changes any series of more than one space to a single space. Thus, if you use TRIM() on the text string " Hello There " the altered text becomes "Hello There." TRIM() can be quite handy for fixing erratic spacing.

Using PROPER() to change Names in All Caps to Initial Caps

Usually, functions like UPPER(), LOWER(), and PROPER() transform the appearance of text that's already in your spreadsheet. But you could have a tricky time figuring out exactly how to do this transformation.

Say you've got a list of first and last names in column A (beginning in cell A1) whose letters are all uppercase. You want to change these names so that only the first letter of each name's capitalized. Here's what to do. First, insert a new column B. Next, enter the formula =PROPER(A1) in cell B1, and then copy this formula to the rest of the cells in column B. Because this formula uses a *relative* cell reference (as explained on page 487), Excel automatically adjusts the formula for each cell that you paste it into.

Once you've taken this step, Excel displays the properly capitalized names in column B. But you can't just copy and paste these cells into column A (because they hold formulas that reference the cells you'd be pasting them into). Instead, you need to select the corrected names from column B, copy them (Home→Clipboard→Copy, move to cell A1, and then select Home→Clipboard→Paste→Values (not the plain-vanilla Home→Clipboard→Paste command).

This technique provides a quick way to clean up a number of problems. For example, you can also use this approach with many other text functions like TRIM(), CLEAN(), SUBSTITUTE(), TEXT(), FIXED(), DOLLAR(), all of which are explained in this chapter.

CLEAN() simply removes non-printable characters from a text string. Non-printable characters, which usually appear as empty-box icons in your text, tend to appear only if you import some text from another file format that Excel has difficulty understanding.

SUBSTITUTE(): Replacing One Sequence of Characters with Another

The SUBSTITUTE() function replaces a sequence of characters in a string with another set of characters. The function has three parts: the text you want to modify, the characters you're looking to replace, and the replacement text you want to insert. In addition, you can supply an optional *occurrence number* parameter, which Excel uses if it finds more than one match. For example, if your search text's matched three times, and you supply 2 for your occurrence number, Excel changes only the second occurrence. If you don't supply the occurrence number, Excel changes all occurrences. Here's what the function looks like:

```
SUBSTITUTE(text, old_text, new_text, [occurrence_number])
```

Consider the case where cell A1 contains the text: *It was the best of times; it was the worst of times.* You could use the following formula:

```
=SUBSTITUTE(A1, "times", "nanoseconds")
```

The result is the string: *It was the best of nanoseconds; it was the worst of nanoseconds.*

On the other hand, the following formula explicitly replaces just the second occurrence. The resulting string is: *It was the best of times; it was the worst of crimes.*

```
=SUBSTITUTE(A1, "times", "crimes", 2)
```

Solving Formula Errors

Errors… they happen in the most unexpected places, transforming rows of calculations into unhelpful error codes like *#NAME?*, *#VALUE!*, and *#MORON!* (OK, that last one doesn't actually appear in Excel, but it might as well, given the sense of defeat and frustration these error codes can give you.) In some cases, you can see how to fix an error just by looking at the formula. However, sometimes the problem isn't so easy to solve, especially if your formulas perform calculations using the results of *other* formulas. In such cases, you can have a tough time tracking down where the original error happened.

Excel provides some interesting *formula auditing tools*—a handful of features that you can use to inspect broken formulas or figure out what's going on in really complex ones. These tools make it much easier to fix errors.

With any error, your first step is to identify the error code by using the information listed in Table 17-2 on page 476. If the problem isn't immediately obvious, then you can use the Formula Auditing tools to perform the following tasks:

- Evaluate an expression step-by-step, until you hit the error. That way, you know exactly what part of the formula's causing the error.

- Trace the *precedents* of a formula that's causing an error. Precedents are the cells that a particular formula references. In the formula =*A1+B1*, both A1 and B1 are precedents. If either one of these cells contains an error, then the error gets fed into—and trips up—the formula.

- Trace the *dependents* of a cell. Dependents are other cells that use the current cell. If one cell has the formula =*A1+B1*, and another cell contains =*A1*10*, both these cells are dependents of cell A1. If A1 has an error, it infects both formulas.

- Perform an error check on the entire worksheet. Excel's error check is like a spell check. One by one, it takes you to each cell that has an unresolved problem.

To perform any of these tasks, you'll need the Formulas tab's Formula Auditing section. The following sections explain how you use it to find errors, evaluate formulas piece-by-piece, and trace relationships.

Step-by-Step Evaluation

Complex formulas usually include multiple *sub-expressions*. Each sub-expression is a piece of any formula that's evaluated separately. It may be an arithmetic operation in parentheses, a nested function, or even just a cell reference. In order to understand what's causing an error in your formula, you need to know which sub-expression caused the problem.

Excel's solution is to provide a feature—called the Evaluate Formula tool—that evaluates your formula one sub-expression at a time. Using this tool, you can watch as Excel computes your formula, up until the point where the error appears.

To watch the step-by-step execution of a formula that contains an error, follow these steps:

1. **Move to the cell that contains the formula that's producing the error.**

   You don't need to highlight the formula, you just need to be in the offending cell.

2. **Choose Formulas→Formula Auditing→Evaluate Formula.**

   The Evaluate Formula dialog box appears (Figure 18-1), with the formula in a large, multiline textbox.

Figure 18-1:
The first two arguments in this formula have been evaluated. (The second argument [60] is italicized, indicating that Excel calculated it in the last step.) The next time you click Evaluate, Excel evaluates the third argument, which is underlined. If you want to show the contents of this cell before evaluating it, you can click Step In.

3. **Excel underlines the part of the formula that it's about to evaluate. Click the Evaluate button.**

   Excel evaluates the sub-expression and replaces it with the calculated value. It might replace a cell reference with the cell's actual value, evaluate an arithmetic operator, or execute a function. The value appears in italics, indicating that it's the most recent value that Excel has calculated.

4. **Repeat step 3 until the sub-expression that generates the error occurs.**

   When the error occurs, you'll see the error code appear in your formula. When you click Evaluate again, the error code spreads, encompassing the whole expression or the function that uses it. Consider the ill-fated formula =1+5/0. The first step (the division) creates a divide-by-zero error, and the formula appears as =1+#DIV/0!. But you can't add 1 to an error, so, in the next step, the error spreads to the whole formula, which becomes =#DIV/0! in the end.

5. **When the calculation process ends, you can click Restart to repeat the calculation from the beginning.**

   You can also click Close to stop evaluating the formula and return to your worksheet at any time.

Digging Deeper into Linked Formulas

Even when you've discovered the sub-expression that's causing the trouble, you still may not have found the root of the problem. If the sub-expression that's causing the error is a reference, it may point to another cell that contains another formula. If it does, then you need to evaluate *that* formula step-by-step in order to find the real mistake.

To evaluate the second formula, you can move to the appropriate cell and start the step-by-step evaluation process by clicking the Evaluate Formula button. However, Excel also provides a useful shortcut that lets you jump from one formula into another. The secret is the Step In and Step Out buttons in the Evaluate Formula dialog box (Figure 18-2).

When you're using the Evaluate Formula dialog box, the Step In button becomes available just before you evaluate a sub-expression containing a cell reference. If you click the Step In button at this point, Excel adds a new text box to the dialog box underneath the first one. This new text

box shows the contents of the referenced cell. Excel also informs you if the cell contains a formula or a constant (just read the label at the bottom of the Evaluate Formula dialog box). If the cell contains a constant or there's no calculation left to perform, you need to click Step Out to return to the original formula. If the cell does contain a formula, you can click the Evaluate button to start evaluating it—one sub-expression at a time—and then click Step Out once you're finished.

In fact, Excel lets you dig even deeper into chains of linked formulas. Every time you find a cell reference that points to another formula-holding cell, you can click Step In to show the formula in a new text box. You can continue this process with no practical limit. If you exceed the space available in the Evaluate Formula dialog box, Excel just adds a scroll bar to help you out.

Figure 18-2:
In this example, the Step In button has taken you three levels deep into a formula. The formula it's evaluating is in the first box; it's A3+A4+A5. However, clicking Step In adds a second box, which reveals that cell A3 itself contains a formula (B3+C3). Finally, another click of Step In shows a third box, which zooms in on the first part of the second formula (B3), and shows that the cell it points to holds the number 84.

Tip: Step-by-step evaluation isn't just for solving errors. It can also help you understand *why* a formula doesn't produce the result you expect. You can use the Evaluate Formula dialog box with a formula that doesn't cause an error in exactly the same way as one that does. By watching the calculation proceed step-by-step, you may realize that the order of operations Excel follows is subtly different from the order you expected. You can then edit the formula accordingly.

Tracing Precedents and Dependents

The Evaluate Formula dialog box is one way you can examine complex formulas' anatomy. However, depending on the complexity of your formulas, you can end up having to move through a long series of steps before you find the problem. In this case, you may be interested in using a different approach, one that uses Excel's ability to graphically trace linked cells. This feature isn't any better or worse than the Evaluate Formula dialog box—it's just another tool that you can use to resolve problems, depending on the situation and your own preference.

First, here's a quick review of how Excel thinks about precedents and dependents. Consider the following formula:

    =A1+B1

If this formula is in cell C1, that makes A1 and B1 *precedents* of C1. In other words, C1 relies on the values in A1 and B1 in order to do its work. If either of these cells contains an error value, the problem spreads into C1. You can say that C1 is the *dependent* of both A1 and B1.

Excel's tracing features let you see a graphical representation of these relationships—in the form of blue arrows—right on your worksheet without needing to look in another window or dialog box.

To see tracing in action, move to a cell that contains one or more cell references, and then choose Formulas→Formula Auditing→Trace Precedents. Excel displays solid blue arrows that link the cells together. If you click Trace Precedents in the cell C1 that contains that formula *=A1+B1*, you see two arrows. One points from A1 to C1, and the other points from B1 to C1. Figures 18-3 and 18-4 show examples.

Note: If a formula references a cell in another worksheet or workbook, Excel draws a dotted line linking your cell to a small grid icon. This icon represents the other worksheet or workbook and can't see the actual cell that the formula links to.

Figure 18-3:
This example shows the direct precedents of cell H2. As you can see, H2 calculates the student's final grade based on the test results that are stored in cells C2 and F2. Because these two arrows overlap, they appear as one arrow, but you can clearly see two circles, each of which represents the starting point of an arrow (one each on cells C2 and F2).

Figure 18-4:
Excel also lets you trace multiple levels of relationships. Just click the Trace Precedents button again to see whether the precedent cells have other precedents. Here you can see that the test result cells are themselves calculations that rely on other cells. C2 makes its calculations using cells B2 and B12.

The first time you click Trace Precedents, you see the *direct precedents*. These cells are the ones directly referenced by the current formula. However, these precedents may themselves refer to other cells. To see *these* cells, click Trace Precedents again.

There's no limit to how many times you can click Trace Precedents. As long as there are more indirect precedents, Excel continues adding arrows. At any point, you can remove a single level of arrows by clicking the Remove Precedent Arrows button, or you can clear everything by choosing Formulas→Formula Auditing→ Remove Arrows.

Tip: Nothing prevents you from tracing the precedents for a bunch of different cells: just move to another cell and repeat the process for each cell you want to trace, one after the other. You can see all the arrows at once, which can make for a tangled worksheet. When you click Remove Arrows, Excel removes all the precedent arrows and any dependent arrows for every cell you've traced. You can remove the arrows for just one cell by moving to it, and then choosing Formulas→Formula Auditing→Remove Precedent Arrows.

You can trace dependents in the same way that you trace precedents—just choose Formulas→Formula Auditing→Trace Dependents (see Figure 18-5). If you click Trace Dependents and cell A1 is selected, Excel adds an arrow connecting A1 to any other cells that *refer* to A1.

Figure 18-5: *If you click Trace Dependents on cell H2, Excel indicates that this cell is used in the average calculation in cell H15. However, it isn't the only value that cell H15 uses. To see all the precedents, you'd need to move to H15, and then click Trace Precedents.*

There really isn't a difference between precedent and dependent arrows—they're just two different ways of looking at the same idea. In fact, every arrow Excel draws connects one precedent to one dependent. Finally, Excel's tracing tools also work with formulas that *aren't* working (which is important, after all, when it comes to troubleshooting). Figure 18-6 shows how the tool works when your formulas are generating error codes.

Error Checking

Sometimes, you may have a large worksheet containing a number of errors that are widely distributed. Rather than hunt for these errors by scrolling endlessly, you can jump straight to the offending cells using Excel's error-checking feature.

Figure 18-6:
Excel's tracing features work with any formulas—whether or not they contain an error. But Excel also includes a related feature, Trace Error, which works only with formulas that result in error values. When you select a cell with an error code, and then choose Trace Error, Excel traces all the precedents that lead back to the error by using blue arrows. Then, Excel uses red arrows to indicate how the error spread. In this example, two blue arrows show the precedents of cell C2, where the error occurred. The error then spread to cell H2 and, finally, to the current cell, H15.

To perform an error check, follow these steps:

1. **Move to the position where you want to start the error check.**

   If you want to check the entire worksheet from start to finish, click the first cell. Otherwise, go to the location where you want to start checking. As with a spell check, Excel moves from column to column first, and then from row to row. However, the error checker automatically loops back to the beginning of your worksheet, making sure to check every cell before it stops.

2. **Choose Formulas→Formula Auditing→Error Checking.**

If Excel doesn't find any errors in your worksheet, it displays a message indicating that its work's complete. Otherwise, you see the Error Checking dialog box, as shown in Figure 18-7, which indicates the offending cell and formula. This box also provides a number of options.

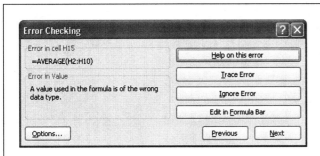

Figure 18-7:
Excel's error checker helps you scan through a worksheet and quickly jump to the cells that contain errors. You can click the Trace Error button to quickly jump to the Evaluate Formula dialog box and start analyzing the problem.

The Error Checking dialog box contains the following options:

- **Next** and **Previous**. Use these buttons to move from one error to the next.

- **Help on this Error**. Click this button to jump to Excel's online help, which lists common causes of specific errors. It may give you some insight into your own troubles.

- **Trace Error**. Use this button to open the Evaluate Formula dialog box, where you can move one step at a time through the evaluation of the formula.

- **Ignore Error**. Click this button to skip the error, and ignore the cell from this point onward. If you want the error checker to pay attention to a cell you've previously decided to ignore, click the Options button, and then click Reset Ignored Errors.

- **Edit in Formula Bar**. Use this button to start editing the formula. This choice doesn't close the error checker—instead, you can click Resume to get back to checking other errors once you've made your change.

- **Options**. Click this button to open the Excel Options dialog box, with the Formulas section selected. The Formulas section includes a small set of error-checking options under the headings "Error checking" and "Error checking rules". Ordinarily, you don't need to change any of these error checking options, as the factory settings are stringent enough to ensure that Excel catches all problems.

Follow the Arrow

If you have a complex number-laden spreadsheet with formulas that pull values from all over the place, you may need to scroll around to find the precedents or dependents that interest you. Excel has a trick to help you out—just double-click the appropriate arrow to follow it back to its source cell, no matter where it lies.

If you've got a particularly tricky worksheet, it may contain formulas that draw upon values in other worksheets or workbooks. If you double-click the arrow in this situation, then Excel pops up the Go To dialog box, with the information about the source cell already filled in at the top of the list. If you want to follow the arrow to the new worksheet or file, just select the reference (something like, [*SuperSecret-Values.xlsx]Sheet1!$A$3*), and then click OK.

Creating Charts

A s you become more skilled with Excel, you'll realize that entering numbers, organizing your layout, and formatting cells aren't the most important parts of spreadsheet creation. Instead, the real work lies in *analyzing* your data—in other words, figuring out a way to tell the story that lies *behind* your numbers. Excel's charting tools may be just what you need.

Charts depict data visually, so you can quickly spot overall trends. They're a fabulous way to help you find the meaning hidden in large amounts of data. You can create many different types of charts in Excel, including pie charts that present polling results, line charts that plot rising or declining assets over time, and three-dimensional area charts that show relationships between environmental conditions in a scientific experiment.

Excel's charting tools are enormously flexible: You can generate a simple chart with standard options in a couple of mouse clicks, or painstakingly customize every aspect of a chart's appearance (including colors, scale, titles, and even 3-D perspective). This chapter takes the first approach and explains how to generate straightforward charts, giving you all the tools you need to move from plain numbers to pretty pictures.

Charting 101

Excel provides a dizzying number of chart types, but they all share a few things. In this section, you'll learn about basic Excel charting concepts that apply to almost all types of charts; you'll also create a few basic charts. At the end of this chapter, you'll take a tour of Excel's most useful chart types.

To create a chart, Excel needs to translate your numbers into a graphical representation. The process of drawing numbers on a graph is called *plotting*. Before you plot your information on a chart, you should make sure your data's laid out properly. Here are some tips:

- Structure your data in a simple grid of rows and columns.

- Don't include blank cells between rows or columns.

- Include titles, if you'd like them to appear in your chart. You can use category titles for each column of data (placed in the first row, atop each column) and an overall chart title (placed just above the category-title row).

Tip: You can also label each row by placing titles in the far-left column, if it makes sense. If you're comparing the sales numbers for different products, list the name of each product in the first column on the left, with the sales figures in the following columns.

If you follow these guidelines, you can expect to create the sort of chart shown in Figure 19-1.

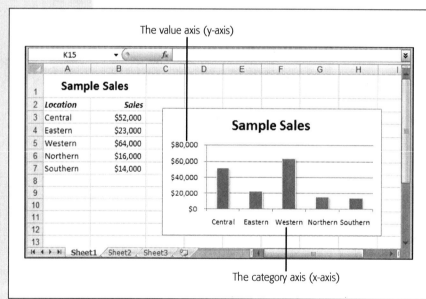

The value axis (y-axis)

The category axis (x-axis)

Figure 19-1:
This worksheet shows a table of data and a simple column chart based on Excel's standard chart settings. Nothing fancy, but it gets the job done.

To create the chart in Figure 19-1, Excel performs a few straightforward steps (you'll learn the specifics of how to actually create this chart in the next section). First, it extracts the text for the chart title from cell A1. Next, it examines the range of data (from $14,000 to $64,000) and uses it to set the value—or Y-axis—scale. You'll notice that the scale starts at $0, and stretches up to $80,000 in order to give your data a little room to breathe. (You could configure these numbers manually, but Excel automatically makes common-sense guesses like these by looking at the data you're asking it to chart.) After setting the vertical scale, Excel adds the labels along the bottom axis (also known as the X-axis or category axis), and draws the columns of appropriate height.

Embedded and Standalone Charts

The chart in Figure 19-1 is an *embedded* chart. Embedded charts appear in a worksheet, in a floating box alongside your data. You can move the chart by dragging the box around your worksheet, although depending on where you put it, you may obscure some of your data.

Your other option is to create a *standalone* chart, which looks the same but occupies an entire worksheet. That means that your chart data and your chart are placed on separate worksheets.

Usually, you'll use an embedded chart if you want to create printouts that combine both your worksheet data and one or more charts. On the other hand, if you want to print the charts separately, it's more convenient to use standalone charts. That way, you can print an entire workbook at once and have the charts and the data on separate pages.

Note: If you use embedded charts, you still have the option of printing just the chart, sized so that it fills a full sheet of paper. Simply select the chart, and then choose File→Print. If you create a standalone chart, you don't have a choice—Excel always prints your chart on a separate page.

Creating a Chart with the Ribbon

So how do you create a chart like the one shown in Figure 19-1? Easy—all it takes is a couple of clicks in the ribbon. Here's how it works:

1. **Select the range of cells that includes the data you want to chart, including the column and row headings and any chart title.**

    If you were using the data shown in Figure 19-1, you'd select cells A1 to B7.

    For speedier chart building, just position your cursor somewhere inside the data you want to chart. Excel then automatically selects the range of cells that it thinks you want. Of course, it never hurts to remove the possibility for error by explicitly selecting what you want to use before you get started.

2. **Head to the ribbon's Insert→Charts section. You'll see a separate button for each type of chart (including column charts, line charts, pie charts, and so on). Click the type you want.**

    When you choose a chart type, you get a drop-down list of subtypes (Figure 19-2).

Excel is loaded with different chart types, some of which are explained in more detail later in this chapter. For now, it's best to stick to some of the more easily understood choices, like Bar, Column, or Pie. Remember, the chart choices are just the starting point, as you'll still be able to configure a wide range of details that control things like the titles, colors, and overall organization of your chart.

3. **Click the subtype you want.**

   Excel inserts a new embedded chart alongside your data, using the standard options (which you can fine-tune later).

Note: If you don't want to make *any* choices, you can actually build a chart with one key press. Just highlight your data and press F11. This step creates a column chart on a new worksheet. Although you can't undo this operation, you can always delete the new chart worksheet and start over.

Figure 19-2:
Under each chart choice are yet more subtypes, which add to the fun. If you select the Column type (shown here), you'll get subtypes for two- and three-dimensional column charts, and variants that use cone and pyramid shapes. If you hover over one of these subtypes, a box appears with a brief description of the chart.

The Chart Tools Ribbon Tabs

When you select a chart, Excel adds three new tabs to the ribbon under the Chart Tools heading. These tabs let you control the details of your charts, and they are:

- **Design.** This tab lets you change the chart type (page 525) and the linked data that the chart uses (page 515). It also lets you choose a chart style and layout, two ways to improve the appearance of a chart that you'll consider starting on page 531.

POWER USERS' CLINIC

Browsing Excel's Chart Gallery

Excel pros sometimes find that the ribbon approach is a bit awkward when you're trying to find a less commonly used chart type. In this situation, you may prefer to look at the full list of chart types and subtypes. To do so, head to the ribbon's Insert→Charts section, and then click the dialog launcher (the square-with-an-arrow icon in the bottom-right corner). You see the Insert Chart dialog box (Figure 19-3).

The Insert Chart dialog box doesn't just let you create charts. You can also designate the default chart type (the one that's used if you select some cells, and then press F11 to create a chart in a single bound). To designate a default chart, select it, and then click "Set as Default Chart".

Figure 19-3:
The gallery on the Insert Chart dialog box's right side has a thumbnail of every chart sub-type, grouped by type. You can scroll through them all, or you can choose a type from the list on the left to jump straight to a specific section. When you find what you want, click OK to create it.

- **Layout**. This tab lets you configure individual parts of the chart. You can add shapes, pictures, and text labels, and you can configure the chart's gridlines, axes, and background.

- **Format**. This tab lets you format individual chart elements, so you can transform ordinary items into eye candy. You can adjust the font, fill, and borders uses for chart titles and shapes, among other things.

Basic Tasks with Charts

Unlike the orderly rows of numbers and labels that fill most worksheets, charts float *above* your data, locked inside special box-like containers. To take advantage of these chart boxes, you need to understand a little more about how they work.

Moving and Resizing a Chart

When you insert a chart into an existing worksheet, it becomes a floating object, hovering above your worksheet. Depending on where Excel puts it, it may temporarily obscure your data. The chart box doesn't damage your data in any way, but it can end up hiding your worksheet's numbers and text (both onscreen and in your printouts).

You have to learn to grab hold of these floating boxes and place them where you really want them. The process is pretty straightforward:

1. **Click the chart once to select it.**

   You'll notice that when you select a chart, Excel highlights the worksheet data the chart uses, as shown in Figure 19-4. At the same time, three new tabs appear in the ribbon, under the Chart Tools heading.

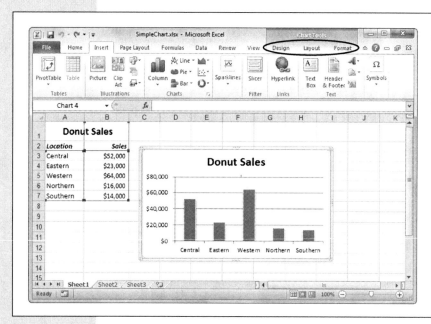

Figure 19-4:
You'll know you've selected the chart when three new charting tabs appear in the ribbon under the Chart Tools heading.

2. **Hover over the chart border until your cursor changes to a four-way arrow.**

   Figure 19-5 shows what you're looking for.

3. **Click and drag with your mouse to move or resize the chart.**

   Using the four-way arrow, you can drag the chart anywhere on your worksheet, releasing the mouse button when it's in the right spot.

   Using the two-way arrow, you can drag the border to make the chart larger or smaller. Once you make a chart box larger, you may also want to resize the individual components inside the chart to better use the available space. Page 516 tells you how to select chart elements and resize them.

4. **When you're finished, click a cell anywhere in the worksheet to go back to your data.**

   At this point, life returns to normal, and the Chart Tools tabs disappear.

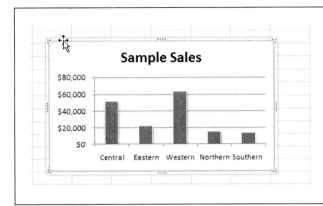

Figure 19-5:
The four-way arrow is a signal that you can click here to move the chart. If you move to one of the corners, you'll see an angled two-way arrow, which lets you resize the chart.

Tip: To remove a chart in one fell swoop, just select it with the mouse, and then press Delete.

UNDER THE HOOD

How Excel Anchors Charts

Although charts appear to float above the worksheet, they're actually anchored to the cells underneath. Each corner of the chart is anchored to one cell (these anchor points change, of course, if you move the chart around). This fact becomes important if you decide to insert or delete rows or columns anywhere in your worksheet.

For example, consider the chart shown in Figure 19-1. Its top edge is bound to row 2, and its bottom edge is bound to row 12. Similarly, its left edge is bound to column C, and its right edge to column I. That means if you insert a new row above row 2, the whole chart shifts down one row. If you insert a column to the left of column C, the whole chart shifts one column to the right.

Even more interesting is what happens if you insert rows or columns in the area that the chart overlaps. For example, if you insert a new row between the current row 10 and row

11, the chart stretches, becoming one row taller. Similarly, if you delete column D, the chart compresses, becoming one column thinner.

If it bugs you, you can change this sizing behavior. First, select the chart, and then head to the ribbon's Chart Tools | Format→Size section. Click the dialog launcher (the square-with-an-arrow icon in the bottom-right corner). When the Size and Properties dialog box appears, choose Properties in the list on the left. You'll see three "Object positioning" options. The standard behavior is "Move and size with cells", but you can also create a chart that moves around the worksheet but never resizes itself ("Move but don't size with cells") and a chart that's completely fixed in size and position ("Don't move or size with cells").

Tip: You can resize a chart in another, slightly more circuitous way. You can set the Height and Width boxes in the Chart Tools | Format→Size section of the ribbon. Although this isn't as quick as dragging the chart edge, it lets you set the size exactly, which is indispensable if you have several charts on the same worksheet and you need to make sure they're all the same size.

Creating a Standalone Chart

Even without your input, Excel usually makes common-sense choices, so you can often build a chart without needing to tweak any of these options.

You have two options for placing charts in a workbook. You can create an embedded chart, which appears in an existing worksheet (usually next to the appropriate data), or you can create a standalone chart, which appears in a new worksheet of its own (Figure 19-6).

Figure 19-6:
A standalone chart lives in a separate worksheet that doesn't have any other data and doesn't include the familiar grid of cells.

Ordinarily, when you pick a chart type from the ribbon, Excel creates an embedded chart. However, you can easily switch your chart over to a new worksheet if you're running out of room—just follow these steps:

1. **Right-click the chart, and then choose Move Chart (or, select the chart, and then choose Chart Tools | Design→Location→Move Chart).**

   The Move Chart dialog box appears (Figure 19-7).

Figure 19-7:
Using the Move Chart dialog box, you can transfer the chart to a standalone worksheet (as shown here) or shuffle it over to another worksheet and keep it as an embedded worksheet. (If you want the latter option, it's just as easy to select the chart, and then use a cut-and-paste operation to move it to a new worksheet.)

2. Choose "New sheet", and then enter the name for the new worksheet.

3. Click OK.

   Excel creates the new worksheet and places the chart on it. The new worksheet goes in front of the worksheet that contains the chart data. (You can always move the worksheet to a new position in your workbook by dragging the worksheet tab.)

Note: You can move or resize only embedded charts—the ones that appear in floating boxes inside other worksheets. If you've created a standalone chart, you can't move or resize it. Instead, it automatically shrinks or enlarges itself to match the Excel window's display area.

Editing and Adding to Chart Data

Every chart remains linked to the source data you used to create it. When you alter the data in your worksheet, Excel refreshes the chart with the new information automatically. As long as Excel is set to automatic recalculations (and it almost always is), there's no such thing as an out-of-date chart.

Note: Excel has no restriction on linking multiple charts to the same data. So, you can create two types of charts (like a pie and a column chart) that show the same data. You can even create one chart that plots all the data and another chart that just uses a portion of the same information.

However, there's one tricky point. Any range you define for use in a chart is *static*, which means it doesn't grow as your data grows. That means that if you add a new row at the bottom of the range, it doesn't appear on the chart because it's outside of the chart range.

If you do want to insert additional data to a range of data used in a chart, you have several options:

- You can use the Home→Cells→Insert→Insert Sheet Rows command. If you do, Excel notices the change, and automatically expands the range to include the newly inserted row. However, this command works only if you add a row into the middle of your data. If you try to tack a row onto the end, Excel still ignores it, and you'll need to use the solution described in the next bullet point.

- After you insert new rows, you can modify the chart range to include the new data. This approach is the most common, and it's quite painless. First, select your chart by clicking the edge of the chart box, or a blank space in the chart. Excel highlights the linked worksheet data with a colored border. Click this colored border, and drag it until it includes all the new data you want. When you release the mouse button, Excel refreshes the chart with the new information.

Excel is smart enough to adjust your chart range in some situations. If you drag your chart data to a new place on your worksheet, Excel updates the chart to match automatically.

Changing the Chart Type

When you create a chart, you choose a specific chart type. However, in many situations you may want to try several chart types with the same data to see which visualization tells your story better. Excel makes this sort of experimentation easy. All you need to do is click your chart to select it, and then make a different choice from the ribbon's Insert→Charts section. You can use this technique to transform a column chart into a pie chart.

You can also choose Chart Tools | Design→Type→Change Chart Type to make a choice from the Change Chart Type dialog box, which looks just like the Insert Chart dialog box shown in Figure 19-3.

Printing Charts

How you print a chart depends on the type of chart you've created. You can print embedded charts either with worksheet data or on their own. Standalone charts, which occupy separate worksheets, always print on separate pages.

Embedded charts

You can print embedded charts in two ways. The first approach is to print your worksheet exactly as it appears in the Excel window, with its mix of data and floating charts. In this case, you need to take special care to make sure your charts aren't split over a page break or positioned over some data you want to read in the printout. You can check for both issues using Page Layout view (choose View→Workbook Views→Page Layout View) or the smaller print preview that's shown in backstage view when you're about to print your worksheet (make sure the chart isn't selected, and then choose File→Print).

You can also print an embedded chart on a separate page, which is surprisingly easy. Just click the chart to select it, and then choose File→Print. When you do so, Excel's standard choice is to print your chart using landscape orientation, so that the long edge of the page is along the bottom, and the chart's wider than it is tall. Landscape is usually the best way to align a chart, especially if it holds a large amount of data, so Excel automatically uses landscape orientation no matter what page orientation you've configured for your worksheet. Of course, you can change this as you would with any other printout; just choose Portrait Orientation in the list of print settings before you click the big Print button.

Excel also includes two print options that are specific to charts. To see these options, click the Page Setup link at the bottom of the list of print settings. When the Page Setup dialog box appears, choose the Chart tab. You'll see an option to print a chart using lower print quality ("Draft quality"), and in black and white instead of color ("Print in black and white").

Standalone charts

If you're using a standalone chart, your chart always prints out on a separate page, sized to fit the whole page. To print out just the chart page alone (rather than the whole workbook), switch to the chart's worksheet, and then choose File→Print. Excel automatically sets all chart worksheets to Landscape orientation, which orients the page so that the long edge runs horizontally across the bottom. If this layout isn't what you want, change the orientation setting to Portrait Orientation before you print.

If you want to print the entire workbook, choose File→Print from any worksheet. Then, change the first print setting from Print Active Sheets to Print Entire Workbook.

Practical Charting

Figure 19-1 showed how to chart a list that contains two columns you want to graph—one with text labels and one with numeric data. But, in real life, you'll probably need to deal with many types of data that occupy many different configurations on your worksheet.

Consider all the possible variations on that simple two-column sales chart. You may need to compare the sales figures but, rather than showing region-to-region comparisons, you want to show how well (or poorly) each of your firm's products sold. Or perhaps you want to chart the quarterly performance of different stores over a five-year period, or determine the relationship between sales and profitability. All these charts require a slightly different arrangement of data. In the next section, you'll get a quick introduction to all these possibilities, using just the simple column chart and line chart.

Charts with Multiple Series of Numbers

A *series* is the sequence of numbers that you plot on a graph. In the simple chart example (Figure 19-1), there's one series of numbers, which represents the sales figures for a company's different regions. Of course, a real chart usually adds extra layers of detail. You may want to compare the sales figures from several different years. In this case, you'd add a separate column to your worksheet data for each year. Then you'd add each column to your chart as a separate series.

It doesn't take any extra expertise to create a chart that uses multiple series—you just select the right range of cells, and then pick a chart option from the ribbon, just as you would for a chart that has a single series. Different types of charts handle multiple series in different ways. The clustered column chart creates a separate bar for each value in a row, as shown in Figure 19-8. A line chart, on the other hand, shows a separate line for each series (as shown in the next section).

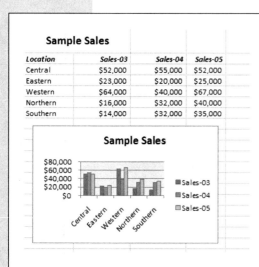

Figure 19-8:
This chart has three series of sales figures (one for each year) and five sets of columns (one for each region). Each of the five sets has three bars, one for each data series. The regions are labeled on the category axis, but you'll need to consult the legend to determine which year each column represents.

Sample Sales

Location	Sales-03	Sales-04	Sales-05
Central	$52,000	$55,000	$52,000
Eastern	$23,000	$20,000	$25,000
Western	$64,000	$40,000	$67,000
Northern	$16,000	$32,000	$40,000
Southern	$14,000	$32,000	$35,000

Tip: You can add multiple series to an existing chart without starting over from scratch. First, select the chart to highlight the linked data. Then, click the rightmost edge, and drag it to the right to expand the range so that it includes the new columns (which, of course, you've already added to your worksheet).

Controlling the Data Excel Plots on the X-Axis

Excel's charting tool has a dirty little secret. You may not realize it right away, but sooner or later, whether it's your first chart or your 40th, you'll stumble onto the fact that Excel makes a fairly important decision for you about what data shows up in your chart's X-axis. Unfortunately, this decision may not be what you want. Fortunately, you can change it.

But what causes the situation in the first place? Excel creates your charts according to the way the data's organized in your worksheet. A simple example shows you the effect.

The worksheet in Figure 19-9 looks at sales based on two factors: the year when the sales were recorded, and the region where the sales were made. In technical charting terms, the regions form the *category axis*, while the sales figures form the *value axis*. In other words, Excel creates a separate series for each year. But it makes just as much sense to organize the table in a different way, by making the year the category axis and creating a separate series for each region! Figure 19-9 contrasts these two different ways of looking at the same data, and shows how they affect the way Excel groups your data in a column chart.

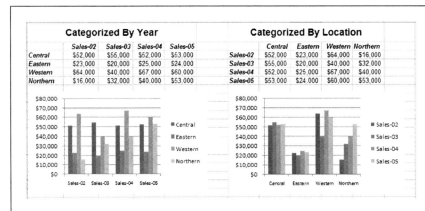

Figure 19-9:
This worksheet shows the same data charted in two different ways. In the first table (left), the category axis lists the sales years, which are used to group the regions. In the second table (right), the category axis lists the regions, which are used to group the years.

The column chart example is fairly innocent. Although you may prefer one way of looking at the data over the other, they're relatively similar. However, most Excel charts aren't as forgiving. The line chart is a classic example.

In a line chart, each line represents a different series. If you list the sales years on the category axis (as shown on the left side of Figure 19-10), you end up with a separate line for each region that shows how the region has performed over time. But if you invert the table (shown on the right side), you end up with a chart that doesn't make much sense at all: a series of lines that connect different regions in each year. Figure 19-10 shows the problem.

Clearly, when you create a line chart, you need to make sure the chart ends up using the data in a way that makes the most sense. So, how does Excel decide how to plot the data? Essentially, Excel makes a best guess about your data. If you have more rows than columns, Excel assumes that the first column represents the category axis. If you have more columns than rows (or if you have the same number of rows and columns), Excel assumes that the first *row* represents the category axis, as in Figure 19-10.

Fortunately, you have the power to override Excel's choice if you need to. Just select your chart, and then choose Chart Tools | Design→Data→Switch Row/Column. If you try this action on the charts in Figure 19-10, you reverse the results. Thus, the chart on the left would group the data into yearly series, and the chart on the right would group the data into regional series. To return them to normal, you can select each chart, and then click Switch Row/Column again.

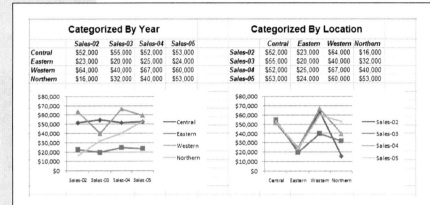

Figure 19-10:
The chart on the left is pretty straightforward. The chart on the right shows a line for each year, which makes sense if you concentrate on what's being depicted, but mostly shows how people can use computers to complicate things.

The Difference Between a Column and a Line

With simple column charts, life is easy. It doesn't matter too much what data you choose to use for your category axis because your choice simply changes the way data's grouped. Other chart types that follow the same principle include pie charts (which only allow one series), bar charts (like column charts, but oriented horizontally instead of vertically), and donut charts (where each series is a separate ring).

The same isn't true for line charts and most other types of Excel charts. The category axis you use for a line chart is important because the values in each series are connected (in this case, with a line). This line suggests some sort of "movement" or transition as values move from one category to another. That means it makes sense to use a line to connect different dates in a region (showing how sales have changed over time), but it probably doesn't make sense to use a line to connect different regions for each date. Technically, this latter scenario (shown on the right side of Figure 19-10) should show how yearly sales vary as you move from region to region, but it's just too counterintuitive for anyone to interpret it properly.

As a general rule of thumb, use time or date values for the category axis. You should do this *especially* for chart types like line and area, which usually show how things change over time.

Data That Uses a Date or Time Scale

As the previous example shows, using time or date values for the category axis makes a lot of sense for charting progress or spotting long-term trends. However, the example does cheat a little. Even though any sentient human knows that the labels

Sales-03, Sales-04, and Sales-05 represent consecutive years, Excel is oblivious to what these labels actually mean. You could chart a bunch of years that are far from sequential (like Sales02, Sales04, and Sales08) and Excel would obediently (and misleadingly) place each value on the category axis, spaced out evenly.

This snafu doesn't present a problem in the previous example, but it's an issue if you need to chart years that aren't spread out evenly. Fortunately, Excel offers an easy solution. Instead of entering text labels, you can enter actual dates or times. Because Excel stores dates and times as numbers, it can scale the chart accordingly (this process is sometimes called *category axis scaling*). Best of all, Excel automatically notices when you're using real dates, and kicks into action, making the appropriate adjustments, as shown in Figure 19-11.

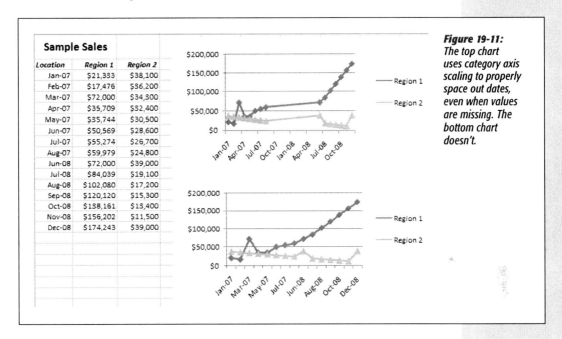

Figure 19-11:
The top chart uses category axis scaling to properly space out dates, even when values are missing. The bottom chart doesn't.

What's happening in Figure 19-11 is worth examining in a bit of detail. The pictured worksheet shows two charts that show the exact same data: a series of monthly sales figures from two regions (covering the time period between January 2010 and December 2011). The diamonds and triangles on the line charts indicate the data points for which sales data is available. The twist is that a big chunk of data (the months between August 2010 and June 2011) is missing. To make sure Excel handles this omission correctly, you have to enter real date values (rather than text labels) for the category axis. If you take that step, the chart Excel creates automatically uses a continuous timescale, as shown in the top chart. (As you can see by looking at the data points, no values fall in the middle of the series.)

On the other hand, if you enter the labels as text (as was done when creating the bottom chart), you'll see an incorrect result: The data from August 2010 and June 2011 are placed close together—even though they record months that are almost a year apart.

Optionally, you have the ability to tell Excel to disregard any values you've used in your column or row labels, thereby spacing the dates out evenly, as though they're ordinary text labels. That's how the incorrect chart in Figure 19-11 was created. (Why you'd want to do it is another question, but someone, somewhere, is probably in desperate need of this feature.) To change how Excel scales the category axis, select the chart, and then choose Chart Tools | Layout→Axes→Axes→Primary Horizontal Axis→More Primary Horizontal Axis Options to show the Format Axis dialog box. Next, change the Axis Type setting, as shown in Figure 19-12.

Figure 19-12:
Under the Axis Type heading, pick one of the following: "Text axis" (treat the category values as labels), "Date axis" (treat the category values as date vales), or "Automatically select based on the data" (let Excel decide based on what it thinks is best).

Category axis scaling works with more than just dates. You can scale any category axis values, as long as they're numeric, which is particularly useful if you're trying to determine the relationship between two different values.

Non-Contiguous Chart Ranges

So far, all the chart examples have assumed the data you want to chart is placed in a single, tightly packed table. But what if your information is actually scattered across your worksheet? This scenario may seem unlikely, but it actually happens quite often when you need to chart only *part* of the data in a table. Say you want to create a chart using two or three columns, and these columns aren't next to each other. In this case, you need to take a few extra steps when you create your chart.

Imagine you have a table that records the monthly sales of 10 different regional offices. However, you want to create a chart that compares only two of these offices. Your chart will use the category information in column A (which contains the month in which the sales were recorded), along with the values in column C and column D (which contain the total amount of sales for the two regions in which you're interested).

The easiest way to create this chart is to start by selecting the noncontiguous range that contains your data. Here's what you need to do:

1. **First, use the mouse to select the data in column A.**

   Excel surrounds the data with a marquee. Don't click anywhere else yet.

2. **Then, hold down the Ctrl key while you drag to select the data in columns C and D.**

   Because you're holding down the Ctrl key, column A remains selected (see Figure 19-13).

Figure 19-13:
This worksheet shows a noncontiguous selection that ignores the numbers from region 1. When you create the chart, Excel includes only two series in the chart: one for region 2, and one for region 3.

3. Now choose Insert→Charts, and then pick the appropriate chart type.

   Excel creates the chart as usual, but uses only the data you selected in steps 1 and 2, leaving out all other columns.

This approach works most of the time. However, if you have trouble, or if the columns you want to select are spaced *really* far apart, then you can explicitly configure the range of cells for any chart. To do so, follow these steps:

1. **Create a chart normally, by selecting part of the data, and then, from the Insert→Chart section of the ribbon, choosing a chart type.**

2. **Select the chart, and then choose Chart Tools | Design→Data→Select Data.**

   The Select Data Source dialog box appears (Figure 19-14).

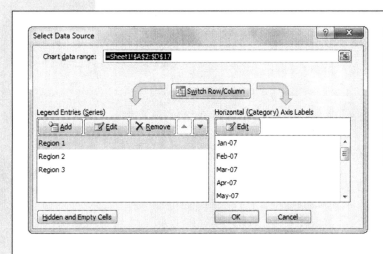

Figure 19-14:
This dialog box shows a handy secret about Excel charting. Excel not only records the whole range of cells that contain the chart data (as shown in the "Chart data range" text box), it also lets you see how it breaks that data up into a category axis and one or more series (as shown in the Legend Entries (Series) list).

3. **Remove any data series you don't want and add any new data series you do want.**

   To remove a series, select it in the Legend Entries (Series) list, and then click Remove.

To add a new series, click Add, and then specify the appropriate cell references for the series name and the series values.

You can also click Switch Row/Column to change the data Excel uses as the category axis (page 508) and you can adjust some more advanced settings, like the way Excel deals with blank values, and the order in which it plots series (as explained in the following sections).

Changing the Order of Your Data Series

If your table has more than one series, Excel charts it in the order it appears on your worksheet (from left to right if your series are arranged in columns, or from top to bottom if they're arranged in rows). In a basic line chart, it doesn't matter which series Excel charts first—the end result is still the same. But in some charts, it *does* make a difference. One example is a stacked chart (Figure 19-20), in which Excel plots each new series on top of the previous one. Another example is a 3-D chart, where Excel plots each data series behind the previous one.

You can easily change your data series' order. Select your chart, and then choose Chart Tools | Design→Data→Select Data. Now select one of the series in the Legend Entries (Series) list, and then click the up or down arrow buttons to move it. Excel plots the series from top to bottom.

Changing the Way Excel Plots Blank Values

When Excel creates a chart, its standard operating procedure is to *ignore* all empty cells. The value of 0 doesn't count as an empty cell and neither does text (Excel plots any cells that contains text as a 0).

So what's the difference between an ignored cell and a cell that contains the number 0? In some types of charts, there's no difference. In a bar or pie chart, the result is the same—you don't see a bar or a pie slice for that data. However, in some charts, there *is* a difference. In a line chart a 0 value is plotted on the chart, but an empty cell causes a break in the line. In other words, the line stops just before the missing data, and then starts again at the next point. This broken line indicates missing information.

If you don't like this behavior (perhaps because your empty cells really do represent 0 values), you can change it. Select your chart, and then choose Chart Tools | Design→Data→Select Data to get to the Select Data Source dialog box. Then, click the Hidden and Empty Cells button, which pops open a dialog box with three choices:

- **Gaps**. Excel leaves a gap where the information should be. In a line chart, this breaks the line (making it segmented). This option is the standard choice.

- **Zero**. Excel treats all blank cells as though they contain the number 0.

- **Span with line**. Excel treats all blank cells as missing information and tries to guess what should go in between. If a line chart goes from 10 to 20 with a blank cell in between, Excel interpolates the data point 15 and plots it.

You can also switch on or off the "Show data in hidden rows and columns" setting to tell Excel whether it should include hidden cells when creating a chart. This setting determines how Excel deals with data when you use filtering in a table, or when you explicitly hide rows or columns using the Home→Cells→Format→Hide & Unhide menu. Ordinarily, Excel treats these missing values just like blank values, and ignores them.

Chart Types

Although there's a lot to be said for simple column charts—they can illuminate trends in almost any spreadsheet—there's nothing quite as impressive as successfully pulling off the exotic bubble chart. This section offers a "greatest hits" tour of the most popular charts that Excel offers.

Column

By now, column charts probably seem like old hat. But column charts actually come in several different variations (technically known as *subtypes*). The main difference between the basic column chart and these subtypes is how they deal with data tables that have multiple series. The quickest way to understand the difference is to look at Figure 19-15, which shows a sample table of data, and Figure 19-16, which charts it using several different types of column charts.

Number of Students in Each Room		
	Male	Female
Cafeteria	42	24
Lounge	13	16
Games Room	73	40
Lecture Hall	31	40
Library	19	18

Figure 19-15:
This simple table of data records the number of female and male students in several rooms at a university. The category is the room name, and there are two data series: the numbers of male students, and the numbers of female students. This data is perfect for a column chart, but different subtypes emphasize different aspects of the data, as you can see in Figure 19-16.

Figure 19-16:
The Clustered Column makes it easy to compare the gender of students in each room, but makes it somewhat more difficult to compare different rooms. The Stacked Column is an elegant way to compress the data, and it lets you compare the total number of students in each room without losing the gender information. The 100% Stacked Column makes each column the same height, so it's useless for comparing total student numbers but perfect for comparing how the gender breakup varies depending on the room. (Notice the scale also changes to reflect that you're comparing percent-age values.) Finally, the 3-D chart shows you all the data at once by placing the male student counts in front of the female student counts.

Note: In order to learn about a chart subtype, you need to know its name. The name appears when you hover over the subtype thumbnail, either in the Insert→Charts list (Figure 19-2) or the Insert Chart dialog box (Figure 19-3).

Here's a quick summary of your column chart choices:

- **Clustered Column**. In a clustered column, each value's shown in its own separate column. To form a cluster, the columns are grouped together according to category.

- **Stacked Column**. In a stacked column, each category has only one column. To create this column, Excel adds together the values from every series for each category. However, the column is subdivided (and color-coded), so you can see the contribution each series makes.

- **100% Stacked Column**. The 100% stacked column is like a stacked column in that it uses a single bar for each category, and subdivides that bar to show the proportion from each series. The difference is that a stacked column always stretches to fill the full height of the chart. That means stacked columns are designed to focus exclusively on the percentage distribution of results, not the total numbers.

- **3-D Clustered Column, Stacked Column in 3-D, and 100% Stacked Column in 3-D**. Excel's got a 3-D version for each of the three basic types of column charts, including clustered, stacked, and 100% stacked. The only difference between the 3-D versions and the plain-vanilla column charts is that the 3-D charts are drawn with a three-dimensional special effect, that's either cool or distracting, depending on your perspective.

- **3-D Column**. While all the other 3-D column charts simply use a 3-D effect for added pizzazz, this *true* 3-D column chart actually uses the third dimension by placing each new series *behind* the previous series. That means, if you have three series, you end up with three layers in your chart. Assuming the chart is tilted just right, you can see all these layers at once, although it's possible that some bars may become obscured, particularly if you have several series.

Along with the familiar column and three-dimensional column charts, Excel also provides a few more exotic versions that use cylinders, cones, and pyramids instead of ordinary rectangles. Other than their different shapes, these chart types work just like regular column charts. As with column and bar charts, you can specify how cylinder, cone, and pyramid charts should deal with multiple series. Your options include clustering, stacking, 100% stacking, and layering (true 3-D). See Figure 19-17 for an example.

Figure 19-17:
Though a cone chart looks a little different, it's really just a column chart in disguise.

Bar

The venerable bar chart is the oldest form of data presentation. Invented sometime in the 1700s, it predates the column and pie chart. Bar charts look and behave almost exactly the same as column charts—the only difference being that their bars stretch horizontally from left to right, unlike columns, which rise from bottom to top.

Excel provides almost the same set of subtypes for bar charts as it does for column charts. The only difference is that there's no true three-dimensional (or layered) bar chart, although there are clustered, stacked, and 100% stacked bar charts with a three-dimensional effect. Some bar charts also use cylinder, cone, and pyramid shapes.

Tip: Many people use bar charts because they leave more room for category labels. If you have too many columns in a column chart, Excel has a hard time fitting all the column labels into the available space.

Line

People almost always use line charts to show changes over time. Line charts emphasize trends by connecting each point in a series with a line. The category axis represents a time scale or a set of regularly spaced labels.

Excel provides several subtypes for line charts:

- **Line.** The classic line chart, which draws a line connecting all the points in the series. The individual points aren't highlighted.

- **Stacked Line.** In a stacked line chart, Excel displays the first series just as it would in the normal line chart, but the second line consists of the values of the first and second series added together. If you have a third series, it displays the total values of the first three series, and so on. People sometimes use stacked line charts to track things like a company's cumulative sales (across several different departments or product lines), as Figure 19-18, bottom, shows. (Stacked area charts are another alternative, as shown later in Figure 19-20.) Stacked line charts aren't as common as stacked bar and column charts.

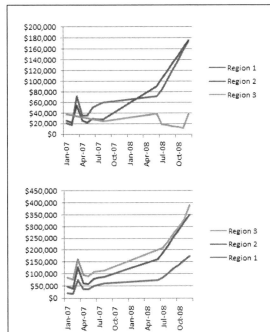

Figure 19-18:
Here are two different line chart variations—both of which show the same information, although you'd never be able to tell that from looking at them quickly.

Top: This chart is a regular line chart that compares the sales for three different regions over time.

Bottom: This chart is a stacked line chart, which plots each subsequent line by adding the numbers from the earlier lines. That makes the stacked line chart a great vehicle for showing cumulative totals. For example, sales in Region 3 for April of 2010 appear to top $150,000. That's because the Region 3 line is stacked. It shows a total made up from three components—$72,000 (Region 1), $54,000 (Region 2), and $34,300 (Region 3). In this example, the stacked line chart clearly shows that sales spiked early on, but have risen overall, which isn't clear in the top chart. However, the stacked line chart also obscures the differences between the regions. You'd never guess that Region 3 is the underperforming region because this chart reflects the total of all three regions.

Note: Lines can never cross in a stacked line chart because Excel adds each series to the one (or ones) before it. You can change which line is stacked at the top by changing the order of the series. To do this, rearrange your table of data on the worksheet (Excel places the rightmost column on top).

- **100% Stacked Line**. A 100% stacked line chart works the same as a stacked line chart in that it adds the value of each series to the values of all the preceding series. The difference is that the last series always becomes a straight line across the top, and the other lines are scaled accordingly so that they show percentages. The 100% stacked line chart is rarely useful, but if you do use it, you'll probably want to put totals in the last series.

- **Line with Markers, Stacked Line with Markers, and 100% Stacked Line with Markers**. These subtypes are the same as the three previous line chart subtypes, except they add markers (squares, triangles, and so on) to highlight each data point in the series.

- **3-D Line**. This option draws ordinary lines without markers but adds a little thickness to each line with a 3-D effect.

Pie

Pie charts show the breakdown of a series proportionally, using "slices" of a circle. Pie charts are one of the simplest types of charts, and one of the most recognizable.

Here are the pie chart subtypes you can choose from:

- **Pie**. The basic pie chart everyone knows and loves, which shows the breakup of a single series of data.

- **Exploded Pie**. The name sounds like a Vaudeville gag, but the exploded pie chart simply separates each piece of a pie with a small amount of white space. Usually, Excel charting mavens prefer to explode just a single slice of a pie for emphasis.

- **Pie of Pie**. With this subtype, you can break out one slice of a pie into its own, smaller pie (which is itself broken down into slices). This chart is great for emphasizing specific data.

- **Bar of Pie**. The bar of pie subtype is almost the same as the pie of pie subtype. The only difference is that the breakup of the combined slice is shown in a separate stacked bar, instead of a separate pie.

- **Pie in 3-D** and **Exploded Pie in 3-D**. This option is the pie and exploded pie types in three dimensions, tilted slightly away from the viewer for a more dramatic appearance. The differences are purely cosmetic.

Note: Pie charts can show only one series of data. If you create a pie chart for a table that has multiple data series, you'll see just the information from the first series.

Area

An area chart is very similar to a line chart. The difference is that the space between the line and the bottom (category) axis is completely filled in. Because of this difference, the area chart tends to emphasize the sheer magnitude of values rather than their change over time; see Figure 19-19.

Area charts exist in all the same flavors as line charts, including stacked and 100% stacked. You can also use subtypes that have a 3-D effect, or you can create a true 3-D chart that layers the series behind one another.

Stacked area charts make a lot of sense. In fact, they're easier to interpret than stacked line charts because you can easily get a feeling for how much contribution each series makes to the total by judging the thickness of the area. If you're not convinced, compare the stacked charts in Figure 19-18 (bottom) and Figure 19-20. In the area chart, it's much clearer that region 3 is making a fairly trivial contribution to the overall total.

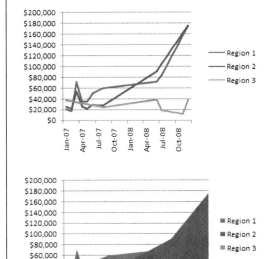

Figure 19-19:
This example compares a traditional line chart (top) against the area chart (bottom). As you can see, the area chart makes a more dramatic point about the rising sales in region 2. However, it also obscures the results in region 1.

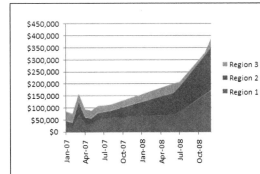

Figure 19-20:
You can create an area chart that doesn't obscure any data, but it needs to be a stacked (as shown here) or 3-D area chart. The stacked area chart shows the combined total of all regions, but it still lets you pick out the most important series. For example, it's clear that Region 3 (the narrow sliver on top of the stack) contributes relatively little to the total, while Region 1 and Region 2 are more important.

Chart Styles and Layouts

Earlier in this book, you learned how Word styles let you take ready-made formatting and apply it to your prose to glitz up the dullest document. In the same way, Excel provides a set of *chart* styles that you can use to give the plainest chart a makeover.

Chart styles draw from the colors, fonts, and shape effects that are part of an overall theme (see the following Note). If you use the Trek theme, your chart styles draw upon a palette of earthy tones, while the Verve theme gives you a much more vivid set of colors. If you use cell styles, table styles, and chart styles, the fonts and colors are consistent everywhere. You can also swap in a new palette for all these elements just by choosing a new theme.

Tip: Before you choose a chart style, it helps to pick the theme you want to use so you can see the real, final result. To change the theme, make a selection from the Page Layout→Themes→Themes list.

Chart Styles

Chart styles give you a way to apply shake-and-bake formatting to ordinary charts. Excel includes a wide range of chart styles that vary from simple, flat charts with minor accents (like colored borders) to showier styles that include bevel effects and shadows. You can quickly create plain or opulent charts, depending on your needs.

Before you use a chart style, it's important to understand what it changes (and what it doesn't). Every chart style includes settings that determine:

- The background color.
- The colors for each series (which may be displayed as bars, lines, points, or something else). Some colorful chart styles use all the colors from the current theme. Other chart styles take a single color from the current theme and use multiple shades of that color for a more refined look.
- Shape effects, like softly curved or beveled edges, shadows, and glow.
- Marker styles (for line charts) that distinguish the points in one series from those in another.

Note: Some chart styles use a heavy black background with bold colors. This sort of style isn't designed for worksheets because it can tie the best color printer in knots. But these high-contrast styles look good on computer monitors and projection screens, so use them if you want to cut and paste your chart into a PowerPoint presentation.

On the other hand, chart styles don't change the font Excel uses for the chart title and labels; instead Excel bases these elements on the current theme. Chart styles also don't change the layout of the chart or the chart settings Excel uses for the legend, scale, axis titles, error bars, and so on.

To choose a style, select the chart, and then head to the ribbon's Chart Tools | Design→Chart Styles section, which gives you a gallery of choices (Figure 19-21).

Note: If you've resized your Excel window to be very small, the chart styles don't fit in the ribbon and you see a Quick Styles button instead. Click this button to see the full list of styles.

Scroll buttons: see more choices

Down arrow: see all choices

Figure 19-21:
Click any of the Chart Style options to dress your chart up in different colors. The scroll bars (circled) let you move through the style options not currently shown, or click the down arrow to see a drop-down window with all your choices.

A chart can use only one style at a time, so if you choose a new style, Excel wipes out the existing formatting.

Chart Layouts

Chart styles make it easy for you to change the colors and visual styling in a chart. Chart layouts are complementary—they let you control the presence and placement of various chart elements, like the chart and axis titles, and the legend.

As you'll learn in the next section, Excel lets you tweak each of these ingredients separately. However, you can choose a prebuilt layout to do it all in one shot. To try it out, head to the ribbon, and then make a choice from the Chart Tools | Design→Chart Layouts section. As with styles, the list of available charts depends on the chart type. Figure 19-22 shows an example.

Note: To make chart layouts as practical as possible, the creators of Excel reviewed thousands of professional charts and identified the most common arrangements. Most Excel pros still want to customize the various parts of their chart by hand. However, a chart layout can provide a great starting point.

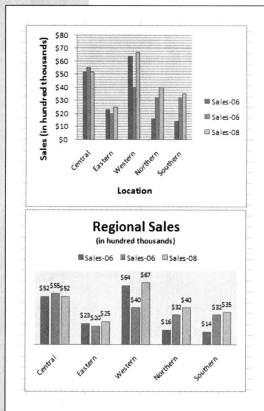

Figure 19-22:
This worksheet shows two copies of the same chart, each with a different layout. The chart at the top includes heavy gridlines, axis titles, and a legend on the right. The chart below has a chart title and places the legend at the top. It also has no gridlines and instead displays the series value above each column.

Adding Chart Elements

You build every chart out of small components, like titles, gridlines, axes, a legend, and the bars, points, or exotic shapes that actually represent the data. And Excel lets you manipulate each of these details separately. That means you can independently change the format of a label, the outline of bar, the number of gridlines, and the font and color of just about everything.

Figure 19-23 shows the different elements that make up a chart. They include:

- **Title.** The title labels the whole chart. In addition, you can add titles to the axes. If you do, then you can select these titles separately.

- **Legend.** The legend identifies each data series on the chart with a different color. A legend's useful only when the chart contains more than one series.

- **Horizontal and Vertical Axes.** An axis runs along each edge of the chart and determines the scale. In a typical two-dimensional chart, you have two axes: the category axis (typically on the bottom of the chart, running horizontally), and the value axis (typically on the left, running vertically).

- **Plot Area**. The plot area is the chart's background, where the gridlines are drawn. In a standard chart, the plot area is plain white, which you can customize.

- **Chart Area**. The chart area is the white space around the chart. It includes the space that's above, below, and to either side of the plot area.

- **Gridlines**. The gridlines are the lines that run across the plot area. Visually, you line the data up with the gridlines to get an idea of the value of each data point. Every chart starts out with horizontal gridlines, but you can remove them or add vertical gridlines. You can tell Excel how many gridlines to draw, and even how to format them.

- **Data Series**. The data series is a single set of data plotted on the chart across the category axis. In a line chart, for example, the data series is a single line. If a chart has multiple series, you'll often find it useful to format them separately to make them easier to differentiate or to emphasize the most important one.

- **Data Point**. A data point is a single value in a data series. In a line chart, a data point is a single dot, and in a column chart, a data point is a single column. If you want to call attention to an exceptionally important value, you can format a data point so it looks different from the rest of the series.

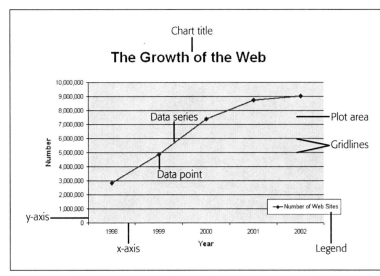

Figure 19-23:
Before you can begin tweaking your chart's formatting, you need to know the names of the different elements you'll find on a chart, all of which are labeled here.

Not all charts include all these elements; the layout you pick determines whether you begin with a chart title, a legend, gridlines in the background, and so on. However, in many cases you'll want to pick and choose exactly the elements you want. Excel lets you do this with the buttons on the ribbon's Chart Tools | Layout tab. The following sections show you how.

Adding Titles

It doesn't matter how spectacular your chart looks if it's hard to figure out what the data represents. To clearly explain what's going on, you need to make sure you have the right titles and labels.

An ordinary chart can include a main title (like "Increase in Rabbit Population vs. Decrease in Carrot Supplies") and titles on each axis (like "Number of Rabbits" and "Pounds of Carrots"). To show or hide the main title, make a selection from the Chart Tools | Layout→Labels→Chart Title list. Your options include:

- **Above Chart** puts a title box at the very top and resizes the chart smaller to make room.

- **Centered Overlay Title** keeps the chart as is but superimposes the title over the top. Assuming you can find a spot with no data, you get a more compact display.

- **None** hides the title altogether.

Once you select one of those options, you see the title box; click inside it, and then type in new text, as shown in Figure 19-24.

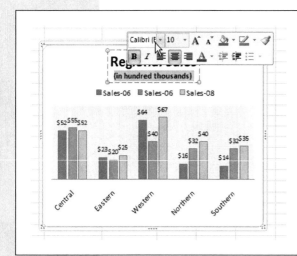

Figure 19-24:
You can type in whatever text you'd like for a chart title. If you select part of the text, a mini bar appears, with formatting options for changing the font, size, color, and alignment. These commands are the same as in the Home→Font section of the ribbon, but it's way more convenient to reach them here.

You can just as easily add a title to each axis using the Chart Tools | Layout→ Labels→Axis Titles→Primary Horizontal Axis Title and Chart Tools | Layout→ Labels→Axis Titles→Primary Vertical Axis Title lists. You'll find options for showing your title, hiding it, and (in the case of a vertical axis), showing a title that's rotated to run neatly along the side of your chart.

Note: As with almost all chart elements, you can also format titles by adding a border, a shadow effect, and a fancy background fill. To get these options, right-click the title, and then choose Format Chart Title.

Adding a Legend

Titles help explain a chart's overall purpose. Usually, titles indicate what a chart is comparing or analyzing. You may add a chart title like "Patio Furniture Sales" and the axis labels "Gross Revenue" and "Month of Sale" to a chart that shows how patio furniture sales pick up in the summertime. However, the category labels don't help you single out important data. They also don't let you point out multiple series (like the sales results in two different stores). You can fix this problem by adding additional labels or a *legend*. A legend is a separate box off to the side of the chart that contains one entry for each data series in a chart. The legend indicates the series name, and it adds a little sample of the line style or fill style that you've used to draw that series on the chart.

Excel automatically adds a legend to most charts. If you don't already have a legend, you can choose a layout that includes one, or you can make a selection from the Chart Tools | Layout→Labels→Legend list. Different selections let you position the legend in different corners of the chart, although true Excel pros just drag the legend box to get it exactly where they want it.

Legends aren't always an asset when you need to build slick, streamlined charts. They introduce two main problems:

- **Legends can be distracting**. In order to identify a series, the person looking at the chart needs to glance away from the chart to the legend, and turn back to the chart again.

- **Legends can be confusing**. Even if you have only a few data series, the average reader may find it hard to figure out which series corresponds with each entry in the legend. This problem becomes more serious if you print your chart out on a printer that doesn't have the same range of colors as your computer monitor, in which case different colored lines or blocks may begin to resemble each other.

If you don't want to use a legend for these reasons, you can use data labels instead, as described in the next section.

Adding Data Labels to a Series

Data labels are labels that you attach to every data point in a series. This text floats just above the point, column, or pie slice that it describes, clearly identifying each piece of information. Data labels have unrivalled explaining power—they can identify *everything*. The only possible drawback is that adding data labels to a chart that's already dense with data may lead to an overcrowded jumble of information.

To apply data labels, choose a position from the Chart Tools | Layout→Labels→Data Labels list. If you choose Chart Tools | Layout→Labels→Data Labels→Center on a column chart, each bar's value appears as a number that's centered vertically inside the bar. On the other hand, if you choose Chart Tools | Layout→Labels→Data Labels→Outside End, the numbers appear just above the top of each column, which is usually more readable (Figure 19-25).

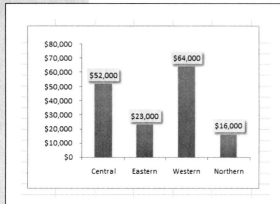

Figure 19-25:
Here, you can see how a value label adds information to a column chart. Even without the labels, you could still get this information by eyeing where the bar measures up to on the value axis on the left, but the labels make it a whole lot easier to get the information with a single glance. The labels have been customized slightly via the Format Data Labels dialog box to shrink their font size and add a simple box border with a shadow effect.

Tip: No matter how you choose to label or distinguish a series, you're best off if you don't add too many of these elements to the same chart. Adding too many labels makes for a confusing overall effect, and it blunts the effect of any comparison.

If you're in an adventurous mood, you can create even more advanced labels by choosing Chart Tools | Layout→Labels→Data Labels→More Data Label Options. The Format Data Labels dialog box appears, with a number of options for customizing data labels (Figure 19-26).

Figure 19-26:
The Format Data Labels dialog box is divided into several sections of settings. (You can see one setting at a time by picking from the list on the left.) For now, you're interested in the Label Options section.

Using the Format Data Labels dialog box, you can choose the data label's position (just like you could from the Chart Tools | Layout→Labels→Data Labels list). But the options under the Label Contains heading are more interesting, as they let you chose the information that appears in the label. Ordinarily, the information is simply the value of the data point. However, you can also apply a *combination of* values. Your exact options depend on the type of chart you've created, but here are the most common choices:

- **Series name**. The series name identifies the series each data point comes from. Because most series have multiple data points, using this option means the same text repeats again and again. In a line chart that compares sales between two stores, using this option would put the label "Store 1" above each data point for the first store, which is probably overkill.

- **Category name**. The category name adds the information from the category axis. If you're using a line chart to compare how sales fluctuated month by month, then this option adds the month above every data point. Assuming you have more than one line in your line chart, this option creates duplicate labels, which crowds out the important information in your form. For that reason, category labels don't work very well with most charts, although you can use them to replace the legend in a pie or donut chart.

- **Value**. Value labels insert the data that corresponds with a data point. This data is the actual information in the corresponding cell in your worksheet. If you're plotting changing sales, this data is the dollar amount of sales for a given month. Value labels are probably the most frequently used type of label.

- **Percentage**. Percentage labels apply only to pie charts and donut charts. They're similar to value labels, except they divide the value against the total of all values to find a percentage.

Note: In some charts, the checkboxes "Category name" and "Value" are renamed as "X Value" and "Y Value", although they have the same effect as "Category name" and "Value."

When you use multiple items, you can also choose a character from the Separator list box to specify how to separate each piece of text in the full label (with a comma, space, semicolon, new line, or a character you specify). And if you want to display a mini square with the legend color next to the label, then choose "Include legend key in label" (although most people don't bother with this feature).

Figure 19-27 shows more advanced data labels at work.

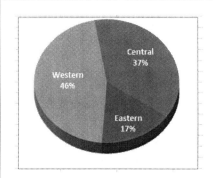

Figure 19-27:
Here's how you can combine percentage and category information to make a pie chart more readable and eliminate the legend altogether.

Note: Wondering what your chart will look like? As you make changes, Excel updates the chart on the worksheet using its handy live preview feature. Just move the Format Data Labels dialog box out of the way to get a sneak peak before you confirm your choices.

Adding Individual Data Labels

In simple charts, data series labels work well. But in more complex charts, data series labels can be more trouble than they're worth because they lead to chart overcrowding, particularly with line charts or any chart that has multiple series. The solution is to add labels to only a few data points in a series—those that are most important. Figure 19-28 shows the difference.

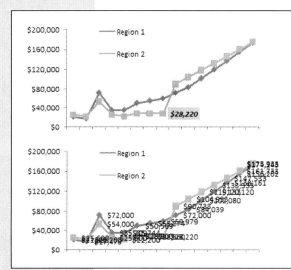

Figure 19-28:
Data point labels work particularly well with line charts because both chart types are dense with information. The two examples here underscore that fact.

Top: Here, a single data point label indicates the point where the sales changed dramatically for the Region 1 office.

Bottom: Here's the mess that results if you add data labels to the whole Region 1 and Region 2 series. No amount of formatting can clear up this confusion.

To add an individual data label, follow these steps:

1. **Click the precise data point that you want to identify. This point could be a slice in a pie chart, a column in a column chart, or a point in a line chart.**

   Selecting a data point is a little tricky. You need to click twice—the first click selects the whole series, and the second click selects just the data point you want. You'll see the handles appear around the specific column or point to indicate you've selected it, as shown in Figure 19-29.

2. **When you have the right data point selected, choose an option from the Chart Tools | Layout→Labels→Data Labels list.**

   These options work the same way they do when you format the whole series, except now they apply only to the currently selected value.

   To remove a data label, click to select it, and then press Delete. If you want to add several data labels, you're best off adding all the data labels (as described in the previous section), and then deleting the ones you don't want.

Figure 19-29:
Top: To select a single data point, click it twice. The first click selects the whole Sales-05 series.

Bottom: The second click gets just the data point you want, which is the Sales-05 data in the Western sales office. In some cases, you may not be able to tell which data point's the one you want. When that happens, just hover over the data point briefly to see a tooltip with the category, series, and value information.

Tip: If a data label doesn't have exactly what you want, you can click inside it and edit the text, just as you do with a chart title.

Right-clicking a data label gives you a choice of formatting options (choose Format Data Labels). It's almost always a good idea to format your labels so they stand out and don't crowd other information on the chart.

Tip: Instead of using data labels, you can add arrows and text boxes anywhere on a chart to call out important information. To do so, you need Excel's drawing features, explained in the next chapter.

Part Four: PowerPoint

4

Creating a Presentation

Since it first came on the scene in the late 1980s, PowerPoint has forever transformed the way we conduct meetings. Its slick slides can illustrate your points so much more clearly and efficiently than stacks of printed handouts or scrawls on a dusty chalkboard. PowerPoint presentations can contain images, charts, tables, videos—all of which are ready to come to life thanks to a slew of built-in animations and transition effects. PowerPoint also gives you flexibility in your delivery options: Give your slideshow in person or remotely over the Internet, set it up to run continuously (in a trade-show kiosk, for example), or put it on a website for people to find and view at their own pace.

Meetings have come a long way—and so has PowerPoint. PowerPoint 2010 features the same enhanced, customizable ribbon you find throughout Office 2010, as well as an improved Animations ribbon, new slide transitions, the ability to divide your presentation into sections, and better photo and video editing options. And that's just for starters. The next several chapters show you what PowerPoint 2010 can do to make your presentations more exciting. This chapter gets you up to speed, covering the basics of creating, saving, viewing, and printing a presentation.

Creating a New Presentation

When you first open the program from the Windows Start menu, PowerPoint has already created a new, blank presentation for you, as shown in Figure 20-1. Center stage is the working area for the active slide. To the left is the Slides pane, which gives an overview of your slideshow as you create it, showing smaller versions of your slides in order. Across the bottom is a pane where you can add notes—reminders to yourself about what to say when you're presenting.

Tip: If you have trouble finding PowerPoint on the Windows Start menu, try this route: Start→All Programs→Microsoft Office→Microsoft PowerPoint 2010.

If you're already working on something in PowerPoint and you want to create a new presentation, the quickest way is to press Ctrl+N. Or select File→New→Create (Alt, F, N, N). A new presentation opens, ready for you to start adding content to slides.

Click this tab to see an outline of your presentation.

The Ribbon

The Slides pane

The active slide

View buttons

The Notes pane

The name of your presentation's theme

Figure 20-1:
PowerPoint opens in Normal view, which has a large workspace for creating and editing slides. On the left side is the Slides pane, which shows an overview of your presentation as you add slides.

Creating a New Presentation from a Template

Like other Office programs, PowerPoint comes with built-in templates that make slideshow creation and formatting a snap. When you use one of these babies, someone else has already done all the design work for you. To create a presentation from a template, just pick the style you want, such as a photo album or a project status report, and then add your content. Templates let you focus on the purpose and substance of your presentation, not on designing slides. Here's what to do:

1. Select File→New→"Sample templates" (Alt, F, N, A). If you're looking for a template you've used before, try "Recent templates" (R) or "My templates" (M).

   PowerPoint opens a page like the one shown in Figure 20-2, with lots of choices to browse through. To get a better look at a template, click it; a preview appears in the pane at right.

2. Click a template to select it, and then click Create.

   Your new, template-based presentation has a number of slides, with placeholder content, to give you ideas for your own presentation. You can delete the content and add your own. (Keep reading to find out how to do that.)

Figure 20-2:
Creating a new presentation from a template can give you a head start on designing a presentation for a particular purpose.

Choosing a Theme

When creating a new presentation from scratch, sure, you can go with plain vanilla slides—black text on a white background. But why not add a touch of flair? Unlike templates (see previous section), themes don't contain multiple slides or placeholder content. Instead, they apply a single design scheme to all the slides you create within a presentation. Here's how to use 'em:

1. Select File→New→Themes (Alt, F, N, I).

   PowerPoint displays its built-in themes. Each theme has its own background design, font styles, and color scheme. Browse through the choices until you see one that looks good; click it to see a larger version in the right preview pane.

2. Click the theme you want to select it, and then click Create.

   Your presentation now has a theme to unify its design.

Tip: You can apply a theme to a slideshow you've already created. Just go to the Design tab and choose a new theme from the Themes gallery there (Alt, G, H). Click the theme you want, and PowerPoint applies it to your presentation.

Adding Text to a Slide

The first thing you'll probably want to do with your newly created presentation is add some text. The first slide in your new presentation is a title slide, which has text boxes in place for a title and a subtitle. (PowerPoint offers several different built-in slide types, as explained in the next section.)

PowerPoint adds placeholder text to show where the text boxes are. (This text appears only on the active slide in the PowerPoint workspace; it doesn't actually show up when you play the slideshow.) Click inside a text box; the placeholder text disappears, and the mouse pointer turns into a cursor. Type to add your text, which is already formatted—for example, on a title slide, the title is larger and more prominent than the subtitle.

If necessary, the text box expands as you type. If your text goes onto a second line, for example, the box gets taller to accommodate it.

When you're done typing, click outside the text box. The box disappears, showing only your nicely formatted and positioned text.

What if you want to put text in a spot where there's no text box? You've got two options:

- **Move an existing text box to where you want it.** Click inside the text box to display its dotted-line outlines, and then hover your mouse pointer over any border. When the pointer becomes a four-way arrow, click and drag the text box (along with its text) to a new position. Let go of the mouse button to drop it in place.

- **Insert a new text box.** You can create and position your own text box from the Insert tab. Select Insert→Text Box (Alt, N, X). Position the cursor where you want a corner of the text box to be, and then click and drag to create a rectangle of the approximate width you want for the text area, as shown in Figure 20-3. When you let go of the mouse button, PowerPoint inserts the text box and puts the cursor inside it, ready for you to start typing.

Note: Page 565 shows you how to format text you've added to a slide.

Figure 20-3:
Click the Insert tab's Text box button (circled), and then click and drag to create a text box of the approximate width you want for your text. Don't worry about the exact size of the box; you can always change it, as described on page 565.

Creating a New Slide

A title slide is a good start, but a presentation needs a lot more than just a title. To add a new slide with text boxes already in place for more of your best ideas, press Ctrl+M or click Home→New Slide. A new slide appears in the workspace as the active slide (it also shows up in the left-hand Slides pane). You've got a variety of slide types to choose from, as the following steps explain:

1. **On the Home tab, click the down arrow at the bottom of the New Slide button (or press Alt, H, I).**

    A menu opens, as shown in Figure 20-4, displaying a gallery of the different types of slides you can add:

    — **Title Slide** has text boxes for a title and a subtitle. This kind of slide doesn't *have* to come at the beginning of a presentation—you can add whatever text you want to its text boxes—but the text boxes are preformatted to look just right for a title slide.

    — **Title and Content** has a text box for a title and a *content box,* which lets you easily insert just about anything you can think of: text, a table, a chart, SmartArt, a photo, clip art, or a video or audio file. The next section tells you more about adding all these items.

Figure 20-4:
When you insert a new slide into your presentation, you can choose from a variety of preformatted slide types.

Note: What's the difference between a text box and a content box? A text box holds text—letters, numbers, and symbols like & or $—and that's it. A content box holds *any* kind of content. You can click inside a content box and start typing to add text, or you can click a picture of the kind of content you want to insert.

— **Section Header** has two text boxes: one for a title and one for regular text. This is a good choice to mark divisions in a long presentation that you've divided into several sections. Page 604 gives you the lowdown on working with sections, a brand-new feature in PowerPoint 2010.

— **Two Content** has a text box for a title and two content boxes, arranged into side-by-side columns.

— **Comparison** looks a lot like a two-content slide, with a text box for a title and two side-by-side content boxes. Above each content box, though, is a text box where you can add commentary on whatever you're comparing in the content boxes.

— **Title Only** has a text box for a title at the top of the slide. The rest of the slide is blank.

— **Blank** has no boxes for text or content. Instead, you add and arrange your own.

— **Content with Caption** has a title box across the top, text box on the left side, and a large content box on the right side.

— **Picture with Caption** has a large box for a picture, which takes up most of the screen, with two text boxes beneath it: one for a title and one for regular text.

Choosing a slide type can save you time. But, as Chapter 21 explains, editing slides and moving around their content is easy, so you never have to worry about choosing the "wrong" slide type—there's really no such thing.

2. **Click the kind of slide you want to insert.**

PowerPoint puts the slide in your presentation, ready for you to add whatever you like.

Adding Content

Page 548 shows you how to add text to a slide. But mere text alone makes for a boring presentation. When it's time to add things like images, audio or video clips, tables, and charts, follow these steps:

1. **Insert a new slide with a content box into your presentation by going to the Home tab and clicking the New Slide button's down arrow (or pressing Alt, H, I).**

The menu that opens includes four slide types with space for content: Title and Content (shown in Figure 20-5), Two Content, Comparison, and Content with Caption.

2. **Select the kind of slide you want to insert.**

PowerPoint adds the new slide to your presentation and presents it front and center in your workspace.

3. **In the slide's content box, click the icon that represents whatever you want to add: table, chart, SmartArt, Picture, clip art, or media clip.**

For a table, PowerPoint asks how many columns and rows you want. For the other kinds of content, PowerPoint opens a dialog box that lets you find and select the image or media clip you want.

4. **Make your selections, and then click OK or Insert (depending on the dialog box where you're working).**

Now it's time to edit, if necessary (see Chapter 21 for more about that).

Note: You don't have to use a slide with a content box to add a picture, SmartArt, a table, or whatever. On any slide, go to the Insert tab (Alt, N) to add any kind of content you want.

Type here to add text.   Click any type of content to insert it.

Figure 20-5:
A content box lets you add text (just start typing) or any of the six kinds of items shown here: table, chart, SmartArt, picture, clip art, or media clip. Click any of the icons shown to open a dialog box where you can do things like specify the number of rows in a table, select an audio file to add, and so on.

Deleting Content

How you give the heave-ho to items on a slide depends in part on what you want to get rid of:

- **To delete text** but keep the text box in which it resides, select the text and then press Delete or Backspace (or type over the text to replace it). If you want to delete both the text and the text box that holds it, then move your mouse pointer to any border of the text box. When the cursor becomes a four-way arrow, click to select the box. Then press Delete or Backspace.

- **To delete a picture, clip art, or a video,** click the image to select it, and then press Delete or Backspace.

- **To delete a table, a chart, or SmartArt,** click the content to reveal the frame that holds it, as shown in Figure 20-6. Next, click the frame to select it, and then press Delete or Backspace.

Tip: If you want to edit or delete content within a table, a chart, or some SmartArt, rather than getting rid of the whole thing, flip to Chapter 21.

Figure 20-6:
Click a chart to show its frame, and then click the frame to select it. (You select a table or SmartArt the same way.)

Saving a Presentation

As you might expect, saving a PowerPoint presentation works just like saving any other kind of Office file:

1. **Select File→Save (Alt, F, S), or press Ctrl+S.**

    The Save As dialog box opens. If your presentation has a title slide, PowerPoint grabs the title and plunks it in the "File name" box. You can change the name if you like.

2. **Navigate to the folder where you want to save the presentation, and then select the file type you want. For most presentations, you'll probably choose one of these:**

    — **PowerPoint Presentation.** This saves your presentation with the file extension .pptx. Starting with PowerPoint 2007, Microsoft introduced this format as the default for PowerPoint files, so it's what you get when you simply save a file.

    — **PowerPoint Macro-Enabled Presentation.** *Macros* are mini-programs you can record to automate tasks you do frequently. If you want to use macros within your presentation, then save it with this option, which gives it the .pptm file extension.

— **PowerPoint 97–2003 Presentation.** If you need to share a copy of your presentation with others who have an older version of PowerPoint, choose this option, which saves the presentation as a .ppt file.

Tip: The box on page describes a few other, less common options to consider when saving a Power-Point presentation.

3. **Click Save.**

    PowerPoint saves the file in your chosen folder, using the filename and format you selected.

File Types and PowerPoint

Most of the time, you'll probably save your PowerPoint presentation as a .pptx, .pptm, or .ppt file. These formats let you open and edit your files in PowerPoint 2010 or 2007 or (for .ppt files) in PowerPoint 97–2003. But you do have other choices, all of which are worth knowing a bit about:

*   **PowerPoint Template.** If you've designed a presentation that you want to use as the basis for future presentations, you can save it as a template. File types are .potx (PowerPoint 2010 or 2007 template), .potm (macro-enabled PowerPoint 2010 or 2007 template), and .pot (PowerPoint 97–2003 template).

*   **PowerPoint Show.** A PowerPoint Show is like a read-only version of your presentation. When someone opens the presentation, PowerPoint immediately launches its slideshow. It's a great choice when you want people simply to view your finished presentation, not work on it. (Just remember to save a regular .pptx, .pptm, or .ppt version, too, in case you want to work on the presentation later.) You can save as a PowerPoint Show (.ppsx), a macro-enabled Power-Point Show (.ppsm), or a PowerPoint Show for earlier versions of PowerPoint (.pps).

*   **PowerPoint Picture Presentation.** This option, new in PowerPoint 2010, adds a layer of security when you distribute a presentation to others. Pow-erPoint makes each slide a single picture instead of multiple objects on the slide's background. This means that others can't modify, rearrange, or "borrow" the slides' content. This option converts slides to pictures and saves a copy of the presentation as a .pptx file.

*   **Windows Media Video.** This option converts your presentation to a .wmv video that's viewable in Windows Media Player, RealPlayer, QuickTime, and other video players.

*   **Office Theme.** If you've created your own theme for a presentation, selecting fonts and colors you like, you can save that theme for use in other PowerPoint presentations and Office programs. PowerPoint saves the file as a .thmx file (that's an Office Theme) and stores it in your Themes folder.

*   **Outline/RTF.** This option saves the text of your slides in outline form as an .rtf file, which you can open in Word and most other word-processing programs. None of the images or themes come along for the ride, but it's a good way to grab all the text in a slideshow.

*   **PDF or XPS file.** This converts your presentation to a Portable Document Format (PDF) or XML Paper Specification (XPS) file, which allow others to view the slides in Adobe Acrobat or the Windows XPS Viewer. If you convert a presentation to one of these file types, it becomes a document—not a presentation—so there's no animation or slide transitions.

Note: As with other Office 2010 programs, PowerPoint temporarily saves the last autosaved version of your file, even if you tell it not to save your changes. To find and open one of these "unsaved" files, click Files→Recent→Recover Unsaved Presentations (Alt, F, R, R), select the file you want to open, and then click the Open button.

Opening an Existing Presentation

So far you've learned how to create, add material to, and save your slideshows. Next up: opening one of your creations. Microsoft gives you a handful of options; this section starts with a few of the quickest.

Open a Recent Presentation from the Windows Start Menu

If you've viewed or worked on a file recently, you can open it right from the Windows Start menu. That way, when you open PowerPoint, your presentation opens, too.

Click Start. When the Start menu opens, hover your mouse pointer over the Microsoft PowerPoint 2010 menu item. A fly-out menu appears listing recent presentations— up to 10 of them. Click the one you want.

Tip: You can pin PowerPoint to the top of your Start menu: Click Start, right-click Microsoft PowerPoint 2010, and then select Pin to Start Menu from the shortcut menu.

Open a Recent Presentation in PowerPoint

If you've already got PowerPoint open, head over to the Recent area in the Backstage section to see a list of shortcuts to files you've recently worked on. Select File→Recent (Alt, F, R) to see the Recent Presentations list. Click the filename you want, and it opens.

Tip: If there's a presentation you use frequently, make it easy to find by pinning it to the top of the Recent Presentations list. Just click the pushpin icon to the right of the file you want, and PowerPoint keeps it at the top of the list. To unpin a pinned file, do the same—click its pushpin icon.

A related option: Tell PowerPoint to display files you've worked on recently right on the Backstage File menu itself; this saves you a click or two by letting you open these presentations directly from that menu. If you don't see any recent files on the File menu, do this:

1. Select File→Recent (Alt, F, R).

    The Backstage view shows you its list of recently opened files.

2. **Scroll down to the bottom of the screen and turn on the checkbox labeled "Quickly access this number of Recent Presentations"**

   Now PowerPoint shows any recent files on the File menu, just above where it says Info.

Open Any Saved Presentation in PowerPoint

Finally, you can always find and open any saved presentation, by pressing ol' reliable Ctrl+O to summon the Open dialog box. (Or take one of these routes: File→Open or Alt, F, O.) Just navigate to the slideshow you want to open, select it, and then click Open. And there it is.

Adding Notes

Not too many people are comfortable giving an off-the-cuff presentation without notes in hand. PowerPoint is ready to help by letting you add notes to individual slides as you create a presentation. These memory aids can do whatever you want them to do: Serve as a sketchy outline of points to cover or provide detailed commentary written out in full. You can add notes as you create slides, one at a time, or go ahead and create the presentation and then return to add notes to it later. You can print out your notes and have them in hand as you give the presentation, look at them in Normal view, or (if you're using two monitors during the presentation) see the notes in Presenter view (page 668).

Adding notes is simple: In Normal view (that's the view you use to work on individual slides, as shown back in Figure 20-1), click the Notes pane below the active slide. The cursor appears, and all you have to do is type. When you're done with your notes for this slide, click outside the Notes pane. If you want to move on to add notes to the next slide, click it in the left Slides pane. PowerPoint opens that slide; click its Notes pane to add your note.

Tip: If the Notes pane feels too cramped to work in, move the mouse pointer to the top border. When the pointer becomes two parallel lines with arrows pointing up and down, click and drag to resize the pane.

You can edit your notes at any time in Normal view by clicking inside the Notes pane, or you can read and edit them in Notes Page view (View→Notes Page or Alt, W, T), which shows each slide on its own page, with a roomy text box for notes beneath it. The next section tells you more about PowerPoint's different views.

Viewing a Presentation

Building a good presentation requires more than just polishing each slide you've created. You also need to pull back and get a bird's-eye view. Only then can you judge (and tweak, if necessary) how the collection is shaping up. Does your argument flow smoothly? Are the slides arranged in the best possible order? Would a new slide help?

Fortunately, PowerPoint is loaded with different ways to view your presentation, from focused takes on individual slides to top-down looks at the entire collection. The following sections give you the grand tour.

Normal View

When you're creating slides, you'll probably spend most of your time working in Normal view, shown in Figure 20-1. It gives you plenty of room to compose, offers an area for notes at the bottom of the screen, and comes with a left-hand pane that shows a scrolling list of all the slides in your presentation. This pane comes in two flavors: the Slides tab, which shows a miniature of each slide, and the Outline tab, shown in Figure 20-7, which shows the text of each slide in outline form.

When you launch PowerPoint, it opens in Normal view. If you switch to a different view, like any of the ones described next, you can get back to Normal by clicking its button on the status bar or clicking View→Normal (Alt, W, L).

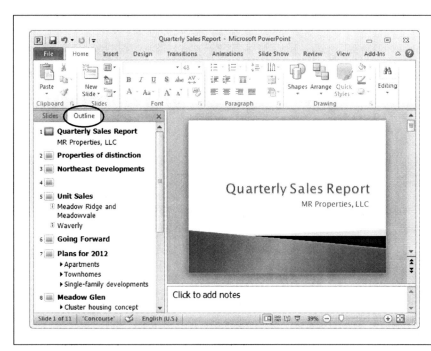

Figure 20-7:
In Normal view, click the Outline tab (circled) to see your presentation's text in outline format.

Slide Sorter View

Here's where to head when you want the big-picture view. Not only do you get an at-a-glance overview (see Figure 20-8), but this view is also perfect for things like plunking in new slides and rearranging the slide order—you can even apply transitions across the entire collection. Here are your options:

- **Insert a new slide.** Click between any two slides and then press Ctrl+M to insert a Title and Content slide. Or use the Home tab's New Slide button (Alt, H, I) to select the kind of slide you want to insert. When PowerPoint inserts the slide, you can leave it there as a placeholder or double-click it to switch to Normal view for editing.

- **Move slides.** Seeing slides in the context of the whole slideshow helps you organize a presentation. Click the slide you want to move (hold down Shift or Ctrl to select multiple slides) and drag it to its new position.

- **Change a presentation's theme.** Head for the Design tab to apply a new look from the Themes gallery (Alt, G, H). Doing this in Slide Sorter view gives you a feel for how a theme looks across your entire presentation.

- **Create or Edit transitions between slides.** A *transition* is how one slide moves to the next during a slideshow. In Slide Sorter view, you can apply the same transition to all the slides in your presentation; press Ctrl+A to select all the slides (or simply choose the ones you want) and then head to the Transitions tab to choose a transition. Page 653 tells you all about working with transitions.

To edit any slide, double-click it. PowerPoint whisks you over to Normal view, with the slide you selected ready and waiting as the active one.

Figure 20-8:
In Slide Sorter view, you see small versions of the slides in your presentation, laid out in order. Click and drag any slide to move it to a different spot in the presentation.

Reading View

New in PowerPoint 2010, Reading view (Figure 20-9) gives you a preview of your slides, just like Slide Show view (coming up). PowerPoint hides the ribbon, and the current slide takes up most of the screen. You can move through your presentation one slide at a time, seeing effects and transitions, just as you would during an actual presentation. But Reading view is a *working* view of your slideshow. Unlike in Slide Show view, the task bar remains visible, so you can switch to another program without ending the slideshow. This comes in handy when you want to check a fact on the company website or ask a colleague a question via instant message, and you don't want to exit the slideshow to do it.

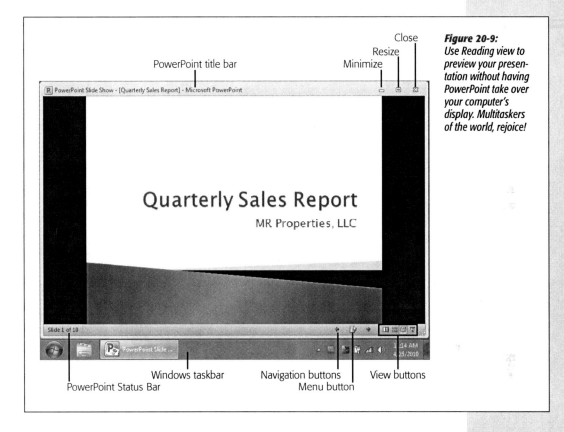

Figure 20-9:
Use Reading view to preview your presentation without having PowerPoint take over your computer's display. Multitaskers of the world, rejoice!

To fire up this view, click the status bar's Reading View button or select View→Reading View (Alt, W, D). PowerPoint quickly launches your show in most of the screen, with these additional elements visible:

- **The PowerPoint title bar** appears above the slide, so you can resize the window or close PowerPoint. If you want to check the spelling of a vice president's name on slide 34, for example, you can resize the PowerPoint window and open the company directory in Word, and then compare the two.

- **The status bar**, the horizontal band directly under the slide, shows which slide you're on. On the right side, arrows let you move forward or backward through the presentation. The Menu button also lets you navigate or end the presentation, print it (page 562), edit individual slides (which switches you to Normal view), or see the slides on the full screen (switching you to Slide Show view).

- **The Windows task bar** displays the Windows Start button and any other programs you have running. This is great news for multitaskers—you can open a different window without ending your slideshow first. So if you need to pause and send an email, you can do that without quitting the slideshow.

Notes Page View

If you've added notes to your slides (page 556), this view shows the goods and the accompanying slide together on one page (see Figure 20-10). As the figure shows, Notes Page view offers a good-sized text box—helpful if you need to refine those notes. To magnify the text, click the View tab's Zoom button (Alt, W, Q) and select the zoom percentage you want;100% zoom is a good size for editing notes.

There's no Notes Page button on the status bar; to summon this view, select View→ Notes Page (Alt, W, T). And to print your notes, skip ahead to page 563 for instructions.

Figure 20-10:
Notes Page view bundles together a slide and its notes on the same page—great for printing and editing during the commute home from work. If you're working on your computer and need a closer look, click the Zoom button (circled) and choose a magnification percentage. Then click the text to edit it.

Click here to add or edit notes.

Slide Show View

Professional speakers know that it's a smart idea to give your presentation a few trial runs before the big event. Practicing lets you familiarize yourself with the flow of the slides and gives you a chance to iron out kinks before going live. In PowerPoint, the best way to practice a presentation is to use Slide Show view. It also happens to be the view you'll use to *give* the presentation. In fact, there's so much you can do in Slide Show view that it gets its own tab, as shown in Figure 20-11.

When you click the status bar's Slide Show button or select Slide Show→From Beginning (Alt, S, B), your presentation occupies center stage and takes over the entire screen. The first slide appears, and there's nothing to divert viewers' attention from your slides. Your slides proceed according to how you've set them up: Click or press Enter to move to the next slide or, if you've added automatic transitions, the slide-show advances on its own.

If you need to go back or jump to a different slide, right-click and choose the option you want from the shortcut menu that appears. To end the presentation, press Esc.

Note: Chapter 24 takes you through setting up and actually giving a slideshow.

Use these buttons to begin your slideshow.

Prepare for and manage your slideshow with these buttons.

Set screen resolution or work with multiple monitors here.

Figure 20-11:
When you click the Slide Show tab, the ribbon changes to display the buttons labeled here. From left to right, the ribbon groups buttons for starting a slideshow, for setting up a slideshow before you give it, and for dealing with the monitors that will display your presentation.

Zooming In and Out

If you need to take a closer look at a slide, the easiest way to zoom in is to go to the status bar's right side and use the Zoom slider. Either click and drag the slider or click the plus or minus sign at either end to change the size of the active slide in Normal view. After you've tinkered with the Zoom slider, you can resize things so the whole slide appears by clicking the "Fit slide to current window" button to the right of the slider.

The View tab's Zoom section also lets you resize slides. Select View→Zoom (Alt, W, Q) and choose a zoom percentage from the dialog box that opens; then click OK. To return the slide to its default size, select View→Fit to Window (Alt, W, F).

In Normal view, you can increase or decrease the size of the slides by resizing the Slides pane. Move your mouse pointer to the border between the Slides pane and the active slide's workspace. When the pointer changes to the resizing cursor, click and drag to resize the pane. When you let go of the mouse button, PowerPoint adjusts the slides in that pane to fit it.

Printing a Presentation

As with other Office 2010 programs, you go Backstage to print a PowerPoint presentation. Press Ctrl+P or select File→Print (Alt, F, P) to open Print, as shown in Figure 20-12. Here you get the following printing options (these are the factory-set options; after you've printed a few slideshows, the buttons reflect what you chose last time):

- **Copies.** Choose the number of copies you want to print from this drop-down list.

- **Printer.** This button displays your default printer. To add a printer or to choose a different one, click this button and select the printer you want to use, or click Add Printer.

Note: Page 138 tells you how to set your default printer.

Figure 20-12:
In PowerPoint 2010, you select your printing options Backstage, in the File menu's Print section.

- **Printer Properties.** Click this link to tweak settings like paper orientation and which printer tray to get paper from. The options depend on the printer you select.

- **Print All Slides.** Here's where you select what you want to print: the whole presentation, a range of slides, or just the current slide.

- **Slides per page.** The name of this button reflects what you did the last time you printed slides: Full Page Slides, Notes Pages, and so on. When you click this button, the menu that appears gives you quite a few options:

  — **Print Layout.** In this section, select what you want to print:

    ▪ **Full Page Slides** prints one slide per page—just the slide, no notes.

    ▪ **Notes Pages** prints your presentation as it appears in Notes Page view: one slide per page, with the slide at the top of the page and the notes below. This is handy when you want to have a hard copy of your notes to consult as you go through the presentation.

    ▪ **Outline** prints an overview of your presentation. It doesn't print the slides, just the text on them, arranged in an outline format. When you select this option, the printed document looks like what you see in the Outline tab (page 557).

  — **Handouts.** If you're creating printed handouts for your audience, here's where you set up how those handouts will look. You can print one to nine slides per page.

Note: Some of the options in the Handouts section specify horizontal or vertical. This doesn't refer to page orientation; it sets the order of the slides. In other words, horizontal prints the slides in *rows,* so readers read across from left to right to follow the presentation. Vertical prints the slides in *columns,* so readers follow the slides from top to bottom.

  — **Frame Slides.** A checkmark next to this option tells PowerPoint to draw a border around each slide when you're printing multiple slides per page. This helps define each slide when you have multiple slides on a page.

  — **Scale to Fit Paper.** To automatically adjust the size of the slides you're printing to fit the paper size you've selected, turn on this option.

  — **High Quality.** Turning on this option sharpens the images of the slides you're printing. Be aware that choosing this option may mean that your slides take longer to print and use up more ink.

  — **Print Comments and Ink Markup.** When you collaborate with others on a presentation, each person working on the presentation can mark up slides and leave comments. If you want those to show in the printed presentation, turn on this option.

- **Collated.** If you're printing multiple copies of the presentation, pick whether you want those copies to be collated (1,2,3; 1,2,3; 1,2,3 order) or uncollated (1,1,1; 2,2,2; 3,3,3 order).

- **Color.** If you're using a color printer, select whether you want to print the presentation in full color, in grayscale (different shades of gray), or in pure black and white.

- **Edit Header & Footer.** If you want your printed pages to have a header or footer or show page numbers, then click this link and then select the Notes and Handouts tab. Here you can create a timestamp that shows when you printed the presentation, write a header or footer, or turn page numbers on or off.

After you've waded through all these choices, there's only one thing left to do: Click the big Print button at the top of the page. That familiar whirring sound means your presentation is on its way to the printer.

Editing Slides

Y ou *could* create a presentation, shovel in some text and images, and leave it at that. Lots of people do. You've probably sat through slideshows that were little more than one poorly formatted slide after another. But when PowerPoint makes it so easy to make your slides look good, why settle for boring or, worse, confusing?

In PowerPoint, whatever you put on a slide—text, photo, table, or chart—is an object. That means it lives inside a frame, such as a text box or a content box, and everything inside the frame comprises the object. So when you move a frame, you also move its contents. When you resize a frame, its contents automatically adjust to the new space. And when you delete a frame, you delete the whole object—not just the frame but everything inside it. Understanding objects makes it easier to make your slides look good.

This chapter shows you how to edit the objects on a slide, including text, tables, pictures, clip art, SmartArt diagrams, and more. If you're familiar with Word, you'll be happy to know that you work with many of these objects in PowerPoint just as you do in Word. As with Word, PowerPoint 2010 has better photo-editing capabilities, including background removal and the ability to take screenshots. Read on for the full scoop.

Editing Text

If you're used to Word, editing text in PowerPoint is both familiar and a little different: familiar because the Mini Toolbar and the Font and Paragraph sections of the Home tab look pretty similar, and different because you're working in a text box inserted into a slide, rather than directly on the page. This section tells you everything you need to know about making your PowerPoint prose look good.

Formatting Text

If you choose a theme for your presentation (page 547 shows you how), you may never need to worry about formatting text, since those prefab collections of designer-chosen styles take care of that task for you. Each theme has text formatting already built in: fonts, sizes, colors, and even special formatting in some text, like bold letters for titles. But if you want to add your own formatting—whether to make a word or phrase stand out or as part of a template you're designing—you can do that, too.

PowerPoint gives you two ways to format text:

- **Head to the Home tab (Alt, H).** The Font and Paragraph sections, shown in Figure 21-1, have buttons, most of them familiar from Word, for formatting text and paragraphs. What's the difference? The Font section is all about formatting characters and words—the buttons here apply fonts, colors, sizes, and other formatting to any text you select. The Paragraph section affects paragraphs (in PowerPoint, as in Word, that's all the text that comes before you press Enter, like a line in a bulleted list), aligning spacing, indenting, and so on.

Tip: Use the Text Shadow button (Home→Text Shadow or Alt, H, 5) to put a shadow behind selected text, adding a bit of depth and making your words stand out from the slide.

- **Use the Mini Toolbar.** When you select text, a ghostly, semitransparent Mini Toolbar hovers just above your selection. Move the mouse pointer toward this floating toolbar to bring it into focus, as shown in Figure 21-1, and then use its buttons to format the text you selected.

Adjusting Character Spacing

Typography is the art of making text readable. One simple control in any typographer's toolkit is *kerning,* better known to non-publishing-geeks as the spacing between characters. You might, for example, want to space a caption so it matches the width of a picture above it.

To adjust character spacing, select the text whose spacing you want to change, and then navigate to Home→Character Spacing (Alt, H, 6). From the menu that appears, choose the spacing you want, from Very Tight to Very Loose (Figure 21-2 shows a few examples).

For even more control, open the Font dialog box to its Character Spacing tab; select Home→Character Spacing→More Spacing (Alt, H, 6, M). Then tell PowerPoint whether you want the spacing expanded or condensed and by how many points. You'll probably want to leave the Kerning checkbox turned on—it tells PowerPoint to adjust the spacing between letters to make the characters look evenly spaced. Click OK to apply your custom character spacing.

Text Shadow

Character Spacing

Text Direction, Align Text, and SmartArt Graphic buttons

Mini Toolbar

Bring Forward/ Send Backward buttons

Figure 21-1:
PowerPoint's Mini Toolbar gives you on-the-spot formatting choices, no matter which tab you have selected, including the ability to move text in front of or behind other objects on the slide. The Home tab has some formatting options specific to PowerPoint—things like adding a shadow to text, adjusting character spacing, positioning text on a slide, and converting text to SmartArt.

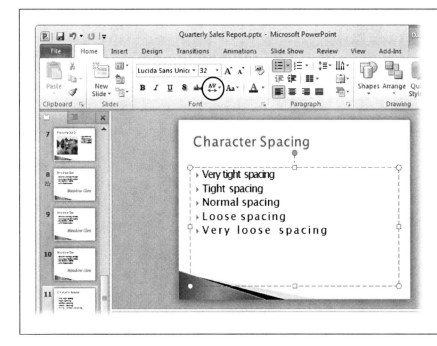

Figure 21-2:
Click the Character Spacing button (circled) to squeeze or stretch your text.

Positioning Text

When you insert a new slide (page 549), most of PowerPoint's slide types have boxes in place to hold your words. Just click inside a text or content box and start typing. If you want to move the text to a different part of the slide, click the text box's border and then drag the box (and the text along with it) to its new location.

If you want your text to appear at an angle, click the text box's rotation handle (the green circle above the box) and drag it in a circular direction. As you drag, the text changes its angle. When you've positioned the text as you want it, let go of the mouse button.

The Home tab's Paragraph section also gives you a couple of options for positioning text. Besides the line spacing, indentation, alignment, and column buttons that you also find in Word, there are a couple of buttons to help position text inside a text box:

- **Text Direction.** Here's where you give the text an orientation *within* the text box. Click Home→Text Direction (Alt, H, AX), and pick one of these options, illustrated in Figure 21-3:

    — **Horizontal (Alt, H, AX, H).** The text reads from left to right, just like a normal line in a book.

    — **Rotate all text 90° (Alt, H, AX, R).** This flips text on its side, so it reads from top to bottom.

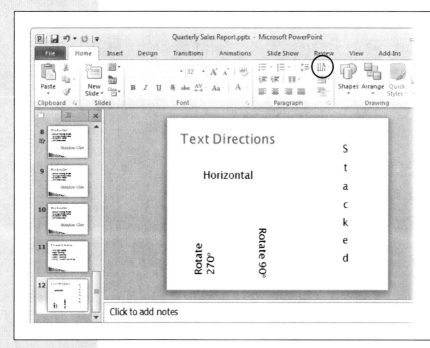

Figure 21-3:
You can position your text in any of these directions using the Text Direction button (circled).

— **Rotate all text 270° (Alt, H, AX, O).** This also flips text on its side, but you read it from bottom to top.

— **Stacked (Alt, H, AX, S).** This turns your text into columns that are one letter wide. Words read from top to bottom, and when your text reaches the bottom of the text box, it starts at the top of a new column.

- **Align Text.** Unlike the Left, Center, Right, and Justify buttons, which align text relative to the left and right borders of a text box, the Align Text button positions text in relation to the top and bottom borders. Click this button (Alt, H, AT) and choose one of these alignments:

— **Top (Alt, H, AT, T).** This puts the first line of text close to the top border of the text box.

— **Middle (Alt, H, AT, M).** This puts text in the middle of the text box, with the first line equidistant from the top and bottom borders. As you type, the middle line of your text stays aligned with the text box's midpoint.

— **Bottom (Alt, H, AT, B).** This lines up text along the bottom border of the text box, so that the last line is always aligned with that border.

Formatting a Text Box

Text Direction and Align Text, explained in the previous section, are two ways to format text boxes. But PowerPoint gives you some other options as well, so you can fine-tune how your text appears inside its box. To see them, right-click the text in a text box and then select Format Text Effects from the shortcut menu; the dialog box shown in Figure 21-4 appears. (You can also choose More Options from the menus associated with the Home tab's Text Direction and Align Text buttons.) Either way, here's what you can tweak:

- **Text layout.** This section has vertical alignment and text direction settings, similar to those buttons on the Home tab.

- **Autofit.** If the words you're typing fill up their text box, PowerPoint normally resizes the text to fit within the box. If you prefer, you can tell PowerPoint to expand the text box instead or to refrain from autofitting the text and text box at all. (In that case, the text spills beyond the text box's borders.)

- **Internal margin.** This sets the distance between the text and the text box borders.

- **Wrap text in shape.** This checkbox, on by default, tells PowerPoint to keep text inside its text box, automatically starting a new line when text reaches the left border of the text box. (If you turn this checkbox off, you have to press Enter to start a new line of text.)

- **Columns.** Want columns inside a text box? Click this button, set the number of columns and the spacing between them, and then click OK.

After you've chosen your text box settings, click Close to make the Format Text Effects box go away.

Figure 21-4:
Set your preferences for text box formatting in the Text Box section of this dialog box.

Creating Lists

Bulleted lists, for better or for worse, are at the heart of many PowerPoint presentations. They structure the presentation, underline your points, and help the audience follow what you're saying. So it's not surprising that PowerPoint assumes that you'll use bulleted lists in your presentation. When you insert a new slide that has a pre-formatted content box, the upper-left corner of the box has a bulleted list ready and waiting for you to add the first line. Just click and type. To add a new bullet item, press Enter to move to the next line.

If you insert your own text box, it's easy to format the words inside it as a list. Just go to the Home tab and, in the Paragraph section, select Bullets (Alt, H, U) or Numbering (Alt, H, N). The drop-down menus for these buttons let you choose a list style or open the Bullets and Numbering dialog box, shown in Figure 21-5, to customize your list.

In the Bullets and Numbering dialog box, you can resize the bullets or numbers and assign them a color. Depending on the kind of list you're working with, you also get these options:

- **On the Bulleted tab,** click the Picture button to select a picture, such as your company logo or a custom checkmark, to use as a bullet. Click the Customize button to choose an icon from the Symbol dialog box.

- **On the Numbered tab,** if you want your list to start with a number other than 1, use the "Start at" dialog box to assign an initial number.

Click OK to apply your selections to your text.

Figure 21-5:
When formatting a list, you can choose a color for your bullets or numbers and specify their size in relation to the text they introduce.

Linking Text to a Web Page

Presentations don't have to be linear, plodding inexorably from one slide to the next. You can insert hyperlinks into your text (or into any object on a slide) to jump somewhere else, such as a web page, another slide, or even a file in another program. Chapter 22 shows how to use links to navigate the slides in your presentation (page 607) and to open a file in another program (page 613). Here's how to insert a link that fires up your web browser and opens a specific web page:

1. **Select the text that you want to contain the hyperlink, and then click the Insert tab's Hyperlink button (Alt, N, I).**

   The Insert Hyperlink dialog box, shown in Figure 21-6, opens. In the left "Link to" list, Existing File or Web Page is already selected.

2. **In the Address box, type or paste in the web address of the page you're linking to. If you want a ScreenTip to appear when you hover the pointer over the link, click the ScreenTip button, write the ScreenTip text in the dialog box that opens, and then click OK. Click OK to close the Insert Hyperlink dialog box.**

   PowerPoint closes the dialog box and inserts the link in your text.

During a slideshow, you can click the link to open a web browser and go straight to the web page you linked to. (For this to work, of course, the computer displaying the slideshow must be connected to the Internet.)

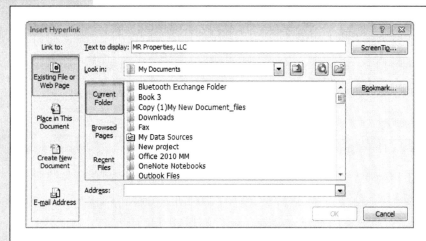

Figure 21-6:
When you insert a hyperlink, the text you selected to hold the link appears in the "Text to display" box. The address of the web page you're linking to goes in the Address box. If you want, click the ScreenTip button to display text when the pointer hovers over the link.

After you've inserted a link, right-click the linked text to perform any of these actions:

- **Edit Hyperlink** opens the Edit Hyperlink dialog box, which looks just like Figure 21-6, except that it has the information for the current hyperlink already filled in. Make the changes you want, and then click OK.

- **Open Hyperlink** tests the link you inserted by opening the web page in your default web browser.

- **Copy Hyperlink** copies the text and its inserted link so you can paste them elsewhere.

- **Remove Hyperlink** deletes the hyperlink, while leaving the text in place.

Checking Your Spelling

Nothing distracts your audience like an obvious typo or a spelling goof in the middle of a slide. But PowerPoint, like other Office programs, has you covered with a built-in spell checker. The first line of defense is AutoCorrect. As in Word, PowerPoint has a list of built-in AutoCorrections that fix common misspellings and typos as you type. So if you accidentally type *taht* instead of *that*, PowerPoint automatically corrects the mistake.

Tip: You set PowerPoint's AutoCorrect and AutoFormat options the same way you do for Word. Check out the how-tos starting on page 122.

PowerPoint also checks your spelling as you type, throwing a squiggly red line under any word that's not in its dictionary. Right-click an underlined word and choose the correct spelling from the suggestions in the shortcut menu. PowerPoint replaces the error with the correct word.

Spell checking in PowerPoint works in the same way it does in Word, with one exception: PowerPoint has no grammar checker. (When you consider that many presentations consist of bulleted lists made up of sentence fragments, that makes sense.) Table 21-1 tells you where in this book to find instructions for using Office's proofing and research tools—they're the same in PowerPoint as in Word.

Table 21-1. *Where to find instructions for Office's proofing and research tools*

Topic	Page Number
Turning off automatic spell checking	116
Hiding spelling errors while you work	117
Using contextual spelling	117
Checking an entire document's spelling	117
Undoing an AutoCorrect change	121
Setting AutoCorrect options	122
Making an exception to autocorrection	124
Adding custom corrections	124
Deleting an AutoCorrect correction	121
AutoFormatting	125
Using Office's research tools	128

Turning Text into WordArt

WordArt and PowerPoint are a natural fit. The big, bold formatting that makes WordArt stand out is a great way to emphasize titles or other phrases on your slides (especially if you add animation—page 638 tells you how to do that).

In PowerPoint, WordArt works the same way it does in Word. You create WordArt by going to the Insert tab (Insert→WordArt or Alt, N, W) and picking the style of WordArt you want. PowerPoint inserts a text box with placeholder text in the WordArt style you chose. Type inside the text box to replace the placeholder text.

If you want to make your WordArt look even snazzier, select the contents of your text box (click inside the box and press Ctrl+A) and select Drawing Tools | Format→Text Effects (Alt, JD, TX). From the menu that opens, choose the effect you want to add: shadow, reflection, glow, bevel, 3-D rotation, or transform (which bends and twists WordArt into circles, waves, and other shapes). For each type of effect, you've got many options to play with; hover the pointer over an effect to see them. PowerPoint shows a live preview as you browse the options. When you see an effect you like, click it to apply it to the WordArt on your slide.

Tip: To learn more about working with WordArt, see page 109.

Embedding Other Files in Slides

If you've ever thought life would be a lot easier if you could just plunk a Word document or an Excel chart directly into a PowerPoint slide, rejoice! Life just got easier. You can embed files from other programs (and even other PowerPoint files) in a slide. It happens through the magic of something called *object linking and embedding* (OLE). The box on page 576 gives you a primer on what OLE is, but in a nutshell it lets you work with another Office program from inside PowerPoint. That means you can use all the features of, say, Word or Excel in a file that lives in a PowerPoint slide.

Embedding an Existing File in a Slide

If you've got a file that would enhance your presentation—a worksheet you created in Excel, say—you can tack that file directly onto a slide. Just follow these steps:

1. **Insert a new blank slide. Then select Insert→Object (Alt, N, J).**

   The Insert Object dialog box, shown in Figure 21-7 opens.

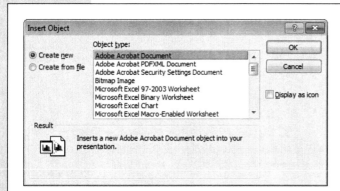

Figure 21-7:
The Insert Object dialog box is where you embed another kind of file in a PowerPoint slide. The "Create new" radio button (selected here) lets you choose the kind of file you want to create and embed on your slide. Turn on the "Create from file" radio button to embed and link to a file you've already created in another program.

2. **Turn on the "Create from file" radio button.**

   The Insert Object dialog box morphs into the same kind of file-finding window you see anytime you want to open a file.

3. **Click the Browse button.**

   The Browse dialog box opens.

4. **Navigate to and select the file you want to insert; click Open.**

   PowerPoint puts the filename in the Insert Object dialog box.

5. **If you want the object on the PowerPoint slide to reflect any changes that get made to the original document, then turn on the Link checkbox. Click OK.**

   PowerPoint inserts the file into your slide.

Tip: If the file you're embedding is too big to fit on the slide, then turn on the Insert Object dialog box's "Display as icon" checkbox. This inserts an icon that represents the kind of file you're embedding. When you're working in PowerPoint's Normal view, double-click the icon to open the file.

After you've embedded the file as an icon, insert a hyperlink (page 613) into the icon that links to the file. During a presentation, you can click the icon and open the file in its original program. Obviously, for this to work, the computer you're using to give the presentation must have access to the linked file wherever it happens to live (such as on the company network).

Updating Links

When you open a presentation that contains a linked file, PowerPoint asks whether you want to update the link. In other words, do you want PowerPoint to fetch the latest and greatest version of the embedded file? To update the embedded file, click Update Links. To open the presentation without updating links, click Cancel.

Creating a New Embedded File

As the box on page 576 explains, embedding a file is like opening another program from within PowerPoint. You can then take advantage of all the bells and whistles of Word or Excel, for example, as you create and edit a file that lives on a PowerPoint slide. You don't even need to open Word or Excel. Here's how to create an embedded file in PowerPoint:

1. **Insert a new blank slide. Then select Insert→Object (Alt, N, J).**

   The Insert Object dialog box, shown in Figure 21-7, opens. The "Object type" box shows the different kinds of files you can insert as objects, including Adobe Acrobat documents, Excel worksheets, PowerPoint presentations, Word documents, and Microsoft Works and OpenDocument files.

2. **Make sure the "Create new" radio button is turned on, and then select the kind of file you want to create. Click OK.**

   PowerPoint inserts a frame for the object, and the ribbon changes to reflect the type of document you chose. If you picked a Word document, for example, the ribbon changes to the Word ribbon.

3. **Work inside the frame to create your document. When you're finished, click outside the frame.**

   PowerPoint switches the ribbon back to its own familiar layout. Your work is now an object on the slide.

To resize the object, click it so its frame appears, and then click and drag the frame. If you need to edit the embedded file, double-click anywhere inside its frame; the ribbon changes, and you can work on it again.

OLE!

OLE (pronounced *oh-lay*) may bring to mind dashing tore-adors, swirling capes, and charging bulls, but the reality is a bit more prosaic—and a lot more useful to your PowerPoint presentations. OLE stands for *object linking and embed-ding,* and it's a way to make two programs work together to share information.

Embedding a file in a PowerPoint slide is like opening a ver-sion of a different program from inside PowerPoint. When you click an embedded Word document, for example, you no longer see the PowerPoint ribbon at the top of your screen; instead, you see the Word tabs and buttons you need to work with a document. When you click outside the embedded file, the PowerPoint ribbon returns.

Linking goes one step beyond embedding by keeping your embedded file in sync with a version of the same file that lives in another program. So if you create a worksheet in

Excel, embed the worksheet in a PowerPoint slide, and then link the embedded worksheet to its Excel version, you can update the linked file to reflect any changes made to it in Excel. That way you can be sure that your presentation has up-to-the-minute data.

OLE is useful when you want to take advantage of the power of other Office programs as you work in PowerPoint, such as using a complex Excel formula on spreadsheet data. It's also great for making sure that your linked files stay up to date, so you know you're presenting the very latest sales data, for example. But OLE does have some limitations. Embedding a file in a slide can increase a presentation's size dramatically. And moving a file you've linked to, or emailing someone a copy of the presentation, breaks any links. Still, OLE is a handy tool to have in your PowerPoint toolbox, letting you work with a program-within-a-program.

Note: OLE works in other programs besides PowerPoint. Word, Excel, Outlook, and Publisher all let you embed objects from the Insert tab. Select Insert→Object (Alt, N, J) to begin.

Adding Tables to Slides

Tables are a good visual for slides because they present a lot of information in a compact space. PowerPoint automatically formats tables according to your presenta-tion's theme, so their color scheme, style, and fonts fit perfectly with other slides. (Of course, you can adjust the formatting if you like.)

Working with tables in PowerPoint is much like working with them in Word (see page 81 for the full story). This section focuses on the key differences.

Inserting a Table

PowerPoint gives you several different ways to put a table on a slide. Read on to see your options.

Note: In PowerPoint, unlike Word, you can't start with data and then convert your text to a table.

Inserting a table when you add a new slide

To create a brand-new slide and put a table on it in just a few steps, do this:

1. **In the Slides pane, select the slide you want your new table to follow. Click the Home tab, and then click the New Slide button's down arrow (Alt, H, I).**

    PowerPoint shows you its gallery of slide types.

2. **Pick the slide you want. Choose one that has a content box, such as Title and Content.**

    Your new slide appears in the Slides pane and becomes the active slide in the work area.

3. **In the slide's content box, click Insert Table.**

    The Insert Table dialog box opens, asking you to choose the number of columns and rows for the new table.

4. **Set the number of columns and rows (you can always insert and delete them later) and then click OK.**

    PowerPoint inserts a table, preformatted to match your presentation's theme, into the slide.

Tip: Don't try to cram too much information into a table on a slide. Too many rows and columns, or text that's squeezed to fit into a cramped cell, will have your audience squinting as they try to read the table's content.

Inserting a table on an existing slide

Here's how to insert a table on a blank slide:

1. **Go to the Insert tab and click the Table button (Alt, N, T).**

    A menu opens with a 10 × 8 grid, shown in Figure 21-8, that lets you select the number of columns and rows you want in your table.

2. **Use the mouse pointer or arrow keys to choose how many columns and rows you want.**

    As you make your selections, you see a live preview of your table-in-progress on the slide.

3. **When the table looks good, click or press Enter.**

    PowerPoint inserts your new table on the slide.

Insert a table using an Excel-style spreadsheet

As in Word, you can also create a table by entering your data in an Excel-style spreadsheet, which PowerPoint then converts to a table. Select Insert→Table→ Excel Spreadsheet (Alt, N, T, X), type in your data, and then click outside the spreadsheet area to convert the data into a table.

Figure 21-8:
As you select the number of rows and columns you want for the table, Live Preview shows how the table will look, complete with formatting to fit your presentation's theme.

Tip: If the spreadsheet entry area is too small to work with, expand the box that holds the spreadsheet by clicking a corner resizing handle and dragging it outward.

Later, if you want to edit the table's data, double-click the table. PowerPoint changes it back to a spreadsheet, and you can edit the cells.

Drawing a table

You can also draw your table freehand, which is helpful when you need a table with rows or columns of different widths or some cells split into subsections. It's easy:

1. **Make the slide that will hold the table your active slide. Then select Insert→Table→Draw Table (Alt, N, T, D).**

   Your mouse pointer changes to a pencil. Click and drag to draw a rectangle. When it's the size you want your table to be, let go of the mouse button.

2. **The rectangle becomes the frame that holds your table, and PowerPoint opens the Table Tools | Design contextual tab.**

   On the right side of the Table Tools | Design tab, click the Draw Table button (Alt, JT, D).

3. **Again, the pointer turns into a pencil.**

   Draw borders between the rows and columns of your table. If you make a mistake, click the Table Tools | Design tab's Eraser button (Alt, JT, E) to erase a line. Click the Draw Table button (Alt, JT, D) to go back to drawing.

4. When you're finished, click outside the table or click the Draw Table button (Alt, JT, D) to toggle off drawing.

Your custom-drawn table is now part of your slide.

Click inside any cell to start adding data.

Tip: When you draw a table by hand, PowerPoint doesn't format the table according to your presentation's theme. If you want to add some color to your table, apply a table style: On the Table Tools | Design tab, choose a table from the Table Styles gallery (Alt, JT, A). Kepp reading to learn more about giving your PowerPoint tables style.

Adding Information to a Table

After you've inserted a table on a slide, click inside any cell and start typing to fill in information. To move to the next cell, press Tab. You can also use the arrow keys to navigate the table's cells.

Use the Mini Toolbar or Home tab's formatting buttons to format the text you add to a table.

Editing a Table

Much of what you can do to edit a table—add or delete rows and columns, merge or split cells, view or hide gridlines—happens the same way in PowerPoint as in Word, using the Table Tools | Design and Table Tools | Layout contextual tabs. So if you want to work with your table in any of the ways listed in Table 21-2, flip to the page referenced there.

Table 21-2. Where to find information about working with tables

Topic	Page Number
Inserting rows and columns	88
Moving rows and columns	89
Merging and splitting cells	90
Applying a table style	91
Applying shading	93
Working with borders	64

Selecting all or part of a table

Because PowerPoint tables are objects inside a frame, selecting parts of a table may be different from doing the same thing in Word. Here's how to select all or part of a table on a PowerPoint slide:

- **To select a single cell,** move the pointer to the lower-left corner of the cell you want. When the pointer becomes a fat black arrow, click to select that cell.

- **To select a row or column,** move the pointer just outside the frame next to the row or column you want to select (the pointer can be above, below, to the left, or to the right of what you're selecting). When the pointer changes to a fat black arrow pointing to the row or column you want, click to select it.

- **To select a range of cells,** select the first cell of the range, and then hold down the Shift key and select the last cell in the range. PowerPoint selects everything between those two cells. You can also click and drag to select the range you want.

- **To select the entire table,** click inside the table and then press Ctrl+A.

Resizing a table

When you insert a table on a PowerPoint slide, a frame encloses the table. Whenever you click the table, its frame becomes visible. To make the table larger or smaller, look for the frame's resizing points: These appear in the four corners and at the halfway point of each border. When you hover the pointer over a resizing point, the pointer becomes a two-headed arrow. Click and drag to resize the table. The cells stay proportional as you drag.

Tip: If you want to resize cells within a table, point at a border between rows or columns. When the pointer becomes two parallel lines with arrows pointing away from them, click and drag to move the border.

Moving a table

To move a table, click it so you can see its frame. Move the pointer to the frame so it becomes a four-way arrow. Drag to move the table; let go of the mouse button to drop the table in place.

Changing a table's style

For the most part, changing a table's style—coloring rows or columns, giving the first or last row a different appearance from the rest of the table—works the same in PowerPoint as in Word. You apply styles using the Table Tools | Design tab's Table Style Options, Table Styles, and Draw Borders sections. (Flip back to page 91 to learn about working with those sections.)

PowerPoint gives you a couple of options for styling tables that aren't available on Word's Table Tools | Design tab:

- **Effects.** This option, in the Table Styles section, adds visual effects to the table, such as shadowing, reflection, or beveling. To add an effect, select the table (or the group of cells to which you want to apply the effect), and select Table Tools | Design→Effects (Alt, JT, F). From the menu that appears, point at the kind of effect you want, and another fly-out menu opens, as shown in Figure 21-9, so you can choose a specific style. Pass your mouse pointer over the possibilities

to see a live preview on your slide. Click the effect you want, and PowerPoint
applies it to your table.

- **WordArt.** Want to call attention to a particular row, column, or cell? Make it
  pop by converting its contents to WordArt (page 109 tells you more about working with WordArt). Select the cell or cell range you want to convert, and then
  select Table Tools | Design→Quick Styles (Alt, JT, Q). Select a letter style for
  your WordArt, and PowerPoint applies that style to your selection. If you want,
  you can change the Text Fill (Alt, JT, TI), the Text Outline (Alt, JT, TO), or Text
  Effects (Alt, JT, TX) of your WordArt using the options in the Table Tools | De-
  sign tab's WordArt Styles section.

Adding Images to Slides

If you've ever added a picture or a piece of clip art to a Word document, you already
know how to work with images in PowerPoint. And all the cool image-editing capabilities added to Word 2010 are also available in PowerPoint 2010—so you can take a
screenshot or remove a photo's background, for example, without leaving PowerPoint.
Table 21-3 directs you to the pages in this book that explain how to work with photos.

Table 21-3. Where to find information about working with images

Topic	Page Number
Inserting images	96
Inserting clip art	97
Inserting a screenshot	98

Creating a Photo Album

If you've ever come home from vacation or family gathering with a camera full of digital photos and no good way to organize and share them, PowerPoint is here to help. PowerPoint's photo album option lets you create and then edit a presentation based on a set of pictures. Insert anywhere from one to four photos on a slide (Power-Point sizes and lays them out for you). You can give photos captions and add text boxes for your commentary. You can then put your album on the Web or on a CD (page 683) to share with others. For a program that's often associated with work, this feature can turn PowerPoint into a whole lot of fun.

Setting up a photo album

To create a photo-album presentation and show off your snaps, follow these steps:

1. Select Insert→Photo Album→New Photo Album (Alt, N, A, A).

    PowerPoint opens the Photo Album dialog box, shown in Figure 21-10.

2. Click the File/Disk button to choose the pictures you want to insert.

    The Insert New Pictures dialog box opens. Here's where you pick the photos you want to include.

Note: PowerPoint doesn't move the original file when it inserts a picture; that stays wherever you stored it. What you see on a slide is a copy of the original file, and any changes you make to the picture in PowerPoint don't affect the original.

---

3. Navigate to the folder that holds the pictures you want, and select the ones you want in your photo album.

    Select multiple files by holding down the Shift key (to choose a contiguous range) or the Ctrl key (to choose files one by one). As you select files, they appear in the "File name: box at the bottom of the Insert New Pictures dialog box.

4. Click Insert.

    The names of the files you chose appear in the Photo Album dialog box's "Pictures in album" box. Select any file in the box to see its thumbnail in the Preview box.

---

5. **If you want to insert an empty text box in place of a picture, click the New Text Box button where you want a text box to appear.**

   Text boxes are placeholders. As you edit the presentation, you can type the text you want into the text boxes you've inserted. If you want to tell a story about a picture, for example, you might create a slide that has a photo on one side and a text box on the other.

6. **To change the order of the pictures in your presentation, select a picture and use the up and down arrows beneath the "Pictures in album" box to move it.**

   The filename moves up or down the list, one place at a time, as you click.

7. **If you want to rotate or adjust the appearance of any picture, use the picture controls below the Preview pane.**

   From left to right, you can rotate counterclockwise/clockwise; increase/decrease contrast; and increase/decrease brightness.

   The preview image changes when you click the buttons, although its small size makes it a little hard to gauge how the changes affect the image. You can always view the image in the presentation and come back here to adjust it (the next section tells you how to edit a photo album).

8. **In the Picture Options section, turn on the checkbox for either of the two options listed.**

   — **Captions below ALL pictures.** To turn on this checkbox, you need to choose a picture layout (see step 9) *other* than "fit to slide".

Tip: If you want captions below some pictures but not others, turn on this checkbox anyway. After you've created your presentation, you can delete any captions you don't want.

   — **ALL pictures black and white.** This option makes all the photos in the presentation black and white. (It doesn't affect the original photos, only the versions you've inserted into this presentation—and you can change them back to color if you change your mind.)

9. **In the Album Layout section, tell PowerPoint how you want the pictures to appear on your slides.**

   Here are your options:

   — **Picture layout.** You can choose anywhere from one to four pictures, with or without a title text box, for each slide. "Fit to slide" means that the picture takes up the entire slide, with no room for a caption or a title. When you pick an option from the drop-down list, the sample slide at right changes to show how that option looks on a slide.

   — **Frame shape.** For any layout option other than "fit to slide", you choose a frame shape for your photos, such as rounded rectangle, simple frame, or soft-edge rectangle. The sample slide shows a preview of each frame style,

---

but it's small and a little hard to see if you don't have a big screen. If you change your mind about a frame shape, you can always change it later. (The next section tells you how to edit a photo album.)

— **Theme.** Click the Browse button to select an Office theme (page 547) for your presentation.

10. **When all your choices look good, click Create.**

PowerPoint gets busy and whips up your new photo album.

Figure 21-10:
Select, arrange, and even edit photos using the Photo Album dialog box.

In the not-quite-yet finished album, the first slide contains the captivating phrase "Photo Album" as the title and "by [Your Name]" as the subtitle (with your actual Office user name). If you told PowerPoint you wanted the pictures to have captions, each picture's filename is its caption in a text box below the picture. You can edit any of the text in the same way you'd edit any other text in PowerPoint; click inside the text box, select any text you don't want, and type to replace it.

You can also move images and text in the same way you normally would, by clicking and dragging.

Editing a photo album

After you've created a photo album, added some captions and titles, and looked through its slides, you might want to make some changes. For example, you might want to remove a picture, rearrange others, or adjust the brightness or contrast after you've seen the full-size photo on a slide.

To edit a photo album, select Insert→Photo Album→Edit Photo Album (Alt, N, A, E). The Edit Photo Album dialog box opens, looking just like the Photo Album box you used to create the album (Figure 21-10), except that it already displays the current pictures, text boxes, and settings. You can adjust any of these settings.

To remove a picture from your presentation, select it in the "Pictures in album" list, and then click the Remove button.

After you've finished editing the photo album, click Update to apply your changes to the presentation.

Working with Shapes

PowerPoint comes with a plethora of built-in shapes that you can add to your slides, from basic ovals and rectangles to stars, lightning bolts, arrows, and thought bubbles. There are also specialized shapes for flowcharts and basic equations. You can use a shape as a background for text, to show relationships between other elements on the slide, or to just get crazy and add a little pizzazz. This section shows you how to put a shape on your slide and get it looking just the way you want it.

Inserting a shape

To insert a shape on your slide, follow these steps:

1. **With the slide you want as the active slide, select Insert→Shapes (Alt, N, SH).**

    The Shapes menu, shown in Figure 21-11, opens. The top section of this menu shows shapes you've used recently. Beneath that, shapes appear by category: lines, rectangles, basic shapes (a catchall category that includes text boxes, triangles, circles, and other miscellaneous shapes and symbols), block arrows, equation shapes, flowchart sections, stars and banners, callouts, and action buttons. Scroll down to see all the shapes on offer.

2. **Select the shape you want to put on your slide.**

    PowerPoint closes the Shapes menu and changes your mouse pointer to a crosshairs.

3. **Position the crosshairs about where you want the shape to appear, and then click and drag to draw the shape. When the shape is the approximate size you want, let go of the mouse button.**

    The shape appears in a content box on your slide.

Changing a shape's size or position

After you've inserted a shape, you can work with it in these ways:

*   **Move a shape.** Click the shape to show the box that holds it. Move the mouse pointer to a border. When the pointer becomes a four-way arrow, click and drag the shape to its new location.

*   **Rotate a shape.** Click the shape, and then move the mouse pointer to the green rotation handle that appears above the shape's content box. When the pointer turns into a circular arrow, click and drag in a circle to rotate the shape.

Figure 21-11:
PowerPoint comes with a whole library of predesigned shapes for you to add to your slides.

- **Resize a shape.** Click the shape to show its content box. A resizing handle appears at each corner and at the halfway point of each border. When you place the mouse pointer over a resizing handle, the pointer changes to a two-way arrow; click and drag to resize the shape.

Tip: To keep a shape's proportions when you resize it, drag a corner resizing handle diagonally.

Adding text to a shape

To add text to a shape, just click the shape and start typing. To format text, use the Mini Toolbar (page 566) or the Home tab's Font and Paragraph sections. Or turn your text into WordArt using the Drawing Tools | Format WordArt Styles section.

Tip: When you insert a shape, PowerPoint automatically selects a font color for any text you might write on it. To see the shape-and-font color combos, open the Drawing Tools | Format tab and click the lower-right Shape Styles gallery's More button (Alt, JD, SS). Click any color combination you like to apply it to your shape and its text.

Formatting a shape

PowerPoint formats shapes automatically, choosing their fill and outline colors according to your presentation's theme. But you can format a shape however you like.

Right-click the shape and select Format Shape from the shortcut menu. This opens the Format Shape dialog box, shown in Figure 21-12. On the left side of the dialog box, choose the kind of formatting you want to apply to your shape:

- **Fill.** This setting is all about your shape's interior. You can select "No fill" (which makes the shape an outline), "Solid fill", or a range of other options. Experiment with "Gradient fill" (which shades from one color to another), "Picture or texture fill" (select a picture from your computer or choose a texture to apply), "Pattern fill" (choose a pattern and a color to fill the shape), or "Slide background fill" (which makes the shape's fill match the background of the slide). The kind of fill you choose determines what you can do with it: For solid fill, you can choose a fill color and degree of transparency; for pattern fill, you can choose from a gallery of patterns and pick a color; and so on.

Note: What's the difference between "No fill" and "Slide background fill"? "No fill" makes the shape's interior transparent. "Slide background fill" matches the background but is opaque, so the shape blocks any objects that appear behind it.

- **Line Color.** These settings are for the shape's outline. You can choose no line, solid line, or gradient line and select a color for the outline.

Figure 21-12:
The Format Shape dialog box gives you many choices for formatting the shapes in your presentation. Here the dialog box shows the options for formatting a shape's interior (also known as its fill).

- **Line Style.** If your shape has an outline, you can set its width and type here. If you're working with arrows, the Arrow settings section is where you choose a head style and size.

- **Shadow.** Give your shape a shadow here, choosing from preset shadow styles or building your own.

- **Reflection.** To put a reflection under your shape, select one of the preset options or select your own settings.

- **Glow and Soft Edges.** You can give your shape a little or a lot of glow by using the presets or adjusting the glow settings yourself. To soften edges, select the number of points by which PowerPoint blurs the shape's edges (a higher number of points means softer edges).

- **3-D Format.** Here you can add beveling to the shape, increase its depth, and sharpen its contours. You can also select a material and lighting style. (If playing with these choices changes the shape too much, click the Reset button to return it to its original condition.)

- **3-D Rotation.** Give your shape some perspective by making it three-dimensional and adjusting its angle. You can choose from preset options or adjust the shape on your own.

- **Size.** As the previous section explains, you can resize a shape right on the slide by dragging one of its resizing handles. If you want to be more precise, use this option in the Format Shape dialog box. You can select the height and width in inches or by a percentage of its current size, determine its rotation by degrees, and lock the aspect ratio to make sure the shape doesn't get distorted when you resize it.

- **Position.** Instead of dragging a shape around a slide, you can place it precisely by using this option, specifying how far the shape appears (in inches) from the slide's center or top-left corner.

After you've formatted your shape, click Close to save your formatting and close the Format Shape dialog box.

Working with SmartArt

SmartArt made its debut with Office 2007, and since then it's spiced up countless presentations with its bold, attractive graphics. SmartArt makes it easy to add professionally designed graphics to your slides that show how elements within a slide relate to one another. Whether you need a process diagram, an organizational chart, a pyramid, or an eye-catching list, SmartArt will help add some nice visuals to your slides.

Inserting SmartArt

To add some SmartArt *oomph,* follow these steps:

1. **With the slide that's going to host the SmartArt active, select Insert→SmartArt.**

   The Choose a SmartArt Graphic dialog box opens, as shown in Figure 21-13. This dialog box shows a gallery of dozens of lists, charts, and graphs. You can scroll through the gallery to view all types, or choose a category from the dialog box's left side. When you select a piece of SmartArt, the right preview pane shows a full-size example of what it looks like, along with suggestions of when to use it.

2. **Select the type of SmartArt you want, and then click OK.**

   PowerPoint inserts the SmartArt into your slide and opens the SmartArt Tools | Design contextual tab, as shown in Figure 21-14.

Now you can add text to the SmartArt diagram (click any text placeholder and type), adjust the graphic's design, or format the SmartArt.

Tip: Some SmartArt styles have placeholders for pictures, as well as text. You insert a picture into a Smart-Art graphic the same way you'd add a picture to a content box (page 551).

Figure 21-13:
Select a category on the left to see a gallery of SmartArt graphics for that category. Click a graphic to see an example and a description of it on the right.

Tip: If you think best in terms of bulleted lists, use the Text pane to add words to your SmartArt diagram. Choose SmartArt Tools | Design→Text Pane (Alt, JS, X), and a pane opens that shows a bulleted list. Type and use the arrow keys to add items to the list. As you do, your typing appears in the SmartArt diagram.

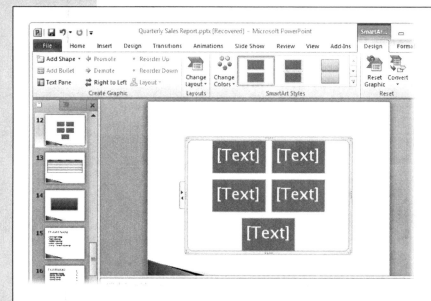

Figure 21-14:
*When you add a
SmartArt graphic to
a slide, each shape
and text placeholder
is an individual object
within that frame.
This lets you animate
SmartArt (see page
638 to learn how to
do that).*

Converting text to SmartArt

If you've got yet another boring bulleted list on yet another slide, you can make the
slide more interesting by converting your existing text to a SmartArt graphic. Just
select the text you want to transform and then follow these steps:

1. **In the Home tab's Paragraph section, click the "Convert to SmartArt Graphic"
    button (Alt, H, M).**

    A menu opens, showing a gallery of SmartArt designs. Point to any design to see
    a live preview of it on your slide. If you don't see a design you like, click More
    SmartArt Graphics to open the "Choose a SmartArt Graphic" dialog box (Figure
    21-13).

2. **Select the SmartArt design you want.**

    PowerPoint converts your text to SmartArt.

Now you can format the SmartArt using the SmartArt Tools | Design tab (Alt, JS)
and the SmartArt Tools | Format tab (Alt, JO). Upcoming sections explain more
about doing that.

Adding a shape

The SmartArt diagram you inserted is just for starters. Just because a process dia-
gram shows three steps doesn't mean that your process is limited to that number.
If you need to add another shape to your diagram, click the SmartArt to open the
SmartArt Tools contextual tabs.

Select a shape adjacent to where you want the new shape to appear. On the SmartArt Tools | Design tab, click the down arrow at the bottom of the Add Shape button, and then select one of these options:

- Add Shape After (Alt, JS, O, A)
- Add Shape Before (Alt, JS, O, B)
- Add Shape Above (Alt, JS, O, V)
- Add Shape Below (Alt, JS, O, W)

PowerPoint inserts a new shape where you specified, adjusting the diagram to accommodate it.

Reordering shapes

You can move shapes around in a SmartArt graphic. You can use the drag-and-drop method you'd use for any object on a slide, but to make sure shapes line up right, select the shape you want to move and open the SmartArt Tools | Design tab. In the Create Graphic section, click one of these options to move the shape:

- **Promote (Alt, JS, P) or Demote (Alt, JS, D).** In a hierarchical diagram (which shows levels), these buttons move the shape up or down a level.
- **Right to Left (Alt, JS, R).** The selected shape and its next-door neighbor swap positions horizontally.
- **Reorder Up (Alt, JS, U) or Reorder Down (Alt, JS, W).** These buttons switch the shape with the one immediately above or below it.

Applying a different layout

After you've chosen and worked with one SmartArt graphic, you might decide that you'd prefer a different look. To change the style of your diagram, head for the Smart-Art Tools | Design tab's Layouts section. Choose a new design, or click the section's lower-right More button (Alt, JS, L) to see other designs in the current diagram's category. (To see even more, select More Layouts—M if you're using keyboard short-cuts—to open the "Choose a SmartArt Graphic" dialog box shown in Figure 21-13.)

Select any layout to apply it to your diagram. Any text or other content you've added appears in the proper place in the new layout.

Adjusting a SmartArt graphic's style

The SmartArt Tools | Design tab's SmartArt Styles section is where you change a diagram's colors or add an effect to its appearance:

- **To change the diagram's colors,** select SmartArt Tools | Design→Change Colors (Alt, JS, C), and a menu opens showing a gallery of color schemes that work with your presentation's theme. As you move your mouse pointer over the pos-sibilities, you see a live preview of the color scheme on your slide. Click an option to apply it to your slide.

- **To add a visual effect to your diagram,** click SmartArt Tools | Design and, in the SmartArt Styles section, click the lower-right More button (Alt, JS, S). The menu that appears shows a variety of 3-D, shading, and beveling effects that you can apply to your diagram, with live previews as you browse them. To apply an effect, click it.

Tip: To edit or format a diagram that has a 3-D effect, click SmartArt Tools | Format→Edit in 2-D (Alt, JO, E). PowerPoint temporarily switches the diagram to 2-D mode. When you're done making changes, click the Edit in 2-D button again to turn the 3-D effect back on.

- **To make plain text into WordArt,** select the text you want to convert and then go to the SmartArt Tools | Format tab's WordArt Styles section (Alt, JO, Q) and choose the WordArt style you want. Use the SmartArt Tools | Format tab's Text Fill (Alt, JO, TI), Text Outline (Alt, JO, TO), and Text Effects (Alt, JO, TX) buttons to adjust the WordArt's style.

Tip: It's easy to get a little carried away as you play with SmartArt options. If that happens, you can go back to square one by clicking SmartArt Tools | Design→Reset Graphic (Alt, JS, E). Resetting your SmartArt affects only its design—not its content.

Formatting shapes within a SmartArt graphic

SmartArt offers so many shapes, layouts, and effects that you may decide to stick with the preformatted designs. But you can customize SmartArt to give it your own personal stamp. The SmartArt Tools | Format tab (Alt, JO) lets you work with the shapes that make up a SmartArt graphic in these ways:

- **Change a shape's size.** In the SmartArt Tools | Format tab's Shapes section, click the Larger (Alt, JO, N) or Smaller button (Alt, JO, D) to increase or decrease a shape's size a bit at a time. Keep clicking until the shape is the size you want.

Tip: Of course, you can also change a shape's size by dragging its resizing handles.

- **Change the shape itself.** When you click SmartArt Tools | Format→Change Shape (Alt, JO, I), a menu of shapes like the one shown in Figure 21-11 appears. Click any shape to convert the selected shape to the shape you choose.
- **Tweak a shape's style.** You can make a shape stand out from the rest of the diagram by giving it a different style. To do that, head for the SmartArt Tools | Format tab's Shape Styles section, which has these options:
    - **Shape Styles (Alt, JO, SS).** Apply borders and colors to your chosen shape. Click to select the one you want. (The ribbon shows only a few options; click the lower-right More button to see the whole gallery.)

— **Shape Fill (Alt, JO, SF).** Change the shape's interior color or make it a picture, a gradient, or a texture.

— **Shape Outline (Alt, JO, SO).** Adjust the color, weight, and style of the shape's outline.

— **Shape Effects (Alt, JO, SE).** Apply visual effects to the shape: shadow, reflection, glow, soft edges, beveling, or 3-D rotation.

Rotating a SmartArt graphic

Think the diagram or one of its shapes would look better upside-down or sideways? Select what you want to rotate and then go to SmartArt Tools | Format→Arrange→ Rotate (Alt, JO, ZA, AY). There you can pick one of these:

- **Rotate Right 90° (R)** turns the selection 90 degrees clockwise.
- **Rotate Left 90° (L)** turns the selection 90 degrees counterclockwise.
- **Flip Vertical (V)** turns the selection 180 degrees on a horizontal axis.
- **Flip Horizontal (H)** turns the selection 180 degrees on a vertical axis.
- **More Rotation Options (M)** opens the Format Shape dialog box to its Size options. Use the Rotation drop-down list to specify a rotation angle for the selection.

Resizing a SmartArt graphic

To make a diagram larger or smaller, you can click and drag one of the resizing areas on its frame. Or you can select SmartArt Tools | Format→Size (Alt, JO, ZZ) and change the height (H) and width (W) settings there.

Working with Charts and Diagrams

Charts and diagrams work well on slides to track trends, to make comparisons, and to show relationships, like the parts that make up a whole. From simple bar, line, and pie charts to more complex scatter charts and surface or radar diagrams, PowerPoint has loads of built-in chart styles.

Creating a chart or diagram using Excel

PowerPoint works with Excel to gather data, organize it into a chart or diagram, and display the results on a slide. This works the same way in PowerPoint as it does in Word, so flip to page 112 for all the how-to details.

Creating a diagram using shapes

To create a flow chart or process diagram, your best bet is SmartArt (page 588). If you've got a diagramming program like Microsoft's Visio, you might draw a diagram in that program and take a screenshot (page 98) to insert it onto your slide as an image.

You can also use PowerPoint's Shapes menu to create this kind of diagram. This menu has lines, arrows, and flow chart shapes you can use to draw your own process diagram. All you need to do is insert text boxes (page 548) and shapes (page 585) and then move and format them as you wish.

Arranging Objects on a Slide

Once you've added text, images, a diagram, and maybe a shape or two to a slide, things can get pretty crowded. You can arrange the objects on your slide by dragging them around, but trying to position things just right can be frustrating. The Home tab's Arrange button (Alt, H, G) is perfect when you're ready to align, order, or group your objects.

Aligning Objects on a Slide

If the text and content boxes look scattered around the slide, select the objects you want to line up, and then select Home→Arrange→Align (Alt, H, G, A). Depending on the relative positions of the objects you've selected, you can choose from these options:

- **Align Left (L).** This lines up the left borders of the selected objects' boxes.
- **Align Center (C).** Choose this option to line up objects along their vertical centerlines.
- **Align Right (R).** This lines up the right borders of the selected objects' boxes.

Tip: You can also select any of these alignment options from the Picture Tools | Format tab (click Arrange→Align or press Alt, JO, AA) or the Drawing Tools | Format tab (click the Align button or press Alt, JD, AA).

- **Align Top (T).** This lines up the top borders of the selected objects' boxes.
- **Align Middle (M).** This option lines up objects along their horizontal centerlines.
- **Align Bottom (B).** This lines up the bottom borders of the selected objects' boxes.
- **Distribute Horizontally (H).** Choose this option when you want to space objects evenly from left to right on the slide.
- **Distribute Vertically (V).** This option spaces objects evenly from top to bottom on a slide.
- **Align to Slide (A).** When you turn on this option, PowerPoint uses the slide's edges or exact center (depending on the kind of alignment you choose—left, center, top, middle, and so on) to align objects.
- **Align Selected Objects (O).** When you turn on this option, PowerPoint lines up objects relative to one another on the slide.
- **View Gridlines (Alt, JD, AA, S).** This overlays an evenly spaced grid on the slide so that you can see how well the objects line up. (Gridlines are visible only

in Normal view.) To remove the gridlines, choose View Gridlines again to turn off its checkmark.

Tip: Adjust grid spacing by selecting Home→Arrange→Align→Grid Settings (Alt, JD, AA, G), and then choosing the amount of space between lines in the grid.

Ordering Objects

PowerPoint lets you stack objects on top of each other. A common reason to do this is to place text boxes on top of a picture—similar to the labels you see in this book's illustrations. Or you might stack up images to have them appear on the slide, one by one, using animation (see page 638 for more about animating objects).

When you add objects to a slide, the most recently inserted object goes on top, obscuring the object behind it. You can reorder objects using the Home tab's Arrange button (Alt, H, G). Its options are also available in the Arrange sections of the Picture Tools | Format tab (Alt, JP) and the Drawing Tools | Format tab (Alt, JD). Select the object whose order you want to change, and then choose the option you want:

- **Bring to Front** moves the object to the top of a stack of objects, in front of all other objects.
- **Send to Back** moves the object to the bottom of the stack, behind all other objects.
- **Bring Forward** moves the object forward one place in the stack.
- **Send Backward** moves the object back one place in the stack.

Tip: To find and select an object in a stack, use the Selection and Visibility pane. Click an object and click its Format contextual tab (such as Picture Tools | Format or Drawing Tools | Format). In the Arrange section, click the Selection Pane button. The Selection and Visibility pane opens, listing all objects on the slide. Click any object on the list to select it. In this pane, you can also rearrange the objects in a stack by selecting one and using the up and down arrows to change its position; each click moves it one place up or down the stack.

If you don't feel like opening the Selection and Visibility pane, you can cycle through the objects in a stack by selecting one and then pressing the Tab key.

Grouping Objects

Grouping takes several separate objects and merges them into a single object. This makes it easier to move objects on the slide, to keep objects in proportion when you resize them, and to add animation effects to a group (page 638).

To group objects, select the objects you want to treat as one, and then select Home→Arrange→Group (Alt, H, G, G). PowerPoint puts a single content box around the objects you selected, making them into a single object. Now you can work with that object in the same way you would any other object on a slide.

If you want to ungroup objects, select the grouped object and then click Home→Arrange→Ungroup (Alt, H, G, U). The big object breaks apart into the individual items that made it up.

Change your mind about ungrouping? Select any of the objects that used to be in the group, and then click Home→Arrange→Regroup (Alt, H, G, E). The old gang is back together again.

Tips for Creating Good Slides

A slideshow is only as good as the slides that make it up. You don't want to give your audience eyestrain or cause their attention to wander. As you create slides, keep these tips in mind:

- **Think visually.** Even when you're the one up on the podium, you need to put yourself in the audience's place as you design your slides. Use color combinations that are easy on the eyes and fonts that are legible from the back of a conference room or auditorium. (Sans serif fonts like Arial and Calibri are generally easier to read than serif fonts like Times New Roman.) And when it comes to fonts, remember that size does matter—if you want the audience to read your text.

- **Use relevant images and illustrations.** Pictures should help your audience grasp and remember the main points of a slide, so look for images that support what you have to say. Don't throw an image on a slide just to fill up space—that sleeping kitten may be cute, but unless it's relevant to the slide's content, it'll distract the audience from what you're saying.

- **Don't crowd your slides.** For maximum impact, keep your slides clean and uncluttered. Four to six bullet points are enough for any slide. If you find yourself reducing the font size to fit everything onto a slide, you should probably cut some words or spread the slide's content over two slides.

- **Use animations to pace your slideshow.** Don't let your audience get ahead of you. If you've got several bullet points on a slide, don't reveal them all at once. Use animations (page 651) to reveal points one at a time to match the pace of your presentation.

- **But don't overdo animations and effects.** As Chapter 23 shows, PowerPoint animations are fun to play with. You might be tempted to use half or more of the available options in a single presentation, having objects zoom in, spin around, and fade out. But too much will make your audience dizzy. (And the same thing goes for sound effects.) Find a few animation styles you like, and apply them consistently.

- **Be consistent.** Speaking of consistency: it's key for all elements of your slides, not just animations. Color scheme, types of illustrations (photos vs. clip art, for example), fonts—all these should work together to unify your slideshow.

- **Have a copy of any web pages you link to.** If your slides have links to web pages (page 571), make sure you have a backup copy in case any Internet connection problems crop up during your presentation. You can use PowerPoint's screenshot capability to have back-up screenshots on hidden slides.

- **Limit the number of slides.** More isn't always better. Keep that point in mind when you design a presentation. Use only as many slides as you need to support the main points of your presentation.

- **Remember: Your slideshow is not your whole presentation.** Have you ever sat through a presentation where the speaker simply read what was on each slide? How long before your eyelids started drooping? Your slides are more like an outline than a script; they should illustrate the main points of your presentation, but the talk you give is the main event.

Editing a Presentation

Getting information onto your slides is only half the battle. The rest of your work lies in organizing the collection. This chapter focuses on your presentation as a whole—how to do things like work with and order the slides you've created; add footers, page numbers, and other recurring elements; and build links that jump between slides. You'll also learn about *sections,* new in PowerPoint 2010, and great for dividing long presentations into separately designed chunks. Finally, if you collaborate with others, you'll see how to make comments on slides and how to compare and merge different versions of the same presentation.

Copying, Rearranging, and Deleting Slides

As your presentation grows, you'll want to work with slides at a bird's-eye level—adding, reordering, cutting, and even temporarily hiding slides (great for trying out variations between Slide A and Slide B). This section explains all.

Copying a Slide

Copying is one of the oldest tricks in the world of digital documents, and PowerPoint makes it just as easy as you'd expect. You can make an exact copy of any slide and insert it wherever you want in the presentation. To copy a slide, first select it in either the Slides pane or the Slide Sorter view. Then follow these quick steps:

1. **Press Ctrl+C.**

   That's the quickest way to copy; menu fans can select Home→Copy or, for those looking for the long keyboard shortcut route, press Alt, H, C, C.

2. **Click where you want the slide to appear.**

   You can click between two slides or after the presentation's final slide.

3. **Press Ctrl+V. (Alternatively, select Home→Paste or Alt, H, V, K.)**

   A copy of the slide you selected appears in the new location.

Note: If you select a slide and press Ctrl+V, PowerPoint doesn't overwrite the selected slide; it inserts the copy immediately after the selection.

Duplicating a Slide

When you duplicate a slide, you insert an exact copy of it immediately after the original. This comes in handy when you want to use a slide as a template for the design of the next few slides. In the Slides pane or Slide Sorter view, select the slide you want to turn into a replica. In the Home tab's Clipboard section, click the down arrow beside the Copy button, and then select Duplicate (Alt, H, C, I). The duplicate appears after the original.

Note: When copying or duplicating a slide, the new slide retains the contents, formatting, animations, and transition (if any) of the original.

Inserting a Slide from a Different Presentation

If a slide from one presentation is just what you're looking for in another, Power-Point makes it easy to copy. One way to do this is to open both presentations. Copy the slide from its original presentation, click the new presentation's taskbar button to switch to it, and paste the slide into its new home. If you want the pasted slide to retain the theme from its original presentation, paste it in this way: On the Home tab, click the down arrow at the bottom of the Paste button, and then select Keep Source Formatting (Alt, H, V, K).

But you don't have to open both presentations to import a slide. You can also do it this way, which is a timesaver when you want to import multiple slides all at once:

1. **Open the presentation into which you want to import the slide, and position the cursor where you want the new slide to appear. On the Home tab, click the down arrow at the bottom of the New Slide button, and then select Reuse Slides (Alt, H, I, R).**

   The Reuse Slides pane appears on the right side of your screen.

2. **In the Reuse Slides pane, click the Browse button, and then select Browse File from the menu that appears.**

   A Browse dialog box opens, showing your folders.

3. **Find and select the PowerPoint file that contains the slide you want. Click Open.**

   The presentation you chose opens inside the Reuse Slides pane, as shown in Figure 22-1. You can look through the presentation using the scroll bar. When you hold the pointer over a slide, it expands so you can get a better look at it.

4. **Click the slide you want to insert.**

   PowerPoint inserts the slide into the presentation.

5. **If you want to insert multiple slides, keep clicking until you've inserted all the slides you want.**

   You can move the cursor to different insertion points in the target presentation as you work.

6. **When you're done, click the Reuse Slides pane's upper-right X.**

   PowerPoint closes the Reuse Slides pane. The new slides are now part of this presentation. If you make changes to them here, those changes won't affect the slides in their original presentation.

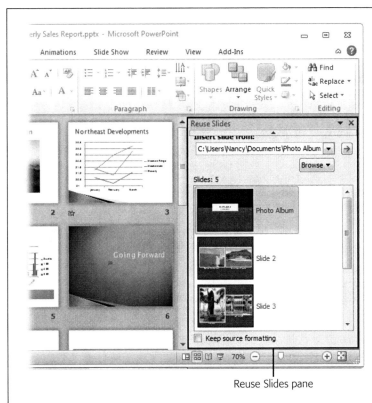

Figure 22-1:
The Reuse Slides pane shows another presentation's slides so you can easily pick and choose the ones you want to import into this presentation.

Reuse Slides pane

Tip: When you import a slide into a presentation, PowerPoint automatically applies the target presentation's theme to the imported slide. If you want imported slides to keep their original theme, turn on the "Keep source formatting" checkbox at the bottom of the Reuse Slides pane.

Rearranging Slides in a Presentation

Moving slides from one spot to another in your presentation is a simple matter of dragging a slide and dropping it into place. In Slide Sorter view, select the slide you want to move, and then drag it to a new spot. As you drag, the cursor jumps between slides to show the insertion point. When the cursor is in the right location, let go of the mouse button. The slide jumps to that spot.

Tip: For an efficient way to move a group of slides, create a section for that group, and then move the section. Page 604 gives you the details on how to do this.

You can also move a slide by cutting and pasting—this can be useful in a large presentation with many slides, where the drag-and-drop method is less efficient. Cutting a slide works just like copying it, except that instead of leaving the original, copied slide in place, PowerPoint deletes the slide from its original spot. (There's a copy on the Clipboard, of course.) To move a slide, switch to an overview of the presentation (the Slides pane or Slide Sorter view) and then do the following:

1. **Select the slide you want to move, and then press Ctrl+X. (If you prefer, you can select Home→Cut or press Alt, H, X.)**

   This deletes the selected slide from the presentation and copies it to the Clipboard.

2. **Click where you want the slide to appear; you can click between two slides or after the presentation's final slide. Press Ctrl+V. (Alternatively, select Home→Paste or Alt, H, V, K.)**

   The slide appears in its new location.

Tip: You can move a group of slides in the same way. To select a range of slides, select the first slide in the range; then hold down the Shift key and select the last slide in the range. When you cut and paste, all the selected slides disappear from their original spot and reappear where you paste them.

Deleting a Slide

To remove a slide, select it in the Slides pane or in Slide Sorter view. Press the Delete or Backspace key. Alternatively, you can right-click the selected slide and choose Delete Slide from the shortcut menu.

Hiding Slides

You might not want to show *every* single slide in a presentation. For example, say you're working on some slides for future versions of the presentation, but you're not ready to show them yet.

Hiding a slide doesn't delete it from the presentation. Instead, it prevents the slide from appearing when you run the presentation as a slideshow. The hidden slide still appears in all of PowerPoint's working views. You can edit a hidden slide and see it in context in Slide Sorter view, but the slide won't appear when you launch a slideshow.

To mark a slide as hidden, select the slide (or group of slides) you want to hide, and then click Slide Show→Hide Slide (Alt, S, H). Alternatively, you can right-click a slide and select Hide Slide from the shortcut menu.

When you hide a slide, the Slides pane and the Slide Sorter view indicate that it's hidden by crossing out its slide number, as shown in Figure 22-2. And in Normal view, the Slide Show tab's Hide Slide button is highlighted for that slide. To make a hidden slide visible again, just select the slide, go back to the Slide Show tab, and then click Hide Slide again (Alt, S, H).

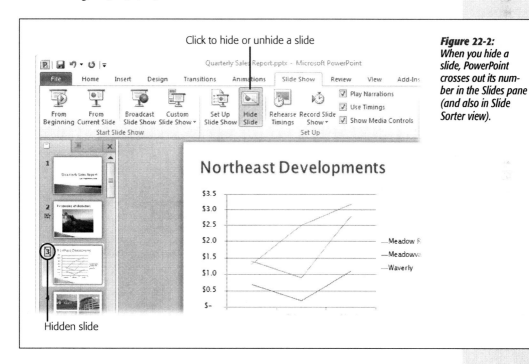

Click to hide or unhide a slide

Hidden slide

Figure 22-2:
When you hide a slide, PowerPoint crosses out its number in the Slides pane (and also in Slide Sorter view).

Tip: You can use a long presentation as the basis for several shorter ones by hiding groups of slides in some versions of the presentation and showing them in others. If you divide your presentation into sections (page 604), you can hide all slides in a section with a single click.

Headers and Footers

If you need boilerplate information to appear on each slide, you can insert it as a footer at the bottom. What you put here is pretty much up to you. Include standard stuff like the date, time, or slide numbers—or whip up a custom footer, featuring your organization's name or finger-pointing confidentiality reminders. For notes and handouts that you print, you can also add a header.

Time-Stamping Your Slides

Let your audience know that your information is up to date by adding the date, time, or both to your slides. On the Insert tab, click the Text section's Header & Footer button (Alt, N, H) to open the Header and Footer dialog box, shown in Figure 22-3. Turn on the "Date and time" checkbox. When you do, these options become available:

- **Update automatically.** Turn on this radio button if you want PowerPoint to update the timestamp whenever someone works on the presentation. Use the dropdown lists to choose the info and format you want (such as 5/1/2010; Saturday, May 5, 2010; May-10; 5/1/2010 10:20 AM; and so on), the language for the timestamp, and (if you choose a non-Western language) the type of calendar.

- **Fixed.** Turn on this radio button if you want the timestamp to stay the same, no matter when the presentation gets updated. Then type the date you want in the text box just below.

If you want your timestamp to show on all slides *except* the first one, turn on the "Don't show on title slide" checkbox.

Click Apply to All to time-stamp the entire presentation or Apply to time-stamp just the current slide.

Figure 22-3:
When there's information you need to add to all slides in a presentation, use the Header and Footer dialog box. The lower-right preview shows where the text you're adding will appear on your slides. The dotted line represents the slide's content area.

Adding a Footer to Your Slides

If you want to add a copyright notice, your name, or other information to the bottom of each slide, here's how:

1. Select Insert→Header & Footer (Alt, N, H).

   The Header and Footer dialog box (Figure 22-3) opens.

2. **Turn on the Footer checkbox. Beneath it, type in the text of your footer.**

   When you turn on the Footer checkbox, the lower-right Preview pane shows where the text will appear.

3. **If you don't want the footer to show on the presentation's first slide, then turn on the "Don't show on title slide" checkbox. Click Apply to All or Apply (if you want the footer only on the current slide).**

   Your footer appears in the presentation.

Tip: A footer doesn't have to appear at the bottom of a slide. If you want footer text to appear elsewhere, open the presentation in Slide Master view (View→Slide Master or Alt, W, M). On the slide master, drag the Footer placeholder wherever you like. Page 616 tells you more about what you can do in Slide Master view.

Numbering Slides

You can always see each slide's number in the Slides pane (where a number appears to the left of each slide) and in Slide Sorter view (where a number appears below each slide). If you want to put numbers on the slides themselves—perhaps to make it easy for your audience to refer back to a previous slide—you can. Just follow these steps:

1. Select Insert→Slide Number (Alt, N, SN).

   The Header and Footer dialog box, shown in Figure 22-3, opens.

2. **Turn on the "Slide number" checkbox. If you want all slides except the first one to show a number, then turn on the checkbox labeled "Don't show on title slide". Click Apply to All.**

   PowerPoint numbers your slides.

Slide numbers usually appear in a slide's lower-right corner, but the precise location depends on your presentation's theme. PowerPoint formats them automatically to make sure they're visible against the slide's background.

Tip: If slide numbers are hard to read because of their size, switch to Slide Master view (View→Slide Master or Alt, W, M) and apply a larger font size to the placeholder. For more about working with slide masters, see page 614.

Adding a Header and Footer to Notes and Handouts

When you're printing out presenter's notes or handouts for the audience, you can add a header, a footer, or both to the printed pages. Here's how:

1. **Select Insert→Header & Footer (Alt, N, H).**

   The Header and Footer dialog box opens.

2. **Click the Notes and Handouts tab, shown in Figure 22-4.**

   This tab looks similar to the Slides tab (Figure 22-3), with a few differences. There's an option to add a header, and the lower-right Preview reflects a page, rather than a slide.

3. **Turn on the checkboxes of the elements you want to add to the printed notes or handouts: date and time, header, page number, and footer. Supply the required information for any checkboxes you turn on.**

   As you make your choices, the Preview shows you where on the page the element will appear.

4. **Click Apply to All.**

   PowerPoint adds your selections to the notes and handouts you print to accompany your presentation.

Figure 22-4:
You can add headers, footers, timestamps, and page numbers to printed handouts and presenter's notes.

Organizing Your Presentation with Sections

Sections are new in PowerPoint 2010, and they're such a great idea that you'll wonder why PowerPoint hasn't had them all along. Use sections to group related slides; then you can move or hide these bunches en masse—perfect for tucking away groups of slides you don't need right now but don't want to delete. Sections make a large presentation more manageable—and any presentation more organized.

Creating a Section

Before you can create a section, you need to insert a slide to mark the section's start. (See page 549 for instructions on inserting a new slide.) You can announce the new section in a slideshow by inserting a Section Header slide, with boxes for a section title and some text (choose Section Header from the New Slide menu), or you can start a new section with any slide.

In the Slides pane or in Slide Sorter view, right-click the slide that will be first in the new section. From the shortcut menu that appears, select Add Section. Now, any slides that come after the section header slide are part of this section; see Figure 22-5.

To end the current section and start a new one, repeat the process: Insert a new section header slide after the last slide in the current section (if you want), right-click the first slide of the new section, and then select Add Section.

Figure 22-5:
Two sections as they appear in Slide Show view. Each new section begins with a section header slide.

Section title bar

Section header slides

Note: When you create your first section, slides from the initial title slide straight through to the first section slide become the presentation's default section. You can rename the default section, but you can't remove it. PowerPoint lets you remove the default section only if you remove the section *and* all its slides (page 607). If you do that, then the first section you created becomes the new default section.

Naming a Section

When PowerPoint creates a section, it simply calls it "Untitled Section" (as you can see in Figure 22-5). To help keep your sections straight, give them more meaningful names. Here's how:

1. **In the Slides pane or in Slide Show view, right-click the title bar of the section you want to rename.**

   A shortcut menu appears.

2. **Select Rename Section.**

   The Rename Section dialog box opens.

3. **Type in the section's new name and click the Rename button.**

   The new name appears in the section's title bar.

Tip: Here's a good reason to name your sections: You can jump straight to any section during a slide-show. To do to that, right-click a slide to open the shortcut menu. Select Go to Section, and a flyout menu appears, showing the names of the presentation's sections. Click any section name to jump to it.

Collapsing and Expanding Sections

In a long presentation, you may not want to see all the slides at once. When your presentation has sections, you can collapse and expand 'em, focusing on only one group of slides at a time. You can collapse or expand any section by clicking the arrow to the left of its name. As Figure 22-6 shows, when a section is collapsed, the arrow is white and points at the section's title; after the title, the number of slides in that section appears in parentheses.

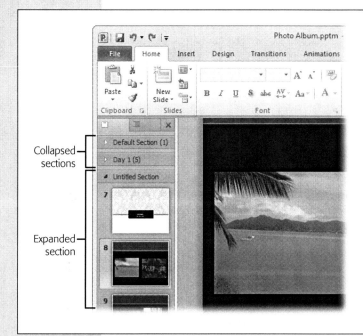

Collapsed sections

Expanded section

Figure 22-6:
Collapsed and expanded sections in Normal view's Slides pane. When you collapse a section, you see how many slides it has thanks to a number in parentheses after the section's name. When you expand a section, you see thumbnail images of its slides.

To collapse all the sections in your presentation, right-click any section's title bar and select Collapse All from the shortcut menu. To expand them all, select Expand All.

Moving a Section Within a Presentation

Sections make it easy to rearrange things, because you can move all the slides in a section, in order, all at the same time. Right click the section header and select Move Section Up or Move Section down. The entire section, with all its slides, plays leap-frog over its adjacent section.

Hiding All Slides Within a Section

One advantage of creating sections is that they make it easy to hide a group of related slides. You can have a single marketing presentation, for example, that has a section for each product line, and then hide sections that aren't of interest to a particular client. Or imagine you've created a presentation to accompany a talk you give to different groups. Sometimes you've got 20 minutes to speak, sometimes 40, and sometimes a whole hour. By dividing your presentation into sections, you can have short, medium, and long versions, all in one presentation, by hiding the sections you skip in shorter versions of the talk.

To hide a section, go to the Slides pane or Slide Show view and click the title bar for the section you want to hide. This selects all slides in that section. On the Slide Show tab, click the Hide Slide button (Alt, S, H). With just one click, you've hidden that section and all its slides.

Removing a Section from a Presentation

If you no longer need a section in a presentation, right-click the section's title bar in the Slides pane or Slide Show view and choose one of these options:

- **Remove Section.** This option gets rid of the section's title bar and ungroups the slides.

Note: Removing a section does not delete the section header slide from that section.

- **Remove Section & Slides.** This removes the section and deletes all its slides.
- **Remove All Sections.** This removes all section title bars and slide groupings, returning the presentation to an ungrouped collection of individual slides.

Navigating with Links and Action Buttons

You can take a journey a step at a time, putting one foot in front of the other. Similarly, you can give a slideshow in a linear manner, clicking from one slide to the next.

But sometimes it's the detours that make the journey. In a presentation, that might mean a table of contents that lets you go straight to any section of the presentation, or it might be a hidden slide that you click only when you want to show more information about a topic.

Inserting a hyperlink lets you jump to another slide anywhere in the presentation—even a hidden slide. Say you're giving a marketing presentation, and you've got a single slide that introduces four new products. You don't want the specifications for each product cluttering up the slide, but you do want to be able to show those specs if someone asks. You could create a slide for each product and stow them in a hidden section, and then create a hyperlink for each product to its specs slide. When someone in the audience asks, "Could you tell me more about your new electric banana peeler?" a single click jumps right to the banana peeler's detailed slide.

Action buttons are also helpful navigation tools—you can use them as buttons to help viewers get around self-run presentations, for example. But they do a whole lot more, too, like playing a sound or opening an embedded file (page 575). Read on to learn more.

Inserting a Hyperlink to Another Slide

You can insert a link that jumps from one slide to another anywhere in the presentation. In the marketing presentation example mentioned earlier, you might create a section at the end of the presentation that contains a series of slides, each one giving more information about a specific product. When someone asks about a product, click the link to jump to its slide. If no one wants more information about the products right now, then you can just move on to the next slide in the presentation (and sharpen your sales pitch for next time).

To insert a link to another slide, follow these quick steps:

1. **Select the text, picture, or other object that will hold the link. Then click Insert→Hyperlink (Alt, N, I).**

   PowerPoint opens the Insert Hyperlink box, shown in Figure 22-7.

2. **In the left "Link to" list, click Place in This Document.**

   The dialog box changes to show a list of slides in your presentation. The list identifies slides by number and title (for slides that have titles). On the right, you can see a preview of the selected slide.

3. **In the list of slides, select the slide you want to link to. Check the preview to make sure it's the right slide, and then click OK.**

   PowerPoint inserts a hyperlink to the selected slide.

Now when you click the hyperlink during a slideshow, the presentation will jump to the slide you indicated. Even if you insert new slides, making slide numbers change, the link stays with the slide you linked to.

Tip: Don't forget to insert a link back to the original slide so you can smoothly get back into the slideshow's flow.

Click this button…

…and choose a slide to link to from this list.

Figure 22-7:
Use this dialog box to create a hyperlink that displays the selected slide when you click it during a slideshow. Slides are identified by number and title (if the slide has one). If a slide is hidden, its number appears in parentheses, like Slide 9 in this example.

Creating a Table of Contents for Your Presentation

A table of contents is useful because it lets you jump straight to any topic in your presentation, without guessing at the slide number. First, create section header slides for the main sections of your presentation. Then, insert a new slide immediately after the presentation's initial title slide. On the new slide, create and format a list that names all the presentation's main sections.

Select the first item on the list, click Insert→Hyperlink (Alt, N, I), and then create a link to the first section header slide. Repeat the process for each item on the list, linking the name of each section to the appropriate section header. When you've linked each section name on the list to its section header, you've got a table of contents for your presentation.

Linking to a Hidden Slide

As page 601 explains, hidden slides don't appear when you run the presentation from the Slide Show tab—that is, unless you create a link to the hidden slide. When you link to a hidden slide, clicking the link tells PowerPoint to move to and display the hidden slide.

For example, a teacher might create a presentation with a multiple-choice quiz at the end of each section. If a student clicks the right answer, a slide congratulates him. If he clicks a wrong answer, a slide explains why that answer is incorrect. If he opts not to take the quiz, the presentation continues without showing any of the answer slides.

Or you might set up a presentation that has hidden slides answering questions you anticipate about various points. If no one asks, you simply move past the hidden slide to the next point. If you do get a question, though, you can reply, "Great question, Fred. I'm glad you asked. Here's a chart that shows how I arrived at that recommendation," and jump to the hidden slide. Fred gets his question answered in detail—and you get to look like a star.

Here's how to set up a slide that links to several hidden slides, bypassing those slides if the viewer continues without clicking a link:

1. **Create the slide that will link to the hidden slides. Then, create as many slides as you'll need for the hidden slides.**

   In the quiz example, you'd create one slide for the quiz and three answer slides to hide.

2. **In the Slides pane, select the slides you want to hide, and then click Slide Show→Hide Slide (Alt, S, H).**

   PowerPoint marks the selected slides as hidden.

3. **Open the slide that will link to the hidden slides. Select the text that will hold the link to the first hidden slide, and then select Insert→Hyperlink (Alt, N, I).**

   The Insert Hyperlink dialog box (Figure 22-7) opens.

4. **In the "Link to" list, select "Place in This Document". In the "Select a place in this document" list, choose the hidden slide you're linking to.**

   You can tell which slides in the list are hidden slides because their slide numbers are enclosed by parentheses.

5. **Click OK.**

   PowerPoint creates a link to the hidden slide.

6. **Next, open the hidden slide and insert a link to the slide that will open after a viewer has seen this slide.**

   In the example, you might link back to the quiz slide (if the answer is wrong and you want the viewer to try again). Or you might link to the first slide of the next section (if the answer is correct and you want the presentation to go forward).

7. **Repeat steps 3–6 until you've linked to all the hidden slides.**

   When you're done, select the first slide in your sequence and switch to Reading view or Slide Show view (use the status bar buttons) to make sure the links work the way you want them to.

Inserting an Action Button

An action button makes something happen when you click it—or even when you pass the mouse over it—during a presentation. The action might be moving to another slide, running a program or macro, opening an embedded object (page 575), or playing a sound. Action buttons are especially useful when your presentation is on a computer or the Web for others to navigate—they help viewers know to click an arrow to move forward or backward in the slideshow.

To insert an action button on a slide, follow these steps:

1. **Select Insert→Shapes.**

    The Shapes menu, shown in Figure 22-8, opens.

2. **Scroll down to the bottom of the menu to the Action Buttons section. Click the button you want to insert.**

    The Shapes menu disappears, and the mouse pointer turns into crosshairs.

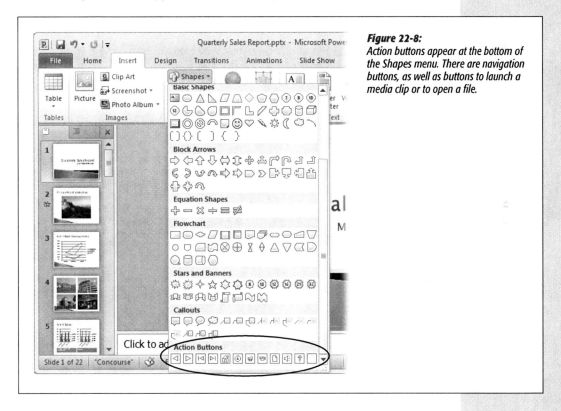

Figure 22-8:
Action buttons appear at the bottom of the Shapes menu. There are navigation buttons, as well as buttons to launch a media clip or to open a file.

3. **Move the crosshairs to where you want to insert the action button. Click and drag to draw a rectangle that's about the size you want the button to be, and then let go of the mouse button.**

   PowerPoint draws your button and opens the Action Settings dialog box, shown in Figure 22-9. This dialog box lists the actions that can happen when someone clicks the action button during a slideshow.

4. **Turn on the radio button for the action you want, and then specify what the action will do.**

   When you select an action, the drop-down list beneath it goes live. So, for example, if you want a click to advance to the next slide, you'd turn on the "Hyperlink to" radio button and select Next Slide from the drop-down list.

5. **If you want to play a sound, turn on the "Play sound" radio button, and then select a sound from the drop-down list.**

   PowerPoint has a list of built-in sounds, from applause to a drumroll to a cash-register "cha-ching" to an explosion. Select any of these sounds, or choose "Other sound" to use an audio file stored on your computer.

6. **Click OK.**

   PowerPoint puts the *action* in your action button. Now, when you click the button (or pass the mouse pointer over it, depending on what you chose), PowerPoint will perform whatever action you specified.

Figure 22-9:
Use the Action Settings dialog box to add an action to a button on your slide. The "Run macro" option is available only if you've recorded a macro in PowerPoint. For the "Object action" option to be available, you must have inserted a file as an object (page 575) in the presentation. If you want the action to happen when someone passes the mouse over the button, click the Mouse Over tab, which has the same settings.

Tip: Actions aren't confined to action buttons. You can add an action to any object on a PowerPoint slide. Just select the object and then click Insert→Action (Alt, N, K) to open the Action Settings dialog box (Figure 22-9). Then follow steps 4–6 in the preceding list.

Opening an Inserted File

If you've inserted an object from another program into a slide, such as a Word document or an Excel spreadsheet, you can open the inserted file (along with the program used to create it) with a click. This is helpful when you've got a document or a spreadsheet that's too big to fit on a slide.

First, insert the object into your slide (page 575 tells you how to do that). When you insert the object, turn on the "Display as icon" checkbox. This shows a small picture on the slide that represents the kind of file you inserted—Adobe PDF file, Excel spreadsheet, Word document, whatever—as shown in Figure 22-10.

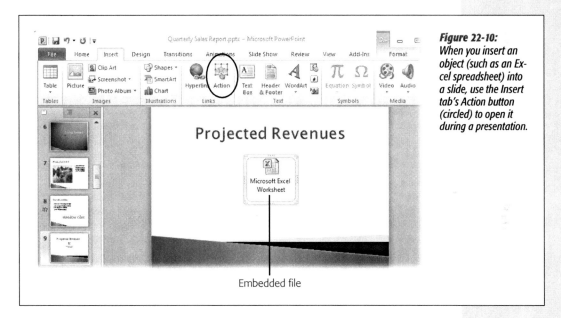

Figure 22-10:
When you insert an object (such as an Excel spreadsheet) into a slide, use the Insert tab's Action button (circled) to open it during a presentation.

Next, set things up so that the file opens when you click the icon:

1. **Select the inserted file's icon, and then click Insert→Action (Alt, N, K).**

   The Action Settings dialog box, shown in Figure 22-9, opens, with the "Object action" option enabled.

2. **Turn on the "Object action" radio button.**

   The drop-down list of actions goes live.

3. From the "Object action" list, select Open. Click OK.

   PowerPoint adds the action to the object.

During a slideshow, just click the icon to open the file.

Slide Masters: Powerful Slide Blueprints

Think of a slide master as the trendsetter for your presentation. When the slide master changes its style, all the other slides follow suit. In that sense, the slide master is a template for individual slides. If you change a font style or move a placeholder on the slide master, all slides in the presentation reflect that change.

Every presentation contains at least one slide master. The slide master contains information about the look of a presentation, including layout, fonts, colors, theme, background, kinds of placeholders, and effects. If you put your company logo on the slide master, for example, that logo appears on all slides in the presentation—even new slides you add later.

And that's the main reason to use PowerPoint's slide masters—by changing one slide, you can easily change every slide in the presentation. New slides also reflect the change. If you're working with a lengthy presentation that has dozens of slides, then using the slide master can save you lots of time and formatting hassles.

Each slide master has a number of layouts associated with it for specific types of slides, such as Title Only slides or Content with Caption slides. You can also change the layout slides. Changes to layout slides don't affect the slide master, but they do affect all slides of that type in the presentation.

Note: Before you start fooling around with slide masters, think about what you want to accomplish. There might be an easier way. If you want to change a presentation's color scheme, fonts, layouts, or background, apply a different theme (see the Tip on page 548) or customize the current theme instead. If you want to apply a theme and placeholder content to use over and over for similar presentations, create a template instead. Use slide masters when you want to customize slides' default layouts or have the same content (like some standard action buttons) on every slide.

Changing the Look of All Slides in Your Presentation

To use the slide master to alter the look of all your slides, follow these steps:

1. Select View→Slide Master (Alt, W, M).

   PowerPoint opens the Slide Master tab, shown in Figure 22-11. When this tab is open, PowerPoint shows the master slide and its associated layouts: title slide, section header, and so on. The first slide in the Slides pane is the slide master, which controls the styles of *all* slides in the presentation. When you make a change to this slide, PowerPoint applies it to all the different slide types.

Figure 22-11:
*The Slides pane shows
the slide master and its
associated layouts.*

Slide master ────

Slide layouts ────
for this
slide master

To change the slide master,
make changes to this slide.

2. If it's not already selected, click the first slide in the Slides pane to display the slide master in the main workspace. Use the Slide Master tab's Edit Theme, Background, and Page Setup sections to make any changes you want to your slides' appearance.

    Here's what's in each section:

    — **Edit Theme.** This section has buttons that let you choose a different theme or alter the theme's color scheme, fonts, or text effects.

    — **Background.** Click this button to see a gallery of background styles that you can add to the presentation. Click the Format Background button to open the Format Background dialog box, which lets you design your own background for the slides. If you use a picture as your slides' background and want to hide it (without deleting it from the presentation), turn on this section's Hide Background Graphics checkbox.

    — **Page Setup.** The buttons here let you specify slide size and orientation (portrait or landscape). If you want slide numbers to begin from a number other than 1, you can change that in the Page Setup dialog box.

3. Click inside the text box that says, "Click to edit Master title styles". Use the Home tab (Alt, H) and the Drawing Tools | Format tab (Alt, JD) to format how titles appear in the presentation.

    Head for the Home tab if you want to change the font or font size, apply special formatting (like bold or italic), change the text's alignment, and so on. The Drawing Tools | Format tab lets you format text as WordArt or add and format shapes, such as a rectangle to serve as a background for titles.

4. **Click inside the content box, and then make whatever changes you want to the text there.**

   You might, for example, select Home→Bullets (Alt, H, U) to change your lists' bullet style. Or if you've made changes to the title style's font, you can change the font here to match.

5. **If you want, click inside the Footer, Date, or Page Number boxes to make changes there.**

   You can move these boxes around if you want; just drag and drop to rearrange them.

6. **When you're finished, click Slide Master→Close Master View (Alt, M, C).**

   PowerPoint applies the changes to all the slides in your presentation, and also to any new slides you create.

Tip: You can have more than one slide master in a presentation. To create a new series of slide layouts based on a second slide master, open Slide Master view and click the Slide Master tab's Insert Slide Master button (Alt, M, N). Set up the new slide master the way you want it; your selections affect the masters for the types of slide layouts that follow it.

Changing the Layout for a Particular Type of Slide

In Slide Master view, the slide master is the big slide at the top of the Slides pane. As the previous section explains, any changes you make to the slide master apply to all slide types, so you can quickly make changes to the look and formatting of the whole presentation.

But what if you want to make changes to one particular type of slide—and *only* that type? Maybe you want section header slides to use a different title style from other slides. Easy. Just open Slide Master view (View→Slide Master or Alt, W, M) and find the type of slide whose layout you want to edit. Then follow the steps listed previously for editing a presentation's slide master.

Tip: If the Slide Master view's Slides pane shows a layout you don't want in the presentation, select that slide and click the Slide Master tab's Delete button (Alt, M, D) to remove it.

Creating a New Layout

Each slide layout serves as a template for creating a particular kind of slide. If there's a layout you use frequently that's not one of the standard layouts, follow these steps to create a new layout and add it to the master list:

1. **Open Slide Master view by selecting View→Slide Master (Alt, W, M). Then, on the Slide Master tab, click the Insert Layout button (Alt, M, I).**

    PowerPoint inserts a new master slide for a specific layout. This slide has text boxes for a title, footer, date, and page number. You can change these elements as you like—move them around, change the font style, and so on.

2. **To add a placeholder for a specific type of content, go to the Slide Master tab's Master Layout section and click the down arrow on the Insert Placeholder button (Alt, M, A).**

    A menu opens, as shown in Figure 22-12, displaying the different kinds of placeholders you can insert: content (which inserts a general content box that accepts any kind of content, like the one shown in Figure 20-5 back on page 552), text, picture, chart, table, SmartArt, media, or clip art.

*Figure 22-12:
The Insert Place-
holder button shows
the different kinds of
placeholders you can
put into a layout.*

3. **Select the type of content for which you're creating a placeholder.**

    The mouse pointer becomes a crosshairs.

4. **Click and drag to create a box that holds the kind of content you chose.**

    Move and resize the placeholder as you like, until it looks the way you want slides of that type to appear.

Tip: To position the new content box precisely, use the Format Shape dialog box's Position section. Select Drawing Tools, and then click the Size section's lower-right Size and Position button (Alt, JD, SZ) to open the Format Shape dialog box. Select Position, and then specify the placeholder's horizontal and vertical positions on the slide. You can also use the Home tab's Arrange button (Alt, H, G, A) to align placeholders.

5. If you want more than one placeholder, repeat steps 2 and 3 until you've placed them all on the slide. Then (with your new master slide selected in the Slides pane), click the Slide Master tab's Rename button (Alt, M, R).

   The Rename Layout dialog box opens.

6. Type in the name you want to give this kind of master slide, such as "Table" or "Four Photos." Click Rename.

   Your custom master slide has a new name.

7. Click Close Master View.

   PowerPoint creates the new master slide and adds it to the menu of slides you can choose from when you insert a new slide into a presentation.

Working with Masters for Handouts and Notes

PowerPoint comes with built-in masters for the handouts and notes you print to go with your presentation. You can alter these masters to print the way you want them—to adjust the number of slides per page on a handout, for example, or to give your notes more room on a notes page.

Modifying the handout master

To change a presentation's handout master, follow these steps:

1. Select View→Handout Master (Alt, W, H).

   PowerPoint opens the Handout Master tab and shows the current handout master, as shown in Figure 22-13.

2. Use the Page Setup section to tell PowerPoint how you want the slides to appear on your handout.

   These buttons adjust how your handout displays slides:

   — **Handout Orientation (Alt, M, R).** Click this button to select Portrait or Landscape for the pages in your handout.

   — **Slide Orientation (Alt, M, O).** This setting lets you select portrait or landscape orientation for the slides printed on the handout.

   — **Slides Per Page (Alt, M, L).** You can display as few as one slide per page or as many as nine. Select Slide Outline if you want your handout to show slides' text in outline form, rather than showing a picture of each slide.

3. **Turn the options in the Placeholders section on or off.**

   You can choose to display or hide headers, footers, dates, and page numbers. (See page 604 for instructions on how to create these elements for your handouts.)

4. **When you're finished, click Close Master View (Alt, M, C).**

   PowerPoint closes the Handout Master tab and saves your new handout master.

Figure 22-13:
The handout master shows the number of slides that will print on each page.

Modifying the notes master

To change the appearance of notes that you print out to use with a presentation, go to the Notes Master tab:

1. **Select View→Notes Master (Alt, W, K).**

   The Notes Master tab opens, with the presentation's notes master displayed, as shown in Figure 22-14.

2. **On the Notes Master tab, make any adjustments you want.**

   Here are the sections you're most likely to use:

   — **Page Setup.** Here, you can adjust the orientation of pages or of the slides on the pages.

   — **Placeholders.** Turn the checkboxes in this section on or off to show or hide headers, footers, dates, page numbers, slide images, or body (the written notes).

   — **Background.** If slides have a background image that make them hard to read when printed, turn on the Hide Background Graphics checkbox.

3. **If you want, resize the placeholders for the slide image and text on the page. Click the slide image or the text box, and resize them as you normally would.**

   If you have extensive notes, for example, you might make the slide image smaller and the text box bigger.

4. **When you're done revising the notes master, click Close Master View.**

   PowerPoint closes the Notes Master tab and uses your new notes master to format notes pages.

Figure 22-14:
You can change the appearance of your printed notes by editing the notes master.

Collaborating with Others

Whether it's work, school, or volunteering, it's common practice for people to band together to create group presentations. Collaboration splits up the workload and lets people lend their unique expertise to a presentation. PowerPoint's collaboration tools include comments and a new approach to comparing and merging different versions of the same document.

Tip: In PowerPoint, unlike Word, you can't restrict the styles others can use when they're working on your presentation. To keep the slideshow consistent, it's a good idea to agree ahead of time on the theme, SmartArt, animations, and transitions everyone will use. That way, your presentation looks coordinated as it moves from one section to the next.

Adding and Reading Comments

Whether you're working with others to create a presentation or just want some feedback on your work, comments are a handy feature. Each commenter gets assigned a different color, and the notes are signed with the commenter's name and initials, so it's easy to see who said what. PowerPoint comments work like sticky notes—you can move them around and stick them to whatever part of a slide they pertain to.

Note: In PowerPoint, comments appear only in Normal view.

Inserting a comment

To insert a comment on a slide, go to the Review tab, and then click New Comment (Alt, R, C). PowerPoint labels the slide with a comment marker in the upper-left corner and opens a box where you can type what you want to say, as shown in Figure 22-15. The cursor is already blinking away, waiting, so just start typing.

When you're finished, click outside the comment box; it disappears, leaving a marker to show that there's a comment on the slide.

Tip: You can move the marker: Just drag and drop. That way you can put the comment on the part of the slide it refers to.

Comment marker

Figure 22-15:
When you insert a new comment, PowerPoint puts it in the slide's upper-left corner. Your initials and the comment number appear on the comment marker; your name and the date appear on the comment itself.

Reading comments

To read a comment, hover the mouse pointer over the comment marker. The text appears as a ScreenTip until you move the mouse pointer away. If you want the comment to stay visible, click its marker. This opens it up for reading; it stays open until you click elsewhere or move to another slide.

To find the comments in a presentation, go to the Review tab's Comments section and click the Next button (Alt, R, N) or Previous button (Alt, R, V) to move forward or backward between comments. Clicking Next, for example, jumps to the next comment in the presentation and opens it so you can read it.

Editing a comment

To edit a comment, double-click its marker. Alternatively, you can select Review→Edit Comment (Alt, R, T) or right-click the marker and select Edit Comment from the shortcut menu. The comment box opens, looking like the one in Figure 22-15. Make whatever changes or additions you want, and then click outside the comment box to close it.

Hiding comments

When you add a comment to a presentation, PowerPoint automatically turns on the Review tab's Show Markup button (you can see this button in Figure 22-15). If you don't want comment markers cluttering up your slides in Normal view, select Review→Show Markup. This turns off the Show Markup button and hides the markers.

Be aware, though, that hiding comment markers doesn't make comments impossible to find. Even when you've turned off the Show Markup button, the Previous and Next buttons in the Review tab's Comments section are still active. So anyone looking at the presentation in Normal view can find, open, and edit comments.

Deleting comments

After you've dealt with the issue raised by a comment, there are several different ways to delete it:

- **To delete a single comment,** right-click the comment marker and select Delete Comment from the shortcut menu. Or select the comment and then click the Review tab's Delete button (Alt, R, D, D).

- **To delete all comments on a slide,** go to the Review tab's Comments section and click the Delete button's down arrow. Then choose "Delete All Markup on the Current Slide" (Alt, R, D, A).

- **To delete all the comments in an entire presentation,** click the Review tab, then the Delete button's down arrow, then "Delete All Markup in this Presentation" (Alt, R, D, P). PowerPoint asks if you're sure you want to nix all the presentation's comments and annotation. Click Yes if this is what you want.

Tip: You can restrict a presentation's permissions in PowerPoint—limiting who can view or edit the presentation—much as you can in Word. To set permissions, select File→Info→Protect Presentation (Alt, F, E, P), then choose one of these options (described in detail starting on page 236): Mark as Final, Encrypt with Password, Restrict Permission by People, or Add a Digital Signature.

Comparing Versions of a Presentation

PowerPoint 2010 has a powerful new compare and merge feature. Although you can't track changes in PowerPoint as you can in Word, comparing and merging is the next best thing. When you compare two versions of the same presentation, Power-Point points out and describes the changes, which you can accept or reject, and then merges the two versions. Multiple versions of the same presentation become a single, definitive version, so you're never left wondering which version is the latest one.

To compare and merge two versions of a presentation, follow these steps:

1. **Select Review→Compare (Alt, R, G).**

   A dialog box opens so you can select the version of the presentation that you want to compare and merge with this one.

2. **Find and select the file you want to compare with this one. Click Merge.**

   PowerPoint merges the two slideshows, keeping track of what's changed, and opens the Revisions pane, shown in Figure 22-16. This pane has two tabs:

   — **Slides.** If the current slide has changes, this tab shows a thumbnail of the slide and lists who made the changes. The reviewer's name has a checkbox to its left; turn on the checkbox to accept all changes on the slide from that reviewer.

   — **Details.** This tab has two lists: "Slide changes", which describe the changes on the currently displayed slide, and "Presentation changes", which describe changes made to more than one slide. Click a change to open a box describing the change and containing a checkbox (you can see an example in Figure 22-16). Turn on the checkbox to accept the change in the merged presentation.

Tip: You can also use the Previous (Alt, R, F) and Next (Alt, R, J) buttons in the Review tab's Compare section to jump from one change to the next. This is probably the easiest way to find and review changes to slides.

3. **When you see a change that you want to accept in the merged presentation, select it and then click the Review tab's Accept button (Alt, R, A, A). To accept all changes on a slide, go to the Review tab and, in the Compare section, click the Accept button's down arrow and select "Accept All Changes to the Current Slide" (Alt, R, A, S).**

Note: If you don't accept a change, it doesn't merge with the current presentation.

When you accept a change, PowerPoint puts a checkmark on that slide in the Slides pane.

4. **If you've accepted a change and then have second thoughts about merging it into the presentation, you can reject the change. Select the change you want to reject, and then click the Review tab's Reject button (Alt, R, J, R). When you click the Reject button's down arrow, you can also choose to Reject All Changes to the Current Slide (Alt, R, J, S) or Reject All Changes to the Presentation (Alt, R, J, P).**

Rejecting a change removes that slide's checkmark in the Slides pane.

5. **When you're finished accepting and rejecting changes, click the Review tab's End Review button (Alt, R, W).**

PowerPoint displays a dialog box that warns you that it will discard any changes you haven't merged into the document and asks if you're sure you want to end the review.

6. **Click Yes.**

PowerPoint merges the presentations, incorporating the changes you've accepted, and closes the Revisions pane.

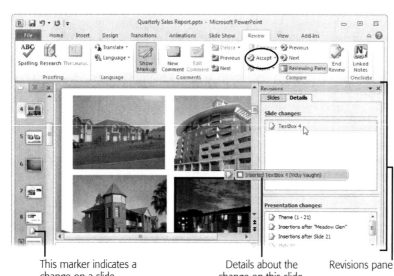

Figure 22-16:
Compare two versions of a presentation and keep only the changes you want when you merge them. Select a change in the Revisions pane's "Slide changes" list to get details about it; to accept a change, turn on the checkbox in its description or click the Accept button (circled).

This marker indicates a change on a slide.

Details about the change on this slide.

Revisions pane

Tip: When you're collaborating with others on a PowerPoint presentation, divide the slideshow into sections (page 604) to make it easier to keep track of who's working on what. Assign each collaborator a section (you can name the section after the person responsible for it). After everyone has completed a section, merge the different versions of the presentation.

Adding Multimedia and Movement

Here's where PowerPoint gets fun—livening up your slides with video, sound, and motion. Although content is always king, you can grab and keep your audience's attention by adding video and audio clips, animating text and images, and creating transitions between slides.

PowerPoint 2010 makes snazzing up your presentations easier than ever. You can now edit media clips right within the program, doing things like trimming clips and adding bookmarks to help get straight to the point. And animating objects on your slides is a snap. The Animations tab now displays a gallery of options right on the ribbon. Transitions get their own tab, too, along with some cool new styles—including 3-D effects—for these between-slide effects. This chapter will teach you to use PowerPoint to make your presentations will snap, crackle, and pop.

Putting Media Clips in a Presentation

Just because it's you up on the podium doesn't mean you need to do all the talking. Videos and sound recordings give you (and your audience) a break. And if you're creating a presentation for viewers to watch on their own, media clips can add a soundtrack and provide a break from reading what's on the screen.

This section tells you how to add, format, and edit media clips—including how to bookmark and trim clips so you can play exactly the parts you want.

Adding Video from Your Hard Drive

The quickest route to getting that video on a slide goes like this: Insert a new slide with a content box; click the Insert Media Clip button (it looks like a reel of film);

and, from the dialog box that opens, navigate to the video file and click Insert. PowerPoint pops the video onto your slide, as shown in Figure 23-1. Select the video to see its controls; click the Play button to preview the video in Normal view; or switch to Reading or Slide Show view to see how the video will look during a slideshow.

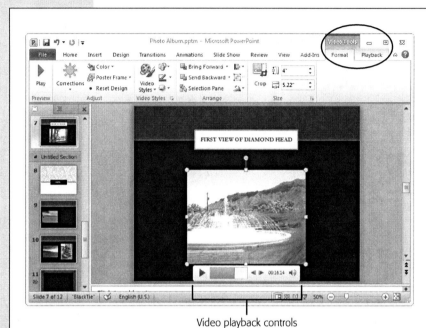

Figure 23-1:
When inserting a video from your computer, you can watch it from any tab in Normal view: Just click the Play button in the player controls. PowerPoint has two contextual tabs for working with videos (circled) Video Tools | Format and Video Tools | Playback.

Video playback controls

Tip: If you prefer—or if you're working with a slide that doesn't have a content box—you can also open the Insert Video dialog box by selecting Insert→Video (Alt, N, V, F).

Adding Video from a Website

Plenty of times that video you want to add isn't on your computer; instead, it's on the company website or a video-sharing site like YouTube. PowerPoint makes it easy to grab and incorporate such external files right into your slides. Start by inserting the slide to hold the video (this might be a blank slide or a title only slide), and then do this:

1. **Open your web browser, find the video you want, and then look for an Embed button.**

   The Embed button is your one-click path to code that describes how to display and play the video. (The code is what you're going to copy and paste into PowerPoint.) On YouTube, the code appears as preselected when you click the Embed button. (Other sites may open a new page.)

2. **Select the embed code (if it's not already selected), and then press Ctrl+C.**

Windows copies the code to your computer's Clipboard.

Note: Some online videos may have embedding disabled—in that case, you won't find any embed code. Your best bet is to find a different video or to just create a link to the video's web page. Copy what's in your web browser's address bar and use it to create a hyperlink (page 571) on the slide. When you click the link, the computer's web browser will open to the page that contains the video.

---

3. **Now head to PowerPoint. In the Insert tab's Media section, click the Video button's down arrow, and then select "Video from Web Site" (Alt, N, V, W).**

A dialog box opens, as shown in Figure 23-2, asking for the video's embed code.

4. **Paste the code into the dialog box (it'll look something like the gobbledygook in Figure 23-2) and click Insert.**

A black box appears on the slide as a placeholder for your video, and PowerPoint opens the Video Tools | Format and Video Tools | Playback contextual tabs.

5. **To play the video, you can use either of the contextual tabs. Click Video Tools | Format→Play (Alt, JN, P) or Video Tools | Playback→Play (Alt, JH, P).**

The video appears in a player on your slide.

6. **Click the Play button to watch the video.**

The video you saw online plays on your slide!

Tip: To preview how the video will look in an actual slideshow, use the buttons on the status bar to switch to Reading or Slide Show view.

If the video player looks too small on the slide, switch back to Normal view and click the placeholder box to reveal its resizing handles. Click a corner handle and then drag to resize the video. Drag the placeholder or use the Video Tools | Format tab's Align button (Alt, JN, AA) to put the video where you want it on the slide. When you view the video, the player is the size of the placeholder in Normal view.

Figure 23-2:
To insert a video from a website, you need the video's embed code. Video-sharing sites like YouTube and Hulu have an Embed button or a link that provides this code.

Note: After you've inserted a video from a website, you may see a yellow bar with this security warning the next time you open the presentation: "References to external media objects have been blocked." That's to protect you from possibly malicious websites that want to put viruses or other nasties on your computer, and it means that it won't play the video unless you explicitly okay it. If you trust the site where you found the video, then click the Enable Content button.

Adding Animated Clip Art

Office (the suite of programs) and Office.com have tons of animated clip art that can enliven your slides. These aren't high-quality video, just animated, cartoonish images that move—kind of like a flip book. Inserting these animated doodads works the same way as inserting a regular clip art drawing: On the slide where you want to insert the animated clip art, open the Clip Art pane using one of these paths:

- In a slide with a content box, click the Clip Art button.
- Select Insert→Clip Art (Alt, N, F).
- On the Insert tab, click the Video button's down arrow, and then select Clip Art Video (Alt, N, V, C).

In the Clip Art pane, limit your search results by making sure you're searching only for animated clip art: From the "Results should be" drop-down list, turn on the Videos checkbox. (If you don't see this option, click the + sign next to "All media types" to see the categories that are available.)

To find animated clip art related to a particular theme or topic, type a keyword in the search box at the top of the pane. (If you just want to browse clip art options, you can leave this box empty.) Click Go, and then scroll through the results that appear. If you're searching in more than one category of clip art, you can tell which results are animated because they're marked with a small star in the bottom-right corner. Click a piece of clip art to insert it on your slide, and resize or move it as you like.

Note: When you insert animated clip art, the Video Tools context tabs don't appear. Instead, you see the Picture Tools context tab. (That's because moving clip art isn't a full-blown video; it's an animated GIF, a small animation based on several pictures displayed one after the other.) To see the animated clip art in action, click the status bar's Reading View or Slide Show button.

Adding Sound from Your Hard Drive

Got a favorite MP3 file you want to lay down as background music during your presentation? Or maybe there's a recording of that Help Center call gone horribly wrong? Whatever your purpose, audio can give your presentation a whole new dimension. Adding an audio clip works like adding a video clip. Insert or select the slide to hold the clip, and then follow these steps:

1. Select Insert→Audio (Alt, N, O, F).

   The Insert Audio dialog box opens, ready to find a variety of audio files, including MP3s, MP4s, Windows Audio Files (.wav), and Window Media Audio files (.wma and .wax), among others.

2. Find and select the audio file you want, and then click Insert.

   PowerPoint inserts the audio clip on your slide, displaying an audio icon and controls, as shown in Figure 23-3.

3. Click Play to hear the audio clip.

   You can also play an audio clip by selecting Audio Tools | Playback→Play (Alt, JH, P).

Figure 23-3:
The audio icon indicates that there's an audio clip on the slide. When you select the icon, the audio playback controls appear.

Audio icon   Playback controls

Tip: The audio icon is a well-known symbol that indicates to viewers that there's an audio clip to play. But you're not limited to this icon for your audio clip. If you'd prefer a different picture, then click the audio icon and go to the Audio Tools | Format tab. In the Adjust section, click the Change Picture button (Alt, JN, G). This opens a dialog box where you can find and select any picture you want to replace the audio icon.

Adding Clip Art Audio

Office also has a rich collection of sound clips, both built in and available on Office.com, to add sound effects to your slides. If you want to add a little mood music or play applause, chirping birds, sirens—just about any sound you can think of—you'll probably find what you're looking for in Office's audio clip art library.

Note: The term "audio clip art" may be a little confusing, because there are no images to go with the sound clips. Inserting a sound clip just gives you the usual audio icon. Microsoft must have found the term "clip art" a convenient, catch-all category for all kinds of media clips: graphics, photos, animated GIFs— and audio.

The instructions for inserting these audio snippets are the same as for inserting clip art video (page 97). The only difference is the kind of file you select from the "Results should be" drop-down menu: Instead of videos, turn on the Audio checkbox.

After you've inserted an audio clip, click the audio icon to see the controls. Press Play to listen.

Recording Audio

Recording your own voice and adding it to your slideshow is a great customization option. Imagine, for example, that you're creating a presentation for others to view on their computers. You could record instructions or read from the same script you might use at a live presentation. Similarly, foreign language lessons could include audio files that demonstrate correct pronunciation. You can record whatever sound clips enrich your slides.

The only special equipment you need is a microphone connected to your computer; many recent-model PCs have a microphone built in. When you've got that set up, follow these steps:

1. **On the slide where you're inserting the audio, select Insert, click the Audio button's down arrow, and then select Record Audio (Alt, N, O, R).**

   The Record Sound dialog box, shown in Figure 23-4, opens. This box has three control buttons: Play, Stop, and Record.

Change this default name to one that identifies your clip.

Play Stop Record

Figure 23-4:
To record your own audio clip, use the Record and Stop buttons. To preview the result, press Play.

2. **Type a name for your sound clip in the Name box, and get ready to speak into the microphone. Click the Record button and start talking.**

   As you record, the dialog box keeps track of the passing time in seconds.

3. **When you're finished, click Stop, and then click OK.**

   PowerPoint puts the audio clip on your slide.

To listen to the clip you've inserted, click the audio icon to bring up the controls, and then press the Play button.

Note: If you need to pause while recording, press Stop. When you're ready to resume, click Record again. PowerPoint doesn't end the recording until you click OK to insert it in your presentation.

Formatting Video Clips

PowerPoint can't duplicate the power of a full-blown video editing program like Adobe Premiere Pro or Sony Vegas Movie Studio, but you can make some minor tweaks to a video's appearance right from PowerPoint. By heading to the Video Tools | Format tab, shown in Figure 23-5, you can adjust brightness and contrast, add color and video effects, crop the video player, and more. The following sections show you ways you can format video clips.

Figure 23-5:
Use the Video Tools | Format tab to change the appearance of your video. Apply an effect and then click the left Play button to test it out.

Adjust brightness and contrast

If the video seems too bright or too dark when you preview it, head to the Video Tools | Format tab and, in the Adjust section, click the Corrections button (Alt, JN, CO). A menu opens that shows different degrees of brightness and contrast, with your video's current setting selected.

Move the mouse pointer over the different settings to see a live preview in your video. Click any setting to apply it to the video.

Tip: If you prefer to adjust brightness and contrast settings manually, using sliders, then open the Corrections menu and select Video Corrections Options (Alt, JN, CO, C). This opens the Format Video dialog box to its Video section, where you can adjust brightness and contrast or restore the video to its original settings.

Add a frame or border

The Video Styles section of the Video Tools | Format tab has a gallery of frames you can add to your video. Some styles add other effects as well, like a shadow or a reflection. If the ribbon doesn't show the effect you want, click the gallery's lower-right More button (Alt, JN, V) to see the whole array.

If you just want to throw a border around the video, use the Video Border button (Alt, JN, SO), which lets you add a border and choose its color, style, and thickness.

Add effects

You can also add and format these effects for a video:

- **Color effects.** To tint the video with a wash of color or change it to stark black and white, click the Color button (Alt, JN, L) and choose an option from the Recolor menu (you get a live preview of the options as you move your mouse over them). Don't see a color effect you like? Click More Variations (M) or Video Color Options (C) to broaden your choices.

- **Video shape.** Click this button (Alt, JN, I) to open the Shapes menu. The shape you select defines the video's area. If you select a cloud, for example, PowerPoint imposes a cloud shape over the video, and the video plays inside the cloud.

- **Video effects.** You can add the same effects to videos that you add to pictures: shadows, reflections, glow, soft edges, beveling, and 3-D rotation. (Page 106 tells you more about these effects.) To select and apply an effect to your video, click the Video Effects button (Alt, JN, F).

Tip: It's easy to go overboard when you're formatting a video. If you decide you don't like the effects you've added, click Video Tools | Format→Reset Design (Alt, JN, Q). PowerPoint removes all the effects, and you're back at square one.

Crop the player

If you want to focus on a small area of the video playback, you can crop the size of the player. Cropping a video player works the same way as cropping a photo (page 101). Select Video Tools: Format→Crop (Alt, JN, C1) to make cropping handles appear at the corners and midpoints of the video's borders. Drag and drop any cropping handle to show only part of the player.

Formatting Audio Clips

The Audio Tools | Format tab, shown in Figure 23-6, doesn't format the sound of your audio clip; it formats the appearance of the audio icon (or whatever picture you insert to show that there's an audio clip to play). The options are nearly identical to those on the Video Tools | Format toolbar, with a few exceptions:

- **Remove Background.** If you insert a picture to replace the audio icon (see the Tip on page 629), you can remove its background to show only the main image. Select Picture Tools | Format→Remove Background (Alt, JN, E) and see page 102 for step-by-step instructions.

- **Corrections.** Adjust brightness and contrast or sharpen/soften your image by clicking this button (Alt, JN, R).

- **Artistic Effects.** Get artsy with your image by clicking the Audio Tools | Format tab's Artistic Effects button (Alt, JN, X) and choosing the texture or visual effect you want.

- **Change Picture.** If you want to insert a different image while keeping any formatting you've applied to the current image, click this button (Alt, JN, G) to open the Insert Picture dialog box.

Figure 23-6:
The Audio Tools | Format tab formats the appearance of the audio icon (or whatever image you use to replace it). Its options are the same as those on the Picture Tools | Format tab (page 101).

Tip: Because you're formatting an image when you use the Audio Tools | Format options, its ribbon options are the same as those on the Picture Tools | Format tab. Page 100 tells you all about formatting pictures in Word—and it works the same way in PowerPoint.

Editing Media Clips

PowerPoint 2010 has some cool new tools that let you work with videos and audio clips right inside PowerPoint. Fade in and out like a professional director. Bookmark certain points in the playback, and use the bookmarks to jump to those points. You can also trim a video by changing its starting and ending points so you can show what's relevant and leave out the rest.

Note: You can't trim, add bookmarks, or add fade effects to a video that you got from the Web and embedded in your presentation.

Using bookmarks

When you insert a bookmark into a media clip, you can jump straight to that bookmark as you play the clip during a presentation. Imagine that you've inserted a video of the CEO's speech, for example. But the Big Cheese is a wordy guy and had an awful lot to say, so only a couple of parts are relevant to your presentation. Bookmark the start of those relevant parts, and when you play the video during your presentation, you can make the video jump right to where you want it—so Mr. Cheese gets right to the point for a change.

Inserting a bookmark. Here's how to insert a bookmark into a media clip:

1. **Select the clip and, depending on the kind of clip you're working with, select the Video Tools or Audio Tools|Playback contextual tab (Alt, JH). Click Play.**

   The clip starts to play. As it does, a gray bar moves from left to right in the controls to show what percentage of the clip has played.

2. **When the playback reaches the spot you want to bookmark, click the Playback tab's Add Bookmark button.**

   The clip pauses, and a dot appears on the playback bar to bookmark the spot, as shown in Figure 23-7.

An audio clip can hold only one bookmark, so if you're working with audio, you're done. If you're working with a video, you can insert more bookmarks by repeating the steps.

Figure 23-7:
Add bookmarks to jump to a particular spot in the video or to serve as a trigger for an animation.

Tip: You can use a bookmark to trigger animation, causing text or an image to appear when the video reaches a certain point. The Tip on page 647 tells you how.

Jumping to a bookmark during playback. To jump to a bookmark, bring up the clip's controls (in Normal view, select the clip object; in Reading or Slide Show view, pass the mouse pointer over the video). Find the bookmark you want and click it. The clip jumps to the bookmarked spot. Click Play to start from there.

Removing a bookmark. To remove a bookmark, select the one you want to delete, and then click the Playback contextual tab's Remove Bookmark button (Alt, JH, R). The bookmark disappears from the clip's controls.

Trimming a media clip

Often, a video or audio clip is longer than you need to make your point. So you can edit down the clip to play only the part you want. It's easy, and a big help in making a presentation go smoothly—you no longer have to guesstimate where the relevant part of a clip starts or rush to stop playback when that part's over.

Whether you're trimming an audio or a video clip, the process is the same:

1. **Select the clip to bring up its controls. On the contextual Playback tab, click the Trim Audio or Trim Video button (Alt, JH, T—the keyboard shortcut is the same whether you're trimming audio or video).**

   The Trim Audio (Figure 23-8) or Trim Video (Figure 23-9) dialog box opens, showing a playback timeline. The green handle at the left of the timeline represents the clip's starting point, and the red handle on the right represents its end point. If there are any bookmarks in the clip, they appear in the timeline.

2. **Adjust the video's start time and end time.**

   You've got two options for doing this:

   — Drag the green handle to the point where you want the clip to begin, and drag the red handle to its ending point. If you've bookmarked these points, simply drag the handles to line up with your bookmarks.

   — Enter playback times in the Start Time and End Time boxes. To get precise times, use the controls to start and stop the clip: Play/Pause, Previous Frame, and Next Frame. When you stop at the point you want, note its time. Type that time into the Start Time or End Time box.

3. **When you're finished, click OK.**

   PowerPoint trims the clip as you've specified.

Trimming a media clip doesn't delete any part of it. So if you need to adjust a clip's starting or ending point later on, go back to the contextual Playback tab and click the Trim button (Alt, JH, T). The Trim dialog box appears, showing the clip's current settings, and you can make whatever adjustments you need.

Name of
audio file

Start
handle

Length of trimmed file

Length of full audio file

End
handle

Previous Frame

Next Frame

Play/Pause

Figure 23-8:
*In the Trim Audio dialog
box, drag the start and
end handles to shorten the
audio clip. Or enter spe-
cific times in the Start Time
and End Time boxes.*

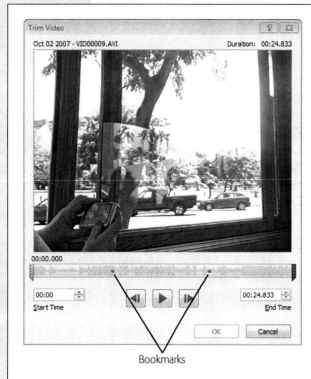

Bookmarks

Figure 23-9:
*The Trim Video dialog box has the same controls
as the Trim Audio dialog box. As you drag the
start or end handle, the image changes so you
can see where you are in the video.*

Fading in and fading out

Unleash your inner Hollywood director by getting creative with fade effects at the beginning or end (or both) of your media clips. To make your clip fade in or fade out, use the Fade Duration controls in the Editing section of the contextual Playback tab:

- **Fade In** (Alt, JH, N) creates a fade effect at the start of the clip.
- **Fade Out** (Alt, JH, O) creates a fade effect at the end of the clip.

Set the number of seconds you want the effect to last, and then click the Play button to test it out.

Hide a clip until you want it to play

You may not want the video player to appear on the slide until you're ready to play the video. When that's the case, you can hide the video player, and then trigger it when it's showtime. (You can do the same for an audio clip.)

Make sure that the slide has a media clip inserted and something to trigger playback of the clip—an image, piece of text, or some other object. Then follow these steps:

1. **Select the media clip and, on the Animations tab (Alt, A), select Play from the animations gallery.**

   This tells PowerPoint to launch the clip as an animation. In other words, you don't have to click the Play control to make the clip start playing.

2. **Still on the Animations tab, click Trigger→"On Click of" (Alt, A, AT, C).**

   A menu flies out, listing the objects on the slide.

3. **Select the object you want as a trigger to play the media clip.**

   A lightning bolt appears by the media object to show it now has a trigger.

4. **Switch over to the contextual Playback tab and turn on the Hide While Not Playing checkbox (Alt, JH, I).**

   You've just told PowerPoint not to display the media clip on the slide unless it's playing.

Test out your trigger in Reading or Slide Show view. Here's how it should work: When the slide opens, the video or audio player isn't visible. When you click the trigger, the clip plays; when it's done playing, the clip disappears.

Other media clip settings

The contextual Playback tab also offers these settings for adjusting how your media clip plays:

- **Adjust the volume.** To limit how loudly a media clip plays, adjust its volume by using the contextual Playback tab's Volume button (Alt, JH, V). The Volume button's options are Low, Medium, High, and Mute.

Tip: During a slideshow, you can also adjust a media clip's volume by using its playback controls: Click the speaker icon to mute or unmute the volume, or hover the mouse pointer over the icon to make the volume slider appear. Move the slider up to increase volume or down to lower it.

- **Start a media clip automatically.** If you want the clip to start as soon as its slide opens, go to the contextual Playback tab and, from the Start drop-down list (Alt, JH, U), select Automatically. (The other option, On Click, is the default.)

- **Hide the clip when it's not playing.** The Hide While Not Playing checkbox does just what it says—it makes the video or audio clip disappear from the slide when it's not playing. If you turn on this checkbox, make sure you've also chosen Automatically in the Start box or set up a trigger for the clip (as described in the steps on page 646). Otherwise, you won't be able to find the clip to play it.

- **Create a loop.** If you want the video or audio to play in a continuous loop, then turn on the contextual Playback tab's Loop until Stopped checkbox.

- **Rewind when done.** Normally, when a media clip ends, it stops at the ending point and stays there, showing the final frame. If you want the played-out clip to jump back to the first frame, then choose this option.

- **Play a video in full-screen mode.** To make your video visible even to those in the back of the room, play it in full-screen mode. Rather than being part of a slide, the video takes up the whole screen. When the video is over, the presentation switches back to slides.

Animating Objects

Ready to have your bullet points zip across the screen, your pictures bounce in, your favorite text spin or pulse for emphasis? Here are all the kinds of animation you can add to the objects on a slide:

- **Entrance** effects determine how an object arrives on your slide, such as flying in from the left side or bottom of the slide.

- **Emphasis** effects animate an object that's already visible on the slide. For example, you might have a headline pulse, spin, or change color when you click the mouse to call viewers' attention to it.

- **Exit** effects determine how an object disappears from the slide, such as fading out or bouncing off the slide.

- **Motion path** effects move objects from one part of the slide to another. Objects can move in a straight line, arc, loop, or other path that you determine.

You can apply animations to any object on a slide—text, lists, photos, clip art, other images, even media clips. This section shows how to animate an object and how to choreograph groups of these movements to give your slideshow professional polish.

Tip: If you're going to be giving your slideshow on a different computer than the one you created it on, make sure your media clips will play the way they're supposed to. Select File→Info→Optimize Compatibility (Alt, F, E, MP). PowerPoint automatically adjusts the file to make it widely compatible with different computers.

Animating an Object

Start by selecting the object you want to set in motion and then do the following:

1. **Click the Animations tab.**

   The Animations section has a gallery showing effects you've used recently, as shown in Figure 23-10. PowerPoint uses a color scheme to let you know what kind of animation you're looking at:

   — Entrance effects are green.

   — Emphasis effects are yellow.

   — Exit effects are red.

2. **To see more effects, click the More button in the lower-right part of the animation gallery (Alt, A, S).**

   A menu opens that shows you a wider range of effects, as shown in Figure 23-11.

Click to see an animation in action

Animation gallery

After you've applied an animation, adjust its effects here.

Add more animations to an object

Open or close the Animation pane

See more animations

Figure 23-10:
The Animations tab is packed with options for adding and adjusting animations. You can apply an animation effect right from the Animations tab, or click the More button (circled) to see a larger gallery of options.

Tip: If you want to browse through even more effects, choose one of the More Effects options on the list, available for entrance, emphasis, exit, and motion path effects. This opens the Change Entrance Effect dialog box, which lists all available effects for the animation you chose, dividing them into categories of Basic, Subtle, Moderate, and—brace yourself—Exciting.

3. **Choose the effect you want. If you select an effect from the Animations tab, all you need to do is click the effect. If you select it from the Change Entrance Effect dialog box, click the effect and then click OK.**

   PowerPoint applies the animation and shows you a preview of the effect. It also adds an animation number to the slide to indicate where this animation happens in the sequence of animations for that slide.

If you want to see an animation again after you've added it, select Animations→Preview (Alt, A, P).

Figure 23-11:
This menu shows you a variety of animation choices. Scroll down or choose one of the More Effects options (circled) to see even more.

Changing an Animation

You're not stuck with the first animation you try. Say you had a few objects bounce in and then decided you wanted a more subtle entrance effect, like Wipe. To change an animation, select the object whose animation you want to change, zip over to the Animations tab, and select the new animation. PowerPoint exchanges the old animation for the new one.

For a slide that has multiple animations, select the one you want to change by clicking its animation number. When you do, PowerPoint highlights the relevant effect in the Animations tab's gallery. Check to make sure you're changing the correct animation, and then select its replacement.

Tip: As your animations grow more complex, with animation numbers crowding the slide, use the Animation pane to find and change a particular animation. Page 648 shows how to navigate the Animation pane.

Adjusting Effect Options

After you've animated an object, you can fine-tune it by applying Effect Options. Select the object and click Animations→Effect Options (Alt, A, O). The options you see here depend on the kind of animation you're working with. For example, if you're having the object enter by wiping or flying in, the Effect Options button lets you choose the direction of the object's movement. If you've chosen an animation that uses color, Effect Options let you select the color. Click the Effect Options button to see your choices for tweaking the animation you've applied.

Tip: Good news, animation fans! PowerPoint 2010 debuts Animation Painter, a feature that's been on a lot of people's wish lists for a long time. If you have several objects that you want to animate in the same way, set up the animation for one object, and then use the Animation Painter to apply that same animation to other objects. Select the object whose animation you want to copy and click Animations→Animation Painter (Alt, A, AP). The mouse pointer becomes an arrow with a paintbrush. Click another object, and Animation Painter applies the animation to it.

To apply the same formatting to several objects, double-click the Animation Painter button, which leaves it turned on as you click different objects on the slide. When you're done applying formatting, click the button again to turn it off.

Adding sound to an animation

There's no button for adding a sound to an animation on the ribbon. Instead, if you want to play a sound when the animation occurs, apply the animation first, and then open a dialog box that shows extra effect options:

1. **Select the animation you're adding a sound to, and then click Animations→ Show Additional Effect Options (it's the pop-out button in the Animations section's lower-right corner) or press Alt, A, M.**

   The Effect Options dialog box for the specified effect opens (the actual name of the box reflects the kind of animation you're working with). Figure 23-12 shows effect options for a Fade animation.

2. **On the Effect tab, use the Sound drop-down list to select the sound you want.**

   If you want, use the Volume button to the list's right to make the sound louder or softer. (If you don't want to play animation sounds for a particular presentation, you can also mute an animation sound here without removing it.)

Figure 23-12:
This dialog box has additional animation effect options that don't appear on the Animations tab: Add a sound effect, dim an object after animation, or animate text.

3. Click OK.

4. **PowerPoint plays a preview of the animation, complete with your new sound effect.**

If you want to adjust the volume, choose a different sound, or remove the sound effect, then reopen the dialog box, make your adjustments, and then click OK.

Dimming text

Well-designed presentations focus viewers' attention on the current point. And the Dim feature can help you there. This feature dims the previous object when a new one enters. So if you're discussing items on a bulleted list, point by point, the previous bullet dims (but is still visible) when a new bullet enters. This makes it clear to your audience which point you're now discussing.

Note: Use dimming for text, not images. You can make black text dim to gray, for example. If you try to dim a picture in the same way, though, the picture gets replaced by a gray shape. If you want to dim a picture, use the workaround in the box on page 644.

Here's how to dim some text when the next object enters:

1. **Apply animation to the text that will dim. You might have the text dissolve or wipe in, for example. Select the text box and, in the Animations section of the Animations tab, click the lower-right Show Additional Effect Options button (Alt, A, M).**

    The Effect Options dialog box (Figure 23-12) for that effect opens.

2. From the "After animation" drop-down list, choose the color you want the text to dim to—the text changes to this color when the next object enters the slide.

   Choose a color that's close to the slide's background but still visible, such as gray on a white or black background or pale blue on a dark blue background. Figure 23-13 shows an example of dimmed text.

3. Click OK.

   PowerPoint shows you a preview of how your dimmed text will look. In the preview, the text dims immediately. In an actual slideshow, however, it waits until the next object enters.

Repeat these steps until you've applied the effect to all the text you want to dim. To test that dimming works the way you want it to, take a look at the slide in Reading or Slide Show view.

Tip: Dimming works great when you're animating a bulleted or numbered list. Page 651 shows you how to animate a list so that each item on the list enters separately.

> ⟩ Dimmed text
>
> ⟩ Dimmed text
>
> ⟩ **Text of current topic**

Figure 23-13:
Dim previously discussed text to keep the focus on the current topic.

Note: If you *really* want to focus the audience's attention, use the "After animation" drop-down menu to make the previous object disappear when the next object enters or when you click the mouse. Choose Hide After Animation or Hide on Next Mouse Click.

Animating paragraphs and words

When you animate a text box, the text inside that box usually enters all at once. So if you have a short paragraph, for example, that's flying in from the left, the whole paragraph flies in together. If you'd rather have the text enter word by word or even letter by letter, select the animated text box and open the Additional Effect Options dialog box (Figure 23-12) by clicking Animations→Show Additional Effect Options (Alt, A, M).

In the dialog box, go to the "Animate text" drop-down list and select one of these options:

- **By word.** The text enters one word at a time.
- **By letter.** The text enters one letter at a time.

When you select one of these options, you activate the "% delay between words" (or "letters", depending on your choice) drop-down list. The default is 10, which makes the words or letters enter pretty fast. You can make the entrance a little quicker by choosing a smaller number or stretch it out by choosing a larger number. Click OK to apply the animation to your selected text.

Adding More Animation

You can apply more than one animation to an object. For example, you might want to have an object fly in from the left side when it enters and fly off to the right side when it exits. Or a picture might enter by fading in and, later, follow a motion path to move over and make room for the next picture that enters.

To add more animation to an animated object, select the object and then choose Animations→Add Animation (Alt, A, AA). This opens a menu of animations like the one shown in Figure 23-11. Click the animation you want, and PowerPoint adds it to the animations for your selected object.

WORKAROUND WORKSHOP

Dimming a Photo with Animation

The Dim effect that you can apply from the Additional Effect Options dialog box (Figure 23-12) works for text, but not for photos or other images. If you want to apply a dimming effect to a photo, you've got to get a little creative with your animation. Here's how:

1. Insert the photo you're going to dim on a slide. Select the photo and press Ctrl+C to make a copy of it. Press Ctrl+V to paste that copy onto the same slide.

2. The pasted copy appears on top of the original. Move it so that it lines up precisely on top of the original. With the copy selected, go to Picture Tools | Format→Color (Alt, JP, I). From the menu that opens, select a dimmer version of the photo.

3. Now it's time to animate the dimming effect. With the dimmed photo selected, go to the Animations tab and choose an entrance effect for the dimmed photo. Fade and Dissolve In are both good options for this effect. Because the dimmed photo is on top of the original, it hides the original when it enters.

4. Click the Preview button to see how the animation looks. Test out how it will look in a slideshow by switching to Reading or Slide Show view.

You can get fancier with the animation if you like. For example, you might have the original photo exit by dissolving or fading out at the same time the dimmed photo enters.

Note: PowerPoint assigns an order to the animations on a slide based on the order you apply those animations. So the first animation you apply is the first animation to happen on the slide, the next animation you apply comes second, and so on. To change this order, use the Animation pane. Page 648 tells you how.

Creating a Motion Path

A *motion path* moves an object from one part of the slide to another. So you could have an object—say a picture or some text—appear in the center of the slide and then move to the side when the next object appears. Motion paths come in all shapes, from a straight line or simple arc to spirals, S-curves, waves, figure 8s, and zigzags. And if you don't find a predesigned motion path that moves your object in exactly the way you want, you can choose something close and tweak it as you like.

You apply a motion path to an object the same way you apply any other kind of animation: Select the object and, from the Animations tab's animation gallery, select the motion path you want—you've got dozens of options to choose from. PowerPoint shows you a preview of the path and draws a line to indicate the path on the working version of the slide, as shown in Figure 23-14.

The motion path arrow has two heads: green to indicate the object's starting point and red to show where the object ends up. The line that connects the arrows shows the shape of the path the object takes.

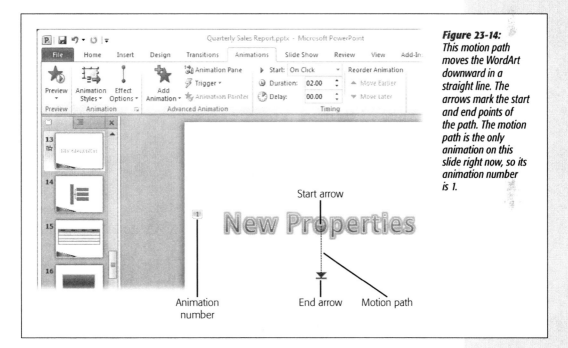

Figure 23-14:
This motion path moves the WordArt downward in a straight line. The arrows mark the start and end points of the path. The motion path is the only animation on this slide right now, so its animation number is 1.

You can tweak a motion path in these ways:

- **To change the length of the path,** hover your mouse pointer over the motion path's red arrow. When the pointer becomes a two-headed arrow, click and drag to lengthen or shorten the path.

- **To move the path's end point,** hover over the red arrow to make the pointer a two-way arrow. Click and drag the red arrowhead to its new location.

- **To change the direction of a motion path,** select Animations→Effect Options (Alt, A, O). A menu opens, showing the direction options for the path. If you want to reverse the direction of the motion path, making the green and red arrows switch places, choose Reverse Path Direction (Alt, A, O, R).

- **To change the shape of a motion path,** select Animations→Effect Options→Edit Points (Alt, A, O, E). When you do, handles appear along the motion path—the more complex the path, the more handles. Click and drag a handle to change the shape of the path.

Triggering an Animation

An *animation trigger* is an object on the screen that causes something to happen when you click it. For example, a slide might show a list of different products. When you click the name of a product (the trigger), a picture of that product appears.

To add an animation trigger, you need two things: an animated object and another object to trigger the animation. The trigger might be some text, for example, and the animated object a picture that enters the slide when you click the trigger. Figure 23-15 shows an example.

Figure 23-15:
Click the Trigger button (circled) and select "On Click of" to see a fly-out menu of objects you can use to trigger an animation. In this example, clicking the text will cause the picture to enter by zooming in.

When you've got the animated object and its trigger in place, follow these steps to make the trigger start the animation:

1. **Select Animations→Trigger→"On Click of"** (Alt, A, AT, C).

   A flyout menu lists the objects on your slide. Objects are numbered according to the order in which you put them on the slide.

2. **Choose the object that will serve as the trigger—when you click that object, the animation happens.**

   PowerPoint makes the object you chose the animation's trigger. You can tell an animation has a trigger because its number changes to a lightning-bolt icon.

To test the animation, switch to Reading or Slide Show view. When you point at the trigger, the mouse pointer becomes a hand. Click to see if the animation does what you want it to.

Tip: Here's an impressive effect: Use a bookmark in a media file—a video or audio clip—to trigger an animation. First add a bookmark to the media clip (page 634 tells you how to do that). Then select the animated object that the bookmark will trigger. Select Animations→Trigger→On Bookmark (Alt, A, AT, B). A menu opens listing bookmarks in the media clip. Select the one you want as a trigger. During playback, when the clip reaches the bookmark, it starts the animation. Kind of like the "Pow!" "Bam!" "Biff!" that zoomed in during fights in the old *Batman* TV show.

Timing Animations

Normally, the way you start an animation is to click the mouse. If you've got multiple animations, the first one happens with the first mouse click, the second one happens with the second mouse click, and so on. And that works fine for many purposes.

But sometimes you want more complex animation. Maybe you'd like to see the title fly in from the top at the same time a picture flies in from the bottom. Or you'd like to have a picture of a customer appear, followed a second later by a thought bubble.

You can achieve these and other effects by setting your animations' timing. You do this in the Animations tab's Timing section, using these options:

- **Start (Alt, A, T).** Use this drop-down list to choose when you want the animation to start:
  - **On Click.** This is the default option. The animation waits until you click the mouse.
  - **With Previous.** When you choose this option, the animation happens concurrently with the previous animation, no mouse click needed. If the animation is the first one on the slide, it happens automatically when the slide opens.
  - **After Previous.** This option automatically starts the animation after the previous animation has occurred. How long after depends on the Delay setting.
- **Duration (Alt, A, DU).** Use this setting to speed up or slow down an animation. Choose a number, in seconds, to specify how long the animation lasts. So for an image that fades in, for example, a duration of 00.50 means that it takes half a second for the image to fully appear. A duration of 01.00 means a slower fade-in, taking a full second.

- **Delay (Alt, A, DE).** This setting specifies, in seconds, how long PowerPoint waits before the animation happens.

Select the object whose timing you're adjusting, and then pick the settings you want.

Reordering Animations

PowerPoint keeps track of animations in the order you create them and plays them in that order. Say you have a slide with a title, a line of text, and two pictures. If you animate the title first, then picture 1, then the text, and then picture 2, that's the order PowerPoint uses to play the animations when it's showtime.

Note: When you select the Animations tab, animation numbers appear on the slide to show the animation sequence; click any number to select that animation.

Now imagine that when you preview the slide's animation, you decide you want the text to appear *before* picture 1, not after. To swap the orders of these animations, select one of the objects whose animation you want to reorder. On the right side of the Animations tab is the Reorder Animation section; click Move Earlier (Alt, A, E) or Move Later (Alt, A, L) to change when the animation occurs relative to other animations on the slide. When you do, the animation numbers of the affected objects change. If you need to move the animation by several places, keep clicking the button until you've got it positioned where you want it.

Tip: For a slide with a lot of animations, you may find it easier to reorder animations using the Animation pane, described below.

Removing an Animation

To remove an animation from an object, select it and then open the Animations tab. In the Animations gallery (Alt, A, S), select None. (It's the very first animation in the gallery.) The object is now animation-free.

Note: If an object has multiple animations, selecting None removes them all. If you want to zap just one animation from the object but leave the others in place, use the Animation pane (explained in the next section).

Using the Animation Pane

If you've worked with earlier versions of PowerPoint, you're already familiar with the Animation pane, shown in Figure 23-16. Click Animations→Animation Pane (Alt, A, C) to open it. As you add animations to a slide, the Animation pane lists them, in order. This is extremely helpful when you have complex animations, because you get an overview of all of them: What they are, their order, and any effects you've applied. Click an animation to select it. When you do, a drop-down arrow appears to its right. Click this arrow to open a menu of animation effects and options.

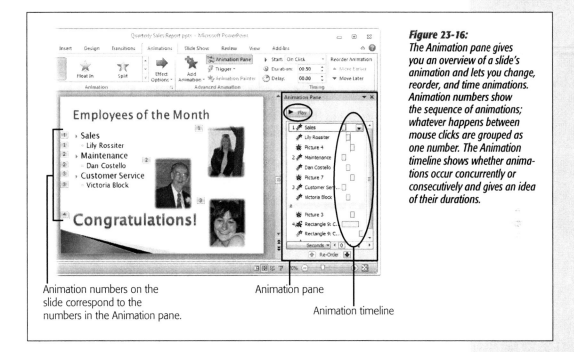

Figure 23-16:
The Animation pane gives you an overview of a slide's animation and lets you change, reorder, and time animations. Animation numbers show the sequence of animations; whatever happens between mouse clicks are grouped as one number. The Animation timeline shows whether animations occur concurrently or consecutively and gives an idea of their durations.

Animation numbers on the slide correspond to the numbers in the Animation pane.

Animation pane

Animation timeline

Here's what you can do in the Animation pane:

- **View a timeline of animations.** To the right of each animation, a block appears. This block represents when the animation starts and how long it lasts. If an animation begins with the previous animation, its block appears underneath the previous animation's block; if the animation appears after the previous animation, its block is indented. The wider the block, the longer the animation's duration.

Tip: If you don't need to see animation starts and durations, then select any animation and click its drop-down arrow. From the menu that appears, select Hide Advanced Timeline. To bring the timeline back, click a drop-down arrow, and then select Show Advanced Timeline.

- **Change an animation.** Select the animation you want to change. PowerPoint shows it in the Animations tab's animation gallery. Select a different animation from the gallery, and PowerPoint applies it to the object.

- **Reorder animations.** Select the animation you want to move, and click the up and down arrows at the bottom of the pane to change its order in the animation sequence.

- **Change when the animation starts.** Select an animation and click its drop-down arrow. From the menu that opens, select when you want the animation to begin: on click, with the previous animation, or after the previous animation.

- **Apply effect options.** Click an animation's drop-down arrow and choose Effect Options to open the options dialog box for that effect (like the one back in Figure 23-12).

- **Adjust an effect's timing.** When you click an animation's drop-down arrow and select Timing, the options dialog box opens to the Timing tab, shown in Figure 23-17. Change when the animation starts, its delay before starting, or how long it lasts. If you want the animation to repeat, use the Repeat drop-down list to play the animation a set number of times, until the next click, or until you advance to the next slide. You can also select an animation trigger on this tab.

- **Preview animations.** Click the Play button at the top of the animation pane to see your animations in action. As the animation proceeds on the slide, the pane highlights which animation or group of animations is happening, and a vertical line measures the duration of each.

- **Remove an animation.** If you don't like a particular animation, select it, click its drop-down arrow, and then click Remove.

Keeping the Animation pane open as you work helps you keep track of complex animations-in-progress. When you're done applying and fine-tuning your animations, close the Animation pane by clicking its upper-right X or toggle it off by clicking the Animations tab's Animation Pane button (Alt, A, C).

Figure 23-17:
The Timing tab of an effect's options box lets you set the start and duration of an effect or choose a trigger for the animation. You can also have the effect repeat here.

Animating Lists

When you animate a bulleted or numbered list, you probably want the list items to enter one at a time, so you can discuss each item at the appropriate moment in your presentation. PowerPoint makes doing that a breeze. When you select a list to animate, PowerPoint assumes that you want the list items to enter one at a time.

To make this happen, first create a list and then select its text box. On the Animation pane, find and apply the entrance animation you want (Alt, A, S, or Alt, A, S, E for a menu of all entrance effects). PowerPoint applies the animation and puts an animation number next to each item on the list, showing the order in which items will enter.

Adjusting animation for individual list items

When you apply animation to a list, PowerPoint gives each item on the list the same animation. If you want to give different list items different effects, open the Animation pane (Figure 23-16). Here the animations list shows only the first animation in the sequence. Click the expansion arrow just below that animation to see each item in the sequence. Now you can select any list item and adjust its animation effects individually.

Giving subitems their own animation

If a list has subitems, such as subbullets indented under a main bullet, PowerPoint treats those subbullets as part of the main bullet. When you animate the list, the subbullets enter with the main bullet they belong to.

To break up this unit and have subbullets enter one by one, open the Animation pane (Figure 23-16). Expand the list animation if necessary. Click the first subbullet to select it. On the menu that opens, Start With Previous is selected. Change this setting to Start On Click.

PowerPoint assigns the subbullet its own animation number. Now, during a slideshow, the subbullet won't enter until you click the mouse. Repeat the process for any other subbullets you want to enter separately.

Tip: Here's another way to animate a list's subitems separately. Select the list and then, in the Animations tab's Animations section, click the lower-right Show Additional Effect Options button (Alt, A, M). In the dialog box that opens, click the Text Animation tab. From the "Group text" drop-down list, select "By 2nd Level Paragraphs". (If your list has lots of subbullet levels, you can choose a deeper level—all the way up to fifth.) Click OK. This breaks up the list for animations at the level you chose.

Animating a list as a single block of text

You might want a list to act as a single block of text, rather than a collection of separate items. Maybe you're repeating a list that appeared earlier for emphasis, for example, and you don't need the teaser of one-item-at-a-time entry.

To make a list enter all at once, animate the list and then select the text box that contains it. On the Animations tab, click Effect Options (Alt, A, O). In the menu that opens, find the Sequence section (depending on the animation you've chosen, you may have to scroll down to find it). Select As One Object: PowerPoint "glues" the list together, treating all its lines as a single object.

Stacking Objects

A slide can easily get crowded, especially when you've got a number of different images or graphics to support five or six different points on a bulleted list. Instead of trying to cram all the different images onto the slide, you can stack them up. When a new image enters, it covers the previous one. (Or you can have the previous image exit as the new one comes on the slide—for example, you can have the new object fly in from the left while the previous object flies out to the right.) Stacking objects maximizes your use of slide real estate. And it looks cool, too.

To animate and stack objects, insert the first object (say it's a photo) onto the slide and add its animation effects, such as its entrance and exit effects. Then insert the next photo and apply its animations. Drag the second photo on top of the first; the new photo will cover the old one. Repeat the process until you've animated and stacked all the photos you plan to use on this slide.

Use the Animations tab (Alt, A) or the Animation pane (Alt, A, C) to reorder and time animations as necessary. For example, you'll probably want to time animations so that the new animation enters as the old one exits.

If you need to change the position of an object in the stack, right-click the object and select Bring to Front, Bring Forward, Send to Back, or Send Backward. These options also appear on the contextual Format tabs (Picture Tools | Format; Drawing Tools | Format; Video Tools | Format; and so on).

Tip: When you've got a bunch of objects all stacked up, it can be hard to select and work with an object at the bottom or in the middle of the pile. In that situation, the Tab key is your friend. Pressing Tab cycles through all the objects on your slide, selecting them one by one. That way you can find the object you're looking for without messing up the stack.

Animating SmartArt Graphics

SmartArt graphics are designed for high impact. You can make them even more impressive by animating them. Just like a bulleted list, SmartArt can be broken up and animated in separate segments. So you can serve up a pie chart one slice at a time, for example, or animate a process diagram to bring its steps to life. Here's how:

1. **Click the SmartArt graphic to select it. Go to the Animations tab's Animations section (Alt, A, S) and select the animation you want to apply.**

   PowerPoint applies the animation and shows you a preview.

2. Next, with the SmartArt still selected, click the Animations tab's Effect Options button (Alt, A, O).

   A menu appears, showing these sequence options:

   — **As One Object (N).** This option animates all elements of the SmartArt in the same way and makes them happen at the same time.

   — **All at Once (A).** This option breaks the SmartArt into separate elements (pieces in a pie chart, for example). It animates all those elements in the same way and makes them happen at the same time. But because Power-Point treats each part of your diagram as its own, separate element, you can open the Animation pane (click Animations→Animation Pane or press Alt, A, C) and apply whatever entrances and timings you want.

   — **One by One (Y).** Choose this option to break the SmartArt into separate elements, apply the same animation to each, but have the animations happen consecutively. Open the Animation pane to adjust these animations.

3. Select the option you want.

   PowerPoint adjusts your SmartArt animation accordingly.

If you select All at Once or One by One, you can open the Animation pane and tweak or reorder animations as you wish.

Creating Transitions Between Slides

Out with the old and in with the new! Transitions add pizzazz to the movement from one slide to the next, giving your presentation another level of polish. Without transitions, slides blink out and blink in on a mouse click. Bo-o-o-o-ring. When you select a transition, you can have the incoming slide push the outgoing one out of the way or wipe it from the screen. Transitions makes slides ripple, flash, glitter, shred, flip, or appear from and disappear into a vortex. They're a fun way to catch the audience's eye when a new slide comes on the scene.

Adding a Transition

You apply a transition to the slide that's *entering;* the transition tells it how to come onto the screen. To add a transition to a slide, just go to the Transitions tab, shown in Figure 23-18, and choose what you want from the transition gallery (Alt, K, T). When you select a style, PowerPoint applies it to the slide and shows you a preview. (To see it again, click the Preview button or press Alt, K, P).

Tip: If you've set up a transition you like for a slide—and adjusted its effect options and duration to get them just right—you can apply that transition to all slides in the presentation. Select the slide with the transition you want, and then click Transitions→Apply to All (Alt, K, L). With that one click, PowerPoint gives all the slides in your presentation the exact same transition.

See a transition in action

Transition gallery

Click here to see more transition styles.

Create automatic, timed transitions here.

Northeast Developments

Figure 23-18:
The Transitions tab displays a gallery of transition styles, which govern how a slideshow moves from one slide to the next. Click the More button (circled) to open a menu of even more transitions. PowerPoint 2010 has some new transitions, like Vortex, Ripple, Switch, and Ferris Wheel, so check them out.

Tweaking Transition Effects

The Effect Options button works the same way for transitions as it does for animations. Apply a transition to a slide, and then click Transitions→Effect Options (Alt, K, O). The menu that appears shows the options available for the kind of transition you're using. For example, if you're using a Push transition, in which the new slide appears to push the previous slide out of the way, Effect Options let you specify whether you want the new slide to push its way in from the left, right, bottom, or top.

Adding Sound to a Transition

Transitions can play a sound as they switch from one slide to the next. You could have a cash register ring when the slide with quarterly profits appears, for example, or applause for a slide naming the employee of the month. Cute.

To add a sound to a slide's transition, go to the Transitions tab's Timing section and then click the Sound drop-down list (Alt, K, U). Choose the sound you want from the list (click Other Sound at the bottom of the list to see more). If you want the sound to keep playing until another sound takes its place (such as a sound that plays when the next slide enters), then turn on Loop Until Next Sound at the bottom of the menu.

Timing Transitions

There are two ways you can time the transitions between your slides, both on the Transitions tab:

- **Duration (Alt, K, E).** This setting determines how long the transition takes to move, in seconds, from one slide to the next. You can stick with PowerPoint's default, which varies according to the transition, or adjust the time yourself.

- **Advance Slide.** In this section, you tell PowerPoint how to move to the next slide (the one *after* the selected slide). The default setting is On Mouse Click (Alt, K, M)—PowerPoint waits for your go-ahead (in the form of a mouse click) before it advances to the next slide. If you want the transition to happen automatically, turn of the On Mouse Click checkbox and turn on the After checkbox (Alt, K, F). Then tell PowerPoint how long to wait before it moves on to the next slide.

It's Showtime! Giving a Presentation

This book can't get up on stage for you, but this chapter can certainly help—it's all about setting up, practicing, and delivering a slideshow.

If you've never given a PowerPoint presentation before, you'll learn basics like launching the show, moving through its slides, and drawing the virtual curtain. But even if you're a slide deck veteran, there's plenty here to help avoid the dreaded Death by PowerPoint: how to rehearse and check a presentation's timing, how to record narration, and how to make sure your slides looks good on the big screen. And if you give different versions of the same talk to different groups, this chapter will show you how to generate custom presentations from a single, master file.

You may also be surprised to learn how many options you have for delivering a slideshow that don't involve you standing in front of a group of people. PowerPoint makes it easy to create a kiosk-style show that runs by itself or an interactive show that viewers play on their own, at their own pace. And new in PowerPoint 2010, you can broadcast your slideshow online or turn it into a video, which you can then put on a website or burn to a DVD. You've got tons of options, and this chapter covers them all.

Start, Navigate, End: Tips and Shortcuts

Before you find yourself in front of an audience, muttering about how to get your slideshow going, make sure you're familiar with how to launch the darn thing and move through its slides. When you've got that down, you can practice your timing and double-check animations, transitions, and media clips.

Starting a Slideshow

Start the slideshow by using either of these methods:

- Select Slide Show→From Beginning (Alt, S, B).

- Select the presentation's first slide, and then click the status bar's Slide Show button.

Tip: You can start a slideshow from any slide. Select the one you want to start with and then click Slide Show→Current Slide (Alt, S, C) or click Slide Show on the status bar.

PowerPoint opens the presentation in Slide Show view. Here, a slide takes up nearly the full screen. There's not a tab or a toolbar in sight—just the first slide of your presentation and some nearly-invisible slide controls, as you can (just about) see in Figure 24-1.

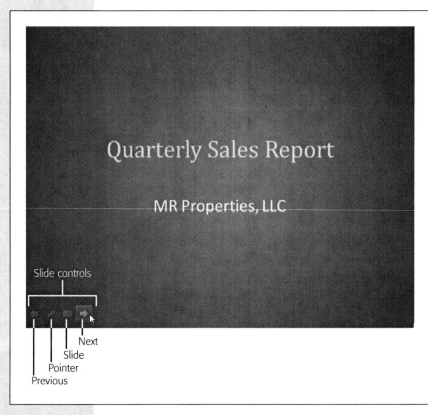

Figure 24-1:
Here's a title slide in action. Move the mouse pointer to the lower-left part of the screen to use the presentation's slide controls.

Moving From Slide to Slide

Depending on your presentation's animations, (page 638), its transitions (page 653), and their settings, you can click the mouse to move through each slide's animation sequence. Then, when you've gone through all animations on a slide, clicking the mouse advances to the next slide. If you've made animations and transitions automatic, however, the slideshow progresses on its own as soon as you launch it.

Note: If you've added action buttons (page 611) to your slides, you can click those to move through the presentation.

In addition, you can always count on these navigation methods:

- **Click the Next button.** The lower-left section of each slide has four buttons—Previous, Pointer, Slide, and Next—but you might not realize they're there unless you look for them. (More on what the Slide button does in the next bullet point; see page 672 for details on the pointer.) Move the mouse pointer toward a slide's lower-left corner, and the buttons appear. Click the right-pointing Next arrow to advance to the next slide.

- **Click the Slide button, and then select Next.** This button opens a menu, shown in Figure 24-2, that lets you jump to any slide in the presentation.

- **Right-click anywhere on the screen, and then select Next.** When you right-click during a slideshow, PowerPoint opens the same menu that appears when you click the lower-left Slide button. Choose Next to move to the next slide.

- **Use a keyboard shortcut.** You don't need a mouse to navigate a slideshow. In Slide Show view, PowerPoint gives you multiple navigation options using the keyboard. To advance, you can press N (for Next), the space bar, Enter, Page Down, the down arrow key, or the right arrow key—all of 'em take you to the next slide. Table 24-1 lists all the keyboard shortcuts you can use during a slideshow.

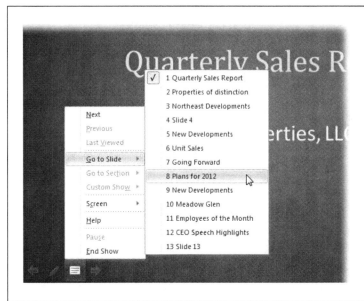

Figure 24-2:
When you click the Slide button or right-click anywhere on a slide, a shortcut menu appears. Select Go to Slide for a fly-out menu that lets you choose the slide you want to jump to. Find any slide by its number or title (if it has one).

Note: If your slides have animations that are triggered by a click, any of the methods just listed will move through the animation sequence before advancing to the next slide.

Table 24-1. Keyboard shortcuts for navigating a slideshow

To do this	Press one of these keys or keystroke combinations
Advance to the next slide	N, space bar, Enter, Page Down, ↓, or →
Return to the previous slide	P, Backspace, Page Up, ↑, or ←
Jump to a specific slide	Press Ctrl+S to open the All Slides dialog box, choose a slide from the list, and then press Alt+G. Or press a slide number and then press Enter.
Jump to the presentation's first slide	Home
Jump to the presentation's final slide	End
End the presentation	Esc, hyphen (-), or Ctrl+Break

Ending a Slideshow

When you reach the last slide, click one final time. The screen goes black, with this message at the top: "End of slideshow, click to exit." Why'd Microsoft include this? To spare you from the rookie maneuver of baring your presentation file's innards to your audience. Now you can wait till the resident techie (or you) unplugs your laptop from the projector and *then* click the exit prompt. When you do so, PowerPoint ends the slideshow and returns you to Normal view. (Pressing any of the keyboard shortcuts to advance to the next slide does the same thing.)

You can also end the slideshow at any point by using one of these methods:

* Click the lower-left Slide button, and then select End Show.
* Right-click anywhere on the screen, and then select End Show.
* Press Esc, the hyphen key (-), or Ctrl+Break.

That's it—show's over. PowerPoint takes you back to Normal view.

Before the Show: Prep Work

Remember this corny old joke:

> "Excuse me, how do I get to Carnegie Hall?"

> "Practice, practice, practice."

That punch line is also the answer to the question of how to give a good PowerPoint presentation. The more you rehearse ahead of time, the better things will go when you do the show for real.

Here's another benefit to rehearsing: You can time it. If you've got only half an hour for your talk, you don't want to find yourself barely halfway through the slides at the

27-minute mark. By rehearsing ahead of time, you can streamline a long presentation—or flesh out a short one.

During rehearsal, you're not the only one who's working. PowerPoint records how much time you spend on each slide and how long it takes to get through the entire presentation. You can use this info to adjust your presentation or to use the timings for a slideshow that runs automatically, without any clicks or other input. (To see how to set up an auto-run slideshow, flip to page 678.)

Tip: Have ready the notes you'll use when giving the presentation for real. And ask a colleague, friend, or family member to serve as your practice audience. They can give you feedback on the presentation, and their reactions will help with your timing.

To test out a practice run-through, open the presentation, take a deep breath, and then follow these steps:

1. **In the Slide Show tab's Set Up section, click the Rehearse Timings button (Alt, S, T).**

   PowerPoint immediately opens the presentation in Slide Show view and starts recording using the Recording toolbar, shown in Figure 24-3. The Recording toolbar appears in the upper-left corner. It includes a timer that tracks how much time is passing, as well as these buttons:

   — **Next.** Click this button to go to the next slide. When you use this button to advance from one slide to the next, PowerPoint notes how much time you spent on each slide.

   — **Pause Recording.** If you need to take a break from the presentation—maybe the phone's ringing or you need more coffee—click this button. When you do, a dialog box (Figure 24-3) appears to let you know recording has paused. When you're ready to continue, click Resume Recording to start the timer ticking again.

   — **Repeat.** If you make a mistake, you don't have to start all over again from the beginning. Click this button, and the recorded time for the current slide resets to 0:00:00 (but there's no effect on the recorded time for the slides you've already done), so you can give it another go.

2. **Click Next whenever you're ready to move forward in the presentation by activating an animation or making a transition to the next slide.**

   As you practice, try not to get distracted by the ticking timer. Focus on your notes, make sure the animations and transitions are working as you expect, and look at the Recording toolbar only when it's time to click the Next button. Make the practice presentation as much like the real thing as you can. If you plan to pause and ask for questions before moving on, for example, allow time for that. And don't forget to leave plenty of time for the audience to crack up over your jokes.

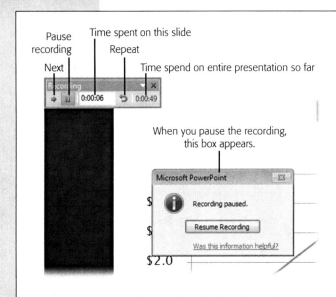

Pause recording

Next

Repeat

Time spent on this slide

Time spend on entire presentation so far

When you pause the recording, this box appears.

Figure 24-3:
The Recording toolbar keeps track of your timing as you practice a presentation. Use its buttons to start on-click animations and advance to the next slide. If you pause while recording, a dialog box opens so you can start again when you're ready.

3. **To end the presentation, click the final slide or press Esc.**

   PowerPoint displays a dialog box showing the time recorded for the entire presentation and asks whether you want to keep the slide timings it recorded when you view the slideshow.

4. **Choose one of these options:**

   — **Yes.** When you click Yes, PowerPoint saves the timings it recorded for each slide. To see how long you spent on a slide, look at the presentation in Slide Sorter view; the recorded time for a slide appears below it on the left.

   — **No.** Click No if you don't want to save the times recorded for this run-through.

   After you've finished your rehearsal, PowerPoint returns you to the view you were in before you began the slideshow.

If you save rehearsed timings, PowerPoint assumes you want to use those timings when giving the presentation. That means when you launch the slideshow, the Power-Point timer starts ticking again. You can advance slides by clicking the mouse, but if you don't, PowerPoint moves forward for you, using the recorded timings.

If you've saved rehearsal timings and *don't* want PowerPoint to advance automatically in this way, go to the Slide Show tab and turn off the Use Timings checkbox (Alt, S, U toggles it off and on). To clear recorded timings entirely, go to the Slide Show tab and, in the Set Up section, click the Record Slide Show button's down arrow (Alt, S, N). From the menu that appears, select Clear→Clear Timing on All Slides (C, A).

Adding Narration to Your Presentation

In PowerPoint, *narration* is an audio recording that plays automatically when a new slide opens. Most commonly, narrations provide commentary for a self-running, kiosk-style slideshow (page 678) or an interactive, user-run slideshow (page 680). PowerPoint 2010 simplifies the audio recording process; in fact, it's a lot like rehearsing slide timings (see previous section), but instead of talking to yourself, you speak into a microphone and record your words.

Tip: If you want to include audio in a presentation that you give live before an audience, your best bet is to record and insert an audio clip. Unlike narration, which plays automatically, audio clips start when you tell them to play, so you retain control over the slideshow's flow. Page 628 has the full scoop on audio clips.

Recording a narration

First you need to connect a microphone to your computer or use its built-in mic, if you've got one. (You can adjust the microphone's settings through the Windows Control Panel.) When you're ready to record, open the presentation and follow these steps:

1. **Select Slide Show→Record Slide Show (Alt, S, N).**

   The Record Slide Show dialog box, shown in Figure 24-4, opens, giving you these options:

   — **Slide and animation timings** records how long you spend on each slide, including each slide's animations. Saving these timings lets the slideshow play on its own—PowerPoint knows when to start the next animation or advance to the next slide.

   — **Narrations and laser pointer** records your voice as you speak about each slide and anything you highlight with the PowerPoint laser pointer. Use the laser pointer (more on that in a moment) to call attention to different parts of the slide as your narration speaks about them.

2. **Make sure the checkboxes for the options you want are on. (If you're recording the presentation to use at a kiosk or to turn into a movie, turn both on.) Click Start Recording.**

   The slideshow begins with your first slide. The Recording toolbar (Figure 24-3) appears in the upper-left corner, just like when you rehearse timings. An audio icon appears in the lower-right corner to indicate that you're recording sound. Speak into the microphone to record your narration. If you want to emphasize something on the slide using a laser-pointer effect, click your mouse while pressing the Ctrl key. A red dot appears onscreen, resembling a laser pointer's beam hitting the slide. Keep holding down the Ctrl key, and you can drag the dot around the screen.

Tip: If you want to start recording at a point *other than* the beginning, here's how to start recording: First, select the slide you want to begin with. Then, go to the Slide Show tab, click the Record Slide Show button's down arrow, and select Start Recording from Current Slide (Alt, S, N, R). PowerPoint opens the Record Slide Show dialog box (Figure 24-4); when you click Start Recording, PowerPoint starts the slideshow on your selected slide.

3. **Go through your presentation, saying what you want to record for each slide. Use the Recording toolbar's Next, Pause Recording, and Repeat buttons as you would when rehearsing timings. If you trip over your tongue while narrating a slide, press Pause Recording to start over again with that slide. When you're done, press Esc.**

Tip: If you're narrating a long presentation and need to take a break, press Esc to finish recording for now. When you're ready to record again, start with the first slide after the one where you took your break.

PowerPoint ends the slideshow, saves your recording, and applies it to your slides. Any slide that has a narration attached to it displays an audio icon in the lower-right corner.

Tip: PowerPoint treats your recorded narrations as animations. To adjust a narration's effect options or to change its order in a slide's animation sequence, open the Animation pane (page 648) and work with it there. Instead of beginning narration as soon as the slide opens, you can start it after a delay, for example, on a mouse click, or on a trigger (page 646).

Figure 24-4:
To attach a recording of your own voice, make sure the checkbox labeled "Narrations and laser pointer timing" is on. If you want the slides to advance automatically, turn on the "Slide and animation timings" checkbox, too.

Playing back a narrated slideshow

To see—and hear—how the recording turned out, head for the Slide Show tab. In the Set Up section, make sure the Play Narration (Alt, S, P) and the Use Timings checkboxes (Alt, S, U) are both on. Then click the From Beginning button (Alt, S, B) to watch and listen to the presentation as you've recorded it.

If the narration on one slide doesn't sound right to your ears, you can record another take. In Normal or Slide Sorter view, select the slide you want to do over and clear its audio: On the Slide Show tab, click the Record Slide Show button's down arrow and select Clear→Clear Narration on Current Slide (Alt, S, N, C, N). Next, with the slide still selected, click the Record Slide Show button's down arrow again and select "Start

Recording from Current Slide". In the Record Slide Show dialog box (Figure 24-4), tell PowerPoint you want to record both the narrations and the timings, to make sure your narration stays in sync with what's happening on the slide.

As you record, the new recording overwrites the previous one. When you're done, *don't* move to the next slide, or you'll overwrite its recordings, too. Instead, when you're done with the slide you're re-recording, press Esc.

Turning off narration

If you don't want narrations to play during a slideshow, you have these options:

- **Turn off narration for this slideshow.** On the Slide Show tab, turn off the Play Narrations checkbox (Alt, S, P toggles it off and on). This keeps narrations as part of the presentation but silences them when you start a slideshow.

- **Remove narration from a slide.** Select the slide (or group of slides) whose narration you want to delete. On the Slide Show tab, click the Record Slide Show button's down arrow, and then select Clear→Clear Narration on Current Slide (Alt, S, C, N) to remove the narration.

- **Get rid of narrations.** To remove narrations completely from your presentation, open the Slide Show tab, click the Record Slide Show button's down arrow, and then select Clear→Clear Narrations on All Slides (Alt, S, C, A). No more narrations on any slide in the presentation.

Creating a Custom Slideshow

A single presentation can serve more than one purpose. For example, you might have a short and a long version of the same slideshow. PowerPoint lets you pick and choose the slides you want in each version, and you can create as many custom slideshows as you want from a single "parent" presentation.

Start by opening the presentation you want to use as the basis for the new custom version, and then follow these steps:

1. **On the Slide Show tab, click Custom Slide Show→Custom Shows (Alt, S, M, W).**

   The Custom Shows dialog box, shown in Figure 24-5, opens. After you've created a custom show or two, they appear in a list here.

2. **Click the New button.**

   This opens the Define Custom Show dialog box, shown in Figure 24-6. The left side displays a list of all the slides in your presentation. On the right is a box that lists the slides in the custom show as you create it.

3. **Start by naming your custom slideshow in the "Slide show name" text box. In the left-hand "Slides in presentation" box, select a slide that you want in the custom presentation. (You can use the Shift and Ctrl keys to select multiple slides.) Click Add.**

   The selected slide appears in the right-hand "Slides in custom show" box.

4. **Continue picking slides and adding them to your custom show.**

   As you work, you can remove any slide from your custom show by selecting it in the right-hand list and then clicking the Remove button. Change the slide order by using the up and down arrows to the right of the custom list.

5. **When you're done creating and organizing the custom presentation, click OK.**

Figure 24-5:
When you want to create or work with a custom version of a slideshow, open this box. You can launch, edit, copy, or delete custom shows from here.

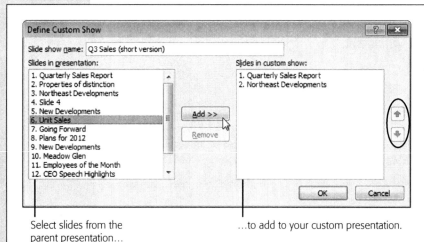

Figure 24-6:
Choose the slides you want from the parent presentation, and add them to a custom version. Use the up and down arrows (circled) to rearrange slides within the custom show.

Select slides from the parent presentation…

…to add to your custom presentation.

After you've put together a special edition of your show, you can work with it in these ways:

• **Open it.** To find a custom show you've created, open the parent presentation (the one from which you created the custom show) and select Slide Show→Custom Slide Show. On the menu that appears, look for the custom slideshow you want; if it's there, select it. If you've saved a lot of custom shows and you don't see the one you're looking for on that menu, select Custom Shows to open the Custom Shows dialog box (Figure 24-5). Find the show you want in the list, select it, and then click Show. Your custom show opens in Slide Show view.

- **Edit it.** To add, remove, or reorganize the slides in a custom slideshow, open the Custom Shows box (Figure 24-5), select your show, and then click the Edit button. This opens the Define Custom Show dialog box (Figure 24-6) for that show. Make the changes you want; when you're finished, click OK to save them.

Note: If you want to make changes to a slide's content, change the slide in the parent presentation. Any change you make there affects all custom slideshows associated with the parent presentation.

- **Copy it.** To make an exact copy of a custom presentation, open the Custom Shows box (Figure 24-5), select the custom show you want to duplicate, and then click the Copy button. PowerPoint adds this new version to the list, with a name that begins "Copy of". If you want, select the copy and then click Edit to customize it further.

- **Delete it.** If you're finished with a custom slideshow and won't need it again, you can remove it from your list of custom shows. In the Custom Shows dialog box (Figure 24-5), select the show you want to get rid of and click Remove.

Creating a Handout

Whether you give them out before, during, or after your slideshow, handouts are a great way to help an audience remember your main points. If you plan to give people printed handouts, PowerPoint works with Word to create them. Select File→Share→Create Handouts (Alt, F, H, H). On the page that opens is a Create Handouts button; click that (or press A if you've got keyboard shortcuts turned on).

PowerPoint opens the Send To Microsoft Word dialog box, shown in Figure 24-7. This dialog box shows a variety of layouts for your handout, each illustrated with an example. You can print one or more slides on a page, along with your presentation's notes or blank lines for audience members to write their own notes. Turn on the radio button of the layout you want, and choose one of these options:

- **Paste.** This pastes an image of each slide into the Word document.

- **Paste link.** When you choose this option, each slide image in the Word document is also a link to that slide in the PowerPoint presentation. You might choose this if you're putting your presentation and the handout on a website.

Click OK, and your presentation opens as a Word document. Now you can edit, format, and print the document in Word.

Note: Turning your presentation into a Word document and then editing and printing a handout from there is only one of your options for printing a handout. You can also set up a handout using PowerPoint's handout master (page 618) and print directly from PowerPoint (page 562).

Figure 24-7:
If you want to print handouts from Word, choose a layout option and then click OK. When you do, PowerPoint sends your presentation to Word, which converts it to a document.

Setting Up Your Show

You're almost ready to deliver your presentation. To make sure your slideshow looks its best—and zips along briskly—take a minute to adjust the screen resolution on the computer showing the presentation. Lots of animations can slow a presentation down, so balancing the speed of the presentation with the sharpness of the screen can be a good compromise.

To adjust the screen resolution, go to the Slide Show tab's Monitors section and click the Resolution drop-down list. You see a variety of options, ranging from low to high. At lower resolutions, slides and animations display faster, but you lose some sharpness and visual detail. At higher resolutions, the slides look good, but your slideshow may be sluggish. Many projectors work with a resolution of 1024 × 768 at most, so if you're not sure about the equipment you'll be using for your presentation, don't go above this setting.

Tip: For other ways to improve your slideshow's performance, see the box on page 669.

Following your notes in Presenter view

You can print out notes and have them in hand, reading from the printed pages, when you give a presentation. If you don't want to keep looking down at your notes and back at the slides, though, you'll love Presenter view. When you use it, you see each slide and its notes on one monitor (perhaps your laptop's screen) and your audience sees the slides—without the notes—on a different monitor.

For Presenter view to work, you need to be able to hook up two monitors to the computer that runs the slideshow. Next, follow these steps to set up PowerPoint to use both those monitors:

1. **In the Slide Show tab's Monitors section, turn on the Use Presenter View checkbox.**

   The Windows Control Panel's Display Settings dialog box opens.

2. **On the Monitor tab, select the monitor you want to use to view your notes as you give the presentation. Turn on the "This is my main monitor" checkbox.**

   This tells Windows which monitor will display your notes along with the slides.

3. **Select the second monitor (the one whose display your audience will see) and turn on the checkbox labeled "Extend my Windows Desktop onto this monitor." Click OK.**

   PowerPoint can now display your slideshow on both monitors.

Now that you've done the setup work, head back to PowerPoint to start your slideshow. On the Slide Show tab, check the Monitors section to make sure the Show On list shows the monitor whose display the audience will see. Then start the slideshow in the usual way. On your monitor, your presentation's notes appear along with the relevant slides—but the audience sees only the slides.

Tuning Up Your Presentation's Performance

If your slideshow is acting sluggish, the first thing to try is adjusting the screen resolution (page 668). If the slideshow still seems slow, try these options for speeding things up:

- **Shut down other programs.** Running several programs simultaneously can slow down your computer's performance.

- **For large objects, avoid gradients and transparency.** Choose solid fills instead.

- **Make animated images smaller.** Just select the picture, click a resizing handle, and drag to resize it.

- **Avoid certain kinds of animations.** Instead of animations that rotate, fade, or scale an object (change its size), try other animation styles.

- **Don't have too many animations happen at the same time.** Instead, have some of the animations start on the next mouse click, or run them one after another.

- **Reduce the overall number of animations.** Animated effects are fun, but not if they make your slideshow drag.

- **Compress media clips.** If you have audio or video clips in your presentation, compressing them saves disk space and speeds up playback (although it might diminish quality). To compress the media files in your presentation, select File→Info→Compress Media (Alt, F, E, MC) and choose a compression option: Presentation Quality (best quality), Internet Quality (comparable to streaming media you play over the Internet), and Low Quality (most compressed). You can come back to this page later and click Undo to return to the previous quality level.

At the Event

You've probably done at least a few practice runs before it's time to get up in front of a real audience. So you know what to say, when to say it, and how animations and transitions work in practice. This section holds your hand on the day of the dance, offering up an assortment of timely tricks that'll help make your presentation (and you!) look good.

Settings to Check

Before starting your show, check the Set Up Show dialog box, shown in Figure 24-8, to confirm that the slideshow's settings are what you want. To open this dialog box, click Slide Show→Set Up Show (Alt, S, S). Check these settings before you start the show:

- **Show type.** For a live presentation, make sure the "Presented by a speaker (full screen)" radio button is on. That shows your slides at their full size and puts you in control of the show.

- **Show options.** If the "Loop continuously until 'Esc' " checkbox is on, turn it off. For a live presentation, you probably want the "Show without narration" and "Show without animation" checkboxes turned off, too. If you want to change the pen or laser pointer color (more about these tools in a page or two), you can do that here.

- **Show slides.** Here's where you can choose any custom shows you've created or select a limited range of slides to show for this presentation. If you're showing the whole presentation from start to finish, then turn on the All radio button.

- **Advance slides.** To stay in control of the show's pacing, make sure the Manually radio button is on.

Figure 24-8:
The Set Up Show dialog box is where you choose the settings that determine how your slideshow will run. Give it a quick check before you launch a live slideshow.

- **Multiple monitors.** If you're using Presenter view (page 668) to see your notes on one monitor while your audience sees just the slides on another, check this section to make sure that the Show Presenter View checkbox is on and that the drop-down list displays the correct monitor for showing the audience's version of the show.

Once you've reviewed this list, click OK. You're ready to get the show on the road.

Launching a Slideshow

You already know how to open a presentation and view it in Slide Show view (if not, flip back to page 658 for a quick refresher). And you can launch your slideshow the same way when you present it to an audience. But if you'd rather not fumble around with starting PowerPoint, finding the presentation you want, opening it, and then switching to Slide Show view, here are some ways to launch your presentation quickly:

- **From the Windows 7 or Windows Vista Start menu.** Click the Start button. In the search box at the bottom of the Start menu, type in the presentation's name. As you type, Windows searches for matches to the filename. Right-click the file you want to open and select Show from the shortcut menu. PowerPoint opens the file in Slide Show view.

- **From Windows Explorer.** In Windows Explorer, find your presentation and right-click it. From the menu that appears, select Show. The first slide appears in Slide Show view.

- **From your computer's desktop.** If you know you'll be giving the presentation from your own computer, save the presentation to the desktop. When it's show-time, right-click the file's desktop icon and select Show to open the first slide.

When you launch a presentation using any of these methods, ending the presentation closes PowerPoint, revealing your computer's desktop.

Tip: It's not a bad idea to double-check what's showing on your desktop before hooking your laptop up to the big screen; you may love Pekingese puppies or Justin Bieber, but do you really want the 200 people in your audience seeing that stuff?

During the Show

When you give a live presentation, you probably want to interact with your audience—emphasizing points, encouraging questions and discussion, maybe pausing the presentation to address a side issue that arises. PowerPoint gives you a whole bunch of tools to help get your points across and make the slideshow appear just so.

Hiding or showing the pointer

During a slideshow, PowerPoint hides the pointer until you move the mouse; then the arrow magically appears. (When the arrow is invisible, so are the lower-left slide controls.) But you can tell PowerPoint to keep the pointer visible or to never show it at all.

Right-click any slide during the slideshow and select Pointer Options→Arrow Options. The fly-out menu has three choices:

- **Automatic.** This is the default, which hides the arrow pointer when you're not using the mouse and shows it when you move the mouse. The lower-left slide controls go into hiding when the pointer does.

- **Visible.** When you select this option, the arrow pointer stays visible all the time (and so do the slide controls).

- **Hidden.** If you use keyboard shortcuts, rather than the mouse, to move through a presentation, you might want this option. It hides both the pointer and the slide controls. (The mouse still gives input when you hide the pointer. You can right-click to bring up the shortcut menu, for example, or click to start the next animation sequence. You just won't see the arrow onscreen.)

Marking up slides

PowerPoint may have replaced chalkboards and whiteboards as the main tool for giving a presentation, but there are still times when you want to write comments or mark up slides to emphasize a point. No problem. Turn the mouse pointer into a pen or a highlighter, and mark up your slides to your heart's content.

To write on your slides during a presentation, click the lower-left Pointer button to bring up the menu shown in Figure 24-9. Select the writing option you want:

- **Pen** produces a thin line, like a ballpoint pen.
- **Highlighter** produces a thick line, like a marker.

Tip: Here's another path to changing the pointer: Right-click a slide, select Pointer Options, and then choose the pointer style you want from the fly-out menu.

To bring back the arrow, press the Esc key. (Don't press it twice, or you'll end the slideshow.) Or you can open the Pointer Options menu and select Arrow.

Changing markup color

If you're marking up slides during a presentation, you may want to change the markup color—to highlight one kind of information in yellow and another in green, for example. To change pen color during a presentation, right-click and select Pointer Options→Ink Color. A menu flies out, showing a palette of colors, with the current color selected. Click any color to change it.

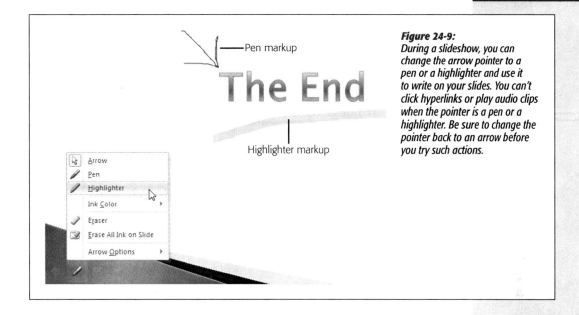

Pen markup

The End

Highlighter markup

Figure 24-9:
During a slideshow, you can change the arrow pointer to a pen or a highlighter and use it to write on your slides. You can't click hyperlinks or play audio clips when the pointer is a pen or a highlighter. Be sure to change the pointer back to an arrow before you try such actions.

Tip: Changing the pen's color during a slideshow lasts only as long as that slideshow. The next time you run the slideshow, the pen reverts back to its default color (red). If you want to change the default color (maybe your eighth-grade English teacher left you with a fear of red pens), you can do so on the Slide Show tab. Click Set Up Slide Show (Alt, S, S). In the Set Up Show dialog box (Figure 24-8), click the "Pen color" drop-down list to choose a different color.

Erasing markup

You've written all over the slide, and now it's hard to read through your annotations. Or maybe you wrote in a blank spot, but now it's time for a new bullet point to appear there. To erase marks you made on a slide with the pen or the highlighter, click the lower-left Pointer button, or right-click the slide and select Pointer Options.

The menu that appears has two eraser options:

- **Eraser.** This option turns the pointer into an eraser. Touch the eraser to any piece of markup and click, and that piece disappears. So if you underlined a word, click any part of the line to erase it.

- **Erase All Ink on Slide.** This option gets rid of all the pen and highlighter marks on the slide.

You don't have to erase the marks you've made on slides as you go along. If markup remains on any slide when you close the presentation, PowerPoint asks if you want to keep your ink annotations. Click Keep if the answer is yes; click Discard if you want to erase them all when the presentation closes.

Note: If you select Keep, the markup becomes an object on the slide. (So the eraser won't work on it during future slideshows.) After an annotation becomes an object, you can delete it from the slide in the same way you'd delete any other object: Select the box that holds it and then press Delete or Backspace.

Making the mouse pointer a laser pointer

Forget your laser pointer on presentation day? No problem. You can turn your mouse pointer into a red dot that looks like a laser pointer by pressing the Ctrl key as you click and move the mouse. When you let go of the mouse button or stop pressing Ctrl, the pointer changes back to an arrow.

Your virtual laser pointer doesn't have to be red. To change its color, select Slide Show→Set Up Slide Show (Alt, S, S) and select the color you prefer from the "Laser pointer color" drop-down list. Click OK to save your choice.

Making the screen go blank

If you need to pause the presentation—to take a coffee break, perhaps, or to focus the audience's attention on something besides the slideshow—you can make the screen temporarily go blank using one of these methods:

- **Black out the screen.** Press B or the period (.) key. Or right-click and select Screen→Black Screen. This makes the current slide disappear and the entire screen go black.

- **White out the screen.** Press W or the comma (,) key. Alternatively, you can right-click and select Screen→White Screen. The current slide disappears, replaced by a block of white space.

To bring back the current slide and continue your slideshow, press any key.

Switching to another program (and back)

If you're giving a presentation that involves more than one program—maybe you've got a spreadsheet that's too big to put on a slide—you can switch from PowerPoint to another program without ending the slideshow. Just do this:

1. **At any point in the presentation, right-click and select Screen→Switch Programs.**

   The Windows taskbar appears at the bottom of the screen, displaying open programs. If the program you want isn't currently open, click the Start button to launch it.

2. **To switch to an open program, click its taskbar button.**

   Windows switches to the program you selected. Now you can work in that program as you normally would.

3. **To get back to your presentation, in the taskbar, find the PowerPoint button labeled PowerPoint Slide Show, along with the filename of your presentation.**

   If you have several programs open, hover the pointer over a taskbar button to see the program's full name, as well as the name of its currently open file.

4. **Click the taskbar button you want.**

PowerPoint returns you to your slideshow already in progress. The slideshow is at the point where you left it, so you can continue from that point.

Ending the Show

If you click Next after your slideshow's final slide, PowerPoint blacks out the screen and puts a notice in small letters at the top: "End of slideshow, click to exit." If you launched the presentation in one of the ways described at the beginning of this section (page 671), clicking ends your slideshow, closes PowerPoint, and shows the computer's desktop. (If you launched the slideshow by starting PowerPoint, opening the presentation, and switching to Slide Show view, clicking now switches the presentation back to Normal or Slide Sorter view—whichever you were in when you started the slideshow.)

Tip: You don't have to click past the last screen when you finish the presentation. If the final screen has your contact information, for example, you may want that to remain on the screen until your audience packs up and leaves.

Other Presentation Options

Giving your presentation in front of a live audience is one way to deliver your message. But it's not the only way—not by a long shot. You can give a live slideshow over the Internet to remote viewers, a kiosk-style slideshow that (once you start it) runs by itself, or a slideshow that viewers interact with at their own pace, on their own computers. In PowerPoint 2010, you can even turn a slideshow into a video and save it on a DVD or post it on a website.

Broadcasting a Slideshow

If you can't gather everyone in the same conference room, don't fret. When your audience is far-flung, you can broadcast a slideshow online. When you send audience members your slideshow's web address, they can click a link to view the show in their web browsers. As you move through the presentation, the broadcast does, too, so viewers can follow your slides as you present them. Set up a conference call, and they can hear your commentary and ask questions—you actually have to do it this way because narrations and audio don't work in a broadcasted slideshow. (The box on page 679 describes a few other limitations of broadcasted slideshows.)

Note: To broadcast a slideshow, you need a Windows Live ID. If you've used SkyDrive or you have a Hotmail, Messenger, or Xbox Live account, you've already got one. Otherwise, head to *http://home.live.com*, click the Sign Up button, and follow the steps to create an account. Do this well before your slideshow's scheduled start time, so your audience won't be kept waiting while you set up your Live ID.

Here's how to broadcast your slideshow in real time:

1. **Make sure your computer is connected to the Internet. Open the presentation you want to broadcast and select Slide Show→Broadcast Slide Show (Alt, S, D).**

   The Broadcast Dialog box opens. This box reminds you that you need a Windows Live ID to broadcast your presentation. It also has a link to the terms you must agree to. (Click the Service Agreement link to find out what they are.)

2. **Click Start Broadcast.**

   PowerPoint connects to the Internet and asks for your Live ID and password.

3. **Supply the requested account information. If you want to store your username and password for future use, turn on the "Remember my credentials" checkbox. Click OK.**

   PowerPoint connects to the PowerPoint Broadcast Service. A progress bar keeps track of how it's going. When you're connected, PowerPoint prepares the broadcast and then gives you a link that you can share with your remote audience, as shown in Figure 24-10.

Figure 24-10:
PowerPoint gives you a web address for your broadcasted slideshow. Share it as a link that remote viewers can use to watch the show in real time. Click Send in Email to open a ready-to-go email message in Outlook—just add addresses. To copy the link and send it in a different email program or via an instant message, click Copy Link.

Note: Audience members don't need a Windows Live ID to view your broadcast.

4. **Share the link with viewers who'll watch the broadcast.**

   You can copy the link and paste it into an email or an instant message, or click the Send in Email link to open Outlook with an email message that's ready to go—it's got a prefilled subject line and a message that contains the link. Just fill in recipient email addresses in the To line and then click Send. As viewers click the link and join your slideshow, they see a message that says "Waiting for broadcast to begin" until you start the show.

5. **When you're ready to begin the show, click Start Slide Show.**

   Your slideshow launches. What appears on your screen also appears in the web browsers of viewers who went to the web address you sent. As you move through the presentation, they see what you do, with a couple of exceptions. If you right-click, they don't see the shortcut menu that appears on your screen. If you switch to another program (page 674), that program isn't part of the broadcast. And if you temporarily duck out of the slideshow, they'll never know—the current slide stays on their screens.

Tip: If you need to send out more invitations during a broadcast, press Esc to stop the show temporarily on your computer. (Remote viewers continue to see the slide that was onscreen when you pressed Esc.) You see the presentation in Broadcast view (Figure 24-11). To send more invitations, click the Broadcast tab's Send Invitations button, and then repeat steps 4 and 5. When you click Start Slide Show, PowerPoint takes you back to the broadcast, with the currently selected slide displayed.

---

6. **When you reach the end of the show, press Esc to close it.**

   PowerPoint ends the slideshow and displays your presentation in Broadcast view, shown in Figure 24-11. Your audience doesn't see this view.

7. **To end the broadcast, click the Broadcast tab's End Broadcast button (Alt, B, E).**

   A dialog box asks if you're sure you want to disconnect all viewers from your broadcast.

8. **Click End Broadcast.**

   On your computer, PowerPoint displays its usual tabs. Your viewers see a notice that the broadcast is over.

The web address you used for this broadcast lasts only until you end the broadcast, so you can't tell people to go to the same address the next time you broadcast the slideshow. When you broadcast the slideshow again, you get a new link to share.

Tip: If you want to put a copy of your slideshow on the Web so people can view it whenever they want, then make it a video (see page 681) and upload it to your website or a video-sharing site such as YouTube.

During a broadcast, you can end the show temporarily. Ending the show doesn't end the broadcast. It takes you to Broadcast view, shown in Figure 24-11. While you see Broadcast view on your screen, remote viewers see the most recent slide. To return to the in-progress broadcast, click From Current Slide (or start all over from the beginning by clicking From Beginning). PowerPoint connects again, and you can proceed with your slideshow.

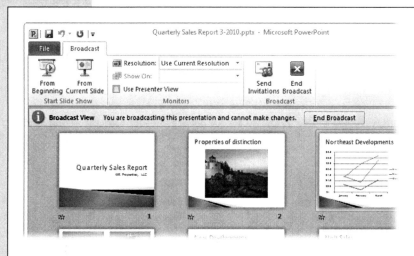

Figure 24-11:
You can't make changes to a presentation when a broadcast is in progress, so if you exit the slideshow you see only two tabs: File and Broadcast. On the Broadcast tab, you can adjust the screen resolution, switch to Presenter view (if you have two monitors hooked up to your computer; see page 668), send more viewers a link to the slideshow, or end the broadcast.

Creating a Slideshow that Runs by Itself

You've seen it at trade shows and conventions: a presentation set up in a booth or kiosk that plays all by itself in a continual loop. Passersby don't have to interact with the computer; they just stop and watch as the show runs. When it reaches the end, it starts all over again from the first slide.

Tip: Before you create a kiosk-style slideshow, make sure that any animations in your presentation happen automatically and don't require a mouse click. To check, open the Animation pane (Alt, A, C) and work your way through each slide's animations. When you select an animation, it should start with previous or start after previous, *not* start on click. Adjust as necessary.

When you want a presentation to run as a kiosk-style slideshow, your first step is to let PowerPoint know the timings for all the animations and transitions in your presentation. The easiest way to do this is to rehearse your slideshow's timings (page 660) by going to the Slide Show tab and clicking Rehearse Timings (Alt, S, T). As you go through the slideshow, move forward at the same pace you want for the kiosk-style slideshow. When you're finished and PowerPoint asks if you want to save the timings, click Yes. PowerPoint applies the new timings to each slide.

Note: If you've already rehearsed a slideshow and saved the timings, going through the process again overwrites the old timings when you save the new ones.

Broadcasting Caveats

Broadcasting is a great tool and makes PowerPoint a lot more flexible. But it's not perfect. Before you broadcast a slideshow over the Internet, there are a few things you should know:

- Slideshow broadcasting works with Internet Explorer, Firefox, and Safari Web browsers. (Sorry, Chrome fans.)

- Some presentations are too big to broadcast. The maximum size depends on the service you're using to broadcast the show; for the PowerPoint broadcast service, for example, the upper limit is 20 MB.

- Media clips (both audio and video) and narrations don't broadcast. If you play a video as you present the slideshow, for example, your audience doesn't see or hear it.

- Most transitions and a few animations won't appear on your audience's screens. In those cases, Power-Point uses Fade.

- You can't use a pen or a highlighter to mark up slides during a slideshow that you're broadcasting.

- If you click a hyperlink that goes to a website or opens a file, your audience doesn't see the webpage or file you opened. Instead, they continue to see the slide that holds the link.

- The same thing is true if you switch to another program during the slideshow—your audience can't see the other program, just the current PowerPoint slide.

- There will probably be some lag time between what appears on your screen and what the members of your audience see on theirs. Pace yourself accordingly.

If you prefer, you can set the amount of time between transitions manually. In Slide Sorter view, select the first slide and click the Transitions tab. In the Advance Slide section, make sure the On Mouse Click checkbox is turned off (Alt, K, M toggles this checkbox off and on). In the same section, turn on the After checkbox (if it isn't already) and type in the amount of time you want the slide to stay on the screen. If you want the slide to stay on screen for 30 seconds, for example, the number in the After box would be "00:30:00."

If you want all slides to have the same timing, click Transitions→Apply to All (Alt, K, L). If you want different slides to be onscreen for different amounts of time, type in the timings individually. (You can also apply the same timing to all slides and then select and adjust only certain slides.)

So far so good. Now each slide has an amount of screen time assigned to it. Your next step is to identify the presentation as one that runs itself. Here's how:

1. **Select Slide Show→Set Up Slide Show (Alt, S, S).**

    The Set Up Show dialog box (Figure 24-8) opens.

2. **In the "Show type" section, turn on the "Browsed at a kiosk (full screen)" radio button.**

    When you turn on this radio button, PowerPoint automatically turns on the checkbox labeled "Loop continuously until 'Esc' ", and grays it out so you can't turn it off. That's because you want a self-running presentation to keep going for as long as people are around to watch it.

3. **In the "Advance slides" section, make sure the "Using timings, if present" radio button is on. Then click OK.**

    Now your presentation will run all by itself. The next time you start it up, it will advance automatically and keep playing until you press Esc to stop it.

Creating an Interactive Slideshow

It's common to create a presentation that you distribute to others, by email (page 681) or on a CD (page 683), so they can go through the slideshow at their own pace. In this scenario, the viewer moves from slide to slide, taking her time on this slide or zipping past that one; clicking its links (or not), maybe jumping back to take another look at an earlier slide. It's all up to the viewer.

When you set up the slideshow to run this way, it appears in Reading view (page 558), which shows the status bar at the bottom of the screen. The lower-left slide controls don't appear. Instead, viewers can use the status bar's Previous, Next, and Menu buttons to move through the slideshow. (The Menu button opens a navigation menu that lets the viewer move to the next or previous slide or to any slide or section in the presentation.)

Also, a viewer-run slideshow doesn't let the viewer mark up the slides. If a viewer right-clicks a slide, Pointer Options don't appear on the shortcut menu. Same goes for Screen Options: Viewers can't black out or white out the screen during the show.

Tip: The box on page 684 shares tips for creating a good viewer-run presentation.

Here's how to make a slideshow viewer-run:

1. **Open the presentation and select Slide Show→Set Up Slide Show (Alt, S, S).**

    The Set Up Show dialog box (Figure 24-8) appears.

2. **In the "Show type" section, turn on the radio button labeled "Browsed by an individual (window)". In the "Advance slides" section, turn on the Manually radio button.**

    The first setting tells PowerPoint to run the slideshow in Reading view. The second turns off automatic transitions, letting viewers move through the slideshow at their own pace.

3. **Adjust any other settings you want for this slideshow.**

    For example, you might want to select a custom version of the slideshow, limit the slides shown, or turn off narration.

4. **When your settings look good, click OK.**

    PowerPoint makes the presentation viewer-run.

If you want the presentation to launch as a slideshow when a viewer opens it, save the presentation as a PowerPoint Show. When you save the file (page 553), select PowerPoint Show (.ppsx), PowerPoint Macro-Enabled Show (.ppsm), or PowerPoint 97–2003 Show (.pps). If some of your viewers might have older versions of PowerPoint that can't open 2007 or 2010 .ppsx files, your best bet is to save the file in 97–2003 format (.pps).

Tip: Viewers can edit a presentation whose show type is set as "Browsed by an individual." To discourage viewers from messing around with your presentation, you can mark it as final (page 236).

Turning Your Presentation into a Video

It used to be that when you wanted to put a PowerPoint presentation on the Web, you had to make do with a static presentation—no animations or transitions, just pictures of your slides. No more. New in PowerPoint 2010, you can quickly and easily turn a slideshow into a video. From there, you can post it on a website or save it on a DVD to distribute.

Before you repackage your presentation as a video, it's a good idea to record timings and narration. That way you can be sure that the slideshow moves at the pace you want and contains all the information you want it to convey. (Page 663 tells you how to record a slideshow with timings and narration.) When you're ready to create your video, put on your director's hat and follow these steps:

1. **Select File→Share→Create a Video.**

   The Create a Video page, shown in Figure 24-12, opens.

2. **Select a resolution.**

   Here's where you ensure that your presentation will look good on the devices people will be using to view it. Choose from these options:

   — **Computer & HD Displays.** If viewers will look at your presentation on a computer monitor, on a high-definition screen, or using a projector, then go with this setting.

   — **Internet & DVD.** If you plan to post the video on the Web or save it as a DVD, this is the resolution you want.

   — **Portable Devices.** For handheld devices like smartphones or iPods, choose this option.

3. **Tell PowerPoint how to time the presentation.**

   This setting determines how to pace the slideshow and whether or not to use narration. Choose one of these options:

   — **Don't Use Recorded Timings and Narrations.** When you choose this option, PowerPoint spends the same number of seconds on each slide. The default is 5 seconds, but you can change it using the drop-down list just under this setting.

— **Use Recorded Timings and Narrations.** This option gives you the most control over your slideshow. If you've recorded narration and timings, pick this.

4. **When you're happy with your settings, click Create Video.**

   PowerPoint creates the video as a Windows Media Video (.wmv) file and opens the Save As dialog box.

5. **Tell PowerPoint where you want to save the video.**

   Now you can play your new video on a media player, burn it to a DVD, attach it to an email, or post it to a website.

Figure 24-12:
Go Backstage to turn your slideshow into a video. Choose a resolution based on how people will view the video and tell PowerPoint whether to use your recorded timings or to move to a new slide after a certain interval. When you're all set, click Create Video (circled).

Sharing Your Presentation

You can share a PowerPoint presentation in many of the same ways you can share a Word document. Table 24-2 lists topics elsewhere in this book related to sharing Office files.

Table 24-2. Where to find instructions for sharing Office files

Topic	Page Number
Sending a file using email	216
Emailing a link to a file	217
Saving a file to SkyDrive	218
Saving a file to SharePoint	219
Restricting permissions	236
Removing hidden data and personal information	230

Packaging Your Presentation on a CD or DVD

One popular way to share a PowerPoint video is to save it on a CD or DVD, where you can package it with other presentations or relevant files. (These steps refer to CDs and DVDs that store data files, not the kind you'd put into a DVD player to watch a movie.) PowerPoint makes it easy to package a presentation on a disc. Start by putting a blank disc into your computer's writeable CD/DVD drive, and then follow these steps:

1. **Open the presentation you want to share via CD and select File→Share Package Presentation for CD (Alt, F, H, G).**

   The Backstage view changes to give you information about packaging a presentation to save it on a disc.

2. **Click Package for CD (or press A if you're using keyboard shortcuts).**

   The Package for CD dialog box opens, with a placeholder name for the disc you're creating and the current presentation appearing in the "Files to be copied" list.

3. **Give the disc a name that reflects what the presentation is about. If you want to add any other files to the CD, click the Add button.**

   Clicking Add opens the Add Files dialog box, where you can locate any other files you want to put on the same disc with the current presentation. Select a file (use the Shift or Ctrl key to select multiple files) and then click Add.

4. **If you want to protect the presentation, limiting who can view or edit it (or both), click Options.**

   The Options dialog box has two text boxes:

   Password to open each presentation

   Password to modify each presentation

   Type in a password for either or both (and don't forget to write down the passwords and share them with recipients who need them). Also, if you haven't had Power-Point look over the presentation for personal or other information you may not want to share, turn on the checkbox labeled "Inspect presentations for inappropriate or private information", and then click OK to run an inspection of the file.

5. **In the Package for CD dialog box, use the up and down arrows to the left of the file list if you want to package the files in a different order. When you're happy with the settings you've chosen, click Copy to CD.**

If a presentation in your package has linked files, PowerPoint shows a dialog box asking you to confirm that it's OK to include them. Click Yes. PowerPoint copies the files to the blank disc.

WORD TO THE WISE

Tips for Creating a Viewer-Run Slideshow

When you create a viewer-run slideshow, you give up some control over the show. Unlike shows that, say, play on a kiosk, you're no longer in charge of the pace at which the slideshow proceeds. This is a good thing, because you want a person viewing your slideshow to go through it at his own speed.

Creating a viewer-run slideshow, therefore, requires you to think a bit differently about the presentation than you would if you were giving it yourself. These tips will help make sure that individual viewers get the most out of your slides:

- **Don't use timed transitions.** Think how annoying it would be if a slide moved forward all by itself before you were done with it. Sure, you could use the Previous button to go back, but the switch has already interrupted your concentration. Don't do this to your viewers. In the Transitions tab's Timing section, make sure all transitions have On Mouse Click (Alt, K, M) turned on and After (Alt, K, F) turned off.

- **Make navigation controls clear.** You can't assume that viewers are PowerPoint pros like you. They might not notice the navigation buttons in the status bar, for example. The last thing you want is for them to waste time scratching their heads about how to move to the next slide—or to even give up on viewing the show. Use action buttons (page 607) to indicate viewers' options for moving around the presentation. Buttons like Next, Previous, Home, Beginning of Section, and Next Section are super-helpful for getting around.

- **Don't rely on narration and media clips to make your main points.** In a viewer-run presentation, media clips are optional. Even if you set the clip to play automatically, the viewer can always jump to the next slide if she doesn't feel like watching the video. And while narration is great for a slideshow that loops in a kiosk, an individual viewer can always turn off the sound. For these reasons, make sure the text of your presentation covers all the main points. Make media effects optional and supplemental.

- **Don't let a slide be blank when it enters.** You don't want a viewer to sit there, confused, staring at an empty slide and waiting for something to happen. Each new slide should have some visible content when it enters.

- **Let the viewer control animation sequences.** Don't have text and other objects appear and disappear at random; make sure the viewer controls them—and knows when to click to start the next sequence. It's a good idea to create a symbol to indicate when an animation sequence is done, such as a small arrow—an object whose appearance says, "Click again and the slide will change." Have the symbol appear at the end of each animation sequence on a slide, except the last one, when clicking advances to the next slide.

- **Make sure the presentation is appropriate for any environment.** A loud soundtrack and goofy sound effects might be fun when you present a slideshow to a large audience, but if a viewer is going through the presentation surrounded by coworkers, they might wonder about the boings and drumrolls and applause emanating from his cubicle.

Part Five: Access

5

Creating Your First Database

Although Microsoft won't admit it, Access can be intimidating—intimidating enough to trigger a cold sweat in the most confident office worker. Even though the company has spent millions of dollars making Access easier to use, most people still see it as the most complicated Office program on the block. They're probably right.

Access seems more daunting than any other Office program because of the way databases work. Quite simply, databases *need strict rules*. Other programs aren't as obsessive. For example, you can fire up Word, and start typing a letter straightaway. Or you can start Excel, and launch right into a financial report. But Access isn't nearly as freewheeling. Before you can enter a stitch of information into an Access database, you need to create that database's *structure*. And even after you've defined that structure, you'll probably want to spend more time creating other useful tools, like handy search routines and friendly forms that you can use to simplify data lookup and data entry. All of this setup takes effort and a good understanding of how databases work.

In this chapter, you'll conquer any Access resistance you have, and learn to create a simple but functional database. Along the way, you'll get acquainted with the slick Access user interface, and learn exactly what you can store in a database. You'll then be ready to tackle the fine art of database design, which is covered in the next chapter.

Note: Access is by far the most complex (and powerful) program in the Office suite. The four chapters in this book contain the basics that most readers will need to design and fire up their first database. On this book's Missing CD page (*www.missingmanuals.com/cds*), you'll find three additional chapters, covering the next stage in any Access learner's journey: creating queries (Appendix C), creating reports (Appendix D), and creating forms (Appendix E).

Using Someone Else's Database

Can I use an Access database I didn't design?

Sure. Although every database follows the same two-step process (first somebody creates it, and then people fill it with information), the same person doesn't need to perform both jobs. In fact, in the business world, different people often work separately on these two tasks.

For example, a summer student whiz-kid at a beer store may build a database for tracking orders (task #1). The sales department can then use the database to enter new orders (task #2), while other employees look up orders and fill them (also task #2). Warehouse staff can make sure stock levels are OK (again, task #2), and the resident accountant can keep an eye on total sales (task #2).

If task #1 (creating the database) is done well, task #2 (using the database) can be extremely easy. In fact, if the database is well designed, people who have little understanding of Access can still use it to enter, update, and look up information. Amazingly, they don't even need to know they're running Access at all!

Understanding Access Databases

As you already know, a database is a collection of information. In Access, every database is stored in a single file. That file contains *database objects,* which are simply the components of a database. Database objects are the main players in an Access database. Altogether, you have six different types of database objects:

- **Tables** store information. Tables are the heart of any database, and you can create as many tables as you need to store different types of information. A fitness database could track your daily running log, your inventory of exercise equipment, and the number of high-protein whey milkshakes you down each day, as three separate tables.

- **Queries** let you quickly perform an action on a table. Usually, this action involves retrieving a choice bit of information (like the 10 top-selling food items at Ed's Roadside Diner or all the purchases you made in a single day). But you can also use queries to apply changes.

- **Forms** are attractive windows that you create, arrange, and colorize. Forms provide an easy way to view or change the information in a table.

- **Reports** help you print some or all of the information in a table. You can choose where the information appears on the printed page, how it's grouped and sorted, and how it's formatted.

- **Macros** are mini-programs that automate custom tasks. Macros are a simple way to get custom results without becoming a programmer.

Access gurus refer to all these database ingredients as objects because you manage them all in essentially the same way. If you want to use a particular object, then you add it to your database, give it a name, and then fine-tune it. Later on, you can view your objects, rename them, or delete ones you don't want anymore.

Note: Designing a database is the process of adding and configuring database objects. For those keeping score, an Access database can hold up to 32,768 separate objects.

In this chapter, you'll consider only the most fundamental type of database object: *tables*. But first, you need to create a blank database you can work with.

Getting Started with Your First Database

When you start Access, you begin in backstage view, with the New command already selected. From there, you're just a few clicks away from generating a database of your very own.

In this chapter, you'll slap together a fairly straightforward database. The example is designed to store a list of prized bobblehead dolls. (For those not in the know, a bobblehead doll is a toy figure with an oversized head on a spring, hence the signature "bobbling" motion. Bobblehead dolls usually resemble a famous celebrity, politician, athlete, or fictional character.)

Here's how to create a blank new database:

1. **If you're currently working with a database, choose File→New. If you've just started Access, you're there already.**

    The Access window now has three columns (Figure 25-1). At left is a narrow strip of backstage commands. In the middle section, you choose the type of database you want. At far right is an optional picture that previews your choice, a text box for you to pick the file name, and the all-important Create button.

2. **At the far right, in the File Name box, type a file name for the database you're about to create.**

    Access stores all the information for a database in a single file with the extension *.accdb* (which stands for "Access database"). Don't stick with the name Access picks automatically (like "Database1.accdb"). Instead, pick something more suitable. In this example, Bobblehead.accdb does the trick.

    As with any other file, Access files can contain a combination of letters, spaces, numbers, parentheses, hyphens (-), and underscores (_). It's generally safest to stay away from other special characters, some of which aren't allowed.

Note: Depending on your computer settings, Windows may hide file extensions. Instead of seeing the Access database file MyScandalousWedding.accdb in file-browsing tools like Windows Explorer, you may just see the name MyScandalousWedding (without the *.accdb* part on the end). In this case, you can still tell the file type by looking at the icon. If you see a small Access icon (which looks like a key) next to the file name, that's your signal that you're looking at an Access database.

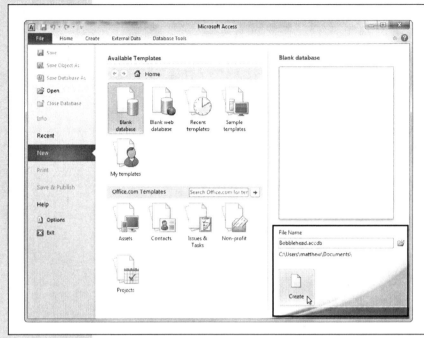

Figure 25-1:
This database is named Bobblehead.accdb. As you can see by the file path below the File Name box, it will be saved in the folder C:\Users\matthew\Documents. You can edit the file name by typing in the File Name box or browse to a different folder by clicking the folder icon.

3. **Choose a folder.**

   Like all Office programs, Access assumes you want to store every file you create in your personal Documents folder. If this isn't what you want, click the folder icon to show the File New Database dialog box, browse to the folder you want (Figure 25-2), and then click OK.

4. **In the middle of the window, choose "Blank database".**

   When you choose to create a blank database, that's exactly what you get—a new, empty database file with no tables or other database objects. Starting from scratch is the best way to learn about Access. It's also the favorite choice of database experts, who prefer to create everything themselves so it's exactly the way they like it. That said, you can click one of the other pictures under the Available Templates heading to build a database based on a template. The box on page 691 has more about this approach.

5. **Click the big Create button (under the File Name box).**

   Access creates your database file and then shows a datasheet where you can get to work creating your first table.

Figure 25-2:
The File New Database dialog box lets you choose where you'll store a new Access database file. It also gives you the option to create your database in the format used by older versions of Access (.mdb), instead of the more modern format used by Access 2010 and Access 2007 (.accdb). To do so, you need to choose either the 2000 or 2002-2003 format options from the "Save as type" list, as shown here.

Templates: One Size Fits Some

The example in this section shows you how to create a blank database. However, you've probably noticed a number of other options in the Available Templates section in the middle of the File→New page. These options let you browse dozens of prebuilt databases, which are known as *templates*. Templates aim to save you the work of creating a new database and let you jump straight to the fine-tuning and data-entry stage.

As you might expect, there's a price to be paid for this convenience. Even if you find a template that stores the type

of information you want to track, you might find that the predefined structure isn't quite right. For example, if you choose to use the Home Inventory template to track all the stuff in your basement, you might find that it's missing some information you want to use (like the projected resale value of your stuff on eBay) and includes other details you don't care about (like the date you acquired each item). To make this template work, you'll need to change the design of your table, which involves the same Access know-how as creating one.

Once you create or open a database, the Access window changes quite a bit. An impressive-looking toolbar (the *ribbon*) appears at the top of your screen, and a navigation pane shows up on the left. You're now in the control center where you'll perform all your database tasks (as shown in Figure 25-3).

The ribbon

The
navigation
pane

The document window

Figure 25-3:
*The navigation pane
on the left lets you
see different items
(or objects) in your
database. You can
use the navigation
pane to jump from
a list of products to
a list of customers
and back again. The
ribbon along the top
groups together every
Access command.
This ribbon is the
control center that lets
you perform various
tasks with your data-
base. The document
window in the middle
takes up the rest of
the window. This win-
dow is where you'll
do your work, such as
designing tables and
entering data.*

Now it's time to consider how you can make use of your brand-new, empty database
by adding a table.

Understanding Tables

Tables are information containers. Every database needs at least one table—without
it, you can't store any data. In a simple database, like the Bobblehead database, a
single table (which we'll call Dolls) is enough. But if you find yourself wanting to
store several lists of related information, then you need more than one table. In the
database BigBudgetWedding.accdb, you might want to keep track of the guests that
you invited to your wedding, the gifts that you requested, and the loot that you actually received. Figure 25-4 shows a sample table.

Before you start designing this table, you need to know some very basic rules:

- **A table is a group of** *records*. A record is a collection of information about
  a single thing. In the Dolls table, for example, each record represents a single
  bobblehead doll. In a Family table, each record would represent a single relative. In a Products table, each record would represent an item that's for sale. You
  get the idea. When you create a new database, Access starts you out with a new
  table named *Table1,* although you can choose a more distinctive name when
  you decide to save it.

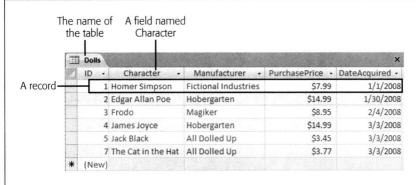

The name of the table

A field named Character

A record

Figure 25-4:
In a table, each record occupies a separate row. Each field is represented by a separate column. In this table, you can see entries for six bobblehead dolls. You're storing information for each doll in five fields (ID, Character, Manufacturer, PurchasePrice, and DateAcquired).

- **Each record is subdivided into *fields*.** Each field stores a distinct piece of information. For example, in the Dolls table, one field stores the person on whom the doll is based, another field stores the price, another field stores the date you bought it, and so on.

- **Tables have a rigid structure.** In other words, you can't bend the rules. If you create four fields, *every* record must have four fields (although it's acceptable to leave some fields blank if they don't apply).

- **Newly created tables get an ID field for free.** The ID field stores a unique number for each record. (Think of it as a reference number that will let you find a specific record later on.) The best part about the ID field is that you can ignore it when you're entering a new record. Access chooses a new ID number for you and inserts it in the record automatically.

UP TO SPEED

Database Planning for Beginners

Many database gurus suggest that before you fire up Access, you should decide exactly what information you want to store by brainstorming. Here's how it works. First, determine the type of list you want by finishing this sentence "I need a list of…." (One example: "I need a list of all the bobblehead dolls in my basement.")

Next, jot down all your must-have pieces of information on a piece of paper. Some details are obvious. For example, for the bobblehead doll collection, you'll probably want to keep track of the doll's name, price, and date you bought

it. Other details, like the year it was produced, the company that created it, and a short description of its appearance or condition may require more thought.

Once you've completed this process and identified all the important bits of data you need, you're ready to create the corresponding table in Access. The bobblehead doll example demonstrates an important theme of database design: First you plan the database, and then you create it using Access.

Creating a Simple Table

When you first create a database, it's almost empty. But in order to get you started, Access creates your first database object—a table named Table1. The problem is, this table begins life completely blank, with no defined fields (and no data).

If you followed the steps to create a new database described earlier, you're already at the *Datasheet view* (Figure 25-4), which is where you enter data into a table. All you need to do is customize this table so that it meets your needs.

There are two ways to customize a table:

- **Design view** lets you precisely define all aspects of a table before you start using it. Almost all database pros prefer Design view, and you'll start using it in the next chapter.

- **Datasheet view** is where you enter data into a table. Datasheet view also lets you build a table on the fly as you insert new information. You'll use this approach in this chapter.

The following steps show you how to turn a blank new table (like Table1) into the Dolls table using the Datasheet view:

1. **To define your table, you need to add your first record.**

   In this case, that means choosing a bobblehead doll to add to the list. For this example, you'll use a nifty Homer Simpson replica.

Note: It doesn't matter which doll you enter first. Access tables are *unsorted*, which means they have no underlying order. However, you can sort them any way you want when you need to retrieve information later on.

Putting Big Values in Narrow Columns

A single field can hold entire paragraphs of information. But if you have lengthy values, you may find yourself running out of viewing space while you're typing them into a narrow column. And although you're free to scroll forward and backward through your field, this gets annoying fast. Most people prefer to see the entire contents of a column at once.

Fortunately, you don't need to suffer in silence with cramped columns. To expand a column, just position your mouse at the right edge of the column header. (To expand a column named Field1, move your mouse to the right edge of the Field1 box.) Then, drag the column to the right to resize it as big as you want.

If you're just a bit impatient, there's a shortcut. Move the mouse over the right edge of the column, so that it turns into a two-way arrow. Then, double-click the column edge. This resizes the column to fit its largest piece of information (provided this doesn't stretch the column beyond the edge of the Access window).

2. **In the datasheet's rightmost column, under the "Click to Add" heading, type the first piece of information for the record (see Figure 25-5).**

   Based on the simple analysis you performed earlier (see the box on page 693), you know that you need to enter four fields of information for every doll. For the Homer Simpson doll, this information is "Homer Simpson" (the name), "Fictional Industries" (the manufacturer), "$7.99" (the price), and today's date (the purchase date). Although you could start with any field, it makes sense to begin with the name, which is clearly an identifying detail.

Start entering info here. . .   . . .then enter the next piece of info here

Figure 25-5:
To fill in your first record, start by entering something in the first field of information (like the doll name "Homer Simpson"). Then, press Tab to jump to the second column, and enter the second piece of information. Ignore the ID column for now—Access adds that to every table to identify your rows.

3. **Press Tab to move to the next field, and return to step 2.**

   Repeat steps 2 and 3 until you've added every field you need, being careful to put each separate piece of information into a different column.

   If you want to get a little fancier, include the currency symbol ($) when you enter the price, and make sure you put the date in a recognized date format (like *January 1, 2010* or *01-01-2010*). These clues tell Access what type of information you're putting in the column. (In the next chapter, you'll learn how to take complete control of the type of data in each column and how to avoid possible misunderstandings.) Figure 25-6 shows the finalized record.

Note: If you press Tab without entering any information, you'll move to the next row and start inserting a new record. If you make a mistake, you can backtrack using the arrow keys.

4. **It's time to fix your column names. Double-click the first column title (like Field1).**

   The field name switches into Edit mode.

5. **Type in a new name, and then press Enter. Return to step 4.**

Repeat this process until you've cleaned up all the field names. The proper field names for this example are Character, Manufacturer, PurchasePrice, and Date-Acquired. Figure 25-7 shows how it works.

Figure 25-6:
The only problem with the example so far is that as you enter a new record, Access creates spectacularly useless field names. You'll see its choices at the top of each column (they'll have names like Field1, Field2, Field3, and so on). The problem with using these meaningless names is that they might lead you to enter a piece of information in the wrong place. You could all too easily put the purchase price in the date column. To prevent these slipups, you need to set better field names.

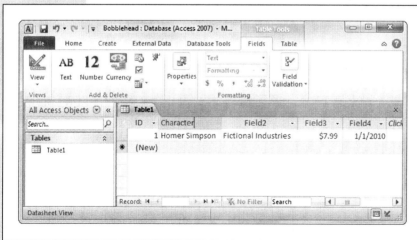

Figure 25-7:
To specify better field names, double-click the column title. Next, type in the real field name, and then press Enter. In general it's best to stick to short, text-only titles that don't include any spaces, as shown here.

Tip: Don't be too timid about tweaking your table. You can always rename fields later, or even add entirely new fields. (It's also possible to *delete* existing fields, but that has the drawback of also clearing out all the data that's stored in that field.)

6. **Choose File→Save (or press Ctrl+S) to save your table.**

   Access asks you to supply a table name (see Figure 25-8).

7. **Type a suitable table name, and then click OK.**

   Congratulations! The table is now a part of your database.

Figure 25-8:
A good table name is a short text title that doesn't have any spaces (like Dolls here).

Note: Technically, you don't need to save your table right away. Access prompts you to save it when you close the datasheet (by clicking the X at the document window's top-right corner), or when you close Access.

As you can see, creating a simple table in Access is almost as easy as laying out information in Excel or Word. If you're itching to try again, you can create *another* table in your database by choosing Create→Tables→Table from the ribbon. But before you get to that stage, it makes sense to take a closer look at how you edit your table.

Editing a Table

You now have a fully functioning (albeit simple) database, complete with one table, which in turn contains one record. Your next step is filling your table with useful information. This often-tedious process is *data entry.*

To fill the Dolls table, you use the same datasheet you used to define the table. You can perform three basic tasks:

- **Editing a record.** Move to the appropriate spot in the datasheet (using the arrow keys or the mouse), and then type in a replacement value. You may also want to use Edit mode, which is described in the next section.

- **Inserting a new record.** Move down to the bottom of the table to the row that has an asterisk (*) on the left. This row doesn't actually exist until you start typing in some information. At that point, Access creates the row and moves the asterisk down to the next row underneath. You can repeat this process endlessly to add as many rows as you want (Access can handle millions).

- **Deleting a record.** You have several ways to remove a record, but the easiest is to right-click the margin immediately to the left of the record, and then choose Delete Record. Access asks you to confirm that you really want to remove the selected record, because you can't reverse the change later on.

WORD TO THE WISE

When in Doubt, Don't Delete

Most seasoned database designers rarely delete records from their databases. Every ounce of information is important.

For example, imagine you have a database that lists the products that a mail-order origami company has for sale. You might think it makes sense to delete products once they've been discontinued and can't be ordered anymore. But it turns out that it makes sense to keep these old product records around. For example, you might want to find out what product categories were the best sellers over the previous year. Or maybe a manufacturer issues a recall of asbestos-laced paper, and you need to track down everyone who ordered it. To perform either of these tasks, you need to keep your product records.

This hang-onto-everything rule applies to any kind of database. For example, imagine you're tracking student enrollment at a top-flight culinary academy. When a class is finished, you can't just delete the class record. You might need it to find out if a student has the right prerequisites for another course, what teachers she's had in the past, and so on.

The same is true for employees who retire, sales promotions that end, items that you used to own but you've sold, and so on. You need them all (and you probably need to keep them indefinitely).

In many cases, you'll add extra fields to your table to help you separate old data from the new. For example, you can create a Discontinued field in the Products table that identifies products that aren't available anymore. You can then ignore those products when you build an order-placement form.

Edit mode

You'll probably spend a lot of time working with the datasheet. So settle in. To make your life easier, it helps to understand a few details.

As you already know, you can use the arrow keys to move from field to field or row to row. However, you might have a bit of trouble editing a value. When you start typing, Access erases any existing content. To change this behavior, you need to switch into *Edit mode* by pressing the F2 key; in Edit mode, your typing doesn't delete the stuff that's already in that field. Instead, you get to change or add to it. To switch out of Edit mode, press F2 again. Figure 25-9 shows a closeup look at the difference.

Edit mode also affects how the arrow keys work. In Edit mode, the arrow keys move through the current field. For example, to move to the next cell, you need to move all the way to the end of the current text, and then press the right arrow key again. But in Normal mode, pressing the arrow keys always moves you from cell to cell.

Datasheet shortcut keys

Power users know the fastest way to get work done is to use tricky keyboard combinations like Ctrl+Alt+Shift+*. Although you can't always easily remember these combinations, a couple of tables can help you out. Table 25-1 lists some useful keys that can help you whiz around the datasheet.

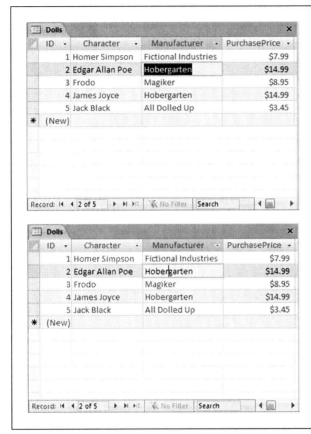

Figure 25-9:
Top: Normal mode. If you start typing now, you'll immediately erase the existing text ("Hobergarten"). The fact that all the text in the field is selected is a big clue that you're about to wipe it out.

Bottom: Edit mode. The cursor shows where you're currently positioned in the field. If you start typing now, you'll insert text in between "Hober" and "garten".

Table 25-1. *Keys for moving around the datasheet*

Key	Result
Tab (or Enter)	Moves the cursor one field to the right, or down when you reach the edge of the table. This key also turns off Edit mode if it's currently switched on.
Shift+Tab	Moves the cursor one field to the left, or up when you reach the edge of the table. This key also turns off Edit mode.
→	Moves the cursor one field to the right (in Normal mode), or down when you reach the edge of the table. In Edit mode, this key moves the cursor through the text in the current field.

←	Moves the cursor one field to the left (in Normal mode), or up when you reach the edge of the table. In Edit mode, this key moves the cursor through the text in the current field.
↑	Moves the cursor up one row (unless you're already at the top of the table). This key also turns off Edit mode.
↓	Moves the cursor down one row (or it moves you to the "new row" position if you're at the bottom of the table). This key also turns off Edit mode.
Home	Moves the cursor to the first field in the current row. This key brings you to beginning of the current field if you're in Edit mode.
End	Moves the cursor to the last field in the current row. This key brings you to the end of the current field if you're in Edit mode.
Page Down	Moves the cursor down one screenful (assuming you have a large table of information that doesn't all fit in the Access window at once). This key also turns off Edit mode.
Page Up	Moves the cursor up one screenful. This key also turns off Edit mode.
Ctrl+Home	Moves the cursor to the first field in the first row. This key doesn't do anything if you're in Edit mode.
Ctrl+End	Moves the cursor to the last field in the last row. This key doesn't do anything if you're in Edit mode.

Table 25-2 lists some convenient keys for editing records.

Table 25-3. *Keys for editing records*

Key	Result
Esc	Cancels any changes you've made in the current field. This key works only if you use it in Edit mode. Once you move to the next cell, the change is applied. (For additional cancellation control, try the Undo feature, described next.)
Ctrl+Z	Reverses the last edit. Unfortunately, the Undo feature in Access isn't nearly as powerful as it is in other Office programs. For example, Access allows you to reverse only one change, and if you close the datasheet, you can't even do that. You can use Undo right after you insert a new record to remove it, but you can't use the Undo feature to reverse a delete operation.
Ctrl+"	Copies a value from the field that's immediately above the current field. This trick is handy when you need to enter a batch of records with similar information. Figure 25-10 shows this often-overlooked trick in action.
Ctrl+;	Inserts today's date into the current field. The date format is based on computer settings, but expect to see something like "24-12-2010". You'll learn more about how Access works with dates on page 727.
Ctrl+Alt+Space	Inserts the default value for the field. You'll learn how to designate a default value on page 731.

Figure 25-10:
An Access user has been on an eBay buying binge and needs to add several doll records. With a quick Ctrl+" keystroke, he can copy the date from the previous record into the Date-Acquired field of the new record.

Cut, copy, and paste

Access, like virtually every Windows program, lets you cut and paste bits of information from one spot to another. This trick is easy using just three shortcut keys: Ctrl+C to copy, Ctrl+X to cut (similar to copy, but the original content is deleted), and Ctrl+V to paste. When you're in Edit mode, you can use these keys to copy whatever you've selected. If you're not in Edit mode, the copying or cutting operation grabs all the content in the field.

GEM IN THE ROUGH

Copying an Entire Record in One Step

Usually, you'll use copy and paste with little bits and pieces of data. However, Access has a little-known ability that lets you copy an *entire record*. To pull it off, follow these steps:

1. Click the margin to the left of the record you want to copy.

   This selects the record. (If you want to copy more than one adjacent record, hold down Shift, and then drag your mouse up or down until they're all selected.)

2. Right-click the selection, and then choose Copy.

   This copies the content to the Clipboard.

3. Scroll to the bottom of the table until you see the new-row marker (the asterisk).

4. Right-click the margin just to the left of the new-row marker, and then choose Paste.

   Presto—an exact duplicate. (Truth be told, one piece of data doesn't match exactly. Access updates the ID column for your pasted record, giving it a new number.)

Saving Databases

Unlike other programs, Access doesn't require that you save your data. It automatically saves any edits you make to the records in a table. This automatic-saving process takes place every time you change a record, and it happens almost instantaneously. It

---

also takes place behind the scenes, and you probably won't notice anything. But don't be alarmed when you exit Access and it doesn't prompt you to save changes, as *any change to your data is saved the moment you make it.*

Note: The rules are a bit different for database objects (page 710). When you add or edit a database object, Access waits until you finish and close the object, at which point it prompts you to save or discard your changes. If you're a bit paranoid and can't stand the wait, just choose File→Save to save the current database object immediately.

Making Backups

The automatic save feature can pose a problem if you make a change mistakenly. If you're fast enough, you can use the Undo feature to reverse your last change (Figure 25-11). However, the Undo feature reverses only your most recent edit, so it's no help if you edit a series of records and then discover the problem. It also doesn't help if you close your table and then reopen it.

Figure 25-11:
The Undo command appears in the Quick Access toolbar at the top left of the Access window, so it's always available.

For these reasons, it's a good idea to make frequent database backups. To make a database backup, you simply need to copy your database file to another folder, or make a copy with another name (like Bobblehead_Backup1.accdb). You can perform these tasks with Windows Explorer, but Access gives you an even easier option. First, choose File→Save & Publish. Then, under the File Types heading, choose Save Database As. Finally, under the Save Database As heading, double-click Back Up Database. This opens to create a copy of your database, in the location you choose (Figure 25-12).

Of course, it's still up to you to remember to copy your database backup to another location (like a network server) or to a different type of storage (like a DVD or a USB memory stick), so you're ready when disaster hits. You can use any number of different backup tools to safeguard your computer, including the Backup and Restore Center included in Windows Vista and Windows 7.

Figure 25-12:
When you choose to create a backup, Access fills in a suggested file name that incorporates the current date. That way, if you have several backup files, you can pick out the one you want.

What's with the .laccdb File?

I see an extra file with the extension .laccdb. What gives?

So far, you've familiarized yourself with the .accdb file type. But if you're in the habit of browsing around with Windows Explorer, you may notice another file that you didn't create, with the cryptic extension .laccdb. Along with Bobblehead. accdb, you may spot the mysterious Bobblehead.laccdb.

Access creates a .laccdb file when you open a database file and removes it when you close the database, so you'll see it only while you or someone else is browsing the database.

Access uses the .laccdb to track who's currently using the database. The *l* stands for *lock*, and it's used to make sure that if more than one person is using the database at once, people can't make changes to the same record at the same time (which could cause all manner of headaches). It's safe to ignore the .laccdb file. You don't need to include it in your backups.

Saving a Database with a Different Name or Format

You've probably already noticed the File→Save Database As command. When you click it, you can save your database with a new name. With this command, however, you're limited to the standard .accdb format used in Access 2010 and Access 2007, which isn't compatible with older versions of Access. If you try to open Bobblehead.accdb in Access 2003, you'll get nothing more than a blank stare and an error message.

Instead, Access 2003 uses the *.mdb* file format (which stands for Microsoft database) which actually comes in *three* versions: the really, really old original format, a re-tooled version that appeared with Access 2000, and the improved-yet-again version that Microsoft introduced with Access 2002 and reused for Access 2003.

To save the current database using an older Access file format, you have to use File→Save & Publish, and then, under the File Types heading, click Save Database As. The standard .accdb format is the best choice if you don't need to worry about compatibility, because it has the best performance and a few extra features. But if you need to share databases with people running much older versions of Access, the .mdb format is your only choice.

Keep in mind that once Access creates the new database file, that file is the one it keeps using. In other words, when you create a table or edit some data, Access updates the *new* file. (If you want to go back to the old file, you either need to open it in Access, or need to use File→Save Database As to save it again.)

You can also use the old-style .mdb format when you first create a database. Choose File→New and then click the folder icon next to the File Name box. Access opens the File New Database dialog box (which you saw back in Figure 25-2). It includes a "Save as type" box where you can choose the Access 2002-2003 file format or the even older Access 2000 format. (If you're set on going back any further, say the Access 95 format, your best bet is a time machine.)

Opening Databases

Once you've created a database, it's easy to open it later. The standard approach is to choose File→Open, and then to browse for your database file, select it, and click Open.

You can also open a database file from outside Access. For example, you can browse to the folder that holds your database file using Windows Explorer and double-click it. Or, just save the file on your desktop so it's easy to find when you need it.

Designating a Database as Trusted

When you open a database for the first time, you'll notice something a little bizarre. Access pops up a message bar with a scary-sounding security warning (Figure 25-13).

If you're opening your own recently created database, this security warning is a bit confusing, because right now your database doesn't even *attempt* to do anything risky. However, if you ever start building databases using certain types of advanced queries (online Appendix C), it's a different story. In those situations, you need to know if Access trusts your database and will allow it to run code and action queries.

Figure 25-13:
This security warning tells you that Access doesn't trust your database—in other words, it's opened your file in a special safe mode that prevents your database from performing any risky operations.

In the meantime, you're probably wondering what you should do about the message bar. You have two options:

- Click the X at the right side of the message bar to banish it. (But it'll reappear the next time you open the database.)

- Click Enable Content to tell Access that it can trust this database. Access won't bother you again about this file.

In previous versions of Access, the security warning would appear *every* time you opened a database, unless you took additional steps to configure Access's security settings. Access 2010 tries to be less annoying. If you click Enable Content, Access remembers that you trust this database, and it won't ask you again.

Opening Recent Databases

You can find the most recently opened databases in Access's Recent Databases list. To see this list, just choose File→Recent (Figure 25-14).

Ordinarily, Access tracks the previous 17 databases in the File→Recent list, but you can tell it to keep a shorter or longer list. To change this setting, choose File→Options, choose Client Settings, scroll down to the Display section, and change the number for "Show this number of Recent Documents". You can pick any number from 0 to 50.

The Recent Databases list isn't the only way to return to a database that you've worked on recently. Access places the four most recently opened database files in an even more accessible place: the column of commands in backstage view. For example, if you've recently worked on Bobbleheads.accdb, you can open it in a jiffy by choosing File→Bobbleheads.accdb, as highlighted in Figure 25-14.

Pin a recent database to the
list permanently

The three
"quick access"
databases

See all
recent
databases

Choose the number
of "quick access"
databases

Figure 25-14:
*The Recent Databases
list's biggest advantage
is the way it lets you
keep important files at
your fingertips by using
pinning. To try it, click the
thumbtack next to the
database file you want
to keep. Access moves
your database to the
top of the list and keeps
it there. From this point
on, that database won't
leave the list, no matter
how many databases
you open. If you decide
to stop working with
the database later on,
just click the thumbtack
again to release it.*

If you want Access to place more (or fewer) recent databases in this superconve-
nient spot, choose File→Recent, and modify the number for the "Quickly access this
number of Recent Databases" setting at the bottom of the window. You can also clear
the checkbox next to this setting to stop adding recent databases to the command list
altogether, which is useful if you find they're just getting in the way.

Tip: Want to hide your recent work? You can remove any file from the Recent Databases list by right-
clicking it and choosing "Remove from list". And if the clutter is keeping you from finding the databases
you want, just pin the important files, then right-click any file, and choose "Clear unpinned items". This
action removes every file that isn't pinned down.

Opening More Than One Database at Once

Every time you use the File→Open command, Access closes the current database
and then opens the one you chose. If you want to see more than one database at a
time, you need to fire up more than one copy of Access at the same time. (Computer
geeks refer to this action as starting more than one *instance* of a program.)

It's almost embarrassingly easy. If you double-click another database file while Access is already open, then a second Access window appears in the taskbar for that database. You can also launch a second (or third, or fourth…) instance of Access from the Start menu, and then use File→Open to load up a different database in each one.

The Navigation Pane

It's time to step back and take a look at what you've accomplished so far. You've created the Bobblehead database, and added a single database object: a table named Dolls. You've filled the Dolls table with several records. You don't have the fancy windows, reports, and search routines that make a database work really smoothly, but you do have the most important ingredient—organized data.

One issue you haven't tackled yet is how you manage the objects in your database. For example, if you have more than one table, you need a way to move back and forth between the two. That tool is the navigation pane, shown in Figure 25-15.

Figure 25-15:
Unhappy with the space consumed by the navigation pane? Click the Open/Close button in the top-right corner (top), and the navigation bar slides out of the way to give more room for the datasheet (bottom). Click the button again to expand it back into view.

Browsing Tables with the Navigation Pane

The navigation pane shows the objects that are part of your database, and it lets you manipulate them. However, you don't necessarily see all your database objects at all times. The navigation pane has several different viewing modes, so you can home in on exactly what interests you.

When you first create a database, the navigation pane shows only the tables in your database. That's good enough for now—after all, your database doesn't contain anything but the tables you've created.

To really try out the navigation pane, you need a database with more than one table. To give it a whirl, choose Create→Tables→Table from the ribbon to add a new blank table. Follow all the steps on page 694 to define the table and insert a record or two.

Tip: Not sure what table to create? Try creating a Collectors table that tracks all the friends you know who share the same bobbleheaded obsession. Now try to come up with a few useful fields for this table (while remembering that there's no need to go crazy with the details yet), and then compare your version to the example in Figure 25-16.

Once you've added the new table, you see both the new table and the old in the navigation pane at the same time. If you want to open a table, just double-click it in the navigation pane. If you have more than one datasheet open at once, then Access organizes them into tabs (see Figure 25-16).

The tab for the
Collectors table

The tab for the
Dolls table

Close the current tab
(Collectors)

Figure 25-16:
Using the navigation pane, you can open as many tables at once as you want. Access gives each datasheet a separate tabbed window. To move from one window to another, you just click the corresponding tab. If you're feeling a bit crowded, just click the X at the far right of the tab strip to close the current datasheet.

If you open enough tables, eventually all the tabs you need won't fit. In this situation, Access adds tiny scroll buttons to the left and right of the tab strip. You can use these buttons to move through all the tabs, but it takes longer.

Collapsing the Ribbon

Most people are happy to have the ribbon sit at the top of the Access window, with all its buttons on hand. However, serious data crunchers demand maximum space for their data. They'd rather look at another record of information than a pumped-up toolbar. If this preference describes you, then you'll be happy to find out you can *collapse* the ribbon, which shrinks it down to a single row of tab titles, as shown in Figure 25-17. To do so, just double-click the current tab title.

Even when the ribbon is collapsed, you can still use all its features. Just click a tab. If you click Home, the Home tab pops up over your worksheet. As soon as you click the button you want in the Home tab (or click somewhere else in the Access window), the ribbon collapses itself again. The same trick works if you trigger a command in the ribbon using the keyboard.

If you use the ribbon only occasionally, or if you prefer to use keyboard shortcuts, it makes sense to collapse the ribbon. Even when collapsed, the ribbon commands are available; it just takes an extra click to open the tab. On the other hand, if you make frequent trips to the ribbon, or if you're learning about Access and you like to browse the ribbon to see the available features, don't bother collapsing it. The extra space that you'll lose is well worth it.

Figure 25-17:
Want to use every square inch of screen space for your data? You can collapse the ribbon (as shown here) by double-clicking any tab. Click a tab to pop it open temporarily, or double-click a tab to bring the ribbon back for good. And if you want to perform the same trick without raising your fingers from the keyboard, then you can use the shortcut key Ctrl+F1.

Managing Database Objects

So far, you know how to open a table using the navigation pane. However, opening tables isn't all you can do with the navigation pane. You can actually perform three more simple tasks with any database object that shows up in the navigation pane:

- **Rename it.** Right-click the object, and then choose Rename. Type in the new name, and then press Enter. Go this route if you decide your Dolls table would be better off named DollsInMyWorldRenownedCollection.

- **Create a copy.** Right-click the object, and then choose Copy. Right-click anywhere in the navigation pane, and then choose Paste. Access prompts you to supply the new copy's name. The copy-an-object feature is useful if you want to take an existing table and try redesigning it, but you're not ready to remove the original copy just yet.

- **Delete it.** Right-click the object, and then choose Delete. Access asks you to confirm this operation, because you can't reverse it with the Undo command.

Access gives you a few more options for transferring database objects and tucking them out of sight.

TIMESAVING TIP

Creating a Shortcut to a Table

You probably already know that you can place a Windows shortcut on your desktop that points to your database file. To do so, just right-click your desktop, choose New→Shortcut, and then follow the instructions to pick your database file and choose a shortcut name. Now, anytime you want to jump back into your database, you can double-click your shortcut.

You probably don't know that you can create a shortcut that opens a database *and* navigates directly to a specific table. In fact, this maneuver is even easier than creating a plain-vanilla shortcut. Just follow these steps:

1. Resize the Access window so it doesn't take up the full screen, and then minimize any other programs. This way, you can see the desktop behind Access, which is essential for this trick.

2. Find the table you want to use in the navigation pane. Drag this table out of Access and over the desktop.

3. Release the mouse button. Access creates a shortcut with a name like "Shortcut to Dolls in Bobblehead. accdb". Double-click this shortcut to load the Bobblehead database and to open a datasheet right away for the Dolls table.

Building Smarter Tables

In the previous chapter, you learned how to dish out databases and pop tables into them without breaking a sweat. However, there's bad news. The tables you've been creating so far aren't up to snuff.

Most significantly, you haven't explicitly told Access what *type* of information you intend to store in each field of your table. A database treats text, numbers, dates, and other types of information differently. If you store numeric information in a field that expects text, then you can't do calculations later on (like find the average value of your bobblehead dolls), and you can't catch mistakes (like a bobblehead with a price value of "fourscore and twenty").

To prevent problems like these, you need to define the *data type* of each field in your table. You'll tackle that task in this chapter. Once you've mastered data types, you're ready to consider some of the finer points of database design. Finally, you'll also spend a few pages learning about a favorite pastime of seasoned database pros: keeping bad data out of your tables.

Understanding Data Types

All data is not created equal. Consider the Dolls table you created in the previous chapter. Its fields actually contain several different types of information:

- **Text.** The Character and Manufacturer fields.
- **Numbers.** The ID and PurchasePrice fields.
- **Dates.** The DateAcquired field.

You may naturally assume that the PurchasePrice field always includes numeric content and that the DateAcquired field always includes something that can be interpreted as a date. But if you haven't set the data types correctly, Access doesn't share your assumptions and doesn't follow the same rules.

When you create a new field in Datasheet view, Access makes an educated guess about the data type by examining the information you've just typed in. If you type *44*, then Access assumes you're creating a number field. If you type *Jan 6, 2010*, then Access recognizes a date. However, it's easy to confuse Access, which leads to the problems shown in Figure 26-1.

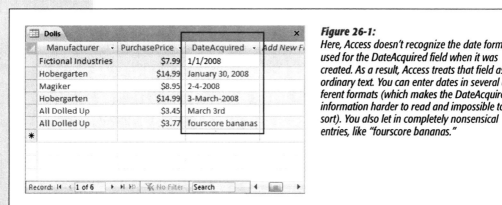

Figure 26-1:
Here, Access doesn't recognize the date format used for the DateAcquired field when it was created. As a result, Access treats that field as ordinary text. You can enter dates in several different formats (which makes the DateAcquired information harder to read and impossible to sort). You also let in completely nonsensical entries, like "fourscore bananas."

To prevent invalid entries, you need to tell Access what each field *should* contain. Once you set the rules, Access enforces them rigorously. You put these requirements in place using another window—the Design view of your table.

Design View

When you create a new database, Access starts you off with a single table and shows that table in Datasheet view. (As you learned last chapter, Datasheet view is the grid-like view where you can create a table *and* enter data.) To switch to Design view, right-click the tab name (like "Dolls: Table"), and then choose Design View. (Or you can use the Home→Views→View command or the View buttons at the bottom of the Access window. Figure 26-2 shows all your options. All of these commands do the same thing, so pick whichever approach seems most convenient.)

___

Note: If you've opened an old Access 2003 database, you won't see any tabs. Instead, you'll get a bunch of overlapping windows. You can remedy this problem and get your tabs back by following the instructions on page 704. Or, if you want to keep the overlapping windows, just use the view buttons or the ribbon to change views (instead of the right-click-the-tab-title approach described in Figure 26-2).

___

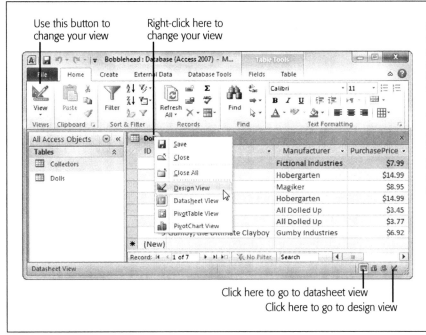

Use this button to change your view

Right-click here to change your view

Figure 26-2:
Right-click the tab name to see this menu. You can switch to Design view (choose Design View) and back again (choose Datasheet View). Alternatively, you can use the tiny view buttons in the window's bottom-right corner to jump back and forth.

Click here to go to datasheet view
Click here to go to design view

If you switch to Design view on a brand-new table that you haven't saved yet, Access asks you for a table name. Access then saves the table before switching you to Design view.

While Datasheet view shows the content in your table, Design view shows only its *structure* (see Figure 26-3).

You can use Design view to add, rearrange, and remove fields, but you can't use it to add new records. In the Dolls table, you can use Design view to add a Quantity field to keep track of doll duplicates. However, you can't add your newly purchased Bono bobblehead without switching back to the Datasheet view. In other words, Design view isn't intended for data entry.

If the Property Sheet box is open on the window's right side, you may want to close it to reclaim more space. (The Property Sheet lets you set a few highly technical table settings, none of which you need to consider right now.) To banish it, choose Table Tools | Design→Show/Hide→Property Sheet. If you want to bring it back later, then just repeat the same command.

Organizing and Describing Your Fields

Design view lets you rearrange the order of your fields, add new ones, rename the existing ones, and more. You can also do all these things in Datasheet view, but Access gurus usually find it's easier to make these changes in Design view, because you won't be distracted by the data in the table.

The list of fields (columns) in your table The data type of each field Settings that affect your entire table

The properties (additional settings) for the currently selected field (Character)

Figure 26-3:
Design view lists the fields in your table, putting each in a separate row. Fields here are listed from top to bottom, but they appear in Datasheet view ordered from left to right. Next to each field is its data type and an optional description. Underneath the field list, the Field Properties section shows more information about the currently selected field. Here, the navigation pane has been collapsed to provide extra space.

Here are a few simple ways you can change the structure of your table in Design view:

- **Add a new field to the end of your table.** Scroll to the last row of the field list, and then type in a new field name. This action is equivalent to adding a new field in Datasheet view.

- **Add a new field between existing fields.** Move to the field that's just *under* the place where you want to add the new field. Right-click the field, and then choose Insert Rows. Then, type a field name in the new, blank row.

- **Move a field.** Click the gray square immediately to the left of the field you want to move, and release the mouse button. This selects the field. Then, click the gray square, and drag the field to the new position.

Note: Remember, the order of your fields isn't all that important, because you can change the order in which you view the fields in Datasheet view. However, most people find it's easier to design a table if they organize the fields from the start.

- **Delete a field.** Right-click the gray square immediately to the left of the field you want to remove, and then choose Delete Rows. Keep in mind that when you remove a field, you also wipe out any data that was stored in that field. This action isn't reversible, so Access prompts you to confirm that it's really what you want to do (unless the table is completely empty).

- **Add a description for a field.** Type in a sentence or two in the Description column next to the appropriate field. (You might use "The celebrity or fictional character that this bobblehead resembles" as the description for the Character field in the Dolls table, as shown in Figure 26-4.)

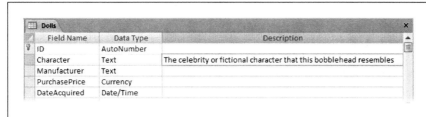

Figure 26-4:
Descriptions can help you remember what's what if you need to modify a table later. Descriptions are a great idea if more than one person maintains the same database, in which case you need to make sure your fields are as clear as possible. Descriptions also appear in the status bar when you're entering information in a table (see Figure 26-5).

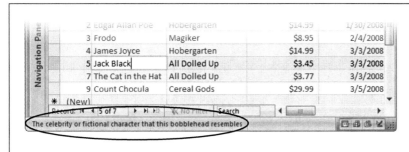

Figure 26-5:
The status bar text tells you what goes in this column, based on the field description. Sadly, this feature isn't as useful as it seems, because most people never think to look down at the status bar.

How Updates Work in Design View

Access doesn't immediately apply the changes you make in Design view. Instead, it waits until you close the table or switch back to Datasheet view. At that point, Access asks whether you want to save the table. (The answer, of course, is Yes.)

Sometimes, you may apply a change that causes a bit of a problem. You could try to change the data type of a field so that it stores numbers instead of text. In this situation, you won't discover the problem until you close the table or switch back to the Datasheet view, which might be a little later than you expect.

If you've made a potentially problematic change and just can't take the suspense, you're better off applying an update *immediately,* so you can see if there's a problem before going any further. To do so, click the Quick Access toolbar's Save button (it's the diskette icon in the Access window's top-left corner), or just use the keyboard shortcut Ctrl+S. Access applies your change and then saves the table. If it runs into a problem, Access tells you about it (and lets you choose how you want to fix it) before you do anything else with the table.

Access Data Types

Design view is a powerful place for defining a table. Design view lets you tweak all sorts of details without jumping around the ribbon (as you would if you were creating a table in Datasheet view).

One of the details is the *data type* of each field—a setting that tells Access what type of information you're planning to store in it. To change the data type, make a selection in the Data Type column next to the appropriate field (Figure 26-6). Here's where you separate the text from numbers (and other data types). The trick is choosing the best data type from the long list Access provides—you'll get more help in the following section.

Figure 26-6:
To choose a data type, click the Data Type column next to the appropriate field. A drop-down list box appears, with 12 choices.

Depending on the data type you choose, you can adjust other *field properties* to nail down your data type even more precisely. If you use a text data type, then you use field properties to set the maximum length. If you choose a decimal value, then you use field properties to set the number of decimal places. You set field properties in the Field Properties part of the Design view, which appears just under the field list. You'll learn more about field properties throughout this chapter.

The most important decision you make for any field is choosing its data type. The data type tells Access what sort of information you plan to store in that field. Access uses this information to reject values that don't make sense (see Figure 26-7), to perform proper sorting, and to provide other features like calculations, summaries, and filtering.

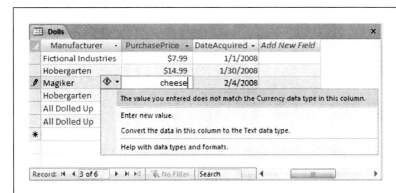

Figure 26-7:
This currency field absolutely does not allow text. Access lets you fix the problem by entering a new value (the right choice) or changing the field data type to text so that it allows anything (the absolutely wrong choice).

Note: A field can have only one data type. You can't create a field that can store two or three different data types, because Access wouldn't have enough information to manage the field properly. (Instead, in this situation, you probably need two separate fields.)

As you learned earlier, there are three basic types of data in the world: text, numbers, and dates. However, Access actually provides a whopping *12* data types, which include many more specialized choices. Before picking the right data type, it's a good idea to review all your choices. Table 26-1 shows an overview of the menu options in the Data Type list. (The Lookup Wizard choice isn't included, because it isn't a real data type. Instead, this menu option launches the Lookup wizard, which lets you set a list of allowed values. You'll learn more about this on page 756.)

Table 26-1. *Access data types*

Data Type	Description	Examples
Text	Numbers, letters, punctuation, and symbols, up to a maximum of 255 characters (an average-sized paragraph).	Names, addresses, phone numbers, and product descriptions. This data type is the most common.

Memo	Large amounts of unformatted text, up to 65,536 characters (an average-sized chapter in a novel).	Articles, memos, letters, arrest warrants, and other short documents.
Number	Different kinds of numbers, including negative numbers and those that have decimal places.	Any type of number except currency values (for example, dollar amounts). Stores measurements, counts, and percentages.
Currency	Similar to Number, but optimized for numbers that represent values of money.	Prices, payments, and expenses.
Date/Time	A calendar date or time of day (or both). Don't use this field for time *intervals* (the number of minutes in a song, the length of your workout session)—instead, use the Number data type.	Birthdates, order dates, ship dates, appointments, and UFO sighting times.
Yes/No	Holds one of two values: Yes or No. (You can also think of this as True or False.)	Fields with exactly two options, like male/female or approved/unapproved.
Hyperlink	A URL to a website, an email address, or a file path.	*www.FantasyPets.com, noreplies@ antisocial.co.uk, f:\Documents\ Report.doc*.
Attachment	One or more separate files. The content from these files is copied into the database.	Pictures, Word documents, Excel spreadsheets, sound files, and so on.
AutoNumber	Stores a unique, identifying number that Access generates when you insert a new record.	Used to uniquely identify each record; typically set as the primary key (page 740). Usually, every table has a single AutoNumber field named ID.
Calculated	Generates the value automatically, based on an expression you supply. You can perform simple math and combine the values from other fields.	Values that depend on other fields. For example, if you already have a UnitCost and a Quantity field, you can add a TotalCost calculated field that multiplies them together.
OLE Object	Holds embedded binary data, according to the Windows OLE (object linking and embedding) standard. Rarely used, because it leads to database bloat and other problems. The Attachment field is almost always a better choice.	Some types of pictures and documents from other programs. Mostly used in old-school Access databases. Nowadays, database designers use the Attachment data type instead of the OLE Object data type.

The following sections describe each data type except for OLE Object, which is a holdover from the dark ages of Access databases. Each section also describes any important field properties that are unique to that data type.

Changing the Data Type Can Lose Information

The best time to choose the data types for your fields is when you first create the table. That way, your table is completely empty, and you won't run into any problems.

If you add a few records, and *then* decide to change the data type in one of your fields, life becomes a little more complicated. You can still use Design view to change the data type, but Access needs to go through an extra step and *convert* the existing data to the new data type.

In many cases, the conversion process goes smoothly. If you have a text field that contains only numbers, you won't have a problem changing the data type from Text to Number. But in other cases, the transition isn't quite so seamless. Here are some examples of the problems you might run into:

- You change the data type from Text to Date, but Access can't interpret some of your values as dates.

- You change the data type from Text to Number, but some of your records have text values in that field (even though they shouldn't).

- You change the data type from Text to Number. However, your field contains non-integer numbers (like 4.234), and you forget to change the Field Size property (page 724). As a result, Access assumes you want to use only whole numbers and chops off all your decimal places.

The best way to manage these problems is to make a backup (page 702) before you make any drastic changes, and to be on the lookout for changes that go wrong. In the first two cases in the list above, Access warns you that it needs to remove some values because they don't fit the data type rules (see Figure 26-8). The third problem is a little more insidious—Access gives you a warning, but it doesn't actually tell you whether a problem occurred. If you suspect trouble, switch to Datasheet view, and then check out your data before going any further.

Figure 26-8:
Don't say you weren't warned. Here, Access lets you know (in its own slightly obscure way) that it can't make the change you want—modifying the data type of the field from Text to Date—without throwing out the values in four records. The best course of action is to click No to cancel the change, and then to take a closer look at your table in Datasheet view to track down the problematic values.

Text

Text is the all-purpose data type. It accepts any combination of letters, numbers, and other characters. So you can use a text field for a word or two (like "Mary Poppins"), a sentence ("The candidate is an English nanny given to flights of song."), or anything else ("@#$d sf_&!").

Note: Because text fields are so lax, you can obviously enter numbers, dates, and just about anything else in them. However, you should use text only when you're storing some information that can't be dealt with using another data type, because Access always treats the contents of a text field as plain, ordinary text. In other words, if you store the number 43.99 in a text field, Access doesn't realize you're dealing with numbers, and it doesn't let you use it in a calculation.

Text length

Every text field has a *maximum length.* This trait comes as a great surprise to many people who aren't used to databases. After all, with today's gargantuan hard drives, why worry about space? Can't your database just expand to fit whatever data you want to stuff inside?

The maximum length matters because it determines how *densely* Access can pack your records together. For performance reasons, Access needs to make sure that an entire record is stored in one spot, so it always reserves the maximum amount of space a record might need. If your table has four fields that are 50 characters apiece, Access can reserve 200 characters' worth of space on your hard drive for each record. On the other hand, if your fields have a maximum 100 characters each, Access holds onto twice as much space for each record, even if you aren't actually using that space. The extra space isn't a major issue (you probably have plenty of room on your computer), but the more spread out a database, the slower your searches.

The standard maximum length is 50, a good starting point. The box on page 721 has some more recommendations.

To set the maximum length, go to the Field Properties section, and enter a number in the Field Size box (Figure 26-9). The largest maximum you're allowed is 255 characters. If you need to store a large paragraph or an entire article's worth of information, then you need the Memo data type instead (see the next section).

Tip: It's worthwhile being a little generous with maximum lengths to avoid the need to modify the database later.

Memo

Microsoft designed the Memo data type to store large quantities of text. If you want to place a chapter from a book, an entire newspaper article, or just several paragraphs into a field, you need the Memo data type. The name is a little odd—although a memo field could certainly store the information from an interoffice memorandum, it's just as useful anytime you have large blocks of text.

When creating a memo field, you don't need to supply a maximum length, because Access stores the data in a memo field differently from other data types. Essentially, it stuffs memo data into a separate section, so it can keep the rest of the record as compact and efficient as possible, but accommodate large amounts of text.

The field you're using

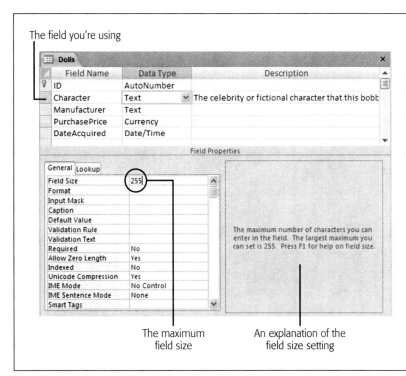

Figure 26-9:
To set a maximum length, choose your field, and then click the Field Size box in the Field Properties list (shown here). (All the field properties you need in this chapter are on the General tab.) When you click a field property box, that field property's description appears on the right.

The maximum field size

An explanation of the field size setting

UP TO SPEED

Maximum Length Guidelines

Here are some recommended maximum lengths:

- **First names and last names.** Usually, 25 characters handles a first name, while 50 characters plays it safe for a long, hyphenated last name.

- **Middle initial.** One character. (Sometimes common sense is right.)

- **Email address.** Go with 50 characters. Email addresses closer to 100 characters have turned up in the wild (Google "world's longest email address" for more), but they're unlikely to reach your database.

- **Cities, states, countries, and other places.** Although a Maori name for a hill in New Zealand tops out at over 80 characters (see *http://en.wikipedia.org/wiki/Longest_word_in_English*), 50 is enough for most practical purposes.

- **Street address.** A street address consists of a number, followed by a space, then the street name, another space, and the street abbreviation (like Rd or St). Fifty characters handles it, as long as you put postal codes, cities, and other postal details in other fields.

- **Phone numbers, postal codes, credit card numbers, and other fixed-length text.** Count the number characters and ignore the placeholders, and set the maximum to match. If you want to store the U.S. phone number (123) 456-7890, make the field 10 characters long. If you plan to accept international numbers, you'll need to allow for up to 15 digits.

- **Description or comments.** Specifying 255 characters fits three or four average sentences of information. If you need more, consider the Memo data type instead (page 720).

A memo field tops out at 65,536 characters. To put it in perspective, that's about the same size as this chapter. If you need more space, then add more than one memo field.

Note: Technically, the 65,536-character limit is a limitation in the Access user interface, not in the database. If you program an application that uses your database, it could store far more—up to a gigabyte's worth of information in a memo field.

If you need to edit a large amount of text while you're working on the datasheet, use the Zoom box (Figure 26-10). Just move to the field you want to edit, and then press Shift+F2.

The value that's being edited

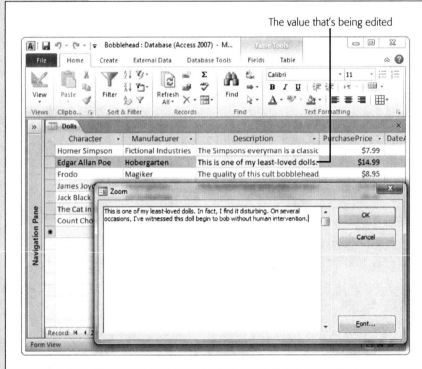

Figure 26-10:
If you have lengthy text in a field, it's hard to see it all at once without a lot of scrolling. By opening a Zoom box (Shift+F2), you can see more content and edit it more easily. You'll need to click OK (to accept your edits) or Cancel (to abandon them) to get back to the datasheet.

Formatted text

Like a text field, the memo field stores *unformatted* text. However, you can also store *rich text* in a memo field—text that has different fonts, colors, text alignment, and so on. To do so, set the Text Format field property to Rich Text (rather than Plain Text).

To format part of your text, you simply need to select it and then choose a formatting option from the ribbon's Home→Text Formatting section. However, most of the time you won't take this approach, because it's difficult to edit large amounts of text in the datasheet's narrow columns. Instead, use Shift+F2 to open a Zoom box, and then use the minibar (Figure 26-11).

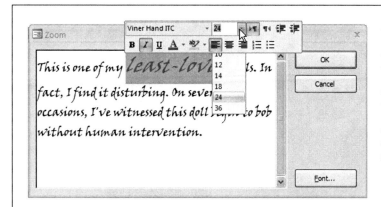

Figure 26-11:
To show the minibar (sadly, of the nonalcoholic variety), select some text, and then hover over it with the mouse. The minibar—a compact toolbar with formatting options—gradually fades into view. The minibar is sometimes a little finicky, and you may need to reselect the text more than once to get it to appear.

Tip: There's another, even easier way to get formatted text into a Memo field. Create the text in a word-processing program (like Word), format it there, and then copy and paste it into the field. All the formatting comes with it.

As neat as this feature may seem at first glance, it's rarely worth the trouble. Database purists believe that tables should store raw information and let other programs (or fancy forms) decide how to format it. The problem is that once you've created your formatted text, it can be quite a chore to maintain it. Just imagine having to change the font in 30,000 different records.

If you really do want to store formatted content, then consider linking your database to a separate document, like a Word file. In Access, you can do this in two ways:

- **Create a field that points to the file.** For example, *c:\myfile\BonoBobblehead-Description.docx*. For this trick, use the Text or Hyperlink data type (page 731).

- **Embed the file inside your database.** This way, it's impossible to lose the file (or end up pointing to the wrong location). However, you'll need to pull the file out every time you want to update it. To do this, you need to use the Attachment data type (page 733).

Number

The Number data type includes a wide variety of differently sized numbers. You can choose to allow decimal numbers, and you can use negative values (just precede the value with a – sign). You should use the Number data type for every type of numeric information you have—except currency amounts, in which case the Currency data type (page 726) is a better match.

When you use numeric fields, you don't include information about the units you're using. You may have a field that represents a Weight in Pounds, a Height in Meters, or an Age in Years. However, these fields contain only a number. It's up to you to know what that number signifies. If you think other people may be confused, consider explaining the units in the description (page 715), or incorporate it into the field name (like HeightInMeters).

Note: Your field should *never, ever* contain values like "44 pounds." Access treats this value as a text value, so if you make this mistake, you can't use all of Access's number-crunching tools.

Number size

As with a text field, when you create a number field, you need to set the Field Size property to make sure Access reserves the right amount of space. However, with numbers your options are a little more complicated than they are for ordinary text.

Essentially, numbers are divided into several subgroups, depending on whether they support non-integer values (numbers to the right of a decimal point) and on how many *bytes* of space Access uses to store them.

Note: A *byte* is a group of eight bits, which is the smallest unit of storage in the computer world. For example, a megabyte is approximately one million bytes.

Table 26-2 lists the different Field Size options you can choose for the Number data type and explains when each one makes most sense. Initially, Access chooses Long Integer for all fields, which gives a fair bit of space but requires whole numbers.

Table 26-2. *Field size options for the Number data type*

Field Size	Contains	When to Use It
Byte	An integer (whole number) from 0 to 255. Requires just one byte of space.	This size is risky, because it fits only very small numbers. Usually, it's safer to use Integer for small numbers and give yourself a little more breathing room.
Integer	An integer (whole number) from −32,768 to 32,767. Requires two bytes of space.	Useful if you need small numbers with no decimal part.
Long Integer	An integer (whole number) from −2,147,483,648 to 2,147,483,647. Requires four bytes of space.	The Access standard. A good choice with plenty of room. Use this to store just about anything without hitting the maximum, as long as you don't need decimals.

Single	Positive or negative numbers with up to 38 zeroes and 7 decimal places of accuracy. Requires four bytes of space.	The best choice if you need to store non-integer numbers or numbers that are too large to fit in a Long Integer.
Double	Positive or negative numbers with up to 308 zeroes and 15 decimal places of accuracy. Requires eight bytes of space.	Useful if you need ridiculously big numbers.
Decimal	Positive or negative numbers with up to 28 zeroes and 28 decimal places of accuracy. Requires eight bytes of space.	Useful for numbers that have lots of digits to the right of the decimal point.

Note: Table 26-2 doesn't include Replication ID, because you use that option only with the Number data type (page 723).

Number formatting

The Field Size determines how Access stores your number in the table. However, you can still choose how it's *presented* in the datasheet. For example, 50, 50.00, 5E1, $50.00, and 5000% are all the same number behind the scenes, but people interpret them in dramatically different ways.

To choose a format, you set the Format field property. Your basic built-in choices include:

- **General Number.** Displays unadorned numbers, like 43.4534. Any extra zeroes at the end of a number are chopped off (so 4.10 becomes 4.1).

- **Currency and Euro.** Both options display numbers with two decimal places, thousands separators (the comma in $1,000.00), and a currency symbol. These choices are used only with the Currency data type (page 726).

- **Fixed.** Displays numbers with the same number of decimal places, filling in zeroes if necessary (like 432.11 and 39.00). A long column of numbers lines up on the decimal point, which makes your tables easier to read.

- **Standard.** Similar to Fixed, except it also uses thousands separators to help you quickly interpret large numbers like 1,000,000.00.

- **Percent.** Displays numbers as percentages. For example, if you enter 0.5, that translates to 50%.

- **Scientific.** Displays numbers using scientific notation, which is ideal when you need to handle numbers that range widely in size (like 0.0003 and 300). Scientific notation displays the first nonzero digit of a number, followed by a fixed number of digits, and then indicates what power of ten that number needs to be multiplied by to generate the specified number. For example, 0.0003 becomes 3.00×10^{-4}, which displays as 3.00E–4. The number 300, on the other hand, becomes 3.00×10^2, or 3.00E2.

Note: When using Fixed, Standard, Percent, or Scientific, you should also set the Decimal Places field property to the number of decimal places you want to see. Otherwise, you always get two places.

- **A custom format string.** This is a cryptic code that tells Access exactly how to format a number. You need to type the format string you need into the Format box. For example, if you type in the weird-looking code #,##0, (including the comma at the end) Access hides the last three digits of every number, so 1,000,000 appears as 1,000 and 15,000 as 15.

Note: Custom number formats aren't terribly common in Access (they're more frequently used with Excel).

Currency

Currency is a slight variation on the Number data type that's tailored for financial calculations. Unlike with the Number data type, here you can't choose a Field Size for the Currency data type—Access has a one-size-fits-all policy that requires eight bytes of storage space.

Tip: The Currency data type is better than the Number data type because it uses optimizations that prevent rounding errors with very small fractions. The Currency data type is accurate to 15 digits to the left of the decimal point, and 4 digits to the right.

You can adjust the number of decimal places that Access shows for currency values on the datasheet by setting the Decimal Places field property. Usually, it's set to 2.

The formatting that Access uses to display currency values is determined by the "Regional and Language" settings on your computer. However, these settings might produce results you don't want—for example, say you run an artisanal cereal business in Denmark that sells all its products overseas in U.S. dollars (not kroner). You can control exactly how currency values are formatted by setting the Format field property, which gives you the following options:

- **Currency.** This option is the standard choice. It uses the formatting based on your computer's regional settings.
- **Euro.** This option always uses the Euro currency symbol (€).
- **A custom format string.** This option lets you use any currency symbol you want (as described below). You need to type the format string you need into the Format box.

There's a simple recipe for cooking up format strings with a custom currency symbol. Start by adding the character for the currency symbol (type in whatever you want), and then add #,###.##, which is Access code for "give me a number with thousands separators and two decimal places."

For example, the Danish cereal company could use a format string like this to show the U.S. currency symbol:

```
$#,###.##
```

Whereas a U.S. company that needs to display a Danish currency field (which formats prices like *kr 342.99*) would use this:

```
kr #,###.##
```

Note: Enterprising users can fiddle around with the number format to add extra text, change the number of decimal places (just add or remove the # signs), and remove the thousands separators (just take out the comma).

Date/Time

Access uses the Date/Time data type to store a single instant in time, complete with the year, month, day, and time down to the second. Behind the scenes, Access stores dates as numbers, which lets you use them in calculations.

Although Access always uses the same amount of space to store date information in a field, you can hide some components of it. You can choose to display just a date (and ignore time information) or just the time (and ignore date information). To do this, you simply need to set the Format field property. Table 26-3 shows your options.

Table 26-3. Date/time formats

Format	Example
General Date	2/23/2010 11:30:15 PM
Long Date	February 23, 2010 11:30:15 PM
Medium Date	23-Feb-10
Short Date	2/23/2010
Long Time	11:30:15 PM
Medium Time	11:30 PM
Short Time	23:30

Note: Both the General Date and Long Date formats show the time information only if it's not zero.

The format affects only how the date information is displayed—it doesn't change how you type it in. Access is intelligent enough to interpret dates correctly when you type any of the following:

- 2010-2-23 (the international year-month-day standard always works)
- 2/23/2010 (the most common approach, but you might need to flip the month and day on non-U.S. computers)

- 23-Feb-10
- Feb 23 (Access assumes the current year)
- 23 Feb (ditto)

To add date and time information, just follow the date with the time, as in 23-Feb-10 5:06 PM. Make sure to include the AM/PM designation at the end, or use a 24-hour clock.

If it's too much trouble to type in a date, then consider using the calendar smart tag instead. The smart tag is an icon that appears next to the field whenever you move to it, as shown in Figure 26-12. You can turn this feature off by setting the Show Date Picker field property to Never.

UP TO SPEED

Dating Your Computer

Windows has regional settings for your computer, which affect the way Microsoft programs display things like dates and currencies. In Access the regional settings determine how the different date formats appear. In other words, on a factory-direct U.S. computer, the Short Date format shows up as 2/23/2010. But on a British computer, it may appear as 23/2/2010. Either way, the information that's stored in the database is the same. However, the way it appears in your datasheet changes.

You can change the regional settings, and they don't have to correspond to where you live—you can set them for your company headquarters on another continent, for instance. But keep in mind that these settings are global, so if you alter them, you affect all your programs.

To make a switch, head to Control Panel. (In Windows XP, click the Start menu and choose Settings→Control Panel. In Windows Vista or Windows 7, click Start and look for

the Control Panel option on the right side.) Once you've opened the Control Panel, double-click "Region and Language", which brings up a dialog box. The first tab has all the settings you want. The most important setting is in the first box, which has a drop-down list you can use to pick the language and region you want to use, like English (United States) or Swedish (Finland).

You can fine-tune the settings in your region, too. This makes sense only if you have particular preferences about how dates should be formatted that don't match the standard options. To do so, you click a button whose name varies depending on your operating system. In Windows XP click the Customize button; in Windows Vista look for the "Customize this format" button; and in Windows 7, click the Additional Settings button. Then, click the Date tab in the new dialog box that appears (Figure 26-13).

Custom date formats

If you're not happy with the seven standard date options that Access provides, you can craft your own date format string and type in the Format property. This format string tells Access how to present the date and time information.

A date format string is built out of pieces. Each piece represents a single part of the date, like the day, month, year, minute, hour, and so on. You can combine these pieces in whatever order you want. For example, consider the following format string:

```
yyyy-mm-dd
```

Figure 26-12:
Access automatically pops up the calendar smart tag for all date fields. Click the calendar icon to pop up a mini-calendar where you can browse to the date you want. However, you can't use the calendar to enter time information.

Figure 26-13:
Your computer settings determine how dates appear in applications like Access. Use the drop-down lists to specify the date separator; order of month, day, and year components in a date; and how Access should interpret two-digit years. You can mix and match these settings freely, although you could wind up with a computer that's completely counterintuitive to other people's perspectives.

This string translates as the following instructions: "Display the four-digit year, followed by a dash, followed by a two-digit month number, followed by another dash, followed by a two-digit day number." You're free to put these components in any order you like, but this example defines them according to the ISO date standard. You can also control how to display the year, day, and month components. You can use month abbreviations or full names instead of a month number (just replace the *mm* code with something different).

If you apply this format string to a field that contains the date January 1, 2010, then you see this in the datasheet:

    2010-01-01

Remember that regardless of what information you choose to display or hide, Access stores the same date information in your database. Table 26-4 shows the basic placeholders that you can use for a date or time format string.

Table 26-4. *Date and time formatting codes*

Code	Description	Displays (January 1, 2010, 1:05:05 p.m.)...
d	The day of the month, from 1 to 31, with the numbers between 1 and 9 appearing without a leading 0.	1
dd	The day of the month, from 01 to 31 (leading 0 included for 1 to 9).	01
ddd	A three-letter abbreviation for the day of the week.	Fri
dddd	The full name of the day of the week.	Friday
m	The number value, from 1 to 12, of the month (no leading 0 used).	1
mm	The number value, from 01 to 12, of the month (leading 0 used for 01 to 09).	01
mmm	A three-letter abbreviation for the month.	Jan
mmmm	The full name of the month.	January
yy	A two-digit abbreviation of the year.	10
yyyy	The year with all four digits.	2010
h	The hour, from 0 to 23 (no leading 0 used).	13
hh	The hour, from 00 to 23 (leading 0 used for 00 to 09).	13
:n	The minute, from 0 to 59 (no leading 0 used).	5

:nn	The minute, from 0 to 59 (leading 0 used for 00 to 09).	05
:s	The second, from 0 to 59 (no leading 0 used).	5
:ss	The second, from 0 to 59 (leading 0 used for 00 to 09).	05
AM/PM	Tells Access to use a 12-hour clock, with an AM or PM indication.	PM
am/pm	Indicates a 12-hour clock, with an am or pm indication.	pm
A/P	Tells Access to use a 12-hour clock, with an A or P indication.	P
a/p	Tells Access to use a 12-hour clock, with an *a* or *p* indication.	p

Yes/No

A Yes/No field is a small miracle of efficiency. It's the leanest of Access data types, because it allows only two possible values: Yes or No.

When using a Yes/No field, imagine that your field poses a yes or no question by adding an imaginary question mark at the end of your field name. You could use a field named InStock to keep track of whether a product is in stock. In this case, the yes or no question is "in stock?" Other examples include Shipped (in a list of orders), Male (to separate the boys from the girls), and Republican (assuming you're willing to distinguish between only two political affiliations).

Although every Yes/No field is essentially the same, you can choose to format it slightly differently, replacing the words "Yes" and "No" with "On" and "Off" or "True" and "False." You'll find these three options in the Format menu. However, it doesn't make much difference because on the datasheet, Yes/No fields are displayed with a checkbox, as shown in Figure 26-14.

Hyperlink

The Hyperlink data type comes in handy if you want to create a clickable link to a web page, file, or email address. You can mix and match any combination of the three in the same table. Access handles hyperlinks a little differently in Datasheet view. When you type text into a hyperlink field, it's colored blue and underlined. And when you click the link, Access pops it open in your browser (Figure 26-15).

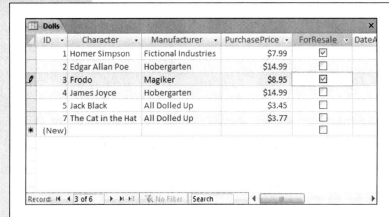

Figure 26-14:
In this example, ForResale is a Yes/No field. A checked checkbox represents Yes (or True or On). An unchecked checkbox represents No (or False or Off).

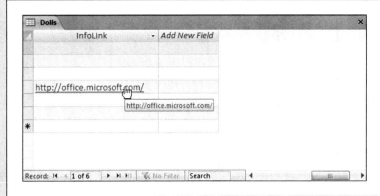

Figure 26-15:
Click this hyperlink, and you'll head straight to the welcoming arms of Office Online.

Note: Access doesn't prevent you from entering values that aren't hyperlinks in a Hyperlink data field. This trait leads to problems if you click the hyperlink. If you put the text "saggy balloons" in a hyperlink field and click it, then Access tries to send your browser to *http://saggy balloons*, which obviously doesn't work.

One hyperlink field feature isn't immediately obvious. Hyperlink fields actually store more than one piece of information. Every hyperlink includes these three components:

- The text you see in the cell.

- The text you see when you hover over the link with your mouse (the tooltip).

- The destination you go to when you click the cell (the URL or file path).

When you type a link into the datasheet, the first two are set to the same value—whatever you've just typed in. For example, when you type *www.FantasyPharmacologists.com*, the text you see and the tooltip are both set to hold the same content, which is *www.FantasyPharmacologists.com*.

To set the third piece of information—the URL or file path—Access examines your entry and makes a reasonable guess. For example, if you type *www.FantasyPharmacologists.com*, Access assumes you want the URL to be the web location *http://www.FantasyPharmacologists.com*, so it adds the *http://* sequence at the beginning. Similarly, if you type an email address like *dr.z@b-store.com*, Access creates the full email link *mailto:dr.z@b-store.com*. When you click a link like this in Access or in a web browser, your email program starts a new message. Finally, if you enter a file path or a URL that already starts with *http://* (or some other URL prefix), Access doesn't make any changes.

Most of the time, Access's approach gives you the result you want. However, you aren't limited to this strategy. You can set these three components to have different values—for example, so your URL has a website address (like *www.zyqcorp.com*) but your display text has a more approachable name ("The ZYQ Corporation"). To do so, move to the value, and then press Ctrl+K to pop up the Edit Hyperlink window (see Figure 26-16). Or right-click it, and then choose Hyperlink→Edit Hyperlink.

Figure 26-16:
Using the Edit Hyperlink window, you can change the text that appears in the cell (at the top of the window) and the page that Access opens when you click it (at the bottom). You can also create links that use email addresses (in which case Access opens the email program that's configured on your computer) or links to file paths (use the folder-browsing area to pick the file you want).

Attachment

The Attachment data type lets you add one or more files to your database record in much the same way that you tack on attachments to your email messages. Access stores the files you add to an attachment field as part of your table, embedded inside your database file.

The Attachment data type is a good choice if you need to insert a picture for a record, a short sound file, or even a document from another Office application like Word or Excel. You could create a People table with a picture of each person in your contact list, or a product catalog with pictures of the wares you're selling. In these cases, attachments have an obvious benefit—because they're stored inside your database file, you never lose track of them.

However, attachments aren't as graceful with large files, or files you need to modify frequently. If you place a frequently modified document into an Access database, it isn't available on your hard drive for quick editing, printing, and searching. Instead, you need to fire up Access, and then find the corresponding record before you can open your document. If you want to make changes, then you also need to keep Access open so it can take the revised file and insert it back into the database.

Tip: Think twice before you go wild with attachments. As you've already learned, an Access database is limited to two gigabytes of space. If you start storing large files in your tables, you just may run out of room. Instead, store large documents in separate files, and then record the file name in a text or hyperlink field.

When you use the Attachment data type, make sure you set the Caption field property, which determines the text that appears in the column header for that field. (Often, you'll use the field name as the caption.) If you don't set a caption, the column header shows a paper clip but no text.

You'll recognize an attachment field in the datasheet because it has a paper-clip icon next to it (Figure 26-17).

ID	Character	Picture	Manufacturer	PurchasePrice
1	Homer Simpson	ⓤ(0)	Fictional Industries	$7.99
2	Edgar Allan Poe	ⓤ(0)	Hobergarten	$14.99
3	Frodo	ⓤ(0)	Magiker	$8.95
4	James Joyce	ⓤ(0)	Hobergarten	$14.99
5	Jack Black	ⓤ(0)	All Dolled Up	$3.45
7	The Cat in the Hat	ⓤ(0)	All Dolled Up	$3.77
9	Count Chocula	ⓤ(2)		
(New)		ⓤ(0)		

Figure 26-17:
Attachments are flagged with a paper-clip icon and a number in brackets, which tells you how many files are attached. In this example, all the values in the Picture attachment field are empty except Count Chocula, which has two.

To attach a file or review the list of attached files, double-click the paper-clip icon. You'll see the Attachments dialog box (see Figure 26-18).

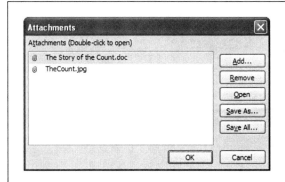

Figure 26-18:
The Attachments dialog box shows you all the files that are linked to your field.

Here's what you can do in the Attachments window:

- **Add a new attachment.** Click the Add button. Then browse to a new file and click OK. You'll see the file appear at the bottom of the list.

- **Delete an attachment.** Select the attachment in the list and then click Remove.

- **Save a copy of an attachment.** Select the attachment, click Save As, and then browse to a location on your computer. Or, click Save All to save copies of all the attachments in this field. If you change these copies, you don't change the attachment in the database.

- **View an attachment.** Select the attachment and then click Open. Access copies the attachment to a temporary folder on your computer, where Internet content is cached, and then opens it in the associated program. For example, .doc files get opened in Microsoft Word.

- **Edit an attachment.** This process is similar to viewing an attachment. First, select the attachment and click Open. Begin editing the document, but make sure you don't close the Attachments window in Access. When you're finished, save the temporary document (without changing its name or moving it to a new folder), switch back to Access, and click OK in the Attachments window. Access notices your changes and asks if it should copy the updated version of the file to your database, replacing the original (Figure 26-19, top).

Unfortunately, the Attachment data type doesn't give you a lot of control. Here are some of its limitations:

- You can't restrict the number of attachments allowed in an attachment field. All attachment fields allow a practically unlimited number of attachments (although you can't attach two files with the same name).

- You also can't restrict the types of files used for an attachment.

- You can't restrict the size of the files used for an attachment.

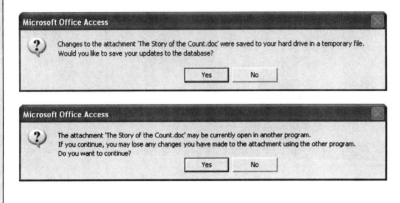

Figure 26-19:
Top: In this example, Access notices that you've updated the attachment file "The Story of the Count. doc" in Word. When you close the At- tachments window, Access asks if you want to update the database with the new saved version.

Bottom: This system only works if you keep the Attachments window open while you edit. If you close the Attachments window while the attachment file is still open, you get a warning message like this one. If you continue, then any changes you make (or any changes you've made so far and haven't saved) won't be reflected in the database. (To avoid such headaches, attach only files that you don't plan to edit.)

AutoNumber

An AutoNumber is a special sort of data type. Unlike with all the other data types you've seen, you can't fill in the value for an AutoNumber field. Instead, Access does it automatically whenever you insert a new record. Access makes sure that the AutoNumber value is unique—in other words, it never gives two records the same AutoNumber value.

Note: Every table can have up to one AutoNumber field.

Ordinarily, the AutoNumber field looks like a *sequence* of numbers—Access tends to give the first record an AutoNumber value of 1, the second an AutoNumber of 2, and so on. However, the truth isn't so straightforward. Sometimes, Access skips a number. This skipping could happen when several people are using a database at once, or if you start adding a new record, and then cancel your action by pressing Esc. You may also delete an existing record, in which case Access never reuses that

AutoNumber value. As a result, if you insert a new record and you see it's assigned an AutoNumber value of 401, then you can't safely assume that there are already 400 records in the table. The actual number is probably less.

An AutoNumber value doesn't represent anything, and you probably won't spend much time looking at it. The AutoNumber field's sole purpose is to make sure you have a unique way to point to each record in your table. Usually, your AutoNumber field is also the primary key for your table, as explained on page 741.

Using AutoNumbers without revealing the size of your table

AutoNumber values have one minor problem: They give a clue about the number of records in a table. You may not want a customer to know that your brand-new food and crafts company, Better Butter Sculptures, hasn't cracked 12 customers. So you'll be a little embarrassed to tell him he's customer ID number 6.

The best way to solve this problem is to start counting at a higher number. You can fool Access into generating AutoNumber values starting at a specific minimum. For example, instead of creating customer IDs 1, 2, and 3, you could create the ID values 11001, 11002, 11003. This approach also has the advantage of keeping your IDs a consistent number of digits, and it lets you distinguish between IDs in different tables by starting them at different minimums. Unfortunately, to pull this trick off, you need to fake Access out with a specially designed query, which you can learn about in the online Appendix C.

Alternatively, you can tell Access to generate AutoNumber values in a different way. You have two choices:

- **Random AutoNumber value.** To use random numbers, change the New Values field property from Increment to Random. Now you'll get long numbers for each record, like 212125691, 1671255778, and -1388883525. You might use random AutoNumber to create values that other people can't guess. (For example, if you have an Orders table that uses random values for the OrderID field, you can use those values as confirmation numbers.) However, random AutoNumbers are rarely used in the Access world.

- **Replication IDs.** Replication IDs are long, obscure codes like 38A94E7B-2F95-4E7D-8AF1-DB5B35F9700C that are statistically guaranteed to be unique. To use them, change the Field Size property from Long Integer to Replication ID. Replication IDs are really used only in one scenario—if you have separate copies of a database and need to merge the data together in the future. The next section explains that scenario.

Both of these options trade the easy-to-understand simplicity of the ordinary AutoNumber for something a little more awkward, so evaluate them carefully before using these approaches in your tables.

Using replication IDs

Imagine you're working at a company with several regional sales offices, each with its own database for tracking customers. If you use an ordinary AutoNumber field, then you'll end up with several customers with the same ID, but at different offices. If you ever want to compare data, you'll quickly become confused. And you can't combine all the data into one database for further analysis later on.

Access gives you another choice—a *replication ID*. A replication ID is a strange creation—it's an extremely large number (16 bytes in all) that's represented as a string of numbers and letters that looks like this:

```
38A94E7B-2F95-4E7D-8AF1-DB5B35F9700C
```

This ID is obviously more cumbersome than an ordinary integer. After all, it's much easier to thank someone for submitting Order 4657 than Order 38A94E7B-2F95-4E7D-8AF1-DB5B35F9700C. In other words, if you use the AutoNumber value for tracking or bookkeeping, then the replication ID is a bad idea.

However, the replication ID solves the problem described earlier, where multiple copies of the same database are being used in different places. That's because replication IDs are guaranteed to be *statistically unique.* In other words, there are so many possible replication IDs that it's absurdly unlikely that you'll ever generate the same replication ID twice. So even if you have dozens of separate copies of your database, and they're all managing hundreds of customers, you can rest assured that each customer has a unique customer ID.

Note: A replication ID is also called a GUID (short for "globally unique identifier"). In theory, the chances of two GUIDs being identical are one in 2, which is small enough that you could set one billion people to work, ask them to create one billion GUIDs a year, and still be duplicate-free for the next decade or two. In practice, the real limitation is how good the random number generator is in Access.

Figure 26-20 shows a table that uses replication IDs.

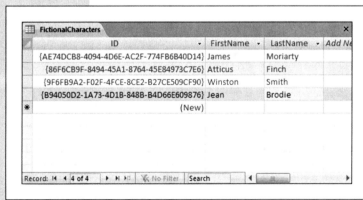

Figure 26-20:
This figure shows four records in the FictionalCharacters table, each with a statistically unique AutoNumber value.

Calculated

A *calculated* field is one that shows the result of a calculation. You provide the formula (known as the *expression*) that produces the result. Access does all the calculating work. For example, imagine you have a table of products with a Price field and a CostToManufacture field. You can add a calculated field named Profit that uses the expression *[Price] – [CostToManufacture]* to arrive at its result. (Technically, the square brackets are required only for field names that have spaces in them, but Access likes to add them in every expression just to be safe.) When you create a calculated field, you type the expression into the Expression field property. It's impossible to create a calculated field without an expression—if you try it, Access won't let you save the table.

Like an AutoNumber field, a calculated field is a hands-off affair. In the current example, whenever you update a record's Price or CostToManufacture, Access automatically performs the profit calculation and stores the result in the Profit field. You don't need to—and can't—edit the Profit field by hand.

GEM IN THE ROUGH

Setting Field Data Types in Datasheet View

Although Access pros favor Design view, it's not the only game in town. You can create exactly the same table, with exactly the same data types, using Datasheet view.

There are actually two techniques you can use to create fields with proper data types in Datasheet view (as shown in Figure 26-21). The first approach is to click the "Click to Add" column header, which appears on the right side of your table. When you do, Access pops open a list of the different field types. Choose one, type a field name, and you're ready to start entering information in the new field.

The second technique is to use the ribbon, which gives you more field-creation options. To try this approach, move to the column that falls just *before* the position where you want to insert the new field. Then, pick an option from the Table Tools | Fields→Add & Delete section of the ribbon. The most popular field types (for example, Text, Number, Currency, and Date & Time) have buttons of their own, but many more options are tucked just out of sight in the Table Tools | Fields→Add & Delete→More Fields list. In fact, the More Fields list is a bit cleverer than the Data Type list in Design view. Rather than just including the basic data types, it includes a much larger collection of data type *presets*. For

example, rather than seeing one Date/Time data type, you find a list of differently formatted date options, including Short Date, Medium Date, Long Date, Medium Time, and so on. These options all use the same Date/Time data type, but with the field properties adjusted to get the desired formatting.

At the very bottom of the More Fields list, under the Quick Start heading, are a small number of more unusual presets. These are field building-blocks—readymade fields like Phone and Status—that pair a basic data type with some field properties tailored for a specific type of information. A few actually insert several related fields. (For example, choose Address and you get the following fields: Address, City, State Province, ZIP Postal, and Country Region.)

Access fans are divided on whether this feature is a true timesaver or just another distraction. But if you like it, you can even create your own presets for the More Fields list. Just select your fully configured field (or group of fields), and choose Table Tools | Fields→Add & Delete→More Fields→Save Selection As New Data Type. Supply a name for your preset, and pick a category for the More Fields list.

Figure 26-21:
Left: For quick field creation, use the data type list that pops up when you click the column header on the right side of the datasheet.

Right: Another option is to use a field preset from the ribbon. Each preset combines a basic data type with common field property settings.

When you choose the Calculated data type, the Expression Builder dialog box appears, where you can type your expression into the topmost text box, and click OK to seal the deal.

Before you get too excited and start adding calculated fields all over the place, here's a word of caution. Calculated fields like the Profit example usually aren't a good idea. If you need to have this sort of information easily at hand (and often you do), you're better off creating a *query* that can run the calculation. Using a query helps you avoid bulking up your table with unnecessary information. Instead, your query calculates the information whenever you need it. Online Appendix C has the full scoop on queries.

Note: So if calculated fields make more sense in queries than in tables, why does Access offer the Calculated data type? It's for special situations where calculations are extremely slow, you have lots of records, and performance is critical. In this situation, it *may* make sense to use a calculated field to avoid the time-consuming calculating query when you need the calculated result. But unless you're a database pro and you're certain you need this frill, you're better off keeping your tables for raw data and letting other database objects handle the number crunching.

The Primary Key

Design view also lets you set a table's *primary key,* which is a field (or a combination of fields) that's unique for each record. Every table should have a primary key.

The purpose of a primary key is to prevent duplicate records (that is, records with *exactly* the same information) from slipping into your table. Databases are notoriously fussy, and they definitely don't like this sort of sloppiness.

The challenge of preventing duplicates isn't as easy as it seems. Access is designed to be blisteringly fast, and it can't afford to double-check your new record against every other record in the table to see if there's a duplicate. So instead, it relies on a *primary key*. As long as every record in a table has a unique, never-duplicated primary key, you can't have two identical records. (At worst, they'll be two almost-identical records that have the same information in all their other fields, but have different primary keys. And this is perfectly acceptable to Access.)

Choosing a primary key is trickier than it seems. Imagine you have a list of friends (and their contact information) in a table named People. You may logically assume that you can create a primary key using a combination of first and last name. Unfortunately, that just won't do—after all, many are the address books that have two Sean Smiths.

Your best solution is to *invent* a new piece of information. For example, you can label every individual in your contact list with a unique ID number. Best of all, you can get Access to automatically create this number for you (and make sure that no two people get the same number), so you don't even need to think about it. That way, if you have two Sean Smiths, each one has a different ID. And even if Ferris Wheel Simpson decides to change his first name, the ID remains the same.

This approach is exactly the one Access uses when you create a table using Datasheet view. Consider the Dolls table you built in the previous chapter. Notice that it includes a field named ID, which Access fills automatically. You can't set the ID value in a new record, or change it in an existing record. Instead, Access takes complete control, making sure each bobblehead has a different ID number. This behavior is almost always what you want, so don't try to change it or delete the ID field.

However, there's one exception. If you *create* a table in Design view by choosing Create→Tables→Table Design, then Access assumes you know what you're doing, and it doesn't create an ID field for you. You need to add an ID field (or something like it).

Creating Your Own Primary Key Field

If your database doesn't have an ID field (perhaps because you created it using the Create→Tables→Table Design command), it's up to you to create one and set the primary key. Here's how to do it:

1. **Create a new field by typing a name in the Field Name column.**

   For automatically generated values, the name "ID" is a good choice. Some people prefer to be a little more descriptive (for example, BobbleheadID, CustomerID, and so on), but it's unnecessary.

2. **In the Data Type column, choose AutoNumber.**

   By choosing the AutoNumber data type, you make sure that Access generates a unique ID value for every new record you insert. If you don't want this process to happen, you can choose something else (like the Text or Number data type).

You'll be responsible for entering your own unique value for each record, which is more work than it seems.

3. **Right-click the field and then choose Primary Key.**

   This choice designates the field as the primary key for the table. Access doesn't allow duplicate values in this field.

Tip: If you want to make a primary key that includes more than one field, then you need to take a slightly different approach. Hold down the Ctrl key, and click each field you want to include, one after the other. Then, while holding down Ctrl, right-click your selection and choose Primary Key.

Six Principles of Database Design

With great power comes great responsibility. As a database designer, it's up to you to craft a set of properly structured tables. If you get it right, you'll save yourself a lot of work in the future. Well-designed databases are easy to enhance, simpler to work with, and lead to far fewer mind-bending problems when you need to extract information.

Sadly, there's no recipe for a perfect database. Instead, a number of recommendations can guide you on the way. In the following sections, you'll learn about a few of the most important.

Note: Few database rules can't be broken. Sometimes, there's tension between clear, logical design and raw performance. Other times, database designers adopt personal quirks and conventions that make their lives a little easier. But even though an experienced database designer can bend, warp, and—on occasion—limbo right under some of these rules, they're still an excellent starting point for newbies. If you follow them, they'll never steer you into a bad decision. Finally, remember this: Building a good database is an art that takes practice. For best results, read these guidelines, and then try building your own test databases.

---

1. Choose Good Field Names

Access doesn't impose many rules on what field names you can use. It lets you use 64 characters of your choice. However, field names are important. You'll be referring to the same names again and again as you build forms, create reports, and even write code. So it's important to choose a good name from the outset. Here are some tips:

- **Keep it short and simple.** The field name should be as short as possible. Long names are tiring to type, more prone to error, and can be harder to cram into forms and reports. (Of course, you don't want a table name that's been abbreviated into nothingness either. The cryptic name FinCSalesReg isn't good for anyone.)

- **CapitalizeLikeThis.** It's not a set-in-stone rule, but most Access fans capitalize the first letter of every word (known as CamelCase), and then cram them all together to make a field name. Examples include UnitsInStock and DateOf-Expiration.

- **Avoid spaces.** Spaces are allowed in Access field names, but they can cause problems. In SQL (the database language you'll use to search for data), spaces aren't kosher. That means you'll be forced to use square brackets when referring to a field name that includes spaces (like "[Number Of Guests]"), which gets annoying fast. If you really must have spaces, then consider using underscores instead.

- **Be consistent.** You have the choice between the field names Product_Price and ProductPrice. Either approach is perfectly reasonable. However, it's not a good idea to mingle the two approaches in the same database—doing so is a recipe for certain confusion. Similarly, if you have more than one table with the same sort of information (for example, a FirstName field in an Employees table and in a Customers table), use the same field name.

- **Don't repeat the table name.** If you have a Country field in a Customers table, it's fairly obvious that you're talking about the Country where the customer lives. The field name CustomerCountry would be overkill.

- **Don't use the field name "Name."** Besides being a tongue-twister, Name is an Access keyword. Instead, use ProductName, CategoryName, ClassName, and so on. (This is one case where it's OK to violate the previous rule and incorporate the table name in the field name.)

Also give careful thought to naming your tables. Once again, consistency is king. For example, database nerds spend hours arguing about whether to pluralize table names (like Customers instead of Customer). Either way is fine, but try to keep all your tables in line.

2. Break Down Your Information

Be careful that you don't include too much information in a single field. You want to have each field store a single piece of information. Rather than have a single Name field in a table of contacts, it makes more sense to have a FirstName and a LastName field.

There are many reasons for breaking down information into separate fields. First of all, it stops some types of errors. With a Name field, the name could be entered in several different ways (like "Last, First" or "First Last"). Splitting the name avoids these issues, which can create headaches when you try to use the data in some sort of automated task (like a mail merge). But more importantly, you can more easily work with data that's broken down into small pieces. Once the Name field is split into FirstName and LastName, you can perform sorts or searches on just one of these two pieces of information, which you couldn't otherwise do. Similarly, you should split address information into columns like Street, City, State, and Country—that way, you can far more easily find out who lives in Nantucket.

Figure 26-22 (top) shows an example of proper separation. Figure 26-22 (bottom) shows a dangerous mistake—an attempt to store more than one piece of information in a single field.

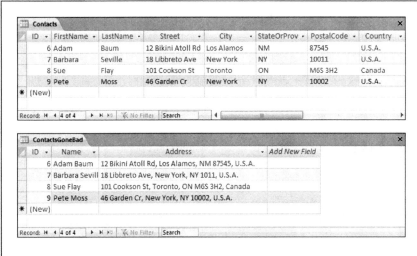

Figure 26-22:
This example shows the right way to subdivide information in the Contacts table (top), and the wrong way (bottom). Notice that it's technically still possible to break the information down further—the street address information could theoretically be split into StreetNumber, StreetName, and StreetType. However, that added bit of complexity doesn't add anything useful, so database gurus rarely go to the extra trouble.

3. Include All the Details in One Place

Often, you'll use the same table in many different tasks. You may use the Dolls table to check for duplicates (and avoid purchasing the same bobblehead twice), to identify the oldest parts of your collection, and to determine the total amount of money you've spent in a given year (for tax purposes). Each of these tasks needs a slightly different combination of information. When you're calculating the total money spent, you aren't interested in the Character field that identifies the doll. When checking for a duplicate, you don't need the DateAcquired or PurchasePrice information.

Even though you don't always need all these fields, it's fairly obvious that it makes sense to put them all in the same table. However, when you create more detailed tables, you may not be as certain. It's not difficult to imagine a version of the Dolls table that has 30 or 40 fields of information. You may use some of these fields only occasionally. However, you should still include them all in the same table. As you'll see in later chapters, you can easily filter out the information you don't need from the datasheet, as well as from your forms and printed reports.

4. Avoid Duplicating Information

As you start to fill a table with fields, it's sometimes tempting to include information that doesn't really belong. This inclusion causes no end of headaches, and it's a surprisingly easy trap to fall into. Figure 26-23 shows this problem in action with a table that tries to do too much.

Figure 26-23:
This table lists the available pets at an exotic animal breeder. It also lists some helpful information about the life expectancy, temperament, and meal requirements of each type of animal. Initially, this design seems fairly reasonable. However, a problem appears when you have several of the same type of animals (in this case, three elephants). Now the elephant-specific details are repeated three separate times.

Duplicate data like that shown in Figure 26-23 is inefficient. You can easily imagine a table with hundreds of similar records, needlessly wasting space repeating the same values over and over again. However, this concern is minor compared to the effort of updating that information, and the possibility of inconsistency. What happens if you want to update the life expectancy information for every elephant based on new studies? Based on the current design of the table, you need to change each record that has the same information. Even worse, it's all too easy to change some records but leave others untouched. The overall result is inconsistent data—information in more than one spot that doesn't agree—which makes it impossible to figure out the correct information.

This problem occurs because the information in the Pets table doesn't all belong. To understand why, you need to delve a little deeper into database analysis.

As a rule, every table in a database stores a single *thing*. In the Pets table, that thing is pets. Every field in a table is a piece of information about that thing.

In the Pets table, fields like Name, Animal, and Weight all make sense. They describe the pet in question. But the LifeSpan, Temperament, and Diet fields aren't quite right. They don't describe the individual pet. Instead, they're just standards for that species. In other words, these fields aren't based on the *pet* (as they should be)—they're based on the *animal type*. The only way to solve this problem is to create two tables: Pets and AnimalTypes (Figure 26-24).

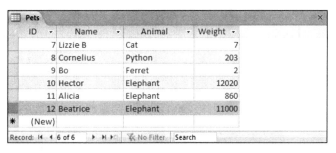

Figure 26-24:
Now the animal-specific information is maintained in one place, with no duplicates. It takes a little more work to get all the pet information you need—for example, to find out the life expectancy for Beatrice (top), you need to check out the Elephant record in the AnimalTypes table (bottom)—but the overall design is more logical.

It takes experience to spot fields that don't belong. And in some cases, breaking a table down into more and more subtables isn't worth the trouble. You could theoretically separate the address information (contained in fields like Street, City, Country, and PostalCode) from a Customers table, and then place it into a separate Addresses table. However, it's relatively uncommon for two customers to share the same address, so this extra work isn't likely to pay off.

Tip: Many database gurus find the best way to plan a database is to use index cards. To do this, start by writing down all the types of information you need in your database. Then, set aside an index card for each table you expect to use. Finally, take the fields you wrote on the scrap paper, and write them down on the appropriate index cards, one at a time, until everything is set into neat, related groups.

---

5. Avoid Redundant Information

Another type of data that just doesn't belong is redundant information—information that's already available elsewhere in the database, or even in the same table, sometimes in a slightly different form. As with duplicated data, this redundancy can cause inconsistencies.

Calculated data is the most common type of redundant information. An Average-OrderCost field in a Customers table is an example. The problem here is that you can determine the price of an average order by searching through all the records in the Orders table for that customer and then averaging them. By adding an Average-OrderCost field, you introduce the possibility that this field may be incorrect (it may not match the actual order records). You also complicate life, because every time a customer places an order, you need to recalculate the average, and then update the customer record.

Here are some more examples of redundant information:

- **An Age and a DateOfBirth field (in a People table).** Usually, you'll want to include just a DateOfBirth field. If you have both, then the Age field contains redundant information. But if you have only the Age field, you're in trouble—unless you're ready to keep track of birthdays and update each record carefully, your information will soon be incorrect.

- **A DiscountPrice field (in a Products table).** You should be able to calculate the discount price as needed based on a percentage. In a typical business, markups and markdowns change frequently. If you calculate 10 percent discounts and store the revised prices in your database, then you'll have a lot of work to do when the discount drops to 9 percent.

Note: As you've already learned, Access 2010 gives you one acceptable way to use calculated data: by creating a calculated field (page 739). This dodges the problems of inconsistency and maintenance, because Access maintains the calculated data for you. However, calculated data still makes for awkward database design. As a general rule, don't use calculated fields unless you're absolutely sure you need this particular compromise to boost performance, and you've ruled out the alternatives (like queries).

---

6. Include an ID Field

As you learned earlier, Access automatically creates an ID field when you create a table in Datasheet view and sets it to be the primary key for the table. But even now that you've graduated to Design view, you should still add an ID field to all your tables. Make sure it uses the AutoNumber data type so Access fills in the numbers automatically, and set it to be the primary key.

In some cases, your table may include a unique field that you can use as a primary key. *Resist the temptation.* You'll always buy yourself more flexibility by adding an ID field. You never need to change an ID field. Other information, even names and Social Security numbers, may change. And if you're using table relationships, Access copies the primary key into other tables. If a primary key changes, you'll need to track down the value in several different places.

Blocking Bad Data

Even the best database designer has spent a sleepless night worrying about the errors that could be lurking in a database. Bad data is a notorious problem—it enters the database, lies dormant for months, and appears only when you discover you've mailed an invoice to customer "Blank Blank" or sold a bag of peanuts for $499.99. Once bad data has entered your database, it's harder to spot than a plastic bag in a swimming pool.

The best way to prevent these types of problems is to stop bad data from making it into your database in the first place. Ahead you'll read about two essential classes of tools in this fight:

- **Duplicates, required fields, and default values** are the basics of data integrity.

- **Lookups** limit values to a list of preset choices.

Data Integrity Basics

All of Access's data validation features work via the Design view you learned about in earlier in this chapter. To put them in place, you choose a field and then tweak its properties. The only trick is knowing what properties are most useful. You've already seen some, but the following sections fill in a few more details.

Tip: Remember, Access gives you three ways to switch to Design view. Once you right-click the table tab title, you can then choose Design View from the menu, use the Home→View button on the ribbon, or use the tiny view buttons at the Access window's bottom-right corner. And if you're really impatient, then you don't even need to open your table first—just find it in the navigation pane, right-click it there, and then choose Design View.

Preventing Blank Fields

Every record needs a bare minimum of information to make sense. However, without your help, Access can't distinguish between critical information and optional details. For that reason, every field in a new table is optional, except for the primary-key field (which is usually the ID value). Try this out with the Dolls table from the previous chapter; you'll quickly discover that you can add records that have virtually no information in them.

You can easily remedy this problem. Just select the field that you want to make mandatory in Design view, and then set the Required field property to Yes (Figure 26-25).

Access checks the Required field property whenever you add a new record or modify a field in an existing record. However, if your table already contains data, there's no guarantee that it follows the rules.

Imagine you've filled the Dolls table with a few bobbleheads before you decide that every record requires a value for the Character field. You switch to Design view, choose the Character field, and then flip the Required field property to Yes. When you save the table (by switching back to Datasheet view or closing the table), Access gives you the option of verifying the bobblehead records that are already in the table (Figure 26-26). If you choose to perform the test and Access finds the problem, it gives you the option of reversing your changes (Figure 26-27).

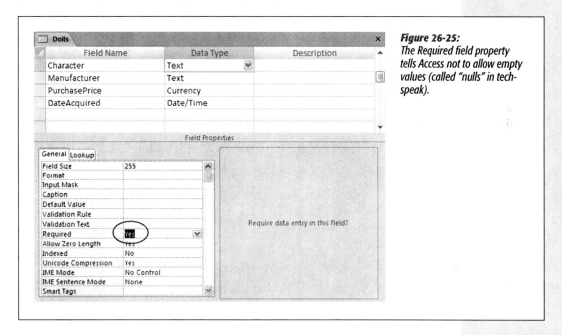

Figure 26-25:
The Required field property tells Access not to allow empty values (called "nulls" in tech-speak).

Figure 26-26:
It's a good idea to test the data in your table to make sure it meets the new requirements you put into place. Otherwise, invalid data could still remain. Don't let the message scare you—unless you have tens of thousands of records, this check doesn't take long.

Figure 26-27:
If Access finds an empty value, it stops the search and asks you what to do about it. You can keep your changes (even though they conflict with at least one record)—after all, at least new records won't suffer from the same problem. Your other option is to reset your field to its more lenient previous self. Either way, you can track down the missing data by performing a sort on the field in question (page 768), which brings empty values to the top.

Blank values and empty text

Access supports this Required property for every data type. However, with some data types you might want to add extra checks. That's because the Required property prevents only blank fields—fields that don't have any information in them at all. However, Access makes a slightly bizarre distinction between blank values and something called *empty text*.

A blank (null) value indicates that no information was supplied. Empty text indicates that a field value was supplied, but it just happens to be empty. Confused yet? The distinction exists because databases like Access need to recognize when information is missing. A blank value could indicate an oversight—someone might just have forgotten to enter the value. On the other hand, empty text indicates a conscious decision to leave that information out.

Tip: To try this out in your datasheet, create a text field that has Required set to Yes. Try inserting a new record and leaving the record blank. (Access stops you cold.) Now, try adding a new record, but place a single space in the field. Here's the strange part: Access automatically trims out spaces, and by doing so, it converts your single space to empty text. However, you don't receive an error message because empty text isn't the same as a blank value.

The good news is that if you find this whole distinction confusing, then you can prevent both blank values *and* empty text. Just set Required to Yes to stop the blank values, and set Allow Zero Length to No to prevent empty text.

Setting Default Values

So far, the fields in your tables are either filled in explicitly by the person who adds the record or are left blank. But there's another option—you can supply a *default value.* Now, if someone inserts a record and leaves the field blank, Access applies the default value instead.

You set a default value using the Default Value field property. For a numeric Added-Cost field, you could set this to be the number 0. For a text Country field, you could use the text "U.S.A." as a default value. (All text values must be wrapped in quotation marks when you use them for a default value.)

Access shows all your default values in the new-row slot at the bottom of the datasheet (Figure 26-28). It also automatically inserts default values into any hidden columns (page 765). But default value settings don't affect any of your existing records—they keep whatever value they had when you last edited them.

Access inserts the default value when you create a new record. (You're then free to change that value.) You can also switch a field back to its default value by using the Ctrl+Alt+Space shortcut while you're editing it.

Figure 26-28:
This dating service uses four default values: a default height (5.9), a default city (New York), a default state (NY), and a default country (U.S.A.). This system makes sense, because most of the example new entries have this information. On the other hand, there's no point in supplying a default value for the name fields.

ID	FirstName	LastName	HeightInFeet	City	StateOrProv	Country
6	Josh	Smith	5.8	Chicago	IL	U.S.A.
7	Elbarah	Zahari	6.1	New York	NY	U.S.A.
8	Hans	Vanderlay	4.6	Toronto	ON	Canada
9	Roy	Sacamato	5.5	New York	NY	U.S.A.
10	Rany	Dorkavikin	5.7	Plank	AL	U.S.A.
11	Rick	MacDougal	6.1	New York	NY	U.S.A.
12	Doug	Sacamato	5.9	New York	NY	U.S.A.
13	Hank	Andersen	5.9		DC	Canada
18	Noah	Hudson	6	Vanier	HI	U.S.A.
19	Stan	Rialti	5.3	Littleton	NC	U.S.A.
20	Zack	Sabadash	5.8	New York	NY	U.S.A.
21	Dan	Yu	6.3	Aurora	OH	U.S.A.
* (New)			5.9	New York	NY	U.S.A.

Record: 13 of 13   No Filter   Search

Tip: One nice feature is that you can use the default value as a starting point for a new record. For example, when you create a new record in the datasheet, you can edit the default value, rather than replacing it with a completely new value.

You can also create more intelligent *dynamic* default values. Access evaluates dynamic default values whenever you insert a new record, which means that the default value can vary based on other information. Dynamic default values use *expressions* (specialized database formulas) that can perform calculations or retrieve other details. One useful expression, *Date()*, grabs the current date that's set on your computer. If you use Date() as the Default Value for a date field (as shown in Figure 26-29), then Access automatically inserts the current date whenever you add a new record.

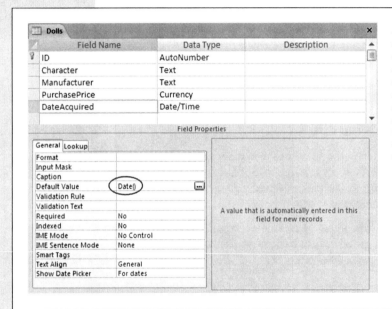

Figure 26-29:
If you use the Date() function as the Default Value for the DateAcquired field in the bobblehead table, then every time you add a new bobblehead record, Access fills in the current date. You decide whether you want to keep that date or replace it with a different value.

Preventing Duplicate Values with Indexes

In a properly designed table, every record must be unique. To enforce this restriction, you should choose a primary key (page 740), which is one or more fields that won't be duplicated.

Here's the catch. As you learned earlier in this chapter, the safest option is to create an ID field for the primary key. So far, all the tables you've seen have included this detail. But what if you need to make sure *other* fields are unique? Imagine you create an Employees table. You follow good database design principles and identify every record with an automatically generated ID number. However, you also want to make sure that no two employees have the same Social Security number (SSN), to prevent possible errors—like accidentally entering the same employee twice.

You can force a field to require unique values with an *index*. A database index is analogous to the index in a book—it's a list of values (from a field) with a cross-reference that points to the corresponding section (the full record). If you index the SocialSecurityNumber field, Access creates a list like this and stores it behind the scenes in your database file:

SocialSecurityNumber	Location of Full Record
001-01-3455	...
001-02-0434	...
001-02-9558	...
002-40-3200	...

Using this list, Access can quickly determine whether a new record duplicates an existing SSN. If it does, then Access doesn't let you insert it.

UP TO SPEED

How Indexes Work

It's important that the list of SSNs is *sorted*. Sorting means the number 001-01-3455 always occurs before 002-40-3200 in the index, regardless of where the record is physically stored in the database. This sorting is important, because it lets Access quickly check for duplicates. If you enter the number 001-02-4300, then Access needs to read only the first part of the list. Once it finds the next "larger" SSN (one that falls later in the sort, like 001-02-5010), it knows the remainder of the index doesn't contain a duplicate.

In practice, all databases use many more optimizations to make this process blazingly fast. But there's one key principle—without an index, Access would need to check the entire table. Tables aren't stored in sorted order, so there's no way Access can be sure a given SSN isn't in there unless it checks every record.

So how do you apply an index to a field? The trick is the Indexed field property, which is available for every data type except Attachment and OLE Object. When you add a field, the Indexed property is set to No, which means Access doesn't create an index. To add an index and prevent duplicates, you can change the Indexed property in Design view to Yes [No Duplicates]. The third option, Yes [Duplicates OK], creates an index but lets more than one record have the same value. This option doesn't help you catch repeated records, but you can use it to speed up searches (see the box above for more).

Note: As you learned earlier (page 740), primary keys also disallow duplicates, using the same technique. When you define a primary key, Access automatically creates an index on that field.

When you close Design view after changing the Indexed field property, Access prompts you to save your changes. At this point, it creates any new indexes it needs.

You can't create a no-duplicates index if you already have duplicate information in your table. In this situation, Access gives you an error message when you close the Design window and it attempts to add the index.

Multifield indexes

You can also use indexes to prevent a *combination* of values from being repeated. Imagine you create a People table to track your friends and their contact information. You're likely to have entries with the same first or last name. However, you may want to prevent two records from having the same first *and* last name. This limitation prevents you from inadvertently adding the same person twice.

Note: This example could cause endless headaches if you honestly *do* have two friends who share the same first and last names. In that case, you'll need to remove the index before you're allowed to add the name. You should think carefully about legitimate reasons for duplication before you create any indexes.

To ensure that a combination of fields is unique, you need to create a *compound index,* which combines the information from more than one field. Here's how to do it:

1. **In Design view, choose Table Tools | Design→Show/Hide→Indexes.**

   The Indexes window appears (Figure 26-30). Using the Indexes window, you can see your current indexes and add new ones.

Figure 26-30:
The Indexes window shows all the indexes that are defined for a table. Here, there's a single index for the ID field (which Access created automatically) and a compound index that's in the process of being created.

2. **Choose a name for your index. Type this name into the first blank row in the Index Name column.**

   The index name has no real importance—Access uses it to store the index in the database, but you don't see the index name when you work with the table. Usually, you'll use the name of one or both of the fields you're indexing (like LastName+FirstName).

3. **Choose the first field in the Field Name column in the same row (like Last-Name).**

   It doesn't matter which field name you use first. Either way, the index can prevent duplicate values.

4. **In the area at the bottom of the window, set the Unique box to Yes.**

   This creates an index that prevents duplicates (as opposed to one that's used only for boosting search speeds).

   You can also set the Ignore Nulls box to Yes, if you want Access to allow duplicate blank values. Imagine you want to make the SSN field optional. In this case, you should set Ignore Nulls to Yes. If you set Ignore Nulls to No, then Access lets only one record have a blank SSN field, which probably isn't the behavior you want.

Tip: You can also disallow blank values altogether using the Required property, as described on page 750.

Ignore the Primary box (which identifies the index used for the primary key).

5. **Move down one row. Leave the Index Name column blank (which tells Access it's still part of the previous index), but choose another field in the Field Name column (like FirstName).**

   If you want to create a compound index with more than two fields, then just repeat this step until you've added all the fields you need. Figure 26-31 shows what a finished index looks like.

   You can now close the Indexes window.

Figure 26-31:
Here's a compound index that prevents two people from sharing the same first and last names.

Lookups

In a database, minor variations can add up to big trouble. Suppose you're running International Cinnamon, a multinational cinnamon bun bakery with hundreds of orders a day. In your Orders table, you have entries like this:

```
Quantity Product
10       Frosted Cinnamon Buns
24       Cinnamon Buns with Icing
16 Buns, Cinnamon (Frosted)
120 FCBs
...
```

(Other fields, like the ID column and the information about the client making the order, are left out of this example.)

All the orders shown here amount to the same thing: different quantities of tasty cinnamon and icing confections. But the text in the Product column is slightly different. This difference doesn't pose a problem for ordinary human beings (for example, you'll have no trouble filling these orders), but it does create a small disaster if you want to analyze your sales performance later. Since Access has no way to tell that a Frosted Cinnamon Bun and an FCB are the same thing, it treats them differently. If you try to total up the top-selling products or look at long-range cinnamon sales trends, then you're out of luck.

Note: This example emphasizes a point that you've seen before. Namely, databases are strict, no-nonsense programs that don't tolerate minor discrepancies. For your databases to be useful, you need to make sure you store topnotch information in them.

Lookups are one more tool to help standardize your data. Essentially, a lookup lets you fill a value in a field by choosing from a readymade list of choices. Used properly, this tool solves the problem in the Orders table—you simply need a lookup that includes all the products you sell. That way, instead of typing the product name in by hand, you can choose Frosted Cinnamon Buns from the list. Not only do you save some time, but you also avoid variants like FCBs, thereby ensuring that the orders list is consistent.

Note: The only data types that support lookups are Text and Number.

Creating a Simple Lookup with Fixed Values

Simple lookups make sense if you have a simple, short list that's unlikely to change. The state prefix in an address is a perfect example. In this case, there's a set of just 50 two-letter abbreviations (AL, AK, AZ, and so on).

To try out the process in the following list of steps, you can use the Bachelors table included with the online examples for this chapter (look for the DatingService.accdb database file). Or, you can jump straight to the completed lookup by checking out the DatingServiceLookup.accdb file:

1. **Open the table in Design view.**

    If you're using the DatingService.accdb example, then open the Bachelors table.

2. **Find the field where you want to add the lookup.**

    In the Bachelors table, it's the State field.

3. **Make sure your field has the correct data type.**

    Text and Number are the most common data types that you'll use in conjunction with the lookup feature.

4. **Choose Lookup Wizard from the data type list.**

    This action doesn't actually change your data type. Instead, it tells Access you want to run the Lookup wizard based on the current data type. When you select this option, the first step of the Lookup wizard appears (Figure 26-32).

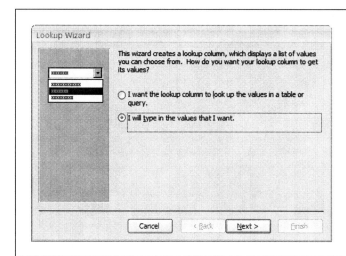

Figure 26-32:
First you choose the source of your lookup: data from another table or fixed values.

5. **Choose "I will type in the values that I want".**

    The box on page 759 describes your other choice: drawing the lookup list from another table.

6. **Click Next.**

    The second step of the wizard gives you the chance to supply the list of values that should be used, one per row (Figure 26-33). In this case, it's a list of abbreviations for the 50 U.S. states.

    You may notice that you can supply multiple columns of information. For now, stick to one column.

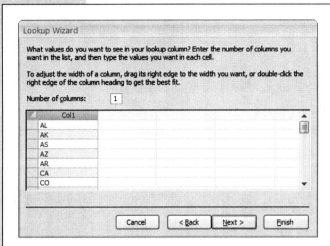

Figure 26-33:
This lookup includes the abbreviations for all the American states. This list is unlikely to change in the near future, so it's safe to hard-code this rather than store it in another table.

7. **Click Next.**

   The final step of the Lookup wizard appears.

8. **Choose whether you want the lookup column to store multiple values.**

   If you allow multiple values, then the lookup list displays a checkbox next to each item. You can select several values for a single record by choosing more than one item.

Tip: Once you configure a field to allow multiple values and you save your table, you can't back out. Access won't let you modify the field's Allow Multiple Values setting to convert it back to a single-value field.

In the State field, it doesn't make sense to allow multiple values—after all, a person can physically inhabit only one state (discounting the effects of quantum teleportation). However, you can probably think of examples where multiple selection does make sense. For example, in the Products table used by International Cinnamon, a multiple-value lookup would let you create an order for more than one product.

9. **Click Finish.**

   Switch to Datasheet view (right-click the tab title, and then choose Datasheet View), and then save the table changes. Figure 26-34 shows the lookup in action.

ID	FirstName	LastName	HeightInFeet	City	State
6	Josh	Smith	5.82	Chicago	IL
7	Elbarah	Zahari	6.10	New York	
8	Hans	Vanderlay	4.60	Toronto	
9	Roy	Sacamato	5.50	New York	
10	Randy	Dorkavikin	5.70	Plank	
11	Rick	MacDougal	6.10	New York	
12	Ernestp	Sacamato	5.91	New York	
13	Hank	Andersen	5.90	Washington	
18	Noah	Hudson	6.02	Vanier	
19	Stanley	Rialti	5.30	Littleton	
20	Zack	Sabadash	5.85	New York	
21	Dan	Yu	6.30	Aurora	

Record: 1 of 12 · No Filter · Search

Dropdown list: IL, IN, IA, KS, KY, LA, ME, MH, MD, MA, MI, MN

Figure 26-34:
When you move to a field that has a lookup, you'll see a down arrow on the right side. Click this arrow, and a drop-down list appears with all your possibilities. Choose one to insert it into the field.

Creating a Lookup That Uses Another Table

In the previous example (page 757), you created a lookup list that's stored as part of your field settings. This is a good approach, but it's not the best solution. A much more flexible approach is to store the lookup list in a separate table.

There are several reasons to use a separate table:

- **It lets you add, edit, and remove items, all by simply editing the lookup table.** Even if you think you have a set of fixed, unchanging values, it's a good idea to consider a separate table. For example, the set of state abbreviations in the previous section seems unlikely to change—but what if the dating service goes international, and you need to add Canadian provinces to the list?

- **It lets you reuse the same lookup list in several different fields** (either in the same table, or in different tables). That beats endless copy-and-paste operations.

- **It lets you store extra information.** For example, maybe you want to keep track of the state abbreviation (for mailing purposes) but show the full state name (to make data entry easier).

Table-based lookups are a little trickier, however, because they involve a table *relationship*: a link that binds two tables together and (optionally) enforces new restrictions. Chapter 28 is all about relationships, which are a key ingredient in any practical database.

Adding New Values to Your Lookup List

When you create a lookup that uses fixed values, the lookup list provides a list of *suggestions.* You can choose to ignore the lookup list and type in a completely different value (like a state prefix of ZI), even if it isn't on the list. This design lets you use the lookup list as a timesaving convenience without limiting your flexibility.

In many cases, you don't want this behavior. In the Bachelors table, you probably want to prevent people from entering something different in the State field. In this case, you want the lookup to be an error-checking and validation tool that actually stops entries that don't belong.

Fortunately, even though this option is mysteriously absent in the Lookup wizard, it's easy enough to add after the fact. Here's what you need to do:

1. **In Design view, go to the field that has the lookup.**

2. **In the Field Properties section, click the Lookup tab.**

   The Lookup tab provides options for fine-tuning your lookup, most of which you can configure more easily in the Lookup wizard. In the Row Source box, for example, you can edit the list of values you supplied. (Each value's on the same line, in quotation marks, separated from the next value with a semicolon.)

3. **Set the "Limit to List" property to Yes.**

   This action prevents you from entering values that aren't in the list.

4. **Optionally, set Allow Value List Edits to Yes.**

   This action lets people modify the list of values at any time. This way, if something's missing from the lookup list, you can add it on the fly (Figure 26-35).

Figure 26-35:
If you set Allow Value List Edits to Yes, an icon appears under the lookup list when you use it (left). Click this icon to open an Edit List Items dialog box (right) where you can edit the items in the lookup list and change the default value.

Mastering the Datasheet: Sorting, Searching, Filtering, and More

I n Chapter 25, you took your first look at the *datasheet*—a straightforward way to browse and edit the contents of a table. As you've learned since then, the datasheet isn't the best place to build a table. (Design view is a better choice for database control freaks.) However, the datasheet is a great tool for reviewing the records in your table, making edits, and inserting new data.

Based on your experience creating the Dolls table (page 694), you probably feel pretty confident breezing around the datasheet. However, most tables are considerably larger than the examples you've seen so far. After all, if you need to keep track of only a dozen bobbleheads, then you really don't need a database—you'll be just as happy jotting the list down in any old spreadsheet, word processor document, or scrap of unused Kleenex.

On the other hand, if you plan to build a small bobblehead empire (suitable for touring in international exhibitions), you need to fill your table with hundreds or thousands of records. In this situation, it's not as easy to scroll through the mass of data to find what you need. All of a sudden, the datasheet seems more than a little overwhelming.

Fortunately, Access is stocked with datasheet goodies that can simplify your life. In this chapter, you'll become a datasheet expert, with tricks like sorting, searching, and filtering at your fingertips. You'll also learn a quick-and-dirty way to print a snapshot of the data in your table.

Datasheet Customization

Tip: It's entirely up to you how much time you spend using datasheets. Some Access experts prefer to create *forms* for all their tables (as described in online Appendix E). With forms, you can design a completely customized window for data entry. Designing forms takes more work, but it's a great way to satisfy your inner Picasso.

Datasheet Customization

Getting tired of the drab datasheet with its boring stretch of columns and plain text? You can do something about it. Access lets you tweak the datasheet's appearance and organization to make it more practical (or to suit it to your peculiar sense of style). Some of these customizations—like modifying the datasheet font—are shameless frills. Other options, like hiding or freezing columns, can genuinely make it easier to work with large tables.

Note: Access doesn't save formatting changes immediately (unlike record edits, which it stores as soon as you make them). Instead, Access prompts you to save changes the next time you close the datasheet. You can choose Yes to keep your customizations or No to revert to the table's last look and feel (which doesn't affect any edits you've made to the *data* in that table).

Formatting the Datasheet

Access lets you format the datasheet with eye-catching colors and fonts. Do these options make any difference to the way the datasheet works? Not really. But if your computer desktop looks more like a '60s revival party than an office terminal, then you'll enjoy this feature. To find the formatting features, look at the ribbon's Home→Font section (see Figure 27-1).

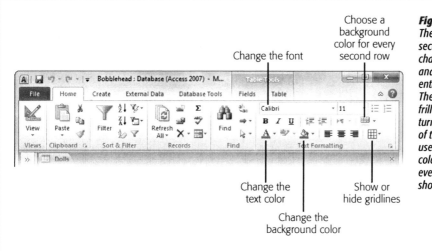

Choose a background color for every second row

Change the font

Change the text color

Change the background color

Show or hide gridlines

Figure 27-1:
The Home→Font section lets you change the text font and colors in the entire datasheet. The most practical frill is the ability to turn off some or all of the gridlines and use alternating row colors to highlight every other row, as shown here.

Every formatting change you make affects the entire table. You may think it's a nifty idea to apply different formatting to different columns, but Access doesn't let you. If this limitation is frustrating you, be sure to check out forms (online Appendix E) and reports (online Appendix D). Both are more complicated to set up, but give you more formatting power.

Tip: There's one other way you can use the ribbon's Home→Font section. If you have a field that uses the Memo data type and you've set your field to use rich text (page 722), then you can select some text inside your field, and change its formatting using the ribbon.

GEM IN THE ROUGH

Customizing All Your Datasheets

Access lets you format only one table at a time. So if you find a formatting option you really like, you'll need to apply it separately to every table in your database.

However, you can set formatting options so that they automatically apply to every table in every database by configuring Access itself. To pull off this trick, follow these steps:

1. Choose File→Options to show the Access Options window.

2. Choose Datasheet from the list on the left.

3. On the right, you see the standard font, gridline, and column width options, which you can change to whatever you want.

When you change the datasheet formatting settings in the Access Options window, you change the *defaults* that Access uses. These settings determine the formatting that Access uses for new tables and any tables that aren't customized. When you customize a table, you override the default settings, no matter what they are.

Rearranging Columns

The fields in the datasheet are laid out from left to right, in the order you created them. Often, you'll discover that this order isn't the most efficient for data entry.

Imagine you've created a Customers table for a novelty pasta company. When a new customer registration ends up on your desk, you realize that the registration form starts with the name and address information, and then includes the customer's pasta preferences. Unfortunately, the fields on the datasheet are laid out in a completely different order. From left to right, they're arranged like this: ID, FreshPasta-Preference, DriedPastaPreference, FirstName, LastName, Street, City, State, Country. (This organization isn't as crazy as it seems—it actually makes it easier for the people filling pasta orders to quickly find the information *they* want.) Because of this ordering, you need to skip back and forth just to enter the information from a single registration.

Fortunately, you can solve this problem without redesigning the table. Drag the columns you want to move to new positions, as shown in Figure 27-2.

Figure 27-2:
To move a column, click the column header once to select that column. Then, drag the column header to its new location. In this example, the FirstName field is about to be relocated so that it's just before the Fresh-PastaPreference field.

The best part of this approach is that you don't need to modify the database's actual structure. If you switch to Design view after moving a few columns, you'll see that the field order hasn't changed. In other words, you can keep the exact same physical order of fields (in your database file), but organize them differently in Datasheet view.

Note: *Rearranging columns is a relatively minor change. Don't worry about shifting columns around to suit a specific editing job and then switching them back later on. Your changes don't affect the data in the database. If you want to use a particular column order for a one-time job, simply refrain from saving your changes when you close the datasheet.*

Resizing Rows and Columns

As you cram more and more information into a table, your datasheet becomes wider and wider. In many cases, you'll be frustrated with some columns hogging more space than they need and others being impossibly narrow.

As you'd expect, Access lets you tweak column widths. But you probably haven't realized how many different ways you can do it:

- **Resize a single column.** Move the mouse to the column's right edge, so that the mouse pointer changes into a vertical bar. Then click the edge and drag it to the left (to shrink the column) or to the right (to make it larger).

- **Resize a column to fit its content.** Double-click the right column edge. Access makes the column just wide enough to fit the field name or the largest value (whichever's larger). However, it doesn't make the column so wide that it stretches beyond the bounds of the window.

- **Resize several adjacent columns.** Drag the first column's header across the columns until you've selected them all. Then, drag the right edge of your selection to the left or the right. All the selected columns shrink or expand to fit the available space, sharing it equally.

- **Resize a column with pinpoint accuracy.** Right-click the column header, and then choose Field Width. You'll see the Column Width dialog box, which lets you set an exact width as a number (Figure 27-3).

Figure 27-3:
The Column Width dialog box lets you set an exact width as a number. (The number doesn't actually have a concrete meaning—it's supposed to be a width in characters, but because modern Access uses proportional fonts, different characters are different sizes.) You can also turn on the Standard Width checkbox to reset the width to the standard narrow size, or click Best Fit to expand the column to fit its contents (just as when you double-click the edge of the column).

Tip: Remember, a column doesn't need to be wide enough to show all its data at once. You can scroll through a lengthy text field using the arrow keys, and if that's too awkward, use the Shift+F2 shortcut to show the full contents of the current field in a Zoom box.

Just as you can resize columns, you can also resize rows. The difference is that Access makes sure all rows have the same size. So when you make one row taller or shorter, Access adjusts all the other rows to match.

You'll mainly want to shrink a row to cram more rows into view at once. You'll want to enlarge a row mostly to show more than one line of text in each text field (see Figure 27-4).

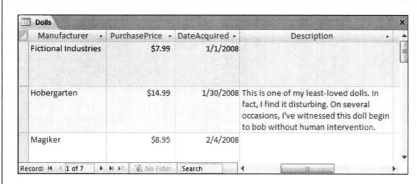

Figure 27-4:
If a row is large enough, Access wraps the text inside it over multiple lines, as shown here with the Description column.

Hiding Columns

Many tables contain so many columns that you can't possibly fit them all into view at the same time. This quality is one of the drawbacks to the datasheet, and often you have no choice but to scroll from side to side.

However, in some situations, you may not need to see all the fields at once. In this case, you can temporarily hide the columns that don't interest you, thereby homing in on the important details without distraction. Initially, every field you add to a table is out in the open.

To hide a column, select the column by clicking the column header. (You can also select several adjacent columns by clicking the column header of the first, and then dragging the mouse cursor across the rest.) Then, right-click your selection, and then choose Hide Fields. The column instantly vanishes from the datasheet. (This sudden disappearance can be a little traumatic for Access newbies.)

Fortunately, the field and all its data remain just out of sight. To pop the column back into view, right-click any column header and choose Unhide Fields. Access then shows the Unhide Columns dialog box (Figure 27-5).

Note: You'll notice that Access uses the words "column" and "field" almost interchangeably. This leads to strange cases where the command uses one word (like Unhide *Fields*) while the window uses the other (Unhide *Columns*). But don't let this quirk throw you off.

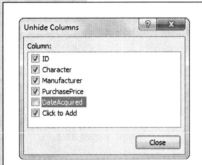

Figure 27-5:
Using the Unhide Columns dialog box, you can choose to make hidden columns reappear, and (despite the dialog box name) you can hide ones that are currently visible. Every column that has a checkmark next to it is visible—every column that doesn't is hidden. As you change the visibility, Access updates the datasheet immediately. When you're happy with the results, click Close to get back to the datasheet.

At the bottom of the field list in the Unhide Columns dialog box, you'll see an entry named "Click to Add". This "field" isn't really a field—it's the placeholder that appears just to the right of your last field in Datasheet view, which you can use to add new fields. If you're in the habit of adding fields using Design view, then you can hide this placeholder to free up some extra space.

If you add a new record while columns are hidden, you can't supply a value for that hidden field. The value starts out either empty or with the default value (if you've defined one for that field, as described on page 751). If you've hidden a required field (page 748), you receive an error message when you try to insert the record. All you can do is unhide the appropriate column, and then fill in the missing information.

Freezing Columns

Even with the ability to hide and resize columns, you'll probably need to scroll from side to side in a typical datasheet. In this situation, you can easily lose your place. You might scroll to see more information in the Contacts table, but then forget exactly which person you're looking at. Access has one more feature that can help you by making sure important information is always visible—*frozen* columns.

A frozen column remains fixed in place at the Access window's left side at all times. Even as you scroll to the right, all your frozen columns remain visible (Figure 27-6). To freeze a column (or columns), select them, right-click the column header, and then choose Freeze Fields.

Figure 27-6:
Top: In this example, the First-Name and LastName field are frozen. They appear initially at the left.

Bottom: When you scroll to the side to see more information, the FirstName and LastName columns stay put.

Tip: If you want to freeze several columns that aren't next to each other, start by freezing the column that you want to appear at the very left. Then, repeat the process to freeze the column that you want to appear just to the right of the first column, and so on.

Frozen columns must always be positioned at the left side of the datasheet. If you freeze a column that's somewhere else, Access moves it to the left side and then freezes it. You can move it back after you unfreeze the column by using the column reordering trick on page 763. Keep in mind that while a column is frozen, you can't drag it to a different place.

To unfreeze columns, right-click a column header, and then choose Unfreeze All Fields.

Datasheet Navigation

In Chapter 25, you learned the basics of moving around the datasheet. Using your mouse and a few select keystrokes, you can cover a lot of ground. (Refer back to page 699 (Table 25-1) for a review of the different keys you can use to jump from place to place and perform edits.)

However, you haven't seen a few tricks yet. One is the timesaving record navigation buttons at the bottom of the datasheet (Figure 27-7).

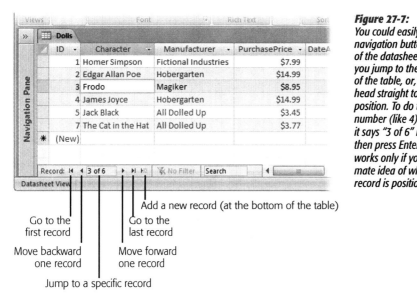

Figure 27-7:
You could easily overlook the navigation buttons at the bottom of the datasheet. These buttons let you jump to the beginning and end of the table, or, more interestingly, head straight to a record at a specific position. To do this, type the record number (like 4) into the box (where it says "3 of 6" in this example), and then press Enter. Of course, this trick works only if you have an approximate idea of where in the list your record is positioned.

Go to the
first record

Move backward
one record

Jump to a specific record

Add a new record (at the bottom of the table)

Go to the
last record

Move forward
one record

Several more datasheet features help you orient yourself when dealing with large amounts of data, including *sorting* (which orders the records so you can see what you want), *filtering* (which cuts down the data display to include only the records you're interested in), and *searching* (which digs specific records out of an avalanche of data). You'll try out all these features in the following sections.

Sorting

In some cases, you can most easily make sense of a lot of data by putting it in order. You can organize a customer list by last name, a product catalog by price, a list of wedding guests by age, and so on. Sorting doesn't change how Access stores records, but it does change the way they're displayed.

To sort your records, pick a column you want to use to order the records. Click the drop-down arrow at the right edge of the column header, and then choose one of the sort options at the top of the menu (see Figure 27-8).

Figure 27-8:
This text field gives you the choice of sorting alphabetically from the beginning of the alphabet (A to Z) or backward from the end (Z to A). The menu also provides filtering options, which are described on page 771.

Depending on the data type of the field, you'll see different sorting options, as explained in Table 27-1. (You can also apply the same types of sort by using the commands in the ribbon's Home→Sort & Filter section.)

Tip: Use the Home→Sort & Filter→Remove Sort command to return your table to its original, unsorted order.

Table 27-1. Sorting options for different data types

Data Type	Sort Options	Description
Text, Memo, and Hyperlink	Sort A to Z Sort Z to A	Performs an alphabetic sort (like the dictionary), ordering letter by letter. The sort isn't case-sensitive, so it treats "baloney" and "Baloney" the same.
Number, Currency, and AutoNumber	Sort Smallest to Largest Sort Largest to Smallest	Performs a numeric sort, putting smaller numbers at the top or bottom.
Date/Time	Sort Oldest to Newest Sort Newest to Oldest	Performs a date sort, distinguishing between older dates (those that occur first) and more recent dates.
Yes/No	Sort Selected to Cleared Sort Cleared to Selected	Separates the selected from the unselected values.

Sorting is a one-time affair. If you edit values in a sorted column, then Access doesn't reapply the sort. Imagine you sort a list of people by FirstName. If you then edit the

FirstName value for one of the records, changing "Frankie" to "Chen", Access *doesn't* relocate the row to the C section. Instead, the changed row remains in its original place until you re-sort the table. Similarly, any new records that you add stay at the end of the table until the next sort (or the next time the table is opened). This behavior makes sense. If Access relocated rows whenever you made a change, you'd quickly become disoriented.

Note: The sorting order is one of the details that Access stores in the database file. The next time you open the table in Datasheet view, Access automatically applies your sort settings.

Numbers and Special Characters in Text Fields

Text sorts can be a little counterintuitive, especially if you have a text field that includes numeric content.

Ordinarily, when you sort two numbers (like 153 and 49), the numbers are arranged from smallest to largest (49, 153). However, a text sort doesn't work this way. When Access performs a text sort, it examines the text character by character, which means it sorts numbers based on the first *digit.* If the first digit is the same, then it checks the second digit, and so on. As a result, if you sort 49 and 153 alphabetically, you get 153, 49, because 4 (the first digit in 49) is larger than 1 (the first digit in 153).

Life gets even more interesting if you throw punctuation and other special characters into the mix. Here's the order in which Access sorts everything (in a standard A-to-Z sort):

1. Blank (empty) values
2. Space
3. Special characters (like punctuation)
4. Numbers
5. Letters

Sorting on multiple fields

If a sort finds two duplicate values, there's no way to know what order they'll have (relative to one another). If you sort a customer list with two "Van Hauser" entries in it, then you can guarantee that sorting by last name will bring them together, but you don't know who'll be on top.

If you want more say in how Access treats duplicates, then you can choose to sort based on more than one column. The traditional phone book, which sorts people by last name and *then* by first name, is a perfect example of this. People who share the same last name are thus grouped together and ordered according to their first name, like this:

```
...
Smith, Star
Smith, Susan
Smith, Sy
Smith, Tanis
...
```

In the datasheet, sorts are *cumulative,* which means you can sort based on several columns at the same time. The only trick is getting the order right. The following steps take you through the process:

1. **Choose Home→Sort & Filter→Remove Sort.**

   Access reverts your table to its original, unsorted order.

2. **Use the drop-down column menu to apply the subsort that you want for duplicates.**

   If you want to perform the phone book sort (names are organized by last name, then first name), you need to turn on sorting for the FirstName field. "Datasheet Navigation" later in this chapter explains the sorting options you'll see, depending on the data type.

3. **Use the drop-down column menu to apply the first level sort.**

   In the phone book sort, this is the LastName field.

You can extend these steps to create sorts on more fields. Imagine you have a ridiculously large compendium of names that includes some people with the same last *and* first name. In this case, you could add a third sort—by middle initial. To apply this sort, you'd switch sorting on in this order: MiddleInitial, FirstName, LastName. You'll get this result:

```
...
Smith, Star
Smith, Susan K
Smith, Susan P
Smith, Sy
...
```

Filtering

In a table with hundreds or thousands of records, scrolling back and forth in the datasheet is about as relaxing as a pneumatic drill at 3:00 a.m. Sometimes, you don't even need to see all the records at once—they're just a finger-tiring distraction from the data you're really interested in. In this case, you should cut the datasheet down to just the records that interest you, with *filtering.*

To filter records, you specify a condition that the record must meet to be included in the datasheet. For example, an online store might pick out food items from a full product catalog, a shipping company might look for orders made last week, and a dating service might hunt down bachelors who don't live with their parents. When you apply a filter condition, you end up hiding all the records that don't match your requirements. They're still in the table—they're just tucked neatly out of sight.

Access has several different ways to apply filters. In the following sections, you'll start with the simplest, and then move on to the more advanced options.

Quick filters

A *quick filter* lets you choose what values you want to include and which ones you want to hide, based on the current contents of your table. To apply a quick filter, choose the column you want to use, and then click the drop-down arrow at the column header's right edge. You'll see a list of all the distinct values in that column. Initially, each value has a checkmark next to it. Clear the checkmark to hide records with that value. If you want to hide everything except for a few specific values, click to remove the checkmark next to "(Select All)", and then add a checkmark next to the ones you want. Click OK to apply your filter.

Figure 27-9 shows an example where a sort and filter are being used at the same time. When a column is using filtering, Access adds a funnel icon to the right side of the column header.

Figure 27-9:
This list of eligible bachelors is sorted first by height (in descending largest-to-smallest order), and then filtered to include only those hopefuls who live in the state of New York. A checkmark indicates that records that have this value are included in the datasheet. Others are hidden from view.

Tip: To remove all the filters on a column (and show every record in the datasheet), click the drop-down button at the right edge of the column header, and then choose "Clear filter from".

Not all data types support filtering. Data types that do include Number, Currency, AutoNumber, Text, Hyperlink, Date/Time, and Yes/No. Memo fields don't support quick filters (because their values are typically too large to fit in the drop-down list), but they do support other types of filters.

You can apply quick filters to more than one column. The order in which you apply the filters doesn't matter, because all filters are *cumulative*, which means you see only records that match all the filters you've set. You can even use quick filters in combination with the other filtering techniques described in the following sections. To temporarily remove a filter, choose Home→Sort & Filter→Toggle Filter. Click Toggle Filter again to put your filter back into action.

Note: Quick filters work best if you have a relatively small number of distinct values. Limiting people based on the state they live in is a great choice, as is the political party they support or their favorite color. It wouldn't work as well if you wanted to cut down the list based on birth date, height, or weight, because there's a huge range of different possible values. (You don't need to give up on filtering altogether—rather, you just need to use a different type of filter.)

Filter by selection

Filter by selection lets you apply a filter based on any value in your table. This choice is handy if you've found exactly the type of record you want to include or exclude. Using filter by selection, you can turn the current value into a filter without hunting through the filter list.

First, find the value you want to use for filtering in the datasheet. Right-click the value, and then choose one of the filter options at the bottom of the menu (see Figure 27-10).

Figure 27-10:
Depending on the data type, you see slightly different filtering options. For a text field (like the City field shown here), you have the option to include only the records that match the current value (Equals "Chicago"), or those that don't (Does Not Equal "Chicago"). You also have some extra filtering options that go beyond what a quick filter can do—namely, you can include or exclude fields that simply contain the text "Chicago". That filter condition applies to values like "Chicagoland" and "Little Chicago".

All data types that support filtering let you filter out exact matches. But many also give you some additional filtering options in the right-click menu. Here's what you'll see for different data types:

- **Text-based data types.** You can filter values that match exactly, or values that contain a piece of text.

- **Numeric data types.** You can filter values that match exactly, or numbers that are smaller or larger than the current number.

- **Date data types.** You can filter values that match exactly, or dates that are older or newer than the current date.

Finally, to get even fancier, you can create a filter condition using only *part* of a value. If you have the value "Great at darts" in the Description field in your table of hopeful bachelors, you can select the text "darts", and then right-click just that text. Now you can find other fields that contain the word "darts". This ability is what gives the filter "by selection" feature its name.

Access makes it easy to switch filtering on and off at a moment's notice. Figure 27-11 shows how.

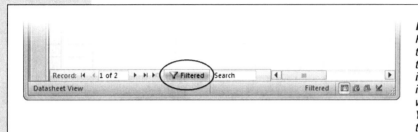

Figure 27-11:
Right next to the navigation controls at the bottom of your datasheet is a Filtered/Unfiltered indicator that tells you when filtering is applied. You can also use this box to quickly switch your filter on and off—clicking it once removes all filters, and clicking it again reapplies the most recent set of filters.

Filter by condition

So far, the filters you use have taken the current values in your table as a starting point. But if you're feeling confident with filters, you may be ready to try a more advanced approach: *filtering by condition*. When you use a filter by condition, you can define exactly the filter you want.

Imagine you want to find all the rare wine vintages in your cellar with a value of more than $85. Using the filter-by-selection approach, you need to start by finding a wine with a value of $85, which you can use to build your condition. But what if there isn't any wine in your list that has a price of exactly $85, or what if you just can't seem to find it? A quicker approach is defining the filter condition by hand.

Here's how it works. First, click the drop-down arrow at the right edge of the column header. But instead of choosing one of the quick filter options, look for a submenu with filtering options. This menu is named according to the data, so text fields include a Text Filters option, number fields have a Number Filters option, and so on. Figure 27-12 shows an example.

Here's a quick overview that describes the extra options you get using filter by condition, depending on your data type:

- **Text-based data types.** All the same options as filter by selection, plus you can find values that start with specific text, or values that end with certain text.

Figure 27-12:
Top: With a numeric field like this PurchasePrice field, filtering by condition lets you look at values that fall above a certain minimum.

Bottom: Once you've chosen the type of filter you want, you need to supply the information for that filter. If you choose Greater Than, then you need to supply the minimum number. Records that are equal to or larger than this value are shown in the datasheet.

- **Numeric data types.** All the same options as filter by selection, plus you can find values that are in a range, meaning they're greater than a set minimum but smaller than a set maximum.

- **Date data types.** All the same options as filter by selection, plus you can find dates that fall in a range, *and* you can choose from a huge list of built-in options, like Yesterday, Last Week, Next Month, Year to Date, First Quarter, and so on.

Searching

Access also provides a *quick search* feature that lets you scan your datasheet for specific information. Whereas filtering helps you pull out a batch of important records, searching is better if you need to find a single detail that's lost in the mountains of data. And while filtering changes the Datasheet view by hiding some records, searching leaves everything as is. It just takes you to the data you want to see.

The quickest way to search is through the search box near the record navigation controls (see Figure 27-13). Just type in the text you want to find. As you type, the first match in the table is highlighted automatically. You can press Enter to search for subsequent matches.

When performing a search, Access scans the table starting from the first field in the first record. It then goes left to right, examining every field in the current record. If it reaches the end without a match, then it continues to the next record and checks all of its values, and so on. When it reaches the end of the table, it stops.

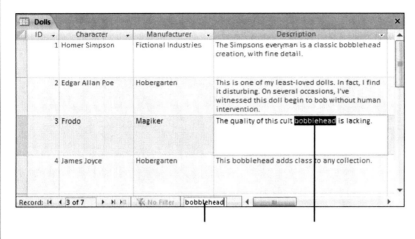

Figure 27-13:
Here, a search is being performed for the word "bobblehead". If you find a match, you can keep searching—just press Enter again to jump to the next match. In this example, pressing Enter sends Access to the next record's Description field.

POWER USERS' CLINIC

Filters vs. Queries

If you use filters frequently, you're sure to run into a problem. Access stores only one set of filters—the filters you're currently using. In other words, once you apply a different filter, your original filter is gone, and you need to reapply it from scratch the next time you need it. In most cases, reapplying a filter isn't difficult. But if you've spent a considerable amount of effort crafting the perfect set of filter conditions, and you know you want to use them later, it's frustrating.

If you find yourself in this situation, you're overusing filters. Instead of relying on filters to show the information you're interested in, you'd be better off creating a separate, reusable *query*. Like filters, queries let you see a subset of your data based on certain conditions. Unlike filters, queries can contain much more sophisticated logic, they can leave out columns you're not interested in, and Access saves them as separate database objects so you can always reuse them later. If you're up for diving into queries, check out online Appendix C.

If you want to change the way Access performs a search, you'll need to use the Find feature instead:

1. **Choose Home→Find→Find. (Or, just use the shortcut Ctrl+F.)**

   The "Find and Replace" dialog box appears (Figure 27-14).

2. **Specify the text you're searching for in the Find What box, and then set any other search options you want to use:**

   — **Find What.** The text you're looking for.

   — **Look In.** Allows you to choose between searching a single field (choose "Current field") or the entire table (choose "Current document").

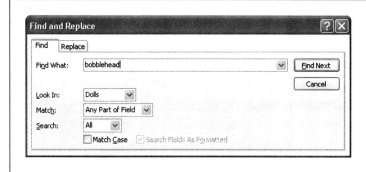

Figure 27-14:
*The "Find and Replace" dialog box
is the perfect tool for hunting for lost
information.*

— **Match.** Lets you specify whether values need to match exactly. Use Whole Field to require exact matches. Use "Start of Field" if you want to match beginnings (so "bowl" matches "bowling"), or "Any Part of Field" if you want to match text anywhere in a field (so "bowl" matches "League of extraordinary bowlers").

— **Search.** Sets the direction Access looks: Up, Down, or All (which loops from the end of the table to the beginning, and keeps going until it has traversed the entire table).

— **Match Case.** If selected, finds only matches that have identical capitalization. So "banana" doesn't match "BANANA".

— **Search Fields As Formatted.** If selected, means Access searches the value as it appears on the datasheet. For example, the number 44 may appear in a Currency field as $44.00. If you search for 44, you always find what you're looking for. But if you search for the formatted representation $44.00, you get a match only if you have Search Fields As Formatted switched on. In extremely large tables (with thousands of records), searches may be faster if you switch off Search Fields As Formatted.

Tip: To turn off Search Fields As Formatted, you must choose to search a single field in the Look In box. If you are searching the entire table, then you must search the formatted values.

---

3. **Click Find Next.**

   Access starts searching from the current position. If you're using the standard search direction (All), Access moves from left to right in the current record, and then down from record to record until it finds a match.

   When Access finds a match, it highlights the value. You can then click Find Next to look for the next match, or Cancel to stop searching.

Find and Replace

The search feature doubles as a powerful (but somewhat dangerous) way to modify records.

Initially, when the "Find and Replace" dialog box appears, it shows the Find tab. However, you can click the Replace tab to be able to find specific values and replace them with different text. All the settings for a replace operation are the same as for a find operation, except you have an additional text box, called Replace With, to supply the replacement text.

The safest way to perform a replace operation is to click the Find Next button to jump to the next match. At this point, you can look at the match, check that you really *do* want to modify it, and then click Replace to change the value and

jump to the next match. Repeat this procedure to move cautiously through the entire table.

If you're a wild and crazy skydiving sort who prefers to live life on the edge, you can use the Replace All button to change every matching value in the entire table in a single step. Although this procedure is ridiculously fast, it's also a little risky. Replace operations *can't be reversed* (the Undo feature is no help here because it can reverse only a single record change), so if you end up changing more than you intend, there's no easy way back. If you're still seduced by the ease of a Replace All, consider creating a backup of your database file before going any further.

Printing the Datasheet

If you want to study your data at the dinner table (and aren't concerned about potential conflicts with non-Access-lovers), nothing beats a hard copy of your data. You can dash off a quick printout by opening your datasheet, choosing File→Print to enter backstage view, and then clicking the big Print button. However, the results you get will probably disappoint you, particularly if you have a large table.

The key problem is that Access isn't bothered about tables that are too wide to fit on a printed page. It deals with them by splitting the printout into separate pages. If you have a large table and you print it using the standard Access settings, you could easily end up with a printout that's four pages wide and three pages long. Assembling this jigsaw is not for the faint of heart. To get a better printout, it's essential to *preview* your table before printing it, as described in the next section.

Print Preview

The print preview feature in Access gives you the chance to tweak your margins, paper orientation, and so on, before you send your table to the printer. This way, you can make sure the final printout is genuinely usable. To preview a table, open it (or select it in the navigation pane), choose File→Print, and then click the Print Preview button.

The print preview shows a picture of what your data will look like once it's committed to paper. Ordinarily, the print preview shows you a single page of your printout at a time. But to get an overall sense of what's going on—for example, to see whether all your columns can fit on a single page—it's a good idea to lay two or more sheets side by side. To see two pages at once, choose Print Preview→Zoom→Two Pages (Figure 27-15). To see more, choose Print Preview→Zoom→More Pages, and then choose the number of pages you want to see at once from the list.

Figure 27-15:
Unlike the Datasheet view, the print preview paginates your data. You see exactly what fits on each page and how many pages your printout requires (and what content shows up on each page). Print preview shows you that this table is too wide to fit on one sheet of paper, so some of the columns will be relocated to a second page.

Move to a different page

Return to the datasheet view

Change the zoom

If you decide you're happy with what you see, then you can fire off your printout by clicking the Print button on the ribbon (Print Preview→Print→Print). The familiar Windows Print dialog box opens so you can pick a printer and seal the deal.

When you're finished looking at the print preview window, click the ribbon's Close Print Preview button (Print Preview→Close Preview→Close Print Preview), or click one of the view buttons at the Access window's bottom-right corner to switch to Datasheet view or Design view.

Moving around the print preview

You can't change any data while viewing a table in the print preview window. However, you can browse through the pages of your virtual printout and see if it meets your approval.

Here's how you can get around in the preview window:

- Use the scroll buttons to move from one page to another. These buttons look the same as the scroll buttons in the datasheet, but they move from page to page, not record to record.

- To move from page to page, you can use the Page Up and Page Down keys.

- To jump in for a closer look, click anywhere on the preview page (you'll notice that the mouse pointer has become a magnifying glass). This click magnifies the sheet to 100 percent zoom, so you can more clearly see the text and details. To switch back to full-page view, click the page or click the mouse pointer again.

- To zoom more precisely, use the zoom slider that's in the status bar's bottom-right corner. Slide it to the left to reduce your zoom (and see more at once), or slide it to the right to increase your zoom (and focus on a smaller portion of your page).

Changing the page layout

Access provides a small set of page layout options that you can tweak using the ribbon's Print Preview→Page Layout section in the print preview window. Here are your options:

- **Size.** Lets you use different paper sizes. If you're fed up with tables that don't fit, you might want to invest in some larger stock (like legal-sized paper).

- **Portrait and Landscape.** Let you choose how the page is oriented. Access, like all Office programs, assumes you want to print text using standard *Portrait* orientation. In portrait orientation, pages are turned upright so that the long edge is along the side and the short edge is along the top. It makes perfect sense for résumés and memos, but it's pure madness for a wide table, because it guarantees at least some columns will be rudely chopped off and relocated to different pages. *Landscape* orientation makes more sense in this case, because it turns the page on its side, fitting fewer rows per page but many more columns.

- **Margins.** Lets you choose the breathing space between your table and the edges of the page. Margins is a drop-down button, and when you click it, you see a menu with several common margin choices (Normal, Narrow, and Wide). If none of those fit the bill, then click the Page Setup button, which opens a Page Setup dialog box where you can set the exact width of the margin on each side of the page.

Fine-Tuning a Printout

Based on the limited page layout options, you might assume that you can't do much to customize a printout. However, you actually have more control than you realize. Many of the formatting options that you've learned about in this chapter also have an effect on your printout. By applying the right formatting, you can create a better printout.

Here are some pro printing tips that explain how different formatting choices influence your printouts:

- **Font.** Printouts use your datasheet font and font size. Scale this down, and you can fit more in less space.

- **Column order and column hiding.** Reorder your columns before printing to suit what you want to see on the page. Even better, use column hiding (page 765) to conceal fields that aren't important.

- **Column widths and row height.** Access uses the exact widths and heights that you've set on your datasheet. Squeeze some columns down to fit more, and expand rows if you have fields with large amounts of text and you want them to wrap over multiple lines.

- **Frozen columns.** If a table is too wide to fit on your printout, then the frozen column is printed on each part. For example, if you freeze the FirstName field, you'll see it on every separate page, so you don't need to line up the pages to find out who's who.

- **Sort options.** They help you breeze through data in a datasheet—and they can do the same for a printout. Apply them before printing.

- **Filter options.** These are the unsung heroes of Access printing. Use them to get just the important rows. That way, your printout has exactly what you need.

The only challenge you face when using these settings is the fact that you can't set them from the print preview window. Instead, you have to set them in the datasheet, jump to the print preview window to see the result, jump back to the datasheet to change them a little bit more, jump back to the print preview window, and so on. This process can quickly get tiring.

Tip: Don't spend too much time tweaking the formatting options to create the perfect printout. If you have a large table that just can't fit gracefully into a page, you probably want to use *reports*, which are described in online Appendix D. They provide much more formatting muscle, including the ability to split fields over several lines, separate records with borders, and allow large values to take up more space by gently bumping other information out of the way.

Linking Tables with Relationships

The tables you've seen so far lead lonely, independent lives. You don't find this isolation with real-world databases. Real databases have their tables linked together in a web of *relationships*.

Suppose you set out to build a database that can manage the sales of your custom beadwork shop. The first ingredient is simple enough—a Products table that lists your merchandise—but before long you'll need to pull together a lot more information. The wares in your Products table are sold in your Orders table. The goods in your Orders table are mailed out and recorded in a Shipments table. The people in your Customers table are billed in your Invoices table. All these tables—Products, Orders, Shipments, Customers, and Invoices—have bits of related information. As a result, if you want to find out the answer to a common question (like, "How much does Jane Malone owe?" or "How many beaded wigs did we sell last week?"), you'll need to consult several tables.

Based on what you've learned so far, you already know enough to nail down the design for a database like this one. But relationships introduce the possibility of inconsistent information. And once a discrepancy creeps in, you'll never trust your database the same way again.

In this chapter, you'll learn how to *explicitly* define the relationships between tables. This process lets you prevent common errors, like data in different tables that doesn't sync up. It also gives you a powerful tool for browsing through related information in several tables.

Relationship Basics

One of any database's key goals is to break information down into distinct, manageable pieces. In a well-designed database, you'll end up with many tables. Although each table records something different, you'll often need to travel from one table to another to get all the information you want.

To better understand relationships (of the nonromantic kind, anyway), consider an example. The following section demonstrates two ways to add information to the bobblehead database: one that risks redundant data, and one that avoids the problem by properly using a relationship.

Redundant Data vs. Related Data

Think back to the Dolls table you created in Chapter 25 to store a list of bobblehead dolls. One of the pieces of information in the Dolls table is the Manufacturer field, which lists the name of the company that created each doll. Although this seems like a simple-enough detail, it turns out that to properly assess the value of a bobblehead, you need to know a fair bit more about the manufacturing process. You may want to know things like where the manufacturing company is located, how long it's been in business, and if it's had to fight off lawsuits from angry customers.

If you're feeling lazy, you could add all this information to the Dolls table, like so (the shaded columns are the new ones):

ID	Character	Manufacturer	Manufacturer-Location	Manufacturer-OpeningYear	Manufacturer-Lawsuits	Purchase-Price
342	Yoda	MagicPlastic	China	2003	No	$8.99

Your first reaction to this table is probably to worry about the clutter of all these fields. But don't panic—in the real world, tables must include all the important details, so they often grow quite wide. (That's rule #3 of data design, from page 744.) So don't let the clutter bother you. You can use techniques like column hiding (page 765) to filter out the fields that don't interest you.

Although column clutter isn't a problem, another issue lurks under the surface in this example—redundant data. A well-designed table should list only one type of thing. This version of the Dolls table breaks that rule by combining information about the bobblehead *and* the bobblehead manufacturer.

This situation seems innocent enough, but if you add a few more rows, things don't look as pretty:

ID	Character	Manufacturer	Manufacturer-Location	Manufacturer-OpeningYear	Manufacturer-Lawsuits	Purchase-Price
342	Yoda	MagicPlastic	China	2003	No	$8.99
343	Dick Cheney	Rebobblicans	Taiwan	2005	No	$28.75
344	Tiger Woods	MagicPlastic	China	2003	No	$2.99

Once you have two bobbleheads that were made by the same company (in this case, MagicPlastic), you've introduced duplicate data, the curse of all bad databases. (You'll recognize this as a violation of rule #4 of good database design, from page 745.) The potential problems are endless:

- If MagicPlastic moves its plants from China to South Korea, you'll need to update a whole batch of bobblehead records. If you were using two tables with related data (as you'll see next), you'd have just one record to contend with.

- It's all too easy to update the manufacturer information in one bobblehead record but to miss it in another. If you make this mistake, you'll wind up with *inconsistent* data in your table, which is even worse than duplicate data. Essentially, your manufacturer information will become worthless because you won't know which record has the correct details, so you won't be able to trust anything.

- If you want to track more manufacturer-related information (like a contact number) in your database, you'll have to update your Dolls table and edit *every single record*. Your family may not see you for several weeks.

- If you want to get information about manufacturers (but not dolls), you're out of luck. For example, you can't print a list of all the bobblehead manufacturers in China (at least not easily).

It's easy to understand the problem. By trying to cram too many details into one spot, this table fuses together information that would best be kept in two separate tables. To fix this design, you need to create two tables that use *related data*. For example, you could create a Dolls table like this:

ID	Character	Manufacturer	PurchasePrice
342	Yoda	MagicPlastic	$8.99
343	Dick Cheney	Rebobblicans	$28.75
344	Tiger Woods	MagicPlastic	$2.99

And a separate Manufacturers table with the manufacturer-specific details:

ID	Manufacturer	Location	OpeningYear	Lawsuits
1	MagicPlastic	China	2003	No
2	Rebobblicans	Taiwan	2005	No

This design gives you the flexibility to work with both types of information (dolls and manufacturers) separately. It also removes the risk of duplication. The savings are small in this simple example, but in a table with hundreds or thousands of bobblehead dolls (and far fewer manufacturers), the difference is dramatic.

Now, if MagicPlastic moves to South Korea, you need to update the Location field for only one record, rather than for many instances in an overloaded Dolls table. You'll also have an easier time building queries (online Appendix C) that combine the information in neat and useful ways. (For example, you could find out how much you've spent on all your MagicPlastic dolls and compare that with the amounts you've spent for dolls made by other manufacturers.)

Tip: Access includes a tool that attempts to spot duplicate data in a table and help you pull the fields apart into related tables. (To try it out, choose Database Tools→Analyze→Analyze Table.) Although it's a good idea in theory, this tool really isn't that useful. You'll do a much better job of spotting duplicate data and creating well-designed tables from the start if you understand the duplicate-data problem yourself.

Matching Fields: The Relationship Link

This bobblehead database shows you an example of a *relationship*. The telltale sign of a relationship is two tables with matching fields. In this case, the tip-off is the Manufacturer field, which exists in both the Dolls table and the Manufacturers table.

Note: In this example, the fields that link the two tables have the same name in both tables: Manufacturer. However, you don't have to do it this way. You can give these fields different names, so long as they have the same data type.

Using these linked fields, you can start with a record in one table and look up related information in the other. Here's how it works:

- **Starting at the Dolls table,** pick a doll that interests you (let's say Yoda). You can find out more information about the manufacturer of the Yoda doll by looking up "MagicPlastic" in the Manufacturers table.

- **Starting at the Manufacturers table,** pick a manufacturer (say, Rebobblicans). You can now search for all the products made by that manufacturer by searching for "Rebobblicans" in the Dolls table.

In other words, a relationship gives you the flexibility to ask more questions about your data and to get better answers.

Linking with the ID Column

In the previous example, the Dolls and Manufacturers tables are linked through the Manufacturer field, which stores the name of the manufacturing company. This seems like a reasonable design—until you spend a couple of minutes thinking about what might go wrong. And databases experts are known for spending entire weeks contemplating inevitable disasters.

Here are two headaches that just may lie in store:

- **Two manufacturers have the same company name.** So how do you tell which one made a doll?

- **A manufacturer gets bought out by another company and changes its name.** All of a sudden, there's a long list of records to change in the Dolls table.

You might recognize these problems, because they're similar to the challenges you faced when you tackled primary keys (page 740). As you learned, it's difficult to find information that's guaranteed to be unique and unchanging. Rather than risk problems, you're better off just relying instead on an AutoNumber field, which stores an Access-generated ID number.

Interestingly enough, you use the same solution when linking tables. To refer to a record in another table, you shouldn't use just any piece of information—instead, you should use the unique ID number that points to the right record. Here's a redesigned Dolls table that gets it right by changing the Manufacturer field to ManufacturerID:

ID	Character	ManufacturerID	Purchase-Price
342	Yoda	1	$8.99
343	Dick Cheney	2	$28.75
344	Tiger Woods	1	$2.99

If you take a look back at the Manufacturers table (page 786), then you can quickly find out that the manufacturer with the ID value 1 is MagicPlastic.

This design is the universal standard for databases. However, it does have two obvious drawbacks:

- The person adding records to the Dolls table probably doesn't know the ID of each manufacturer.

- When you look at the Dolls table, you can't tell what manufacturer created each doll.

To solve both these problems, use a *lookup*. Lookups show the corresponding manufacturer information in the Dolls table, and they also let you choose from a list of manufacturers when you add a record or edit the ManufacturerID field in the Dolls table.

The Parent-Child Relationship

No, this isn't a detour into feel-good Dr. Phil psychology. Database nerds use the labels *parent* and *child* to identify the two tables in a relationship and to keep track of which one is which.

Here's the analogy. In the real world a parent can have any number of children. However, a child has exactly one set of parents. The same rule works for databases. In the bobblehead database, a single manufacturer record can be linked to any number of doll records. However, each doll record refers to a single manufacturer. So according to the database world's strange sociology, Manufacturers is a parent table and Dolls is a child table. They're linked by a *parent-child relationship*.

Note: Don't think too hard about the parent-child analogy. It's not a perfect match with biological reality. For example, in the bobblehead database, you may create a manufacturer that doesn't link to any dolls (in other words, a parent with no children). You still call that record a parent record, because it's part of the parent table.

It's important to realize that you can't swap the parent and child tables around without changing your relationship. It's *incorrect* to suggest that Dolls is the parent table and Manufacturers is the child table. You can see that such a suggestion would break the parent-child analogy: A single doll can't have more than one manufacturer, and a manufacturer isn't limited to creating a single doll. To prevent problems and all-around fuzzy thinking, you need to know exactly which table is the parent and which one is the child.

Tip: If you have trouble identifying which table is the parent, there's a simple rule to steer you right. The child table always contains a piece of identifying information from the parent table. In the bobblehead database, the Dolls table contains the ManufacturerID field. On the other hand, the Manufacturer table doesn't have any doll information.

If you have database-savvy friends, you'll hear the term "parent-child relationship" quite a bit. The same relationship is also called a *one-to-many* relationship (where *one* is the parent and *many* represents the children, because a single parent record in one table can link to several child records in the other). It's the most common relationship, but not the only one—you'll learn about two other types on page 805 and page 806.

Note: Relationships are so common in modern-day databases that software like Access is often described as a *relational database management system* (RDBMS). A database without relationships is about as common as an oceanfront resort in Ohio.

Using a Relationship

The relationship between Dolls and Manufacturers is *implicit,* which is a fancy way of saying that you know the relationship exists, but Access doesn't. Database pros aren't satisfied with this arrangement. Instead, they almost always define their relationships *explicitly.* When you create an explicit relationship, you clearly tell Access how two tables are related. Access then stores the information about that relationship in the database file.

You have good reasons to bring your relationships out into the open. Once Access knows about a relationship, it can enforce better error checking. It can also provide handy features for browsing related data and editing linked fields. You'll see all these techniques in the following sections. But first, you need to learn how to define a relationship.

Defining a Relationship

You can try out the following steps with the Bobblehead.accdb file, which is included with the online examples for this chapter. It contains the Dolls and Manufacturers tables, in their original form (with no relationships defined). The Bobblehead-Relationships.accdb database file shows the final product: two tables with the right relationship.

Here's what you need to do to set up a relationship:

1. **Every relationship links two fields, each in a different table. Your first step is to identify the field you need to use in the parent table.**

   In a well-designed database, you use the primary-key field (page 740) in the parent table. For example, in the Manufacturers table, you use the ID column, which uniquely identifies each manufacturer.

2. **Open the child table in Design view. (The quickest way is to right-click it in the navigation pane, and then choose Design View.)**

   In this example, the child table is Dolls.

3. **Create the field you need in the child table, if it's not there already.**

   Each child record creates a link by storing a piece of information that points to a record in the parent table. You need to add a new field to store this information, as shown in Figure 28-1.

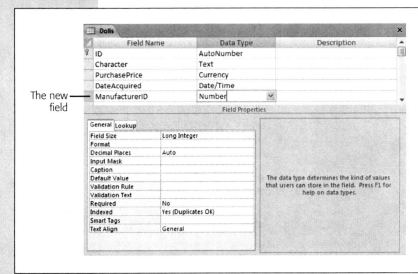

Figure 28-1:
In the Dolls table, you need a field that identifies the manufacturer for that doll. It makes sense to add a new field named ManufacturerID. Set the data type to Number, and the Field Size to Long Integer, so it matches the ID field in the Manufacturers table. After you add this field, you need to fill it with the right information. (Each doll record should have the ID number of the corresponding manufacturer.)

The new field

Note: The fields that you link in the parent and child tables must have consistent data types. However, there's one minor wrinkle. If the parent field uses the AutoNumber data type, then the child field should use the Number data type instead (with a Field Size of Long Integer). Behind the scenes, an AutoNumber and a Long Integer actually store the same numeric information. But the AutoNumber data type tells Access to fill in the field with a new, automatically generated value whenever you create a record. You obviously don't want this behavior for the ManufacturerID field in the Dolls table.

---

4. **Close both tables.**

   Access prompts you to save your changes. Your tables are now relationship-ready.

5. **Choose Database Tools→Relationships→Relationships.**

   Access opens a new tab named Relationships. This tab is a dedicated window where you can define the relationships between all the tables in your database. In this example, you'll create just a single relationship, but you can use the Relationships tab to define many more.

   Before Access lets you get to work in the Relationships tab, it pops up a Show Table dialog box for you to choose what tables you want to work with (see Figure 28-2).

6. **Add both the parent table and child table to your work area.**

   It doesn't matter which one you choose first. To add a table, select it in the list, and then click Add (or just double-click it).

   Access represents each table in the Relationships tab by a small box that lists all the table fields. If relationships are already defined between these tables, they'll appear as connecting lines.

7. **Click Close.**

You can now arrange the tables in the Relationships tab (see Figure 28-3). The Relationships tab shows a *database diagram*—it's the canvas where you add relationships by "drawing" them on.

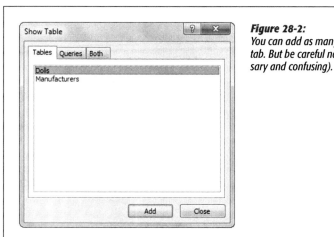

Figure 28-2:
You can add as many tables as you want to the Relationships tab. But be careful not to add the same table twice (it's unnecessary and confusing).

Figure 28-3:
You can drag the tables you've added to any place in the window. If you have a database that's thick with relationships, this ability lets you arrange them so that the relationships are clearly visible. To remove a table from the diagram, right-click it, and then choose Hide Table. To add another table, right-click the blank space, and then choose Show Table to pop up the Show Table dialog box.

Tip: Access gives you a shortcut if you need to rework the design of a table that's open in the Relationships tab. Just right-click the table box, and choose Table Design.

8. **To define your relationship, find the field you're using in the child table. Drag this field to the field you want to link it to in the parent table.**

In this case, you're linking the ManufacturerID field in the Dolls table (the child) to the ID field in the Manufacturers table (the parent). So drag ManufacturerID (in the Dolls box) over to ID (in the Manufacturers box).

Tip: You can drag the other way, too (from the parent to the child). Either way, Access creates the same relationship.

When you release the mouse button, the Edit Relationships dialog box appears (see Figure 28-4).

Figure 28-4:
Access is clever enough to correctly identify the parent table (shown in the Table/Query box) and the child table (shown in the Related Table/Query box) when you connect two fields. Access identifies the field in the parent table because it has a primary key (page 740) or a unique index (page 752). If something isn't quite right in the Edit Relationships dialog box, then you can swap the tables or change the fields you're using to create the relationship before continuing.

9. **If you want to prevent potential errors, then put a checkmark in the Enforce Referential Integrity option. (It's always a good idea.)**

This setting turns on enhanced error checking, which prevents people from making a change that violates the rules of a relationship (like creating a doll that points to a nonexistent manufacturer). You'll learn more about referential integrity and the two settings for cascading changes on page 795. For now, it's best to switch on the Enforce Referential Integrity option and leave the others unchecked.

10. **Click Create.**

This action creates the relationship that links the two tables. It appears in the diagram as a line (Figure 28-5).

If you receive an error that says "the database engine could not lock your table because it is already in use by another person or process," it means you still have your table—or a database object that uses your table—open in another tab. But in order to create a relationship, Access needs exclusive control over both tables. To fix this problem, cancel the current operation, close all the tabs except the Relationships tab, and repeat the process starting at step 8.

Figure 28-5:
Access uses a line to connect related fields in the Relationships tab. The tiny "1" and infinity (∞) symbol let you distinguish between the "one" and the "many" side in this one-to-many relationship. To edit the relationship, double-click the line. To remove it altogether, right-click the line, and then choose Delete.

Tip: If you chose Enforce Referential Integrity (in step 9), Access checks to make sure any existing data in the table follows the relationship rules. If it finds some that doesn't, then it alerts you about the problem and refuses to continue. At this point, the best strategy is to create the relationship without referential integrity, correct the invalid data, and then edit the relationship later to turn on referential integrity.

11. **Close the Relationships tab. (You can click the X in the tab's top-right corner, or choose Relationship Tools | Design→Relationships→Close.)**

    Access asks whether you want to save the Relationships tab's layout. Access is really asking you whether you want to save the relationship diagram you've created. No matter what you choose, the relationship remains in the database, and you can use it in the same way. The only difference is whether you'll be able to quickly review or edit the relationship in the Relationships tab.

    If you choose to keep the relationship diagram, the next time you switch to the Relationships tab (by choosing Database Tools→Relationships→Relationships), you see the same arrangement of tables. This feature is handy.

If you choose not to keep the relationship diagram, it's up to you to recreate the diagram next time by adding the tables you want to see and arranging them in the window (although you won't need to redefine the relationships). This process takes a little more work.

Tip: Many database pros choose to save their database diagram, because they want to see all their relationships at once in the Relationships tab, just the way they left them. However, real-world databases often end up with a tangled web of relationships. In this situation, you may choose *not* to save a complete diagram so you can focus on just a few tables at once.

Editing Relationships

The next time you want to change or add relationships, you'll follow the same path to get to the Relationship window (choose Database Tools→Relationships→Relationships).

Every database can store a single relationship diagram. If you chose to save the relationship diagram for your tables (in step 11 in the previous section), the tables will appear automatically, just as you left them. If you want to work with tables that aren't in any relationships yet, you can add them to the diagram by right-clicking anywhere in the blank area, and then choosing Show Table.

If you chose *not* to save your relationship diagram, you can use a few shortcuts to put your tables back on display:

- Drag your tables right from the navigation pane, and then drop them in the Relationships tab.

- Choose Relationship Tools | Design→Relationships→All Relationships to show all the tables that are involved in *any* relationships you've created previously.

- Add a table to the diagram, select it, and then choose Relationship Tools | Design→Relationships→Direct Relationships to show the tables that are linked to *that* table.

You can also use Relationship Tools | Design→Relationships→Clear Layout to remove all the tables from the current relationship diagram. This way, you have a clear surface and can add back just a few select tables. Clearing the layout doesn't remove the underlying table relationships; they remain even though they aren't on display in your diagram.

As you already know, you can use the Relationships tab to create new relationships. You can also edit the relationships you've already created. To do so, right-click the line that represents the relationship, and then choose Edit Relationships. (This takes some deft mouse-clicking. If you don't see the Edit Relationships option in the menu, you've just missed the line.) To remove a relationship, right-click the relationship line, and then choose Delete.

Note: Usually, you edit a relationship to change the options for referential integrity, which you'll learn about in the next section.

Switching Off Referential Integrity

Are there any situations where you don't want to enforce referential integrity?

In most cases, referential integrity is the ultimate database safety check, and no one wants to do without it—especially if the database includes mission-critical information for your business. Remember, referential integrity prevents only inconsistent data. It still lets you leave a field blank if there's no related record that you want to link to.

The only time you may decide to dodge the rules of referential integrity is when you're using *partial copies* of your database. This situation usually happens in a large business that's using the same database at different sites.

Consider an extremely successful pastry sales company with six locations. When a customer makes an order at your downtown location, you add a new record in the Orders table and fill in the CustomerID (which links to a full record in the Customers table). But here's the problem: The full customer record may not be in your copy of the database—instead, it's in one of the databases at another site, or at company headquarters. Although the link in the Orders table is valid, Access assumes you've made a mistake because it can't find the matching customer record.

In this situation, you may choose to turn off referential integrity so you can insert the record. If you do, then be sure to enter the linked value (in this case, the CustomerID) very carefully to avoid errors later on.

Referential Integrity

Now that you've gone to the work of defining your relationship, it's time to see what benefits you've earned. As in the real world, relationships impose certain restrictions. In the database world, these rules are called *referential integrity*. Taken together, they ensure that related data is always consistent.

Note: Referential integrity comes into action only if you switched on the Enforce Referential Integrity option (page 792) for your relationship. Without this detail, you're free to run rampant and enter inconsistent information.

In the bobblehead example, referential integrity requires that every manufacturer you refer to in the Dolls table must exist in the Manufacturers table. In other words, there can never be a bobblehead record that points to a nonexistent manufacturer. That sort of error could throw the hardiest database software out of whack.

To enforce this rule, Access disallows the following three actions:

- Adding a bobblehead that points to a nonexistent manufacturer.

- Deleting a manufacturer that's linked to one or more bobblehead records. (Once this record is removed, you're left with a bobblehead that points to a nonexistent manufacturer.)

- Updating a manufacturer by changing its ID number, so that it no longer matches the manufacturer ID in the linked bobblehead records. (This updating isn't a problem if you use an AutoNumber field, because you can't change AutoNumber values once you've created the record.)

Note: If you need to add a new doll made by a new manufacturer, you must add the manufacturer record first, and *then* add the doll record. There's no problem if you add manufacturer records that don't have corresponding doll records—after all, it's perfectly reasonable to list a manufacturer even if you don't have any of the dolls they've made.

Along with these restrictions, Access also won't let you remove a table if it's in a relationship. You need to delete the relationship first (using the Relationships window) and *then* remove the table.

Blank values for unlinked records

It's important to realize that there's one operation you can perform that doesn't violate referential integrity: creating a bobblehead that doesn't point to *any* manufacturer. You do this by leaving the ManufacturerID field blank (which database nerds refer to as a *null value*). The only reason you'll leave the ManufacturerID field blank is if the manufacturer record doesn't exist in your database, or if the information doesn't apply. Perhaps the bobblehead wasn't created by any manufacturer but was created by an advanced space-faring alien race and left on this planet for you to discover.

If this blank-value back door makes you nervous, then you can stop it. Just set the Required field property (page 748) on the ManufacturerID field in the Dolls table. This setting ensures that every bobblehead in your Dolls table has legitimate manufacturer information. This technique is important when related information isn't optional. A sales company shouldn't be able to place an order or create an invoice without linking to the customer who made the order.

Cascading deletes

The rules of referential integrity stop you cold if you try to delete a parent record (like a manufacturer) that other child records (like dolls) link to. However, there's another option—and it's much more drastic. You can choose to blow away all related child records whenever you delete a parent. For example, this would allow you to remove a manufacturer and wipe out all the dolls that were produced by that manufacturer.

Warning: Cascading deletes are risky. It's all too easy to wipe out way more records than you intend, and if you do, there's no going back. Even worse, the Undo feature can't help you reverse this change. So proceed with caution.

To turn on this option, you need to switch on the Cascade Delete Related Records setting when you create your relationship (Figure 28-4). You can also modify the relationship later on to add this setting.

Once you've switched on this option, you can try it by deleting a manufacturer, as shown in Figure 28-6.

Microsoft Office Access

Relationships that specify cascading deletes are about to cause 9 record(s) in this table and in related tables to be deleted.

Are you sure you want to delete these records?

[Yes]   [No]   [Help]

Figure 28-6:
In this example, the Dolls-Manufacturers relationship uses the Cascade Delete Related Records setting. When you delete a manufacturer, Access warns you that you'll actually end up deleting every linked doll record, for a total of nine records.

WORD TO THE WISE

Use Cascading Deletes with Care

Cascade Delete Related Records is the nuclear option of databases, so think carefully about whether it makes sense for you. This setting makes it all too easy to delete records when you should really be *changing* them.

If you're dropping a customer from your customer database, then it doesn't make sense to remove the customer's payment history, which you need to calculate your total profit. Instead, you're better off modifying the customer record to indicate that this record isn't being used anymore. You could add a Yes/No field named Active to the customer record, and set this field to No to flag customer accounts that aren't currently in use, without removing them.

Also keep in mind that cascading deletes are just a convenience. They don't add any new features. If you don't switch on Cascade Delete Related Records, you can still remove linked records, as long as you follow the correct order. If you want to remove a manufacturer, then start by removing any linked bobbleheads, or by changing those bobbleheads to point to a different manufacturer (or have no manufacturer at all) by modifying the ManufacturerID values. Once you've taken this step, you can delete the manufacturer record without a problem.

Cascading updates

Access also provides a setting for cascading updates. If you switch on this feature (by going to the Edit Relationships dialog box, and then choosing Cascade Update Related Fields), Access copies any change you make to the linked field in the parent record to all the children.

CHAPTER 28: LINKING TABLES WITH RELATIONSHIPS

With the bobblehead database, a cascading update lets you change the ID of one of your manufacturers. When you change the ID, Access automatically inserts the new value into the ManufacturerID field of every linked record in the Dolls table. Without cascading updates, you can't change a manufacturer's ID if there are linked doll records.

Cascading updates are safer than cascading deletes, but you rarely need them. That's because if you're following the rules of good database design, you're linking based on an AutoNumber ID column (page 787). Access doesn't let you edit an AutoNumber value, and you don't ever need to. (Remember, an AutoNumber simply identifies a record uniquely, and it doesn't correspond to anything in the real world.)

On the other hand, cascading updates come in handy if you're working with a table that hasn't been designed to use AutoNumber values for links. If the Dolls and Manufacturers table were linked based on the manufacturer name, then you need cascading updates—it makes sure that child records are synchronized whenever a manufacturer name is changed. Cascading updates are just as useful if you have linked records based on Social Security numbers, part numbers, serial numbers, or other codes that aren't generated automatically and are subject to change.

Navigating a Relationship

Relationships aren't just useful for catching mistakes. Relationships also make it easier for you to browse through related data. In the next chapter, you'll learn to create search routines that pull together information from related tables. But even without this technique, Access provides some serious relationship mojo in the datasheet.

Here's how it works. If you're looking at a parent table in the datasheet, then you can find the related child records for any parent record by clicking the + box that's just at the left of the row (Figure 28-7).

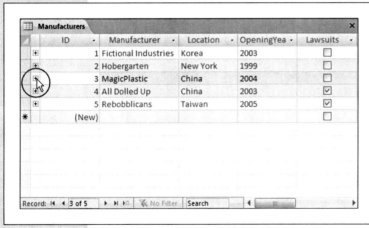

Figure 28-7:
Curious to find out what dolls you have from MagicPlastic? Just click the + box (circled).

This drops a *subdatasheet* into view, which shows just the related records (Figure 28-8). You can use the subdatasheet to edit the doll records here in exactly the same way as you would in the full Dolls datasheet. You can even add new records.

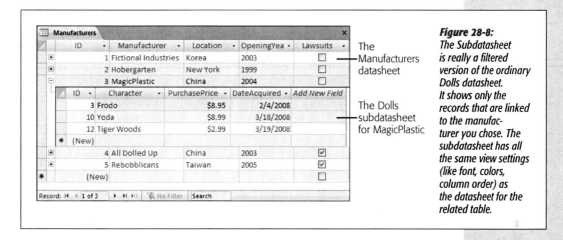

The Manufacturers datasheet

The Dolls subdatasheet for MagicPlastic

Figure 28-8:
The Subdatasheet is really a filtered version of the ordinary Dolls datasheet. It shows only the records that are linked to the manufacturer you chose. The subdatasheet has all the same view settings (like font, colors, column order) as the datasheet for the related table.

Tip: You can open as many subdatasheets as you want at the same time. The only limitation is that the records in a subdatasheet don't show up if you print the datasheet (page 778).

A parent table may be related to more than one child table. In this case, Access gives you a choice of what table you want to use when you click the + box. Imagine you've created a Customers table that's linked to a child table of customer orders (Orders), and a child table of billing information (Invoices). When you click the + box, Access doesn't know which table to choose, so it asks you (see Figure 28-9).

Figure 28-9:
When Access doesn't know which table to use as a sub-datasheet, it lets you pick from a list of all your tables. In this case, only two choices make sense. Choose Orders to see the customer's orders, or Invoices to see the customer's invoices. When you select the appropriate table in the list, Access automatically fills in the linked fields in the boxes at the bottom of the window. You can then click OK to continue.

Tip: You have to choose the subdatasheet you want to use only once. Access remembers your setting and always uses the same subdatasheet from that point on. If you change your mind later on, you'll need to tweak the table settings, as described in the box below.

As you create more elaborate databases, you'll find that your tables are linked together in a chain of relationships. One parent table might be linked to a child table, which is itself the parent of another table, and so on. This complexity doesn't faze Access—it lets you drill down through all the relationships (see Figure 28-10).

The Customers datasheet

The Orders subdatasheet for Lisa Limone

The OrderDetails subdatasheet for Order #1

Figure 28-10:
There are two relationships at work here. Customers is the parent of Orders (which lists all the orders a customer has placed). Orders is the parent of OrderDetails (which lists the individual items in each order). By digging through the levels, you can see what each customer bought.

POWER USERS' CLINIC

Changing Subdatasheet Settings

You can tweak a few more details that affect how subdatasheets are shown for your table. To show these settings, switch your table to Design view. Then, choose Table Tools | Design→Show/Hide→Property Sheet (assuming the Property Sheet isn't currently visible). This action shows the Property Sheet box at the right side of the window.

The Property Sheet has a collection of miscellaneous settings that apply to your whole table. Here are the ones that relate to subdatasheets:

- **Subdatasheet Name.** The linked table used for the subdatasheet. If you have several linked tables, you may choose to adjust this to the one you want to work

with. Or set it to "(Auto)" so that Access prompts you for the subdatasheet you want to use the next time you click the + box, as shown in Figure 28-9.

- **Subdatasheet Height.** Sets the height, in inches, given to the subdatasheet to display its data. If all the related rows don't fit into this space, then you'll need to scroll through them. The standard setting is 0, which allows the subdatasheet to take as much space as it needs.

- **Subdatasheet Expanded.** Lets you choose whether the subdatasheets should start off hidden until you click the + box (the default setting), or automatically expand when you open the table (choose Yes).

Lookups with Related Tables

So far, you've seen how relationships make it easier to review and edit your records. But what about when you add your records in the first place? Relationships are usually based on an unhelpful AutoNumber value. When you create a new doll, you probably won't know that 3408 stands for Bobelle House O' Dolls. Access stops you from entering a manufacturer ID that isn't linked to anyone, but it doesn't help you choose the ID value you want.

Fortunately, Access has a technique to help you. In Chapter 26, you learned about *lookups* (page 756), a feature that provides you with a list of possible values for a column. When creating a lookup, you can supply a list of fixed values, or you can pull values from another table. You could create a lookup for the ManufacturerID field in the Dolls table that uses a list of ID values drawn from the Manufacturers table. This type of lookup helps a bit—it gives you a list of all the possible values you can use—but it still doesn't solve the central problem. Namely, the befuddled people using your database won't have a clue what ID belongs to what manufacturer. You still need a way to show the manufacturer name in the lookup list.

Happily, *lookup lists* provide just this feature. The trick is to create a lookup that has more than one column. One column holds the information (in this case, the manufacturer name) that you want to display to the person using the database. The other column has the data you want to use when a value is picked (in this case, the manufacturer ID).

Note: Access is a bit quirky when it comes to lookups. It expects you to add the lookup, and *then* the relationship. (In fact, when you set up a lookup that uses a table, Access creates a relationship *automatically.*) So if you've been following through with the examples on your own, then you'll need to *delete* the relationship between the Dolls and Manufacturers tables (as described on page 794) before you go any further.

The following steps show how you can create a lookup list that links the Dolls and Manufacturers tables:

1. **Open the child table in Design view.**

   In this example, it's the Dolls table.

2. **Select the field that links to the parent table, and, in the Data Type column, choose the Lookup Wizard option.**

   In this example, the field you want is ManufacturerID.

3. **Choose "I want the lookup column to get values from another table or query" and then click Next.**

   The next step shows a list of all the tables in your database, except the current table.

4. **Choose the parent table, and then click Next.**

   In this case, you're after the Manufacturers table. Once you select it and move to the next step, you'll see a list of all the fields in the table.

---

5. **Add the field you use for the link and another more descriptive field to the list of Selected Fields (Figure 28-11). Click Next to continue.**

   In this case, you need to add the ID field and the Manufacturer field.

Tip: In some cases, you might want to use more than one field with descriptive information. For example, you might grab both a FirstName and LastName field from a FamilyRelatives table. But don't add too much information, or the lookup list will become really wide in order to fit it all in. This looks a bit bizarre.

---

6. **Choose a field to use for sorting the lookup list (Figure 28-12), and then click Next.**

   In this example, the Manufacturer field is the best choice to sort the list.

Figure 28-11:
The secret to a good lookup is getting two pieces of information: the primary key (in this case, the ID field) and a more descriptive value (in this case, the manufacturer's name). The ID field is the piece of information you need to store in the doll record, while the Manufacturer field is the value you'll show in the lookup list to make it easier to choose the right manufacturer.

Figure 28-12:
It's important to sort the lookup list, so that the person using it can find the right item quickly.

7. **The next step shows a preview of your lookup list (Figure 28-13). Make sure the "Hide key column" option is selected, and then click Next.**

   Although the primary-key field has the value that links the two tables together, it doesn't mean much to the person using the database. The other, descriptive field is more important.

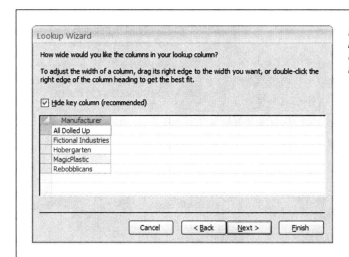

Figure 28-13:
Here, the lookup list shows the manufacturer name (the Manufacturer field) and hides the manufacturer ID (the ID field).

8. **Choose a name for the lookup column.**

   Usually, it's clearest if you keep the name of the field that uses the lookup (in this case, ManufacturerID).

   The final step also gives you two additional options:

   - **Allow Multiple Values.** If you turn on this option, the lookup list shows a checkbox next to each item, so that you can pick several at once. (In this example, you can create a doll that has more than one manufacturer.) You'll learn more about the Allow Multiple Values option on page 809.

   - **Enable Data Integrity.** This choice plays the same role as the Enforce Referential Integrity setting in the Relationships tab (page 792). If you turn it on, Access prevents you from violating the rules of referential integrity (like creating a doll that points to a nonexistent manufacturer). You can also choose a suboption called Cascade Delete, which matches the Cascade Delete Related Records setting you learned about earlier (page 796).

9. **Click Finish.**

   Now, Access creates the lookup for the field and prompts you to save the table. Once you do, Access creates a relationship between the two tables you've linked with your lookup column. Here, Access creates a parent-child relationship between Manufacturers and Dolls, just as you did yourself on page 789.

Now, if you switch to the datasheet view of the Dolls table, you can use your lookup when editing or adding records (Figure 28-14).

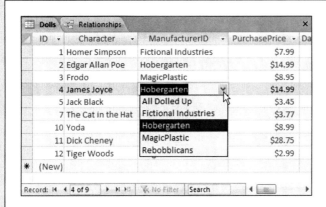

Figure 28-14:
Even though the Dolls table stores an ID value in the ManufacturerID field behind the scenes, that's not how it appears on your datasheet. Instead, you see the related manufacturer name (both onscreen and in any printouts you make). Even better, if you need to add a new record or change the manufacturer that's assigned to an existing one, then you can pick the manufacturer from the list by name.

FREQUENTLY ASKED QUESTION

Refreshing a Lookup

I just added a record, but it doesn't appear in my lookup. Why not?

Access fills in your lookup lists when you first open the table. For example, when you open the Dolls table, Access gets a list of manufacturers ready to go. However, sometimes you might have both the table that *uses* the lookup and the table that *provides* the lookup data open at the same time. In this situation, the changes you make in the table that provides the lookup won't appear in the table that uses the lookup.

To see how this works, open both the Dolls and Manufacturers tables at once. (They'll appear in separate tabs.) In the Manufacturers table, add a new manufacturer. Now, switch back to the Dolls table and try using the ManufacturerID lookup. You'll notice that the lookup list doesn't show the new record.

Fortunately, there's an easy to solution. You can tell Access to refresh the lookup list at any time by choosing Home→Records→Refresh All. Try that out in the Dolls table, and you'll see the updated list of manufacturers appear in the lookup.

More Exotic Relationships

As you learned on page 788, a one-to-many (a.k.a. *parent-child*) relationship that links a single record in one table to zero, one, or more records in another table is the most common relationship. A single manufacturer could be linked to one bobblehead, several bobbleheads, or no bobbleheads at all.

Along with one-to-many relationships, there are two subtly different types of relationships: one-to-one relationships and many-to-many relationships. You'll learn about both in the following sections.

One-to-One Relationships

A *one-to-one relationship* links one record in a table to zero or one record in another table. People sometimes use one-to-one relationships to break down a table with lots of fields into two (or more) smaller tables.

A Products table may include detailed information that describes the product and its price, and additional information that describes how it's built. This information is important only to the people in the engineering department, so you may choose to split it into a separate table (named something like ProductsEngineering). That way, sales folks don't need to think about it when they're making an order. Other times, you might break a table into two pieces because it's simply too big. (Access doesn't let any table have more than 255 fields.)

You create a one-to-one relationship in the same way you create a one-to-many relationship—by dragging the fields in the Relationships tab (Figure 28-15). The only difference is that the linked fields in *both* tables need to be set to prevent duplicates. This way, a record in one table can (at most) be linked to a single record in the other table.

Note: A field prevents duplicates if it's set as the primary key for a table (page 740), or if it has an index that prevents duplicates (page 752).

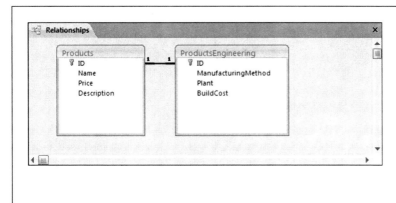

Figure 28-15:
When you link two fields that don't allow duplicates (and you have the Enable Referential Integrity option switched on), Access realizes that you're creating a one-to-one relationship. Access places the number 1 at each side of the line to distinguish it from other types of relationships. In this example, the ID column in the Products table and the ID column in the ProductsEngineering table are both primary keys of their respective tables, so there's no way to link more than one record in ProductsEngineering to the same record in Products.

When you create a design like the one shown in Figure 28-15, make sure that the ID column is not configured to be an AutoNumber field in both tables. Otherwise, Access will try to generate a new AutoNumber when you insert the first record and when you insert the second, linked record.

If you want to use an AutoNumber ID field (and there's no reason you shouldn't), use it in the *parent* table. In this example, the Products table contains the AutoNumber ID. The ID field in the ProductsEngineering table uses the Number data type. That way, each record in the ProductsEngineering table can link itself to a record in the Products table using a matching ID value.

WORD TO THE WISE

Approach One-to-One Relationships with Caution

One-to-one relationships are extremely rare in Access. Usually, features like column hiding (page 765) and queries (online Appendix C) are better choices if you want to see only some of the fields in a table.

Splitting a table into two pieces complicates the design of your database, and you'd generally do it only if you have other reasons to separate the tables. Some possible examples include:

- The two parts of the table need to be placed in separate databases (page 805) so that different people can copy them to separate computers and edit them independently.
- You want to stop prying eyes from seeing sensitive data. One way to do this is to put the information that should be secure into a separate table, and to put that separate table in a different, more secure database file.
- You have a table that stores huge amounts of data, like an Attachment field (page 733) with large documents. In this case, you might get better performance by splitting the table. You might even choose to put one half of the table in a separate database.
- Some of the data in your table is optional. Rather than include a lot of blank fields, you can pop it into a separate table. If you don't need to include this information, then you don't need to add a record to the linked table.

If you don't have these requirements, then you're better off creating a single large table.

Many-to-Many Relationships

A *many-to-many relationship* links one or more records in one table to one or more records in another table. Consider a database that tracks authors and books in separate tables. Bestselling authors seldom stop at one book (so you need to be able to link one author to several books). However, authors sometimes team up on a single title (so you need to be able to link one book to several authors). A similar situation occurs if you need to put students into classes, employees into committees, or ingredients into recipes. You can even imagine a situation where this affects the bobblehead database, if more than one manufacturer can collaborate to create a single bobblehead doll.

Many-to-many relationships are relatively common, and Access gives you two ways to deal with them.

Junction tables

Junction tables are the traditional approach for dealing with many-to-many relationships, and people use them throughout the database world (including in industrial-strength products like Microsoft SQL Server). The basic idea is that you create an extra table that has the sole responsibility of linking together two tables.

Each record in the junction table represents a link that binds together a record from each table in the relationship. In the books and authors database, a single record in the junction table links together one author with one book. If the same author writes three books, then you need to add three records to the junction table. If two authors work on one book, then you need an additional record to link each new author.

Suppose you have these records in your Authors table:

ID	FirstName	LastName
10	Alf	Abet
11	Cody	Pendant
12	Moe	DeLawn

And you have these records in your Books table:

ID	Title	Published
402	Fun with Letters	January 1, 2007
403	How to Save Money by Living with Your Parents	February 24, 2008
404	Unleash Your Guilt	May 5, 2007

Here's the Authors_Books table that binds it all together:

ID	AuthorID	BookID
1	10	402
2	11	403
3	12	403
4	11	404

Authors_Books is a junction table that defines four links. The first record indicates that author #10 (Alf Abet) wrote book #402 (*Fun with Letters*). As you traverse the rest of the table, you'll discover that Cody Pendant contributed to two books, and two authors worked on the same book (*How to Save Money by Living with Your Parents*).

Tip: The junction table often has a name that's composed of the two tables it's linking, like Authors_Books.

The neat thing about a junction table is that it's actually built out of two one-to-many relationships that you define in Access. In other words, the junction table is a child table that has two parents. The Authors table has a one-to-many relationship with the Authors_Books table, where Authors is the parent. The Books table also has a one-to-many relationship with Authors_Books, where Books is the parent. You can define these two relationships in the Relationships tab to make sure referential integrity rules the day (Figure 28-16).

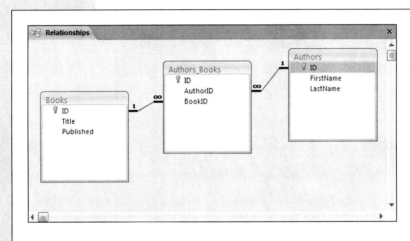

Figure 28-16:
The many-to-many relationship between Authors and Books is really two one-to-many relationships that involve the Authors_Books table. Once you've defined these relationships, you can't link to an author or book that doesn't exist, and you can't delete an author or book that has a record in the Authors_Books table.

Although junction tables seem a little bizarre at first glance, most database fans find that they quickly become very familiar. As with the one-to-many relationships you used earlier, you can create lookups (page 756) for the AuthorID and BookID fields in the Authors_Books table. However, you'll always need to add the Authors_Books record by hand to link an author to a book.

Multi-value fields

For most of database history, junction tables were the only option for many-to-many relationships. But Access 2007 added another approach, called *multi-value fields*.

As its name suggests, a multi-value field can store more than one value. This capacity neatly solves the problem of many-to-many relationships. The trick is to configure the linked field in the child table as a multi-value field. Reconsider the authors and books example. Without the junction table, you'd need to add an AuthorID column to the Books table to indicate which author wrote a given book:

ID	Title	Published	AuthorID
402	Fun with Letters	January 1, 2006	10
403	How to Save Money by Living with Your Parents	February 24, 2005	11
404	Unleash Your Guilt	May 5, 2006	11

But an ordinary field holds a single value. Thus, this table can indicate only one of the two authors for book #403.

However, if you change AuthorID to allow multiple values, you can enter a list of authors, like this:

ID	Title	Published	AuthorID
403	How to Save Money by Living with Your Parents	February 24, 2005	11, 12

Behind the scenes, a multi-value field actually uses a junction table. However, Access hides that detail from you, which makes it a bit easier to link related records.

To create a multi-value field, you need to use a lookup. As you've already seen, you can choose to turn on this option in the last step of the Lookup wizard. Alternatively, if you already have a lookup in a field, you just need to make one minor modification. Open the table in Design view, choose the field that has the lookup (like ManufacturerID), and then, in the Field Properties section, click the Lookup tab. Look for the Allow Multiple Values property, and change it from No to Yes.

Note: Once you change your field to support multiple values, you can't switch back.

FREQUENTLY ASKED QUESTION

Dealing with Many-to-Many Relationships

Which approach is better: junction tables or multi-value fields?

Most database purists will stick with junction tables for years to come. They're accepted, established, and don't hide your database's inner workings. Junction tables are particularly useful if you want to add extra bits of information about the relationship between these two tables. Suppose you create a Students_Classes table to keep track of the classes every student is taking at a popular school. In the Students_Classes table, you could insert additional fields like EnrollmentDate, ConfirmationLetterSentDate, and PrerequisitesChecked.

On the other hand, junction tables have a downside—you can't work with them as easily in the datasheet. If your database uses the Authors_Books junction table, then you

need to edit at least two tables just to add one new book to your system. First, you need to insert a record into the Books table. Then, you need to open the Authors_Books table, and add a new record there that maps this book to an author. (You can use lookups in the Authors_Books table to make this process easy, but it still requires a separate step.) But if the Books table includes a multi-value Authors field, then you can add the book and assign all the authors in one step, which is more convenient.

If you've decided to go with junction tables and you want to make your life a bit easier, then Access has a great solution. You can build a customized *form* that deals with more than one table at once. You can create a form that lets the person using the database insert a record in the Books and Authors_Books tables at the same time. Best of all, your form can make it look like there's only one table involved.

Figure 28-17 shows a multi-value lookup list in action.

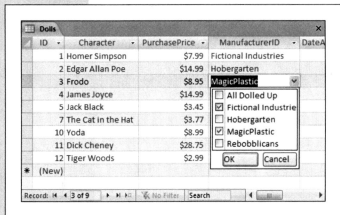

Figure 28-17:
This lookup list uses checkboxes, because it's on a multi-value field. You can select several values for a single record by checking more than one item. So you can indicate that a single doll was created by a two-manufacturer partnership.

Multi-value fields are available only if you're using the new .accdb database format (page 689). You can't use them with an .mdb file (a database that was created in Access 2003 and hasn't been converted yet).

Multi-value fields also cause headaches if you want to upsize your database to SQL Server, because SQL Server doesn't support them. So if there's a possibility that you'll need to share your database with lots of people (say, in a large company), and you might move your data to a high-powered SQL Server database someday, avoid multi-value fields.

FREQUENTLY ASKED QUESTION

Printing Your Relationship

Why is the File→Print command disabled when I'm looking at the Relationships tab?

Once you've created your relationships, you might want to have a printed copy at your fingertips. You can't print the contents of the Relationships tab directly, but you *can* convert the tab data into a *report*, which is a specialized database object that lets you create a printout whenever you want. (You can learn how to create reports in online Appendix D.)

To create a report for your relationships, first arrange all the tables to your liking in the Relationships tab. Then, choose Relationship Tools | Design →Tools →Relationship Report.

A preview window appears, which looks more or less the same as the current contents of the Relationships tab. You can then choose File→Print to send it to the printer.

When you close the relationship report, Access asks you if you want to save it permanently in your database. Usually, you won't bother, because you can easily regenerate the report whenever you need it. However, if you have a complex database and you want to print several different diagrams (each showing a different group of relationships), you may decide to save your relationship report for later use.

Part Six: Other Office Tools

6

Publisher

When you need to lay out a document for publication, Publisher is the program for you. It helps create everything from simple greeting cards and postcards to complex multipage newsletters and catalogs. You can write directly in Publisher—using it as a kind of souped up word processor—or polish your prose in Word and then copy and paste your text into Publisher.

This chapter introduces this low-profile yet high-powered program and shows you how to lay out a publication, from creation straight through to adding text and storing your business information so you don't have to enter it over and over again. It also includes design advice like unifying the look of your document with color and font schemes, using Publisher's layout guides, and adding and formatting images. Finally, when you're ready to send your baby off to the Land of Print, you can run Document Checker to look for (and fix) design problems, and then use a desktop printer or package it up for a commercial printer.

Creating a New Publication

To open Publisher, click the Windows Start button, and then select Microsoft Publisher 2010. (If you don't see that option on the Start menu, look for it here: Start→All Programs→Microsoft Office→Microsoft Publisher 2010.)

To get started on a new publication, select File→New (Alt, F, N) to open the Available Templates page. You can build your publication based on one of Publisher's built-in templates or start it from scratch.

Tip: If you've already got a publication open, selecting File→New (Ctrl+N) closes the current publication to open a new one in a new window.

Creating a Publication from a Template

The Available Templates page lists a wide range of ready-to-use designs for every conceivable print job—from business cards, brochures, and calendars to flyers, invitations, and newsletters. (And if that's not enough, scroll down the page and click More Categories, where you'll find templates for bookmarks, coupons, coloring pages for kids, charts, and all kinds of things you may never even have thought of printing.)

Note: Templates include some created by Microsoft and others added to Office.com by other entities—designers, companies, and Publisher users who came up with cool ideas.

Select a category to see its templates. Figure 29-1 shows some options for creating a calendar. When you click a template, a preview appears on the right.

Figure 29-1:
Publisher has dozens of built-in templates for creating just about any kind of document. Many of them let you customize the color or font scheme before you start working.

Customization section

For many of the Microsoft-built templates, you can start customizing the template before you use it to create a new publication. Beneath the preview is a Customize section; use its drop-down lists to choose a color and a font scheme. The preview reflects your selections. To go back to the template's original look, select "default template colors" and "default template fonts"—they're at the top of their respective lists. (You can always adjust the colors and fonts to your liking after you've created the publication.)

If you want to add business information *before* creating the publication, many templates now let you do that, too. As page 825 explains, you can store things like your name, job title, and contact info in Publisher and then automatically insert it into publications. When you're creating a new publication from a template, the "Business information" drop-down list lets you select information you've already added, or you can click "Create new" to add that info now. (The box on page 821 tells you more about storing business information in Publisher.)

When you're ready to get started on your new publication, click the Create button. In the document that opens, click an image or a text box to start adding content.

Tip: If you launch a document from a template and then decide it's not what you want, select Page Design→Change Template (Alt, P, C) to open a dialog box showing available templates. That way you can choose a different design.

Creating a Publication from Scratch

If you're the do-it-yourself type, you can start with nothing but a blank page and build your new publication from the ground up. On the Backstage Available Templates page, click a blank page in portrait or landscape orientation to open a new publication based on that page. If you don't see the paper size you want, click More Blank Page Sizes to see a whole range of possibilities.

Tip: Working with a nonstandard page size? Click More Blank Page Sizes and, in the Custom section, select "Create new page size". This opens a dialog box for you to specify the width, height, layout, and margins you want for your page. Give your page size a name and click OK, and Publisher adds it to your blank page options.

Viewing the Page

When you create a new publication, it appears in the Publisher workspace, as shown in Figure 29-2. To the left is the Navigation pane, which shows all the pages in your document; click any page to see it in the main workspace. Vertical and horizontal rulers appear around the active page to help you place its objects precisely. The page itself is zoomed out, which is great for getting an overview of its layout, but not so helpful for working with content. Use the status bar's Zoom slider to zoom in on the page, increasing its magnification, or click the View tab to adjust the page's size:

- **100% (Alt, W, J).** Choose this option to zoom in on the page and see its text and illustrations at the size they'll print.

- **Page Width (Alt, W, I).** This option matches the page's width to the width of the window where you're working.

- **Zoom (Alt, W, O).** Choose this option to set the percentage you want: a smaller percentage zooms out, showing more of the page, and a higher percentage zooms in, giving you a closer look.

To go back to an overview of the entire page, like the view in Figure 29-2, select View→Whole Page (Alt, W, 1).

Tip: Multipage publications that you fold over to create pages, like programs and some newsletters, can appear as individual pages or in two-page spread format. Head to the View tab and click Single Page (Alt, W, SP) or Two-Page Spread (Alt, W, 2) to switch between these views.

Rulers

Navigation
pane

Figure 29-2:
When you first create a new publication, it's in whole-page view. Use the buttons in the View tab's Zoom section (circled) to get a closer look at the page. The left-hand Navigation pane gives an overview of your publication and lets you move from page to page.

Tip: Some desktop printers don't work with all of Publisher's features. To avoid frustration later, select the printer you plan to use for this publication as soon as you create a new publication. Publisher turns off any features that your selected printer doesn't support.

Entering Text

In Publisher, as in PowerPoint, text boxes hold the words you add to a page. One great advantage of starting with a template is that its text boxes are already in place, laid out and ready for you to add content. When you start a publication with a blank page, you have to add a text box before you can actually write anything.

If you're working with a template, click inside any text box and start typing to replace the placeholder text. If you created the publication from scratch, then you first need to insert a text box to hold your text. Zoom in to get a good view of the page, and then take one of these actions:

- **To draw a basic text box,** select Insert→Draw Text Box (Alt, N, TB). The mouse pointer becomes crosshairs; click and drag to create a rectangle to hold your text. As you drag, markers on the rulers show the text box's horizontal and vertical position on the page. When the text box is the size you want, let go of the mouse button.

- **To insert a preformatted text box,** select Insert→Page Parts (Alt, N, G). A menu opens, showing text boxes for different purposes: headings, sidebars, pull quotes, stories, and so on. Select a text box from the list, or select More Page Parts (M) to open Publisher's building blocks library, which has a gallery of text boxes. Click any text box in the building blocks library, and then click Insert to put it on your page.

After you've inserted a text box, you can type inside it; format the text (use the buttons on either the Home tab or the Text Box Tools | Format tab); drag and drop to move it to a new location; resize it (click and drag any resizing handle); or rotate it (click the green rotation handle and drag in a circle to tilt the text box). Page 826 gives you the lowdown on working with text boxes in Publisher.

Inserting an Image

Inserting an image into a Publisher page is like inserting an image into any Office program: On the page where you want the image to appear, select Insert→Picture (Alt, N, PI). The Insert Picture dialog box opens; find and select the image you want and then click Insert.

Publisher puts the picture on your page and opens the Picture Tools | Format tab. You can drag and drop the picture into position and adjust its appearance. (Flip to page 830 to read about formatting images in Publisher.)

You can also insert these kinds of images from the Insert tab:

- **Clip Art (Alt, N, V).** This button opens the Clip Art pane (page 97), where you can search for clip art related to a keyword. When you see a result you like, click its down arrow and select Insert to put it on your page.

- **Shapes (Alt, N, SH).** Click this button to open a menu of shapes. Select one and drag the pointer to position and size it on your page. Page 585 tells you more about working with shapes.

- **WordArt (Alt, N, W).** Click the WordArt button and choose a style (if you've never used WordArt, page 581 explains what it is). A dialog box opens for you to type whatever words you're making into art. Type your text and click OK. Publisher inserts the WordArt and opens the WordArt Tools | Format tab, where you can format the WordArt by changing its color, spacing, outline, fill, shape, or effects.

Tip: If you're creating a publication to use as a template for *other* publications (as described in the Tip on page 820), then insert a picture placeholder to mark where an image should go. Select Insert→Picture Placeholder (Alt, N, I1)—that's the letter I (as in Indiana) and the number 1. Publisher inserts an empty content box for an image. Make this box the approximate size you want the image to be, and then drag it into place to save a spot for a picture in your layout. Later, to insert a picture, click inside the placeholder frame to open the Insert Picture dialog box.

Adding Pages

To add a new, blank page to your publication, press Ctrl+Shift+N or go to the Insert tab and click Page (Alt, N, NP, P). Publisher inserts the new page immediately after the current page.

You've also got a couple of related options when inserting a page:

- **Insert a duplicate page (Alt, N, NP, L).** This one's helpful when you've got a page all laid out and want to create a similar page. In the Navigation pane, select the page you want to duplicate, and then click the Page button's down arrow; choose Insert Duplicate Page. Publisher inserts an exact copy of the page immediately after it. Move the page and tweak its layout as you like.

- **Insert a custom page (Alt, N, NP, G).** When you click the Page button's down arrow and select Insert Page from the menu, the Insert Page dialog box, shown in Figure 29-3 opens. Use this to select the number of new pages you want to insert, their location (before or after the current page), and whether you want any objects or text boxes on them. Click OK to insert your new page(s).

Figure 29-3:
Use the Insert Page dialog box to create a new page or to duplicate the current page; then tell Publisher where you want the page to go.

Note: For some templates, the Insert Page box is tailored to the kind of template you're working with. If you're creating a newsletter, for example, the template lets you select elements, like story boxes and calendars, to lay out on the page.

Navigating Pages

Some publications, like flyers and brochures, aren't more than a single sheet of paper; others, like a newsletter or catalog, may be many pages long. To move through a publication's pages, use the Navigation pane on the left side of the screen. But this pane is useful for plenty more than just its namesake mission. Here's what else you can do:

- **Insert a page.** Right-click any page in the navigation pane and select Insert Page (to open the Insert Page dialog box shown in Figure 29-3) or Insert Duplicate Page (to insert a copy of this page right after it).

- **Delete a page.** Right-click the page you want to delete and choose Delete. If the page is blank, Publisher deletes it immediately. If it has text boxes, images, or other objects on it, Publisher asks for confirmation.

- **Move a page.** The quick way to move a page is to drag it up or down the Navigation pane to its new location. Alternatively, right-click the page you want to move and select Move Page. The Move Page dialog box opens, listing the pages in your publication. Select a page, and turn on the Before or After radio button. Click OK, and the page jumps to its new location.

- **Name a page.** Page titles don't appear on the actual pages. Instead, they help you keep track of pages when working with them. For example, the Move Page dialog box lists a publication's pages by title and page number. For a short publication, it's easy to find a page by its number, but in longer publications, page titles are helpful in identifying the page you want. To name (or rename) a page, right-click the page and select Rename. In the Rename Page dialog box, type in the page's new title, and then click OK.

Tip: Another option for working with pages is the Page Design tab (Alt, P), where you can Delete (D), Move (V), or Rename (N) the current page.

Saving a Publication

This works pretty much like saving a file in any other Office program. You can save the current publication in any of these ways:

- Press Ctrl+S.
- Click the Quick Access toolbar's Save button.
- Select File→Save (Alt, F, S).
- Select File→Save As (Alt, F, A).

The first time you save a publication, Publisher opens the Save As dialog box. Navigate to the folder where you want to store the file, give it a name, and select Publisher Files (.pub) as the file type. Click Save to save the file.

Tip: If you've laid out a publication that you want to use as the basis for future publications, save it as a template; when you save the file, put "template" in its name (*newsletter_template*, for example) and then choose Publisher Template as the file type. Publisher still saves the file as a .pub file, but it stores it in your Templates folder, so it appears in the My Templates section of your Available Templates page.

Adding Text

Text boxes are the basic building blocks for any document you create with Publisher. They hold your words—an article, a list, a greeting, you name it—and make laying out a page a breeze.

Tip: Use the layout guides described on page 834 to line up your text boxes on the page. Baseline guides are particularly helpful in making sure that text in adjacent boxes appears even, not skewed horizontally.

Editing and Formatting Text

When you click inside a text box, the Text Box Tools | Format contextual tab appears. From that control center, all sorts of text tweaking maneuvers are possible.

Aligning text within a text box

The best way to position text inside the text box that holds it is to use the alignment buttons on the Text Box Tools | Format tab. These nine buttons let you line up text along the top, bottom, right, left, or center of a text box.

Fitting text to a text box

If you're used to working with Word documents, where your words automatically wrap from one line to the next, then text boxes can take a little getting used to. You might find yourself typing or pasting in text, for example, and all of a sudden you've run out of text box to contain it. The Text Box Tools | Format tab has the following options to make text fit into its text box:

- **Best Fit (Alt, JX, I, B).** This option bumps up or scales back the font size to fit the text box as you type. So you might start off with very large letters but, as you type more and more, the text gets smaller to fit the box. This one is a good option to choose when you want the largest size that will fit in the box—for an eye-catching headline, perhaps.

Adding Your Business Information to Publisher

Help! I hate having to add things like my company's name, address, and phone number every time I create a document. There's got to be a better way, right?

You bet. Publisher lets you store all that information (plus a few similar items) in what it calls a *business information set*. When you create and save one of these timesavers, you can pull up the set and automatically insert its contents. Just follow these steps:

1. Select Insert→Business Information→Edit Business Information (Alt, N, BI, E) to open the Create New Business Information Set dialog box, shown in Figure 29-4.

2. Type in the information you want to save in this set. You can add all or some of these items: your name, job title, and email address; your company's name,

address, and phone numbers; and your company's tagline and logo. To add a logo, click the Change button to open the Insert Picture dialog box. If you don't want any logo at all, click Remove to clear the Logo box.

3. When you've entered the information you want to save, give the set a name, and then click Save.

Publisher creates this info package and opens the Business Information dialog box, showing the details of the set you just saved. If you want, edit the details or create another set now. (Multiple sets come in handy if you need to create one for yourself, another for your boss, and perhaps a third for an organization you volunteer for.)

Figure 29-4:
Type in any business information you want to store and insert into publications. Delete any placeholder text you don't need.

- **Shrink Text on Overflow (Alt, JX, I, S).** This option decreases font size rather than letting text overflow its text box. So if you start off specifying a 12-point font, for example, and then select this option, Publisher automatically reduces the text size by small, gradual increments if the text you type threatens to overflow the box's boundaries.

Note: Select a font size and then select Shrink Text on Overflow. If you change a text box's font size, Publisher automatically changes the Text Fit selection to Do Not Autofit.

- **Grow Text Box to Fit (Alt, JX, I, G).** Instead of shrinking text to fit your text box, you can expand the text box to accommodate the text. If you've already got a page all laid out in columns and boxes, don't choose this option, because expanding the text box will mess up your layout.

- **Do Not Autofit (Alt, JX, I, D).** This is Publisher's default text-fitting option. If you put more text into a text box than it can hold, any overflow doesn't appear. You'll need to flow it into another text box (read on to find out how to do that).

Adjusting hyphenation

Publisher automatically hyphenates words that fall within a preset hyphenation zone (the default is 0.25"). When you click Text Box Tools | Format→Hyphenation (Alt, JX, H), you open a dialog box that lets you adjust the hyphenation zone, turn automatic hyphenation off or on, or apply hyphenation manually.

Working with character spacing

Adjusting the spacing between characters can help fit text better into its space, making your words easier to read (or just look that much better). To tweak your text character spacing, head to the Character Spacing button—you can find it on the Home tab (Alt, H, M) or the Text Box Tools | Format tab (Alt, JX, M1).

Clicking the Character Spacing button shows a menu of options for spacing your text, from Very Tight to Very Loose. (PowerPoint also has this button; Figure 21-2 on page 567 shows how each character spacing option looks.)

To fine-tune character spacing more than the quick options on the Character Spacing menu allow, select that menu's More Spacing option. This opens the Character Spacing box, shown in Figure 29-5. Go to this dialog box to adjust character spacing in these ways:

- **Scaling.** This squeezes or expands the characters in selected text without changing their height. The scaling for normal text is 100%; a lower number squeezes text, and a higher number stretches it.

- **Tracking.** Go to this section to adjust the spacing between characters by a percentage you specify. Again, normal is 100%; a lower number reduces spacing, and a higher number expands it.

- **Kerning.** *Kerning* adjusts the spacing between two characters. Some character pairs, such as "WA" or "VA" can look "off" compared to other characters in the text, as Figure 29-6 shows. Kerning lets you fine-tune spacing between such pairs so they don't stick out from the rest of the text.

Figure 29-5:
Make your text easy on the eyes by using the options in this dialog box to adjust character spacing.

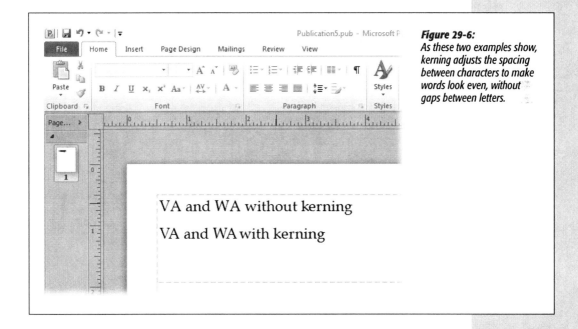

Figure 29-6:
As these two examples show, kerning adjusts the spacing between characters to make words look even, without gaps between letters.

- **Automatic pair kerning.** You don't have to fiddle with kerning between each pair of letters (although you can if you've got that kind of time to kill). The bigger the characters, the more noticeable kerning is. So let Publisher take care of kerning for you in text above a certain size. Turn on the "Kern text at" checkbox and set a font size (the default is 14 points). Publisher automatically kerns text at the selected size or bigger.

Tip: If you work with character spacing a lot, click the Show Toolbar button to open the Measurement toolbar, which lets you fine-tune character spacing even further.

Formatting text

Publisher gives you three ways to format text: the Mini Toolbar (page 50) for quick formatting of selected text, and the Font sections on the Home tab (Alt, H) and the Text Box Tools | Format tab (Alt, JX). So you're never far from buttons to change the font, adjust its size or color, or add formatting like boldface or italics.

Adding some style to your text

The Text Box Tools | Format tab's Typography section, shown in Figure 29-7, has a toolbox of neat tricks that add interest to your text, giving it a professional flourish. Here's what you'll find there:

- **Drop Cap (Alt, JX, DC).** Sometimes an article starts off with an extra-large capital letter or word. This formatting, called a drop cap, calls attention to a story's beginning, as shown in Figure 29-7. To create a drop cap, click inside the text box where your story begins and click the Drop Cap button. A menu opens, showing numerous styles of drop caps. Point at different options, and Live Preview applies each to your text. Click a drop cap style to apply it to your text.

  You can also tweak a drop cap's style or create your own. From the Drop Cap menu, select Custom Drop Cap (C) to open a dialog box where you can adjust the letter's position, size, and height; specify the number of letters to include; and adjust the font, style, and color of the drop cap.

- **Number Style (Alt, JX, U).** Some fonts offer a range of styles for the numbers in your text. Click this button to see a menu of options for the font you're working with. If you see one you like, click it to apply it to your selected text.

- **Ligatures (Alt, JX, L1).** Ligatures join two characters together for a smoother appearance (like the *ff* combinations in Figure 29-7). Publisher uses ligatures by default; if you don't want them in some text, select that text, click Ligatures, and then choose No Ligatures from the menu.

- **Stylistic Sets (Alt, JX, L2).** Some fonts come with different style sets built in, giving the same basic font a range of appearance tweaks, such as the swashes described in the next item. (Figure 29-7 shows an example of two different looks from the same stylistic set.) Click this button to see the style tweaks available for your chosen font.

- **Swash (Alt, JX, SW).** A swash is a textual flourish. When you turn on swashes by clicking this button, you can decorate your text with all sorts of swoops and swirls, as shown in Figure 29-7.

- **Stylistic Alternatives (Alt, JX, A).** Some fonts have alternative shapes for certain characters, such as different styles for the lowercase *a* and *g*. (The two *a*'s on the button show an example.) Click this button to give selected text a slightly different look.

Note: Not all fonts include all these typographical options. When you select a font, Publisher grays out any options that aren't available for that font.

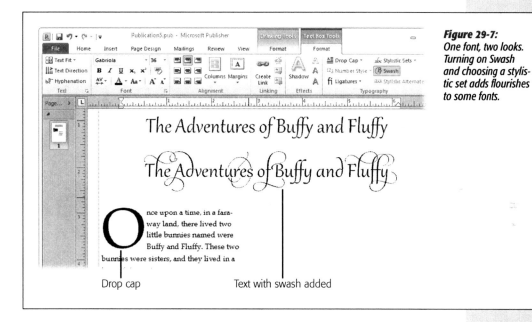

Figure 29-7:
One font, two looks. Turning on Swash and choosing a stylistic set adds flourishes to some fonts.

Drop cap   Text with swash added

Inserting Your Business Information

If you've saved a business information set (as described in the box on page 821), you can save yourself some typing and automatically add any of that info to your publication. This works is thanks to the magic of *fields*—data placeholders that pipe in items from these saved sets. Many templates have fields built in, so you can insert a set's entire contents at once. Even if your publication doesn't have fields, though, you can place stored business information into regular text boxes. This section covers both methods.

When you create a publication that has fields for business information, you can insert the info from a business information set in just a couple of clicks:

1. Select Insert→Business Information→Edit Business Information (Alt, N, BI, E).

   This opens the Business Information box, shown in Figure 29-8. The main part of the dialog box shows the current business information set.

2. If you've saved more than one set, choose the one you want from the "Select a Business Information set" drop-down list. Click Update Publication.

   Publisher checks the publication for fields that match those in the set and inserts the content where appropriate.

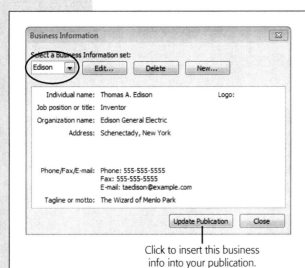

Figure 29-8:
When you've stored more than one business information set, select the set you want from the drop-down list (circled) to see its information in the dialog box. To insert the information in your publication, click the Update Publication button.

Click to insert this business info into your publication.

If you want to insert just a single piece of information into a text box (which can help protect against typos), you can do that, too:

1. Draw a text box or click inside an existing one (delete any placeholder text). Select Insert→Business Information (Alt, N, BI).

   A menu opens with the information from the current set.

2. Scroll down the menu to find the information you want to insert; click it.

   Publisher inserts the information into the text box.

Flowing Text from One Box to Another

Stories in newspapers and magazines often don't fit on a single page. You may read part of a story on page 1, for example, and then flip over to page 4, where the story continues, to read the rest. Similarly, in Publisher a story or article might not fit into a single text box. Starting a story in one text box and finishing it in another is called *flowing* text. Effectively, you pour any overflow text from one text box into another, empty text box.

Publisher offers two ways to flow text: manually and automatically. When you flow text manually, you choose a second text box (or more) to take on the overflow text. (This is probably the way you'd deal with overflow in a one-off publication.) When you autoflow text, you set up links between text boxes so that when you paste text into the first box, it automatically flows into the linked box (or boxes). Autoflowing text is useful in a template you use frequently, such as to produce a monthly newsletter.

Flowing text manually

If you find that your text won't fit into its text box, you can continue it in another box by following these steps:

1. **Create the text boxes that will hold your story or article.**

   You can draw them yourself (page 817) or use a template that has text boxes already laid out (page 814).

2. **Copy the text of your article from its source, such as a Word file or your blog. (You can type in Publisher, of course, but many people find it easier to compose their text in a word processor and then paste it into Publisher.)**

   Use Ctrl+A to select an entire document and then Ctrl+C to copy the document to the Clipboard.

3. **Back in Publisher, click inside the text box that will hold the *beginning* of your article. Press Ctrl+V to paste in your text.**

   If the story is too long to fit in the text box, Publisher indicates this by showing an Overflow indicator: a small box containing an ellipsis on the border of the text box, as shown in Figure 29-9.

Tip: If you haven't yet created a second text box to hold the overflow, do it before clicking on the Overflow indicator.

---

4. **Click the Overflow indicator.**

   The pointer turns into a pitcher, as shown in Figure 29-9, indicating that you can "pour" the overflow text into another text box.

5. **Click inside the text box where you want to continue the article.**

   The text flows into the new text box, picking up right where it left off in the previous box. If the article overflows the second text box, repeat steps 4 and 5 until your publication shows the whole article.

After you've flowed text into one or more text boxes, take a look at the text itself. Make sure it breaks at a good spot (for example, you don't want to direct readers to another page in the middle of a word). Adjust as needed by editing the text, adjusting the font size, or tweaking the character spacing to make the text break where you want it to.

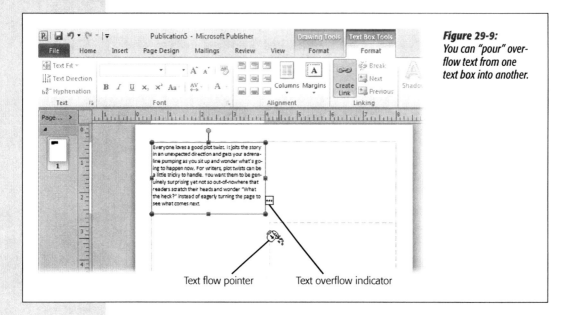

Figure 29-9:
You can "pour" overflow text from one text box into another.

Text flow pointer   Text overflow indicator

Connecting text boxes to autoflow text

You can tell Publisher to flow text from one box to another automatically. In other words, you can connect the text boxes *before* typing or pasting text into the first text box. When you create this kind of link between text boxes, Publisher automatically continues your article in the next text box. You might want to connect text boxes in this way in a newsletter template, for example, where the lead story always begins on page 1 and then continues on a later page.

Here's how to create a link between text boxes:

1. **Create the text boxes you want to link (they can be on different pages). Select the first one, where the article will begin, and then select Text Box Tools | Format→Create Link.**

   Your pointer turns into a pitcher, like the one shown in Figure 29-9. As you move the pointer through your publication, text boxes appear with a dotted-line outline.

2. **Click inside the text box you want to link *to* (the box that will continue the article that begins in the first text box).**

   Publisher links the boxes, and an arrow appears on the border of the selected text box, as shown in Figure 29-10, indicating that the box is connected to another text box. You can repeat these steps to link as many text boxes as you need, linking from the second box to the third, and so on.

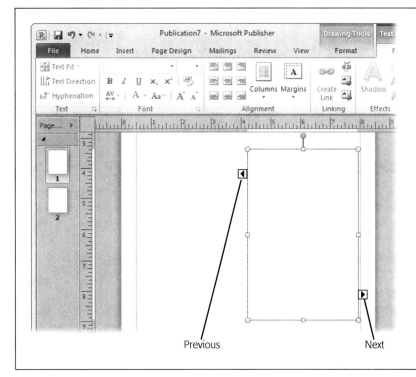

Figure 29-10:
This text box is linked to
two other text boxes; one
before it and one after it.
Click an arrow to jump to
the previous or next text
box in the chain.

Now when you add text to the first text box, any overflow automatically appears in the second text box to which it's linked.

To move between linked text boxes, use the Next and Previous arrows on the boxes themselves, or go to the Text Box Tools | Format tab and click the Linking section's Next (Alt, JX, N) and Previous (Alt, JX, P) buttons.

If you need to break a link between text boxes—maybe because you're reusing a publication as a template and you don't need the text to flow into a new box—click the first box in the chain and select Text Box Tools | Break (Alt, JX, K). Poof—the link is gone.

Flowing Text Around an Object

You can wrap text around pictures, clip art, and other objects in a Publisher document, just as you can in Word. In Publisher, however, if you insert a picture into a text box, the text automatically wraps around it. (Try it and see.)

To adjust text wrapping in Publisher, click the Wrap Text button on the Home tab (Alt, H, TW) or the Picture Tools | Format tab (Alt, JP, TW). As you point at the different wrapping options, Live Preview shows how each looks on the page. Click the option that looks best to apply it to your publication.

Tip: Page 107 tells you about the different ways you can wrap text around an image.

Adding Pictures, Shapes, and Other Objects

In Publisher, objects are the elements you place on a page, such as text boxes, pictures, shapes, and WordArt. This chapter gives text boxes their own section (page 820); here you can read about working with all the non-text objects you can add to a publication.

Formatting Objects

Controlling the appearance of objects in Publisher works pretty much the same way as it does in other Office programs. When you add an object to a page (page 817), a contextual toolbar appears, packed with special commands that lets you do things like add shadow effects, align objects, and crop photos. This section looks at all those maneuvers—and plenty more—in depth.

Formatting pictures

When you insert a picture into a document, Publisher opens the Picture Tools | Format tab, shown in Figure 29-11. Use the buttons on this tab to adjust the picture's brightness, contrast, or color. You can also apply picture styles (page 106) and crop the photo (page 101) right in Publisher.

Publisher's Picture Tools | Format tab has a couple of sections that are different from other Office programs:

- **Swap.** If you lay out two pictures on the same page and then decide things would look better if you switched their positions, select the pictures and then click Swap (Alt, JP, SW, S).

Tip: You can also swap two pictures' formatting. This leaves them in place but applies the formatting of one to the other and vice versa. Click the Swap button's down arrow and then select Swap Formatting Only (Alt, JP, SW, F).

- **Shadow Effects.** Other Office programs let you apply shadow effects to images, but Publisher puts these effects front and center. Click the Shadow Effects button (Alt, JP, V) to select the shadow style you want, then use the four nudge shadow buttons beside it to push the shadow up (Alt, JP, 1), down (Alt, JP, 4), left (Alt, JP, 2), or right (Alt, JP, 3). After you've added a shadow effect, you can toggle it off and on (Alt, JP, 0).

Tip: Sometimes you insert a picture where the subject is looking left, but the image would fit your layout better if only she were looking right. To flip an image in this way, select Picture Tools | Format→Rotate→Flip Horizontal (Alt, JP, R, H).

Figure 29-11:
*Publisher's Picture
Tools | Format tab
has all the commands
you'd expect for
working with images.
The Swap button
(circled) lets you
change pictures' posi-
tions, formatting, or
both. You can apply
shadow effects with
precision by nudging
the shadow up, down,
left, or right (also
circled).*

Formatting shapes and WordArt

The Drawing Tools | Format tab and the WordArt Tools | Format tab both offer buttons for changing an object's style, including adjusting its fill and outline colors, adding shadow effects, and rotating and aligning the object. Click the 3-D Effects button (Alt, JD, Z3, F for shapes; Alt, JW, Z3, F for WordArt) to apply 3-D formatting to an object—your choices here are more extensive than in other Office programs. And you can nudge 3-D effects up, down, left, or right, as you can with shadows.

The WordArt Tools | Format tab also has a text section where you can work with the words that make up your WordArt:

- **Edit Text (Alt, JW, E).** Click when you need to change the text of your WordArt.

- **Spacing (Alt, JW, AS).** This adjusts the spacing between characters, from very tight to very loose, and lets you kern (page 822) pairs of characters.

- **Even Height (Alt, JW, AH).** To make all the letters in your WordArt exactly the same height, whether lowercase or uppercase, click this button.

- **WordArt Vertical Text (Alt, JW, AV).** This button stacks the WordArt's letters vertically.

- **Align Text (Alt, JW, AL).** If your WordArt is longer than a single line, click this button to align those lines.

Stacking and Grouping Objects

In Publisher, you can create a complex graphic by stacking objects on top of each other in layers. Publisher puts objects on top of each other based on the order in which you add them to the page; the earliest object goes on the bottom, and later objects get stacked on top. You can change the placement of an object in the stack. When you've arranged objects as you want them, you can group them, so that Publisher treats them as a single object.

To create a graphic by stacking objects, follow these steps:

1. **Insert all the objects you want to appear in the group. Click an object and drag it into position, and then click and drag another object on top of the first.**

   Publisher puts the items in a stack, with the more recently placed objects on top.

2. **If you want to change the order of objects in the stack, select an object, go to the contextual Format tab's Arrange section, and then select an option from the Bring Forward or Send Backward menu.**

   You can bring an object forward one level (Bring Forward) or to the top of the stack (Bring to Front). You can also send the object back one level (Send Backward) or to the bottom of the stack (Send to Back).

3. **Continue stacking objects until you've arranged the overall graphic as you want it. Then press Ctrl as you select each object in the stack, as shown in Figure 29-12. On a Format contextual tab (it may be Drawing Tools, Picture Tools, or WordArt Tools), go to the Arrange section and click Group, or press Shift+Ctrl+G.**

   Publisher merges the objects into a single object.

Figure 29-12:
When you're stacking objects, use the circled buttons in any of the contextual Format tab's Arrange sections to order, group, and ungroup the objects. Right now, this image shows a stack of three objects; grouping them would make them into a single object.

Now whenever you move, resize, or otherwise format the grouped object, you affect all its parts.

To ungroup a grouped object, select the object, head back to the Format contextual tab, and then click Ungroup, or press Shift+Ctrl+G again.

Designing and Laying Out Pages

Publisher is packed with tools to help you produce professional-looking pages. This section walks you through setting up pages, choosing color and font schemes, and using Publisher's layout guides.

Setting up Your Pages

When you create a new publication, the first order of business is deciding how you want the pages to look. Go to the Page Design tab's Page Setup section to adjust these settings:

- **Margins (Alt, P, MR).** Click this button to choose wide (1"), moderate (0.5"), narrow (0.25"), or no margins. Or select Custom Margins to open a dialog box where you can set your own margins.

- **Orientation (Alt, P, OR).** Choose portrait or landscape orientation here.

- **Size (Alt, P, SZ).** Choose a paper size from this button's menu. If you don't see the size you want, try More Preset Page Sizes or select Create New Page Size to open a dialog box where you set page width and height, margins, layout type, and paper size.

Choosing a Color Scheme

In Publisher, color schemes are like themes in other Office programs: Assigning a color scheme to your publication ensures that its colors complement one another. Publisher offers dozens of color schemes with alluring names like Opulent, Tuscany, Meadow, and Summer. (Kinda makes you want to power down your computer and go hiking.) You can view these color schemes in their gallery in the Page Design tab's Schemes section; click the gallery's lower-right More button (Alt, P, TC) to see all the color schemes in one menu.

If you've got an artistic eye, you can create your own color scheme and save it in Publisher. On the Page Design tab, click the Color Scheme gallery's More button and choose Create New Color Scheme (Alt, P, TC, C). The Create New Color Scheme box, shown in Figure 29-13, opens. This dialog box shows the scheme's colors; next to each color is a drop-down list where you can pick a different color. The right side of the box shows a preview of the page and some sample text.

Select a main color (for text), up to five accent colors, and colors to indicate hyperlinks (both unclicked and clicked). As you choose colors, the preview and sample text change to show how the new colors look. When you have a scheme you like, give it a name and click Save. Publisher adds your new scheme to the Color Scheme gallery.

Figure 29-13:
To design your own color scheme, choose a main color and accent colors in the Create New Color Scheme dialog box.

Choosing a Font Scheme

Picking a font scheme for a publication gives you the same advantage as choosing a color scheme—you're already a step ahead in the design game when you choose a group of fonts that go well together for headings and regular text.

On the Page Design tab, click the Fonts button (Alt, P, TF) to see a menu of fonts. Each named option shows two fonts: one for headings and one for body text. As you point at the options, Live Preview shows how each font looks in your document. Click a font scheme to apply it to your publication.

As with color schemes, you can create your own font scheme. Select Page Design→Fonts→Create New Font Scheme (Alt, P, TF, C) to open the Create New Font Scheme dialog box. Choose a heading font and a body font from drop-down lists. The Sample pane shows how the fonts look together. When you're satisfied with your pairing, type a name into the "Font scheme name" text box, and then click Save.

Using Layout Guides

One of the challenges of designing a publication is laying out the pages. It can be tricky to arrange objects—text boxes, columns, images, and shapes—so that they look good and line up correctly. That's why Publisher has *rulers* and *layout guides* to help you position the objects on your pages.

Margins (page 833) are one kind of layout guide; they make sure your text and images don't creep too close to the edges of the page. The Page Design tab's Layout section also offers several other kinds of guides. To see them, select Page Design→Guides (Alt, P, G) to open the menu shown in Figure 29-14.

Figure 29-14:
*Ruler guides help
you get precise about
laying out objects
on a page. Choose
a built-in guide or
click Ruler Guides to
design your own.*

The Guides menu offers several different kinds of layout guides that you're sure to find useful:

- **Ruler guides.** These are green lines that you can put on a page in different configurations—perfect for helping you line up text boxes, images, and other objects. Figure 29-12 shows Publisher's built-in ruler grids. Use one of those, or draw your own using one of these methods:

  — **Position ruler guides on the page.** Select Add Horizontal Ruler Guide (H) or Add Vertical Ruler Guide (V), and Publisher places a horizontal or vertical guide (depending on your choice) across the middle of the page. Click and drag the guide to position it where you want it.

  — **Use the Ruler Guides dialog box.** Select Ruler Guides (H) to open the Ruler Guides dialog box. Choose the Horizontal or Vertical tab, and then type in the position (in inches) for each guide you want to create. Click OK to make the guides appear on the page.

Tip: Ruler guides appear only on the current page. To show the same ruler guides on all pages in a publication, apply them to the publication's master page: Select Page Design→Master Pages (Alt, P, R). In the menu that opens, select Edit Master Pages (E). Go to the Page Design tab and apply ruler guides as just described. Select Master Page→Close Master Page (Alt, JM, C). Now all pages in the publication have the ruler guides you applied to the master page.

- **Grid guides.** You can overlay a grid of lines across each page in your document, and then line up objects by having them snap to the grid (see the next section). In the Guides menu, select Grid and Baseline Guides (G). The Layout Guides dialog box opens to the Grid Guides tab, shown in Figure 29-15. In the dialog box, enter the number of columns and rows you want in your grid. The Spacing boxes indicate how close an object can come to a gridline. You probably don't want a number smaller than 0.2 if you want to keep a reasonable distance between objects. (If you set spacing to 0, objects will touch one another.) Turn on the checkbox labeled "Add center guide between columns and rows" if you want to add red lines that mark the center point between columns and rows. Click OK to apply your grid to the publication (it shows up on all pages).

- **Baseline guides.** These guides are like the horizontal lines in notebook paper, and they're particularly helpful when you need to make sure that text in two adjacent text boxes lines up evenly. In the Guides menu, select Grid and Baseline Guides (G) and, in the Layout Guides dialog box, click the Baseline guides tab. On this tab, shown in Figure 29-16, adjust the Spacing measurement to make lines closer together or farther apart; adjust the Offset measurement to change the distance from the top margin to the top baseline guide. Click OK to apply your baseline guides.

Figure 29-15:
A grid guide lays a visual matrix over your page to assist you with placing objects. When you create a grid guide, the preview gives you an idea of its size.

Tip: To show or hide your publication's guides, go to the View tab (Alt, W) and turn on or off the Guides (D) and Baselines (B) checkboxes. Be aware, though, that turning off the Guides checkbox also hides pages' margins.

Figure 29-16:
A baseline guide helps you align text horizontally, like lined notebook paper.

Tip: To measure objects precisely, shift-click either ruler and drag it onto the page. When you're done using it there, Shift-click again to drag the ruler back to its usual place.

Snapping an Object to a Guide

You can position objects by eye, but a surer way to make them line up on the page is to "snap" them to a grid or ruler guide. When you drag and drop a text box, image, or other object, it lines up with the nearest guide when you let go of the mouse button.

To turn this feature on, go to the Page Design tab's Layout section and turn on the Guides checkbox.

Reviewing Your Design

Carpenters have a saying: Measure twice, cut once. If printers don't have a similar saying, they should, because double-checking before hitting Print is just as important when you're working on a newsletter as when you're building a cabinet.

Publisher makes double-checking easy with its built-in Design Checker. When you run a design check, this tool automatically scours your publication for issues that could (if left unfixed) cause headaches when you try to print. To enlist this paper-and-ink saver, follow these steps:

1. **Select File→Info→Run Design Checker (Alt, F, E, I).**

   Design Checker opens in its own pane, as shown in Figure 29-17, and immediately starts sniffing around your document. At the top of the Design Checker pane are four checkboxes listing the different kinds of inspections Design
   Checker can conduct:

   — **Run general design checks.** This looks for general design issues, such as
   objects that run off the page or overlap some text; empty text boxes or missing pictures; text that's too big for its box; and so on.

   — **Run commercial printing checks.** If you're sending the publication to
   a commercial printer for publishing, it's a good idea to run these checks,
   which look for issues with color models, embedded fonts, and so on. (Page
   839 has some pointers for preparing a publication for a commercial printer.)

   — **Run website checks.** If you plan to save the publication as an HTML file
   (page 205) and publish it on a website, run these checks.

   — **Run e-mail checks (current page only).** You can convert a page in your
   publication to HTML and send it as an email message; these checks looks
   for HTML issues on the current page.

Figure 29-17:
*To deal with issues Design Checker turns up, click any issue and
then choose an action from its menu.*

2. Turn checkboxes on or off to tell Design Checker which checks to run.

   Results appear in the "Select an item to fix" list.

3. Scroll through the list to see the potential problems Design Checker found. Point to an item you want to address.

   When you point to an item, a drop-down arrow appears. Click the arrow to choose one of these options:

   — **Go to this Item.** Click this option to jump to the item so you can fix it by hand.

   — **Fix.** Choose this option, and Publisher tries to fix the problem automatically. Of course, Publisher can't fix every problem—if it's something that needs your input, like an empty text box, clicking this option takes you to the problem so you can fix it yourself.

   — **Never Run this Check Again.** If the issue isn't one that bothers you, tell Design Checker to quit looking for it in future checks.

   — **Explain.** Click this option to open Publisher Help, where you can read about the issue and learn about how to fix it.

4. When you've dealt with all the issues Design Checker has found, click the Close Design Checker button at the bottom of the pane.

Printing a Publication

If you're printing your publication yourself, printing works the same way as in other Office programs: Select File→Print (Alt, F, P) to go to the Backstage Print page. There, select a printer, adjust any settings that need tweaking, and click Print.

Preparing a Publication for a Commercial Printer

If you're sending your document to a commercial printer, you need to do a little prep work before packing it up and send it. Start by heading to File→Info→Commercial Print Settings (Alt, F, E, C) and select any of these options:

- **Choose Color Model.** When you print something on your home or office printer, you probably use the RGB (red, green, blue) model. Commercial printers, however, use either process colors, spot colors, or a combination of the two. Process colors are also called CMYK, which stands for cyan, magenta, yellow, and black (yup, K for black), which combine in different ways to produce full-color publications. Spot colors are premixed colors used for a single print run.

  Check with your printer to find out which color system your print job will use. In general, process-color printing is pricier than spot-color printing, but it's the best method for printing clear, sharp photographs in your publication.

- **Manage Embedded Fonts.** When you embed fonts in a publication, you make the font part of the file, so it displays consistently on whatever computer opens the file. Choose this option and turn on the checkbox labeled "Embed TrueType fonts when saving publication" if you have unusual fonts that may not be installed on your printer's computer. Be aware, though, that embedded fonts can make a file quite large.

- **Registration Settings.** Ask your print shop whether you should use either of these settings:

    — **Trapping.** This smooths out an image by overlapping small areas of adjacent colors to prevent any gaps.

    — **Overprinting.** This allows one layer of ink to print over another.

Tip: When you change a publication's Commercial Print Settings, be sure to have Design Checker run a commercial printing check before you take it to the print shop.

When your publication is ready to package up for the printer, Publisher has a wizard to help. Here's how it works:

1. **Select File→Share→Save for a Commercial Printer→Pack and Go Wizard (Alt, F, H, M, D).**

    The "Pack and Go Wizard" opens and walks you through the steps of preparing and saving the file for commercial printing.

2. **Select the location where you want to save the file. You can burn it to a CD, copy it to removable storage (like a flash drive), or save it to another location. Click Next.**

    The wizard packs up your file and copies it to the location you selected.

Note: If you change a publication you've packed and saved, you must run the "Pack and Go Wizard" again to save those changes.

OneNote

OneNote might sound like the world's shortest song, but it's a lot more useful—and a lot more fun—than that. OneNote 2010 is a place to create, gather,
and store notes. A note can be almost anything you want it to be: a typed
line or several paragraphs, a sketch, a picture, a link to a web page, an audio or video
clip—you name it. You can enter notes directly into a virtual notebook, pull them
in from other Office programs, share them with others, gather them from the Web.
One place, tons of notes—OneNote. Get it?

Previous versions of OneNote had toolbars to hold commands, but OneNote 2010
catches up to its Office siblings with a tabbed ribbon, making it easier and faster to
do the things you want. Another new feature you'll love is Linked Notes, which links
notes (as you take them) to their source in Word, PowerPoint, a web page, or another
OneNote entry.

This chapter introduces the program and shows you how to create and organize
notebooks, and then fill them up with information. It shows you the different kinds
of notes and how to add them to a notebook page. You'll also see how to find and
tag (label) notes, share your notes with others, and make OneNote work with other
Office programs. So get out your pens, scissors, and glue—no wait, with OneNote,
you won't need those to gather and organize pretty much *anything* you run across.

What Is OneNote?

Traditionally, students lug around notebooks, one for each class they're taking.
Each class notebook might be divided into tabbed sections—perhaps one section
for lecture notes, another for reading notes, and a third for research notes for the
big term paper.

OneNote is like a library of such notebooks. The notebook, shown in Figure 30-1, is the main unit of organization, holding notes related to a particular topic—like the notebook a student takes to history, physics, or opera class. To keep your notes organized, each notebook holds these elements:

- **Sections.** Sections are like divider tabs in a paper notebook—and they look like them, too, appearing as a series of tabs above the pages of a notebook. Sections divide a big topic (what the notebook is about) into its main subtopics. For example, if you were compiling notes about opera composers, you might create sections based on nationality: Italian composers, German composers, French composers, and so on. Or you might organize your notes by creating sections for time periods or styles of music—whatever works for you.

- **Section groups.** If you want, you can group related sections into a *section group*. You give this group a name, add sections to it, and then fill up each one with pages and notes. In the opera notebook, for example, you might create section groups by continent: A "European Composers" section group would contain the sections for Italian, German, and French composers.

- **Pages.** Just like a physical notebook, the bulk of your OneNote notebook consists of pages. Pages are where you write, doodle, and paste in your notes. Each page has a name, so you can group related notes on that page. An "Italian Composers" section might have pages for Verdi, Puccini, Donizetti, Bellini, and so on, each page devoted to notes about that composer.

- **Subpages.** If a page is getting full, making it a challenge to find individual notes, you can break it into subpages. OneNote files subpages under their associated "parent" in the Pages pane, as shown in Figure 30-2.

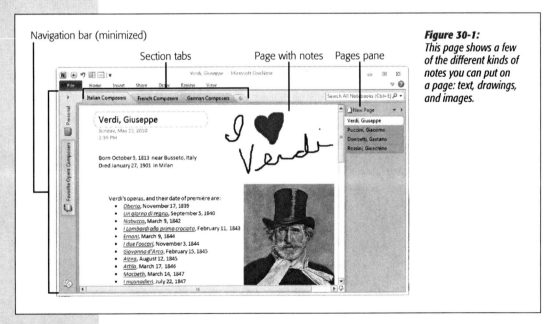

Navigation bar (minimized)

Section tabs   Page with notes   Pages pane

Figure 30-1:
This page shows a few of the different kinds of notes you can put on a page: text, drawings, and images.

- **Notes.** And, finally, here's the main event—the notes themselves. A note can be just about anything—you can type it, draw it, write it freehand, paste it in, or link to a source. Notes can be text, images, tables, screenshots, equations, even audio and video recordings. If it's worth saving or jotting down, you can put it in your notebook.

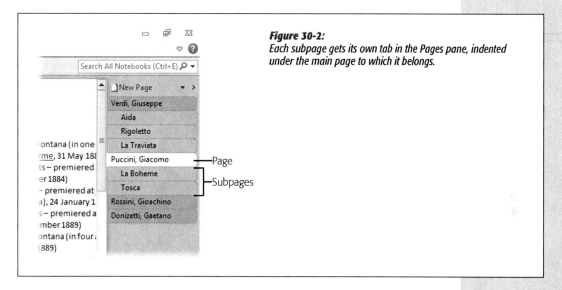

Figure 30-2:
Each subpage gets its own tab in the Pages pane, indented under the main page to which it belongs.

Getting Familiar with the OneNote Workspace

Figure 30-1 shows a notebook page filled with several kinds of notes. The main section of the page is for notes. Above the notes workspace are the notebook's section tabs; click any tab to go to that section. Along the right side of the screen is the Pages pane (Figure 30-2), listing pages and subpages by title. Click any tab in the Pages pane to jump to that page.

To move from one notebook to another, open the Navigation bar, shown in Figure 30-3. (Click the Expand the Navigation Bar button to see it in its full glory.) This pane lists all your notebooks, along with their section groups and individual sections. To move from one notebook to another, click any button in the Navigation bar.

Note: One thing you might wonder when you start working with OneNote is, "Where's the ribbon?" Instead of the familiar band of buttons across the top of the screen, you see what looks like an old-fashioned toolbar. The ribbon is there; it's just hiding. To give you more room to work with your notes, OneNote minimizes the ribbon by default. It appears when you click any tab, and then hides again after you select a command. If you want the ribbon to stay visible, click the upper-right "Expand the Ribbon" button (it's next to the Help button).

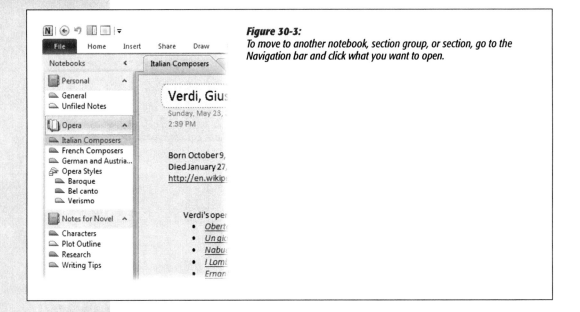

Figure 30-3:
To move to another notebook, section group, or section, go to the Navigation bar and click what you want to open.

Creating and Filling up a Notebook

OneNote comes with one notebook already created for you, called Personal. But one notebook won't get you very far. To create a new one, follow these steps:

1. Select File→New (Alt, F, N).

   The New Notebook page, shown in Figure 30-4, opens.

2. Choose among OneNote's three storage options:

   — **Web.** Click here if you want to save your notebook on SkyDrive (page 875). This lets you access it from anywhere you have an Internet connection. You can share the notebook with others or keep it private—it's up to you.

   — **Network.** If you plan to share this notebook with others in your organization, choose this option to save the data on a network drive.

   — **My Computer.** If your notebook is just for you—research notes for a novel, perhaps—and you always plan to access it from the same computer, go with this.

3. Enter a title for your notebook in the Name box.

   Pick something that identifies what the notebook is about, such as "Research for Novel" or "History Report."

4. In the Location box, enter your notebook's exact storage address.

   The information you give here depends on whether you chose Web, Network, or My Computer in step 2. Wherever you store the notebook, click the Browse button to navigate to and select a folder where you'll store the notebook.

Figure 30-4:
*When you create a
new notebook, give
it a name and tell
OneNote where to
store it.*

5. **Click the Create Notebook button.**

   OneNote opens your notebook, as shown in Figure 30-5.

Right now, the notebook is blank except for the date and time of creation. Start by giving both the first page and section a name:

- **To name your new page,** type a name into the Page Name text box. As you type, the name also appears on the left-hand tab.

- **To name the section,** right-click its tab and select Rename from the shortcut menu (or simply double-click the section name). The current name changes to a text box; type the name you want.

Now that you're done with that bit of housekeeping, you're ready to start taking notes.

Adding Notes to a Page

Now for the fun part. Any empty notebook is full of potential, but not much else, so you'll probably want to start adding notes to your pages right away.

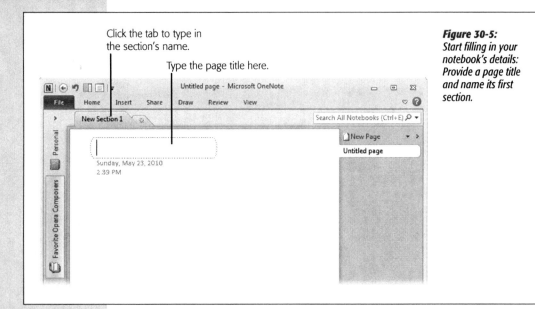

Click the tab to type in
the section's name.

Type the page title here.

Figure 30-5:
Start filling in your
notebook's details:
Provide a page title
and name its first
section.

Typing a note

To type a note onto your page, just click the page and start typing. When you do, a *note container* appears, with the text you're typing inside it. A note container is a frame that holds a particular note. The container may look small when it appears on the page, but it expands as you type. When you're done with this note, click outside its container. To edit the note, click its text and make whatever changes you want.

Pasting in a note

You can copy text to the Clipboard and paste it directly onto a OneNote page. The quickest way to paste in a note is to click your OneNote page and then press Ctrl+V. The pasted-in note appears immediately.

If you prefer, you can paste by going to the Home tab, clicking the Paste button's down arrow, and then choosing one of these Paste options:

- **Keep Source Formatting (Alt, H, V, K).** This preserves the formatting of what you're pasting in, so the font size and style are the same as they were in the original.

- **Merge Formatting (Alt, H, V, M).** This converts the pasted text's format to OneNote's standard formatting (you can see the styles OneNote uses in the Home tab's Styles section).

- **Keep Text Only (Alt, H, V, T).** Choose this option if you want to remove any images and paste only text.

- **Picture (Alt, H, V, U).** This converts what you're pasting into an image. If you paste in text as a picture, you won't be able to edit that text. Choose this if, for example, you want to save a version of the text as it exists at a specific moment in time.

Note: If you paste in some text that you copied from a web page, OneNote adds the source at the end of the note, such as *Pasted from <http://en.wikipedia.org/wiki/Giuseppe_Verdi>*. The web address is a link, so you can easily return to the source where you found the information.

Drawing a note

What good is a notebook if you can't doodle in it? OneNote comes in with a built-in virtual pen and highlighter that you can use to draw on your pages. If you've got a tablet computer, you can use its stylus or pen to draw, but you can also doodle away using a mouse or a touchpad. Here's how to draw using either method:

1. **Click the Draw tab and, in the Tools section, select a pen style from the Pens gallery (Alt, D, P).**

    The Pens gallery, shown in Figure 30-6, offers a variety of pen colors and widths, from fine point to highlighter. The pointer changes to a pen—a dot that indicates the width and the color of the pen you chose.

Figure 30-6:
To draw on a page, choose a pen color and style. Pens you've used in the past appear in the Favorite Pens section at the top of the menu.

2. **Create your note.**

   If you're using a pen or stylus on a tablet PC, go ahead and draw. Otherwise, use your mouse or your laptop's touchpad to draw with the pen. Hold down the mouse button as you move the mouse to draw a line; let go of the button to stop drawing.

3. **When you're done drawing, select Draw→Select & Type (Alt, D, T).**

   The pointer changes back to normal.

If you make a mistake while drawing, click Draw→Eraser (Alt, D, E) to turn the mouse pointer into an eraser, which comes in small, medium, and large sizes (click the Eraser button's down arrow to pick the one you want). Or choose Stroke Eraser, which erases an entire line when you click any part of it.

Tip: Select a handwritten note and click Draw→Ink to Text (Alt, D, X) to change the note into a typed one. OneNote transcribes your handwriting faster than any secretary ever could.

Inserting a screen clipping

A *screen clipping* is a note container that holds a screenshot (a snapshot of whatever is on your display or in one of its windows); you can take the screenshot right from OneNote. These are great, for example, when you want to capture what's on the *New York Times* website *right now* or that adorable message your son just IM'd you.

When you find a screen clipping you want to add to OneNote, follow these steps:

1. **Go straight from the window you want to clip to OneNote and select Insert→ Screen Clipping (Alt, N, R).**

   Windows switches back to the window you were in, and your mouse pointer becomes a crosshairs.

2. **Drag the crosshairs to select the portion of the screen you want to copy. When you've selected the area you want, let go of the mouse button.**

   The screen clipping appears on your page, along with a timestamp that records the date and time you took the screenshot.

You don't have to have OneNote open to take a screen clipping. If you're surfing the Web and come across a page you'd like to stash in your notebook, do this:

1. **In the Windows Navigation tray (on the right side of the taskbar), right-click the OneNote icon (it's a purple N). To get started even faster, press the Windows key+S.**

   A menu opens, showing ways you can work with OneNote from the tray.

Tip: If you don't see the OneNote icon in the Navigation tray, click the tray's Show Hidden Icons button to reveal more icons.

---

2. **Select Create Screen Clipping.**

   The mouse pointer becomes a crosshairs.

3. **Drag to select the portion of the screen you're clipping.**

   The Select Location in OneNote dialog box, shown in Figure 30-7, opens. Here you see a list of your notebooks and their sections.

Tip: If you prefer, click the Copy to Clipboard button instead of selecting a location in OneNote to send to. When you copy your screenshot to the Clipboard, you can open OneNote and paste it onto any page you like.

---

4. **Select the notebook and section where you want to save the clipping. Click Send to Selected Location.**

   Windows opens OneNote and pastes in the screen clipping on a new page.

From there, you can rename the page to reflect what's in the screenshot or copy the image and paste it on a different page.

Recording audio and video notes

Here's something you *can't* do with a paper notebook: If you've got a microphone and a webcam for your computer, you can record audio and video clips, store them in OneNote, and then play them back later. You can record an interview, for example, or a quick thought that you don't have time to write down.

Figure 30-7:
When you take a screenshot to add to One-Note as a screen clipping, select whether you want to copy the screenshot to the Clipboard or save it directly to a particular notebook section.

Tip: Before you start recording an audio or video note, press Ctrl+F1 to maximize the Ribbon, so you can see the Audio & Video: Recording tab as you record. This makes it easier to work with the recording controls.

If your computer doesn't have a built-in microphone and webcam, you'll have to get this equipment and connect it to your computer to take advantage of these features. When you're ready to record, follow these steps:

1. **Click where you want the note to appear. Choose Insert→Record Video (Alt, N, V) to create a video with sound. If you want to make a sound-only recording, select Insert→Record Audio (Alt, N, A).**

   OneNote puts a timestamp on the page, opens the Audio & Video: Recording contextual tab, and starts recording.

2. **Speak, do a dance, sing a song—whatever you want to record for your note.**

   As you record, you can click Audio & Video: Recording→Pause (Alt, JA, U) to take a break; click it again to resume recording.

3. **When you're finished, select Audio & Video: Recording→Stop (Alt, JA, S).**

   OneNote saves your creation and opens the Audio & Video: Playback contextual tab.

OneNote offers several ways to play back a recording:

- Select Audio & Video: Playback→Play (Alt, JA, P).
- Move the mouse pointer over the recording icon. A Play button appears to its left; click the Play button.
- Right-click the recording icon and then select Play from the shortcut menu.

Organizing a Notebook

In a loose-leaf notebook, you snap open the rings and add a divider and some paper when you need to create a new section or expand an existing one. In OneNote, adding new sections or pages is just as quick, and there's no risk of pinching your fingers.

To add a new section or page, open the notebook you want to expand and take one of these actions:

- **Add a new section.** As you learned earlier, sections appear as tabs above the current page. To the far right is a mini-tab showing a starburst icon, the Create a New Section button. Click the starburst, and a new section tab appears, called New Section 1 (the number will be different if you've got other unnamed sections in your notebook). Type the new section's name on the section tab and, if you want, give its first page a title.
- **Add a new page.** The quickest way to add a new page to the current section is to press Ctrl+N. Alternatively, head to the Pages pane. At the top of the pane is the New Page button; click it to add a new page to the end of the section.

- **Add a new page in a specific location.** As you move the pointer over the tabs in the Pages pane, a New Page icon appears to the left, with an arrow pointing between tabs. Point at the New Page icon, and a thick black line appears between tabs, as shown in Figure 30-8. Click the New Page icon, and OneNote inserts a new page between those tabs.

- **Add a new subpage.** When you want to create a subpage to better organize an overcrowded page, select the main page you want. In the Pages pane, click the New Page button's down arrow and select New Subpage. OneNote creates the new subpage and slots it into the Pages pane underneath the main page it belongs to.

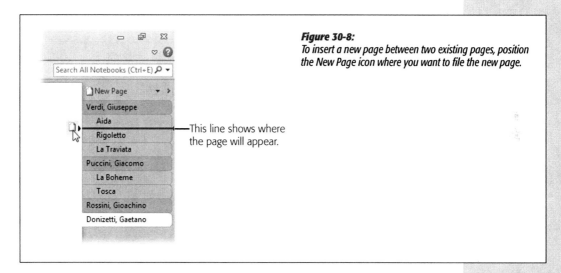

Figure 30-8:
To insert a new page between two existing pages, position the New Page icon where you want to file the new page.

Working with Sections and Pages

You can move a notebook's sections and pages—that's an organizational no brainer. But here are a couple of even more powerful tidying maneuvers: OneNote lets you merge sections or change a page's "level" (from page to subpage or vice versa).

Moving a section

It's easy to rearrange the sections in a notebook. Click a section tab, drag it to its new location, and then drop it there. If your notebook has a lot of sections, head to the Navigation bar when you want to rearrange them. Click a section to select it, and then drag it up or down the list. A black bar shows where the section will land in relation to other sections. When it's in the right spot, let go of the mouse button to drop the section in place.

Merging sections

Merging sections, of course, means combining two sections' pages. It takes just a few steps:

1. **Right-click the tab of the section whose pages you want to move into another section; select Merge into Another Section.**

   The Merge Section dialog box opens, showing a list of all your notebooks.

2. **Select the section you want to transfer this section's pages** *to*. **(It can be in the current notebook or in a different one). Click Merge.**

   OneNote warns that you can't undo a merge and asks if you want to go through with it.

3. **Click Merge Sections.**

   Another dialog box appears, asking whether you want to delete the original section (the one whose pages you just transferred).

4. **Click Delete if you want to get rid of the merged section; click No if you want to leave it in place.**

   OneNote follows your instructions and opens the section to which you transferred the pages.

Moving a page

When you press Ctrl+N or click the New Page button to create a new page, OneNote adds that page to the bottom of the Pages pane's list of tabs. Eventually, you might want to rearrange pages—put them in alphabetical order, for example—to make them easier to find.

To move a page within its section, select it in the Pages pane and drag it up or down the list. As you drag, a black bar keeps track of where you're moving the page. When it's in the location you want, let go of the mouse button.

You can also move a page from one section or one notebook to another:

1. **In the Pages pane, right-click the page you want to move and select Move or Copy.**

   A dialog box opens showing a list of your notebooks, their section groups, and their sections. (You may have to expand a notebook or a section group to see its sections; click the + sign to the left of the notebook or section group's name.)

2. **Select the section you want, and click Move to relocate the page. Or click the Copy button to place a copy of the page in the selected section while leaving the current page in place.**

   The page (or a copy of it) appears in the section you chose.

Changing a page's level

If you work with pages and subpages, you can make a page into a subpage or promote a subpage to full-fledged page. Open the page and right-click it (or right-click
its tab in the Pages pane), and then select one of these options:

- **Make Subpage.** Click this option to make the page a subpage of whatever page
  is above it in the Pages pane.

- **Promote Subpage.** This turns a subpage into an independent page.

Tip: If you've got so many subpages that they're crowding the Pages pane, point at a main page's tab. An
arrow appears on the tab; click it to collapse that section's subpages. When you want to see the subpages
again, repeat the point-and-click operation.

Deleting Notebooks, Sections, and Pages

Before you delete a notebook, think about whether you'll use it again—you might
want to keep the notebook in storage, even if you're not actively using it in OneNote
(the box on page 854 explains how to do that). If you decide you really do want to
dump a notebook, section, or page, here's how:

- **Delete a notebook.** You can't delete a notebook from inside OneNote. Instead,
  open Windows Explorer or Computer, find the folder where you stored the
  notebook, and delete it there—right-click it, select Delete, and then confirm
  that you do want to delete the notebook.

- **Delete a section.** In OneNote's Navigation bar, right-click the name of the section you want to get rid of (or right-click its tab above the Notes workspace)
  and then select Delete. OneNote asks for confirmation; click Yes to send it to
  the Recycle Bin.

- **Delete a page.** In the Pages pane, right-click the tab of the page you want to nix
  and select Delete.

Note: In OneNote, each notebook has its own Recycle Bin, where sections and pages go when you delete
them. (OneNote hangs onto deleted items for 60 days, then tosses 'em for good.) To open a notebook's
Recycle Bin, select Share→Notebook Recycle Bin (Alt, S, B, B). If you want to remove (that is, resurrect) a
deleted page from the Recycle Bin, go to the Pages pane, right-click the page you want to restore, select
Move or Copy, and then choose the section you want to restore it to.

Managing Individual Notes

One advantage OneNote has over physical notebooks is that you can easily move
your notes around without ripping any paper. And when you no longer need a note,
there's no need to scribble over it or tear out its page; just delete it, and leave the rest
of your notebook intact.

Closing the Book on a Notebook

Deleting a notebook is like tossing it in the recycling bin, never to see it again. Closing a notebook, on the other hand, is more like filing it away in a storage cabinet. It's not cluttering up your workspace, but you know where to find it if you need it. So before you delete a notebook, think about closing it instead.

When you close a notebook, you remove it from the Navigation bar, but you save the notebook (and all its contents) wherever you stored it—on your computer's hard drive, for example, or in a network folder. If you need the notebook again later, you can find it in its storage location and open it from there.

To close a notebook, go to the Navigation bar, right-click the notebook, and then select Close This Notebook from the shortcut menu. The notebook and all its sections disappear from the Navigation bar.

If you want another look at the closed notebook, right-click an empty space in the Navigation bar and then select Open Notebook. In the dialog box that opens, find and select the closed notebook, and then click the Open button. The notebook reappears in OneNote's Navigation bar, as though you'd never closed it.

Here's how to select, move, and delete notes:

- **Select a note.** Click the note so its container appears. Move the mouse pointer to the top of the container, and click when it becomes a four-headed arrow.

- **Move a note to another spot on this page.** Select the note and then drag and drop it to its new location.

- **Move a note to another page.** Select the note you want to move. Press Ctrl+C to copy the note or Ctrl+X to cut it. Open the destination page, click where you want the note to appear, and then press Ctrl+V.

- **Delete a note.** To get rid of a note, select it and then press the Backspace or Delete key. Alternatively, you can right-click the top of the note container and then select Delete.

Writing Side Notes

Have you ever had an idea come to you suddenly while you were working on something unrelated? When Archimedes had one of those sudden, brilliant ideas, he leaped out of his bathtub and ran through the streets naked, yelling, "Eureka!" One-Note lets you record your own brilliant ideas with a lot more dignity, thanks to Side Notes.

A side note is a quick way to jot down a thought when you're working in another program and don't have OneNote open. To write a side note, just click the OneNote icon in the Windows Navigation tray (on the right side of the taskbar). Or just press the Windows key+N. A miniature OneNote window opens, like the one shown in Figure 30-9. Type your note, and then click the window's upper-right X to close it.

Later, when you open OneNote, your side notes are filed, paradoxically, under Unfiled Notes. At the bottom of the Navigation bar, click the Unfiled Notes button; the Unfiled Notes section opens, and your note is on a page named after the first few words of your side note. You can move the note from Unfiled Notes to any page in any of your notebooks.

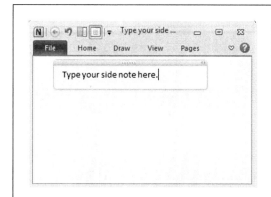

Figure 30-9:
Whatever you're doing, you can open a OneNote window like this one and type in a quick side note.

Linking a Note to its Source

It's worth taking a minute to record *where* the information in your notebook came from. In OneNote, it's fairly easy to insert links that point to your sources. Later, if you need to look up, say, the origin of the term "wharfinger," just click the link (*www. wordnik.com/words/wharfinger*, if you're curious). Whether it's a web page or an Office file, it opens right away. Here's what you need to do:

1. **In the note, select where you want to insert the link.**

   If you select some text, the link will appear as a hyperlink. If you put the cursor on a blank line, the link will appear there—as a web address, for example.

2. **Select Insert→Link (Alt, N, H).**

   The Link dialog box opens (Figure 30-10). Here's where you control the link's appearance and provide information about what you're linking to:

   — **Text to display.** If you selected some text to hold the link, it already appears in this box. You can type a new word or phrase or leave the box blank. If you leave the box blank, the link appears as the web address or filename you're linking to.

   — **Address.** If you're linking to a file or web page outside of OneNote, use this box to indicate its location. Click the Browse the Web button (the icon showing a magnifying glass and a globe) to open your web browser and find the web page you want; copy its address from the browser's address bar and paste it in here. If you're linking to a file on your computer, such as a Word document, click the Browse for File button (the folder icon), select the folder you want, and then click OK.

— **Pick a location in OneNote.** If you're linking to another page in OneNote, select the page from the list in this section. No need to put anything here if you're not linking to another note.

3. **Select the location you're linking to, and then click OK.**

OneNote inserts the link into your note.

Figure 30-10:
Link a note to its source by telling OneNote where to link to: It can be a web page (as in this example), a file on your computer or network, or another page in OneNote.

Tagging a Note

Think of tagging a note like putting a question mark or exclamation point next to information on a physical notebook page. OneNote tags serve the same purpose: They're emphasis markers and action reminders. You can also organize your notes by tag.

Tagging a note is simple: Select the note and, on the Home tab, choose a tag from the Tags gallery (Alt, H, T). OneNote adds the tag's icon to the note (a lightbulb for the Idea tag, a telephone receiver for the Phone tag, a star for the Important tag, and so on) and adds it to the Tags Summary pane (read on to learn about that). Figure 30-11 shows some examples of tagged notes.

Creating a custom tag

You're not limited to the built-in tags that come with OneNote. Go ahead and design whatever kinds of tags you like to suit your own needs.

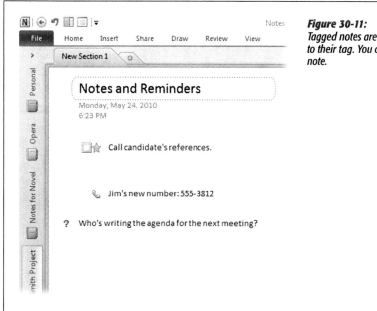

Figure 30-11:
Tagged notes are marked with an icon related to their tag. You can add more than one tag to a note.

To create a new tag, open the Home tab, click the Tags gallery's lower-right More button, and then select Customize Tags. The Customize Tags dialog box opens; click New Tag. From the dialog box that opens (shown in Figure 30-12) make the following choices:

- **Display name.** This is the label for your tag that appears on the Tags menu and in the Tags Summary pane.

- **Symbol.** Click this button to choose a symbol for your tag. The symbol appears in the note itself, as well as in the Tags menu and in the Tags Summary pane.

- **Font color.** If you want the tag to stand out with an eye-catching font color, use this button to select a shade.

- **Highlight color.** To highlight the tag's name, select a highlight color here.

As you make your choices, the Preview pane reflects them. When your tag looks good, click OK to create it and add it to the Tags menu.

Note: Another way to create a custom tag is to modify an existing tag. Open the Customize Tags dialog box, choose a tag, and then click Modify Tag. The Modify Tag dialog box looks just like the New Tag box shown in Figure 30-12; the tag's current formatting is already selected. Customize the tag as you wish; click OK when you're done.

Figure 30-12:
Create your own tag by giving it a name and selecting a symbol, font color, or highlight color (or any combination of these).

Finding tagged notes

You can group notes by tag, making it easy to find related notes or those you've marked as important. On the Home tab, click the Find Tags button (Alt, H, G) to open the Tags Summary pane, shown in Figure 30-13.

To find all notes with a certain tag, make sure the "Group tags by" drop-down list shows "Tag name". (You can also group tags by section, page title, date, or note text.) Tags and a snippet of their associated notes appear in a list in the middle of the Tags Summary pane; scroll down to see more. To open a tagged note, click it—OneNote jumps to that note's page and opens the note.

Choose how you want to group tags.

Look for tagged notes here.

Figure 30-13:
To browse notes by their tags or to find a particular note you've tagged, open the Tags Summary pane.

Removing a tag

To remove a tag from a note, select the note and then go to the Home tab. In the Tags section, click the Tags gallery's lower-right More button to open the Tags menu. At the bottom of the menu, click Remove Tag. No more tag.

Finding a Note

If you need to find a note but can't remember where you tucked it away, click inside the upper-right Search box or press Ctrl+E. Start typing a word or phrase you remember from the note. As you type, OneNote searches all your notebooks, looking for a match, and shows the results immediately. If you spot the note you're looking for in the results list, click it to open the note on its page.

To search through *all* your notebooks, click the upper-right Search box or press Ctrl+E and start typing. As you type, OneNote looks for matches and displays them immediately below the Search box. If you see the result you want, click it to open the relevant page or section.

Searching a page

If you want to quickly find a word or phrase on the page you're on right now, press Ctrl+F. The words "Find on page" appear beside the Search box, and OneNote restricts its search to the current page, highlighting any matches.

Changing the scope of your search

A search doesn't have to be as broad as all notebooks or as narrow as the current page; you can set the scope of your search to any notebook, section group, section, or page and subpages in OneNote. When you click in the Search box or press Ctrl+E, a menu appears immediately below the Search box. This menu lists your notebooks, sections, and pages, as well as each notebook's Recycle Bin.

From the list, select what you want to search, and then type your search term. OneNote looks for the term in the places you specified.

Tip: If the limited-scope search doesn't return the note you're looking for, try Ctrl+E to broaden the search to all notebooks.

Viewing Your Notebooks

Some people like a lot of elbow room when working on the canvas of their notebook pages; others prefer having all of OneNote's tools ready and waiting, even though those tools take up extra screen space. Besides minimizing or expanding the Navigation bar, the ribbon, and the Pages pane, you have these workspace-adjusting options:

- **Normal View (Alt, W, V).** The Navigation bar is on the left, the Page area is in the middle, and the Pages pane is on the right. Figure 30-1 shows an example of Normal View.

- **Full Page View (Alt, W, F).** If you need more room to work with your notes, this view minimizes the ribbon and closes the Navigation and Pages panes.

- **Dock to Desktop (Alt, W, D).** This is a super-convenient way to have OneNote ready and available as you work in other programs. OneNote appears in a pane on the right side of your display; any other program you work with moves over to make room for it. When you dock OneNote in this manner, OneNote automatically links any notes you take to whatever appears in the window that's open next to OneNote. For more about linked notes, see page 862.

Note: You can also change views from the Quick Access toolbar. Both the Dock to Desktop and Full Page View buttons toggle between Normal view and whichever button's view you click.

OneNote also gives you a fair amount of control over how your individual note pages look. Head to the View tab's Page Setup section, where you'll find the following options for changing the appearance of a page:

- **Page Color (Alt, W, PC).** By default, notebook pages have a white background. But OneNote has a range of soft pastel colors you can use as a backdrop for your notes. Because sections are color-coded, you might want a complementary color for that section's pages. Click this button and then select a color from the menu.

- **Rule Lines (Alt, W, R).** If you want your OneNote notebook to look like a real notebook, click this button. Select from among grids and narrow- or wide-ruled lines.

- **Hide Page Title (Alt, W, T).** Click this button if you want to delete the page's title from both the page and its tab in the Pages pane.

Tip: If you want to change a page's title, rather than delete it, click the title to change it both on the page and on the page's tab.

- **Paper Size (Alt, W, PS).** When you click this button, the Paper Size pane opens. This pane is helpful when you plan to print your page and want to make sure its layout is right. Here you can specify the page's size, change its orientation, and adjust its margins.

Sharing Notes

OneNote 2010 makes sharing a notebook easier than ever. To create a shared notebook from scratch, head to the Share tab: Select Share→New Shared Notebook (Alt, S, S). When the Backstage New Notebook page opens, pick Web or Network as the place where you'll store the notebook.

Tip: To find out how to share files in SkyDrive, see page 879.

If you've already got a notebook going and decide you want to share it with others, open it and select Share→Share This Notebook (Alt, S, T). OneNote takes you Backstage to the Share Notebook page. Like the New Notebook page, it has three sections:

- **Select Notebook.** The notebook you had open when you clicked Share This Notebook appears here. If you want to share a different notebook, click the drop-down arrow and pick the notebook from the list.

- **Share On.** Unlike the New Notebook page, this section has only two options: Web and Network. Select where you'll store the shared notebook.

- **Location.** Choose the folder where the shared notebook will reside.

When you've specified the notebook and its location, click Share Notebook.

Finding Changes Others Have Made

When you share a notebook with others, OneNote tracks the changes each person makes to it. Use these buttons (they're all on the Share tab) to see the changes others have made:

- **Next Unread (Alt, S, N).** Click this button to jump to the next page that contains a note you haven't read yet.

- **Mark as Read (Alt, S, R).** If you want to mark a page as read (even if you haven't read every single note on the page), click this button.

- **Recent Edits (Alt, S, E).** When you click this button, a menu displays a list of time periods to show, from today only to all edits from the past six months. Select an option, and OneNote highlights the tabs of pages edited during that time period and opens a Search Results pane listing individual edits. Click any edit to open the page with edits highlighted.

- **Find by Author (Alt, S, F).** When you click this button, the Search Results pane opens, listing edits by the author who made them. Click any edit to open its page.

- **Page Versions (Alt, S, V, V).** Click this button to see previous versions of a page, each listed on its own tab under the page. The tab shows who made changes and when. Click a tab, and the page highlights what changed in that version. To delete all versions of a page except the current one, click the Page Versions button's down arrow and choose to delete all versions in the current section, section group, or notebook.

Emailing a Page

If you want to share a page from your notebook, open the page and select Share→ E-mail Page (Alt, S, M). An Outlook Message window opens with your page's title in the Subject line and the page itself inserted as an image. Fill in the recipients, add a message if you want, and click Send to email the page.

Tip: For more options when emailing a page, open the page and select File→Send (Alt, F, D). The Backstage Send page lets you email the page as an inserted image, as an attached OneNote file, or as an attached PDF file.

Using OneNote with Other Office Programs

Microsoft designed OneNote to work seamlessly with its Office siblings, letting you easily exchange information among these programs and link between documents.

Using Linked Notes

Thanks to the new Linked Notes feature, OneNote can automatically link to and record information about a PowerPoint slide or a web page, for example, that you're writing notes about. It's like having an assistant who keeps track of all your sources as you focus on your notes.

Note: If you want linked notes to record web pages, you have to use Internet Explorer; this feature doesn't work with other web browsers.

Here's how linked notes work:

1. **In Word, PowerPoint, or OneNote, select Review→Linked Notes (Alt, R, ON).**

    Two things happen: OneNote opens in Docked view, and the Select Location in OneNote dialog box opens.

2. **In the dialog box, choose the section or page where you want to take notes about what you're looking at in the other window (a Word document or a PowerPoint presentation, for example). Click OK.**

    OneNote opens the section or page you selected and displays the Linked Notes icon, which looks like three links of chain, in the window's upper-left corner. When you see that icon, it means that any notes you take in the docked One-Note window get automatically linked to whatever appears in the other window. For example, if you're writing a report in Word, any notes you jot down in One-Note get linked to the Word document. If you switch to Internet Explorer to look something up and make a note about it, OneNote links to the website that was showing when you wrote the note.

Tip: Here's an easy way to take some linked notes: Open OneNote and switch to Docked view (click Dock to Desktop on the Quick Access toolbar or press Alt, W, D). Linked Notes turns on automatically when OneNote is in Docked view.

3. **Work as you normally would. You can open another OneNote page or switch to another program (linked notes work with Word, PowerPoint, OneNote, and Internet Explorer).**

Whenever you write a note in the docked OneNote window, that note gets linked to what you see in the other window—a document, a presentation, a web page, or another page in OneNote. OneNote also stores a thumbnail image of the page and a text excerpt from any Word or PowerPoint files you took notes on, so you can easily find that page or slide again.

Tip: If you want to pause automatic linking—maybe you decide to listen to an Internet radio station for a while as you work on your notes—click the Linked Notes icon and select Stop Taking Linked Notes. When you turn on this option, you see a red "No" symbol on the Linked Notes icon; OneNote doesn't record what's in the other window as you work on your notes. To reactivate the bond, click the Linked Notes icon and select Start Taking Linked Notes.

---

4. **When you're done taking linked notes, go to the docked OneNote pane and switch back to Normal view by clicking the Quick Access toolbar's Dock to Desktop button or selecting View→Normal View (Alt, W, C).**

Switching back to Normal View turns Linked Notes off.

Viewing note links

When you open OneNote and view a page with linked notes, the page shows the Linked Notes button in its upper-left corner. Any linked note you select shows a program icon to its left, such as a Word or Internet Explorer symbol, indicating the note's source. Figure 30-14 shows an example. Point at the icon to see a thumbnail image and a snippet of text from the source.

For a list of *all* the links on a page, click the Linked Fields button and select Linked Field(s). A fly-out menu shows all the connections you've made to other sources; select any link to open it.

Removing links from linked notes

How you remove links from linked notes depends on what you're working with:

- **To remove a link from a single note,** right-click the program icon to the left of the note and select Remove Link.

- **To remove links from all notes on a page,** click the upper-left Linked Notes icon, and then select Delete Link(s) on This Page→Delete All Links on This Page.

- **To remove links from all notes in a notebook,** select File→Options (Alt, F, I)→Advanced. In the Linked Notes section, click the Remove Links from Linked Notes button. A box appears to warn you that you're about to remove all links from all notes in the entire notebook. If that's what you want to do, click Remove.

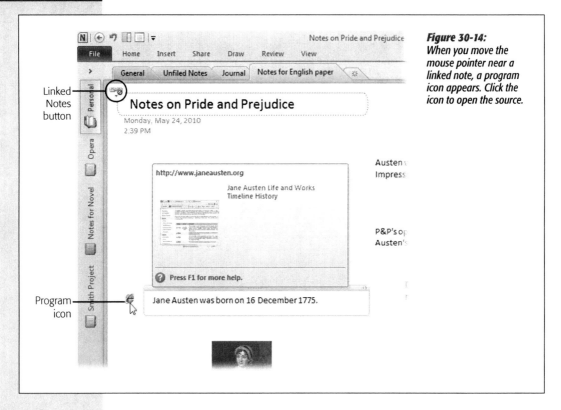

Figure 30-14:
When you move the mouse pointer near a linked note, a program icon appears. Click the icon to open the source.

Linked Notes button

Program icon

Turning off linked notes

If you'd rather not have OneNote ever recording sources, when you have it docked to your desktop, you can disable the Linked Notes feature:

1. Select File→Options (Alt, F, I).

    The OneNote Options dialog box opens.

2. **Select Advanced. In the Linked Notes section, turn off the checkbox labeled "Allow creation of new Linked Notes". Click OK.**

    OneNote no longer records your notes' sources when in Docked view.

Getting Office Files into OneNote

You can keep copies of files from other Office programs in a OneNote notebook by attaching or inserting files into a note.

Attaching a file to a note

To attach a file to a note, follow these steps:

1. **Select the note (or click anywhere on a page) and then click Insert→Attach File (Alt, N, F).**

    The "Choose a file or a set of files to insert" dialog box opens. (How's that for a catchy name?)

2. **Select the file you want to attach. (Hold down the Shift or Ctrl keys to select multiple files.) Click Insert.**

    A file icon from the relevant program (like Word or Excel), along with the file's name, appears in your note, as shown in Figure 30-15.

Double-click the icon to open the file in the appropriate Office program.

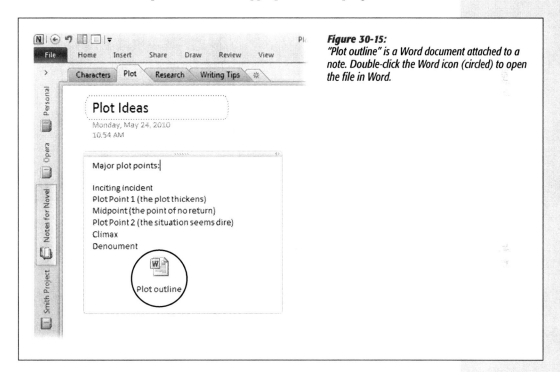

Figure 30-15:
"Plot outline" is a Word document attached to a note. Double-click the Word icon (circled) to open the file in Word.

Inserting a copy of a file into OneNote

If you want to copy a file from Word, Excel, PowerPoint, or Publisher onto a One-Note page, head for the Insert tab and click File Printout (Alt, N, O). A dialog box opens where you can select the file you want to insert. Navigate to the file, select it, and then click Insert.

If you're working on a file in another Office program and want to copy it over to a OneNote page, select File→Print. When the Backstage Print page opens, click the Printer button and select Send to OneNote 2010. Click Print. In the Select Location in OneNote dialog box, choose the location for the file (it can be a section or a page). Click OK. The information you "printed" appears in OneNote.

Tip: You can also copy information from another Office program and paste it directly into a OneNote page, as page 846 describes.

Office Web Apps

In 2010, Microsoft introduced a new way of working with Office—on the Web. Office Web Apps let you create, edit, and store files online. It's free, and you don't have to install Office 2010 on your computer to use it. All you need is an Internet connection, a web browser, and a Windows Live account (that's free, too).

Office Web Apps consists of mini-versions of Word, Excel, PowerPoint, and One-Note. You can use these apps independently of your full-fledged Office 2010 programs, or you can make them work together, easily transferring files back and forth, for example.

This chapter shows you how to get up to speed with Office Web Apps: setting up and getting started, creating and organizing folders, and filling those folders with files. Sharing folders with others is one of the main reasons to use Office Web Apps, so you'll see how to share folders to let others view or work on your files.

In the Department of Related News, this chapter wraps up with an introduction to Docs.com, an online Office program built to work with Facebook. This tool lets you create and share files with your Facebook friends. No word yet on whether Microsoft is planning a Twitter version of Office.

Introducing Office on the Web

Office Web Apps is a group of *web-based applications*. And what are those? Simply put, they're programs you access over the Internet. You point your web browser to the program's online home, sign in, and then work in more or less the same way you would with the Office applications that live on your computer.

Web-based applications offer some serious advantages for getting your work done:

- **Portability.** When a program lives on your computer, you can use the program only on that particular computer. So if you work on your desktop PC in the afternoon and then want to work on your laptop that evening, you have to remember to transfer the files, or you're out of luck. When you store your files on SkyDrive, Windows Live's online file storing and sharing service, you can access those files from *any* Internet-connected computer. So you can work from pretty much anywhere: at work, at home, in a coffee shop, your WiFi-enabled yacht—wherever.

- **Collaboration.** When a file lives on your computer's hard drive, you're the only one who has access to it. If you want to share the file, you have to email or print it. When a document lives on the Web, though, you can share it with lots of people at once. With Office Web Apps, you can invite coworkers to share a folder with you and collaborate on the files it holds. Want to edit and comment on the same Word document? Not a problem. And if you're working in Excel, you can all work on the same file *at the same time* (see page 879 for more on this feature). No more emailing spreadsheets around and getting confused about which version is most current.

- **Flexibility.** Office Web Apps are stripped-down versions of their Office 2010 cousins, so they don't have every single cool feature you've come to know and love in their full-featured kin. For example, you can't create a table of contents or do a mail merge in Word, insert a chart or a pivot table in Excel, or apply a theme to a PowerPoint presentation. Then again, you'll probably use both versions (web- and PC-based) in tandem. You can, for example, store a document in SkyDrive and then open it in Word 2010 with a single click. When you're done editing the document in Word, you can upload it to SkyDrive again to save it there. And for basic editing and formatting, you can work on the file online.

- **Updates and bug fixes.** Because Office Web Apps live on the Web, it's easy for Microsoft to fix bugs, glitches, and add new features—and you don't have to install a thing. You don't have to wait for a new edition to come out to take advantage of new features. As updates become available, they're ready and waiting for you the next time you sign in.

Note: Because it's so easy for Microsoft to update Office Web Apps, what you see on your computer screen may differ somewhat from the images in this chapter. Tweaks and improvements sometimes move things around on the screen.

- **Security.** Office Web Apps support *SSL* (secure sockets layer), which encrypts data to keep it secure. You know you're in a secure mode when the URL in your web browser's address bar starts with "https://" instead of the usual "http://" (think of that added "s" as standing for "security"). Whenever you sign into your Windows Live account (which is how you access Office Web Apps), you do so through a secure connection—one that starts with *https://*—so no one can eavesdrop on your username and password. And you access and work with your online files through a secure connection as well.

In other words, if you leave your laptop in a taxi or drop it in a pool, you know your online files are safe.

Note: It's common sense, but when you store files on the Web, you need to be extra-careful about protecting your account's username and password. If some nefarious person gets their hands on this info, they have access to your files. When creating your Windows Live account, choose a password that's hard to guess—make it a combination of letters and numbers, for example, that *aren't* your birthday or street address.

Setting Up Office Web Apps

Before diving into Office Web Apps, you have a little setup work to do: Create an account, sign in, and get to know SkyDrive, the part of Windows Live where you store your files.

Here are the big-ticket items you need to get started:

- **An Internet connection.** If you want to use Office Web Apps, of course, you need a way to connect to the Web. High-speed connections like cable or DSL are preferable to dial-up.

- **A web browser that works with Office Web Apps.** Internet Explorer, Firefox, and Safari (for the Mac) all work just fine. No such luck for Chrome, Opera, or Safari for Windows—at least not for now.

- **Microsoft Silverlight.** Silverlight is a technology that "plugs in" to your web browser—that is, you install it as a kind of helper program. It's designed to improve the delivery and appearance of media over the Internet. (Basically, it's Microsoft's version of Flash.) You don't *have* to install Silverlight to work with Office Web Apps, but Microsoft recommends it, because your apps work faster and better with it. You can download Silverlight at *www.microsoft.com/silverlight*.

- **A Windows Live account.** If you've got a Hotmail, Messenger, or Xbox Live account, you already have a Windows Live ID. If you don't, go to *http://home.live. com*, click the Sign Up button, and then follow the steps to create an account.

Note: If you're new to Windows Live, it can be confusing to try to figure out the difference between Windows Live, SkyDrive, and Office Web Apps. The box on page 870 clears that up for you.

Signing into SkyDrive

SkyDrive is your home base for all your Office Web Apps fun. To sign in, open a web browser and head to *http://skydrive.live.com*. Enter your Windows Live ID username and password, and then click the "Sign in" button. SkyDrive opens, showing two built-in folders that are waiting for you: My Documents and Public. The first is a repository for any Office files you want to keep private; the second is for files you want to make public. Soon you'll see other folders you create, like the Budget and Class Materials folders shown in Figure 31-1. The SkyDrive home page looks and works pretty much like any folder on your PC. Open any folder, for example, by clicking it (once, not twice).

Note: You can also get to SkyDrive by signing into Windows Live first. Go to *http://home.live.com*. When you want to open SkyDrive, go to the top of the page, click the More link, and then select SkyDrive from its menu.

Click to sign out of Windows Live

Navigation links
Command links

Shared folders

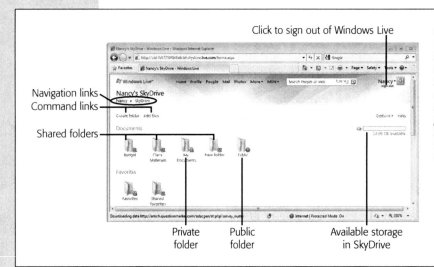

Figure 31-1:
When you sign into SkyDrive, you see folders you've used recently. Each has an icon to show its sharing status: private, shared with select others, or public (available to everyone on the Internet).

Private
folder

Public
folder

Available storage
in SkyDrive

Windows Live, SkyDrive, and Office Web Apps

What's the difference between Windows Live, SkyDrive, and Office Web Apps?

These three entities work together, letting you store and edit your files on the Web, but they're not the same thing. Here's a snapshot of each service's distinct role in life (and, more important, what it does for you):

- **Windows Live** is a group of online programs that includes email, a calendar, photo sharing, and more. You can even create a network of friends and set up your own web page through Windows Live.

- **SkyDrive,** part of Windows Live, is a file storage and sharing service. When you save files on SkyDrive, you can access them online—all you need is an Internet connection and a web browser. SkyDrive lets you choose between keeping your files private or sharing them with others. At this writing, SkyDrive offers 25 generous gigabytes of free storage.

- **Office Web Apps** is an online collection of four Office programs: Word, Excel, PowerPoint, and OneNote. When you open a file you've stored in SkyDrive to view or edit it online, you're using Office Web Apps.

Creating and Editing Files

Once you've found your way to SkyDrive and sniffed around the site, you'll probably want to dive in and play with a new file. Here's how:

1. **Open the folder where you want to store the file.**

   Start with an existing folder, like My Documents, or flip ahead to page 873 to learn how to create a new one. (The short version: Click the "Create folder" link.)

2. **Click New and choose the kind of file you want to create. As Figure 31-2 shows, your options include an Excel workbook, a PowerPoint presentation, a Word document, or a OneNote notebook.**

   The New Microsoft File page opens. (The exact name depends on the file type you selected—Figure 31-3 shows a new PowerPoint presentation).

Figure 31-2:
To create a new Office Web Apps file, open the SkyDrive folder where you want to store the file, click New, and then choose the kind of file you want to create.

3. **Enter a name in the Name box, and then click the Create button.**

   Presto: Your file opens, and you can get to work on it right away.

What you see is a stripped-down version of the program you're used to, as shown in Figure 31-4. The ribbon is there, but with far fewer buttons and tabs. You can do all the basics—type in text, enter data, insert images and hyperlinks, add formatting, and so on. Just don't expect anything fancy.

When you're done editing a file, don't waste your time hunting for a Close button or link—there isn't one. To close the file, use the navigation links at the top of the page to move to a different folder or your SkyDrive home page.

Figure 31-3:
When you create a new file, you see a preview of its first page on the right side of the window.

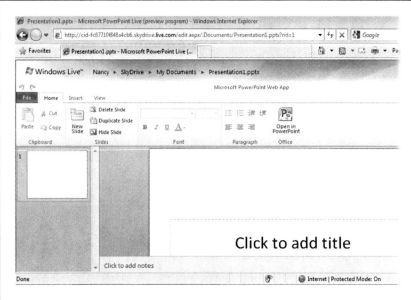

Figure 31-4:
The Office Web Apps version of Power-Point has far fewer commands than the offline version, but you can still insert, duplicate, hide, and delete slides, as well as work with text and images.

Saving a Web Apps File

This has gotta be the shortest topic in this book. To save a Web Apps file…you don't have to do a thing. Office Web Apps automatically saves your file every few seconds as you work. And it saves it again when you switch to a different folder or sign out.

Working with Folders in SkyDrive

As you learned earlier, SkyDrive comes with two built-in folders, but that's only a starting point. Just as you probably already do on your PC, you can furnish your SkyDrive with loads of folders and subfolders. When creating a new folder, you can make it private, keeping its contents to yourself, or share it with others.

Creating a Folder

To create a new top-level folder, start on your SkyDrive page:

1. **Click the Create Folder link.**

    The "Create a folder" page opens, asking for two pieces of information: the new folder's name and the level of sharing you want for it.

2. **In the Name box, type a name. Then click the "Share with" drop-down list and pick any one of the following options:**

    — **Everyone (public).** Anyone who has the folder's web address can view its files.

    — **My network.** If you've created a network of friends on Windows Live, you can share only with people in that network.

    — **Just me.** If you want to keep the contents of your folder private, so no one but you can see or edit its files, choose this option (it's the default).

    — **Select people.** When you select this option, a text box appears so you can type in the email addresses of specific people you want to share with. (If you've created a contact list in Windows Live, you can choose people from that list.)

3. **After you've chosen your "Share with" option (you can always change it later, as page 879 explains), click Next.**

    Office Web Apps creates the folder and opens the "Add files to" page so you can upload some files from your computer to your new folder. (See page 875 for instructions on how to do that.)

Tip: To create a subfolder of an existing folder, open the higher-level folder. On its page, click "Create folder" and then follow the steps just listed. When Office Web Apps creates the new folder, it stores that new folder inside this one.

Viewing Files in a Folder

Start by finding the folder you want to open on your main SkyDrive page; click it and you'll see something like the example shown in Figure 31-5. It's easy to change how the files are displayed onscreen. For example, to view a folder's files as a list, click View→Details. This view shows each file's name, the date someone last modified it, its type, and its size.

Figure 31-5:
This figure shows a folder's contents in Icon view; each icon represents the program used to create the file. Use the View and "Sort by" links (circled) to change how files appear in the folder or to find a particular file.

Whichever view you choose, you can make it easier to find files in a crowded folder by sorting them. Click the "Sort by" command above the files list and tell Office Web Apps what to sort by: name, date, size, or type of file.

Renaming a Folder

To change a folder's name, open its page and then select More→Rename. Type the new name into the text box and then click Save; your folder now has a new name.

Deleting a Folder

Keep in mind that when you delete a folder, you get rid of not just the folder but *all* its contents. If you delete a shared folder, for example, the people you share with will no longer have access to the folder or its files. Bottom line: Think twice before deleting. If you're sure you want to go ahead, open the folder's page and then click More→Delete.

Managing Files in SkyDrive

SkyDrive is all about storing files. This section tells you how to do housekeeping tasks related to the files you store: opening a file, transferring files between your computer and SkyDrive, and managing files within a folder.

Opening a File

When you want to work on a file in Office Web Apps, open the folder that holds the file, find the file you want, and then click it. This opens a window similar to the one shown in Figure 31-6. From here you can either view or edit the file:

- **To view a file,** click the big file icon or the View link above it. The file opens in read-only mode so you can see its contents but not edit them. PowerPoint presentations open in Reading view (page 558).

- **To edit a file,** click the Edit link above its icon. It opens the editor for that kind of file so you can add to or change its contents.

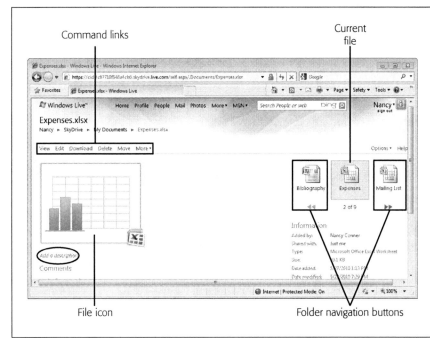

Command links

Current file

Figure 31-6:
The File window is your control center for all your online files. Use the command links above the file's icon to view or edit the file. Click "Add a description" (circled) to remind yourself or others what this file is for.

File icon

Folder navigation buttons

Uploading Files to SkyDrive from Your Computer

When you *upload* a file, you transfer a copy of it from your computer to SkyDrive. How the uploading process works depends on where you start: in SkyDrive or in an Office program installed on your computer.

Note: You can view and edit Office 2007 or 2010 files with Office Web Apps. If you're working with files from Office 2003 or earlier (files that end in .doc, .xls, or .ppt), Office Web Apps only lets you view them.

Starting point: your SkyDrive page

If you're on your SkyDrive page and want to upload a file, click the "Add files" link. On the page that appears, choose a folder (or click "New folder"); the "Add files to" page opens. (The actual page name reflects the folder you're adding files to.)

In the center of the page is a big box labeled "Drop files here". It's really that simple. Open Windows Explorer and resize its window so you can see both Windows Explorer and SkyDrive's "Drop files here" box. In Windows Explorer, find the file you want to upload, drag it to the SkyDrive window, and drop it inside the target box. A program icon indicating the type of file appears, along with the file's name.

If you want to upload more files to this folder now, repeat the process, dropping the files into SkyDrive's target zone. When you've dragged and dropped to your heart's content, click the Upload button, and your computer sends your file(s) over the Internet to your folder on SkyDrive.

Starting point: a SkyDrive folder

If you start from a particular folder in SkyDrive, the process is largely the same as the one just described, except that there's no need to choose a folder (because you're already there).

Click Add Files, open and position Windows Explorer, and drag and drop the files you want to upload. Click the Upload button when you're ready to complete the transfer.

Tip: If you prefer, you can upload files to SkyDrive the old-fashioned way, by browsing in a dialog box. Beneath the "Drop files here" box is a link that says, "Select files from your computer". Click that link to open the "Select files to upload" dialog box. Find and select the file you want to upload, and then click Open. An icon representing the file appears in SkyDrive. Click the Upload button to—you guessed it—upload the file.

Starting point: an Office program

You don't have to have SkyDrive open to save files there; you can do it right from an Office program (although your computer must be connected to the Internet). If you're working in Word, Excel, or PowerPoint and want to save the file you're working on to SkyDrive, select File→Share→Save to SkyDrive→Sign In (Alt, F, H, K, Y3). A dialog box appears, asking for your Windows Live sign-in info; type this in, and then click OK.

Tip: To speed up the sign-in process in the future, turn on the checkbox labeled "Remember my credentials" when you sign in.

Windows signs you into SkyDrive and displays your folders on the Backstage Share page. Pick the SkyDrive folder where you want to store the file, and then click the Save As button.

The Save As dialog box opens, with a SkyDrive location queued up as the place to save the file. Click Save. Your Office program uploads the file to your SkyDrive folder. The next time you open that folder in SkyDrive, there it is.

Note: If you're working with OneNote, the process is a little different. Open the notebook you want to upload, and then select File→Share→Web. In the Location section, select the SkyDrive folder you want, and then click Share Notebook.

Downloading Files from SkyDrive to Your Computer

When you transfer a copy of a file from the Web to your computer, you *download* it. SkyDrive gives you several ways to make this happen:

- **From a File page.** Click the Download link. Your web browser opens a dialog box asking whether you want to open the file or save it on your computer. Make your selection to download the file.

- **From an Office Web Apps editor.** If you're working on a file in Office Web Apps and want to open it in the corresponding Office 2010 program, click the Home tab's "Open in" button. (The name of the button reflects the program you're using—Open in Word, for example.) Windows warns you that some files downloaded from the Internet could harm your computer. Since this is your file, you know you can trust it; click OK to open it in the appropriate program.

Roadblocks and Office Web Apps

If you create files in the regular Office programs and upload them to SkyDrive (page 875), you might occasionally run into the virtual equivalent of a stop sign. That's because there are features in the regular programs that Office Web Apps doesn't support. For example, Office Web Apps can't handle Excel worksheets with inserted comments or shapes. So if you try to open a spreadsheet that contains comments, you get a message from Office Web Apps that the file won't open properly.

If you see that warning, you can convert the Office file to a version that Office Web Apps can work with. So if you really need to hang onto those comments in the worksheet, then be aware that you can't edit it using Office Web Apps. To save the file in a version that Office Web Apps can work with, follow these steps:

1. Select File→Save a Copy.

   A dialog box opens, letting you know which aspects of the original file won't work in Office Web Apps.

2. Click Yes.

   The Save As dialog box appears. You have two choices here:

- **Save the file with its current name and overwrite the existing file in SkyDrive.** Use this option if you want to replace the original Office 2010 file with an Office Web Apps version in SkyDrive, and then work with it in Office Web Apps.

- **Save the file with a new name.** Use this option if you want to store the original Office 2010 file in SkyDrive. (You can't edit it in Office Web Apps, but you can open it in the original program.)

3. Type in a new name, or leave the current name and turn on the "Overwrite existing files" checkbox. Overwriting converts the stored file to a version that's compatible with Office Web Apps. Click Save.

   Office Web Apps saves the file in a version it can work with.

   To view or edit the saved file, go to the folder where you saved it and then click the file. Its File window opens; click View or Edit to work with the file in Office Web Apps.

- **When you're viewing a file.** If you open a file by clicking View on its File page, you can see the file but not edit it. To download a file you're viewing, click the "Open in" link just above the file (it'll say Open in Excel, Open in PowerPoint, and so on). Windows warns you about opening downloaded files; click OK.

- **From a folder.** You can download all files in a folder in the form of a .zip file, a single file that packs multiple files together and compresses them. After you've downloaded the .zip file, you can open it with WinZip or another .zip file utility. Open the folder whose files you want to download, and then select More→"Download as .zip file". SkyDrive creates the .zip file, and your web browser asks whether you want to open or save it—choose one to transfer the file to your computer.

Note: Microsoft wants to do its part to protect your computer from potentially dangerous downloaded files. First there's the warning you get from Windows before downloading a file to open in an Office 2010 program. Then, when you open the file in an Office program, it opens as a read-only file in Protected View, and you see a warning that the file could be unsafe because it came from the Internet. Click the warning bar's Enable Editing button (or select File→Info→Enable Editing or press Alt, F, E, E) to go ahead and edit the file.

Move, Rename, Delete: File Management Tips

Once you've loaded SkyDrive up with a collection of documents, you're bound to want to tweak and manage those files, just as you've always done on a PC. Here's a greatest-hits tour of your options:

- **Moving a file.** To remove a file from its current folder and place it in a different folder, click the Move link. The page that opens shows you a list of folders; click the one you want to move the file to, and another page opens listing the folder and its subfolders (if any). Click the folder you want, and Office Web Apps moves the file there.

- **Copying a file.** Copying a file keeps the original file in its current folder and places a duplicate in another folder that you select. The original and the copy are separate—editing one doesn't change the other.

    To copy a file, select More→Copy. On the page that opens, click the folder where you want to store the copy. Another page opens, letting you store the file in the main folder or in one of its subfolders; select the folder or subfolder you want, and Office Web Apps places a copy there.

- **Renaming a file.** To change a file's name, select More→Rename. The Rename page opens; type in the file's new name, and then click Save.

- **Deleting a file.** To delete a file, click the Delete link and then OK to confirm that you really want to do this. Deletion is permanent and can't be undone, so be extra-sure before you delete.

Sharing Files

A major advantage of Office Web Apps is how easy it is to share files with other people. Instead of emailing documents around or printing out hard copies and stuffing them into mailboxes, you can give your colleagues right-now access to the most up-to-the-minute version of a file. They can look at the file when they have time, whether it's first thing in the morning, between meetings, or in the middle of a sleepless night. And they can leave comments on any file in a folder you've shared with them.

When you share a SkyDrive folder, the people you share it with have access to all the files you store there. You've got control over the kind of access others have, whether they can add, edit, and delete files or just view them.

Note: Sharers don't need a Windows Live ID to view the files in a SkyDrive folder. They do need a Live ID, though, to edit files.

Setting Permissions

Office Web Apps thinks of sharing in terms of giving permission—you grant permission to access a folder and the files it contains. When you create a new folder, Office Web Apps lets you set permissions, as page 873 describes. But you're not stuck with whatever sharing settings you pick at that point; you can change permissions whenever you like.

To set a folder's permissions, open it up and select More→"Edit permissions"; the "Edit permissions" page, shown in Figure 31-7, opens. Here's where you see who has access to the folder and what kind of access they have (read-only or add, edit, and delete). The following sections show you how to change those permissions.

Making a shared folder private

If you've shared a folder and now want to restrict access to yourself and yourself alone, turn off all the checkboxes on the "Edit permissions" page. Click Save to make the folder private.

Note: Making a shared folder private means that people you've shared it with in the past no longer have any access to its files.

Sharing a private folder or changing a shared folder's permissions

If the page says, "You're not sharing this folder", it means the folder is private right now. You can share a private folder or change the permissions of a folder that's currently shared. No matter what the current permissions are, you can share a folder in these ways:

- **Everyone.** Turn on this checkbox if you want the folder available to anyone with Internet access.

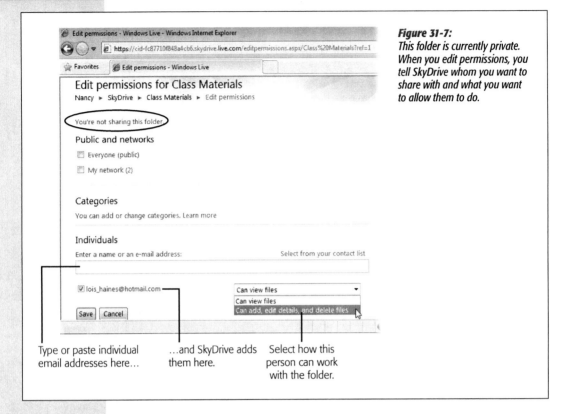

Figure 31-7:
This folder is currently private. When you edit permissions, you tell SkyDrive whom you want to share with and what you want to allow them to do.

Type or paste individual email addresses here…

…and SkyDrive adds them here.

Select how this person can work with the folder.

- **My network.** If you've created a network in Windows Live, turn on this checkbox to share the folder with everyone on that network.

- **Categories.** If you've assembled your Windows Live contacts into groups (called *categories*), you can pick the categories you want to share with here.

- **Individuals.** Type in an email address here and press Enter. Office Web Apps adds the person to your sharing list and clears the text box so you can type in another address.

After you've determined whom you want to share with, set permissions for each person or group with access to your folder. When you turn on a sharing checkbox, a drop-down list appears to its right. Here you can pick from two levels of sharing permission:

- **Can view files.** People on your sharing list can look at the folder's files but not change them in any way.

- **Can add, edit details, and delete files.** Microsoft calls this permission level *coauthoring,* and it gives people you share with full permission to work with the folder's files. They can't, however, move or delete the folder itself.

Select the permission level you want for each category you're sharing with. For example, you might allow everyone to view files, but restrict editing permissions to a few colleagues.

When everything looks good, click Save to put these permissions into effect.

Tip: The people you share with won't know they have access to a folder unless you tell them. When you share with an individual or group, Office Web Apps offers to send a notification that you're sharing the folder, complete with a link to get there. Of you can send a link to the folder by opening the folder and selecting More→Properties→"Send a link".

Leaving Comments

People who share a folder can leave comments for one another on any file in the folder. Comments appear on the File page, under the file icon. To leave a comment, type it into the "Add a comment" text box and then click the Add button.

Comments appear beneath the comment box, along with the name of the commenter. If you own the folder, you can delete any comment left on its files. If someone else has shared one of their folders with you, you can delete only your own comments. To make a comment go away, click its Delete link and then OK to confirm.

Tip: If you make changes to a shared file, it's a good idea to leave a comment outlining those changes so others will know what you've done.

Simultaneous Editing in Excel

Think how much faster you could get your work done if you and your team could all work on that big spreadsheet at the same time. No waiting around for someone to finish before you get your turn. With Office Web Apps Excel, you can do just that.

When you and other people all have editing privileges in a shared folder, you can work on an Excel spreadsheet simultaneously. Say you're working away on a budget spreadsheet in Office Web Apps, and Sarah in the Tulsa office opens the same file to work on it, too. When Sarah changes the data, you see it on screen the next time Office Web Apps saves the file (which is every minute or so), and Sarah sees your changes, too. You can see how many people are editing the spreadsheet right now by looking in its lower-right corner. Click the "x people editing" notice to see a list of who's working on the file, as shown in Figure 31-8.

There's one major drawback to simultaneous editing in Office Web Apps Excel: Although you can see who else is working on a spreadsheet, you can't see who's working *where*. Two people can edit the same cell at the same time, and the later data overwrites the earlier. So if you use simultaneous editing, be clear about who's responsible for which part of the spreadsheet; that way each coauthor stays in her own area.

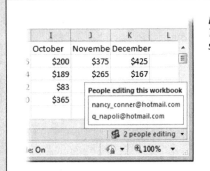

Figure 31-8:
The online version of Excel lets you know who else is working on a spreadsheet at the same time you are.

Note: At this writing, the Office Web Apps versions of Word, PowerPoint, and OneNote don't allow simultaneous editing. If you try to open a shared file that someone else is working on in one of these programs, you see an error message telling you that someone else is using it. You can download the file, but you can't edit it online.

Docs.com: Office Web Apps for Facebook

Facebook, the wildly popular social networking site, has nearly half a *billion* members—so the odds are pretty good that you're one of them. If you have a Facebook account, you can use Docs for Facebook, a Microsoft-created Facebook application that lets you create documents and share them with your Facebook friends. What you get with Docs for Facebook are all the same offerings described earlier in this chapter, but packaged and delivered inside Planet Facebook—that place where so many people now spend so much time. (If you're one of the half-dozen or so people who don't have a Facebook account—what are you waiting for? Head over to *www.facebook.com*, fill in the Sign Up form, and click the green Sign Up button. That's all it takes.)

To get started with Docs for Facebook, point your web browser to *www.docs.com*. If you're already signed into Facebook, you're good to go. If you don't have an active Facebook session going at the moment, click the upper-right Sign In link and enter the email address and password you use for your Facebook account.

Note: At this writing, Docs for Facebook is by invitation only. If you see a notice that there's a wait list to sign up, click the blue "Sign me up!" button to add your name to the list and receive your invitation when one becomes available. Eventually—maybe even by the time you read this—Docs for Facebook will be open to all Facebook users, and you'll just have to sign into your Facebook account to use it.

SharePoint and Office Web Apps

Signing into Windows Live and storing your files on Sky-Drive isn't the only way to work with Office Web Apps. You can also use Office Web Apps through SharePoint 2010, a program that lets people work collaboratively on documents and other files. SharePoint can run Office Web Apps from a server on a local network, such as the one you use at work. If your organization uses SharePoint, it can deploy Office Web Apps on the local network, and you don't have to go on the Web to use them. You don't need a Windows Live ID to use Office Web Apps through SharePoint.

Keeping your stored files on a local network, behind your organization's firewall, adds another layer of security to your files. Ask your network administrator if your Share-Point installation is set up to run Office Web Apps—and then start collaborating with others at work.

Once you've signed in, click the links at the top of the page to see docs your friends have shared with you, add a doc of your own, or view any docs you've stored in Docs for Facebook.

Adding Docs

Docs, in this case, means more than just written documents. You can add, edit, and share Word documents, Excel spreadsheets, and PowerPoint presentations in Docs for Facebook.

Creating a doc from scratch

To create a doc from within Docs for Facebook, go to the top of the page and click Add a Doc. Then choose the kind of file you want to create: document, spreadsheet, or presentation. Docs opens the type of file you chose in the appropriate editor; Figure 31-9 shows an example of a newly created Word file.

Uploading a file from your computer

When you've created and stored a Word, Excel, or PowerPoint file on your computer, you can transfer a copy of that file into Docs for Facebook. Just follow these steps:

1. **On any Docs.com page, select Add a Doc→Upload a Doc.**

    The Upload a Doc page, shown in Figure 31-10, opens. This page has two main sections: choosing a document to upload and setting sharing permissions.

2. **Click the Browse button.**

    The "Choose File to Upload" dialog box opens.

3. **You can upload only Word, Excel, and PowerPoint files. Find the file you want, select it, and then click Open.**

    The file you chose appears in the Choose a Doc box.

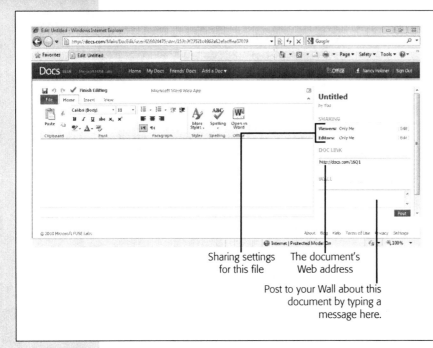

Figure 31-9:
*You can create or edit
a Word document to
share with your Face-
book friends on Docs.
com. The right side of
the page shows your
sharing settings—who
can view or edit this
file.*

Sharing settings
for this file

The document's
Web address

Post to your Wall about this
document by typing a
message here.

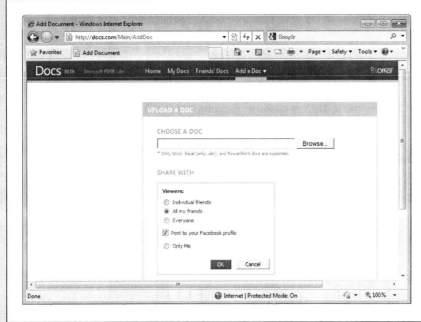

Figure 31-10:
*To upload a file from
your computer to
Docs.com, browse to
the file you want and
choose its sharing
settings.*

4. **Tell Facebook who can see the file.**

   You can choose individual friends (when you do, a text box appears so you can name the individuals you want to share with), all your Facebook friends, everyone on the Internet, or only you (this is the most private option). If you want to put a notification about the file on your Facebook profile, leave the "Post to your Facebook profile" checkbox turned on.

5. **Turn on the radio button that indicates whom you want to share this document with. Then find Editors, below the Share With box, which lists who can edit the file. If that looks fine, then click OK. If you want to change the approved editors for this document, click the Edit link.**

   Docs shows you three choices for who can edit the file: "Individual friends", "All my friends", and "Only Me".

6. **Choose the option you want, and then click OK. Next click the lower-right Upload button.**

   You computer uploads the file you selected to Docs.com.

Note: The first time you upload a file to Docs.com, you may get a notice from your web browser that it has blocked a pop-up. (This depends on your browser's security settings.) If you see this notice, give popups from Docs.com the green light so you can work with the site free of these annoying messages.

Viewing Your Docs

Your docs appear in a list on your My Docs page. To see or open any of your files, click My Docs, and then click the file you want to open. Docs opens it in a reader, like the one shown in Figure 31-11. Above the document are links you can use to work with the document; to its right are your sharing settings. In the document pane, scroll down to read the document.

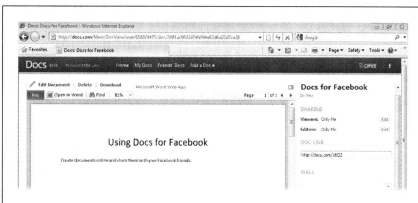

Figure 31-11:
When you view a file in Docs.com, it looks like this. If you don't have permission to edit the file, there's no Edit Document or Delete link above it.

Editing a Doc

To edit a document, open it and then click the Edit Document link above the document pane. Docs opens the document in the appropriate editor (like the Word editor shown in Figure 31-9). Work with it as you would any Office Web Apps file.

Tip: If you want to work on the file in its full, bells-and-whistles Office program, click the Open in Word (or Excel or PowerPoint) link above the document pane. After you've edited the file, upload it to Docs.com again to save your new content there.

Sharing a Doc

You can adjust your sharing settings for each document. So, for example, you can share a PowerPoint photo album of your vacation photos with all your Facebook friends but share your love poems only with your significant other.

To adjust sharing settings for a file, open that document to view or edit it. To the file's right is the Sharing section, listing who can view or edit this file. Click Edit for either setting, select a new sharing level, and click OK.

Tip: If you've set Viewers to Everyone, you can share a doc with anyone—Facebook friend or not—by emailing them a link to the doc's location. Open the doc to view or edit it, and in the pane to its right, find the Doc Link box. Copy the web address in that box, and paste it into an email or insert it on a blog post to share your file.

When you've written or updated a document, you can let your Facebook friends know by posting an announcement on your wall. In the pane to the right of your open doc, type an announcement in the Wall text box. Click Post to put the announcement on your Profile page's Wall.

Viewing Friends' Docs

Tracking down the docs your friends have created and shared with you is easy—you don't have to go any further than your Docs.com Friends' Docs page. Click the Friends' Docs link, and you see a page that looks just like your My Docs page, listing shared docs that you can view and (if your friend has shared permission) edit.

Part Seven: Appendix

7

Appendix A: Customizing Office 2010 Applications

Customizing Office 2010 Applications

Office 2010 is more customizable than ever. Exhibit A: You can now customize the ribbon. That's great news if you sometimes have trouble remembering whether the button you want is on, say, the Review tab or the Reference tab. Now you can outfit the ribbon pretty much any way that makes sense to you—adding or removing buttons, creating new groups, moving things around, even creating your own custom tabs. And, of course, as in Office 2007, you can also handpick what's on the Quick Access toolbar and the status bar.

Customizing the Quick Access Toolbar

The Office Quick Access toolbar sits in the upper-left part of your screen, giving you easy access to the buttons you use most, no matter what's currently on the ribbon. Out of the box, the Quick Access toolbar displays these buttons in most Office programs: Save, Undo, and Redo. Those aren't set in stone; consider them suggestions from Microsoft.

To add *your* favorite buttons, click the button circled in Figure A-1, which displays some of the program's most popular commands. Items already on the toolbar have a checkmark next to their names. Click any command that's not already checked to add its button to the toolbar. The new button appears to the right of those already there. To remove any button, repeat the steps just described, but this time *uncheck* the command's name.

Tip: If you want to see the Quick Access toolbar *below* the ribbon, rather than way up there at the top of the screen, select Customize Quick Access Toolbar→Show Below the Ribbon to move it.

Customize Quick Access Toolbar button

Figure A-1:
Click the circled button to see a menu of popular commands (here, the commands are for Word) that you can add to the Quick Access toolbar. Click More Commands to open a dialog box that lets you add items that aren't on this menu.

What if the command you want isn't on the menu shown in Figure A-1? Go down to the bottom of the menu and click More Commands to open the Options dialog box for your program; Word's version is shown in Figure A-2.

From the "Choose commands from" drop-down list, select a category to choose your button from. Popular Commands, for example, gathers together the most commonly used commands, but you can pick from any tab (including contextual tabs like Table Tools or Header & Footer Tools).

In the list on the left (below the "Choose commands from" drop-down list), select the item you want to add to the toolbar. Click Add, and the command jumps to the list on the right, which shows current Quick Access toolbar commands. To remove a button from the Quick Access toolbar, reverse the process.

Tip: You can customize the Quick Access toolbar for all the files you work with in an Office program or just for a single file. If you want a custom toolbar for just one file, open the file whose toolbar you want to customize and then choose its name from the upper-right Customize Quick Access Toolbar drop-down list.

The top-to-bottom listing of Quick Access toolbar commands corresponds with each button's position on the toolbar, going from left to right. To rearrange the buttons on the Quick Access toolbar, select the button you want to move. This activates the up and down arrows to the right of the list. Click the arrows to move the button.

When you're done customizing, click OK to close the Options dialog box and save your changes.

Tip: Here's a quick way to add a button to the Quick Access toolbar as you work. Right-click any button on the ribbon. From the shortcut menu, choose Add to Quick Access Toolbar.

Figure A-2:
The left-hand list shows commands that you can add to the Quick Access toolbar, and the right-hand list shows items that currently appear there.

Tip: You can undo all customization and go back to the original settings by using the Reset button in the lower-right part of the Options dialog box. Click Reset and then pick whether you want to reset all customizations you've made to the program or only those you've made to the Quick Access toolbar.

Customizing the Ribbon

Start by heading to the Customize Ribbon section of the Options dialog box, such as the PowerPoint Options box shown in Figure A-3. To open this dialog box, right-click the ribbon and then select Customize the Ribbon. Or select File→Options (Alt, F, I) and choose Customize Ribbon.

Here are your ribbon-tweaking options:

- **Add a button to a tab.** On the left, choose the command you want to add (use the "Choose commands from" drop-down list to see your choices). On the right, choose the tab to which you want to add the command. Select a command from the left-hand list, and then click Add to put its button on the ribbon of the tab you chose.

Note: You can't stick a new button anywhere on the ribbon. You can add a button only to a custom group you've created on the ribbon (described a few items down this list).

Figure A-3:
A program's ribbon tabs (here, they're for PowerPoint) appear in the right-hand list. To show or hide a tab, turn its checkbox on or off. To add a button to a custom group you've created, select the button you want from the left-hand list of commands and then select where you want it to appear. Click Add, and then use the up and down arrows to the right of the tabs list to position the new button in the group.

- **Remove a button from a tab.** On the right, choose the tab whose ribbon currently shows the command you want to remove. Select that command and click Remove.

- **Rename a tab.** Select a tab in the right-hand list and click the lower-right Rename tab to open the Rename dialog box. Type in the tab's new name, and then click OK.

- **Create a new group on a tab.** In the right-hand tabs list, select the tab that will display the new group, and then click the New Group button (below the list). A new group appears in the list, with the name New Group (Custom). To give your group a better name, right-click it and then select Rename from the shortcut menu. In the dialog box that opens, enter a name in the "Display name" text box, and then click OK.

- **Remove a group from a tab.** In the right-hand list that displays ribbon tabs, find the group you want to remove and right-click it; choose Remove.

- **Create a new tab.** Under the tabs list, click New Tab. Your new tab appears in the tabs list with the name New Tab (Custom). To rename the tab, right-click it in the tabs list, select Rename, and then enter the new name in the "Display name" text box. Finally, click OK.

- **Hide a tab.** To prevent a tab from showing while still keeping that tab (with all its groups and buttons), go to the tabs list, find the tab you want to hide, and then turn off its checkbox.

- **Remove a tab or group.** To remove a tab altogether, find the tab or group in the tabs list, right-click it, and then select Remove.

- **Move a tab or group.** You can rearrange the ribbon's tabs or the groups that make up a tab. In the tabs list, find the tab or group you want to move, select it, and then use the up and down arrows to the right of the list to move your selection to its new position. Alternatively, you can right-click any tab or group and then select Move Up or Move Down.

- **Reset a tab to its default settings.** If you want to undo customization for a specific tab, click the tab you want to restore in the tabs list, and then (below the list) click Reset. From the shortcut menu, choose "Reset only selected Ribbon tab".

Customizing the Status Bar

The Office status bar appears at the bottom of your screen and gives you information about your file, such as which page you're on, how many words you've written in a Word document, or the results of a formula like Average, Count, or Sum in an Excel worksheet. Here again, you can choose the kind of information that appears.

To customize the status bar, right-click it. The shortcut menu you see in Figure A-4 appears. Elements currently displayed on the status bar have a checkmark next to them. Click any checked element to remove it from the status bar; click any unchecked element to add it to the status bar.

Figure A-4:
Right-click the status bar to see a menu of options for what the status bar displays. Many of these options aren't just FYI—they're also buttons. In Excel, for example, click the lower-left Macro button to create a macro.

Status bar

Note: In Office 2010, the Mini Toolbar (the floating toolbar that appears in Word and other programs when you select some text) still isn't customizable. Maybe in the next version…

Index

H

handouts
    adding headers and footers in PowerPoint, 604
    creating for presentations, 667
    master for, modifying, 618
hanging indent, 57
Header and Footer dialog box
    date and time options, 602
    inserting footer in PowerPoint slides, 603
    Notes and Handouts tab, 604
    numbering slides, 603
headers and footers, 73–79
    adding to PowerPoint notes and handouts, 604
    creating footer for web page in Word, 211
    creating for Excel printouts, 407–409
    creating header for web pages in Word, 208
    editing for Word documents, 75
    editing in PowerPoint presentations, 616
    inserting data and time in Word documents, 76
    inserting images in Word documents, 77
    inserting in Word documents, 73
    inserting page numbers in Word documents, 78
    page number format in Word documents, 78
    in PowerPoint presentation printouts, 564
    in PowerPoint slides, 602
    removing information from shared documents, 232
    removing in Word documents, 78
    removing page numbers from Word documents, 79
headings
    built-in styles, in Word, 127
Help button in Word, 14
Hidden and Empty Cells dialog box, 525
hidden characters in Word documents, 179
hidden data in shared documents, removing, 230–233
hidden slides, inking to, in presentations l, 609
HighBeam Research, 130
highlighting, Text Highlight Color option, 49
home page for website, creating in Word, 206–213
    adding text and images, 212
    footer for page, 211
    header for page, 208
    navigation bar, 209
    saving page as template, 211
    setting up table, 206
Home tab
    Excel, 361
        dialog box launchers for Format Cells, 442

    Font section, 456
    Number section, 447
    PowerPoint
        Arrange button, 594
        character spacing, 566
        Font and Paragraph sections, 566
    Word, 14
        Copy, Cut, and Paste commands, 40
        Font section, 47
        Styles section, 182
horizontal alignment (cells in Excel), 452
.htm (Web Page) files, 24
HTML
    email message format, 257
    generating clean files directly from Word, 214
    saving Excel workbook as, 376
    saving Word document as, 206
    uploading files to your website, 213
Hyperlink data type in Access, 731
hyperlinks
    creating for web page navigation bar, 209
    editing or manipulating in PowerPoint text, 572
    inserting into PowerPoint slides, 608
        creating table of contents, 609
        linking one slide to another, 608
        linking to hidden slide, 609
    inserting into text in PowerPoint slides, 571
    Internet and network paths in Word, 126
hyphenation
    adjusting in Publisher, 822
    in Word, 67
        options for, 68
hyphens, 126

I

Icon view, notes in Outlook, 346
ID field (Access tables), 693, 747
IF() function, 479
images
    adding to PowerPoint slides, 551, 581
        creating a photo album, 582–585
    adding to web page in Word, 212
    adjusting appearance in Word, 105
    in brochures and newsletters, 204
    customizing watermarks with, 69
    deleting from slides, 552
    editing in Word documents, 100
        changing size, 101
        cropping, 101
    inserting and editing in Outlook email, 251
    inserting into Publisher pages, 817
    inserting into Word documents, 96–100
        aligning images with text boxes, 205

Z

Colophon

Adam Witwer provided quality control for *Office 2010: The Missing Manual*. The book was composited in Adobe InDesign CS4 by Franz Buzawa and MPS Content Services.

The cover of this book is based on a series design originally created by David Freedman and modified by Mike Kohnke, Karen Montgomery, and Fitch (*www.fitch. com*). Back cover design, dog illustration, and color selection by Fitch.

David Futato designed the interior layout, based on a series design by Phil Simpson. The text font is Adobe Minion; the heading font is Adobe Formata Condensed; and the code font is LucasFont's TheSansMonoCondensed. The illustrations that appear in the book were produced by Robert Romano using Adobe Photoshop and Illustrator CS.

Office 2010

THE MISSING CD

There's no CD with this book; you just saved $5.00.

Instead, every single Web address, practice file, and piece of downloadable software mentioned in this book is available at *missingmanuals.com* (click the Missing CD icon). There you'll find a tidy list of links, organized by chapter.

Don't miss a thing!
Sign up for the free Missing Manual email announcement list at missingmanuals.com. We'll let you know when we release new titles, make free sample chapters available, and update the features and articles on the Missing Manual website.

39 99

CPSIA information can be obtained at www.ICGtesting.com
Printed in the USA
BVOW041709100212

282641BV00001BA/14/P

9 781449 382407